61st Annual Meeting of the Association for Computational Linguistics (ACL 2023)

Student Research Workshop

Toronto, Canada
10 - 12 July 2023

ISBN: 978-1-7138-8175-9

Printed from e-media with permission by:

Curran Associates, Inc.
57 Morehouse Lane
Red Hook, NY 12571

Some format issues inherent in the e-media version may also appear in this print version.

Printed with permission by Curran Associates, Inc. (2024)

Association for Computational Linguistics
209 N. Eighth Street
Stroudsburg, Pennsylvania 18360

Phone: 1-570-476-8006
Fax: 1-570-476-0860

acl@aclweb.org

Additional copies of this publication are available from:

Curran Associates, Inc.
57 Morehouse Lane
Red Hook, NY 12571 USA
Phone: 845-758-0400
Fax: 845-758-2633
Email: curran@proceedings.com
Web: www.proceedings.com

ACL-SRW 2023

The 61st Annual Meeting of the Association for Computational Linguistics

Proceedings of the Student Research Workshop

July 10-12, 2023

The ACL-SRW organizers gratefully acknowledge the support from the following sponsors.

Gold

Google

Bronze

In cooperation with

NSF

Order copies of this and other ACL proceedings from:

Association for Computational Linguistics (ACL)
209 N. Eighth Street
Stroudsburg, PA 18360
USA
Tel: +1-570-476-8006
Fax: +1-570-476-0860
acl@aclweb.org

Introduction

Welcome to the ACL 2023 Student Research Workshop!

The ACL 2023 Student Research Workshop (SRW) is a forum for student researchers in computational linguistics and natural language processing. The workshop provides a great opportunity for student participants to take part in a mentorship program, present their work and receive valuable feedback from the international research community.

Following the tradition of the previous student research workshops, we accept three kinds of submissions: long and short research papers as well as thesis proposals. The research paper track is a venue for students to describe completed work or work-in-progress along with preliminary results. The thesis proposal track is offered for Ph.D. students who have decided on a thesis topic and are interested in getting feedback on their proposal and ideas about future directions for their work.

Mentoring is at the heart of the SRW. In keeping with previous years, we had a pre-submission mentoring program before the submission deadline. A total of 58 papers participated in the pre-submission mentoring program. This program offered students the opportunity to receive feedback from a mentor to improve the writing style and presentation of their submissions.

The Student Research Workshop again attracted a very large number of submissions this year. We received 145 submissions including 135 research papers (81 long papers and 54 short papers) and 10 thesis proposals. Out of these, 5 were ACL Findings papers whose authors wished to present their work at the SRW. A further 9 submissions were desk rejected and 2 submissions were withdrawn by the authors prior to the completion of the review process. A total of 50 submissions (5 Findings, 2 Thesis Proposals, 28 long papers and 15 short papers) were accepted. 46 of the accepted papers will be presented in person and/or virtually in the poster sessions of the main conference and 4 will be presented as oral presentations.

We are deeply grateful to our sponsors for providing funds for the travel grants that we make available to paper authors. We thank our program committee members for their careful reviews of each paper and all of our mentors for donating their time to provide feedback to our student authors. We are deeply thankful to our faculty advisors, Ivan Vulic and Lu Wang, and to the ACL 2023 organizing committee for their advice and support throughout the process. Finally, we thank each and every one of the authors for their enthusiastic participation!

Organizing Committee

Student Chair

Vishakh Padmakumar, New York University, USA

Student Chair

Gisela Vallejo, University of Melbourne, Australia

Student Chair

Yao Fu, University of Edinburgh, UK

Faculty Advisor

Ivan Vulic, University of Cambridge, UK

Faculty Advisor

Lu Wang, University of Michigan, USA

Program Committee

Chairs

Yao Fu, The University of Edinburgh
Vishakh Padmakumar, New York University
Gisela Vallejo, The University of Melbourne

Program Committee

Omri Abend, The Hebrew University of Jerusalem
Ibrahim Abu Farha, University of Sheffield
Piush Aggarwal, FernUniversität in Hagen, Computational Linguistics
Youssef Al Hariri, University of Edinburgh
Sedeeq Al-khazraji, Rochester Institute of Technology
Abeer Aldayel, King Saud University
Begoña Altuna, Universidad del País Vasco - Euskal Herriko unibertsitatea
Fernando Alva-manchego, Cardiff University
Evelin Amorim, Porto University
Tatiana Anikina, DFKI / Saarland Informatics Campus
Parsa Bagherzadeh, McGill University
Ahsaas Bajaj, University of Massachusetts Amherst
Valerio Basile, University of Turin
Tim Baumgärtner, TU Darmstadt
Rachel Bawden, Inria
Daniel Beck, University of Melbourne
Shabnam Behzad, Georgetown University
Jonas Belouadi, Bielefeld University
Uri Berger, The Hebrew University of Jerusalem, University of Melbourne
Gabriel Bernier-colborne, National Research Council Canada
Terra Blevins, University of Washington
Shikha Bordia, Verisk Analytics
Agostina Calabrese, The University of Edinburgh
Jon Ander Campos, University of the Basque Country (UPV/EHU)
Ronald Cardenas, University of Edinburgh
Silvia Casola, Fondazione Bruno Kessler, University of Padua
Yanda Chen, Columbia University
Jiangjie Chen, Fudan University
Hyundong Cho, USC, Information Sciences Institute
Alessandra Teresa Cignarella, Computer Science Department - University of Turin
Mike Conway, University of Utah
Xiang Dai, CSIRO Data61
Brian Davis, Dublin City University
Alok Debnath, Trinity College, Dublin
Chris Develder, Ghent University
Bonaventure F. P. Dossou, Mila Quebec AI Institute, McGill University
Gabriel Doyle, San Diego State University
Ritam Dutt, Carnegie Mellon University
Micha Elsner, The Ohio State University
Carlos Escolano, Universitat Politècnica de Catalunya

Neele Falk, University of Stuttgart
Antonio Farinhas, Instituto de Telecomunicacoes, IST
Francesca Franzon, Universitat Pompeu Fabra
Jie Fu, Beijing Academy of Artificial Intelligence
Yoshinari Fujinuma, AWS AI Labs
Rena Gao, The University of Melbourne
Iker García-ferrero, HiTZ Basque Center for Language Technologies - Ixa NLP Group, University of the Basque Country UPV/EHU
Aina Garí Soler, LTCI, Télécom-Paris, Institut Polytechnique de Paris
Esam Ghaleb, University of Amsterdam
Anmol Goel, IIIT Hyderabad
Matt Grenander, University of Edinburgh
Jonas Groschwitz, University of Amsterdam (UvA)
Ivan Habernal, Technical University of Darmstadt
Xudong Han, The university of Melbourne
Dirk Hovy, Bocconi University
Dieuwke Hupkes, Facebook AI Research
Joseph Marvin Imperial, National University
Tunazzina Islam, Purdue University
Jeff Jacobs, Columbia University
Labiba Jahan, Augustana College
Jyoti Jha, Ernst and Young
Lavender Jiang, New York University
Abhinav Joshi, Indian Institute of Technology Kanpur
Nitish Joshi, New York University
Jad Kabbara, MIT
Patrick Kahardipraja, University of Potsdam
Ehsan Kamalloo, University of Waterloo
Haoqiang Kang, University of Washington
Sarvnaz Karimi, CSIRO
Borhan Kazimipour, Australian Taxation Office
Anirudh Vishal Khatry, Microsoft
Prashant Kodali, IIIT Hyderabad
Mamoru Komachi, Hitotsubashi University
Fajri Koto, MBZUAI
Maria Kunilovskaya, Saarland University
Mascha Kurpicz-briki, Bern University of Applied Sciences
Alexandra Lavrentovich, Amazon Alexa
Celine Lee, Cornell University
Richard Leibbrandt, Flinders University
Christoph Leiter, Bielefeld University - CITEC NLLG
Manling Li, UIUC
Jasy Suet Yan Liew, School of Computer Sciences, Universiti Sains Malaysia
Zheng Wei Lim, University of Melbourne
Lucy Lin, Spotify
Robert Litschko, LMU Munich
Tatiana Litvinova, Voronezh State Pedagogical University
Chunhua Liu, The University of Melbourne
Robert L Logan Iv, Dataminr
Nicholas Lourie, New York University
Qing Lyu, University of Pennsylvania

Brielen Madureira, University of Potsdam
Rahmad Mahendra, Universitas Indonesia
Lara Martin, University of Maryland, Baltimore County
Sandeep Mathias, Presidency University
Puneet Mathur, University of Maryland College Park
Arya D. Mccarthy, Johns Hopkins University
Nikhil Mehta, Purdue University
William Merrill, New York University
Tsvetomila Mihaylova, Aalto University
Gosse Minnema, University of Groningen
Fatemehsadat Mireshghallah, UC San Diego
Shubhanshu Mishra, shubhanshu.com
Amita Misra, Amazon
Adib Mosharrof, University of Kentucky
Sachin Nagargoje, Microsoft
Masaaki Nagata, NTT Corporation
Nihal V. Nayak, Brown University
Mariana Neves, German Federal Institute for Risk Assessment
Kiet Nguyen, University of Information Technology, VNU-HCM
Vincent Nguyen, Australian National University
CSIRO Data61
Aitor Ormazabal, University of the Basque Country
Maria Leonor Pacheco, University of Colorado Boulder / Microsoft Research
Xiang Pan, New York University
Artemis Panagopoulou, University of Pennsylvania
Sara Papi, Fondazione Bruno Kessler
Tanmay Parekh, University of California Los Angeles
Gabriele Pergola, University of Warwick
Ben Peters, Instituto de Telecomunicações
Ian Porada, Mila, McGill University
Adithya Pratapa, Carnegie Mellon University
Yiyuan Pu, the University of Melbourne
Rajkumar Pujari, purdue.edu
Yusu Qian, Apple
Sunny Rai, University of Pennsylvania
Sree Harsha Ramesh, UMass Amherst
Surangika Ranathunga, university of moratuwa
Shruti Rijhwani, Google
Hayley Ross, Harvard University
Hossein Rouhizadeh, University of Geneva
Shamik Roy, Purdue University
Vlada Rozova, RMIT University
Andreas Rücklé, Amazon
Philipp Sadler, University of Potsdam
Oscar Sainz, University of the Basque Country (UPV/EHU)
Sashank Santhanam, University of North Carolina at Charlotte/ Apple
Abulhair Saparov, New York University
Ryohei Sasano, Nagoya University
Tatjana Scheffler, Ruhr University Bochum
Michael Sejr Schlichtkrull, University of Cambridge
Viktoria Schram, University of Melbourne

Sina Sheikholeslami, KTH Royal Institute of Technology
Manish Shrivastava, International Institute of Information Technology Hyderabad
Chenglei Si, University of Maryland, College Park
Katira Soleyman Zadeh, Ege University
Mayank Soni, ADAPT Centre, Trinity College Dublin
Cesare Spinoso-di Piano, McGill University
Tejas Srinivasan, University of Southern California
Vivek Srivastava, TCS Research
Marija Stanojevic, WinterLightLabs
Ashima Suvarna, UCLA
Stan Szpakowicz, EECS, University of Ottawa
Dage Särg, University of Tartu
Shabnam Tafreshi, UMD:ARLIS
Koichi Takeda, Nagoya University
Zeerak Talat, Simon Fraser University
Chuanqi Tan, Alibaba Group
Hao Tan, Adobe Research
Evgeniia Tokarchuk, University of Amsterdam
Thinh Hung Truong, The University of Melbourne
David Trye, University of Waikato
Sowmya Vajjala, National Research Council
Andrea Varga, Theta Lake
Francielle Vargas, University of São Paulo
Saranya Venkatraman, The Pennsylvania State University
Takashi Wada, The University of Melbourne
Zhiruo Wang, Carnegie Mellon University
Yuxia Wang, The University of Melbourne
Jun Wang, University of Melbourne
Bonnie Webber, University of Edinburgh
Steven Wilson, Oakland University
Patrick Wu, New York University
Zhuohan Xie, The University of Melbourne
Rui Xing, University of Melbourne
Yue Yang, University of Pennsylvania
Wenting Ye, ByteDance Inc
Hiyori Yoshikawa, Fujitsu Limited
Zheng Yuan, Alibaba Group
Zenan Zhai, University of Melbourne
Zixuan Zhang, University of Illinois Urbana-Champaign
Mike Zhang, IT University of Copenhagen
Ran Zhang, University of Bielefeld
Zheng Zhao, University of Edinburgh
Danna Zheng, University of Edinburgh
Zhong Zhou, Carnegie Mellon University
Rongxin Zhu, The University of Melbourne
Elena Zotova, Vicomtech

Table of Contents

ChatGPT vs Human-authored Text: Insights into Controllable Text Summarization and Sentence Style Transfer

Dongqi Pu and **Vera Demberg**
Department of Computer Science
Department of Language Science and Technology
Saarland Informatics Campus, Saarland University, Germany
{dongqipu,vera}@lst.uni-saarland.de

Abstract

Large-scale language models, like ChatGPT, have garnered significant media attention and stunned the public with their remarkable capacity for generating coherent text from short natural language prompts. In this paper, we aim to conduct a systematic inspection of ChatGPT's performance in two controllable generation tasks, with respect to ChatGPT's ability to adapt its output to different target audiences (expert vs. layman) and writing styles (formal vs. informal). Additionally, we evaluate the faithfulness of the generated text, and compare the model's performance with human-authored texts. Our findings indicate that the stylistic variations produced by humans are considerably larger than those demonstrated by ChatGPT, and the generated texts diverge from human samples in several characteristics, such as the distribution of word types. Moreover, we observe that ChatGPT sometimes incorporates factual errors or hallucinations when adapting the text to suit a specific style.[1]

1 Introduction

Generative Pre-trained Transformer (GPT; *e.g.*, ChatGPT) models, which produce results from given conditional input prompts, have exhibited exceptional performance on various natural language understanding (NLU) and generation (NLG) tasks (Jiao et al., 2023; Wang et al., 2023a; Bang et al., 2023b; Zhou et al., 2023; Dai et al., 2023). For instance, in NLU tasks, Qin et al. (2023) have proved that ChatGPT is comparable to state-of-the-art fine-tuning models in language reasoning. In NLG tasks, Yang et al. (2023a) assessed four widely used benchmark datasets, such as QMSum, and confirmed ChatGPT's comparability to traditional fine-tuning methods. Peng et al. (2023) further investigated effective strategies for machine translation using ChatGPT and highlight its strong translation ability. Additionally, ChatGPT can even facilitate multi-modal tasks (Yang et al., 2023b; Shen et al., 2023), as well as the application of data augmentation (Dai et al., 2023). Although the studies mentioned above have demonstrated notable performance of ChatGPT across different domains, there remains a dearth of qualitative and quantitative evaluation of the texts generated by ChatGPT. Such an evaluation is vital to uncover the behavioral differences, potential limitations, and challenges associated with ChatGPT-generated texts, especially when compared with human-authored texts.

Controllable text generation seems to be a task in which ChatGPT-like models could potentially excel. This task is driven by the desire to tailor text for a diverse array of target users (*e.g.,* experts and laypersons) (Kumar et al., 2022; Cao et al., 2020; Luo et al., 2022), and thereby enhancing the accessibility of textual information. In controllable text generation, one delineates a particular set of parameters or provides a prompt that defines the intended target style. This area has recently received growing interest from researchers in the field (Hu and Li, 2021; Li et al., 2022; Zhang et al., 2022; Dathathri et al., 2019a; August et al., 2022; Carlsson et al., 2022; Gu et al., 2022; Li et al., 2022; Keskar et al., 2019; Dathathri et al., 2019b). The traditional natural language generation task (Pu and Sima'an, 2022), which focuses solely on adequately responding with respect to a given input, can be regarded as a special case of controllable natural language generation, wherein the control setting remains unconditioned. Considering ChatGPT as the most recent language generation capability, the assessment of its language generation proficiency, specifically in the realm of controllable language generation, remains largely uncharted. Therefore, our study delves into two distinct applications of ChatGPT, namely controllable summary generation and sentence style trans-

[1]The project information of our study can be accessed at https://dongqi.me/projects/ChatGPT_vs_Human.

Proceedings of the 61st Annual Meeting of the Association for Computational Linguistics - Student Research Workshop, pages 1–18

fer. In the former, we examine ChatGPT's ability to generate summaries that cater to two distinct readerships, namely experts and non-experts, for a given academic literature. Concerning sentence style transfer, we investigate ChatGPT's capability to generate both formal and informal sentences for the task of sentence formality.

The objective of this study is to tackle the research question: **In relation to the human-produced text, to what extent does ChatGPT-generated content demonstrate significant divergence from human behavior and the potential susceptibility to inaccuracies?** Our primary contributions are enumerated below:

- To the best of our knowledge, we are the first to utilize ChatGPT to evaluate its effectiveness in controllable text generation.
- Our findings indicate that there are substantial performance disparities between the text generated by ChatGPT and that generated by humans.
- Our study exposes and quantifies the existence of numerous hard-to-spot errors in the text generated by ChatGPT, which have a tendency to amplify with successive transformations of the text.

2 Related Work

2.1 Controllable Text Summarization

Controllable text summarization is a rapidly evolving field that aims to produce summaries with specific characteristics, such as length, style, or content (Shen et al., 2022b; Chan et al., 2021; Sarkhel et al., 2020; Shen et al., 2022a; Goldsack et al., 2022; Keskar et al., 2019; Dathathri et al., 2019b; He et al., 2022; Earle et al., 2021; Liu et al., 2022b). A range of approaches has been proposed for this task, including the use of sequence-to-sequence models such as the Transformer model (Vaswani et al., 2017). These models have demonstrated promising progress in producing high-quality summaries that can be modulated according to specific requirements (Fan et al., 2018; Wu et al., 2021; Amplayo et al., 2021). Additionally, other techniques also have been proposed to enhance the controllability of the summaries, such as conditional generation (He et al., 2022; Luo et al., 2022), prompt-based summarization (Yang et al., 2022; Liu et al., 2022a; Zhang and Song, 2022), and multi-task learning (Cui and Hu, 2021; Gu et al., 2022).

2.2 Text Style Transfer

Text style transfer is a task that involves transforming an input sentence into a desired style while retaining its style-independent semantics (Jin et al., 2022; Zhu et al., 2021; Dai et al., 2019; Li et al., 2020; Babakov et al., 2022; Mir et al., 2019; Ramesh Kashyap et al., 2022; Tokpo and Calders, 2022). To achieve this, prior research has examined sequence-to-sequence learning strategies that utilize parallel corpora with paired source/target sentences in different styles (Cheng et al., 2020; Hu et al., 2021; Nouri, 2022). Owing to the considerable demand for human resources and material investments in data labeling, parallel data across diverse styles are scarce. This has led to an increased interest in exploring more pragmatic situations where only non-parallel stylized corpora are accessible (Malmi et al., 2020; Reif et al., 2022).

2.3 ChatGPT

ChatGPT[2] is a large language model (LLM), which is built upon the innovations and improvements of its predecessors, such as GPT-3[3]. In terms of training strategies, ChatGPT employs instruction learning and reinforcement learning from human feedback (RLHF; Ouyang et al., 2022) to enhance its overall performance and adaptability.

Upon its emergence, ChatGPT has garnered considerable attention from researchers, who have undertaken initial studies into the model. Scholars such as Baidoo-Anu and Owusu Ansah (2023); Rudolph et al. (2023); West (2023); Sobania et al. (2023); Gilson et al. (2023); Lai et al. (2023); Wang et al. (2023b) have explored the notable strengths of ChatGPT from the fields of education, science, programming, healthcare, and text generation, respectively. However, Bang et al. (2023a) discovered that ChatGPT suffers from hallucination issues in the context of logical reasoning. Due to its immense and inaccessible training corpus and parameters, and the inability to access external knowledge for reliable sources of support, it is imperative to question whether ChatGPT demonstrates the same hallucination issue as other LLMs when performing sentence generation. Based on these clues, we firmly assert that in-depth analysis of the text generated by ChatGPT and its behavioral patterns are both significant and valuable, and can provide meaningful insights to the readers of this paper.

[2] https://openai.com/blog/chatgpt

[3] https://openai.com/research/instruction-following

3 Study on Controllable Summarization

3.1 Prompt Formulation

In this section, our main objective is to test the zero-shot performance of ChatGPT on controllable summarization, with the goal to generate summaries for laymen vs. experts. To this end, we constructed several prompts as natural language instructions for ChatGPT. The prompts we tested include for the layman style: *Please give me a layman / simple / simplified and understandable / easy-to-comprehend / straightforward / general audience summary of X*, where X was replaced by the source text that should be summarized. Similarly, for the expert summary, we experimented with the prompts: *Please give me an expert / a technical / comprehensive and detailed / difficult-to-comprehend / in-depth / complicated summary of X*.

3.2 Experimental Setup

For all experiments, we used ChatGPT *gpt-3.5-turbo*, which was, at the time of experimentation, the best-performing publicly accessible version provided by OpenAI. For the hyper-parameter setting, we set temperature = 0, top p = 1, frequency penalty = 0.2, and presence penalty = 0.2. For summary generation, we configured the maximum number of generated tokens to 512. The remaining hyper-parameters were set to their default values as recommended by OpenAI. It is noteworthy that ChatGPT has the potential to generate empty responses (i.e., empty strings) as the result of network transmission timeouts or API request overloads. Should this arise, we adhere to the established practice of resubmitting the request until ChatGPT provides non-empty responses.

All of our experiments were conducted on the version of ChatGPT between 15 Feb 2023 and 30 Apr 2023 by using the OpenAI's ChatGPT API.[4] We should emphasize that to prevent any potential interference from the prior responses, we cleared the conversation history each time we submit a new query to ChatGPT. Unless otherwise specified, we refrained from engaging in any further conversation with ChatGPT to modify its responses.

3.3 Dataset

We selected ELIFE (Goldsack et al., 2022) dataset for our experiments. It contains summaries of academic literature that exhibit varying levels of readability, tailored to suit either expert or non-expert audiences. By means of this dataset, we can examine to what extent ChatGPT can regulate the summary generation process in accordance with the intended target users, and compare its summaries to human summaries.

3.4 Metrics

In order to assess automatically whether ChatGPT summaries substantially differ in terms of their audience design based on the given prompt, we opted for a set of three automatic readability metrics: Flesch Reading Ease (FRE; Kincaid et al., 1975), Coleman-Liau Index (CLI; Coleman and Liau, 1975), and Dale-Chall Readability Score (DCR; Chall and Dale, 1995).

The Flesch Reading Ease (Kincaid et al., 1975) is a metric that gauges the comprehensibility of a given text. This index relies on the average number of syllables per word and the average number of words per sentence. A higher score signifies an easier-to-understand text. Additionally, the Coleman-Liau Index (Coleman and Liau, 1975) is a measure of the text's difficulty level, which considers the average number of characters per sentence and the average number of sentences per 100 words. A higher score indicates a more challenging text. The Dale-Chall Readability Score (Chall and Dale, 1995) is computed by comparing the number of complex words in the text with a list of common words. A higher score denotes a more challenging text.

We also employed Rouge scores (Lin, 2004) to evaluate the performance of ChatGPT in the task of text summarization, with the aim of comparing its efficacy against the state-of-the-art model. In order to assess the extent to which the summaries re-use word sequences from the original text, we furthermore evaluated N-gram novelty (See et al., 2017; Gehrmann et al., 2019; Pu et al., 2022). Finally, we quantified inconsistency based on factual consistency checking metric SummaC (Laban et al., 2022), as well as hallucination checking metric (Cao et al., 2022; Fischer et al., 2021). SummaC (Laban et al., 2022) uses sentence compression and summarization techniques to extract important information and improve the detection of inconsistencies in NLI models by segmenting documents and aggregating scores. Named entity hallucination (Fischer et al., 2021) flags potential hallucinations

[4]https://platform.openai.com/overview

in named entities if they do not match the original sources. We here used BERT semantic similarity, rather than exact matching, when computing the named entities matching.

3.5 Results on Controllable Summarization

3.5.1 Effect of Prompt Formulation

Table 1 illustrates that different prompt versions are somewhat consistent regarding whether the instructions asking for layman summaries actually lead to more readable texts than those asking for expert summaries, with FRE ranging between scores of 31 and 38 for automatically generated layman summaries, and between 28 and 37 for automatically generated expert summaries. Conversely, human-written summaries exhibit very large differences according to the automatic metrics, with FRE of 53.1 for layman summaries and 22.5 for expert summaries. Similar effects are observed for the CLI and DCR measures. This preliminary test was conducted on a subset of the ELIFE dataset, containing merely 500 random samples; for the rest of the tests, we proceeded to the entire dataset, selecting the prompts asking for "layman" and "expert" summaries, as responses for these prompts seemed to align with the right direction wrt. the readability measures.

Prompt version	FRE	CLI	DCR
layman	37.26†	14.82†	11.21†
simple	31.92†	15.70†	11.54†
simplified and understand.	35.48†	15.17†	11.21†
easy-to-comprehend	36.59†	14.93†	11.32†
straightforward	31.74†	15.58†	11.42†
general audience	35.86†	14.98†	10.96†
human answer (for layman)	53.06	12.36	8.90
expert	29.89†	15.91†	11.88†
technical	36.65†	13.76†	12.20†
comprehensive and detailed	31.62†	15.47†	11.15†
difficult-to-comprehend	28.95†	16.14†	11.71†
in-depth	34.37†	14.93†	10.82†
complicated	29.05†	15.76†	11.40†
human answer (for expert)	22.54	17.65	11.79

Table 1: Reading difficulty on different prompts, tested on a set of 500 randomly selected items from the dataset. † indicates statistical significance ($p<0.05$) against corresponding human answers via paired t-test.

3.5.2 Reading Difficulty Control

Table 2 corroborates that the results of the whole dataset are consistent with the findings from the smaller sample. We conclude that ChatGPT can produce summaries with different levels of reading difficulty to a certain extent based on the provided prompts. Notably, ChatGPT-generated sentences for expert-style summaries show greater complexity than those for layman-style summaries. However, the magnitude of the difference in the reading difficulty scores between the two types of summaries is considerably smaller than that observed in human-written summaries.

Candidate	FRE	CLI	DCR
Human Layman	52.42	12.46	8.93
Human Expert	23.20	17.62	11.78
ChatGPT Layman	37.38†‡	14.78†‡	11.17†‡
ChatGPT Expert	30.38†‡	15.82†‡	11.85†‡

Table 2: Reading difficulty scores by automatic metrics; † and ‡ indicate statistical significance ($p<0.05$) against same-style human answers, and opposite-style ChatGPT answers via paired t-test, respectively.

3.5.3 Comparison to Previous SOTA Model

We also compared summaries generated by ChatGPT to a previous state-of-the-art (SOTA) neural fine-tuned summarization model (Pu et al., 2023). On the same test split, the summaries produced by ChatGPT reached Rouge-1=25.53, Rouge-2=5.48, Rouge-L=13.30 under unsupervised learning, and Rouge-1=47.88, Rouge-2=13.75, Rouge-L=42.44 in few-shot learning use the training samples from the same subset of Section 3.5.1, while the model by Pu et al. (2023) reached Rouge-1=48.70, Rouge-2=14.84, and Rouge-L=46.13.

3.5.4 Disparities in Summarization Behavior

We next examined whether ChatGPT and Humans are consistent with each other regarding the readability of summarization with respect to different items – it could be possible, that some texts simply lead to less readable summaries than others. However, we discovered that Pearson correlations of FRE scores for summaries by humans and ChatGPT were only 0.31 for expert summaries, and 0.2 for layman summaries. (Scores were similarly low for the CLI and DCR metrics.) In addition, the statistical significance test elucidates the noteworthy divergence between the distinctive response styles produced by ChatGPT and the analogous styles of human-generated answers.

Following this, we contrasted the n-gram novelty of human vs. ChatGPT summaries wrt. the original texts. Figure 1 reveals that a significantly higher number of novel 4-grams are present in human-written summaries, particularly those aimed at laymen. This suggests that ChatGPT summaries are slightly more extractive compared to human summaries.

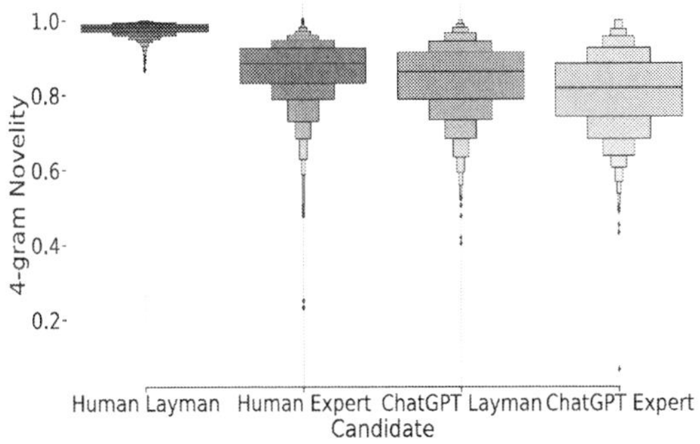

Figure 1: Comparison of abstractiveness between ChatGPT and human-generated summaries

3.5.5 Inconsistencies and Hallucinations

Given that ChatGPT has previously been reported to generate misinformation, we sought to evaluate its risk of hallucinating on our specific task. Figure 2 demonstrates that the SummaC consistency scores are lower for ChatGPT-generated summaries than for human-written summaries. A corresponding phenomenon is verified in the hallucination assessment. Precision scores provided in Table 3 demonstrates the extent to which ChatGPT-generated text contains named entities that are absent in the source text. A lower precision score suggests that the generated text has more named entities that lack support in the source text. The recall scores reflect the ability of ChatGPT to capture named entities from the source text. A lower recall score implies that ChatGPT has missed a considerable number of named entities from the source text. F1 score represents the harmonic mean of the precision and recall scores. By examining Table 3, our findings demonstrate that ChatGPT generates a greater number of named entities that are not present in the source text after undergoing multiple iterations of text conversions and modification. For example, in an expert summary, ChatGPT misinterpreted the meaning of "Geocode" as "regional regulations".

3.6 Intermediary Discussion

Our experiments show that ChatGPT-generated summaries do not adapt as strongly to the target audience as human-authored summaries. One possible reason could be that ChatGPT, given the zero-shot setting, had no way to "know" how strongly the texts should be adapted to the target style. Furthermore, we identified evidence for potential hallucinations generated during summarization. We, therefore, carried out two post-hoc experiments: (1) We modified the prompt to include an example from the dataset, so ChatGPT would have a chance to know the expected level of text adaptation. (2) We subjected the resulting summaries to several re-writing steps and test whether this further intensifies the occurrence of hallucinations.

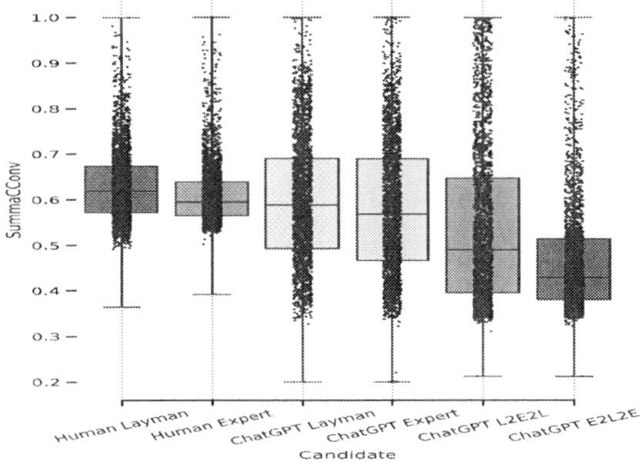

Figure 2: Summary consistency detection. L stands for layman, E for expert.

Candidate	Precision	Recall	F1
Human Layman	0.78	0.63	0.70
Human Expert	0.92	0.61	0.73
ChatGPT Layman	$0.75^{\ddagger}$	$0.47^{\dagger}$	$0.58^{\dagger}$
ChatGPT Expert	$0.90^{\ddagger}$	$0.49^{\dagger}$	$0.63^{\dagger}$
ChatGPT L2E2L	$0.74^{\ddagger}$	$0.39^{\dagger\ddagger}$	$0.51^{\dagger\ddagger}$
ChatGPT E2L2E	$0.88^{\ddagger}$	$0.47^{\dagger\ddagger}$	$0.62^{\dagger\ddagger}$

Table 3: Named entity hallucination on Elife dataset. † and ‡ indicate statistical significance ($p<0.05$) against same-style human answers, and opposite-style ChatGPT answers via paired t-test, respectively. L stands for layman, E for expert.

3.6.1 Follow-up Experiment: Example Inclusion in Prompt

We experimented with prompts that also include a human summary example. Unlike the previous few-shot learning experiment, we do not adjust the parameters of the ChatGPT, but just let the model perform unsupervised reasoning through the contents of the prompt. We observe (see Appendix Table 7) that when guided by a human example from the dataset, the summaries generated by ChatGPT indeed tend to be more aligned with human performance, particularly on the Flesch Reading Ease metric (49.23 for layman, 28.88 for expert summaries). However, no significant changes are detected in other metrics. The degree of control over the summarization style has increased, yet it remains inferior to human capabilities.

3.6.2 Follow-up Experiment: Repeated Re-writing

Summaries are further re-written based on the prompt *Please give me a* ***layman/expert*** *style* <u>*version*</u> *of* X, where X was the previously generated summary. Figure 2 and Table 3 display the performance of ChatGPT after re-writing in the entries "ChatGPT L2E2L" and "ChatGPT E2L2E" which stand for the order in which instructions were given (L stands for layman, and E for expert). The examinations point out that misinformation and hallucinations may be further increased during subsequent rewriting (lower SummaC scores, lower values in the named entity hallucination metric).

4 Study on Text Formality Transfer

4.1 Prompt Formulation and Experimental Setup

Our subsequent set of experiments investigates ChatGPT's capacity for style transfer concerning language formality. Our prompt for this task was formulated as *Please give me a* ***formal*** */ an* ***informal*** <u>*version*</u> *of* X. We utilized the same experimental setup as for the summarization task; however, we restricted the maximum number of generated tokens to 32. We again experimented with various prompts, as shown in Table 4 below. Unless otherwise specified, all experiments used the same configuration.

4.2 Dataset

We investigated whether ChatGPT can proficiently execute style transfer on sentences using data from the GYAFC (Rao and Tetreault, 2018) dataset. The dataset has two branches, Entertainment & Music (EM) and Family & Relationships (FR). With the aid of this dataset, we aim to evaluate ChatGPT's ability for sentence style transfer, examine the differences in vocabulary selection and syntactic structures between ChatGPT and human performance, and identify the limitations of ChatGPT.

4.3 Metrics

To evaluate the level of formality in the generated text, we utilized Text Formality Score (Heylighen and Dewaele, 1999) and MTLD Lexical Diversity (McCarthy and Jarvis, 2010) metric. The Text Formality Score (Heylighen and Dewaele, 1999) is a metric that quantifies the degree of formality in language usage within a text, based on the adherence to formal linguistic norms. Another measure that evaluates language formality is the MTLD Lexical Diversity metric (McCarthy and Jarvis, 2010). This index measures the diversity and richness of the vocabulary used in the text, based on the frequency and number of unique words. A higher MTLD score indicates a greater variety of vocabulary, which typically corresponds to a more formal language style. We also utilized BLEU (Papineni et al., 2002) score to draw a comparison between ChatGPT and SOTA approach. We additionally assessed the distribution of POS tags in the generated different styles, as well as the distribution of dependency labels[5]. For quantifying misinformation and hallucinations, we used DAE and named entity hallucination checking. The DAE algorithm (Goyal and Durrett, 2020) utilizes dependency arcs to identify entailment relationships between propositions and identify inconsistencies in factual information based on syntactic and semantic structures.

4.4 Results on Formality Control

4.4.1 Effect of Prompt Formulation

Table 4 presents the results for a set of 500 random samples from the GYAFC dataset. We observe that the Formality scores are very similar for ChatGPT formal vs. informal texts. We note however that the difference in ratings for human-written texts is also small for this metric. The MTLD metric on the other hand shows higher values for ChatGPT-generated formal texts; in fact, the scores are substantially larger than those of human-written texts, but differ not much from each other. We therefore proceed with the prompts using the formulation formal/informal for the rest of the experiments on the whole dataset.

4.4.2 Sentence Formality Control

Table 5 offers supplementary evidence from the full dataset supporting ChatGPT's capacity to modify the formality level of sentences. By employing the Formality indicator (Heylighen and Dewaele, 1999), it is apparent that the generated text tends to manifest a higher level of formality overall. A primary factor contributing to this result is the pre-

[5]https://spacy.io/

Prompt version	Formality	MTLD
informal	51.09	13.22†
unprofessional	51.20	16.23†
spoken version	51.30†	14.47†
easygoing	51.43†	14.11†
casual	51.00	16.30†
laid-back	51.27	13.94†
human answer (for informal)	50.76	11.42
formal	52.22†	31.23†
professional	51.96†	31.98†
written	51.62†	29.69†
stately	51.30†	34.43†
grandiose	52.85†	30.71†
majestic	52.23†	33.49†
human answer (for formal)	53.92	14.99

Table 4: Text formality on different prompts, tested on a set of 500 randomly selected items from the dataset. † indicates statistical significance ($p<0.05$) against corresponding human answers via paired t-test.

disposition of ChatGPT's training corpus towards written sources, encompassing materials such as books and news articles, as opposed to spoken language corpora (OpenAI, 2023). This perspective is further corroborated by an examination of the generated sentence samples. The MTLD metric underscores that ChatGPT's lexical diversity is considerably lower when generating informal sentences, but shows a marked increase when generating formal sentences.

Dataset	Candidate	Formality	MTLD
GYAFC-FR	Human Informal	49.87	15.20
	Human Formal	53.57	18.70
	ChatGPT Informal	50.77†‡	14.60‡
	ChatGPT Formal	52.06†‡	31.68†‡
GYAFC-EM	Human Informal	50.11	12.11
	Human Formal	53.76	15.82
	ChatGPT Informal	51.02†‡	12.01‡
	ChatGPT Formal	51.98†‡	29.80†‡

Table 5: Text formality scores by automatic metrics; † and ‡ indicate statistical significance ($p<0.05$) against same-style human answers, and opposite-style ChatGPT answers via paired t-test, respectively.

4.4.3 Comparison to Previous SOTA Model

We also find that ChatGPT outperforms the previous supervised SOTA model (Nouri, 2022) by training on the same subset at Section 4.4.1 for few-shot learning, as evident from the higher BLEU score. Specifically, ChatGPT yields superior scores of 0.711 and 0.697 in the EM and FR branches, as compared to the SOTA model's scores of 0.671 and 0.652. However, ChatGPT achieved only 0.07 and 0.06 BLEU scores on the EM and FR branches, respectively, in the unsupervised setting.

4.4.4 Effect of Example Inclusion in Prompt

We again examined the impact of including an example of the dataset into the prompt and find that this again helps ChatGPT slightly with matching the dataset style (with details provided in Table 8). Specifically, the formality score for the informal style is 50.67, while it climbs to 52.13 for the formal style, with the MTLD score also displaying an increase from 14.81 for informal texts to 19.22 for formal texts.

4.4.5 Disparities in Style Transfer Behavior

In terms of controlling the formality of sentence style, ChatGPT's performance still exhibits significant differences compared to human behavior. While the by-item correlation is slightly higher for this dataset than for the summary task (Pearson correlation of around 0.4 for formal style and 0.5 for informal style on the Formality metric; 0.3 for MTLD measure), there are interesting disparities between the distributions of POS tags between ChatGPT and humans. The examination of statistical significance further substantiates our antecedent observation, indicating a substantial disparity between the different response styles engendered by the model, as well as between the answers conforming to the same styles exhibited by humans.

Figure 3 illustrates the absolute differences in the distribution of Part-of-Speech (POS) tags. Based on this figure, it is evident that ChatGPT employs a higher frequency of adjectives, adpositions, determiners, and nouns in the generation of formal sentences when compared to those produced by human writers. Conversely, in the generation of informal sentences, ChatGPT tends to utilize more auxiliary words and punctuation marks. These variances in word choice between formal and informal styles, as exemplified by ChatGPT, are indicative of differences in its selected vocabulary for distinct stylistic modes compare with humans.

By analyzing the distribution of dependency labels (Appendix Figures 5, 6, 7, 8), it is also clear that, in comparison to human-authored sentences, ChatGPT utilizes a greater frequency of adjectival modifiers, auxiliaries, determiners, objects of the preposition, and prepositional modifiers for formal sentences. Contrarily, compounds and dependents are infrequently employed in the generation of informal sentences by ChatGPT.

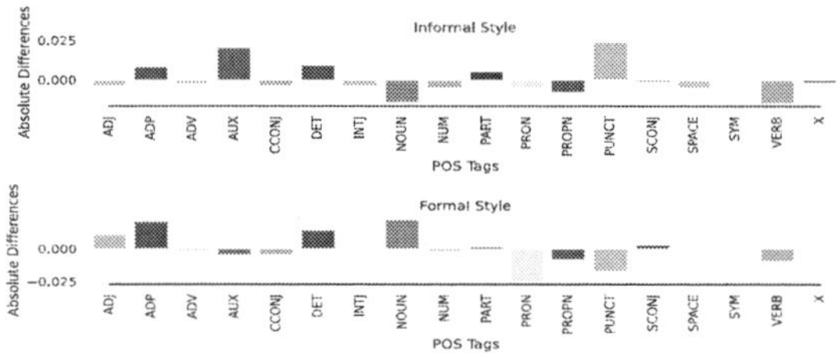

Figure 3: Absolute differences in POS tags distribution of ChatGPT and human-generated sentences: GYAFC - EM

4.4.6 Inconsistencies and Hallucinations

In order to assess the risk of introducing erroneous information when ChatGPT performs sentence style transformation, we employed DAE (Goyal and Durrett, 2020) at the sentence level to examine the factuality after text style transformation, and compare again the effect of multiple re-writes. Similar to before, F denotes formal style, I signifies informal style, and X2X2X ($X \in \{F, I\}$) represents multiple rewriting transformations of the text. The outcomes of our inquiry are depicted in Figure 4, and Appendix Figure 14. We also again scrutinized the potential incorporation of hallucinatory information regarding named entities in the ChatGPT-generated text, and the findings are presented in Appendix Table 9.

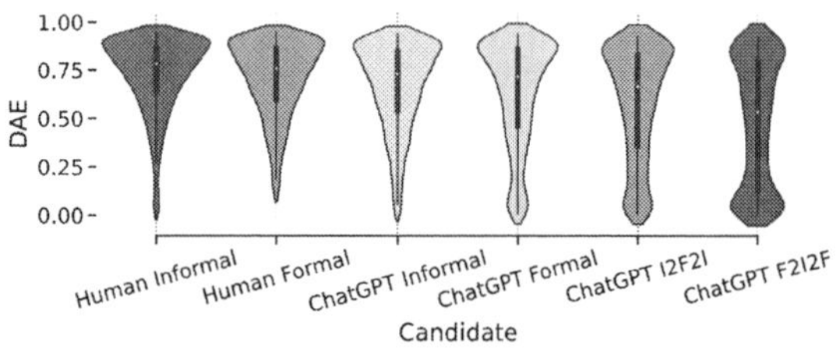

Figure 4: Dependency arc entailment: GYAFC - EM. Data points>0.95≈Accurate. To clarify discrepancies, cutoff point=0.95.

Upon conducting factuality checking (see Figure 4, and Appendix Figure 14), it is discovered that ChatGPT's performance is inferior to that of humans in sentence-style rewriting. Interestingly, with the increase in the number of text conversions and rewritings, ChatGPT's tendency to commit factual errors escalates while the output increasingly deviates from the original text, compromising the fidelity of the final result. In a particular instance, the human-generated formal expression states "She is a poor vocalist", whereas the formal rendition provided by ChatGPT articulates "She does not possess the ability to sing". This discrepancy represents a significant semantic alteration. The degree of dependency arc entailment is low in this case. Similarly, Appendix Table 9 reveals that recall scores on the named entity hallucination metric are lower in ChatGPT sentences than in human sentences.

4.4.7 Qualitative Examples

To explore whether ChatGPT-generated sentences significantly alter the original semantics of the input text, we conducted a case study by randomly selecting 15 samples from each branch of the GYAFC dataset. Our findings indicate that ChatGPT poses a relatively severe risk of modifying the original semantics during sentence style transformation, with approximately 18% of the samples exhibiting noticeable semantic inconsistencies. The examples in Table 6 reveal that during the process of sentence style transfer, ChatGPT erroneously modifies the content words, resulting in significant semantic alterations.

Formal to Informal	
It is such a waste of TV space.	(Reference)
Yes, because it's such a waste of TV space!	(Human)
What a total waste of TV time!	(ChatGPT)
The other boy isn't that great.	(Reference)
The other boy is not that good.	(Human)
The other kid's not so hot.	(ChatGPT)
I really enjoy how the composition has the tec...	(Reference)
I really like how they do like the whole techn...	(Human)
I'm diggin' how the techno beat slows down in ...	(ChatGPT)
Informal to Formal	
Fatboy Slim - Right Here, Right Now Or any oth...	(Reference)
Fatboy Slim is right here and now. He Rocks!	(Human)
Fatboy Slim's "Right Here, Right Now" is an ex...	(ChatGPT)
loved them since their first album.	(Reference)
I have loved them since their first album.	(Human)
I have held a fondness for them since the rele...	(ChatGPT)
if u occasionally doing it then u alrady r add...	(Reference)
If you occasionally do it, then you are already...	(Human)
If you are engaging in the activity on a regul...	(ChatGPT)

Table 6: Case study of ChatGPT generated output

Furthermore, our examination of the visualized dependency tree (see Appendix Figures 11, 12, and 13), which relies primarily on the dependency arc entailment (DAE) algorithm for fact-checking, reveals that the text generated by ChatGPT contains a higher number of dependency arcs lacking support from the original text, when compared to human responses.

5 Conclusion

This paper presents a broad assessment of ChatGPT's proficiency in generating controllable text. We conducted quantitative and qualitative examinations at the document level (summarization task) and sentence level (text style transfer). The empirical findings show that ChatGPT outperforms the previous state-of-the-art models on automatic metrics, but that there are substantial disparities between its generated texts and human-written texts. These disparities are reduced by providing a target example of the human writing style. Furthermore, our investigations also confirm the previously reported problems of hallucinations and inaccuracies in text generated by ChatGPT.

6 Limitations

The primary limitations of the current study pertain to the selection of prompts and evaluation metrics. The experimental cost of requesting API responses from OpenAI to assess ChatGPT's text generation abilities imposes significant constraints on our choice of datasets. Therefore, we have to limit our experimentation to only two related controllable text generation datasets. While we have evaluated ChatGPT's performance at both the document and sentence levels, we cannot extrapolate that ChatGPT has similar performance for other text generation datasets. Additionally, the experimental cost prohibits us from conducting traversal experiments on the selection of hyperparameters. We relied on the default configuration recommended by OpenAI, and we maintain consistency in all hyperparameters to ensure the fairness of the experiments.

Secondly, although we have studied the impact of prompt engineering on ChatGPT, the selection of prompts is mainly affected by human understanding, and the number of potential prompts is infinite. Hence, we cannot guarantee whether other prompts that we did not select will yield the same conclusions as our experiment. Furthermore, ChatGPT is subject to continuous updates and iterations, which may lead to improved performance, making it difficult to predict if future versions of ChatGPT will have similar results to our experiments.

Finally, to select appropriate evaluation metrics, we have included both domain-related evaluation metrics (such as reading difficulty and text formality) and domain-independent evaluation indicators (such as fact-checking and hallucination detection). However, we acknowledge that the automatic metrics may sometimes not capture all aspects of the intended construct correctly.

7 Ethics Considerations

All datasets utilized in this study are publicly available, and we have adhered to ethical considerations by not introducing any additional information into ChatGPT's inputs.

Acknowledgements

This project has received funding from the European Research Council (ERC) under the European Union's Horizon 2020 Research and Innovation Programme (Grant Agreement No. 948878).

References

Reinald Kim Amplayo, Stefanos Angelidis, and Mirella Lapata. 2021. Aspect-controllable opinion summarization. In *Proceedings of the 2021 Conference on Empirical Methods in Natural Language Processing*, pages 6578–6593, Online and Punta Cana, Dominican Republic. Association for Computational Linguistics.

Tal August, Katharina Reinecke, and Noah A. Smith. 2022. Generating scientific definitions with controllable complexity. In *Proceedings of the 60th Annual Meeting of the Association for Computational Linguistics (Volume 1: Long Papers)*, pages 8298–8317, Dublin, Ireland. Association for Computational Linguistics.

Nikolay Babakov, David Dale, Varvara Logacheva, and Alexander Panchenko. 2022. A large-scale computational study of content preservation measures for text style transfer and paraphrase generation. In *Proceedings of the 60th Annual Meeting of the Association for Computational Linguistics: Student Research Workshop*, pages 300–321, Dublin, Ireland. Association for Computational Linguistics.

David Baidoo-Anu and Leticia Owusu Ansah. 2023. Education in the era of generative artificial intelligence (ai): Understanding the potential benefits of chatgpt in promoting teaching and learning. *Available at SSRN 4337484*.

Yejin Bang, Samuel Cahyawijaya, Nayeon Lee, Wenliang Dai, Dan Su, Bryan Wilie, Holy Lovenia, Ziwei Ji, Tiezheng Yu, Willy Chung, Quyet V. Do, Yan Xu, and Pascale Fung. 2023a. A multitask, multilingual, multimodal evaluation of chatgpt on reasoning, hallucination, and interactivity. *ArXiv*, abs/2302.04023.

Yejin Bang, Samuel Cahyawijaya, Nayeon Lee, Wenliang Dai, Dan Su, Bryan Wilie, Holy Lovenia, Ziwei Ji, Tiezheng Yu, Willy Chung, et al. 2023b. A multitask, multilingual, multimodal evaluation of chatgpt on reasoning, hallucination, and interactivity. *arXiv preprint arXiv:2302.04023*.

Meng Cao, Yue Dong, and Jackie Cheung. 2022. Hallucinated but factual! inspecting the factuality of hallucinations in abstractive summarization. In *Proceedings of the 60th Annual Meeting of the Association for Computational Linguistics (Volume 1: Long Papers)*, pages 3340–3354, Dublin, Ireland. Association for Computational Linguistics.

Yixin Cao, Ruihao Shui, Liangming Pan, Min-Yen Kan, Zhiyuan Liu, and Tat-Seng Chua. 2020. Expertise style transfer: A new task towards better communication between experts and laymen. In *Proceedings of the 58th Annual Meeting of the Association for Computational Linguistics*, pages 1061–1071, Online. Association for Computational Linguistics.

Fredrik Carlsson, Joey Öhman, Fangyu Liu, Severine Verlinden, Joakim Nivre, and Magnus Sahlgren. 2022. Fine-grained controllable text generation using non-residual prompting. In *Proceedings of the 60th Annual Meeting of the Association for Computational Linguistics (Volume 1: Long Papers)*, pages 6837–6857, Dublin, Ireland. Association for Computational Linguistics.

Jeanne Sternlicht Chall and Edgar Dale. 1995. *Readability revisited: The new Dale-Chall readability formula*. Brookline Books.

Hou Pong Chan, Lu Wang, and Irwin King. 2021. Controllable summarization with constrained Markov decision process. *Transactions of the Association for Computational Linguistics*, 9:1213–1232.

Yu Cheng, Zhe Gan, Yizhe Zhang, Oussama Elachqar, Dianqi Li, and Jingjing Liu. 2020. Contextual text style transfer. In *Findings of the Association for Computational Linguistics: EMNLP 2020*, pages 2915–2924, Online. Association for Computational Linguistics.

Meri Coleman and Ta Lin Liau. 1975. A computer readability formula designed for machine scoring. *Journal of Applied Psychology*, 60(2):283.

Peng Cui and Le Hu. 2021. Topic-guided abstractive multi-document summarization. In *Findings of the Association for Computational Linguistics: EMNLP 2021*, pages 1463–1472, Punta Cana, Dominican Republic. Association for Computational Linguistics.

Haixing Dai, Zhengliang Liu, Wenxiong Liao, Xiaoke Huang, Zihao Wu, Lin Zhao, Wei Liu, Ninghao Liu, Sheng Li, Dajiang Zhu, et al. 2023. Chataug: Leveraging chatgpt for text data augmentation. *arXiv preprint arXiv:2302.13007*.

Ning Dai, Jianze Liang, Xipeng Qiu, and Xuanjing Huang. 2019. Style transformer: Unpaired text style transfer without disentangled latent representation. In *Proceedings of the 57th Annual Meeting of the Association for Computational Linguistics*, pages 5997–6007, Florence, Italy. Association for Computational Linguistics.

Sumanth Dathathri, Andrea Madotto, Janice Lan, Jane Hung, Eric Frank, Piero Molino, Jason Yosinski, and Rosanne Liu. 2019a. Plug and play language models: A simple approach to controlled text generation. *arXiv preprint arXiv:1912.02164*.

Sumanth Dathathri, Andrea Madotto, Janice Lan, Jane Hung, Eric Frank, Piero Molino, Jason Yosinski, and Rosanne Liu. 2019b. Plug and play language models: A simple approach to controlled text generation. *ArXiv*, abs/1912.02164.

Sam Earle, Maria Edwards, Ahmed Khalifa, Philip Bontrager, and Julian Togelius. 2021. Learning controllable content generators. In *2021 IEEE Conference on Games (CoG)*, pages 1–9. IEEE.

Angela Fan, David Grangier, and Michael Auli. 2018. Controllable abstractive summarization. In *Proceedings of the 2nd Workshop on Neural Machine Translation and Generation*, pages 45–54, Melbourne, Australia. Association for Computational Linguistics.

T. Fischer, C. Biemann, Informatik und Naturwissenschaften Universität Hamburg Fakultät für Mathematik, and Universität Hamburg Fachbereich Informatik. 2021. *Finding Factual Inconsistencies in Abstractive Summaries*. Universität Hamburg.

Sebastian Gehrmann, Zachary Ziegler, and Alexander Rush. 2019. Generating abstractive summaries with finetuned language models. In *Proceedings of the 12th International Conference on Natural Language Generation*, pages 516–522, Tokyo, Japan. Association for Computational Linguistics.

Aidan Gilson, Conrad W Safranek, Thomas Huang, Vimig Socrates, Ling Chi, Richard Andrew Taylor, David Chartash, et al. 2023. How does chatgpt perform on the united states medical licensing examination? the implications of large language models for medical education and knowledge assessment. *JMIR Medical Education*, 9(1):e45312.

Tomas Goldsack, Zhihao Zhang, Chenghua Lin, and Carolina Scarton. 2022. Making science simple: Corpora for the lay summarisation of scientific literature. In *Proceedings of the 2022 Conference on Empirical Methods in Natural Language Processing*, pages 10589–10604, Abu Dhabi, United Arab Emirates. Association for Computational Linguistics.

Tanya Goyal and Greg Durrett. 2020. Evaluating factuality in generation with dependency-level entailment. In *Findings of the Association for Computational Linguistics: EMNLP 2020*, pages 3592–3603, Online. Association for Computational Linguistics.

Yuxuan Gu, Xiaocheng Feng, Sicheng Ma, Lingyuan Zhang, Heng Gong, and Bing Qin. 2022. A distributional lens for multi-aspect controllable text generation. In *Proceedings of the 2022 Conference on Empirical Methods in Natural Language Processing*, pages 1023–1043, Abu Dhabi, United Arab Emirates. Association for Computational Linguistics.

Junxian He, Wojciech Kryscinski, Bryan McCann, Nazneen Rajani, and Caiming Xiong. 2022. CTRLsum: Towards generic controllable text summarization. In *Proceedings of the 2022 Conference on Empirical Methods in Natural Language Processing*, pages 5879–5915, Abu Dhabi, United Arab Emirates. Association for Computational Linguistics.

Francis Heylighen and Jean-Marc Dewaele. 1999. Formality of language: definition, measurement and behavioral determinants. *Interner Bericht, Center "Leo Apostel", Vrije Universiteit Brüssel*, 4.

Zhiqiang Hu, Roy Ka-Wei Lee, and Charu C. Aggarwal. 2021. Syntax matters! syntax-controlled in text style transfer. In *Proceedings of the International Conference on Recent Advances in Natural Language Processing (RANLP 2021)*, pages 566–575, Held Online. INCOMA Ltd.

Zhiting Hu and Li Erran Li. 2021. A causal lens for controllable text generation. *Advances in Neural Information Processing Systems*, 34:24941–24955.

Wenxiang Jiao, Wenxuan Wang, Jen-tse Huang, Xing Wang, and Zhaopeng Tu. 2023. Is chatgpt a good translator? a preliminary study. *arXiv preprint arXiv:2301.08745*.

Di Jin, Zhijing Jin, Zhiting Hu, Olga Vechtomova, and Rada Mihalcea. 2022. Deep learning for text style transfer: A survey. *Computational Linguistics*, 48(1):155–205.

Nitish Shirish Keskar, Bryan McCann, Lav R. Varshney, Caiming Xiong, and Richard Socher. 2019. Ctrl: A conditional transformer language model for controllable generation. *ArXiv*, abs/1909.05858.

J Peter Kincaid, Robert P Fishburne Jr, Richard L Rogers, and Brad S Chissom. 1975. Derivation of new readability formulas (automated readability index, fog count and flesch reading ease formula) for navy enlisted personnel. Technical report, Naval Technical Training Command Millington TN Research Branch.

Sachin Kumar, Biswajit Paria, and Yulia Tsvetkov. 2022. Gradient-based constrained sampling from language models. In *Proceedings of the 2022 Conference on Empirical Methods in Natural Language Processing*, pages 2251–2277, Abu Dhabi, United Arab Emirates. Association for Computational Linguistics.

Philippe Laban, Tobias Schnabel, Paul N. Bennett, and Marti A. Hearst. 2022. SummaC: Re-visiting NLI-based models for inconsistency detection in summarization. *Transactions of the Association for Computational Linguistics*, 10:163–177.

Viet Dac Lai, Nghia Trung Ngo, Amir Pouran Ben Veyseh, Hieu Man, Franck Dernoncourt, Trung Bui, and Thien Huu Nguyen. 2023. Chatgpt beyond english: Towards a comprehensive evaluation of large language models in multilingual learning. *arXiv preprint arXiv:2304.05613*.

Xiang Li, John Thickstun, Ishaan Gulrajani, Percy S Liang, and Tatsunori B Hashimoto. 2022. Diffusion-lm improves controllable text generation. *Advances in Neural Information Processing Systems*, 35:4328–4343.

Xiao Li, Guanyi Chen, Chenghua Lin, and Ruizhe Li. 2020. DGST: a dual-generator network for text style transfer. In *Proceedings of the 2020 Conference on Empirical Methods in Natural Language Processing (EMNLP)*, pages 7131–7136, Online. Association for Computational Linguistics.

Chin-Yew Lin. 2004. ROUGE: A package for automatic evaluation of summaries. In *Text Summarization Branches Out*, pages 74–81, Barcelona, Spain. Association for Computational Linguistics.

Xiaochen Liu, Yang Gao, Yu Bai, Jiawei Li, Yinan Hu, Heyan Huang, and Boxing Chen. 2022a. PSP: Pre-trained soft prompts for few-shot abstractive summarization. In *Proceedings of the 29th International Conference on Computational Linguistics*, pages 6355–6368, Gyeongju, Republic of Korea. International Committee on Computational Linguistics.

Yizhu Liu, Qi Jia, and Kenny Zhu. 2022b. Length control in abstractive summarization by pretraining information selection. In *Proceedings of the 60th Annual Meeting of the Association for Computational Linguistics (Volume 1: Long Papers)*, pages 6885–6895, Dublin, Ireland. Association for Computational Linguistics.

Zheheng Luo, Qianqian Xie, and Sophia Ananiadou. 2022. Readability controllable biomedical document summarization. In *Findings of the Association for Computational Linguistics: EMNLP 2022*, pages 4667–4680, Abu Dhabi, United Arab Emirates. Association for Computational Linguistics.

Eric Malmi, Aliaksei Severyn, and Sascha Rothe. 2020. Unsupervised text style transfer with padded masked language models. In *Proceedings of the 2020 Conference on Empirical Methods in Natural Language Processing (EMNLP)*, pages 8671–8680, Online. Association for Computational Linguistics.

Philip M McCarthy and Scott Jarvis. 2010. Mtld, vocd-d, and hd-d: A validation study of sophisticated approaches to lexical diversity assessment. *Behavior research methods*, 42(2):381–392.

Remi Mir, Bjarke Felbo, Nick Obradovich, and Iyad Rahwan. 2019. Evaluating style transfer for text. In *Proceedings of the 2019 Conference of the North American Chapter of the Association for Computational Linguistics: Human Language Technologies,*

Volume 1 (Long and Short Papers), pages 495–504, Minneapolis, Minnesota. Association for Computational Linguistics.

Nasim Nouri. 2022. Text style transfer via optimal transport. In *Proceedings of the 2022 Conference of the North American Chapter of the Association for Computational Linguistics: Human Language Technologies*, pages 2532–2541, Seattle, United States. Association for Computational Linguistics.

OpenAI. 2023. Gpt-4 technical report. *ArXiv*, abs/2303.08774.

Long Ouyang, Jeffrey Wu, Xu Jiang, Diogo Almeida, Carroll Wainwright, Pamela Mishkin, Chong Zhang, Sandhini Agarwal, Katarina Slama, Alex Ray, et al. 2022. Training language models to follow instructions with human feedback. *Advances in Neural Information Processing Systems*, 35:27730–27744.

Kishore Papineni, Salim Roukos, Todd Ward, and Wei-Jing Zhu. 2002. Bleu: a method for automatic evaluation of machine translation. In *Proceedings of the 40th Annual Meeting of the Association for Computational Linguistics*, pages 311–318, Philadelphia, Pennsylvania, USA. Association for Computational Linguistics.

Keqin Peng, Liang Ding, Qihuang Zhong, Li Shen, Xuebo Liu, Min Zhang, Yuanxin Ouyang, and Dacheng Tao. 2023. Towards making the most of chatgpt for machine translation. *Available at SSRN 4390455*.

Dongqi Pu, Xudong Hong, Pin-Jie Lin, Ernie Chang, and Vera Demberg. 2022. Two-stage movie script summarization: An efficient method for low-resource long document summarization. In *Proceedings of The Workshop on Automatic Summarization for Creative Writing*, pages 57–66, Gyeongju, Republic of Korea. Association for Computational Linguistics.

Dongqi Pu and Khalil Sima'an. 2022. Passing parser uncertainty to the transformer: Labeled dependency distributions for neural machine translation. In *Proceedings of the 23rd Annual Conference of the European Association for Machine Translation*, pages 41–50, Ghent, Belgium. European Association for Machine Translation.

Dongqi Pu, Yifan Wang, and Vera Demberg. 2023. Incorporating distributions of discourse structure for long document abstractive summarization. *arXiv preprint arXiv:2305.16784*.

Chengwei Qin, Aston Zhang, Zhuosheng Zhang, Jiaao Chen, Michihiro Yasunaga, and Diyi Yang. 2023. Is chatgpt a general-purpose natural language processing task solver? *arXiv preprint arXiv:2302.06476*.

Abhinav Ramesh Kashyap, Devamanyu Hazarika, Min-Yen Kan, Roger Zimmermann, and Soujanya Poria. 2022. So different yet so alike! constrained unsupervised text style transfer. In *Proceedings of the 60th Annual Meeting of the Association for Computational Linguistics (Volume 1: Long Papers)*, pages 416–431, Dublin, Ireland. Association for Computational Linguistics.

Sudha Rao and Joel Tetreault. 2018. Dear sir or madam, may I introduce the GYAFC dataset: Corpus, benchmarks and metrics for formality style transfer. In *Proceedings of the 2018 Conference of the North American Chapter of the Association for Computational Linguistics: Human Language Technologies, Volume 1 (Long Papers)*, pages 129–140, New Orleans, Louisiana. Association for Computational Linguistics.

Emily Reif, Daphne Ippolito, Ann Yuan, Andy Coenen, Chris Callison-Burch, and Jason Wei. 2022. A recipe for arbitrary text style transfer with large language models. In *Proceedings of the 60th Annual Meeting of the Association for Computational Linguistics (Volume 2: Short Papers)*, pages 837–848, Dublin, Ireland. Association for Computational Linguistics.

Jürgen Rudolph, Samson Tan, and Shannon Tan. 2023. Chatgpt: Bullshit spewer or the end of traditional assessments in higher education? *Journal of Applied Learning and Teaching*, 6(1).

Ritesh Sarkhel, Moniba Keymanesh, Arnab Nandi, and Srinivasan Parthasarathy. 2020. Interpretable multi-headed attention for abstractive summarization at controllable lengths. In *Proceedings of the 28th International Conference on Computational Linguistics*, pages 6871–6882, Barcelona, Spain (Online). International Committee on Computational Linguistics.

Abigail See, Peter J. Liu, and Christopher D. Manning. 2017. Get to the point: Summarization with pointer-generator networks. In *Proceedings of the 55th Annual Meeting of the Association for Computational Linguistics (Volume 1: Long Papers)*, pages 1073–1083, Vancouver, Canada. Association for Computational Linguistics.

Chenhui Shen, Liying Cheng, Lidong Bing, Yang You, and Luo Si. 2022a. SentBS: Sentence-level beam search for controllable summarization. In *Proceedings of the 2022 Conference on Empirical Methods in Natural Language Processing*, pages 10256–10265, Abu Dhabi, United Arab Emirates. Association for Computational Linguistics.

Chenhui Shen, Liying Cheng, Ran Zhou, Lidong Bing, Yang You, and Luo Si. 2022b. MReD: A meta-review dataset for structure-controllable text generation. In *Findings of the Association for Computational Linguistics: ACL 2022*, pages 2521–2535, Dublin, Ireland. Association for Computational Linguistics.

Yongliang Shen, Kaitao Song, Xu Tan, Dongsheng Li, Weiming Lu, and Yueting Zhuang. 2023. Hugginggpt: Solving ai tasks with chatgpt and its friends in huggingface. *arXiv preprint arXiv:2303.17580*.

Dominik Sobania, Martin Briesch, Carol Hanna, and Justyna Petke. 2023. An analysis of the automatic bug fixing performance of chatgpt. *arXiv preprint arXiv:2301.08653*.

Ewoenam Kwaku Tokpo and Toon Calders. 2022. Text style transfer for bias mitigation using masked language modeling. In *Proceedings of the 2022 Conference of the North American Chapter of the Association for Computational Linguistics: Human Language Technologies: Student Research Workshop*, pages 163–171, Hybrid: Seattle, Washington + Online. Association for Computational Linguistics.

Ashish Vaswani, Noam Shazeer, Niki Parmar, Jakob Uszkoreit, Llion Jones, Aidan N Gomez, Łukasz Kaiser, and Illia Polosukhin. 2017. Attention is all you need. *Advances in neural information processing systems*, 30.

Jiaan Wang, Yunlong Liang, Fandong Meng, Zhixu Li, Jianfeng Qu, and Jie Zhou. 2023a. Cross-lingual summarization via chatgpt. *arXiv preprint arXiv:2302.14229*.

Jiaan Wang, Yunlong Liang, Fandong Meng, Beiqi Zou, Zhixu Li, Jianfeng Qu, and Jie Zhou. 2023b. Zero-shot cross-lingual summarization via large language models.

Colin G West. 2023. Ai and the fci: Can chatgpt project an understanding of introductory physics? *arXiv preprint arXiv:2303.01067*.

Chien-Sheng Wu, Linqing Liu, Wenhao Liu, Pontus Stenetorp, and Caiming Xiong. 2021. Controllable abstractive dialogue summarization with sketch supervision. In *Findings of the Association for Computational Linguistics: ACL-IJCNLP 2021*, pages 5108–5122, Online. Association for Computational Linguistics.

Kexin Yang, Dayiheng Liu, Wenqiang Lei, Baosong Yang, Mingfeng Xue, Boxing Chen, and Jun Xie. 2022. Tailor: A prompt-based approach to attribute-based controlled text generation. *arXiv preprint arXiv:2204.13362*.

Xianjun Yang, Yan Li, Xinlu Zhang, Haifeng Chen, and Wei Cheng. 2023a. Exploring the limits of chatgpt for query or aspect-based text summarization. *arXiv preprint arXiv:2302.08081*.

Zhengyuan Yang, Linjie Li, Jianfeng Wang, Kevin Lin, Ehsan Azarnasab, Faisal Ahmed, Zicheng Liu, Ce Liu, Michael Zeng, and Lijuan Wang. 2023b. Mm-react: Prompting chatgpt for multimodal reasoning and action. *arXiv preprint arXiv:2303.11381*.

Hanqing Zhang and Dawei Song. 2022. DisCup: Discriminator cooperative unlikelihood prompt-tuning for controllable text generation. In *Proceedings of the 2022 Conference on Empirical Methods in Natural Language Processing*, pages 3392–3406, Abu Dhabi, United Arab Emirates. Association for Computational Linguistics.

Hanqing Zhang, Haolin Song, Shaoyu Li, Ming Zhou, and Dawei Song. 2022. A survey of controllable text generation using transformer-based pre-trained language models. *arXiv preprint arXiv:2201.05337*.

Ce Zhou, Qian Li, Chen Li, Jun Yu, Yixin Liu, Guangjing Wang, Kai Zhang, Cheng Ji, Qiben Yan, Lifang He, et al. 2023. A comprehensive survey on pretrained foundation models: A history from bert to chatgpt. *arXiv preprint arXiv:2302.09419*.

Wanrong Zhu, Xin Wang, Tsu-Jui Fu, An Yan, Pradyumna Narayana, Kazoo Sone, Sugato Basu, and William Yang Wang. 2021. Multimodal text style transfer for outdoor vision-and-language navigation. In *Proceedings of the 16th Conference of the European Chapter of the Association for Computational Linguistics: Main Volume*, pages 1207–1221, Online. Association for Computational Linguistics.

A Appendix: One-shot Guidance

B Appendix: Absolute Differences in POS and Dependency Label Distributions

Candidate	FRE	CLI	DCR
Document: {Original Document}, Layman Summary: {Human Layman Summary}.			
Please learn the way of summarization from the previous example, and give me a layman-style summary of X	49.23†	13.26†	10.45†
Human Answer	52.42	12.46	8.93
Document: {Original Document}, Expert Summary: {Human Expert Summary}.			
Please learn the way of summarization from the previous example, and give me an expert-style summary of X	28.88†	15.92†	11.82
Human Answer	23.20	17.62	11.78

Table 7: Reading difficulty of one-shot guidance. † indicates statistical significance ($p<0.05$) against corresponding human answers via paired t-test.

Candidate	Formality	MTLD
Formal: {Formal Sentence}, Informal: {Informal Sentence}.		
Please learn the way of formality conversion from the previous example, and give me an informal version of X	50.67†	14.81
Human Answer	49.87	15.20
Informal: {Informal Sentence}, Formal: {Formal Sentence}.		
Please learn the way of formality conversion from the previous example, and give me a formal version of X	52.13†	19.22
Human Answer	53.57	18.70

Table 8: Text formality of one-shot guidance on GYAFC-FR branch. † indicates statistical significance ($p<0.05$) against corresponding human answers via paired t-test.

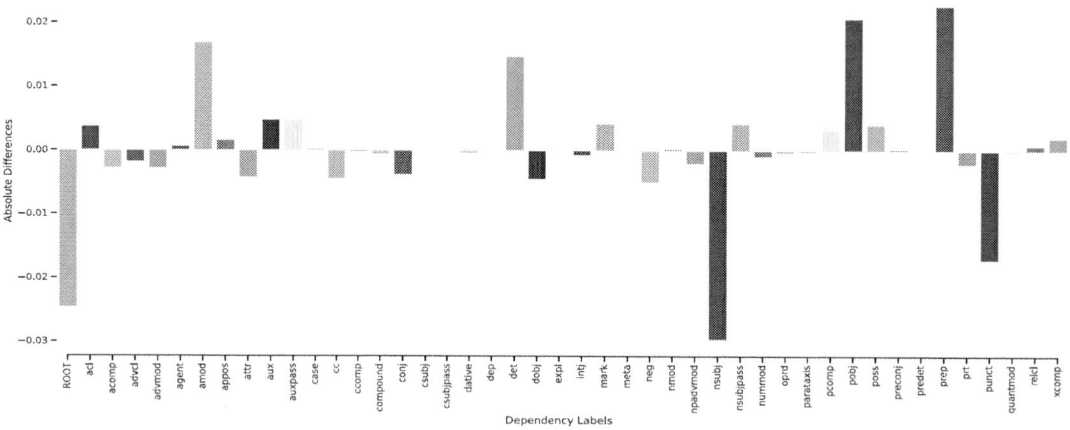

Figure 5: Absolute differences in dependency labels distribution of ChatGPT and human-generated formal style sentences: GYAFC - EM

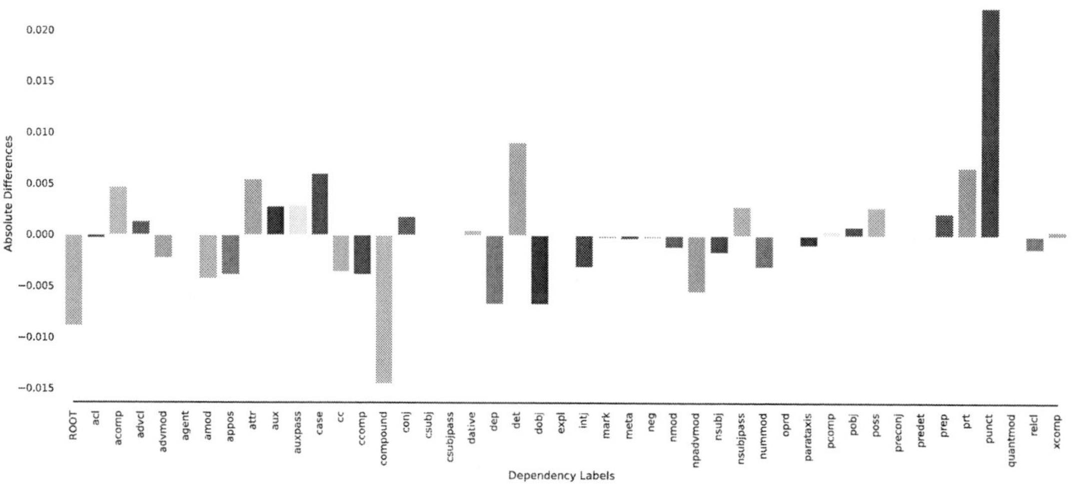

Figure 6: Absolute differences in dependency labels distribution of ChatGPT and human-generated informal style sentences: GYAFC - EM

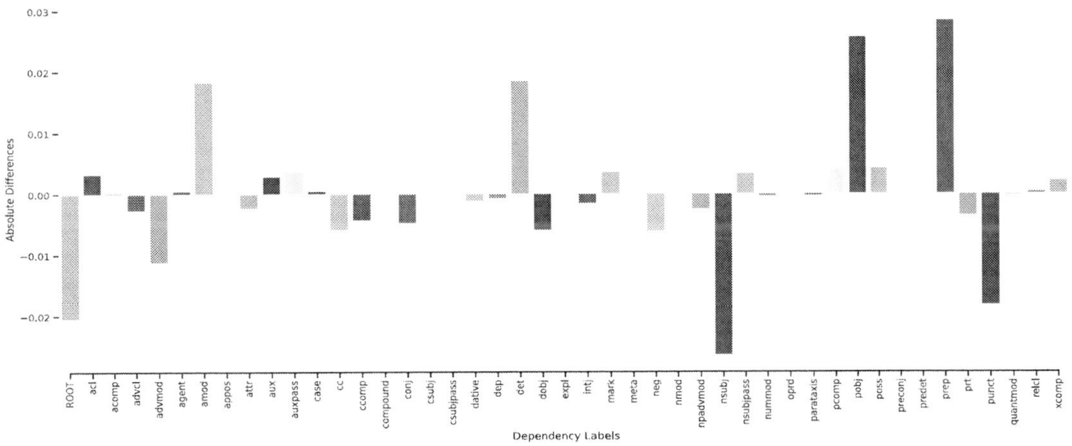

Figure 7: Absolute differences in dependency labels distribution of ChatGPT and human-generated formal sentences: GYAFC - FR

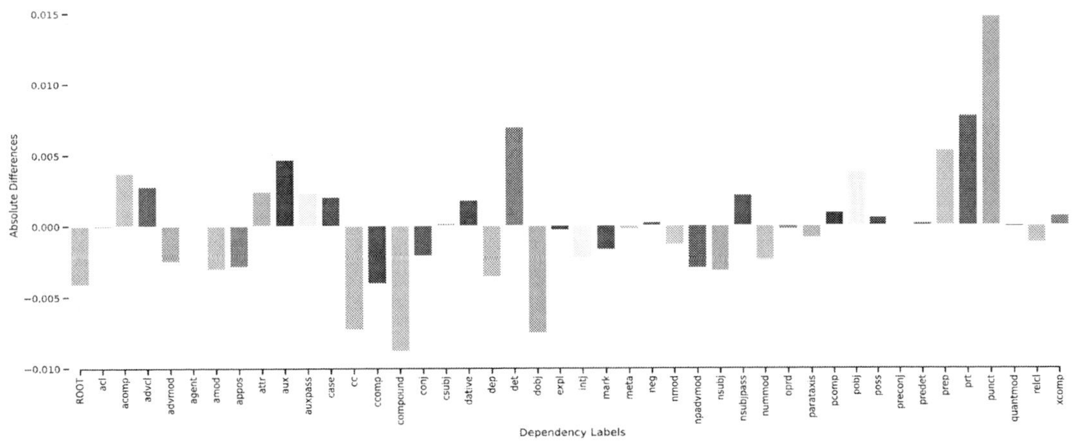

Figure 8: Absolute differences in dependency labels distribution of ChatGPT and human-generated informal sentences: GYAFC - FR

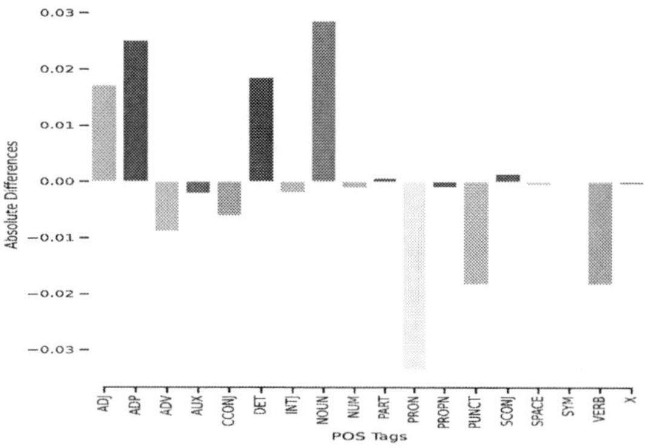

Figure 9: Absolute differences in POS tags distribution of ChatGPT and human-generated formal sentences: GYAFC - FR

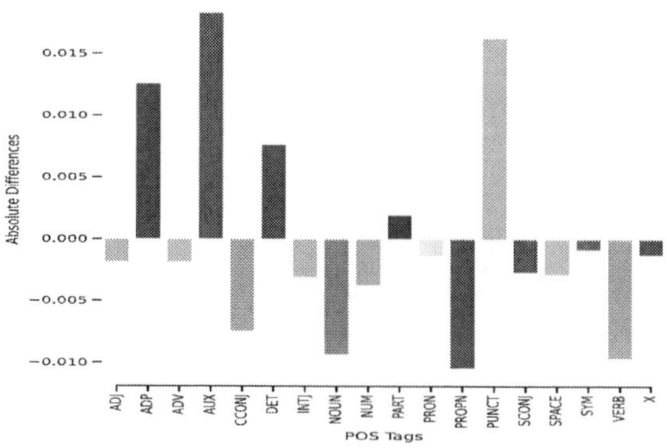

Figure 10: Absolute differences in POS tags distribution of ChatGPT and human-generated informal sentences: GYAFC - FR

C Appendix: Dependency Arc Entailment

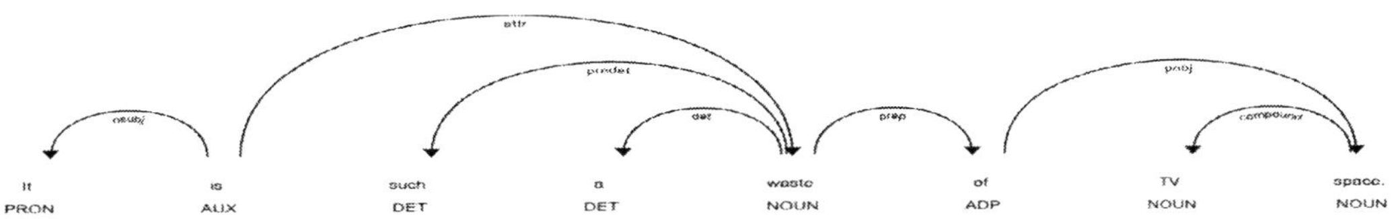

Figure 11: Case study of dependency tree visualization (Reference)

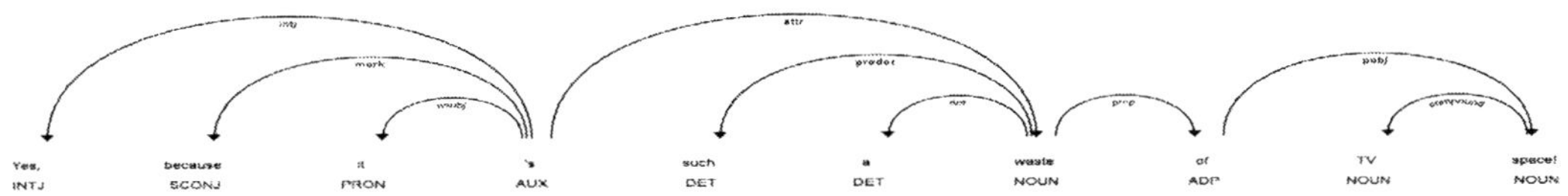

Figure 12: Case study of dependency tree visualization (Human)

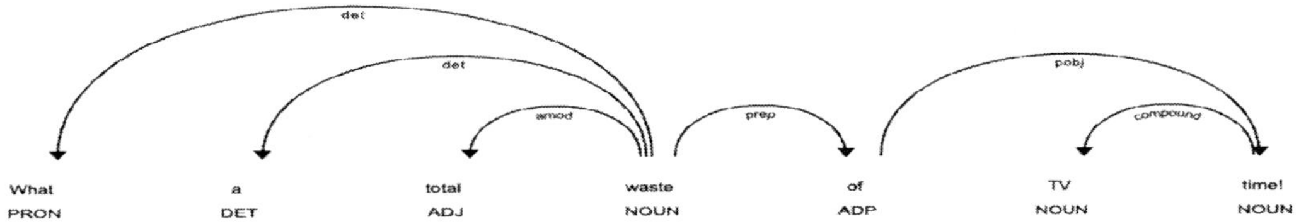

Figure 13: Case study of dependency tree visualization (ChatGPT)

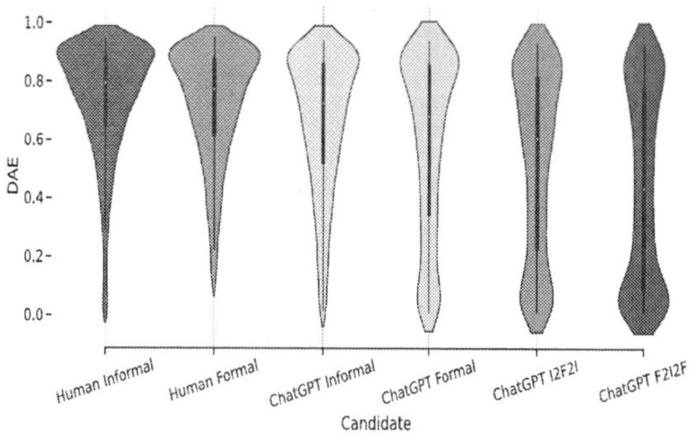

Figure 14: Dependency arc entailment: GYAFC - FR. Data points>0.95≈Accurate. To clarify discrepancies, cutoff point=0.95.

D Appendix: Named Entity Hallucination

Dataset	Candidate	Precision	Recall	F1
GYAFC-FR	Human Informal	0.989	0.988	0.988
	Human Formal	0.988	0.989	0.988
	ChatGPT Informal	0.986	0.985	0.986
	ChatGPT Formal	0.974	0.974	0.974
	ChatGPT I2F2I	0.982	0.982	0.982
	ChatGPT F2I2F	0.974	0.973	0.973
GYAFC-EM	Human Informal	0.979	0.987	0.983
	Human Formal	0.977	0.989	0.982
	ChatGPT Informal	0.975	0.974	0.974
	ChatGPT Formal	0.950	0.952	0.951
	ChatGPT I2F2I	0.970	0.969	0.970
	ChatGPT F2I2F	0.945	0.946	0.945

Table 9: Named entity hallucination - GYAFC

Multi-Dialectal Representation Learning of Sinitic Phonology

Zhibai Jia
No.2 High School of East China Normal University
jiazhibai@proton.me

Abstract

Machine learning techniques have shown their competence for representing and reasoning in symbolic systems such as language and phonology. In Sinitic Historical Phonology, notable tasks that could benefit from machine learning include the comparison of dialects and reconstruction of proto-languages systems. Motivated by this, this paper provides an approach for obtaining multi-dialectal representations of Sinitic syllables, by constructing a knowledge graph from structured phonological data, then applying the BoxE technique from knowledge base learning. We applied unsupervised clustering techniques to the obtained representations to observe that the representations capture phonemic contrast from the input dialects. Furthermore, we trained classifiers to perform inference of unobserved Middle Chinese labels, showing the representations' potential for indicating archaic, proto-language features. The representations can be used for performing completion of fragmented Sinitic phonological knowledge bases, estimating divergences between different characters, or aiding the exploration and reconstruction of archaic features.

1 Introduction

The evolution of languages in the Sinitic family created intricate correspondences and divergences in its dense dialect clusters. Investigating the dynamics of this evolution, through comparison and proto-language reconstruction, is an essential task to Sinitic Historical phonology. However, it may be costly for researchers to manually probe through the groups in search of phonological hints. Hence, it is desirable to accelerate the process with modern algorithms, specifically, representation learning.

Graph-based machine learning (Makarov et al., 2021) have gained increasing attention in recent years, due to their versatility with data with flexible structures. Especially, missing link prediction algorithms for knowledge graphs (Wang et al., 2021) (Zhu et al., 2022) can uncover a latent structure in noisy and incomplete knowledge. In the case for learning phonological representations, using graph-based learning can allow for more comprehensive integration of multi-dialectal evidence. Thus, we propose applying graph-based techniques for multi-dialectal representation learning.

We construct a knowledge graph from the multi-dialectal phonological data, by abstracting unique phonetic components and individual characters into two kinds of nodes. Then, we connect them with edges specific to the dialect type wherein the character is associated with the given component. On the constructed knowledge graph, we train the BoxE algorithm (Abboud et al., 2020), a Box Embedding Model for knowledge base completion. Finally, we evaluate the obtained representations with unsupervised and supervised clustering, as well as MLP probes based on Middle-Chinese-derived labels, to show this tool's value for Sinitic phonological investigation.

2 Background on Sinitic Languages

The analysis of Sinitic languages face a few specific challenges due to unique phonological characteristics. These characteristics define crucial details of our design.

In Sinitic languages, morphemes are primarily monosyllabic. Hence, Chinese writing binds one syllable to each of its glyphs, known as characters. A syllable in Sinitic can be decomposed into an initial, a final and a tone. (Shen, 2020) Initials refer to the consonant-like sounds at the beginning of a syllable, which include both stops (e.g. /p-/, /b-/) and fricatives (e.g. /s-/, /ʃ-/). These initials could be combined with various finals to form syllables. Finals refer to the vowel-like sounds at the end of a syllable, which included both simple vowels (e.g. /-a/, /-i/, /-u/), complex vowels (e.g. /-ai/, /-ao/, /-ei/), and vowels combined with consonant codas (/-m/,/-n/,/-ŋ/,/-p/,/-t/,/-k/). Tones refer to the pitch patterns

Proceedings of the 61st Annual Meeting of the Association for Computational Linguistics - Student Research Workshop, pages 19–29
July 10-12, 2023

associated with syllables in Chinese. Tones could distinguish between words that were otherwise homophonous, and they were an important part of the Chinese phonological system.

Due to the early conception of the Chinese writing system, syllables from different Sinitic languages can usually be aligned to each other through a written form. As this alignment is typically implemented in databases of raw Sinitic data, the difficulty of cognate identification is drastically reduced, facilitating analysis. However, the simple syllable structure introduces large amounts of homophones, words sharing same pronunciations, into Sinitic languages. This hinders the use of the comparative method in reconstructing a Sinitic proto-language. The existence of a supersegmental tone feature also complicates a historical analysis of Sinitic languages.

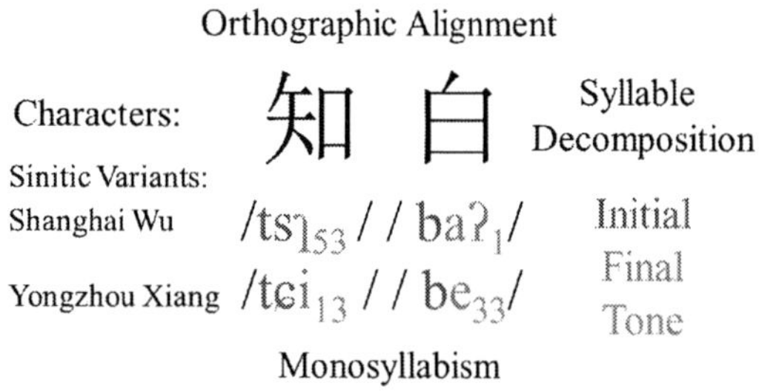

Figure 1: Highlighting key characteristics of Sinitic relevant to our approach. Characters are the central identity in the multi-dialectal representations. The orthographic alignment of sub-syllable components form the structure of data used in this study.

Two factors that motivate the use of a graph-based method include the uniform structure of Sinitic syllables and their intimate relationship with characters. The intuitive syllable decomposition and the glyph-based alignment inspire viewing the components contextualized in various dialects as different "observations" of a single character. Theoretically, these observations are derivable from the reading of the character in the proto-language.

3 Related Work

The practice of computationally-aided proto-language construction, often associated with cognate identification, has been extensively considered in the past two decades (Nerbonne et al., 2007). Examples include (Steiner et al., 2011) which draws insights from bio-informatics and the classical comparative workflow, and (List et al., 2017), which compared many methods for cognate identification. An relevant insight from the latter paper is that language-specific methods often outperform language-general ones, especially for languages like Sinitic. An epitome of neural methods for proto-language reconstruction would be (Meloni et al., 2021), in which Latin is reconstructed from Romance descendent languages with a encoder-decoder structure. Though, our approach differs from their study in many crucial aspects. In Meloni et al. 2021, the reconstruction is supervised, with the proto-language Latin provided at training time. But our method targets not only documented proto-languages like Middle Chinese, but also unknown, intermediate varieties in the development from ancient Sinitic to modern dialects, which requires an unsupervised approach. Additionally, in term of techniques, their use of GRU and attention-based transducers contrasts with our emphasis on a graph-based method.

Considering the representation learning of Sinitic, we found abundant literature on the topic of speech recognition (Ma et al., 2022), segmentation and synthesis, which often yield representations of certain phonological relevance as by-product. Though, these studies devote heavily to a few major languages, specifically Mandarin or Cantonese, and, since they are rarely claim motivation from historical phonology, seldom take a multi-lingual or multi-dialectal approach.

While speech representation learning often serve the aformentioned purposes, the proposals of using neural networks to model phonetics and phonology from either symbolic abstractions or acoustic data in order to examine theories in these fields are relevant to this study. Unsupervised binary stochastic autoencoders were explored in (Shain and Elsner, 2019). GAN (Generative Adversarial Networks) was used in (Begus, 2020). These proposals modeled perception and categorization, in relation to language acquisation. Most interestingly, representation learning has been applied for discovering phonemic tone contours in tonal languages(Li et al., 2020), of which a great portion are Sinitic Languages. However, these proposals again rarely address issues from historical phonology.

Finally, it should be noted that the concept of transforming porous data in a regular, matrix-like form to a loose, graph-like form for flexibility in processing, while essential to the designs of this paper, is not novel in the literature. Rather, it originates with the GRAPE framework in (You et al., 2020). Notably, when the data in question concerns Chinese historical phonology, it coincides with Johann-Mattis List's proposals for introducing network methods into computational linguistics and Chinese historical phonology. Generally, this line of work should be considered most relevant to our study (List, 2018; List et al., 2014; List, 2015). List (2018) approaches issues spanning character formation, Middle Chinese annotation, as well as Old Chinese reconstruction with network methods. List et al. (2014); List (2015) examines dialect evolution with display graphs, with a focus on the complex word-borrowing dynamics between the dialect families. He calls for colleagues to lend more attention to data-driven, quantitative methods. Our proposal answers List's call by bringing together knowledge graphs with Chinese historical phonology. Furthermore, the utilization of SOTA representation learning extends beyond the scope of the aforementioned work.

4 Method

The graph-based method for representing dialect data has the benefit of making the model more flexible, robust, and efficient at using porous, incomplete data. This is particularly important since investigations into dialects are often uncoordinated, resulting in a large amount of partial character entries, where only some columns have pronunciations while others are missing. It could be argued that we can use missing data imputation to alleviate the issue, and continue processing the dialect data in a matrix form, perhaps with feed-forward neural networks or denoising autoencoders(Vincent et al., 2008). However, traditional missing-data imputation techniques may create fictitious syllables that violate the phonotactics of that dialect when imputing initials or finals according to the mode of a type. Conditioning the initials or finals on each other will cause higher-order dependencies that are hard to solve. Therefore, by keeping the spaces untouched and using paired comparisons, the graph formalism circumnavigates the problem. This formulation may also allow for auxiliary input features, such as basic phonological knowledge about the nature of phonemic contrast, to be injected into the model. On this graph, we learn the embeddings with the BoxE algorithm, to be discussed below.

4.1 Construction of a Multi-Dialectal Knowledge Graph

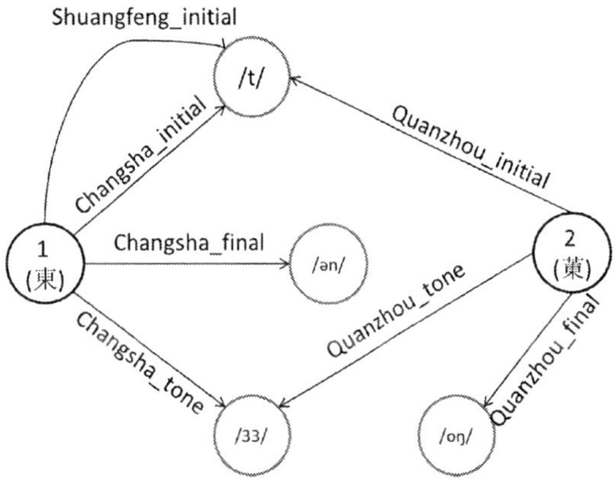

Figure 2: Partial Illustration of the Phonology Knowledge Graph. The numerals represent the indices representing the Chinese characters and the glyphs for what they represent. /33/ is a tone in Chao's notation. The other nodes are segments represented in the International Phonetic Alphabet. The text labels for the edges demonstrate the how edges are categorized according to both dialect and phone type. Note that it is bi-partite by nature, as edges can only occur between "phonemic" nodes and "character" nodes, colored blue and black in the figure.(This is not provided explicitly)

We expressed the data with a knowledge graph and trained the representations through an auxiliary task of completing the multi-dialectal knowledge graph. With a graph-based technique, the representations can be more robust to noisy and porous data. Additionally, the method will be more flexible, allowing for auxiliary input features to be injected.

We construct a graph by leveraging the characters, as well as individual initials, finals and tones from various dialects as nodes. (See Figure 2) .For instance, the fact of character C having an initial I in dialect D is modeled with an edge from C to I. The edge has type specific to the dialect D and the category of the component, which is an initial. This edge type can be denoted as "D-initial". Demonstrated in Fig. 2, C could be character No. 1, when I is /t/ and the edge is "Changsha_initial".

After constructing the graph, character-level and component-level representations are trained simultaneously. The knowledge graph algorithm attempts to model the nodes features as well as a prediction function so that, when given a character node and a type of link, the corresponding pronunciation node can be predicted with maximum likelihood. In this process, the model implicitly generates hypotheses about character pronunciations missing or unseen in training, as well as historical relationships between the syllables.

If there are M characters with readings from N dialects involved in an experiment, the upper bound for the number of edge types will be $3N$. Assuming that $F_1 + F_2 + F_3$ unique initials, finals and tones could be found within the aggregated phonological systems of the N dialects, the upper bound for number of nodes is $M + F_1 + F_2 + F_3$. The graph size scales sub-linearly with the number of dialects, since as more dialects are considered, their phonemic inventories will start to overlap and exhaust.

Following convention in knowledge base research, the graph is presented in Triples of Head-Relation-Tail format.

4.2 The Box Embedding Model

In pilot tests, We considered various algorithms from the field of graph representation learning and knowledge base completion for application. In the process, it is revealed that few algorithms are inherently suitable, as there are many subtle requirements in this context:

1. Models designed for knowledge graphs are more suited to this application than general graph learning algorithms, since the graph to be processed is heterogeneous, besides carrying edge type as information.

2. The model must have strong capacity for modeling multiple unique relations between the same two nodes. It is very common for one character to have the same initial across different dialects. This rules out many translation-based models, that, when given different relations, always predict different tail nodes. Prominent examples of such models include TransE (Bordes et al., 2013) and RotatE (Sun et al., 2019).

3. If the model uses inverse triples as an augmentation technique, then the model should also be expressive in many-to-one and one-to-many relations, because one initial or final will be mapped to numerous characters.

4. Of the applicable algorithms, interpretability should be prioritized, since we hope to extract interpretable phonological knowledge from the obtained representations. This casts doubt on a another large family of knowledge graph models, namely the bi-linear models, epitomized by RESCAL(Nickel et al.) and DistMult(Yang et al., 2015).

After consideration, we chose BoxE for its expressiveness and tolerance to many-to-one relationships, due to its Box embedding designs. Empirically, we also demonstrate that the BoxE is relatively optimal for the phonological task through comparison with RotatE (Sun et al., 2019) and ComplEx (Trouillon et al., 2016) in Table 4.

Here is a brief description of the BoxE algorithm. It is a translational model that embeds each node with two vectors: e_i, which represents the position vector, and $b_i \in \mathbf{R}^d$, which represents the translational bump. These vectors are obtained after incorporating triples into the model. Additionally, each edge type is defined with two hyper-rectangles $r^{(1)}$ and $r^{(2)} \in \mathbf{R}^d$. To satisfy the relation R between entity E_1 and E_2, there is $e_1 + b_2 \in r^{(1)}$ and $e_2 + b_1 \in r^{(2)}$. Intuitively, this means that E_1 and E_2 "bump" each other in hyperspace $\mathbf{R}^d$ by some distance. If the new vectors fall within the bounds of the associated boxes, then the proposition is considered probable. To facilitate gradient descent, the boxes have relaxed borders. It is worth noting that BoxE is also capable of hyper-graph learning as it accepts higher arity relations as input, though we did not exploit this feature for this study.

Our training objective was to maximize the score or probability of given relations. To elaborate, this means maximizing the chance of predicting masked initials/finals/tones of some character in some dialect with the unmasked components associated with that character, from both within and without the dialect. This is analog to the comparative method in Historical Phonology, as the model implicitly reconstructs a latent "proto-language", from which the descendent languages can be deduced (or, "decoded") with maximum likelihood.

5 Data and Experimental Setup

We use pronunciation data from four varieties of Xiang Chinese Changsha 長沙, Shuangfeng 雙峰, Guanyang Wenshi 灌陽文市, and Quanzhou Xiancheng 全州縣城., spoken primarily in Hunan Province, provided by CCR(Huang et al., 2011), and retrived with Comparative analysis toolset for Chinese dialects(Huang, 2021). We also obtain labels of Middle Chinese readings from the same source. In this work, Middle Chinese refers to the phonological system recorded in the dictionary Qieyun, from the year 601 AD. It was supplemented in the Song Dynasty into the dictionary Guangyun, from which this study draws data. Middle Chinese is literary and may not reflect the colloquial speech of China in any time or place. However, most phonological systems of modern Sinitic languages (with the notable exception of the Min Languages) can be derived from the Qieyun system. Thus we treat it as a useful protolanguge model for most Sinitic Languages.

We operate on symbolic abstractions instead of raw acoustic data, as all the data have been transcribed into IPA in the database. One row of data corresponds to readings of one Chinese character. Internally, each character is mapped to a unique identifier, which is the character's serial number in Guangyun. For every variety of Chinese, there are four columns, corresponding to initial value, final value, tonal value and tonal type of a given character's pronuciation. The tone type argument is actually redundant, and it is assigned manually by investigators. In each dialect, there is a one-to-one correspondence between one tone value with one tone type. Between two dialects, tones arising from the same Middle Chinese tone are given same names. Hence, the tone type feature introduces prior expert knowledge about the historical origin of tones. However, we expect the model to derive the historical tones without any diachronic expert knowledge. Hence, we discard the tone type feature, and use only the three values for this study.

5.1 Processing of Duplicate Data

Characters in Sinitic can be polyphonic, that is, sometimes a character will be mapped to multiple readings in one dialect. This results in duplicate data in the dataset. For convenience, we drop the extra pronunciations and keep only the first line for every entry. Though, there can be ambiguity surrounding the correspondence of readings for polyphonic characters. For instance, the first reading entry for a polyphonic character in dialect A might be cognate with the second reading entry for the character in dialect B. However, our naïve approach will match all the first entries to each other. Additionally, two dialects may inherit only partial readings of a polyphonic character in the proto-language. Hence, this procedure potentially introduces erroneous alignment into the model.

5.2 Split of Training, Testing and Validating Datasets

The model was not trained with all the data, so as to examine the robustness of the model. Instead, some triples are diverted to form testing and validating datasets. Unfortunately, assignment in this context is slightly more complicated than simple stochastic choice. There is the scenario where all initial (final/tonal) information about one character is diverted from training. In this case, the model will not be able to correctly embed this character. To circumvent this issue, we mandate that at least one feature from any of the three compositional types is retained in the training set for any character. In the four Xiangyu in this case, the result is empirically a split of 80.50%:12.52%:6.98%.

5.3 Data Statistics

The initials, finals and tones count for the four dialects are listed in Table 1. A total of 2805 characters is included, but not every character has the corresponding phonological data documented in every dialect. In the training set, there are 22300 entries.

5.4 Model Setup

For the parametric size of the model, see Table 2. We employ the BoxE algorithm implemented in the Python library PyKeen (Ali et al., 2021b,a). We did not fine-tune the model or any model parameters, so as to demonstrate the capability of the model in even in a highly suboptimal setting.

	Initials	**Finals**	**Tones**
Changsha	21	38	11
Shuangfeng	28	35	11
Guanyang	28	42	5
Quanzhou	26	43	4

Table 1: Data Statistics

Parameter	**Value**
Vector and hyperbox dimension	64
Number of nodes	2946
Number of edge types	12
Cumulative parameter size	378624
Optimization algorithm	Adam
Number of epochs	2000

Table 2: Model Parameters

6 Experimental Evaluation

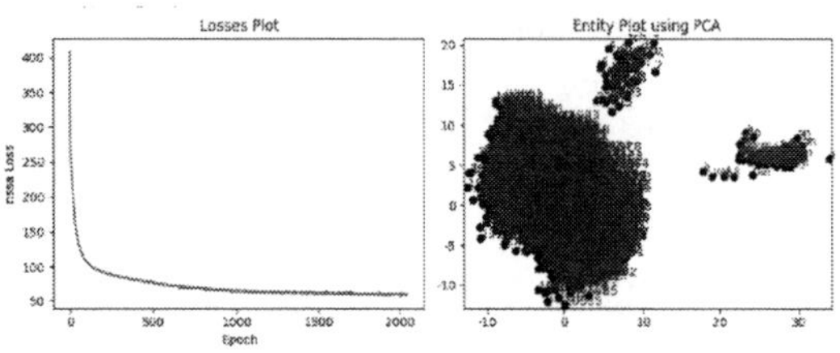

Figure 3: Preliminary Visualization of Training Dynamics and Trained Embeddings.

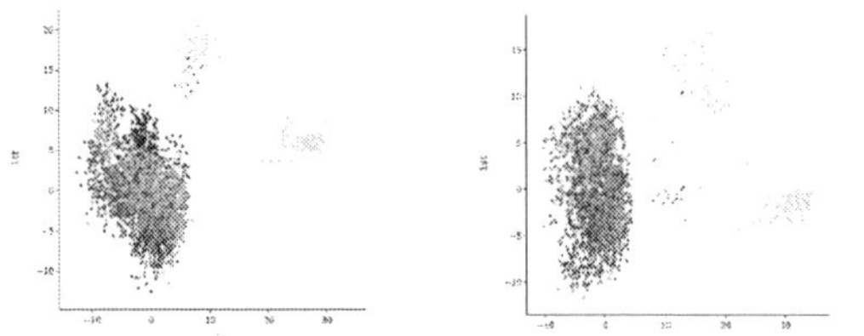

Figure 4: UMAP(McInnes et al., 2018, McInnes et al., 2018,Uniform Manifold Approximation and Projection) decomposed visualizations of the translational bumps (a) and position embeddings (b). The coloring reflects a point's index in the Guangyun, which is sorted according to rhyme.

6.1 Canonical Evaluation of Model

The convergence of the model, and a preview of the spatial distribution of embeddings can be seen in Figure 3. The model quickly converges. The entity plot decomposed with PCA reveals a mass of character readings "ejecting" two groups of entities, respectively the combination of all initials and tones, and all finals, which is in accordance with the bi-partite and heterogeneous nature of this graph.

Canonically, BoxE is evaluated with the hit@n metric and MRR (mean reciprocal rank) for link prediction. On the validation set, our model achieved hit@1:51.25%, hit@5: 87.19%, hit@10: 93.76% on the "tail" batches. The head batches are not relevant because they involve "predicting characters from initials/finals", of which there is many to one. In Table 4, we demonstrate empirically the superiority of the BoxE algorithm over other common knowledge graph algorithms on this phonological task. A clearer visualization of the embedded points can be seen in Figure 4. Guangyun ensures that rhyming characters (having the same final) have similar coloring on the map. The coloring is only a reflection of the point's serial in the dataset and does not have any quantitative interpretation. Presumably, the translational bump for characters will contain more relevant information to historical phonology, as they designate which component types to "bump into the box." Without mention, all experiments are carried out on the bump embeddings and not positions. However, empirically we find that the two kinds of embeddings are interchangeable.

6.2 Examining Contrastive Information

In this section, unsupervised clustering is used to evaluate contrastive information in the embeddings. Based on the hypothesis that the phonological structures of the dialects are co-embedded in the latent structure of embeddings, we determined if the high-dimensional embeddings retain information associated with the theoretic categories of the input dialects, a similar task to Tilsen et al. 2021. After applying a clustering algorithm to the embedded characters, the information yield [1] of the found categories against input categories of initials, finals and tones is computed. A higher information yield indicates that the clusters found by unsupervised clustering were more interpretable with respect to the input phonemic categories. [2] [3]

The clustering algorithms used for dissecting the cloud of embedded characters include HDBSCAN (McInnes and Healy, 2017,A density based method), Affinity Propagation, K-means and Agglomerated Clustering.[4] The results can be seen in Figure 5.

Affinity propagation and HDBSCAN achieved best effects on finding interpretable clusters from the datasets. Though, we find that HDBSCAN is very sensitive to the two parameters: its effect degrades when we allow for smaller clusters but demands greater confidence on the classification. Notably, HDBSCAN achieved an effect similar to affinity propogation with just 29 clusters, while the latter used 130.

The large information yields reflect that the unsu-

[1]Entropy subtracted by conditional entropy, or an empirical estimate of mutual information.

[2]HDBSCAN sometimes refuses to classify points it is not sure of. These points are combined into one category for the aforementioned purpose.

[3]Before using HDBSCAN, UMAP was first used to reduce the 64 embedding dimensions to 8 dimensions, with the neighbour parameter set to 50. This is an advised practice from the HDBSCAN documentation.

[4]The numerous methods were tried sequentially as we do not know which algorithm best recovers the latent structure of representations in accordance with theoretic categories.

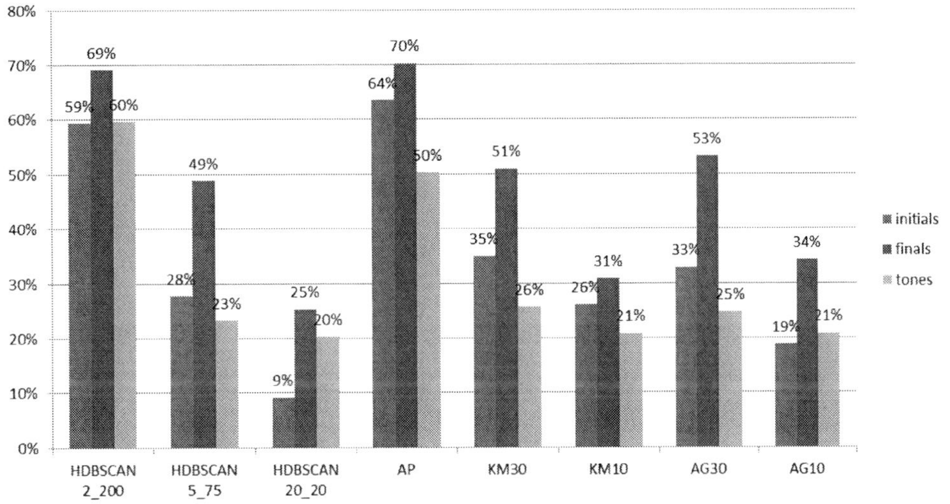

Figure 5: Information yield in percentage averaged across four dialects. For HDBSCAN, the min samples and min cluster size parameters were set to 2 and 200, 5 and 75, 20 and 20 respectively. The other three methods were employed on the original embeddings. For K-means and agglomerative clustering, the number of clusters was specified to be 30 and 10.

pervised algorithms do tend to dissect the character set along latent lines corresponding to phonological opposition in the input dialects, as shown in a partial observation in Table 3. It appears that the distribution of finals in dialects had more influence on the latent structure than initials or tones. Simply put, the characters within each unsupervised cluster are more likely to rhyme than alliterate, though both cases occur in observation of the HDBSCAN Clusters.

There are limitations to this experiment though, which will be discussed below.

6.3 Inference of Proto-language Features

In this section, we investigate the quality of our embeddings with respect to proto-language reconstruction tasks, as an important potential application of this method lies with such work. Hence, we trained classifiers in attempt to infer labels from Middle Chinese, which likely predates proto-Xiang, therefore an accessible surrogate for that proto-language.

The features to infer are Grades (等地), Voice(清濁), Tones(聲調), She (攝, a coarse division of finals), Initials (字母), and Mu(韻目,a fine division of finals).

Grades are believed to be associated with medials, a component in the front of the final (amalgamated with final in Xiangyu data). Voice is a division based on properties of the initial, in which voiced consonants, voiceless unaspirated consonants, voiceless aspirated consonants and nasal consonants are distinguished. For tones, in Middle Chinese, there were four: level, rising, departing, and entering. Of these categorical labels, there are respectively 4, 4, 4, 16, 36 and 206 unique classes. [5]

For this experiment, a train-test split of 0.67-0.33 was instated. Since phonological evolution is quite regular and systematic, we should expect decent results without a great proportion of data used for training. Accuracies below are for the test set. These values are consistently higher than a naïve baseline of guessing the mode of each distribution, proving that proto-language related features were preserved in the retrived embeddings. (See Table 5.)

The MLP generally outperforms Ridge Classification on inference for these characters, with the sole exception of tones, where RC outperforms MLP by 1.1%. The best results are attained for tones and voice, showing these features to be phonologically well preserved from Middle Chinese to Xiang languages.

Interesting observations can be drawn from the confusion matrices generated with such classification. Presumably, these matrices can offer insight

[5] Canonically so, but there are a few erroneous entries in the data we used, resulting in sometimes one or two extra categories containing a few characters. They were kept.

ID	Changsha	Shuangfeng	Guanyang	Quanzhou
0	Initial:/m/	Initial:/m/	Initial:/m/	Initial:/m/
1	Initial:/pʰ/	Initial:/pʰ/	Initial:/pʰ/	Initial:/pʰ/
2	Final:/ĩn/	Final:/ĩ/	Final:/ iɛ̃/	Final:/ ieŋ/
7	Final:/(u)ei/	Final:/ui/	Final:/ uɛi/	Final:/uei/

Table 3: Analysis of Selected HDBSCAN Clusters. In these clusters, characters are predominantly, but not exclusively associated with the listed features.

Alg. (Metric %)	Hit@1	Hit@5	Hit@10
BoxE	**51.25**	**87.19**	**93.76**
RotatE	33.11	57.47	66.18
ComplEx	9.40	24.65	35.37

Table 4: An empirical demonstration of the superiority of the BoxE algorithm for the phonological investigation task among common missing link prediction methods. The models were set to the same embedding dimension. None of the models were fine-tuned or ran for more than a single time, hence all readings should be seen as sub-optimal.

into what categories were blended, which oppositions were lost during the development of some language family. One such example is demonstrated in Figure 6. It could be seen that there is large confusion between the Xian 咸, Dang 宕 and Shan 山 Shes, and also between Xie 蟹 and Zhi 止 Shes. [6] This could indicate that in Proto-Xiang, there is confusion between these categories relative to Middle Chinese.

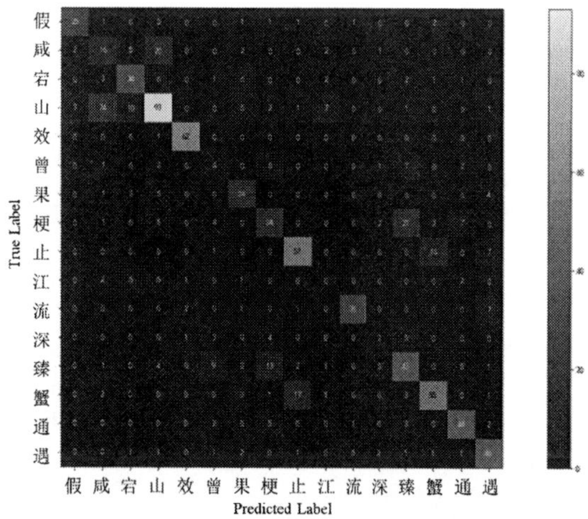

Figure 6: Confusion matrix for She.

[6] In Baxter's transcription, 咸 = *-eam*, 宕 = *-ang*, 山 = *-ean*; 蟹 = *-ea*, 止 = *-i* (Baxter and Sagart, 2014). There are only hypothetical IPA values available for these archaic categories.

7 Discussions

Our current setting only operates on pre-abstracted symbols and lacks incorporation of acoustic or articulatory evidence. Incorporating multi-modal data into a knowledge graph framework could enhance the quality of embeddings and enable more accurate representations of phonological features. Alsp, the proposed method uses shared embeddings for symbolic components across different dialects, which cannot fully capture dialect-specific variations. Investigating contextualized or dialect-specific component embeddings could improve the model's ability to capture finer-grained phonological distinctions. Finally, phonetically similar components are currently treated as independent items, which is too absolute an assumption. However, it is also possible for phonetic cues to override the correct phonological alignment in the model. In many cases, phonetic similarity does not imply diachronic homology. Two phonetically equivalent syllables from two different dialects may have different origins. Conversely, two phonetically distinct syllables from two different dialects may be cognate. The subtle balance between "phonetic" and "phonological" proximity requires further discussion.

Several lines of research may benefit from robust multi-dialectal representations. In dialectology, there is need for estimating divergence between phonological systems. That includes the divergences between its constituents, such as individual characters, phonemes and syllables. With multi-dialectal representations, this divergence can be estimated quantitatively. In historical phonology, the reconstruction of a proto-language demands deep scrutiny of dialect systems whose efficiency can be improved with manipulating the representations. Also, they can be used for completion of the phonological knowledge base. Often knowledge bases for Sinitic phonology are fragmented, due to imperfect surveys and heterogeneity of sources, etc. The representations can be used to infer missing

Algorithm(Acc %)	Grades	Voice	Tones	She	Initials	Mu
Ridge Classification	65.3	76.4	**84.1**	54.6	49.4	18.6
MLP	**70.5**	**81.1**	83.0	**61.4**	**53.2**	**26.9**
Naïve Baseline	48.4	35.4	35.6	15.3	8.1	1.8

Table 5: Comparison of Ridge and MLP probes for proto-language Feature Inference. The baseline is the accuracy obtained by uniformly guessing the most frequent class for each character.

pronunciations in different dialects to improve the quality of observations.

The graph-based method proposed in this paper benefits from phonological characteristics specific to Sinitic languages, but is also limited by these characteristics. Specifically, the process of constructing a phonological graph from words, as proposed in this study, is less natural in languages where words typically have many syllables, and vary in the number of syllables contained. In these languages, the temporal interaction of syllables within a word is a new phenomena that the graph-based method needs to adapt to. Additionally, in these languages, it will be less straightforward to tokenize the words into expressive sub-words to use as nodes in the graph. Presumably, in non-Sinitic languages, the proposed method will be most performant in other languages of the Southeast Asian Sprachbund, such as those in the Hmong-Mien or Austroasiatic families. These languages share phonological features with Sinitic languages that enable our method. On the other hand, this method will likely meet more complications outside of the local sprachbund.

8 Conclusion

This paper demonstrated the potential of graph-based representation learning in Chinese Historical Phonology. The representations are potent in many ways, i.e. facilitating the reconstruction of minor proto-languages.

In the future, more sophisticated techniques such as deep learning models could be explored to further improve the quality of the obtained representations. Furthermore, the proposed method can be integrated with other linguistic resources, such as recordings, articulatory time series, or orthographic corpora, to enrich the knowledge base and improve the accuracy of reconstructions. With the development of modern, massive linguistic datasets such as Nk2028(nk2028, 2020), CogNet(Batsuren et al., 2022) or MorphyNet(Batsuren et al., 2021) as well as improvements in large pre-trained models, we can expect foundational models that possess emergent and meta-generalizing capabilities to arise in historical phonology or morphology. This avenue of research holds great promise for advancing our understanding of the phonology and evolution of Sinitic languages, and potentially other language families as well.

Limitations

This study stems from a novel idea for Chinese Historical Phonology Studies. As few direct predecessors could offer hindsight, there are quite a few limitations to this study that may be addressed with further work.

1. While the initial-final-tone decomposition is convenient in this context, it also limits the transferrability of the proposed tool to languages outside of the Sinosphere. This calls for further exploration of more generalizeable approaches to phonological representation learning.

2. Polyphonic characters were not fully utilized in the study, and their alignment per-reading and tokenization into separate identifiers should be considered in future work.

3. Finally, making full use of the dataset is crucial, and the stochastic train-test split used in this study may leave out important hints. Alternative sampling strategies, such as cross-validation or bootstrapping, could enhance the robustness of the results.

Acknowledgements

We are grateful for the valuable advice and feedback we received from various peers during the course of this work. Without their contributions, this research would not have been possible.

References

Ralph Abboud, Ismail Ceylan, Thomas Lukasiewicz, and Tommaso Salvatori. 2020. BoxE: A Box Embedding Model for Knowledge Base Completion. In *Advances in Neural Information Processing Systems*, volume 33, pages 9649–9661. Curran Associates, Inc.

Mehdi Ali, Max Berrendorf, Charles Tapley Hoyt, Laurent Vermue, Mikhail Galkin, Sahand Sharifzadeh, Asja Fischer, Volker Tresp, and Jens Lehmann. 2021a. Bringing Light Into the Dark: A Large-scale Evaluation of Knowledge Graph Embedding Models under a Unified Framework. *IEEE Transactions on Pattern Analysis and Machine Intelligence*, pages 1–1.

Mehdi Ali, Max Berrendorf, Charles Tapley Hoyt, Laurent Vermue, Sahand Sharifzadeh, Volker Tresp, and Jens Lehmann. 2021b. PyKEEN 1.0: A Python Library for Training and Evaluating Knowledge Graph Embeddings. *Journal of Machine Learning Research*, 22(82):1–6.

Khuyagbaatar Batsuren, Gábor Bella, and Fausto Giunchiglia. 2021. MorphyNet: a Large Multilingual Database of Derivational and Inflectional Morphology. In *Proceedings of the 18th SIGMORPHON Workshop on Computational Research in Phonetics, Phonology, and Morphology*, pages 39–48, Online. Association for Computational Linguistics.

Khuyagbaatar Batsuren, Gábor Bella, and Fausto Giunchiglia. 2022. A large and evolving cognate database. *Language Resources and Evaluation*, 56(1):165–189.

William H. Baxter and Laurent Sagart. 2014. Old chinese: A new reconstruction.

Gasper Begus. 2020. Modeing unsupervised phonetic and phonological learning in Generative Adversarial Phonology. In *Proceedings of the Society for Computation in Linguistics 2020*, pages 38–48, New York, New York. Association for Computational Linguistics.

Antoine Bordes, Nicolas Usunier, Alberto Garcia-Duran, Jason Weston, and Oksana Yakhnenko. 2013. Translating Embeddings for Modeling Multi-relational Data. In *Advances in Neural Information Processing Systems*, volume 26. Curran Associates, Inc.

Rongpei Huang, Xiufang Yang, and Daan He. 2011. Chinese Character Readings. `https://xiaoxue.iis.sinica.edu.tw/ccr/#`. Retrieved March 26, 2023.

Yihua Huang. 2021. Comparative Analysis Toolset for Chinese Dialects. `https://github.com/lernanto/sinetym`. Retrieved March 26, 2023.

Bai Li, Jing Yi Xie, and Frank Rudzicz. 2020. Representation Learning for Discovering Phonemic Tone Contours. In *Proceedings of the 17th SIGMORPHON Workshop on Computational Research in Phonetics, Phonology, and Morphology*, pages 217–223, Online. Association for Computational Linguistics.

Johann-Mattis List. 2015. Network perspectives on chinese dialect history. *Bulletin of Chinese linguistics*, 8:27–47.

Johann-Mattis List. 2018. More on network approaches in historical chinese phonology ().

Johann-Mattis List, Simon J. Greenhill, and Russell D. Gray. 2017. The Potential of Automatic Word Comparison for Historical Linguistics. *PLOS ONE*, 12(1):e0170046.

Johann-Mattis List, Nelson-Sathi Shijulal, William F. Martin, and Hans Geisler. 2014. Using phylogenetic networks to model chinese dialect history.

Han Ma, Roubing Tang, Yi Zhang, and Qiaoling Zhang. 2022. Survey on speech recognition. *Computer Systems and Applications*, 31(1):1–10.

Ilya Makarov, Dmitrii Kiselev, Nikita Nikitinsky, and Lovro ubelj. 2021. Survey on graph embeddings and their applications to machine learning problems on graphs. *PeerJ Computer Science*, 7.

L. McInnes, J. Healy, and J. Melville. 2018. UMAP: Uniform Manifold Approximation and Projection for Dimension Reduction. *ArXiv e-prints*.

Leland McInnes and John Healy. 2017. Accelerated hierarchical density based clustering. In *Data Mining Workshops (ICDMW), 2017 IEEE International Conference on*, pages 33–42. IEEE.

Leland McInnes, John Healy, Nathaniel Saul, and Lukas Grossberger. 2018. Umap: Uniform manifold approximation and projection. *The Journal of Open Source Software*, 3(29):861.

Carlo Meloni, Shauli Ravfogel, and Yoav Goldberg. 2021. Ab antiquo: Neural proto-language reconstruction. In *Proceedings of the 2021 Conference of the North American Chapter of the Association for Computational Linguistics: Human Language Technologies*, pages 4460–4473, Online. Association for Computational Linguistics.

John Nerbonne, T. Mark Ellison, and Grzegorz Kondrak. 2007. Computing and historical phonology. In *Proceedings of Ninth Meeting of the ACL Special Interest Group in Computational Morphology and Phonology on - SigMorPhon '07*, pages 1–5, Prauge, Czech Republic. Association for Computational Linguistics.

Maximilian Nickel, Volker Tresp, and Hans-Peter Kriegel. A Three-Way Model for Collective Learning on Multi-Relational Data.

nk2028. 2020. Qieyun-js. `https://github.com/nk2028`. Retrieved March 26, 2023.

Cory Shain and Micha Elsner. 2019. Measuring the perceptual availability of phonological features during language acquisition using unsupervised binary stochastic autoencoders. In *Proceedings of the 2019 Conference of the North*, pages 69–85, Minneapolis, Minnesota. Association for Computational Linguistics.

Zhongwei Shen. 2020. A phonological history of chinese.

Lydia Steiner, Michael Cysouw, and Peter Stadler. 2011. A Pipeline for Computational Historical Linguistics. *Language Dynamics and Change*, 1(1):89–127.

Zhiqing Sun, Zhi-Hong Deng, Jian-Yun Nie, and Jian Tang. 2019. RotatE: Knowledge Graph Embedding by Relational Rotation in Complex Space. ArXiv:1902.10197 [cs, stat].

Sam Tilsen, Seung-Eun Kim, and Claire Wang. 2021. Localizing category-related information in speech with multi-scale analyses. *PLOS ONE*, 16(10):e0258178.

Théo Trouillon, Johannes Welbl, Sebastian Riedel, Éric Gaussier, and Guillaume Bouchard. 2016. Complex Embeddings for Simple Link Prediction. ArXiv:1606.06357 [cs, stat].

Pascal Vincent, H. Larochelle, Yoshua Bengio, and Pierre-Antoine Manzagol. 2008. Extracting and composing robust features with denoising autoencoders. In *International Conference on Machine Learning*.

Meihong Wang, Linling Qiu, and Xiaoli Wang. 2021. A survey on knowledge graph embeddings for link prediction. *Symmetry*, 13:485.

Bishan Yang, Wen-tau Yih, Xiaodong He, Jianfeng Gao, and Li Deng. 2015. Embedding Entities and Relations for Learning and Inference in Knowledge Bases. ArXiv:1412.6575 [cs].

Jiaxuan You, Xiaobai Ma, Daisy Ding, Mykel Kochenderfer, and Jure Leskovec. 2020. Handling missing data with graph representation learning. *NeurIPS*.

Xiangru Zhu, Zhixu Li, Xiaodan Wang, Xueyao Jiang, Penglei Sun, Xuwu Wang, Yanghua Xiao, and Nicholas Jing Yuan. 2022. Multi-modal knowledge graph construction and application: A survey. *ArXiv*, abs/2202.05786.

Prompt-based Zero-shot Text Classification with Conceptual Knowledge

Yuqi Wang[1,3], Wei Wang[1], Qi Chen[1], Kaizhu Huang[2], Anh Nguyen[3], Suparna De[4]
[1]Xi'an Jiaotong Liverpool University, China
[2]Duke Kunshan University, China
[3]University of Liverpool, United Kingdom
[4]University of Surrey, United Kingdom
yuqi.wang17@student.xjtlu.edu.cn, {wei.wang03,qi.chen02}@xjtlu.edu.cn,
kaizhu.huang@dukekunshan.edu.cn, anh.nguyen@liverpool.ac.uk, s.de@surrey.ac.uk

Abstract

In recent years, pre-trained language models have garnered significant attention due to their effectiveness, which stems from the rich knowledge acquired during pre-training. To mitigate the inconsistency issues between pre-training tasks and downstream tasks and to facilitate the resolution of language-related issues, prompt-based approaches have been introduced, which are particularly useful in low-resource scenarios. However, existing approaches mostly rely on verbalizers to translate the predicted vocabulary to task-specific labels. The major limitations of this approach are the ignorance of potentially relevant domain-specific words and being biased by the pre-training data. To address these limitations, we propose a framework that incorporates conceptual knowledge for text classification in the extreme zero-shot setting. The framework includes prompt-based keyword extraction, weight assignment to each prompt keyword, and final representation estimation in the knowledge graph embedding space. We evaluated the method on four widely-used datasets for sentiment analysis and topic detection, demonstrating that it consistently outperforms recently-developed prompt-based approaches in the same experimental settings.

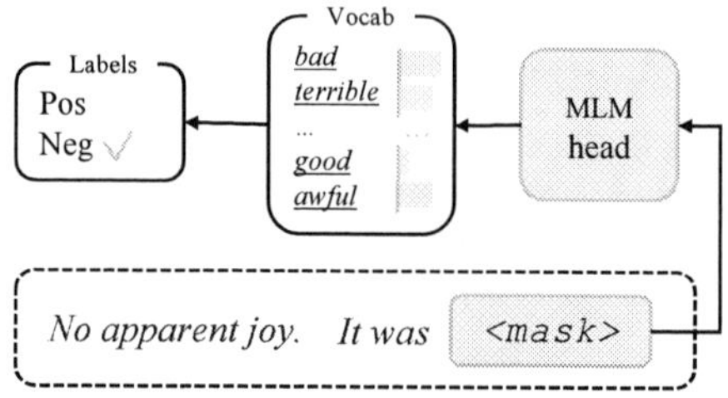

Figure 1: An example of prompt-based text classification for the binary sentiment analysis task.

1 Introduction

Numerous studies have achieved great success in applying supervised natural language processing (NLP) techniques to address a plethora of NLP applications, including text classification (Dong et al., 2019), natural language inference (Wang et al., 2020) and neural machine translation (Mi et al., 2016). However, achieving high accuracy with deep learning models for textual data analysis necessarily requires a large amount of manually annotated samples, which is both time-consuming and labour-intensive.

To address the issues in low-resource settings, considerable attention has been paid to the pre-trained language models (PLMs), such as GPT-3 (Brown et al., 2020), BERT (Devlin et al., 2019), and Roberta (Liu et al., 2019), due to their superior performances on knowledge transfer. The model pre-training stage typically involves language modelling tasks, i.e., word prediction based on the context of the input. Extensive investigations, e.g., knowledge probing, on PLMs show that they have a certain capacity to store both linguistic and relational knowledge from large-scale corpora of general domain data (Petroni et al., 2019).

In recent years, the paradigm of NLP has been shifted from "pre-train and fine-tune" to "pre-train and prompt" (Liu et al., 2023), to fully exploit these PLMs in a gradient-free manner and effectively mitigate the gap between pre-training tasks and downstream tasks for the extreme zero-shot scenario (Yin et al., 2019). Specifically, in the prompt-based approaches (Schick and Schütze, 2021; Min et al., 2022; Gao et al., 2021a), each sample in NLP tasks can be wrapped into cloze-style questions with their corresponding templates, prompting the PLMs to generate the targeted output to solve the problem. For example, in a binary sentiment analysis task (shown in Figure 1), the text "*no apparent joy*" is transformed to the prompt-augmented input "*no apparent joy. It was <mask>.*", where the *<mask>* is a special token to be predicted by the PLMs. This text will then be labelled as positive or negative according to the predicted words. Most existing works utilize a verbalizer to provide the translations

Proceedings of the 61st Annual Meeting of the
Association for Computational Linguistics - Student Research Workshop, pages 30–38
July 10-12, 2023 ©2023 Association for Computational Linguistics

from the predicted vocabulary to the label space in a specific task (Schick and Schütze, 2021). However, these approaches are subject to two significant limitations: (i) by only considering a limited set of pre-defined label words filled in the masked position, some potentially relevant or useful words in the certain domain could be ignored, hindering the model's capacity to generalize; and (ii) the pre-training data of PLMs may contain biases that are reflected in the model's predictions on downstream tasks (Zhao et al., 2021). Some works propose calibration strategies to adjust the distribution of prior probabilities (Hu et al., 2022), which requires access to a large amount of data in specific datasets for true estimation.

In this work, we propose a framework to perform prompt-based zero-shot text classification with conceptual knowledge and overcome the above limitations. The proposed framework includes prompt-based keyword extraction, weight assignment to each keyword in the meaningful semantic space, and final representation estimation. Specifically, in the weight assignment component, by leveraging the contextual relationships captured by SimCSE (Gao et al., 2021b), a powerful contrastive learning model, we refine the probabilities of each keyword being filled in the masked position from the language prompt to mitigate the bias. Additionally, in the final representation, we integrate structured factual data provided by the knowledge graphs (KGs) to include a wider range of semantic relationships between entities in a given domain. By combining their strengths, the proposed framework enables more informed predictions and a richer understanding of the underlying domain. In the experiment, we strictly follow the "label-fully-unseen" setting proposed by Yin et al. (2019) for evaluation. We employ four widely-used text classification datasets and compare the proposed framework with several recently-developed prompt-based approaches under the same experimental settings. The result indicates that our proposed framework brings significant improvement to the model performance.

2 Related Works

Language prompt has been introduced to elicit knowledge from PLMs to solve different NLP tasks, which was inspired by a series of works related to prompt-based approaches, including GPT-3 (Brown et al., 2020) and PET (Schick and Schütze, 2021). However, one issue under the zero-shot setting identified by Chen et al. (2022) is the lack of domain adaptation. They performed prompt-aware continual pre-training based on adaptively retrieved data for better performance on text classification tasks. To widen the coverage of label words, Hu et al. (2022) incorporated external knowledge bases for the verbalizer construction, which greatly improved the stability.

The above-mentioned works used hand-crafted prompt templates, particularly designed by humans for various NLP tasks. While they are carefully constructed, the process requires a considerable amount of human effort. Several automatic prompting techniques were introduced to automatically select a prompt based on the input provided to the PLMs. Gao et al. (2021a) suggested to employ a pre-trained text-to-text transformer, T5 (Raffel et al., 2020), for candidate template generation. The best language prompt can be derived after the evaluation of each candidate template. Shin et al. (2020) proposed a gradient-based approach to search for a set of impactful tokens as the prompts that can cause significant changes in the model's output. Nevertheless, the quality of the automatically generated prompt usually cannot be guaranteed, and this approach lacks sufficient interpretability. Besides discrete prompts, research such as (Li and Liang, 2021) and (Gu et al., 2022) presented continuous prompts as prefixes to the input, which are continuous vectors that can be learned based on patterns and structures from the data. This approach avoids the hassle of explicit prompt design while it introduces a large number of new parameters to be optimized.

3 Methodology

We propose a prompt-based approach to tackle the zero-shot text classification problem. The overall framework is shown in Figure 2. We first extract the keywords to summarize the input text with the prompt-based approach. Then, we assign weights to these keywords based on their semantic relevance to the overall meaning of the text. The weighted embeddings of all extracted keywords in the knowledge graph (KG) embedding space are aggregated to produce the final representation of the input text. Finally, we determine if the text is related to a label in the KG according to their cosine similarity. In the following subsections, we describe the task definition in the extreme zero-shot setting, prompt-based keyword extraction, weight assignment and final representation estimation in the constructed KG embedding space.

3.1 Task Definition

Given n textual inputs $\mathcal{X} = \{x_1, x_2, ..., x_n\}$, the aim of the text classification task is to assign each input x a label y from a fixed label set containing m labels, i.e., $\mathcal{Y} = \{y_1, y_2, ..., y_m\}$. Unlike the label-partially-unseen zero-shot text classification, where a part of labelled data is available for model training or fine-tuning on a specific domain, in this work, all samples are unseen, and only the label names from the label set $\mathcal{Y}$ can be accessed in advance. In order to achieve this goal, it is essential to ensure that the aspect being described in the input text and the meanings of the labels are comprehensible to the framework (Yin et al., 2019).

3.2 Prompt-based Keyword Extraction

To remove noise and preserve the most relevant information, keyword extraction from the input text can summarize its main content and identify the most important concepts. The meaning of an expression, particularly its implicit meaning, can often be inferred from the context in which it is used. Therefore, we first employ a contextualized pre-trained masked language model, denoted as $\mathcal{M}$, for prompt-based keyword extraction. This model has an MLM head on top of the transformer-based architecture, and consequently, it reduces the text classification to the MLM problem with a task-specific template t, which is either added at the beginning or the end of the original input to form a prompt-augmented input. The template includes a mask token <*mask*>, and the probability of each word v from vocabulary $\mathcal{V}$ being filled in this position can be predicted by $\mathcal{M}$. The most likely words generated in this manner are somewhat relevant to the input context, as the model integrates contextual information to make predictions. We then construct a keyword set for x, namely, $\mathcal{V}^x$, i.e.,

$$\mathcal{V}^x = \underset{v \in \mathcal{V}}{\operatorname{top} K} \left[P_{\mathcal{M}} \left(\textit{<mask>} = v | [x; t] \right) \right] \quad (1)$$

where $[x; t]$ is the prompt-augmented input for x. $P_{\mathcal{M}}(|\cdot)$ is the conditional probability generated by the MLM head of $\mathcal{M}$. According to the observations by Meng et al. (2020), the top 50 probable words usually well represent the mask. Hence, we set the parameter K to 50.

3.3 Weight Assignment

To estimate the text representation for the input, each word in the $\mathcal{V}^x$ should be associated with a weight, indicating relevance and importance to the original textual input. Directly using the probability output by the MLM head could be one possible solution. However, the masked language model may produce a biased probability distribution over the keyword set.

To address this issue, we utilize SimCSE (Gao et al., 2021b), a Siamese network for simple contrastive learning, to assign weights to each word. SimCSE employs entailments and contractions from natural language inference (NLI) datasets as supervised signals. In contrastive loss, the premise and entailment hypothesis are considered positive pairs, while in-batch negatives and contradiction hypothesis are treated as negative pairs. This approach helps align semantically similar sentence embeddings while separating contradicted/unrelated sentence embeddings.

We use the encoding function for SimCSE $f_\theta(\cdot)$, parametrized by θ, to transform both the original input x and a template in which the mask token has been replaced by the k-th word in $\mathcal{V}^x$, denoted as $\tilde{t}_k$, into a meaningful semantic space. We then assign the weight w_i to the i-th word in $\mathcal{V}^x$ based on the similarity between $\tilde{t}_i$ and x, i.e.

$$w_i = \frac{e^{\operatorname{sim}\left(f_\theta(x), f_\theta(\tilde{t}_i)\right)}}{\sum_{k=1}^{K} e^{\operatorname{sim}\left(f_\theta(x), f_\theta(\tilde{t}_k)\right)}} \quad (2)$$

where $\operatorname{sim}(\cdot)$ is the cosine similarity function.

3.4 Final Representation in Knowledge Graph Embedding Space

As for the extreme zero-shot scenario in our work, ideally, each label y in the label set $\mathcal{Y}$ should be equipped with auxiliary information, e.g., a textual description and hand-engineered attributes. Nevertheless, such information available for a particular task is usually limited and may not provide a precise description of the label. Fortunately, there is a source of external knowledge that can be applied with little human effort – KGs. ConceptNet (Speer et al., 2017) is a type of KG that organizes and represents linked open data regarding real-world entities and their relations, offering rich structured knowledge at the conceptual level for the labels.

To leverage the knowledge from the ConceptNet, a process called retrofitting (Faruqui et al., 2015) is used to refine the pre-trained distributional word

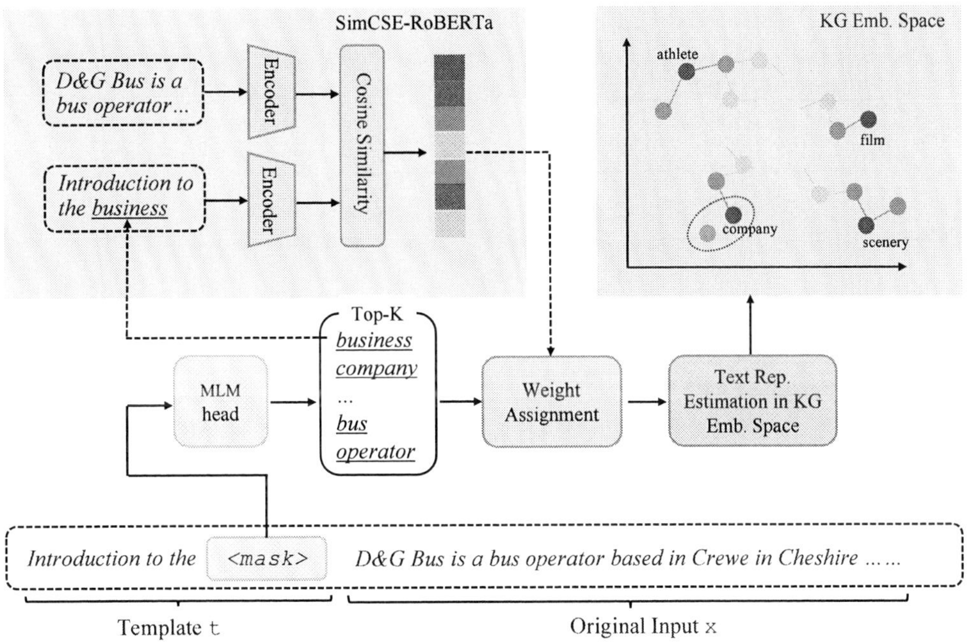

Figure 2: Overall framework of our proposed method

embeddings. The idea is to bring the embeddings of connected entities in the KG closer while maintaining the original distributional ontology (Speer et al., 2017).

The following objective function is minimized to construct the KG embedding space based on the entity set, denoted as $\mathcal{V}^{\text{ent}}$:

$$\sum_{v_i \in \mathcal{V}^{\text{ent}}} \left[\sum_{(v_i, r, v_j) \in \mathcal{E}} \lambda_r (\mathbf{v}_i - \mathbf{v}_j)^2 + \eta_i (\mathbf{v}_i - \hat{\mathbf{v}}_i)^2 \right] \tag{3}$$

where $\mathcal{E}$ is the triplet set of the KG, consisting of two entities v_i and v_j linked by their relation r, i.e., (v_i, r, v_j), and λ_r is the corresponding weight for r. $\mathbf{v}_\mathrm{i}$ is the updated KG graph embedding for the entity v_i. $\hat{\mathbf{v}}_i$ stands for the original word embedding of v_i and η_i controls the associative strength between $\hat{v}_i$ and v_i. For simplicity, we applied the alignment by the name to align the entity in $\mathcal{V}^{\text{ent}}$ with a word in $\mathcal{V}$.

To estimate the final representation in the KG embedding space for input text x, we integrate the conceptual representation of each keyword v_i in $\mathcal{V}^x$ based on semantic relevance between v_i and x. Our assumption for the multi-class classification task is that the content of input text should remain within its desired label and not be relevant to any other labels in the label set. Therefore, the label with the highest similarity to this representation, among all labels in $\mathcal{Y}$, is then selected as the predicted label, denoted by $\hat{y}$, i.e.

$$\hat{y} = \underset{y \in \mathcal{Y}}{\text{argmax}} \left[\text{sim} \left(\mathbf{v}_y, \sum_{v_i \in \mathcal{V}^x} w_i \mathbf{v}_i \right) \right] \tag{4}$$

where $\mathbf{v}_y$ is the label embedding for y in the KG embedding space.

4 Preliminary Results

4.1 Datasets

We conducted experiments on four commonly used text classification datasets, including two sentiment analysis datasets (SST-2 (Socher et al., 2013) and Yelp-polarity (Zhang et al., 2015)) and two topic detection datasets (AG's News (Zhang et al., 2015) and DBPedia (Lehmann et al., 2015)). We adopted the prompt templates from (Chen et al., 2022) for better comparison. For each dataset, we evaluated our method on different templates and reported their average accuracy along with standard deviation. The statistics and example prompt templates of these datasets are listed in Table 1.

4.2 Setup

For the prompt-based keywords extraction and weight assignment, we made use of roberta-large

Datasets	#Samples	#Classes	Type	Example Prompt
SST-2	1,821	2	Sentiment	All in all, it was <*mask*>
Yelp-polarity	38,000	2	Sentiment	All in all, it was <*mask*>
AG's News	7,600	4	Topic	This topic is about <*mask*>
DBPedia	70,000	14	Topic	Introduction to the <*mask*>

Table 1: Statistics of datasets and example prompt templates used in our work.

models with transformers[1] and simcse[2] libraries. We used the latest version of ConceptNet (5.7) [3] for KG embedding space construction.

We implemented our method with PyTorch 1.5.0 and Python 3.6 on IBM Power 9 architecture. The inference process was accelerated on an NVIDIA Tesla V100 Volta GPU card with 32GB of graphics RAM.

4.3 Main Results

We compared the results with those produced by several prompt-based methods for text classification introduced recently, which share the same extreme zero-shot setting. The main results on the four datasets are shown in Table 2. Channel is the noisy channel approach based on GPT-2 proposed by Min et al. (2022). GPT-3 refers to the work of Zhao et al. (2021) that calibrated the probability distribution with a content-free input. The results of applying Roberta for prompt-based text classification were reported by Chen et al. (2022). AdaPrompt (Chen et al., 2022) refers to the method that adaptively retrieves data from large-scale corpora for continual pre-training, and iAdaPrompt is the process of iterative adaption.

It is clear that the proposed method outperformed the baselines on all datasets, providing a performance gain of 13.88% and 5.31% on Yelp-polarity and AG's News datasets, respectively. Another notable observation from the main results is that our method has significantly lower standard deviations in comparison with Roberta, AdaPrompt and iAdaPrompt, suggesting that it is more stable when using different prompt templates for text classification.

4.4 Ablation Study

We also carried out ablation experiments to explore the effectiveness of weight assignment and KG embedding space construction in the proposed framework. The result of the study is shown in Table 3.

Instead of assigning weights to each keyword based on their importance and relevance as explained in Section 3.3, we directly utilized probabilities of masked token output by the MLM head. This resulted in a slight decrease in performance, with an average accuracy drop of 0.87%. Then, we replaced the KG embeddings for text representation estimation with another semantically consistent embedding, GloVe (Pennington et al., 2014), which is solely based on the word co-occurrence in the pre-training corpus. We observe significant decreases in accuracy on AG's News and DBPedia datasets by 19.3% and 14.4%, respectively. This indicates that, compared with distributional semantic embedding space, incorporating knowledge to construct KG embedding space can greatly enhance the performance of text classification, especially on topic detection datasets.

4.5 Visualization

To further understand the weight assignment, we provided the visualization (shown in Figure 3) of each extracted keyword from examples in topic detection datasets. We arranged these words in descending order of probabilities output by the MLM head. The colour depth denotes the importance of each word according to the given context. As can be seen, many of the most significant keywords (indicated as dark colours) were correctly highlighted. For example, "*rocket*", "*space*" and "*launch*" in AG's News example; "store", "company" and "business" in DBPedia example. We also observed that some less related or wrongly-predicted words could be detected by the model. For example, the DBPedia example mainly describes a game company, even though the words like "*author*" and "*blog*" predicted by the MLM head are at the top of the list, they were assigned with low weights (indicated as light colours) in the weight assignment process, which makes reasonable amendments to the prompt-based keywords

[1]https://huggingface.co/transformers

[2]https://pypi.org/project/simcse/

[3]https://github.com/commonsense/conceptnet-numberbatch

Models	SST-2	Yelp-polarity	AG's News	DBPedia
Channel (Min et al., 2022)	77.10 (N/A)	–	61.80 (N/A)	51.40 (N/A)
GPT-3 (Zhao et al., 2021)	75.80 (0.00)	–	73.90 (0.00)	59.70 (0.00)
Roberta (Chen et al., 2022)	64.56 (16.77)	72.63 (6.34)	69.52 (6.96)	56.32 (0.49)
AdaPrompt (Chen et al., 2022)	75.92 (17.36)	75.09 (17.57)	76.55 (7.28)	70.95 (8.80)
iAdaPrompt (Chen et al., 2022)	77.18 (17.96)	75.81 (18.05)	74.28 (9.00)	73.01 (6.70)
Ours	**80.62 (10.08)**	**89.69 (2.81)**	**81.86 (0.75)**	**73.77 (2.55)**

Table 2: Main results on four commonly-used datasets. We report the average accuracy on different templates and the corresponding standard deviation, which is indicated in brackets.

	SST-2	Yelp-polarity	AG's News	DBPedia
Ours	80.62 (10.08)	89.69 (2.81)	81.86 (0.75)	73.77 (2.55)
-WA	79.42 (10.91)	88.82 (3.08)	81.65 (0.79)	72.59 (2.86)
△	-1.20	-0.87	-0.21	-1.18
-KG	77.58 (10.27)	86.61(4.03)	62.35 (16.16)	58.19 (6.49)
△	-1.84	-2.21	-19.3	-14.4

Table 3: Ablation study. "-WA" means that we directly use the output probability from the MLM head, and "-KG" means that, for final representation estimation, we employ the distributional semantic embedding space rather than KG embedding space.

extraction.

We also demonstrated an example of KG embeddings to show how knowledge integration can help language understanding in Figure 4. We randomly selected a number of generated keywords from samples labelled as "sport","politics", "business" and "technology", and utilized the visualization tool, t-SNE[4], to visualize their corresponding entity embeddings in the two-dimensional space. The colour of each point in the figure indicates the label of the sample from which the keywords were generated. It is observable that entity embeddings assigned to different labels are well distributed across the KG embedding space, indicating that knowledge integration can help capture diverse conceptual aspects of the entities. On the contrary, the embeddings assigned to the same label are well clustered, suggesting that entities with similar properties are mapped closely together in the KG embedding space.

5 Conclusion

We proposed a prompt-based framework to tackle the text classification problem in the extreme zero-shot setting. We exploited the PLM to extract keywords from input, assigned their weights in the meaningful semantic space and incorporated conceptual knowledge from ConceptNet to estimate the final representation. Evaluation results showed that the method reduced the biases of the MLM head and generalized well on two topic detection and two sentiment analysis datasets, outperforming several recently-developed prompt-based approaches.

Limitations

The current work has several limitations that warrant further investigation. Firstly, due to time constraints, we did not conduct experiments using the proposed framework on few-shot settings or a more challenging multi-label classification task. Secondly, our ablation study in Section 4.4 showed that the framework with the weight assignment resulted in only a marginal improvement in performance, suggesting that SimCSE may not be the most effective method for addressing prediction bias. Therefore, future work will explore alternative modeling approaches for bias reduction. Thirdly, in Section 4.5, we noticed that several irrelevant words are also generated as keywords with the language prompt, which may negatively impact the final representation. To address this issue, a better solution, such as keyword filtering, should be considered to improve the current framework. Lastly, we treated each word as a single atomic entity in the KG embedding space, regardless of its possible different senses or meanings. A more careful treatment of word meanings is necessary to handle the problem of polysemy.

[4]https://lvdmaaten.github.io/tsne/

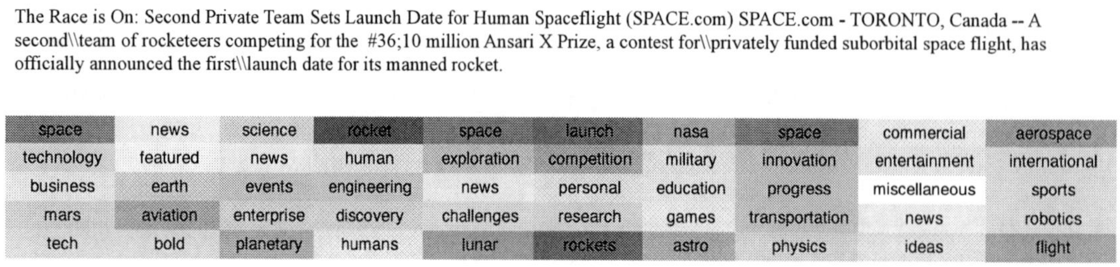

(a) AG's News example

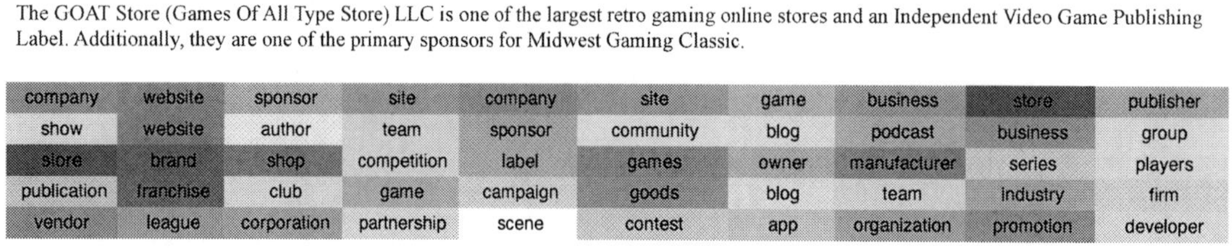

(b) DBPedia example

Figure 3: Weight visualization examples from two topic detection datasets. The Byte-Pair Encoding (BPE) algorithm for the Roberta model may generate words that have their first letters capitalized or a special symbol added as the prefix. After the generation, we replace them with the names of the entities that they actually refer to in the KG. Therefore, there are several duplicates in the keyword set.

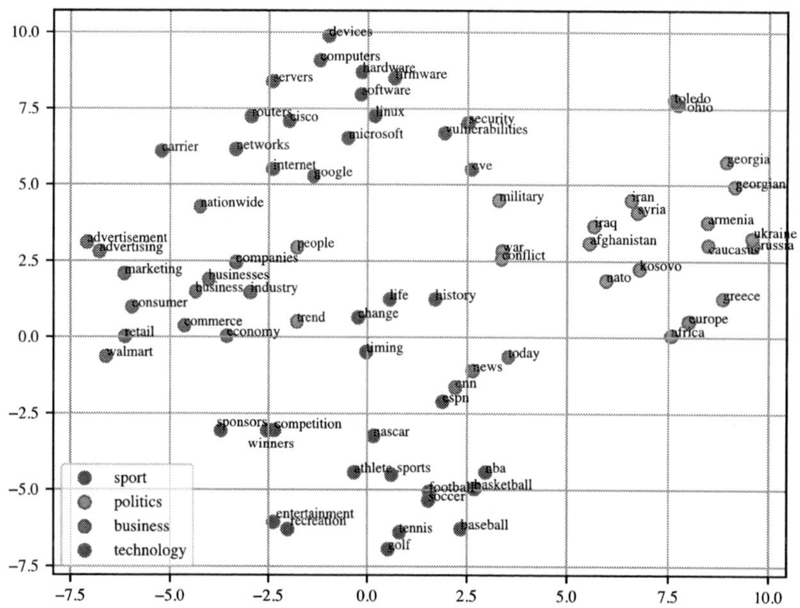

Figure 4: KG embedding visualization. We randomly select several generated keywords from samples labelled as "sport", "politics", "business" and "technology", and utilize the visualization tool, t-SNE, to visualize their corresponding entity embeddings in the two-dimensional space. The colour of each point indicates the label of the sample from which the keyword was generated.

Acknowledgement

We express our sincere gratitude to the matched mentor in the mentoring program, as well as the anonymous reviewers, for their valuable and constructive feedback. Furthermore, we would like to acknowledge the financial support provided by the Postgraduate Research Scholarship (PGRS) at Xi'an Jiaotong-Liverpool University (contract number PGRS2006013). Additionally, this research has received partial funding from the Jiangsu Science and Technology Programme (contract number BK20221260) and the Research Development Fund at Xi'an Jiaotong-Liverpool University (contract number RDF2201132). We are grateful for their support, which has enabled us to carry out this study.

References

Tom Brown, Benjamin Mann, Nick Ryder, Melanie Subbiah, Jared D Kaplan, Prafulla Dhariwal, Arvind Neelakantan, Pranav Shyam, Girish Sastry, Amanda Askell, et al. 2020. Language models are few-shot learners. *Advances in Neural Information Processing Systems*, 33:1877–1901.

Yulong Chen, Yang Liu, Li Dong, Shuohang Wang, Chenguang Zhu, Michael Zeng, and Yue Zhang. 2022. AdaPrompt: Adaptive model training for prompt-based NLP. In *Findings of the Association for Computational Linguistics: EMNLP 2022*, pages 6057–6068, Abu Dhabi, United Arab Emirates. Association for Computational Linguistics.

Jacob Devlin, Ming-Wei Chang, Kenton Lee, and Kristina Toutanova. 2019. Bert: Pre-training of deep bidirectional transformers for language understanding. In *Proceedings of the 2019 Conference of the North American Chapter of the Association for Computational Linguistics: Human Language Technologies, Volume 1 (Long and Short Papers)*, pages 4171–4186.

Hang Dong, Wei Wang, Kaizhu Huang, and Frans Coenen. 2019. Joint multi-label attention networks for social text annotation. In *Proceedings of the 2019 Conference of the North American Chapter of the Association for Computational Linguistics: Human Language Technologies, Volume 1 (Long and Short Papers)*, pages 1348–1354, Minneapolis, Minnesota. Association for Computational Linguistics.

Manaal Faruqui, Jesse Dodge, Sujay Kumar Jauhar, Chris Dyer, Eduard Hovy, and Noah A Smith. 2015. Retrofitting word vectors to semantic lexicons. In *Proceedings of the 2015 Conference of the North American Chapter of the Association for Computational Linguistics: Human Language Technologies*, pages 1606–1615.

Tianyu Gao, Adam Fisch, and Danqi Chen. 2021a. Making pre-trained language models better few-shot learners. In *Proceedings of the 59th Annual Meeting of the Association for Computational Linguistics and the 11th International Joint Conference on Natural Language Processing (Volume 1: Long Papers)*, pages 3816–3830, Online. Association for Computational Linguistics.

Tianyu Gao, Xingcheng Yao, and Danqi Chen. 2021b. SimCSE: Simple contrastive learning of sentence embeddings. In *Proceedings of the 2021 Conference on Empirical Methods in Natural Language Processing*, pages 6894–6910, Online and Punta Cana, Dominican Republic. Association for Computational Linguistics.

Yuxian Gu, Xu Han, Zhiyuan Liu, and Minlie Huang. 2022. PPT: Pre-trained prompt tuning for few-shot learning. In *Proceedings of the 60th Annual Meeting of the Association for Computational Linguistics (Volume 1: Long Papers)*, pages 8410–8423, Dublin, Ireland. Association for Computational Linguistics.

Shengding Hu, Ning Ding, Huadong Wang, Zhiyuan Liu, Jingang Wang, Juanzi Li, Wei Wu, and Maosong Sun. 2022. Knowledgeable prompt-tuning: Incorporating knowledge into prompt verbalizer for text classification. In *Proceedings of the 60th Annual Meeting of the Association for Computational Linguistics (Volume 1: Long Papers)*, pages 2225–2240, Dublin, Ireland. Association for Computational Linguistics.

Jens Lehmann, Robert Isele, Max Jakob, Anja Jentzsch, Dimitris Kontokostas, Pablo N Mendes, Sebastian Hellmann, Mohamed Morsey, Patrick Van Kleef, Sören Auer, et al. 2015. Dbpedia–a large-scale, multilingual knowledge base extracted from wikipedia. *Semantic web*, 6(2):167–195.

Xiang Lisa Li and Percy Liang. 2021. Prefix-tuning: Optimizing continuous prompts for generation. In *Proceedings of the 59th Annual Meeting of the Association for Computational Linguistics and the 11th International Joint Conference on Natural Language Processing (Volume 1: Long Papers)*, pages 4582–4597, Online. Association for Computational Linguistics.

Pengfei Liu, Weizhe Yuan, Jinlan Fu, Zhengbao Jiang, Hiroaki Hayashi, and Graham Neubig. 2023. Pre-train, prompt, and predict: A systematic survey of prompting methods in natural language processing. *ACM Computing Surveys*, 55(9):1–35.

Yinhan Liu, Myle Ott, Naman Goyal, Jingfei Du, Mandar Joshi, Danqi Chen, Omer Levy, Mike Lewis, Luke Zettlemoyer, and Veselin Stoyanov. 2019. Roberta: A robustly optimized bert pretraining approach. *arXiv preprint arXiv:1907.11692*.

Yu Meng, Yunyi Zhang, Jiaxin Huang, Chenyan Xiong, Heng Ji, Chao Zhang, and Jiawei Han. 2020. Text classification using label names only: A language model self-training approach. In *Proceedings of the 2020 Conference on Empirical Methods in Natural Language Processing (EMNLP)*, pages 9006–9017, Online. Association for Computational Linguistics.

Haitao Mi, Zhiguo Wang, and Abe Ittycheriah. 2016. Supervised attentions for neural machine translation. In *Proceedings of the 2016 Conference on Empirical Methods in Natural Language Processing*, pages 2283–2288.

Sewon Min, Mike Lewis, Hannaneh Hajishirzi, and Luke Zettlemoyer. 2022. Noisy channel language model prompting for few-shot text classification. In *Proceedings of the 60th Annual Meeting of the Association for Computational Linguistics (Volume 1: Long Papers)*, pages 5316–5330.

Jeffrey Pennington, Richard Socher, and Christopher Manning. 2014. GloVe: Global vectors for word representation. In *Proceedings of the 2014 Conference on Empirical Methods in Natural Language Processing (EMNLP)*, pages 1532–1543, Doha, Qatar. Association for Computational Linguistics.

Fabio Petroni, Tim Rocktäschel, Sebastian Riedel, Patrick Lewis, Anton Bakhtin, Yuxiang Wu, and Alexander Miller. 2019. Language models as knowledge bases? In *Proceedings of the 2019 Conference on Empirical Methods in Natural Language Processing and the 9th International Joint Conference on Natural Language Processing (EMNLP-IJCNLP)*, pages 2463–2473.

Colin Raffel, Noam Shazeer, Adam Roberts, Katherine Lee, Sharan Narang, Michael Matena, Yanqi Zhou, Wei Li, Peter J Liu, et al. 2020. Exploring the limits of transfer learning with a unified text-to-text transformer. *J. Mach. Learn. Res.*, 21(140):1–67.

Timo Schick and Hinrich Schütze. 2021. Exploiting cloze-questions for few-shot text classification and natural language inference. In *Proceedings of the 16th Conference of the European Chapter of the Association for Computational Linguistics: Main Volume*, pages 255–269, Online. Association for Computational Linguistics".

Taylor Shin, Yasaman Razeghi, Robert L. Logan IV, Eric Wallace, and Sameer Singh. 2020. AutoPrompt: Eliciting Knowledge from Language Models with Automatically Generated Prompts. In *Proceedings of the 2020 Conference on Empirical Methods in Natural Language Processing (EMNLP)*, pages 4222–4235, Online. Association for Computational Linguistics.

Richard Socher, Alex Perelygin, Jean Wu, Jason Chuang, Christopher D. Manning, Andrew Ng, and Christopher Potts. 2013. Recursive deep models for semantic compositionality over a sentiment treebank. In *Proceedings of the 2013 Conference on Empirical Methods in Natural Language Processing*, pages 1631–1642, Seattle, Washington, USA. Association for Computational Linguistics.

Robyn Speer, Joshua Chin, and Catherine Havasi. 2017. Conceptnet 5.5: An open multilingual graph of general knowledge. In *Thirty-first AAAI conference on artificial intelligence*.

Zikang Wang, Linjing Li, and Daniel Zeng. 2020. Knowledge-enhanced natural language inference based on knowledge graphs. In *Proceedings of the 28th International Conference on Computational Linguistics*, pages 6498–6508.

Wenpeng Yin, Jamaal Hay, and Dan Roth. 2019. Benchmarking zero-shot text classification: Datasets, evaluation and entailment approach. In *Proceedings of the 2019 Conference on Empirical Methods in Natural Language Processing and the 9th International Joint Conference on Natural Language Processing (EMNLP-IJCNLP)*, pages 3914–3923, Hong Kong, China. Association for Computational Linguistics.

Xiang Zhang, Junbo Zhao, and Yann LeCun. 2015. Character-level convolutional networks for text classification. In *Advances in Neural Information Processing Systems*, volume 28. Curran Associates, Inc.

Zihao Zhao, Eric Wallace, Shi Feng, Dan Klein, and Sameer Singh. 2021. Calibrate before use: Improving few-shot performance of language models. In *International Conference on Machine Learning*, pages 12697–12706. PMLR.

How do different tokenizers perform on downstream tasks in scriptio continua languages?: A case study in Japanese

Takuro Fujii*
Yokohama National University
tkr.fujii.ynu@gmail.com

Koki Shibata*
University of Tsukuba
s1811496@klis.tsukuba.ac.jp

Atsuki Yamaguchi, Terufumi Morishita and **Yasuhiro Sogawa**
Hitachi, Ltd.
{atsuki.yamaguchi.xn,terufumi.morishita.wp,yasuhiro.sogawa.tp}@hitachi.com

Abstract

This paper investigates the effect of tokenizers on the downstream performance of pretrained language models (PLMs) in *scriptio continua* languages where no explicit spaces exist between words, using Japanese as a case study. The tokenizer for such languages often consists of a morphological analyzer and a subword tokenizer, requiring us to conduct a comprehensive study of all possible pairs. However, previous studies lack this comprehensiveness. We therefore train extensive sets of tokenizers, build a PLM using each, and measure the downstream performance on a wide range of tasks. Our results demonstrate that each downstream task has a different optimal morphological analyzer, and that it is better to use Byte-Pair-Encoding or Unigram rather than WordPiece as a subword tokenizer, regardless of the type of task.

1 Introduction

Tokenization is the first key procedure in current natural language processing when inputting a target sentence to a pretrained language model (PLM). It generally splits an input sequence into subword units, where a subword is a fraction of a word. Previous efforts have proposed several subword-tokenization algorithms (hereafter, subword tokenizers), such as Byte-Pair-Encoding (BPE) (Sennrich et al., 2016), WordPiece (Schuster and Nakajima, 2012), and Unigram (Kudo, 2018), and different PLMs use different subword tokenizers.[1]

It is widely acknowledged that tokenization affects the downstrem performance of PLMs (Rust et al., 2021; Gow-Smith et al., 2022; Bostrom and Durrett, 2020; Park et al., 2020; Toraman et al., 2022). The majority of the previous studies have focused on languages with explicit word boundaries, such as English, while research on *scriptio continua* languages, or languages without word boundaries (like Japanese, Chinese, and Thai), is still understudied. The tokenization process in scriptio continua languages traditionally involves morphological analysis, which splits the input text into morphemes (semantic units similar to words in English) using the dictionary designed by human experts (see Step 1 in Figure 1 for an example). In this case, a tokenizer for a PLM consists of a morphological analyzer and a subword tokenizer. To investigate the impact of tokenization in this scenario, we need to perform a comprehensive study on several sets of the available pairs, which is lacking in the previous work (Bostrom and Durrett, 2020; Inoue et al., 2022; Lowphansirikul et al., 2021).

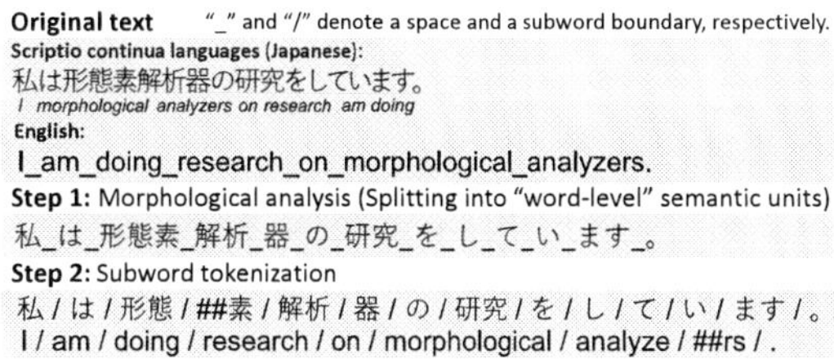

Figure 1: Typical tokenization procedures in both *scriptio continua* languages and English

In this paper, we investigate the effect of tokenizers on the downstream performance of PLMs in scriptio continua languages, focusing on Japanese as a case study. We train an extensive collection of tokenizers consisting of known morphological analyzer and subword tokenizer pairs, use them to pretrain and fine-tune BERT models, and measure their performance on a variety of downstream tasks. On the basis of the experimental results, we address the following three research questions. We first try to answer if we should use a morphological analyzer[2] in a scriptio continua language (Japanese)

[*] Work done while interning at Hitachi, Ltd.

[1] For example, BERT (Devlin et al., 2019) uses WordPiece, and GPT-3 (Brown et al., 2020) uses byte-level BPE.

[2] Not using a morphological analyzer means that we apply subword tokenization directly, the same as in cross-lingual PLMs such as XLM-R (Conneau et al., 2020).

Proceedings of the 61st Annual Meeting of the Association for Computational Linguistics - Student Research Workshop, pages 39–49
July 10-12, 2023

(RQ1). RQ2 and RQ3 each examine whether different morphological analyzers/subword tokenizers perform differently on a downstream task.

Contributions 1) We test a comprehensive set of known morphological analyzer and subword tokenizer pairs and use various downstream tasks to clarify the effect of tokenizers on the downstream performance of Japanese PLMs. 2) Accordingly, we find the followings:

- We should use a morphological analyzer for Japanese.
- Each task seems to have its own optimal morphological analyzer(s).
- It is better to use either BPE or Unigram as a subword tokenizer rather than WordPiece.

3) We publicly release the code and PLMs.[3]

2 Japanese Tokenizer

In this section, we explain the morphological analyzers and subword tokenizers used in this paper.

2.1 Japanese Morphological Analyzers

Japanese morphological analyzers are based on either a pointwise or sequence prediction method. The former tokenizes a sentence by extracting features from the characters within a pre-defined window and then predicting if a boundary exists between each character using a classifier. The latter first constructs a lattice from an input sentence on the basis of a pre-defined dictionary, where each path in the lattice represents a candidate token sequence and has a cost, and then selects the path with the lowest cumulative cost as the analysis result.[4] We obtain a cost for each path using a statistical model(s) or a hand-crafted dictionary.

We test the following four widely used morphological analyzers: MeCab Ⓜ (Kudo et al., 2004), Juman++ Ⓙ (Tolmachev et al., 2018), Sudachi Ⓢ (Takaoka et al., 2018), and Vaporetto Ⓥ (Akabe et al., 2022). The first three adopt sequence prediction while the last uses pointwise prediction.[5]

2.2 Subword Tokenizers

We compare the following three tokenizers: BPE ($\mathcal{B}$), WordPiece ($\mathcal{W}$), and Unigram ($\mathcal{U}$), each of which differs in either vocabulary construction, tokenization algorithms, or both. These tokenizers are empirically known to produce different subword boundaries (Bostrom and Durrett, 2020).

Vocabulary Construction BPE constructs the vocabulary by merging and adding a pair of existing tokens with the highest score in the dictionary until the total number of tokens in the dictionary reaches a pre-defined size. The score is calculated based on the frequency of the existing tokens. WordPiece is similar to BPE but calculates the score based on the frequency of a symbol pair and the individual frequencies. Unigram heuristically builds a large seed vocabulary from a training corpus (e.g., by taking the most frequent substrings) and then iteratively removes the least important symbols from the vocabulary. Specifically, it first fits a unigram LM for the current vocabulary and then computes (i) the log likelihood of the training corpus with the LM and (ii) that of the training corpus with the LM after removing a particular symbol. It then sets (i) − (ii) as the cost, which shows the degradation of the log likelihood when the symbol is removed. Finally, it removes the symbol with the lowest degradation.

Tokenization BPE splits a word into characters and iteratively merges those with the most frequent pair into larger known symbols in the vocabulary. WordPiece[6] splits a word by the longest subword starting at the beginning of the word in the dictionary and continues splitting until its end. Unigram tokenizes a word by performing Viterbi inference to select the maximum likelihood segmentation based on its vocabulary and unigram LM.

3 Experimental Setup[7]

Tokenizers We compared a total of 12 tokenizers (four morphological analyzers and three subword tokenizers), as introduced in §2. We also considered three additional tokenizers not using morphological analyzers. We trained all tokenizers with the vocabulary size of 30k utilizing 10M sentences randomly extracted from Japanese Wikipedia.

Models We used the base configuration of BERT (total parameters: 125M). For each tokenizer, we pretrained BERT for 500k steps with masked language modeling (Devlin et al., 2019) on the Japanese Wikipedia and CC-100 (Conneau et al.,

[3]Available at `https://github.com/hitachi-nlp/compare-ja-tokenizer`.

[4]Since it is intractable to compute costs for all candidate paths, previous studies have used either the Viterbi algorithm (Viterbi, 1967) or beam search to select a path.

[5]For more details, refer to Appendix A.

[6]We follow the longest-match-first strategy used in BERT.

[7]For implementation details, refer to Appendix C.

Tokenizer Subword	 Morphological	MARC-ja Accuracy	JSTS Spearman	JNLI Accuracy	JSQuAD F1	JCQA Acc	NER F1	UD LAS	Avg.
bert-base-japanese		95.5±0.1	85.3±0.3	86.8±0.6	86.4±0.2	76.6±0.8	85.6±0.2	93.3±0.1	87.1
	Ⓜ MeCab	95.4±0.2	84.2±0.1	88.0±0.4	90.1±0.3	74.1±0.7	83.7±0.8	93.6±0.1	87.0
	Ⓙ Juman++	95.5±0.1	84.6±0.4	87.6±0.4	90.1±0.2	73.8±0.3	85.1±0.6	93.6±0.1	87.2
BPE	Ⓢ Sudachi	95.5±0.1	84.2±0.2	88.2±0.3	90.2±0.2	74.2±0.6	83.5±0.6	93.8±0.1	87.1
($\mathcal{B}$)	Ⓥ Vaporetto	95.6±0.1	84.8±0.2	87.5±0.3	89.9±0.2	74.2±1.1	84.1±0.9	93.7±0.1	87.1
	Nothing	95.4±0.2	82.8±0.2	87.2±0.2	88.7±0.3	72.8±0.8	62.9±1.1	93.4±0.1	83.3
	MeCab	95.5±0.1	82.4±0.5	87.5±0.3	89.2±0.3	69.8±0.7	84.0±0.9	93.6±0.1	86.0
	Juman++	95.3±0.3	83.3±0.3	87.7±0.2	89.8±0.3	71.1±0.6	84.7±0.5	93.6±0.1	86.5
WordPiece	Sudachi	95.3±0.2	83.7±0.3	87.2±0.4	89.6±0.1	70.0±0.9	82.4±0.6	94.0±0.1	86.0
($\mathcal{W}$)	Vaporetto	95.3±0.2	83.6±0.1	88.0±0.4	89.7±0.2	71.0±0.4	84.0±0.8	93.8±0.1	86.5
	Nothing	85.5±0.0	N/A	55.3±0.0	10.1±0.1	20.0±0.8	0.0±0.0	63.8±0.9	33.5
	MeCab	95.4±0.3	84.6±0.4	88.3±0.4	89.5±0.3	74.5±0.8	83.1±1.0	93.4±0.2	87.0
	Juman++	95.4±0.2	84.3±0.3	87.8±0.3	89.9±0.2	74.9±1.2	84.1±0.4	93.4±0.1	87.1
Unigram	Sudachi	95.6±0.2	84.8±0.5	88.4±0.3	89.9±0.1	74.5±0.6	83.0±1.3	93.7±0.1	87.1
($\mathcal{U}$)	Vaporetto	95.5±0.3	84.6±0.2	87.9±0.3	89.9±0.1	74.3±0.8	84.1±0.4	93.7±0.1	87.1
	Nothing	95.4±0.4	83.9±0.3	87.7±0.8	89.3±0.1	74.6±0.4	76.9±1.0	93.2±0.2	85.9
Statistical test results: Kruskal-Wallis test (Kruskal and Wallis, 1952). ✓ if $p < .05$ otherwise ✗.									
RQ2: ($\mathcal{B}, \mathcal{W}, \mathcal{U}$)		(✗, ✗, ✗)	(✓, ✓, ✗)	(✓, ✗, ✗)	(✗, ✗, ✗)	(✗, ✓, ✗)	(✓, ✓, ✗)	(✓, ✓, ✓)	
RQ3: (Ⓜ, Ⓙ, Ⓢ, Ⓥ)		(✗, ✗, ✗, ✗)	(✓, ✓, ✓, ✓)	(✗, ✗, ✓, ✗)	(✓, ✗, ✓, ✗)	(✓, ✓, ✓, ✓)	(✗, ✗, ✗, ✗)	(✗, ✗, ✓, ✗)	

Table 1: Results from seven tasks with standard deviations over five runs. JCQA stands for JCommonsenseQA. Values with a wavy line denote the worst results among morphological analyzers with the same subword tokenizer. ✓ indicates that there is statistical significance among (RQ2) morphological analyzers with the same subword tokenizer or (RQ3) subword tokenizers with the same morphological analyzer, while ✗ denotes that there is no statistical significance. For example, (✓, ✗, ✗) in RQ2 indicates that there is statistical significance between different morphological analyzers with BPE, while no statistical significance is observed for WordPiece or Unigram.

2020) datasets, consisting of 2.2 and 1.1M samples each with the maximum length set to 512.

Benchmarks We used the following benchmarks: JGLUE (Kurihara et al., 2022), NER[8], and Universal Dependencies (UD) Japanese-GSD (Asahara et al., 2018).[9] Since the test set for JGLUE is not publicly available, we fine-tuned all models on the training set using five-fold cross-validation and evaluated their performance on the development set. Since the development and test sets are not available for NER, we split the training set into 9:1. We fine-tuned the models with five-fold cross-validation by the former and measured the performance using the latter.

4 Results and Analysis

This section addresses the three RQs raised in §1.

RQ1: Should we use a morphological analyzer? Table 1 lists the results on the seven downstream tasks grouped by subword tokenizer. The average scores across tasks ("Avg.") show that tokenizers without a morphological analyzer ("Nothing") exhibited the worst results among tokenizers with the same subword tokenizer. This trend also generally holds for task-specific results. These results make intuitive sense because a morphological analyzer can provide explicit semantic boundaries of an input text, making the input units for subword tokenization similar to English words (Figure 1). This should help a model to capture the semantic and syntactic information more easily and consequently outperform those that do not use a morphological analyzer. We therefore conclude that we should use a morphological analyzer for Japanese.

In addition to the above, we observe that WordPiece + Nothing produced by far the worst results in all tasks due to the poor tokenization. WordPiece processes a sequence word by word and treats a sequence without a blank as a single word. If it fails to tokenize a particular word, it tokenizes the "whole" as a single `[UNK]` token. Without a morphological analyzer, the length of a word becomes abnormally long, making WordPiece more likely to produce an `[UNK]` token. This means that the majority of an input text will be converted into `[UNK]` tokens, thus losing almost all of the content in the text. In fact, the average sequence length

[8]Dataset: `stockmarkteam/ner-wikipedia-dataset`

[9]We provide the description of each task in Appendix B. For reference, we also measured the performance of `bert-base-japanese`, which uses MeCab and WordPiece.

	JSTS	JNLI	JCQA	NER	UD
BPE	(Ⓥ > Ⓜ) (Ⓥ > Ⓢ)	–	–	(Ⓙ > Ⓢ)	(Ⓢ > Ⓜ) (Ⓢ > Ⓙ)
WordPiece	(Ⓢ > Ⓜ) (Ⓥ > Ⓜ)	–	–	(Ⓙ > Ⓢ)	(Ⓢ > Ⓜ) (Ⓢ > Ⓙ) (Ⓥ > Ⓜ) (Ⓥ > Ⓙ)
Unigram	–	–	–	–	–

Table 2: Combinations of morphological analyzers with statistical significance ($p < .05$, Steel-Dwass test). "–" indicates no statistical significance observed. "Ⓐ > Ⓑ" indicates that morphological analyzer Ⓐ is significantly better than morphological analyzer Ⓑ.

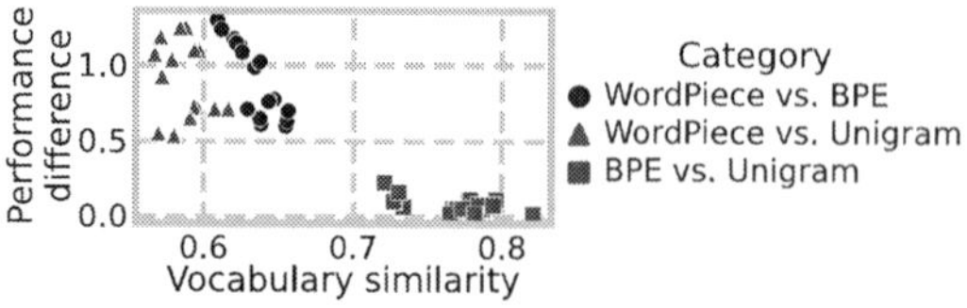

Figure 2: Relationship between vocabulary similarity of subword tokenizers and their performance difference. Samples with the same subword tokenizer are excluded.

and ratio of [UNK] per sample in pretraining were 1.15 ± 3.28 and $99.8 \pm 4.9\%$, respectively. These caused unstable pretraining (see Appendix D).

Compared with other tasks, Nothing in NER showed a considerable performance degradation with a maximum difference of 22.2 (Juman++ vs. Nothing in BPE). In NER, annotations are word-level and tend to align well with morphemes. Since tokenizers with morphological analyzers split a morpheme into subword tokens, they can produce more linguistically motivated subword segmentation than Nothing, thus giving them an advantage.

RQ2: Do different morphological analyzers perform differently on downstream tasks? Looking at the statistical test results for RQ2 in Table 1[10], we can see that there were significant performance differences between different morphological analyzers with the same subword tokenizers in some tasks, e.g., JSTS, NER, and UD. In other words, different morphological analyzers could perform differently on different downstream tasks.

For tasks with statistical significance, we further ran the Steel-Dwass test (Douglas and Michael, 1991) to see which morphological analyzer had a significant performance difference from the others (Table 2). We can observe task-specific trends for an effective morphological analyzer(s). Specifically, for JSTS, Vaporetto performed well. For NER, Juman++ was effective. For UD, Sudachi performed well. Therefore, each task seems to have its own optimal morphological analyzer(s).

RQ3: Do different subword tokenizers perform differently on downstream tasks? From the statistical test results for RQ3 in Table 1, we observe significant performance differences between subword tokenizers with the same morphological analyzers in some tasks, such as JSTS and JCQA. "Avg." in Table 1 indicates that WordPiece performed poorly, while BPE and Unigram achieved similar results. The results of the Steel-Dwass test (Table 3) also confirmed that WordPiece showed significant performance degradation compared with either BPE, Unigram, or both in some tasks. We did not observe a significant difference between BPE and Unigram across all tasks. Therefore, different subword tokenizers could perform on downstream tasks differently, and it is better to use either BPE or Unigram.

We next analyze and discuss which differences in subword tokenizers produced downstream performance differences. First, we look at the difference in the vocabulary of subword tokenizers. We plot the relationship between vocabulary similarity and performance difference between two different subword tokenizers in Figure 2. The vocabulary similarity of two different subword tokenizers is computed as $\frac{|V_1 \cap V_2|}{|V|}$, where $|V|$ is the vocabulary size and V_1 and V_2 are the vocabularies of two subword tokenizers (T_1 and T_2). For each task, we computed the performance difference between the two as $\frac{1}{5}|\sum_i s_{1i} - \sum_j s_{2j}|$, where s_{1i} and s_{2j} are the i-th and j-th observed scores of T_1 and T_2, respectively. We observe that symbols related to WordPiece (● and ▲) are plotted in the upper-left corner, while others (■) are in the lower-right corner, indicating that WordPiece has a different vocabulary composition than BPE and Unigram, and its performance difference is far larger than that between BPE and Unigram. These results are consistent with our finding that WordPiece performed poorly with statistical significance, and both BPE and Unigram showed similar results. Therefore, it is possible that the vocabulary of a subword tokenizer has something to do with the downstream performance.

Further, while WordPiece uses a greedy longest-match-first strategy in tokenizing a word, both BPE

[10]Note that we omit Nothing from the following analyses.

	MARC-ja	JSTS	JNLI	JSQuAD	JCQA	NER	UD
MeCab	–	$(\mathcal{B} > \mathcal{W})$ $(\mathcal{U} > \mathcal{W})$	–	$(\mathcal{B} > \mathcal{W})$	$(\mathcal{B} > \mathcal{W})$ $(\mathcal{U} > \mathcal{W})$	–	–
Juman++	–	$(\mathcal{B} > \mathcal{W})$ $(\mathcal{U} > \mathcal{W})$	–	–	$(\mathcal{B} > \mathcal{W})$ $(\mathcal{U} > \mathcal{W})$	–	–
Sudachi	–	$(\mathcal{U} > \mathcal{W})$	$(\mathcal{U} > \mathcal{W})$	$(\mathcal{B} > \mathcal{W})$ $(\mathcal{U} > \mathcal{W})$	$(\mathcal{B} > \mathcal{W})$ $(\mathcal{U} > \mathcal{W})$	–	$(\mathcal{U} > \mathcal{W})$
Vaporetto	–	$(\mathcal{B} > \mathcal{W})$ $(\mathcal{U} > \mathcal{W})$	–	–	$(\mathcal{B} > \mathcal{W})$ $(\mathcal{U} > \mathcal{W})$	–	–

Table 3: Combinations of subword tokenizers with statistical significance ($p < .05$, Steel-Dwass test). "–" indicates no statistical significance observed. "$\mathcal{X} > \mathcal{Y}$" indicates that subword tokenizer $\mathcal{X}$ is significantly better than subword tokenizer $\mathcal{Y}$.

and Unigram use a more sophisticated approach (as explained in §2.2). This algorithmic difference might also contribute to the performance difference between different subword tokenizers.

5 Conclusion

To investigate the effect of tokenizers on the downstream performance of PLMs in a scriptio continua language (Japanese), we compared extensive sets of tokenizers by evaluating them on a wide range of downstream tasks and addressed the three RQs in §1. Future work will examine how to automatically select the optimal tokenizer pair for a given task.

Limitations

This study has the following limitations:

- We fixed the vocabulary size of each subword tokenizer to 30k. Using a different size might yield different results than those in our paper, though the effect of varying the vocabulary size for a subword tokenizer seemed to be small if the size is sufficiently large (e.g., over 16k or more) (Toraman et al., 2022).
- We have used the BERT architecture for our comparison, while there are other commonly used model architectures such as T5 (Raffel et al., 2020) and GPT-3. The investigation with these architectures is our future work.
- To investigate the impact of tokenizers on the downstream performance of PLMs in scriptio continua languages, we have taken Japanese as a case study. Other scriptio continua languages will be addressed in the future.

Ethics Statement

This study did not involve any sensitive data but only used publicly available data, including Wikipedia, CC-100, JGLUE, Japanese NER, and UD as explained in the paper. Although we plan to release the resulting models, they might perform unfairly in some circumstances, as reported in Baldini et al. (2022). We highly recommend users to refer to studies on debiasing PLMs, such as Guo et al. (2022).

Acknowledgements

We would like to thank anonymous reviewers, Yuta Koreeda, and Yuichi Sasazawa for their insightful comments. We also would like to thank Dr. Masaaki Shimizu for the maintenance and management of the large computational resources used in this paper.

References

Koichi Akabe, Shunsuke Kanda, Yusuke Oda, and Shinsuke Mori. 2022. Vaporetto: Fast japanese tokenizer based on pointwise prediction (in Japanese). In *Proceedings of the 28th Annual Meeting of the Association for Natural Language Processing*.

Masayuki Asahara, Hiroshi Kanayama, Takaaki Tanaka, Yusuke Miyao, Sumire Uematsu, Shinsuke Mori, Yuji Matsumoto, Mai Omura, and Yugo Murawaki. 2018. Universal Dependencies version 2 for Japanese. In *Proceedings of the Eleventh International Conference on Language Resources and Evaluation (LREC 2018)*, Miyazaki, Japan. European Language Resources Association (ELRA).

Ioana Baldini, Dennis Wei, Karthikeyan Natesan Ramamurthy, Moninder Singh, and Mikhail Yurochkin. 2022. Your fairness may vary: Pretrained language model fairness in toxic text classification. In *Findings of the Association for Computational Linguistics: ACL 2022*, pages 2245–2262, Dublin, Ireland. Association for Computational Linguistics.

Kaj Bostrom and Greg Durrett. 2020. Byte pair encoding is suboptimal for language model pretraining. In

Findings of the Association for Computational Linguistics: EMNLP 2020, pages 4617–4624, Online. Association for Computational Linguistics.

Samuel R. Bowman, Gabor Angeli, Christopher Potts, and Christopher D. Manning. 2015. A large annotated corpus for learning natural language inference. In *Proceedings of the 2015 Conference on Empirical Methods in Natural Language Processing*, pages 632–642, Lisbon, Portugal. Association for Computational Linguistics.

Tom B. Brown, Benjamin Mann, Nick Ryder, Melanie Subbiah, Jared Kaplan, Prafulla Dhariwal, Arvind Neelakantan, Pranav Shyam, Girish Sastry, Amanda Askell, Sandhini Agarwal, Ariel Herbert-Voss, Gretchen Krueger, Tom Henighan, Rewon Child, Aditya Ramesh, Daniel M. Ziegler, Jeffrey Wu, Clemens Winter, Christopher Hesse, Mark Chen, Eric Sigler, Mateusz Litwin, Scott Gray, Benjamin Chess, Jack Clark, Christopher Berner, Sam McCandlish, Alec Radford, Ilya Sutskever, and Dario Amodei. 2020. Language models are few-shot learners.

Xinlei Chen, Hao Fang, Tsung-Yi Lin, Ramakrishna Vedantam, Saurabh Gupta, Piotr Dollar, and C. Lawrence Zitnick. 2015. Microsoft coco captions: Data collection and evaluation server.

Alexis Conneau, Kartikay Khandelwal, Naman Goyal, Vishrav Chaudhary, Guillaume Wenzek, Francisco Guzmán, Edouard Grave, Myle Ott, Luke Zettlemoyer, and Veselin Stoyanov. 2020. Unsupervised cross-lingual representation learning at scale. In *Proceedings of the 58th Annual Meeting of the Association for Computational Linguistics*, pages 8440–8451, Online. Association for Computational Linguistics.

Jacob Devlin, Ming-Wei Chang, Kenton Lee, and Kristina Toutanova. 2019. BERT: Pre-training of deep bidirectional transformers for language understanding. In *Proceedings of the 2019 Conference of the North American Chapter of the Association for Computational Linguistics: Human Language Technologies, Volume 1 (Long and Short Papers)*, pages 4171–4186, Minneapolis, Minnesota. Association for Computational Linguistics.

Critchlow E. Douglas and Fligner A. Michael. 1991. On distribution-free multiple comparisons in the one-way analysis of variance. *Communications in Statistics - Theory and Methods*, 20(1):127–139.

Timothy Dozat and Christopher D. Manning. 2017. Deep biaffine attention for neural dependency parsing. In *International Conference on Learning Representations*.

Edward Gow-Smith, Harish Tayyar Madabushi, Carolina Scarton, and Aline Villavicencio. 2022. Improving tokenisation by alternative treatment of spaces. In *Proceedings of the 2022 Conference on Empirical Methods in Natural Language Processing*, pages 11430–11443, Abu Dhabi, United Arab Emirates. Association for Computational Linguistics.

Yue Guo, Yi Yang, and Ahmed Abbasi. 2022. Autodebias: Debiasing masked language models with automated biased prompts. In *Proceedings of the 60th Annual Meeting of the Association for Computational Linguistics (Volume 1: Long Papers)*, pages 1012–1023, Dublin, Ireland. Association for Computational Linguistics.

Seiichi Inoue, Nguyen Tung, Akifumi Nakamachi, Shengzhe Li, and Toshinori Sato. 2022. Investigation of the impact of tokenizers using japanese gpt (in Japanese). In *Proceedings of the 28th Annual Meeting of the Association for Natural Language Processing*.

Phillip Keung, Yichao Lu, György Szarvas, and Noah A. Smith. 2020. The multilingual Amazon reviews corpus. In *Proceedings of the 2020 Conference on Empirical Methods in Natural Language Processing (EMNLP)*, pages 4563–4568, Online. Association for Computational Linguistics.

William H. Kruskal and W. Allen Wallis. 1952. Use of ranks in one-criterion variance analysis. *Journal of the American Statistical Association*, 47(260):583–621.

Taku Kudo. 2018. Subword regularization: Improving neural network translation models with multiple subword candidates. In *Proceedings of the 56th Annual Meeting of the Association for Computational Linguistics (Volume 1: Long Papers)*, pages 66–75, Melbourne, Australia. Association for Computational Linguistics.

Taku Kudo, Kaoru Yamamoto, and Yuji Matsumoto. 2004. Applying conditional random fields to Japanese morphological analysis. In *Proceedings of the 2004 Conference on Empirical Methods in Natural Language Processing*, pages 230–237, Barcelona, Spain. Association for Computational Linguistics.

Kentaro Kurihara, Daisuke Kawahara, and Tomohide Shibata. 2022. JGLUE: Japanese general language understanding evaluation. In *Proceedings of the Thirteenth Language Resources and Evaluation Conference*, pages 2957–2966, Marseille, France. European Language Resources Association.

Ilya Loshchilov and Frank Hutter. 2019. Decoupled weight decay regularization. In *International Conference on Learning Representations*.

Lalita Lowphansirikul, Charin Polpanumas, Nawat Jantrakulchai, and Sarana Nutanong. 2021. Wangchanberta: Pretraining transformer-based thai language models. *CoRR*, abs/2101.09635.

Takashi Miyazaki and Nobuyuki Shimizu. 2016. Cross-lingual image caption generation. In *Proceedings of the 54th Annual Meeting of the Association for Computational Linguistics (Volume 1: Long Papers)*, pages 1780–1790, Berlin, Germany. Association for Computational Linguistics.

Kyubyong Park, Joohong Lee, Seongbo Jang, and Dawoon Jung. 2020. An empirical study of tokenization strategies for various Korean NLP tasks. In *Proceedings of the 1st Conference of the Asia-Pacific Chapter of the Association for Computational Linguistics and the 10th International Joint Conference on Natural Language Processing*, pages 133–142, Suzhou, China. Association for Computational Linguistics.

Adam Paszke, Sam Gross, Francisco Massa, Adam Lerer, James Bradbury, Gregory Chanan, Trevor Killeen, Zeming Lin, Natalia Gimelshein, Luca Antiga, Alban Desmaison, Andreas Kopf, Edward Yang, Zachary DeVito, Martin Raison, Alykhan Tejani, Sasank Chilamkurthy, Benoit Steiner, Lu Fang, Junjie Bai, and Soumith Chintala. 2019. Pytorch: An imperative style, high-performance deep learning library. In H. Wallach, H. Larochelle, A. Beygelzimer, F. d'Alché-Buc, E. Fox, and R. Garnett, editors, *Advances in Neural Information Processing Systems 32*, pages 8024–8035. Curran Associates, Inc.

Colin Raffel, Noam Shazeer, Adam Roberts, Katherine Lee, Sharan Narang, Michael Matena, Yanqi Zhou, Wei Li, and Peter J. Liu. 2020. Exploring the limits of transfer learning with a unified text-to-text transformer. *J. Mach. Learn. Res.*, 21(1).

Pranav Rajpurkar, Jian Zhang, Konstantin Lopyrev, and Percy Liang. 2016. SQuAD: 100,000+ questions for machine comprehension of text. In *Proceedings of the 2016 Conference on Empirical Methods in Natural Language Processing*, pages 2383–2392, Austin, Texas. Association for Computational Linguistics.

Phillip Rust, Jonas Pfeiffer, Ivan Vulić, Sebastian Ruder, and Iryna Gurevych. 2021. How good is your tokenizer? on the monolingual performance of multilingual language models. In *Proceedings of the 59th Annual Meeting of the Association for Computational Linguistics and the 11th International Joint Conference on Natural Language Processing (Volume 1: Long Papers)*, pages 3118–3135, Online. Association for Computational Linguistics.

Mike Schuster and Kaisuke Nakajima. 2012. Japanese and korean voice search. In *2012 IEEE International Conference on Acoustics, Speech and Signal Processing (ICASSP)*, pages 5149–5152.

Rico Sennrich, Barry Haddow, and Alexandra Birch. 2016. Neural machine translation of rare words with subword units. In *Proceedings of the 54th Annual Meeting of the Association for Computational Linguistics (Volume 1: Long Papers)*, pages 1715–1725, Berlin, Germany. Association for Computational Linguistics.

Robyn Speer, Joshua Chin, and Catherine Havasi. 2017. Conceptnet 5.5: An open multilingual graph of general knowledge. *Proceedings of the AAAI Conference on Artificial Intelligence*, 31(1).

Kazuma Takaoka, Sorami Hisamoto, Noriko Kawahara, Miho Sakamoto, Yoshitaka Uchida, and Yuji Matsumoto. 2018. Sudachi: a Japanese tokenizer for business. In *Proceedings of the Eleventh International Conference on Language Resources and Evaluation (LREC 2018)*, Miyazaki, Japan. European Language Resources Association (ELRA).

Alon Talmor, Jonathan Herzig, Nicholas Lourie, and Jonathan Berant. 2019. CommonsenseQA: A question answering challenge targeting commonsense knowledge. In *Proceedings of the 2019 Conference of the North American Chapter of the Association for Computational Linguistics: Human Language Technologies, Volume 1 (Long and Short Papers)*, pages 4149–4158, Minneapolis, Minnesota. Association for Computational Linguistics.

Arseny Tolmachev, Daisuke Kawahara, and Sadao Kurohashi. 2018. Juman++: A morphological analysis toolkit for scriptio continua. In *Proceedings of the 2018 Conference on Empirical Methods in Natural Language Processing: System Demonstrations*, pages 54–59, Brussels, Belgium. Association for Computational Linguistics.

Cagri Toraman, Eyup Halit Yilmaz, Furkan Şahinuç, and Oguzhan Ozcelik. 2022. Impact of tokenization on language models: An analysis for turkish.

Andrew Viterbi. 1967. Error bounds for convolutional codes and an asymptotically optimum decoding algorithm. *IEEE Transactions on Information Theory*, 13(2):260–269.

Thomas Wolf, Lysandre Debut, Victor Sanh, Julien Chaumond, Clement Delangue, Anthony Moi, Pierric Cistac, Tim Rault, Remi Louf, Morgan Funtowicz, Joe Davison, Sam Shleifer, Patrick von Platen, Clara Ma, Yacine Jernite, Julien Plu, Canwen Xu, Teven Le Scao, Sylvain Gugger, Mariama Drame, Quentin Lhoest, and Alexander Rush. 2020. Transformers: State-of-the-art natural language processing. In *Proceedings of the 2020 Conference on Empirical Methods in Natural Language Processing: System Demonstrations*, pages 38–45, Online. Association for Computational Linguistics.

Daniel Zeman, Jan Hajič, Martin Popel, Martin Potthast, Milan Straka, Filip Ginter, Joakim Nivre, and Slav Petrov. 2018. CoNLL 2018 shared task: Multilingual parsing from raw text to Universal Dependencies. In *Proceedings of the CoNLL 2018 Shared Task: Multilingual Parsing from Raw Text to Universal Dependencies*, pages 1–21, Brussels, Belgium. Association for Computational Linguistics.

Daniel Zeman, Martin Popel, Milan Straka, Jan Hajič, Joakim Nivre, Filip Ginter, Juhani Luotolahti, Sampo Pyysalo, Slav Petrov, Martin Potthast, Francis Tyers, Elena Badmaeva, Memduh Gokirmak, Anna Nedoluzhko, Silvie Cinková, Jan Hajič jr., Jaroslava Hlaváčová, Václava Kettnerová, Zdeňka Urešová, Jenna Kanerva, Stina Ojala, Anna Missilä, Christopher D. Manning, Sebastian Schuster, Siva Reddy, Dima Taji, Nizar Habash, Herman Leung, Marie-Catherine de Marneffe, Manuela Sanguinetti, Maria Simi, Hiroshi Kanayama, Valeria de Paiva, Kira

Droganova, Héctor Martínez Alonso, Çağrı Çöltekin, Umut Sulubacak, Hans Uszkoreit, Vivien Macketanz, Aljoscha Burchardt, Kim Harris, Katrin Marheinecke, Georg Rehm, Tolga Kayadelen, Mohammed Attia, Ali Elkahky, Zhuoran Yu, Emily Pitler, Saran Lertpradit, Michael Mandl, Jesse Kirchner, Hector Fernandez Alcalde, Jana Strnadová, Esha Banerjee, Ruli Manurung, Antonio Stella, Atsuko Shimada, Sookyoung Kwak, Gustavo Mendonça, Tatiana Lando, Rattima Nitisaroj, and Josie Li. 2017. CoNLL 2017 shared task: Multilingual parsing from raw text to Universal Dependencies. In *Proceedings of the CoNLL 2017 Shared Task: Multilingual Parsing from Raw Text to Universal Dependencies*, pages 1–19, Vancouver, Canada. Association for Computational Linguistics.

Appendices

A Japanese Morphological Analyzers

MeCab (Kudo et al., 2004) MeCab tokenizes a sentence by first constructing a lattice on the basis of its dictionary and then selecting the combination with the lowest cumulative cost using the Viterbi algorithm (Viterbi, 1967). The cost is calculated using a pre-defined feature function in sequence labeling.

Juman++ (Tolmachev et al., 2018) Juman++ tokenizes a sentence by constructing a lattice in accordance with the dictionary and subsequently selecting the path with the highest score by beam search. The score is calculated using both a RNN-based language model and a feature-based linear model.

Sudachi (Takaoka et al., 2018) Sudachi puts an emphasis on offering a tokenizer and dictionary for business use, enabling us to select tokens of different granularity for each application. We use the "Middle" unit of granularity, which is similar to words in general sense.

Vaporetto (Akabe et al., 2022) Vaporetto tokenizes a sentence by extracting features from the characters within a pre-defined window and subsequently classifying if a boundary exists between each character with a linear classification model.

B Downstream Tasks

We briefly describe the seven downstream tasks used in this paper. The statistics for each task dataset are presented in Table 4.

MARC-ja A binary classification task to predict whether a product review is positive or negative. The dataset is based on the Japanese part of the Multilingual Amazon Reviews Corpus (MARC) (Keung et al., 2020).

JSTS A regression task to predict a semantic similarity score between two sentences. The score ranges from 0 (least similar) to 5 (most similar). The data were sourced from the Japanese version of the MS COCO Caption Dataset (Chen et al., 2015) and the YJ Captions Dataset (Miyazaki and Shimizu, 2016).

JNLI A three-way classification task to predict an inference relation between two sentences. The relation includes "contradiction," "neutral," and "entailment," the same as in SNLI (Bowman et al., 2015). The data source was the same as that for JSTS.

JSQuAD A question answering task to predict a corresponding answer span given a question and context. The data were sourced from Japanese articles in Wikipedia and its construction process is based on SQuAD v1.1 (Rajpurkar et al., 2016).

JCommonsenseQA A multiple-choice question answering task to select the best choice from five choices given a question. JCommonsenseQA is a Japanese version of CommonsenseQA (Talmor et al., 2019), and it was constructed in the same manner as in CommonsenseQA, which used the multilingual knowledge base: ConceptNet (Speer et al., 2017) as seeds.

NER A task to identify and categorize named entities in a given sentence. The data were sourced from Japanese articles in Wikipedia and annotated by Stockmark Inc. The dataset is available at `https://github.com/stockmarkteam/ner-wikipedia-dataset`.

UD A dependency parsing task to predict the syntactic dependency structure of a given sentence (Zeman et al., 2017, 2018). The output is a directed tree originating out of a root node. Each edge in the tree has a label that defines a grammatical relationship between two words.

C Implementation Details

We implemented our tokenizers with the Tokenizers library[11] and our models using the PyTorch (Paszke et al., 2019) and Transformers (Wolf et al., 2020) libraries. We trained our models with four NVIDIA V100 (32GB) GPUs for pretraining and one for fine-tuning. We used automatic mixed precision (FP16) provided by PyTorch as default. The code is available on the GitHub: `https://github.com/hitachi-nlp/compare-ja-tokenizer`, and the models are available on the Hugging Face Hub: `https://huggingface.co/hitachi-nlp`.

C.1 Data

We downloaded Wikipedia data from `https://www.tensorflow.org/datasets/catalog/wikipedia#wikipedia20201201ja`. As its preprocessing step, we excluded sentences with less than 30 characters and those containing "`Category`" or table symbols.

[11] `https://github.com/huggingface/tokenizers`

Dataset		License	Task Type	Number of samples Train	Dev	Test
JGLUE	MARC-ja	CC BY-SA 4.0	Text classification	187,528	5,654	-
	JSTS		Sentence pair classification	12,451	1,457	-
	JNLI		Sentence pair classification	20,073	2,434	-
	JSQuAD		Question answering	62,859	4,442	-
	JCommonsenseQA		Question answering	8,939	1,119	-
Japanese NER		CC-BY-SA 3.0	Named entity recognition	5,343	-	-
UD-Japanese-GSD		CC BY-SA 4.0	Dependency parsing	7,050	507	543

Table 4: Statistics for each dataset used in this paper. Note that the test sets are not currently publicly available for JGLUE. Japanese NER does not have the corresponding development and test sets.

Hyperparameter	Value
Batch size	128
Total training steps	500,000
Adam ϵ	1e-8
Adam β_1	0.9
Adam β_2	0.999
Sequence length	512
Learning rate	1e-4
Learning rate schedule	Linear warmup
Warmup steps	10,000
Weight decay	0.01
Attention dropout	0.1
Dropout	0.1

Table 5: Hyperparameters for pretraining

C.2 Model

We used the base configuration of BERT (12 hidden layers and attention heads, $\text{Dim}_{\text{hidden}} = 768$, $\text{Dim}_{\text{intermediate}} = 3072$, Total parameters = 125M).

C.3 Pretraining

We pretrained all models for 500k steps and optimized them with AdamW (Loshchilov and Hutter, 2019). We mostly followed the configurations of Devlin et al. (2019). Table 5 lists the hyperparameter settings used in pretraining.

C.4 Fine-tuning

Table 6 lists the hyperparameters for fine-tuning models on the JGLUE, NER, and UD datasets. For UD, we trained a deep biaffine attention parser (Dozat and Manning, 2017) built on top of the PLMs. We computed an average for each token over the top four layers of the BERT hidden representations and used it as an input to a biaffine attention parser (BAP). The dimensionalities of arc and relation features given to each biaffine module are 500 and 100, respectively. We used the SuPar library[12] to implement the parser and followed its default hyperparameter configurations.

[12]https://github.com/yzhangcs/parser

Hyperparameter	Value
Batch size	32
Epochs	5 for JGLUE tasks & NER 10 for UD
Adam ϵ	1e-8
Adam β_1	0.9
Adam β_2	0.999
Sequence length	512 for MARC-ja & UD 348 for JSQuAD 128 for JSTS, JNLI & NER 64 for JCQA
Learning rate	3e-5 for JGLUE tasks & NER 5e-5 for BERT in UD 1e-3 for BAP in UD
Learning rate schedule	Linear warmup
Warmup steps	10% of steps
Weight decay	0.01
Attention dropout	0.1
Dropout	0.1

Table 6: Hyperparameters for fine-tuning

D Pretraining Loss

Figure 3 shows the pretraining loss curves for our models grouped by morphological analyzer. We can see that WordPiece + Nothing was unstable in pretraining.

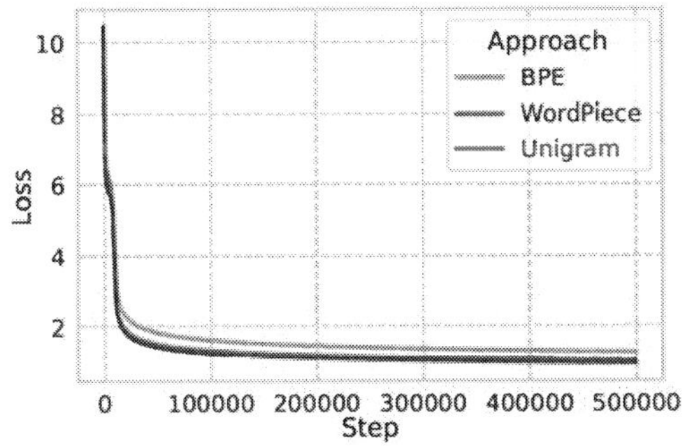

(a) MeCab

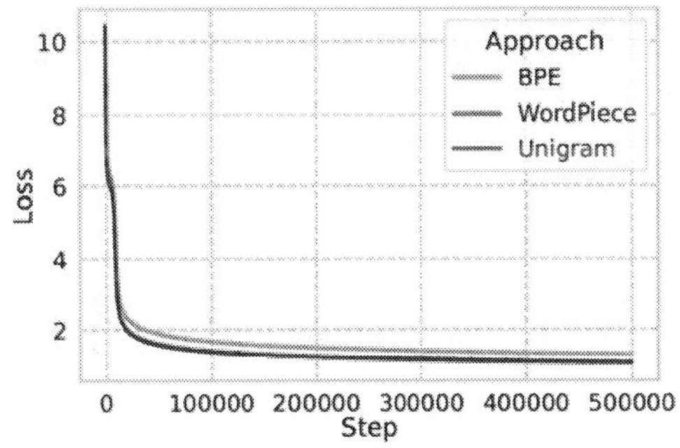

(b) Juman++

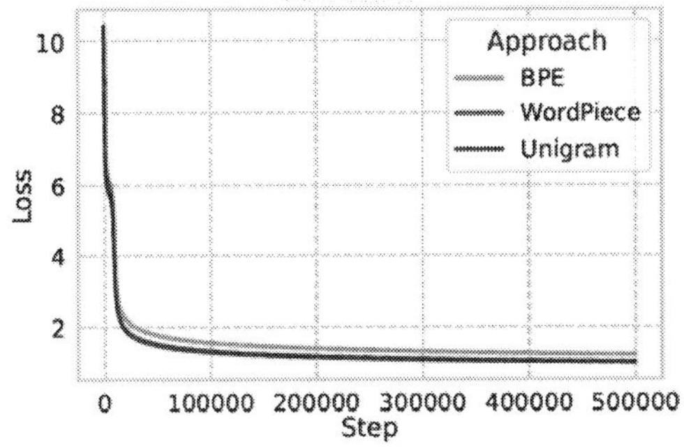

(c) Sudachi

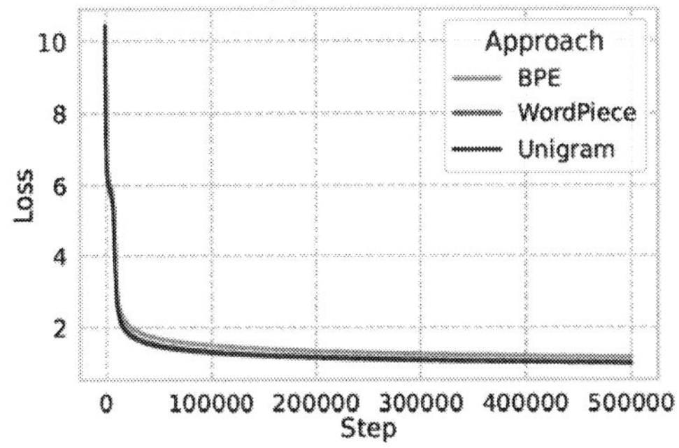

(d) Vaporetto

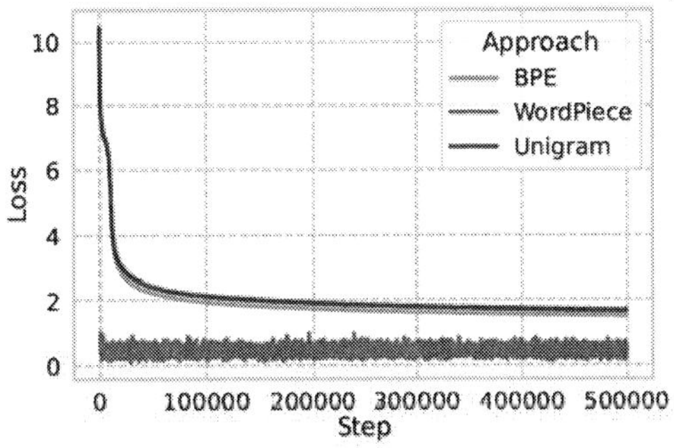

(e) Nothing

Figure 3: Pretraining loss curves

Semantic-aware Dynamic Retrospective-Prospective Reasoning for Event-level Video Question Answering

Chenyang Lyu[†] **Tianbo Ji**[‡*] **Yvette Graham**[¶] **Jennifer Foster**[†]
[†] School of Computing, Dublin City University, Dublin, Ireland
[‡] Nantong University, China
[¶] School of Computer Science and Statistics, Trinity College Dublin, Dublin, Ireland
chenyang.lyu2@mail.dcu.ie, ygraham@tcd.ie, jennifer.foster@dcu.ie
jitianbo@ntu.edu.cn

Abstract

Event-Level Video Question Answering (EVQA) requires complex reasoning across video events to obtain the visual information needed to provide optimal answers. However, despite significant progress in model performance, few studies have focused on using the explicit semantic connections between the question and visual information especially at the event level. There is need for using such semantic connections to facilitate complex reasoning across video frames. Therefore, we propose a semantic-aware dynamic retrospective-prospective reasoning approach for video-based question answering. Specifically, we explicitly use the Semantic Role Labeling (SRL) structure of the question in the dynamic reasoning process where we decide to move to the next frame based on which part of the SRL structure (agent, verb, patient, etc.) of the question is being focused on. We conduct experiments on a benchmark EVQA dataset - TrafficQA. Results show that our proposed approach achieves superior performance compared to previous state-of-the-art models. Our code is publicly available at https://github.com/lyuchenyang/Semantic-aware-VideoQA.

1 Introduction

This paper focuses on one specific variant of Video Question Answering (VQA) (Xu et al., 2016; Yu et al., 2018; Zhong et al., 2022), namely Event-level VQA (EVQA) (Xu et al., 2021). In general, the objective of the VQA task is to provide an answer to a visual-related question according to the content of an accompanying video. Despite significant recent progress in VQA, EVQA still remains one of the most challenging VQA-based tasks since it requires complex reasoning over the *events* across video frames (Sadhu et al., 2021; Zhong et al., 2022; Liu et al., 2022). To tackle the challenges in EVQA, a number of approaches have been proposed (Xu et al., 2021). Luo et al. (2022) propose a temporal-aware bidirectional attention mechanism for improving event reasoning in videos, while Zhang et al. (2022) propose a novel model named Energy-based Refined-attention Mechanism (ERM), which obtains better performance compared to previous approaches with a smaller model size. Liu et al. (2022), on the other hand, incorporate visual-linguistic causal dependencies based on Graph Convolutional Networks (Kipf and Welling, 2017) for enhancing cross-modal event reasoning for EVQA.

Despite recent advances, conventional EVQA approaches generally fail to take into account the explicit semantic connection between questions and the corresponding visual information at the event level. Therefore, we propose a new approach that takes advantage of such semantic connections, using the Semantic Role Labeling (SRL) (Màrquez et al., 2008; Palmer et al., 2010; He et al., 2017) structure of questions. The model uses SRL information to learn an explicit semantic connection between the text-based questions and visual information in videos. Additionally, we carry out a multi-step reasoning mechanism over video frames to avoid adapting to spurious correlation and shortcuts by explicitly learning the reasoning process itself (Yi et al., 2018; Zhang et al., 2021; Picco et al., 2021; Hamilton et al., 2022; Zhu, 2022).

Specifically, in each reasoning step, the model should explicitly decide which frame should be focused on by predicting the reasoning direction (*retrospective* or *prospective*). In terms of the question, in each reasoning step, we focus on one or more specific SRL arguments with high attention weights, and model its connection with the visual information (i.e., video frames) contained within the corresponding video. For example, for a question such as *[**ARG1**: How many cars] were [Verb: involved] [**ARG2**: in the accident?]*, the model con-

*corresponding author

Proceedings of the 61st Annual Meeting of the Association for Computational Linguistics - Student Research Workshop, pages 50–56
July 10-12, 2023 ©2023 Association for Computational Linguistics

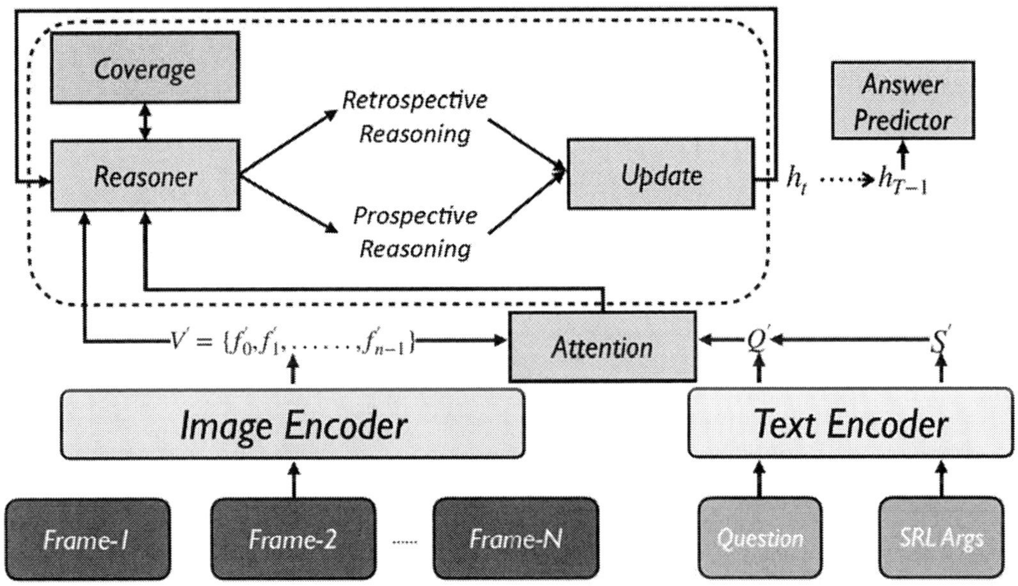

Figure 1: Overview of our approach for multi-step visual reasoning. In each reasoning step, the model predicts the reasoning direction (either *retrospective* or *prospective*) and focuses on a specific SRL argument with high attention weights. A *coverage mechanism* is employed to improve the coverage of SRL arguments in the question.

centrates on the ***ARG2*** when locating the accident, before determining how many cars were involved in the accident (***ARG1***). In a specific reasoning step, t, we inject the relevant visual information based on the semantic connection between the question and video frames by updating a hidden vector. This vector is ultimately expected to contain the necessary information for predicting the correct answer. In the reasoning process, we employ a *coverage mechanism* (Tu et al., 2016) to improve the coverage of the SRL arguments of question. Namely, instead of simply focusing on a small number of specific arguments, the model is capable of including a large range of arguments.

To investigate the effectiveness of the proposed approach, we conduct experiments on a benchmark EVQA dataset: TrafficQA. Results reveal the model to achieve performance superior to that of existing baselines for a range of reasoning types (e.g., counterfactual, prospective).

2 Methodology

An overview of our approach is shown in Figure 1. Suppose the input of our model consists of a video V composed of n image frames sampled from it: $V = \{f_0, f_1, \ldots\ldots, f_{n-1}\}$, and a corresponding question $Q = \{w_0, w_1, \ldots\ldots, w_{m-1}\}$ with associated SRL arguments $S = \{S_0, S_1, \ldots\ldots, S_{N-1}\}$ where $S_i = \{w_i, w_{i+1}, \ldots\ldots, w_k\}$. All frames $V = \{f_0, f_1, \ldots\ldots, f_{n-1}\}$ are fed into an IMAGE ENCODER followed by temporal attention modeling to produce temporal-aware frame representations $V' = \{f'_0, f'_1, \ldots\ldots, f'_{n-1}\} \in \mathbf{R}^{n \times d}$. Meanwhile, we use a TEXT ENCODER to obtain the representations of the question with its corresponding SRL arguments: $Q' \in \mathbf{R}^{1 \times d}$ and $S' \in \mathbf{R}^{N \times d}$. We then perform multi-step reasoning in which we iteratively update the hidden state vector h with the visual information from frame representations based on the attention weights between them and the SRL arguments of the question. h is updated from the initial step h_0 to the final step h_{T-1} where T is the total number of reasoning steps. Finally, we predict the most probable answer a based on h_{T-1}.

2.1 Multi-step Reasoning

Before the first reasoning step, we initialize:

$$h_0 = Attn(Q', V', V') \tag{1}$$

$$j = argmax(AttnWeights(Q', V', V')) \tag{2}$$

where $Attn$ serves as the q, k, v *attention*[1] modeling (Vaswani et al., 2017) and j represents the

[1]In this work, we use a low temperature τ in the *softmax* to encourage the model to assign more attention weights to the most relevant frame.

index of the frame with the highest attention weight. In each specific reasoning step t, we firstly use h_{t-1} as the *attention key* to obtain the relevant SRL argument: $S_t^{'} = Attn(h_{t-1}, S^{'}, S^{'})$. Subsequently, we infer the next focused frame by:

$$V^{focus} = Attn(r_t, V^{'}, V^{'}) \tag{3}$$

where $r_t = g(h_{t-1}, S_t^{'})$. Finally, we update the hidden state vector h_{t-1} based on the currently focused frame (the frame with the largest attention weight):

$$h_t = \delta(h_{t-1}, V^{focus}) \tag{4}$$

2.2 Retrospective-Prospective Reasoning

We propose a *Retrospective-Prospective Reasoning* mechanism for Eq.3 in order to explicitly decide whether the model should move to future frames (*prospective reasoning*) or move back to previous frames (*retrospective reasoning*). We obtain the *retrospective frame* V^{retro} and *prospective frame* V^{prosp} by:

$$V^{retro} = \psi(g(h_{t-1}, S_t^{'}), V^{'}, RetroMask(j)) \tag{5}$$

$$V^{prosp} = \phi(g(h_{t-1}, S_t^{'}), V^{'}, ProspMask(j)) \tag{6}$$

where ψ and ϕ are MASKED ATTENTION that are used to obtain *retrospective* and *prospective* frames, $g(h_{t-1}, S_t^{'})$ and $V^{'}$ serve as *query* and *key, value* respectively. $RetroMask(j)$ means all frames after j ($f_{i>j}$) will be masked whereas $ProspMask(j)$ means that all frames before j ($f_{i<j}$) will be masked. After obtaining V^{retro} and V^{prosp} we generate a probability:

$$p = \sigma(\lambda(V^{retro}, V^{prosp})) \tag{7}$$

If p is larger than a pre-defined threshold α, we update $h_t = \delta(h_{t-1}, V^{retro})$,otherwise we update $h_t = \delta(h_{t-1}, V^{prosp})$ as in Eq. 4. The index for the next-focused frame j is also updated accordingly. The reasoning process is shown in Algorithm 1.

2.3 Coverage Mechanism

We additionally propose to employ a *coverage mechanism* (Tu et al., 2016) to encourage the model to include as many SRL arguments as possible in the reasoning process. Specifically, we track the attention distribution $C_t \in \mathbf{R}^{1\times N}$ of h_{t-1} on all SRL arguments S

$$C_t = C_{t-1} + \frac{AttnWeights([h_{t-1}; C_{t-1}], S^{'}, S^{'})}{\chi} \tag{8}$$

Algorithm 1: Multi-step dynamic retrospective-prospective reasoning with coverage mechanism

$V^{'} = \{f_0, f_1, ..., f_{n-1}\}$: representations of video frames
$Q^{'}$: question
$S^{'}$: SRL representations of Q
T: reasoning steps
χ : normalization factor
α: threshold of the probability for using retrospective frame
$h_0 = Attn(Q^{'}, V^{'}, V^{'})$
$j = argmax(AttnWeights(Q^{'}, V^{'}, V^{'}))$
$C_0 = 0$
for i *in* T **do**
    $S_i^{'} = Attn(h_{i-1}, S^{'}, S^{'}, C_{i-1})$
    $C_i = C_{i-1} + \frac{AttnWeights(h_{i-1}, S^{'}, S^{'}, C_{i-1})}{\chi}$
    $V^{retro} = \psi(g(h_{t-1}, S_t^{'}), V^{'}, RetroMask(j))$
    $V^{prosp} = \phi(g(h_{i-1}, S_i^{'}), V^{'}, ProspMask(j))$
    $p = \sigma(f(V^{retro}, V^{prosp}))$
    if $p > \alpha$ **then**
        $h_i = \delta(h_{i-1}, V^{retro})$
        $j = argmax(\psi(g(h_{t-1}, S_t^{'}), V^{'}, RetroMask(j)))$
    else
        $h_i = \delta(h_{i-1}, V^{prosp})$
        $j = argmax(\phi(g(h_{i-1}, S_i^{'}), V^{'}, ProspMask(j)))$

where χ represents the normalization factor.[2] We obtain the weighted $S_t^{'}$ by $S_t^{'} = Attn([h_{t-1}; C_{t-1}], S^{'}, S^{'})$ where we concatenate C_{t-1} to h_{t-1} as an additional input to the *Attn* function for the purpose of informing the model to assign more attention weights to previously less-focused SRL arguments, in order to improve the coverage for all SRL arguments.

2.4 Training Objective

For the answer prediction, we encode all answer options $A = \{a_0, ..., a_{M-1}\}$ separately and then select the one with the highest similarity with h_{T-1}. We optimize our model parameters θ using *Cross Entropy* loss:

$$J(\theta) = -\sum_i \sum_k log \frac{e^{F(a_k, h_{T-1})}}{\sum_{j=0}^{M-1} e^{F(a_j, h_{T-1})}} y_{i,k} \tag{9}$$

where F is the function measuring the similarity between answer candidate and h_{T-1}, and $y_{i,k}$ represents the answer label for the $i-$th example - if the correct answer for the $i-$th example is the $k-$th answer then $y_{i,k}$ is 1 otherwise it is 0.

[2]In this work, we use the number of SRL arguments of the corresponding question as the normalization factor.

Models	Setting-1/4	Setting-1/2
Q-type (random) (Xu et al., 2021)	25.00	50.00
QE-LSTM (Xu et al., 2021)	25.21	50.45
QA-LSTM (Xu et al., 2021)	26.65	51.02
Avgpooling (Xu et al., 2021)	30.45	57.50
CNN+LSTM (Xu et al., 2021)	30.78	57.64
I3D+LSTM (Xu et al., 2021)	33.21	54.67
VIS+LSTM (Ren et al., 2015)	29.91	54.25
BERT-VQA (Yang et al., 2020)	33.68	63.50
TVQA (Lei et al., 2018)	35.16	63.15
HCRN (Le et al., 2020a)	36.49	63.79
Eclipse (Xu et al., 2021)	37.05	64.77
ERM (Zhang et al., 2022)	37.11	65.14
TMBC (Luo et al., 2022)	37.17	65.14
CMCIR (Liu et al., 2022)	38.58	N/A
Ours	**43.19**	**71.63**

Table 1: Evaluation results on TrafficQA dataset.

3 Experiments

3.1 Dataset

We employ a benchmark dataset for EVQA - TrafficQA (Xu et al., 2021) which contains 62,535 QA pairs and 10,080 videos. We follow the standard split of TrafficQA – 56,460 pairs for training and 6,075 pairs for evaluation. We further sample 5,000 examples from training data as the dev set.

3.2 Experimental Setup

We use CLIP ViT-B/16 (Radford et al., 2021) [3] to initialize our image encoder and text encoder. We evenly sample 10 frames from each video in the TrafficQA dataset. The SRL parser employed in the experiments is from AllenNLP (Gardner et al., 2018; Shi and Lin, 2019). We train our model over 10 epochs with a learning rate of 1×10^{-6} and a batch size of 8. The optimizer is AdamW (Loshchilov and Hutter, 2019). We set the maximum reasoning step T to 3 and we use a temperature τ of 0.2 in *Attention* modeling. The hyper-parameters are empirically selected based on the performance on dev set. There are two experimental settings for TrafficQA (Xu et al., 2021): 1) Setting-1/2, this task is to predict whether an answer is correct for a given question based on videos; 2) Setting-1/4: this task follows the standard setup of multiple-choice task in which the model is expected to predict the correct the answer from the four candidate options.

3.3 Results

The experimental results on the test set of TrafficQA are shown in Table 1, where we also include the previous baseline models for EVQA.[4] The results show that our proposed approach obtains accuracy of 43.19 under the multiple-choice setting, which surpasses previous state-of-the-art approaches including Eclipse (Xu et al., 2021), ERM (Zhang et al., 2022), TMBC (Luo et al., 2022) and CMCIR (Liu et al., 2022) by at least 4.5 points. Furthermore, our approach achieves an accuracy of 71.63 under Setting 1/2, outperforming previous strong baselines by at least 6 points. The results show the effectiveness of our proposed multi-step reasoning approach for event-level VideoQA.

Ablation Study We conduct experiments on the dev set of TrafficQA, investigating the contribution of both the *retrospective-prospective reasoning* and *coverage mechanism* on the performance of our proposed EVQA approach. The results are shown in Table 3, which reveals that multi-step reasoning is critical in terms of model performance while the *coverage mechanism* can provide additional, albeit less substantial, improvements.

Results by Question Type We take a closer look at model performance on different question types, e.g. reverse reasoning, counterfactual reasoning, etc. The results are shown in Table 2. They reveal that our proposed approach outperforms previous state-of-the-art models on all individual question types by a large margin with large improvements seen for *introspection*, *reverse* and *counterfactual* questions.

Effect of Reasoning Steps We study the effect of varying reasoning steps. The results are shown in Table 4. Increasing reasoning steps improves performance, especially from 1 step to 3 steps. Additionally, the performance (both Setting 1/4 and 1/2) is stable with reasoning steps exceeding three.

4 Conclusion and Future Work

In this paper, we propose a multi-step dynamic retrospective-prospective approach for EVQA. Our approach employs a multi-step reasoning model that explicitly learns reasoning based on the semantic connection of the SRL structure of a question and corresponding video frames. We additionally proposed a *coverage mechanism* to improve the coverage of SRL arguments in the reasoning process. Experimental results show that the proposed

[3]https://openai.com/blog/clip/

[4]Some of the baseline results are taken from Xu et al. (2021).

Method	Question Type						
	Basic	Attribution	Introspection	Counterfactual	Forecasting	Reverse	All
HCRN (Le et al., 2020b)	34.17	50.29	33.40	40.73	44.58	50.09	36.26
VQAC (Kim et al., 2021)	34.02	49.43	34.44	39.74	38.55	49.73	36.00
MASN(Seo et al., 2021)	33.83	50.86	34.23	41.06	41.57	50.80	36.03
DualVGR (Wang et al., 2021)	33.91	50.57	33.40	41.39	41.57	50.62	36.07
CMCIR (Liu et al., 2022)	36.10	52.59	38.38	46.03	48.80	52.21	38.58
Ours	**37.05**	**52.68**	**43.91**	**50.81**	**54.26**	**55.52**	**43.19**

Table 2: Results by various *question type* on the dev set of TrafficQA. The highest performance are in bold.

Models	Setting-1/4	Setting-1/2
Model w/o MR and CM	42.53	69.61
Model w/o CM	46.15	74.97
Model	47.38	75.83

Table 3: Ablation study results on TrafficQA dev set, where *MR* represents *Multi-step Reasoning* and *CM* represents *Coverage Mechanism*. MR and CM are coupled in our approach.

Reasoning Steps	Setting-1/4	Setting-1/2
Model w/ 1 step	41.57	71.46
Model w/ 2 steps	44.21	74.95
Model w/ 3 steps	47.38	75.83
Model w/ 4 steps	47.23	75.96
Model w/ 5 steps	47.15	75.87

Table 4: The effect of various reasoning steps.

approach obtains superior performance compared to that of state-of-the-art EVQA models.

Acknowledgements

This work was funded by Science Foundation Ireland through the SFI Centre for Research Training in Machine Learning (18/CRT/6183). We thank the reviewers for helpful feedback.

Limitations

This papers focuses on a variety of VideoQA - event-level VideoQA, we only incorporate *event* information from the question (textual) side as we think that parsing video frames is inaccurate and could introduce unexpected errors, we should also explore how to inject *event-level* information from visual side in the future with more competitive visual parsing models. Our experiments are only conducted on one dataset due to resource constraint, we should also conduct experiments on more datasets to verify the effectiveness of our approach.

References

Matt Gardner, Joel Grus, Mark Neumann, Oyvind Tafjord, Pradeep Dasigi, Nelson F. Liu, Matthew Peters, Michael Schmitz, and Luke Zettlemoyer. 2018. AllenNLP: A deep semantic natural language processing platform. In *Proceedings of Workshop for NLP Open Source Software (NLP-OSS)*, pages 1–6, Melbourne, Australia. Association for Computational Linguistics.

Kyle Hamilton, Aparna Nayak, Bojan Božić, and Luca Longo. 2022. Is neuro-symbolic ai meeting its promise in natural language processing? a structured review. *arXiv preprint arXiv:2202.12205*.

Luheng He, Kenton Lee, Mike Lewis, and Luke Zettlemoyer. 2017. Deep semantic role labeling: What works and what's next. In *Proceedings of the 55th Annual Meeting of the Association for Computational Linguistics (Volume 1: Long Papers)*, pages 473–483, Vancouver, Canada. Association for Computational Linguistics.

Nayoung Kim, Seong Jong Ha, and Je-Won Kang. 2021. Video question answering using language-guided deep compressed-domain video feature. In *Proceedings of the IEEE/CVF International Conference on Computer Vision*, pages 1708–1717.

Thomas N. Kipf and Max Welling. 2017. Semi-supervised classification with graph convolutional networks. In *5th International Conference on Learning Representations, ICLR 2017, Toulon, France, April 24-26, 2017, Conference Track Proceedings*. OpenReview.net.

Thao Minh Le, Vuong Le, Svetha Venkatesh, and Truyen Tran. 2020a. Hierarchical conditional relation networks for video question answering. In *Proceedings of the IEEE/CVF conference on computer vision and pattern recognition*, pages 9972–9981.

Thao Minh Le, Vuong Le, Svetha Venkatesh, and Truyen Tran. 2020b. Hierarchical conditional relation networks for video question answering. In *Proceedings of the IEEE/CVF conference on computer vision and pattern recognition*, pages 9972–9981.

Jie Lei, Licheng Yu, Mohit Bansal, and Tamara Berg. 2018. Tvqa: Localized, compositional video question answering. In *Proceedings of the 2018 Conference on Empirical Methods in Natural Language Processing*, pages 1369–1379.

Yang Liu, Guanbin Li, and Liang Lin. 2022. Cross-modal causal relational reasoning for event-level visual question answering. *arXiv preprint arXiv:2207.12647*.

Ilya Loshchilov and Frank Hutter. 2019. Decoupled weight decay regularization. In *International Conference on Learning Representations*.

Yuanmao Luo, Ruomei Wang, Fuwei Zhang, Fan Zhou, and Shujin Lin. 2022. Temporal-aware mechanism with bidirectional complementarity for video q&a. In *2022 IEEE International Conference on Systems, Man, and Cybernetics (SMC)*, pages 3273–3278. IEEE.

Lluís Màrquez, Xavier Carreras, Kenneth C Litkowski, and Suzanne Stevenson. 2008. Semantic role labeling: an introduction to the special issue.

Martha Palmer, Daniel Gildea, and Nianwen Xue. 2010. Semantic role labeling. *Synthesis Lectures on Human Language Technologies*, 3(1):1–103.

Gabriele Picco, Thanh Lam Hoang, Marco Luca Sbodio, and Vanessa Lopez. 2021. Neural unification for logic reasoning over natural language. In *Findings of the Association for Computational Linguistics: EMNLP 2021*, pages 3939–3950, Punta Cana, Dominican Republic. Association for Computational Linguistics.

Alec Radford, Jong Wook Kim, Chris Hallacy, Aditya Ramesh, Gabriel Goh, Sandhini Agarwal, Girish Sastry, Amanda Askell, Pamela Mishkin, Jack Clark, et al. 2021. Learning transferable visual models from natural language supervision. In *International Conference on Machine Learning*, pages 8748–8763. PMLR.

Mengye Ren, Ryan Kiros, and Richard Zemel. 2015. Exploring models and data for image question answering. *Advances in neural information processing systems*, 28.

Arka Sadhu, Kan Chen, and Ram Nevatia. 2021. Video question answering with phrases via semantic roles. In *Proceedings of the 2021 Conference of the North American Chapter of the Association for Computational Linguistics: Human Language Technologies*, pages 2460–2478, Online. Association for Computational Linguistics.

Ahjeong Seo, Gi-Cheon Kang, Joonhan Park, and Byoung-Tak Zhang. 2021. Attend what you need: Motion-appearance synergistic networks for video question answering. In *Proceedings of the 59th Annual Meeting of the Association for Computational Linguistics and the 11th International Joint Conference on Natural Language Processing (Volume 1: Long Papers)*, pages 6167–6177, Online. Association for Computational Linguistics.

Peng Shi and Jimmy J. Lin. 2019. Simple bert models for relation extraction and semantic role labeling. *ArXiv*, abs/1904.05255.

Zhaopeng Tu, Zhengdong Lu, Yang Liu, Xiaohua Liu, and Hang Li. 2016. Modeling coverage for neural machine translation. In *Proceedings of the 54th Annual Meeting of the Association for Computational Linguistics (Volume 1: Long Papers)*, pages 76–85, Berlin, Germany. Association for Computational Linguistics.

Ashish Vaswani, Noam Shazeer, Niki Parmar, Jakob Uszkoreit, Llion Jones, Aidan N Gomez, Łukasz Kaiser, and Illia Polosukhin. 2017. Attention is all you need. *Advances in neural information processing systems*, 30.

Jianyu Wang, Bing-Kun Bao, and Changsheng Xu. 2021. Dualvgr: A dual-visual graph reasoning unit for video question answering. *IEEE Transactions on Multimedia*, 24:3369–3380.

Jun Xu, Tao Mei, Ting Yao, and Yong Rui. 2016. Msr-vtt: A large video description dataset for bridging video and language. In *Proceedings of the IEEE conference on computer vision and pattern recognition*, pages 5288–5296.

Li Xu, He Huang, and Jun Liu. 2021. Sutd-trafficqa: A question answering benchmark and an efficient network for video reasoning over traffic events. In *Proceedings of the IEEE/CVF Conference on Computer Vision and Pattern Recognition*, pages 9878–9888.

Zekun Yang, Noa Garcia, Chenhui Chu, Mayu Otani, Yuta Nakashima, and Haruo Takemura. 2020. Bert representations for video question answering. In *Proceedings of the IEEE/CVF Winter Conference on Applications of Computer Vision*, pages 1556–1565.

Kexin Yi, Jiajun Wu, Chuang Gan, Antonio Torralba, Pushmeet Kohli, and Josh Tenenbaum. 2018. Neural-symbolic vqa: Disentangling reasoning from vision and language understanding. *Advances in neural information processing systems*, 31.

Youngjae Yu, Jongseok Kim, and Gunhee Kim. 2018. A joint sequence fusion model for video question answering and retrieval. In *Proceedings of the European Conference on Computer Vision (ECCV)*, pages 471–487.

Fuwei Zhang, Ruomei Wang, Fan Zhou, and Yuanmao Luo. 2022. Erm: Energy-based refined-attention mechanism for video question answering. *IEEE Transactions on Circuits and Systems for Video Technology*.

Xi Zhang, Feifei Zhang, and Changsheng Xu. 2021. Explicit cross-modal representation learning for visual commonsense reasoning. *IEEE Transactions on Multimedia*, 24:2986–2997.

Yaoyao Zhong, Wei Ji, Junbin Xiao, Yicong Li, Weihong Deng, and Tat-Seng Chua. 2022. Video question answering: Datasets, algorithms and challenges. *arXiv preprint arXiv:2203.01225*.

Zihao Zhu. 2022. From shallow to deep: Compositional reasoning over graphs for visual question answering. In *ICASSP 2022-2022 IEEE International Conference on Acoustics, Speech and Signal Processing (ICASSP)*, pages 8217–8221. IEEE.

JAMP: Controlled Japanese Temporal Inference Dataset for Evaluating Generalization Capacity of Language Models

Tomoki Sugimoto[1], **Yasumasa Onoe**[2], **Hitomi Yanaka**[1]
[1]The University of Tokyo, [2]The University of Texas at Austin
{sugimoto.tomoki,hyanaka}@is.s.u-tokyo.ac.jp
yasumasa@utexas.edu

Abstract

Natural Language Inference (NLI) tasks involving temporal inference remain challenging for pre-trained language models (LMs). Although various datasets have been created for this task, they primarily focus on English and do not address the need for resources in other languages. It is unclear whether current LMs realize the generalization capacity for temporal inference across languages. In this paper, we present JAMP, a Japanese NLI benchmark focused on temporal inference. Our dataset includes a range of temporal inference patterns, which enables us to conduct fine-grained analysis. To begin the data annotation process, we create diverse inference templates based on the formal semantics test suites. We then automatically generate diverse NLI examples by using the Japanese case frame dictionary and well-designed templates while controlling the distribution of inference patterns and gold labels. We evaluate the generalization capacities of monolingual/multilingual LMs by splitting our dataset based on tense fragments (i.e., temporal inference patterns). Our findings demonstrate that LMs struggle with specific linguistic phenomena, such as habituality, indicating that there is potential for the development of more effective NLI models across languages.

1 Introduction

Natural Language Inference (NLI) is the task of determining whether a set of premises entail a hypothesis. NLI involving temporal inference is a challenging task and remains a significant problem for pre-trained language models (LMs). One line of research has investigated the temporal inference abilities of LMs (Kober et al., 2019; Vashishtha et al., 2020; Thukral et al., 2021; Chen and Gao, 2022). However, existing datasets and analyses primarily focus on English, and more analysis and datasets are required for other languages, including Japanese. Therefore, it is still unclear to what extent current LMs can perform various types of temporal inference across languages. In this paper, we construct JAMP[1], which is a Japanese NLI dataset for temporal inference, and evaluate the generalization capacity of several LMs on our dataset.

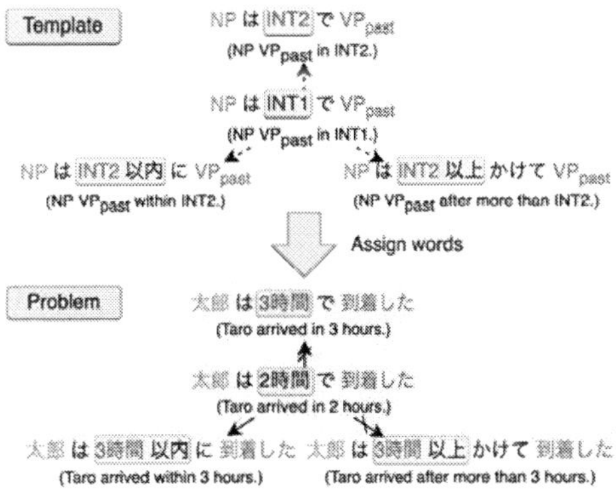

Figure 1: An illustration of our data annotation process. INT in the templates means interval. ⇢ means that the gold label is undetermined, → means that the gold label is *Entailment* and ↛ means that the gold label is *Contradiction*.

Our goal is to construct a temporal inference dataset that precisely assesses the generalization capacities of LMs. Manual annotation is a viable option for achieving this goal, but it does not fully meet our needs based on several limitations described below. Although using crowdsourcing to increase the size of datasets may be cost-effective (Bowman et al., 2015; Williams et al., 2018), managing biases and artifacts in the resulting data can be challenging (Poliak et al., 2018b; Gururangan et al., 2018). In contrast, datasets manually constructed by experts (Cooper et al., 1996; Kawazoe et al., 2015) may have high quality but are potentially expensive to scale. Additionally, manual dataset construction makes it difficult to control the distribution of vocabulary and inference patterns in a dataset because it heavily relies on the prior knowledge of each annotator (e.g., word choice). To address the issues associated with

[1]Our dataset is available on https://github.com/tomo-ut/temporalNLI_dataset

Proceedings of the 61st Annual Meeting of the Association for Computational Linguistics - Student Research Workshop, pages 57–68
July 10-12, 2023

Main Tense Fragment	Sub-tense Fragment		Example Problem
Temporal anaphora	Reference resolution of 昨日 (*yesterday*)	P	昨日、 APCOM は 契約書 に 署名した。 **yesterday** , APCOM wa contract ni sign . (APCOM signed the contract **yesterday**.) 今日 は 7 月 14 日 土曜日 だ。 **today** wa 7 month 14 day Saturday da . (**Today** is Saturday, July 14.)
		H	APCOM は 13 日 の 金曜日 に 契約書 に 署名した。 APCOM wa 13 day no Friday ni contract ni sign . (APCOM signed the contract on Friday the 13th.)
		G	Entailment
Interval	Completion of eventuality	P	スミス は バーミンガム に **2 年** 住んだ。 Smith wa Birmingham ni **2 year** live . (Smith lived in Birmingham **for two years**.)
		H	スミス は バーミンガム に 住んだ。 Smith wa Birmingham ni live . (Smith lived in Birmingham.)
		G	Entailment

Table 1: Examples of tense fragments and corresponding problems. P, H, and G indicate a set of premises, a hypothesis, and a gold label, respectively.

manual annotation, prior work uses template-based approaches that automatically assign diverse vocabulary to templates that are manually created by experts to construct scalable datasets (Richardson et al., 2020; Yanaka and Mineshima, 2021). By using this method, we can strictly manage the vocabulary and inference patterns in a dataset, thus it is a suitable approach for probing LMs.

Figure 1 presents our data annotation process, which consists of two stages: *template creation* and *problem generation*. We first collect Japanese temporal inference examples from JSeM (Kawazoe et al., 2015), which is the Japanese version of FraCaS (Cooper et al., 1996), and manually transform them into templates by masking content words (e.g., nouns and verbs) and temporal expressions (e.g., date and time), producing 46 tense fragments (i.e., temporal inference patterns) based on formal semantics. We then generate examples by assigning content words sampled from a Japanese case frame dictionary (Kawahara and Kurohashi, 2006) and randomly generating temporal expressions to those templates. These techniques ensure that the sentences in JAMP are diverse and cover a wide range of temporal inference patterns. It is important to note that our temporal NLI examples are derived from a diverse set of templates that are classified with tense fragments, allowing us to create different test splits depending on the goal of evaluation, such as generalization across different tense fragments.

We evaluate two Japanese models and one multilingual model on our dataset. We analyze whether they can solve our dataset in a zero-shot setting (trained on existing Japanese NLI datasets) and a fine-tuning setting (trained on a small subset of our dataset). The experimental results demonstrate that the LMs can generalize across different temporal expressions but fail to generalize some tense fragments such as habituality.

2 Background

2.1 Frame

Frame is one of the basic knowledge for language understanding. There are several English resources for frame knowledge, including VerbNet (Schuler, 2005), FrameNet (Baker et al., 1998), and PropBank (Palmer et al., 2005), and previous studies have used these resources to construct datasets (Poliak et al., 2018a; Mitra et al., 2020).

In Japanese, case particles (e.g., が–pronounced *ga*) are attached to verbal arguments (e.g., subject) and determine the case frame. A Japanese case frame dictionary (Kawahara and Kurohashi, 2006) is the largest resource that reflects these characteristics of Japanese language. This case frame dictionary is a set of 110,000 predicates and associated nouns extracted from 10 billion sentences, that are annotated for each predicate usage. Table 2 shows an example of a case frame in the Japanese case frame dictionary.

As shown in Table 2, the case frame dictionary contains information regarding the frequencies of case frames and nouns. In this paper, we use these case frames to generate a dataset containing diverse sentence patterns without grammatical errors.

2.2 Fragments

Some existing datasets (Cooper et al., 1996; McCoy et al., 2019; Yanaka and Mineshima, 2021), including JSeM (Kawazoe et al., 2015), define problem categories for each problem for further analysis. In this study, we systematically defined tense fragments (i.e., temporal inference patterns) based on

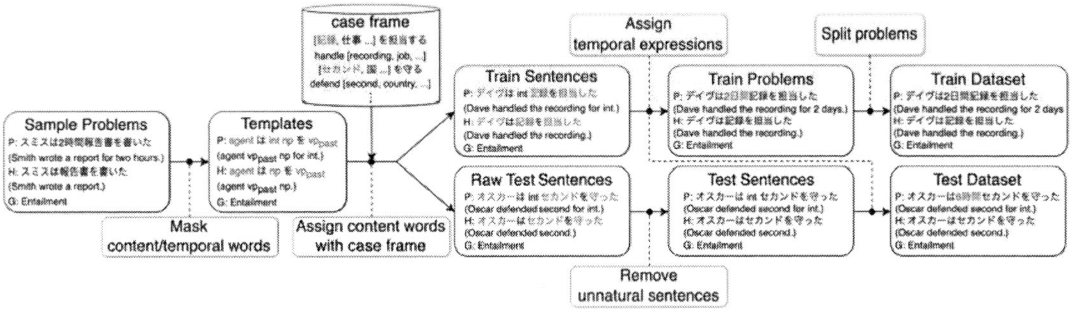

Figure 2: Overview of our data construction pipeline. 1) We first create temporal inference templates from existing examples. 2) We then assign content words using the Japanese case frame dictionary. 3) After isolating train and test examples, we assign temporal expressions to the candidate sentences. Additionally, we manually filter unusable sentences from the test examples.

到着する (arrive): verb, freq=118520	
ga	選手 (athlete)$_{freq=205}$、大統領 (president)$_{freq=114}$、···
ni	空港 (airport)$_{freq=24705}$、ホテル (hotel)$_{freq=9639}$、···
⋮	···
de	飛行機 (airplane)$_{freq=347}$、バス (bus)$_{freq=293}$、···

Table 2: An example of a case frame in the Japanese case frame dictionary.

Template	P:	agent_1 が interval_1 以内に np_1 を vp_1_past。
	H:	agent_1 は interval_2 以内に np_1 を vp_1_past。
	G:	if interval_1 $\leq$ interval_2 then Entailment else Neutral
Generated Problem	P:	エレン が 6 年間 以内 に ゴール を 達成した。 Ellen ga 6 years within ni goal o achieved . (Ellen has achieved her goal within six years.)
	H:	エレン は 5 年間 以内 に ゴール を 達成した。 Ellen wa 5 years within ni goal o achieved . (Ellen has achieved her goal within five years.)
	G:	Neutral

Table 3: An example of a template and a problem generated by our method.

the categories of temporal inference patterns in JSeM.

Table 1 shows some examples of tense fragments (see Appendix A for additional tense fragments). In Table 1, "Main Tense Fragment" represent higher-level classifications, and "Sub-tense Fragment" represent sub-classifications that are subdivided from the main tense fragments. Tense fragments enable a more detailed analysis of LMs' understanding of temporal inference.

3 JAMP

In this paper, we present JAMP, which is a Japanese NLI dataset for temporal inference, and propose a method for automatic construction from templates based on tense fragments. Figure 2 shows the pipeline of our method. First, we create a template by masking content words and temporal expressions in existing temporal NLI problems (§3.1). A template consists of the following triplet: (i) a set of premises in which content words and temporal expressions are masked, (ii) a hypothesis in which content words and temporal expressions are masked, and (iii) a condition for determining a gold label. Here, a gold label can take on three values: *Entailment*, *Contradiction*, and *Neutral*. Next, we generate training and test sentences by assigning content words selected from the vocabulary list to the template (§3.2). We create a vocabulary list by using the Japanese case frame dictionary to make sentences more coherent.[2]

We manually inspect all sentences in the test examples and eliminate any sentences that are unnatural or harmful. We then generate train and test problems by assigning temporal expressions to train and test sentences. Finally, we split the training problems along three axes (e.g., tense fragment, time format, and time span) to create training data for various experimental settings (§3.4). In this section, we describe each of these steps in detail.

3.1 Template Creation

In the first step, we construct templates consisting of a set of premises, a hypothesis, and a gold label. We create templates for temporal problems based on problems in the temporal inference section of JSeM by masking content words such as nouns and verbs (e.g., スミス (*Smith*), 住んだ (*lived*)), and temporal expressions (e.g., 7 月 14 日 (*July 14*), 2 年 (*2 years*)). Additionally, because the gold label depends on the temporal expression in the sentence, we convert the original gold label into a condition in which the gold label is determined by specifying a temporal expression. Table 3 shows

[2]We considered a generation method using masked LMs or generative models but did not adopt them in this study because the generation time was too long, and it was difficult to control the vocabulary and not change inference patterns and syntactic structures.

an example of the template. In the example in Table 3, the condition is "if interval_1 $\leq$ interval_2 then *Entailment* else *Neutral*" and the gold label is determined according to temporal expressions in interval_1 and interval_2.

There can be strong correlations between specific words and labels in examples generated from templates based on certain JSeM problems. Because such correlations could introduce undesired biases into our dataset, we removed these correlations by constructing new challenging templates for some JSeM problems (see Appendix B for examples).

3.2 Problem Generation

We generate problems by filling the masks in templates with various nouns, verbs, and temporal expressions and determining the gold label from these temporal expressions. We use the Japanese case frame dictionary as a vocabulary for selecting verbs and nouns (§2.1). In this study, we manually filter about 30 offensive words from verbs whose frequency in the dictionary is greater than 1000 and nouns whose frequency in the dictionary is greater than 100 extracted from the case frame dictionary and use filtered words.

We target two types of temporal expressions in this study: time points (e.g., 8月16日7時 (*August* 16, 7:00)) and intervals (e.g., 3ヶ月 (3 *months*)). For time points, we use 10 formats combining year/month/day/hour units: Year (Y), Month (M), Day (D), Hour (H), YM, MD, DH, YMD, MDH, and YMDH. For intervals, we use four formats: Year, Month, Day, and Hour.

We assign content words and temporal expressions to templates as follows. First, we randomly select a verb with the case in the template from the case frame dictionary. Next, we randomly select nouns that the selected verb can take as its case in the template. Here, we select a noun for a subjective case from a manually created list of common first names (e.g., *Alice* and *Bob*).

Then, if a temporal expression exists in the original problem corresponding to the template, we generate a new temporal expression as follows and assign it to templates. If the original temporal expression is an interval, we generate an interval by concatenating an integer randomly selected from one to nine according to one of the four formats described above. If the original temporal expression is a time point, we first randomly select a time point within the range of January 1, 2000, at 0:00 to December 31, 2020, at 24:00. Then, one of the ten formats described above is applied to the selected time point. For example, if the MD format is applied to 0:00 on January 1, 2010, then the generated temporal expression will be "January 1."

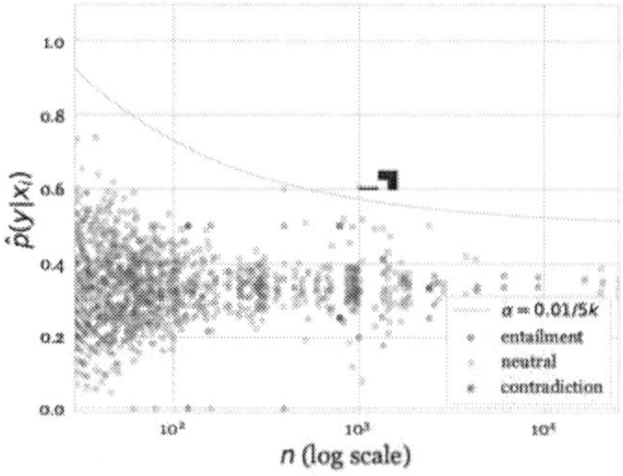

(a) JAMP

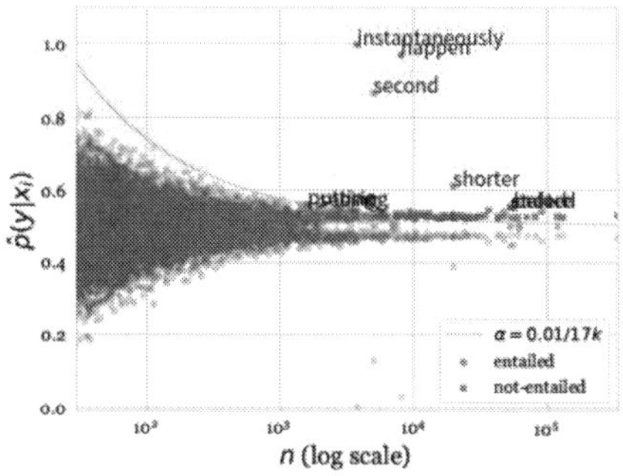

(b) Temporal NLI

Figure 3: The artifact statistics of (a) JAMP and (b) Temporal NLI (Vashishtha et al., 2020) training sets. The majority of words in JAMP, with the exception of "いた," are located below the green line, implying that they do not exhibit spurious correlations with the gold labels. A substantial number of words in Temporal NLI correlate with the gold labels.

Finally, we assign a gold label by evaluating the condition for the gold label in the template. Table 3 shows an example of a template and the problem generated from that template. In Table 3, the condition is "if interval_1 $\leq$ interval_2 then *Entailment* else *Neutral*." Because the generated temporal expressions for interval_1 and interval_2 are 6年間 (*six years*) and 5年間 (*five years*), respectively, its gold label is *Neutral*. To ensure that the distribution of gold labels is approximately uniform, we generate the same number of problems from each pair of a template and a gold label.

Unnatural Sentence	Cause
チャーリー が インク を 吸った。 Charlie ga ink o sucked . (Charlie sucked ink.)	Semantically unnatural
ウォルター は 性格 に 変わった。 Walter wa characteristic ni changed . (Walter changed in character.)	Incomplete sentence
キャロル は 速度 に 生ずるていた。 Carroll wa speed ni arise . (Carroll arose to speed.)	Semantically unnatural Grammatically unnatural

Table 4: Examples of unnatural sentences we filtered.

3.3 Quality Control

3.3.1 Dataset Artifacts

Previous works have demonstrated that existing datasets are often affected by dataset artifacts and spurious correlations between surface features and gold labels (Jia and Liang, 2017; Gururangan et al., 2018; Poliak et al., 2018b). We conduct statistical analysis on our dataset following the method outlined by Gardner et al. (2021) to identify token-level artifacts. Our analysis reveals the extent to which certain words are highly correlated with one of three labels (see Appendix D for details).

Our automatic data annotation approach enables us to effectively manage the examples that we generate. We conduct this statistical analysis during the data generation phase and modify vocabulary words and templates to eliminate shortcuts and spurious correlations between certain words and gold labels. As depicted in Figure 3, the majority of words in JAMP do not exhibit spurious correlations with the gold labels, whereas a significant number of words in Temporal NLI (Vashishtha et al., 2020) correlate with the gold labels.[3] In JAMP, the word "いた"[4] stands out as an exception, but its impact is relatively low because its score is close to the green line.

3.3.2 Dataset Quality

Naturalness We manually check the naturalness of all test examples and filter out disqualified sentences (approx. 40% of all sentences).[5] Table 4 shows examples of sentences we remove from the test set and the reasons for their removal.

Semantically unnatural (e.g., the examples at the top and bottom of Table4) refers to sentences that are grammatically correct but may not be plausible. One reason for the generation of such sentences is that the Japanese case frame dictionary does not describe the correspondence between cases (e.g., ヲ格 (accusative) and ニ格 (dative)). The second case, an incomplete sentence, could be generated since the Japanese case frame dictionary does not describe the essential case for predicates. Other examples, such as the third, show verbs conjugated in the wrong form. This is probably because the verb is not included in the dictionary used to conjugate the verb.

Correctness We randomly sample 100 cases from the constructed test data and manually judge their entailment labels. We check whether the judgement is the same as their gold labels. We confirm that the gold labels in all cases were annotated as intended. However, the gold labels for some problems were debatable. For example, in the sentence *I read a book for three hours*, the meaning of *for three hours* can be interpreted as "just three hours," "about three hours," and "at least three hours". The interpretation depends on the speaker and the context. In such cases, their gold labels depend on the reading, but we confirmed that they are correct in at least one of the possible readings.

3.4 Split Problems

Our controlled data generation method enables us to split problems into seen problems (i.e., problems included in both test and training data) and unseen problems (i.e., problems included only in test data) systematically, which is suitable for investigating the generalization capacity of LMs. In this study, we split our training data to analyze whether LMs can generalize various temporal inference patterns learned from training data. We split the training data based on three axes: tense fragment, time format, and time span. Table 5, 6, and 7 show an example of a seen/unseen problem in each split.

3.4.1 Tense Fragment-Based Split

Tense fragment refers to the categorization of the problems described in Section 2.2. We define two splits based on the tense fragments: FRAGMENT_EASY and FRAGMENT_HARD. These splits aim to test whether LMs can learn temporal inference from basic problems and generalize the acquired inference patterns to more challenging problems. Therefore, both FRAGMENT_EASY and FRAGMENT_HARD include only basic problems in the training data and challenging problems in the test data. FRAGMENT_HARD contains a higher pro-

[3] We sample 100k training examples for this statistical analysis.

[4] This Japanese word has multiple grammatical roles. One is a past stative verb, and another is a past continuous form of a verb.

[5] We ask 3 graduate students studying NLP/linguistics to judge sentence quality.

	Seen problem	Unseen problem
	TF: Order relation - Transitive, Gold label: Entailment	TF: Order relation - Transitive + Before/After, Gold label: Entailment
P	マレット は イブ が 出掛ける 前 に 出掛けた。 Mallett wa Eve ga leave **before** ni leave . (Mullet left **before** Eve left.) イブ は チャーリー が 出掛ける 前 に 出掛けた。 Eve wa Charlie ga leave **before** ni left . (Eve left **before** Charlie left.)	マーヴィン は ペギー が 留学する 前 に 留学した。 Marvin wa Peggy ga study abroad **before** ni study abroad . (Marvin studied abroad **before** Peggy studied abroad.) マーヴィン は キャロル が 留学した 後 に 留学した。 Marvin wa Carol ga studied abroad **after** ni studied abroad . (Marvin studied abroad **after** Carol studied abroad.)
H	マレット は チャーリー が 出掛ける 前 に 出掛けた。 Mallett wa Charlie ga leave **before** ni leave . (Mullet left **before** Charlie left.)	ペギー は キャロル が 留学した 後 に 留学した。 Peggy wa Carol ga study abroad **after** ni study abroad . (Peggy studied abroad **after** Carol studied abroad.)
	TF: Usage of 現在 (*now*) - Present tense, Gold label: Entailment	TF: Usage of 現在 (*now*) - Past tense, Gold label: Neutral
P	マレット は 皆さん に 考え方 を 述べている。 Mallett wa everyone ni thinking o state . (Mallett **is** stating his thinking to everyone.)	アイザック は 見学 に バー を 訪れていた。 Isaac wa tour ni bar o visit . (Isaac **was** visiting the bar for a tour.)
H	マレット は 現在 皆さん に 考え方 を 述べている。 Mallett wa **now** everyone ni thinking o state . (Mallett is **now** stating his thinking to everyone.)	アイザック は 現在 見学 に バー を 訪れている。 Isaac wa **now** tour ni bar o visit . (Isaac is **now** visiting the bar for a tour.)

Table 5: Examples of problems that are in the training data (seen problems) and corresponding problems that are not in the training data (unseen problems) in a tense fragment-based split setting. TF means the tense fragment.

portion of challenging problems and fewer tense fragments in the training data, which is a more difficult setting for models.

We define basic and challenging problems based on the sub-tense fragments in the tense fragment classification. For example, as in the first example in Table 5, suppose a certain tense fragment has sub-tense fragments that are finer than that tense fragment. In this case, the original tense fragment (Order relation – Transitive) is considered as basic, and the subcategories (Order relation – Transitive + Before/After) are considered as challenging. In contrast, as in the second example in Table 5, if there is no such sub-tense fragment, but there are sub-tense fragments with the same granularity as that of the classification, one (Usage of 現在 (*now*) – Present tense) is considered as basic, and the other (Usage of 現在 (*now*) – Past tense) is considered as challenging.

3.4.2 Time Format-Based Split

Time format represents the format of the temporal expression inserted in a problem. In this study, we define ten time formats by combining multiple time units (year, month, day, and hour) for time points and define two splits based on the time formats. This split aims to test whether LMs can learn the size relationships between time units (year > month > day > hour) from a minimal number of combinations of units and generalize the acquired inference patterns to apply them to complex combinations.

The first split is FORMAT_HARD, which contains only a single time unit pattern (i.e., patterns involving only year, only month, only day, or only hour) in a training set and evaluates models on combined patterns of multiple time units.

The other split is FORMAT_EASY, which includes a minimum number of combinations (i.e., year-month pattern, month-day pattern, and day-hour pattern) that allow the models to understand the size relationships between time units, as shown in the second example in Table 6. By comparing the accuracy of FORMAT_EASY and FORMAT_HARD, we can determine whether LMs can learn and generalize the size relationships between time units.

3.4.3 Time Span-Based Split

Time span represents the closeness of temporal expressions when multiple temporal expressions appear in a problem. In this study, we define two time spans: SHORT and RANDOM. In SHORT time span problems, the temporal expressions are generated such that the time points included in the problem are close to each other (see Appendix C), as shown in the unseen problem in Table 7. On the other hand, in RANDOM time span problems, the distance between the time points included in the problem is not predetermined, and the temporal expressions are generated in the same manner as described in Section 3.2. Therefore, the distances between the time points included in a problem are often far apart, as shown in the seen problem in Table 7.

When a model determines the order of two time points, the model must compare the two time points in order, starting with the largest unit. If two time points are far apart, then the model can determine their order by comparing only the larger units, but if two time points are close, then the model must compare additional units to determine their order. For example, the order of January 1, 2010, at 1:00 and October 10, 2020, at 10:00 can be determined by looking only at the year, but the order of January 1, 2010, at 1:00 and January 1, 2010, at 10:00

	Seen problem	Unseen problem
	Format: Year, Gold label: Neutral	Format: Year-Month-Day-Hour, Gold label: Entailment
P	パット が 6 年間 以内 に 代価 を 支払った。 Pat ga 6 year within ni price o paid . (Pat paid the price within 6 years.) パット は **2009** 年 に その 代価 を 支払い 始めた。 Pat wa **2009 year** ni its price o pay began . (Pat began paying the price in **2009**.)	エレン が 2 年間 以内 に 考え を 変えた。 Ellen ga 2 years within ni mind o changed . (Ellen changed her mind within 2 years.) エレン は **2016** 年 **11** 月 **18** 日 **15** 時 に その 考え を 変え 始めた。 Ellen wa **2016 year 11 month 18 day 15 hour** ni its mind o change began . (Ellen began to change her mind at **15:00 on November 18, 2016**.)
H	パット は **2011** 年 までに その 代価 を 支払い 終えた。 Pat wa **2011 year** until ni its price o pay finished . (Pat finished paying the price by **2011**.)	エレン は **2020** 年 **10** 月 **15** 日 **21** 時 までに その 考え を 変え 終えた。 Ellen wa **2020 year 10 month 15 day 21 hour** until ni its mind wo change finished . (Ellen finished changing her mind by **21:00 on October 15, 2020**.)
	Format: Year-Month, Gold label: Entailment	Format: Year-Month-Day-Hour, Gold label: Entailment
P	**2018** 年 **8** 月 以来、 ウォルター は 閣僚 に 指示している。 **2018 year 8 month** since , Walter wa cabinet ni instruct . (Since **August 2018**, Walter has instructed cabinet members.) 現在、 **2018** 年 **11** 月 である。 now , **2018 year 11 month dearu** . (It is now **November 2018**.)	**2008** 年 **2** 月 **27** 日 **0** 時 以来、 ビクター は ソフトバンク に 移籍している。 **2008 year 2 month 27 day 0 hour** since , Victor wa Softbank ni transfer . (Since **0:00 on February 27, 2008**, Victor has been transferred to Softbank.) 現在、 **2008** 年 **2** 月 **27** 日 **4** 時 である。 now , **2008 year 2 month 27 day 4 hour dearu** . (It is now **4:00 on February 27, 2008**.)
H	ウォルター は **2018** 年 **9** 月 には 閣僚 に 指示していた。 Walter wa **2018 year 9 month** niwa cabinet ni instruct . (Walter had instructed the cabinet ministers in **September 2018**.)	ビクター は **2008** 年 **2** 月 **27** 日 **1** 時 には ソフトバンク に 移籍していた。 Victor wa **2008 year 2 month 27 day 1 hour** niwa Softbank ni transfer . (Victor was transferred to Softbank at **1:00 on February 27, 2008**.)

Table 6: Examples of problems that are in the training data (seen problems) and corresponding problems that are not in the training data (unseen problems) in a time format-based split setting.

	Seen problem	Unseen problem
	Span: Random, Gold label: Neutral	Span: Short, Gold label: Contradiction
P	**2002** 年 **8** 月 **16** 日 **7** 時 以来、 ウォルター は 実家 に 泊まっている。 **2018 year 8 month 16 day 7 hour** since , Walter wa parents' house ni stay . (Walter has been staying at his parents' house since **7:00 on August 16, 2002**.) 現在、 **2013** 年 **5** 月 **26** 日 **3** 時 である。 now , **2013 year 5 month 26 day 3 hour** dearu . (It is now **3:00 on May 26, 2013**.)	**2015** 年 **9** 月 **11** 日 **7** 時 以来、 フランク は 細工 に 挑戦している。 **2015 year 9 month 11 day 7 hour** since , Frank wa craft ni try . (Frank has been trying to craft since **7:00 on September 11, 2015**.) 現在、 **2015** 年 **9** 月 **11** 日 **10** 時 である。 now , **2015 year 9 month 11 day 10 hour** dearu . (It is now **10:00 on September 11, 2015**.)
H	ウォルター は **2018** 年 **5** 月 **15** 日 **12** 時 には 実家 に 泊まっていた。 Walter wa **2018 year 5 month 15 day 12 hour** niwa parents' house ni stay . (Walter was staying at his parents' house at **12:00 on May 15, 2018**.)	フランク は **2015** 年 **9** 月 **11** 日 **5** 時 には 細工 に 挑戦していた。 Frank wa **2015 year 9 month 11 day 5 hour** niwa craft ni try . (Frank was trying to craft at **5:00 on September 11, 2015**.)

Table 7: Examples of problems that are in the training data (seen problems) and corresponding problems that are not in the training data (unseen problems) in a time span-based split setting.

requires comparing the year, month, day, and hour in order. Therefore, we consider that determining the order relationships between close time points is more difficult than determining the order relationships between distant time points.

We define a time span-based split that contains only RANDOM in the training data. This split aims to test whether LMs can learn the order relationships of temporal expressions and generalize the acquired inference patterns to apply them to combinations of temporal expressions that require more difficult evaluation.

4 Experiments

We evaluate several NLI models on our dataset. We consider six pre-trained LMs (Japanese BERT-base/large, Japanese RoBERTa-base/large, multilingual XLM-RoBERTa-base/large)[6] available on huggingface/transformers[7] in our experiments. We conduct experiments in three settings: zero-shot (monolingual), zero-shot (cross-lingual), and fine-tuning. Here, zero-shot means that we do not use our training data but use existing Japanese NLI datasets for training data. The statistics of the datasets used in our experiments are provided in Appendix E.

Zero-shot setting (monolingual) We train the LMs on three concatenated NLI datasets: the standard Japanese NLI datasets JSNLI (automatic translation of the English SNLI dataset (Bowman et al., 2015)) (Yoshikoshi et al., 2020) and JSICK (manual translation of the English SICK dataset (Marelli et al., 2014)) (Yanaka and Mineshima, 2022), and the Japanese NLI dataset PLMUTE_ja (Sugimoto and Yanaka, 2022), which involves temporal order. We then evaluate the models on our test data.

Zero-shot setting (cross-lingual) We train the LMs on three concatenated NLI datasets: the standard English NLI dataset SNLI, SICK, and the English NLI dataset PLMUTE (Thukral et al., 2021), which involves temporal order and duration. We then evaluate the models on our test data.

Fine-tuning setting We train and evaluate the LMs on our training data and test data.

Additionally, in the fine-tuning setting, we train the LMs on the split training data described in Sec-

[6] We did not evaluate the prompt-tuning models such as GPT-3 because accurate comparisons with other models in the fine-tuning setting are difficult.

[7] `https://huggingface.co/transformers/`

Model		seen/ unseen	Zero-shot		Fine-tuning						
			Mono lingual	Cross-lingual	IID Split	Tense Fragment		Time Format			Time Span
						Easy	Hard	Easy	Hard	Δ	
BERT	base	seen	-	-	.891±0.02	.879±0.01	.812±0.05	.839±0.02	.800±0.02	.039±0.03	.757±0.03
		unseen	.428±0.02	-	-	.405±0.04	.379±0.02	.897±0.03	.761±0.04	**.136**±0.05	.662±0.05
		Δ	-	-	-	**.474**±0.04	**.433**±0.05	-	-	-	**.095**±0.06
	large	seen	-	-	.955±0.01	.969±0.01	.968±0.02	.920±0.02	.922±0.01	-.002±0.02	.912±0.01
		unseen	.440±0.03	-	-	.457±0.03	.419±0.01	.970±0.02	.893±0.02	**.077**±0.03	.876±0.04
		Δ	-	-	-	**.512**±0.03	**.549**±0.02	-	-	-	**.036**±0.04
RoBERTa	base	seen	-	-	.914±0.02	.898±0.03	.851±0.07	.832±0.03	.754±0.08	.078±0.09	.749±0.06
		unseen	.468±0.03	-	-	.388±0.02	.318±0.02	.846±0.04	.677±0.12	**.169**±0.13	.669±0.05
		Δ	-	-	-	**.510**±0.04	**.533**±0.07	-	-	-	**.080**±0.08
	large	seen	-	-	.937±0.03	.970±0.01	.984±0.01	.914±0.03	.907±0.01	.007±0.03	.819±0.13
		unseen	.460±0.02	-	-	.445±0.03	.399±0.04	.967±0.02	.884±0.01	**.083**±0.02	.799±0.11
		Δ	-	-	-	**.525**±0.03	**.585**±0.04	-	-	-	**.020**±0.17
XLM-RoBERTa	base	seen	-	-	.768±0.05	.683±0.01	.649±0.02	.690±0.09	.607±0.02	.083±0.09	.553±0.06
		unseen	-	.411±0.03	-	.238±0.01	.309±0.02	.678±0.06	.541±0.01	**.137**±0.06	.553±0.06
		Δ	-	-	-	**.445**±0.01	**.340**±0.03	-	-	-	**.000**±0.08
	large	seen	-	-	.941±0.01	.952±0.02	.955±0.03	.883±0.05	.862±0.06	.021±0.08	.761±0.08
		unseen	-	.488±0.03	-	.455±0.04	.383±0.02	.935±0.06	.783±0.08	**.152**±0.10	.735±0.09
		Δ	-	-	-	**.497**±0.04	**.572**±0.04	-	-	-	**.026**±0.12

Table 8: Results on our test data (average accuracy and standard deviation of five runs).

tion 3.4, as well as on all of the training data.

In all experiments, we conduct five trials and calculate the averages and standard deviations of the accuracy of the models. Training details are provided in Appendix F.

5 Results and Discussion

Table 8 shows the results of all our experiments. Overall, monolingual models with larger model sizes tend to perform better. In this section, we describe the results for each setting in detail.

5.1 Zero-shot setting

The two left columns in Table 8 show the results on the zero-shot setting. As Table 8 shows, the accuracy of both the monolingual and cross-lingual models is approximately 40%, and there is no significant difference between them. One possible reason is that SNLI, SICK, and their Japanese versions (JSNLI and JSICK) do not contain temporal inference, and the temporal inference patterns obtained from PLMUTE are only a fraction of the inference patterns required to solve our test set.

5.2 Fine-tuning setting

The right side of Table 8 shows the results on the fine-tuning setting. As expected, all models are highly accurate on the IID split setting (i.e., the setting in which all training data were used). We then discuss the results of the experiments using the splits described in Section 3.4.

Tense Fragment-based Split In the tense fragment-based split, the difference in accuracy between seen and unseen problems was nearly 50% for all models on both FRAGMENT_EASY and FRAGMENT_HARD. This suggests that the models cannot generalize the temporal inferences obtained from the training data.

Table 9 shows an example of unseen problems that RoBERTa-large could not solve on FRAGMENT_EASY and the corresponding seen problems in the training data. Because all models obtained similar results in relation to the generalization ability of LMs for temporal inference, we focus on the RoBERTa-large model, which achieved the best performance on our dataset. For this example, the model gave the same prediction for the both unseen and seen problems. The other tense fragment problems that the model could not solve on FRAGMENT_EASY have the same characteristics. Specifically, the model tended to predict incorrect labels for problems in which the premises and hypotheses of seen and unseen problems were very similar (differences are highlighted in bold), but the gold labels were different, as shown in Table 9. This suggests that this model does not capture the essential meaning of a sentence but determines the entailment relations based only on superficial information (i.e., the model does not generalize temporal inference patterns).

Time Format-based Split As shown in Table 8 shows, all models except XLM-RoBERTa-base achieved 80% accuracies on both unseen problems and seen problems of FORMAT_EASY. Furthermore, detailed analysis revealed that the XLM-RoBERTa-base did not solve problems that required inference of the size relationships between time units. This indicates that XLM-RoBERTa-base only fails to generalize the size relation between time units. One potential reason for this is that this model is cross-lingual and not large. In contrast, on FORMAT_HARD, all models exhibited reduced accuracy for the unseen problems compared to the seen problems. This indicates that the models do not have a priori knowledge regarding the size relationships between time units. There-

	Seen problem	Unseen problem
	TF: Habituality - Unmentioned TP + Always Gold label: Neutral	TF: Habituality + Negation - Unmentioned TP + Always Gold label: Contradiction, Pred label: Neutral
P	イヴァン は いつも 図面 を 遅れて 出す。 Ivan wa always drawing o late submit . (Ivan always submits his drawing late.) 2011 年 11 月 28 日 16 時 に イヴァン は 図面 を 出した。 2011 year 11 month 28 day 16 hour ni Ivan wa drawing o submit . (Ivan submitted his drawing at 16:00 on November 28, 2011.)	デイヴ は いつも マンション を 遅れて 訪れる。 Dave wa always apartment o late visit . (Dave always visits the apartment late.) 2002 年 5 月 11 日 14 時 に デイヴ は マンション を 訪れた。 2002 year 5 month 11 day 14 hour ni Dave wa apartment o visit . (Dave visited the apartment on May 11, 2002 at 14:00.)
H	イヴァン は 2011 年 11 月 28 日 22 時 に 図面 を 遅れて 出した。 Ivan wa 2011 year 11 month 28 day 22 hour ni drawing o late submit . (Ivan submitted his drawing late at 22:00 on November 28, 2011.)	デイヴ は 2012 年 2 月 1 日 0 時 に マンション を 遅れ ず に 訪れた。 Dave wa 2012 year 2 month 1 day 0 hour ni apartment o late **not** ni visit . (Dave visited the apartment on February 1, 2012 at 0:00 **without** delay.)

Table 9: An example of unseen problem that RoBERTa-large could not solve in FRAGMENT_EASY and the corresponding seen problem in the training data. TF means the tense fragment.

fore, we consider that on FORMAT_EASY, BERT and RoBERTa succeeded in generalizing the inference patterns of the size relationships between time units based on minimal combinations of time units in the training data.

Time Span-based Split On the time span-based split, the large models achieved comparable accuracy on both the seen and unseen problems, whereas the base models tended to exhibit lower accuracy on the unseen problems. This suggests that the large models can generalize methods for determining the order relationships between time points, but the base models cannot generalize.

6 Conclusion

In this study, we constructed JAMP, a temporal Japanese NLI dataset, using a template-based approach. Our dataset is controllable in terms of difficulty, vocabulary, and size based on this approach. We conducted experiments using our dataset to probe the generalization ability of pre-trained language models for temporal inference. The experimental results indicated that current LMs can generalize for time format splits and time span splits but fail to generalize for tense fragment splits. Our dataset demonstrates that there is room for improvement in the generalization ability of current standard LMs for temporal inference. Because our method is applicable to the construction of datasets for other linguistic phenomena (e.g., modality, comparative), we plan to investigate the generalization ability of language models for other phenomena using the template-based approach in the future.

7 Limitations

In this section, we discuss two limitations of this study. The first limitation is that aspect and temporal commonsense are outside the scope of our dataset. Here, temporal commonsense refers to knowledge regarding events and the appropriate duration of those events. For example, the event "I washed my face for three years" is unnatural in terms of temporal commonsense, but this study did not consider such unnaturalness.

The second limitation is that the proposed method is currently applicable only to Japanese. In this study, we used a Japanese case frame dictionary to generate natural sentences. However, other languages such as English do not have resources equivalent to such a dictionary. Therefore, to apply our method to additional languages, we must first prepare a case frame dictionary for each language.

Acknowledgements

We thank the two anonymous reviewers for their helpful comments and suggestions, which improved this paper. This work was supported by JST, PRESTO grant number JPMJPR21C8, Japan.

References

Collin F. Baker, Charles J. Fillmore, and John B. Lowe. 1998. The Berkeley FrameNet project. In *36th Annual Meeting of the Association for Computational Linguistics and 17th International Conference on Computational Linguistics, Volume 1*, pages 86–90, Montreal, Quebec, Canada. Association for Computational Linguistics.

Samuel R. Bowman, Gabor Angeli, Christopher Potts, and Christopher D. Manning. 2015. A large annotated corpus for learning natural language inference. In *Proceedings of the 2015 Conference on Empirical Methods in Natural Language Processing*, pages 632–642, Lisbon, Portugal. Association for Computational Linguistics.

Zeming Chen and Qiyue Gao. 2022. Curriculum: A broad-coverage benchmark for linguistic phenomena in natural language understanding. In *Proceedings of the 2022 Conference of the North American Chapter of the Association for Computational Linguistics: Human Language Technologies*, pages 3204–3219, Seattle, United States. Association for Computational Linguistics.

Robin Cooper, Richard Crouch, Jan van Eijck, Chris Fox, Josef van Genabith, Jan Jaspars, Hans Kamp, Manfred Pinkal, David Milward, Massimo Poesio, Stephen Pulman, Ted Briscoe, Holger Maier, and Karsten Konrad. 1996. Using the framework. Technical Report LRE 62-051r, The FraCaS Consortium.

Matt Gardner, William Merrill, Jesse Dodge, Matthew Peters, Alexis Ross, Sameer Singh, and Noah A. Smith. 2021. Competency problems: On finding and removing artifacts in language data. In *Proceedings of the 2021 Conference on Empirical Methods in Natural Language Processing*, pages 1801–1813, Online and Punta Cana, Dominican Republic. Association for Computational Linguistics.

Suchin Gururangan, Swabha Swayamdipta, Omer Levy, Roy Schwartz, Samuel Bowman, and Noah A. Smith. 2018. Annotation artifacts in natural language inference data. In *Proceedings of the 2018 Conference of the North American Chapter of the Association for Computational Linguistics: Human Language Technologies, Volume 2 (Short Papers)*, pages 107–112, New Orleans, Louisiana. Association for Computational Linguistics.

Robin Jia and Percy Liang. 2017. Adversarial examples for evaluating reading comprehension systems. In *Proceedings of the 2017 Conference on Empirical Methods in Natural Language Processing*, pages 2021–2031, Copenhagen, Denmark. Association for Computational Linguistics.

Daisuke Kawahara and Sadao Kurohashi. 2006. A fully-lexicalized probabilistic model for Japanese syntactic and case structure analysis. In *Proceedings of the Human Language Technology Conference of the NAACL, Main Conference*, pages 176–183, New York City, USA. Association for Computational Linguistics.

Ai Kawazoe, Ribeka Tanaka, Koji Mineshima, , and Daisuke Bekki. 2015. An inference Problem Set for Evaluating Semantic Theories and Semantic Processing systems for Japanese. In *JSAI International Symposium on Artificial Intelligence*, volume Technical report LRE 62-051r, FraCaS Consortium. Springer.

Thomas Kober, Sander Bijl de Vroe, and Mark Steedman. 2019. Temporal and aspectual entailment. In *Proceedings of the 13th International Conference on Computational Semantics - Long Papers*, pages 103–119, Gothenburg, Sweden. Association for Computational Linguistics.

Marco Marelli, Stefano Menini, Marco Baroni, Luisa Bentivogli, Raffaella Bernardi, and Roberto Zamparelli. 2014. A SICK cure for the evaluation of compositional distributional semantic models. In *Proceedings of the Ninth International Conference on Language Resources and Evaluation (LREC'14)*, pages 216–223, Reykjavik, Iceland. European Language Resources Association (ELRA).

Tom McCoy, Ellie Pavlick, and Tal Linzen. 2019. Right for the wrong reasons: Diagnosing syntactic heuristics in natural language inference. In *Proceedings of the 57th Annual Meeting of the Association for Computational Linguistics*, pages 3428–3448, Florence, Italy. Association for Computational Linguistics.

Arindam Mitra, Ishan Shrivastava, and Chitta Baral. 2020. Enhancing natural language inference using new and expanded training data sets and new learning models. *Proceedings of the AAAI Conference on Artificial Intelligence*, 34(05):8504–8511.

Hajime Morita, Daisuke Kawahara, and Sadao Kurohashi. 2015. Morphological analysis for unsegmented languages using recurrent neural network language model. In *Proceedings of the 2015 Conference on Empirical Methods in Natural Language Processing*, pages 2292–2297, Lisbon, Portugal. Association for Computational Linguistics.

Martha Palmer, Daniel Gildea, and Paul Kingsbury. 2005. The Proposition Bank: An annotated corpus of semantic roles. *Computational Linguistics*, 31(1):71–106.

Adam Poliak, Aparajita Haldar, Rachel Rudinger, J. Edward Hu, Ellie Pavlick, Aaron Steven White, and Benjamin Van Durme. 2018a. Collecting diverse natural language inference problems for sentence representation evaluation. In *Proceedings of the 2018 Conference on Empirical Methods in Natural Language Processing*, pages 67–81, Brussels, Belgium. Association for Computational Linguistics.

Adam Poliak, Jason Naradowsky, Aparajita Haldar, Rachel Rudinger, and Benjamin Van Durme. 2018b. Hypothesis only baselines in natural language inference. In *Proceedings of the Seventh Joint Conference on Lexical and Computational Semantics*, pages 180–191, New Orleans, Louisiana. Association for Computational Linguistics.

Kyle Richardson, Hai Hu, Lawrence Moss, and Ashish Sabharwal. 2020. Probing natural language inference models through semantic fragments. *Proceedings of the AAAI Conference on Artificial Intelligence*, 34(05):8713–8721.

Karin Kipper Schuler. 2005. Verbnet: A broad-coverage, comprehensive verb lexicon. *Ph. D. Thesis, University of Pennsylvania.*

Tomoki Sugimoto and Hitomi Yanaka. 2022. Compositional semantics and inference system for temporal order based on Japanese CCG. In *Proceedings of the 60th Annual Meeting of the Association for Computational Linguistics: Student Research Workshop*, pages 104–114, Dublin, Ireland. Association for Computational Linguistics.

Shivin Thukral, Kunal Kukreja, and Christian Kavouras. 2021. Probing language models for understanding of temporal expressions. In *Proceedings of the Fourth BlackboxNLP Workshop on Analyzing and Interpreting Neural Networks for NLP*, pages 396–406, Punta Cana, Dominican Republic. Association for Computational Linguistics.

Siddharth Vashishtha, Adam Poliak, Yash Kumar Lal, Benjamin Van Durme, and Aaron Steven White. 2020. Temporal reasoning in natural language inference. In *Findings of the Association for Computational Linguistics: EMNLP 2020*, pages 4070–4078, Online. Association for Computational Linguistics.

Adina Williams, Nikita Nangia, and Samuel Bowman. 2018. A broad-coverage challenge corpus for sentence understanding through inference. In *Proceedings of the 2018 Conference of the North American Chapter of the Association for Computational Linguistics: Human Language Technologies, Volume 1 (Long Papers)*, pages 1112–1122, New Orleans, Louisiana. Association for Computational Linguistics.

Hitomi Yanaka and Koji Mineshima. 2021. Assessing the generalization capacity of pre-trained language models through Japanese adversarial natural language inference. In *Proceedings of the Fourth BlackboxNLP Workshop on Analyzing and Interpreting Neural Networks for NLP*, pages 337–349, Punta Cana, Dominican Republic. Association for Computational Linguistics.

Hitomi Yanaka and Koji Mineshima. 2022. Compositional evaluation on Japanese textual entailment and similarity. *Transactions of the Association for Computational Linguistics*, 10:1266–1284.

Takumi Yoshikoshi, Daisuke Kawahara, and Sadao Kurohashi. 2020. Multilingualization of a natural language inference dataset using machine translation (in japanese). In *Proceedings of the 244th Meeting of Natural Language Processing*.

A Tense Fragment

Table 10 shows the tense fragments we defined.

Tense Fragment	Sub-tense Fragment
Temporal commonsense	Usage of 現在 (*now*)
Temporal ordering	Continuity of state
	Ordering relation
Time point	Mentioned time point
	Unmentioned time point
Temporal anaphora	Reference resolution of 昨日 (*yesterday*)
Interval	Comparison of two intervals
	Completion of eventuality
Habituality	Mentioned time point
	Unmentioned time point
	Negation
	Existential quantification

Table 10: Tense fragments we introduced in this study.

B Problem Creation for Some JSeM Problems

Table 11 shows examples of created problems and corresponding original problems in JSeM. As shown in Table 11, original and new problems are similar but have different gold labels. We also create templates for these created problems.

C Temporal Expression Generation in SHORT Time Span

The temporal expressions in SHORT are generated as follows. In the case of generating intervals, they are generated as described in Section 3.2, except that the integer selection range is one to three instead of one to nine. In the case of generating time points, we first identify the next largest unit after the smallest unit of the time format in the current problem and then calculate the duration of one-third of that unit. We then determine a selection range from a randomly selected time point to a time point that is advanced by the calculated duration. For example, if the smallest unit is "hour," then the next smallest unit is "day," so the selection range is between a specific time point and another time point one-third of a day (eight hours) in the future.

D Details for Dataset Artifacts Analysis

As mentioned in Section ??, dataset artifacts analysis reveals correlations between labels and specific words. Formally, this analysis is a one-side binomial hypothesis test with the null hypothesis $p(y|x_i) = 1/3$, where $y \in \{Entailment, Neutral, Contradiction\}$, and x_i is a

	Original problem	New problem
	Gold label: Entailment	Gold label: Contradiction
P	スミス は ジョーンズ が 去る 前 に 去った。 Smith wa Jones ga leave before ni leave . (Smith left before Jones left.) ジョーンズ は アンダーソン が 去る 前 に 去った。 Jones wa Anderson ga leave before ni leave . (Jones left before Anderson left.)	スミス は ジョーンズ が 去る 前 に 去った。 Smith wa Jones ga leave before ni leave . (Smith left before Jones left.) ジョーンズ は アンダーソン が 去る 前 に 去った。 Jones wa Anderson ga leave before ni leave . (Jones left before Anderson left.)
H	スミス は アンダーソン が 去る 前 に 去った。 Smith wa Anderson ga leave **before** ni leave . (Smith left **before** Anderson left.)	スミス は アンダーソン が 去った 後 に 去った。 Smith wa Anderson ga leave **after** ni leave . (Smith left **after** Anderson left.)
	Gold label: Neutral	Gold label: Entailment
P	スミス が 2 時間 以内 に 報告書 を 書いた。 Smith ga 2 hour **within** ni report o write . (Smith wrote a report **within** two hours.)	スミス が 2 時間 で 報告書 を 書いた。 Smith ga 2 hour **de** report o write . (Smith wrote a report **in** two hours.)
H	スミス は その 報告書 を 書く の に 2 時間 を 費やした。 Smith wa that report o write no ni 2 hour o spent . (Smith spent two hours writing that report.)	スミス は その 報告書 を 書く の に 2 時間 を 費やした。 Smith wa that report o write no ni 2 hour o spent . (Smith spent two hours writing that report.)

Table 11: Examples of created problems and corresponding original problems in JSeM.

Section	Size
Train	9,750 (3,050/3,340/3,360)
Test	344 (114/112/118)

Table 12: JAMP dataset statistics. The lower row in parentheses shows the number of entailment, contradiction, and neutral examples, respectively.

Dataset Name	Size
SNLI (Bowman et al., 2015)	550,152
SICK (Marelli et al., 2014)	9,840
PLMUTE (Thukral et al., 2021)	72,720
JSNLI (Yoshikoshi et al., 2020)	533,005
JSICK (Yanaka and Mineshima, 2022)	5,000
PLMUTE_ja (Sugimoto and Yanaka, 2022)	11,220

Table 13: Statistics of dataset used in our experiments

word included in the vocabulary. For this analysis, we first split the hypothesis and premise sentences into individual words/tokens using Juman++ (Morita et al., 2015). We then count the number of occurrences of the gold label y in the n_i examples for every word x_i present in those examples. $p(y|x_i)$ is estimated based on the fraction of the count of the gold label y over n_i. According to the protocol described in Gardner et al. (2021), the null hypothesis is either accepted or rejected with a significance level of $\alpha = 0.01$ based on the Bonferroni correction.

E Data Statistics

Table 12 shows JAMP dataset statistics. Table 13 shows sizes of datasets used in our experiments.

F Training Details

We select the best learning rate among [6e-6,8e-6,1e-5,1.2e-5,2e-5] based on the development set. We use a batch size of 16 for training and eight for test.

G Data Licensing

Japanese case frame dictionary is distributed by Gengo-Shigen-Kyokai. JSeM is licensed under by BSD-3-Clause license. Our use of these two datasets is consistent with the terms of the license.

Constructing Multilingual Code Search Dataset Using Neural Machine Translation

Ryo Sekizawa[1] **Nan Duan**[2] **Shuai Lu**[2] **Hitomi Yanaka**[1]
[1]The University of Tokyo [2]Microsoft Research Asia
{ryosekizawa,hyanaka}@is.s.u-tokyo.ac.jp
{nanduan,shuailu}@microsoft.com

Abstract

Code search is a task to find programming codes that semantically match the given natural language queries. Even though some of the existing datasets for this task are multilingual on the programming language side, their query data are only in English. In this research, we create a multilingual code search dataset in four natural and four programming languages using a neural machine translation model. Using our dataset, we pre-train and fine-tune the Transformer-based models and then evaluate them on multiple code search test sets. Our results show that the model pre-trained with all natural and programming language data has performed best in most cases. By applying back-translation data filtering to our dataset, we demonstrate that the translation quality affects the model's performance to a certain extent, but the data size matters more.

1 Introduction

Code search is the task of finding a semantically corresponding programming language code given a natural language query by calculating their similarity. With the spread of large-scale code-sharing repositories and the rise of advanced search engines, high-performance code search is an important technology to assist software developers. Since software developers worldwide search for codes in their native language, we expect code search models to be multilingual. Although many previous studies focus on multilingual code tasks other than code search (e.g., code generation, code explanation) (Wang et al., 2021; Ahmad et al., 2021; Fried et al., 2023; Zheng et al., 2023), the existing code search datasets (Husain et al., 2020; Huang et al., 2021; Shuai et al., 2021) contain only monolingual data for search queries.

In this research, we construct a new multilingual code search dataset by translating natural language data of the existing large-scale dataset using a neural machine translation model. We also use our dataset to pre-train and fine-tune the Transformer (Vaswani et al., 2017)-based model and evaluate it on multilingual code search test sets we create. We show that the model pre-trained with all natural and programming language data performs best under almost all settings. We also analyze the relationship between the dataset's translation quality and the model's performance by filtering the fine-tuning dataset using back-translation. Our model and dataset will be publicly available at `https://github.com/ynklab/XCodeSearchNet`. The contributions of this research are as follows:

1. Constructing the large code search dataset consisting of multilingual natural language queries and codes using machine translation.
2. Constructing the multilingual code search model and evaluating it on a code search task using our dataset.
3. Analyzing the correlation between translation quality and the model performance on a code search task.

2 Background

2.1 Code Search Dataset

CodeSearchNet Corpus[1] (CSN; Husain et al., 2020) is a set of code data (**code**) in six programming languages: Go, Python, Java, PHP, Ruby, and Javascript, and natural language data describing them (**docstring**). CSN is created by automatically collecting pairs of function code and its documentation that are publicly available on GitHub and permitted for redistribution. This corpus contains approximately 2.3 million data pairs and 4 million code-only data. The natural language data in CSN is function documentation, which is pseudo data of the texts humans use to search for codes.

[1]`https://github.com/github/CodeSearchNet`

Proceedings of the 61st Annual Meeting of the Association for Computational Linguistics - Student Research Workshop, pages 69–75
July 10-12, 2023

	Pre-training (MLM)	Fine-tuning
PHP	662,907	1,047,406
Java	500,754	908,886
Python	458,219	824,342
Go	319,256	635,652
JavaScript	143,252	247,773
Ruby	52,905	97,580

Table 1: Training data size of CSN for each programming language used for pre-training CodeBERT with MLM and fine-tuning on the code search task.

	Pre-training			Fine-tuning		Test
	Train	Valid	Test	Train	Valid	
Go	316,058	3,198	28,533	635,652	28,482	14,277
Python	453,623	4,596	45,283	824,341	46,212	22,092
Java	495,768	4,986	42,237	908,885	30,654	26,646
PHP	656,277	6,630	54,406	1,047,403	52,028	28,189

Table 2: The sizes of CSN data for training and evaluating the models in our baseline experiments.

In contrast, several datasets are created based on natural language queries used for code search by humans. CodeXGLUE (Shuai et al., 2021), a benchmark for various code understanding tasks, includes two code search datasets: WebQueryTest (WQT) and CoSQA (Huang et al., 2021). The query data of these datasets are collected from the users' search logs of Microsoft Bing and the code from CSN. Given these separately collected data, annotators who have programming knowledge manually map the corresponding query and code to construct the dataset. The common feature of these datasets is that all natural language data, such as docstrings and queries, are limited to English and do not support multiple languages.

2.2 CodeBERT

CodeBERT (Feng et al., 2020) is a model pretrained and fine-tuned with CSN and is based on the RoBERTa (Liu et al., 2019)'s architecture. CodeBERT uses Masked Language Modeling (MLM; Devlin et al., 2019; Lample and Conneau, 2019) and Replaced Token Detection (RTD; Clark et al., 2020) as pre-training tasks. Both docstring and code data in CSN are used in MLM, while only code data are used in RTD. CodeBERT is trained only with English data, thus not available for a code search task with multilingual queries.

3 Dataset Construction Using Machine Translation

A possible way to construct a code search dataset for multiple languages is to translate an existing monolingual dataset. However, CSN's large data size makes manually translating all of its docstrings difficult. Table 1 shows the number of CSN data pairs used for pre-training (MLM) and fine-tuning the CodeBERT.

Therefore, we use a machine translation model to translate the English-only data to generate multilingual data efficiently. By translating CSN docstrings, we create a multilingual dataset consisting of four natural languages (English, French, Japanese, and Chinese) and four programming languages (Go, Python, Java, and PHP). We also translate the queries in the datasets Feng et al. (2020) used for fine-tuning and evaluating CodeBERT for our experiments in Section 4.1 and Section 4.2. In their fine-tuning data, the numbers of positive and negative labels are balanced. Note that we do not use JavaScript and Ruby data, whose sizes are much smaller than those of other programming languages.

As a translation model, we use M2M-100 (Fan et al., 2022), which supports translations in 100 languages.[2] M2M-100 achieved high accuracy in translations of low-resource languages by classifying 100 languages into 14 word families and creating bilingual training data within those families. We use `m2m_100_1.2B` model, which is provided by EasyNMT[3], a public framework of machine translation models. We set the model's beam size to 3.

We manually annotate the labels to some data of our fine-tuning dataset to check the correlation with the original labels, which is found to be 0.911 (see Appendix B for the details).

4 Baseline Experiments

We conduct baseline experiments, where we train the Transformer-based model with our multilingual dataset under various settings of the data sizes and evaluate it on multiple code search test sets.

4.1 Training

We perform pre-training and fine-tuning on a model initialized with the XLM-R (Conneau et al., 2019) architecture and parameters. XLM-R is a model

[2]We compared the translation results of some docstrings by several translation models, including Opus-MT and mBART, and chose M2M-100, which achieved the best performance.

[3]`https://github.com/UKPLab/EasyNMT`

		CSN				CoSQA	WQT
		Go	Python	Java	PHP	Python	Python
No-pre-training	EN	.813	.801	.737	.759	**.526**	.334
	FR	.780	.708	.681	.691	**.463**	.302
	JA	.792	.686	.641	.657	.372	.311
	ZH	.772	.660	.633	.670	.337	.297
All-to-One	EN	.824	**.851**	.763	.790	.494	**.360**
	FR	.798	**.796**	**.733**	.734	.432	**.363**
	JA	.805	**.781**	.700	.711	**.460**	.348
	ZH	.788	**.759**	.712	.731	**.427**	**.359**
All-to-All	EN	**.835**	.848	**.786**	**.809**	.473	.351
	FR	**.808**	.788	.731	**.759**	.420	.346
	JA	**.816**	.778	**.719**	**.730**	.436	**.364**
	ZH	**.804**	**.759**	**.750**	**.745**	.418	**.359**

Table 3: MRR scores of models pre-trained with all natural language data with either one programming language data or all programming language data.

	Go	Python	Java	PHP
RoBERTa	.820	.809	.666	.658
CODEONLY, INIT=S	.793	.786	.657	.617
CODEONLY, INIT=R	.819	.844	.721	.671
MLM, INIT=S	.830	.826	.714	.656
MLM, INIT=R	.838	.865	.748	.689
RTD, INIT=R	.829	.826	.715	.677
MLM+RTD, INIT=R	.840	.869	.748	.706

Table 4: MRR scores of CodeBERT from Feng et al. (2020) for Go, Python, Java, and PHP. CODEONLY is RoBERTa pre-trained only with code data. INIT refers to how the parameters of the model are initialized. S is for training from scratch, and R is for the initialization with those of RoBERTa (Liu et al., 2019).

pre-trained by MLM with the Wikipedia and Common Crawl corpora for 100 languages using Transformer (Vaswani et al., 2017) and achieved high performance on multilingual tasks, such as question answering. Note that we use the term "pre-training" to refer to further training of XLM-R with our dataset. In this paper, we use MLM as the learning objective to pre-train XLM-R and then fine-tune it using data pairs whose query and code languages are monolingual. We use monolingual data pairs for fine-tuning instead of a multilingual combination, given that Feng et al. (2020) clarifies that fine-tuning CodeBERT with six programming languages altogether "performs worse than fine-tuning a language-specific model for each programming language." Query and code data are concatenated to be input to the model, and it predicts their similarity based on the vector representation of the output [*CLS*] tokens. See Appendix C for more details on training settings, including hyper-parameters.

4.2 Evaluation

As with Feng et al. (2020), we use Mean Reciprocal Rank (MRR) as an evaluation metric.

$$\text{MRR} = \frac{1}{|Q|} \sum_{i=1}^{|Q|} \frac{1}{\text{rank}_i}$$

$|Q|$ refers to the total number of queries. When a test set has 1,000 data pairs, given a natural language query$_i$, the model calculates the similarity with the corresponding code$_i$ and the 999 distractor codes. If the similarity score given for code$_i$ is the 2nd highest among 1,000 codes, rank$_i$ equals 2. Then, the average of the inverse of rank$_i$ over all queries and codes is calculated as MRR.

Table 2 shows the sizes of CSN we use in our experiments. Each test set of CSN for MRR evaluation contains 1,000 data pairs randomly sampled from the original test sets. We use CoSQA and WQT as test sets in addition to CSN. As well as CSN, we create CoSQA test sets from the original 20,604 data pairs. We compute the average of MRR scores over three different test sets for CSN and CoSQA. The original WQT test set has 422 data pairs, so we use it as-is without sampling data like CoSQA.

We translate natural language queries in these test sets using the same machine translation model and parameter settings as the translation of the training data.

4.3 Model Settings

We prepare three model settings that differ in the amount and pattern of training data.

No-pre-training An XLM-R model with no further training applied and its initial parameters used.

All-to-One A model that uses data pairs of multilingual queries and monolingual codes for pre-training. The size of pre-training data ranges from 1.2 million to 2.7 million, depending on programming languages.

All-to-All A model that uses data pairs of multilingual queries and multilingual codes for pre-training. The size of pre-training data is over 7.6 million.

4.4 Results

Table 3 shows the scores of the MRR evaluation under all settings. The scores with CSN showed that All-to-All performed best in Go, Java, and PHP in almost all natural languages. On the other hand, All-to-One showed better scores than All-to-All on the Python test set. It is possible that the performance reached the top at All-to-One on the Python test set, given that the difference in scores between All-to-One and All-to-All was relatively small (<0.1). On CoSQA and WQT, there were also cases where model settings other than All-to-All performed better.

The performance of the original CodeBERT on a code search task is shown in Table 4. Overall, All-to-All is on par with the performance of CodeBERT in English data. Especially, All-to-All marks better scores in Java and PHP than CodeBERT. Note that our experiments and those of CodeBERT differ in the number of test sets used. Thus, it is difficult to compare these scores directly to discuss the model's superiority.

We observed a gradual trend that the scores decreased in English and French and increased in Japanese and Chinese as we increased the size of the pre-training data. This phenomenon might be due to the difference in knowledge of these languages acquired during pre-training XLM-R. The XLM-R pre-training data contain approximately 350 GiB for English and French and approximately 69 GiB and 46 GiB for Japanese and Chinese, respectively. As parameters of XLM-R were updated during our pre-training, the knowledge of English and French the model originally had was lost. On the other hand, the scores of Japanese and Chinese, in which the model owned a small amount of data, were improved by increasing the data size.

	Train					
	0.2	0.3	0.4	0.5	0.6	0.7
FR	621,167	613,893	597,092	570,891	530,485	391,897
JA	612,422	594,477	552,979	480,567	388,189	250,028
ZH	607,468	588,808	557,748	500,622	410,369	265,986
	Valid					
	0.2	0.3	0.4	0.5	0.6	0.7
FR	27,881	27,535	26,799	25,621	24,000	20,231
JA	27,433	26,524	24,901	21,981	16,327	10,304
ZH	27,115	26,178	24,971	22,280	18,445	10,792

Table 5: The sizes of our dataset for fine-tuning after back-translation filtering applied.

	0	0.2	0.3	0.4	0.5	0.6	0.7
EN	.835	N/A	N/A	N/A	N/A	N/A	N/A
FR	.808	.810	.808	.805	**.811**	.809	.807
JA	.816	.805	.803	**.817**	.813	.813	.802
ZH	.804	**.818**	**.818**	.807	.798	.802	.802

Table 6: MRR scores with back translation filtering for fine-tuning data. 0 means no filtering applied.

5 Analysis on Translation Quality

5.1 Back-translation Filtering

The translation quality of our dataset must affect the model's task performance. Therefore, we investigate whether there is a difference in the scores of the code search task when we filter out the low-quality data from the fine-tuning dataset.

We apply a back-translation filtering method based on previous studies that used machine translation to automatically build a high-quality multilingual dataset from the English one (Sobrevilla Cabezudo et al., 2019; Dou et al., 2020; Yoshikoshi et al., 2020). We first apply back-translation to French, Japanese, and Chinese docstrings. Then we calculate the uni-gram BLEU (Papineni et al., 2002) score between the back-translated docstrings and the original English ones and collect only data with scores higher than certain thresholds. In our experiments, we conduct filtering to the fine-tuning dataset of Go. Table 5 shows the data sizes after back-translation filtering. We set thresholds to 0.2 to 0.7 in increments of 0.1 and compare the model's performance with each threshold. We choose these values because the sizes of the datasets change relatively hugely when filtered with the threshold 0.3 to 0.6 (Appendix D).

5.2 Results

Table 6 shows the MRR scores of the models whose fine-tuning data are filtered with different thresholds. In every language, the scores peak when we set the threshold between 0.2 to 0.5 and then drop with larger thresholds up to 0.7. This result implies that the filtering successfully removes the low-quality data while maintaining the number of training data and leads to better MRR scores. We assume that the change in size from the original dataset becomes more prominent with thresholds from 0.5 to 0.7 (around 100K-400K), thus eventually resulting in lowering the overall scores.

However, the score changes seem insignificant (± 0.02) among these thresholds. One possible reason is that the data size remains over 250K even after filtering, which should already be enough for fine-tuning in general.

In summary, the results show that filtering out some low-quality data improves the model's performance on the code search task, but removing over 150K data worsens the test scores.

6 Conclusion

We created a large multilingual code search dataset by a neural machine translation model. We then constructed a multilingual code search model using our dataset. We found out that the models pre-trained with all of the multilingual natural language and programming language data achieved the best performance on a code search task almost all the time. We also investigated the relationship between the translation quality of our dataset and the model's performance. The results indicated that the data size contributed more to the model's code search performance than the data translation quality.

Overall, this research introduced that using a publicly available machine translation model helps to translate texts in the programming domain. We can apply our method to extend datasets for languages other than French, Japanese, and Chinese to construct models for various natural languages.

Limitations

We used XLM-R for the baseline model to train with our dataset in our experiments because we wanted to make experimental settings as close as the previous study of CodeBERT but for multilingual data. Since CodeBERT is based on RoBERTa, we chose XLM-R, which is also RoBERTa-based and already trained with multilingual data.

Acknowledgements

We thank the two anonymous reviewers for their helpful comments and suggestions, which improved this paper. This research is supported by JSPS KAKENHI Grant Number JP20K19868 and partially by Microsoft Research Asia (Collaborative Research Sponsorship).

References

Wasi Ahmad et al. 2021. Unified Pre-training for Program Understanding and Generation. In *Proceedings of the 2021 Conference of the North American Chapter of the Association for Computational Linguistics: Human Language Technologies*, pages 2655–2668, Online. Association for Computational Linguistics.

Kevin Clark et al. 2020. ELECTRA: Pre-training Text Encoders as Discriminators Rather Than Generators. In *International Conference on Learning Representations*.

Alexis Conneau et al. 2019. Unsupervised cross-lingual representation learning at scale. *arXiv preprint arXiv:1911.02116*.

Jacob Devlin et al. 2019. BERT: Pre-training of Deep Bidirectional Transformers for Language Understanding. In *Proceedings of the 2019 Conference of the North American Chapter of the Association for Computational Linguistics: Human Language Technologies, Volume 1 (Long and Short Papers)*, pages 4171–4186, Minneapolis, Minnesota. Association for Computational Linguistics.

Zi-Yi Dou, Antonios Anastasopoulos, and Graham Neubig. 2020. Dynamic data selection and weighting for iterative back-translation. In *Proceedings of the 2020 Conference on Empirical Methods in Natural Language Processing (EMNLP)*, pages 5894–5904, Online. Association for Computational Linguistics.

Angela Fan et al. 2022. Beyond english-centric multilingual machine translation. *The Journal of Machine Learning Research*, 22(1):107:4839–107:4886.

Zhangyin Feng et al. 2020. CodeBERT: A Pre-Trained Model for Programming and Natural Languages. In *Findings of the Association for Computational Linguistics: EMNLP 2020*, pages 1536–1547, Online. Association for Computational Linguistics.

Daniel Fried et al. 2023. InCoder: A Generative Model for Code Infilling and Synthesis. In *The Eleventh International Conference on Learning Representations*.

Junjie Huang et al. 2021. CoSQA: 20,000+ Web Queries for Code Search and Question Answering.

In *Proceedings of the 59th Annual Meeting of the Association for Computational Linguistics and the 11th International Joint Conference on Natural Language Processing (Volume 1: Long Papers)*, pages 5690–5700. Association for Computational Linguistics.

Hamel Husain et al. 2020. CodeSearchNet Challenge: Evaluating the State of Semantic Code Search. *arXiv preprint arXiv:1909.09436*.

Guillaume Lample and Alexis Conneau. 2019. Cross-lingual language model pretraining. *arXiv preprint arXiv:1901.07291*.

Yinhan Liu et al. 2019. RoBERTa: A Robustly Optimized BERT Pretraining Approach. *arXiv preprint arXiv:1907.11692*.

Kishore Papineni et al. 2002. BLEU: A method for automatic evaluation of machine translation. In *Proceedings of the 40th Annual Meeting on Association for Computational Linguistics*, ACL '02, page 311–318, USA. Association for Computational Linguistics.

Lu Shuai et al. 2021. CodeXGLUE: A machine learning benchmark dataset for code understanding and generation. *arXiv preprint arXiv:2102.04664*.

Marco Antonio Sobrevilla Cabezudo, Simon Mille, and Thiago Pardo. 2019. Back-translation as strategy to tackle the lack of corpus in natural language generation from semantic representations. In *Proceedings of the 2nd Workshop on Multilingual Surface Realisation (MSR 2019)*, pages 94–103, Hong Kong, China. Association for Computational Linguistics.

Ashish Vaswani et al. 2017. Attention is All you Need. In *Advances in Neural Information Processing Systems*, volume 30. Curran Associates, Inc.

Yue Wang et al. 2021. CodeT5: Identifier-aware Unified Pre-trained Encoder-Decoder Models for Code Understanding and Generation. In *Proceedings of the 2021 Conference on Empirical Methods in Natural Language Processing*, pages 8696–8708, Online and Punta Cana, Dominican Republic. Association for Computational Linguistics.

Takumi Yoshikoshi et al. 2020. Multilingualization of a natural language inference dataset using machine translation. *The 244th meeting of IPSJ Natural Language Processing*, 2020(6):1–8.

Qinkai Zheng et al. 2023. CodeGeeX: A Pre-Trained Model for Code Generation with Multilingual Evaluations on HumanEval-X. *arXiv preprint arXiv:2303.17568*.

A CodeSearchNet

Table 1 shows the size of CSN for each programming language used for pre-training CodeBERT with MLM and fine-tuning on the code search task. The number of data for fine-tuning in Go is listed as 635,635 in Feng et al. (2020), but the dataset publicly provided contains 635,652 data.

B Dataset Translation

We manually evaluate the translation quality of our dataset. Table 7 shows examples of translation of query data from English to Japanese using M2M-100. Since queries of CSN are based on source code descriptions, some of them contain strings that do not necessarily need to be translated, such as variable names, function names, and technical terms (e.g., `SetStatus`, `retrieveCoinSupply`). M2M-100 successfully translates the entire sentence, leaving such domain-specific strings as needed.

On the other hand, we observe some errors, such as translating to unknown words (e.g., "alphanumeric" to "アルファナウマリ") or omitting some texts from the translation.

We also manually annotate the labels of 45 sampled data pairs from the fine-tuning dataset of Japanese queries and Go codes and calculate how much they match the original labels. These 45 data pairs do not contain queries that were not successfully translated and remain in English. Among 45 data pairs, 28 of them have "1" as their labels and 17 for "0". We calculate the correlation with accuracy, and the score is 0.911.

C Training Settings

As hyperparameters for pre-training the model, we set the batch size to 64, the maximum input length to 256, and the learning rate to 2e-4. As hyperparameters for the fine-tuning of the model, we set the batch size to 16, the learning rate to 1e-5, and the number of max training epochs to 3. In both cases, we use Adam as the optimizer.

D Back-translation Filtering

Table 8 shows an example of the removed data by filtering. Table 9 shows the data size of each filtering threshold.

Original (EN)	Translated (JA)	Quality
SetStatus sets the Status field s value .	SetStatus は、Status フィールドの値を設定します。	✓
retrieveCoinSupply fetches the coin supply data from the vins table .	retrieveCoinSupply は、vins テーブルから コイン供給データを取得します。	✓
stateIdent scans an alphanumeric or field .	stateIdent は、アルファナウマリまたは フィールドをスキャンします。	✗ Unknown word
VisitFrom calls the do function starting from the first neighbor w for which w ≥ a with c equal to the cost of the edge from v to w . The neighbors are then visited in increasing numerical order . If do returns true VisitFrom returns immediately skipping any remaining neighbors and returns true .	VisitFrom は、最初の隣人 w から始まる do 関数を 呼び出し、その w ≥ a と c は v から w までの エッジのコストに等しい。 If do returns true VisitFrom returns immediately skipping any remaining neighbors and returns true. もしそうであれば、VisitFromは直ちに 残りの隣人を無視して true を返します。	✗ Wrong translation / Omission

Table 7: Examples of query data from the dataset (Japanese, Go, threshold=0.4). These data are sampled from the top 10 entries of the dataset.

Original (EN)	Translated (JA)	Back-translated (EN)
NoError asserts that a function returned no error (i . e . nil) . **actualObj err : = SomeFunction () if a . NoError (err) { assert . Equal (t actualObj expectedObj) }** Returns whether the assertion was successful (true) or not (false) .	NoError は、関数がエラーを返しません (i. e. nil) を主張します。 まあ、あれ? まあ、あれ? まあ、あれ? まあ、あれ? まあ、あれ? まあ、あれ? 真実(真実)か否かを返す。	NoError claims that the function does not return an error (i.e. nil). Oh well that? Oh well that? Oh well that? Oh well that? Oh well that? It is the truth or the truth.
The original query contains a code-like sequence (bold texts), so the model could not successfully translate it (underline texts).		

Table 8: An example of filtered-out query data (Japanese, Go, threshold=0.4).

	Train								
	0.1	0.2	0.3	0.4	0.5	0.6	0.7	0.8	0.9
FR	626,130	621,167	613,893	597,092	570,891	530,485	391,897	224,928	78,989
JA	621,857	612,422	594,477	552,979	480,567	388,189	250,028	76,965	27,670
ZH	618,904	607,468	588,808	557,748	500,622	410,369	265,986	71,625	20,173
	Valid								
	0.1	0.2	0.3	0.4	0.5	0.6	0.7	0.8	0.9
FR	28,123	27,881	27,535	26,799	25,621	24,000	20,231	11,646	4,647
JA	27,837	27,433	26,524	24,901	21,981	16,327	10,304	5,422	1,806
ZH	27,693	27,115	26,178	24,971	22,280	18,445	10,792	4228	1,002

Table 9: The sizes of our fine-tuning dataset after back-translation filtering with thresholds in increment of 0.1.

Multimodal Neural Machine Translation Using Synthetic Images Transformed by Latent Diffusion Model

Ryoya Yuasa[1] **Akihiro Tamura**[1] **Tomoyuki Kajiwara**[2]
Takashi Ninomiya[2] **Tsuneo Kato**[1]
[1]Doshisha University [2]Ehime University
{ctwh0190@mail4, aktamura@mail, tsukato@mail}.doshisha.ac.jp
{kajiwara, ninomiya}@cs.ehime-u.ac.jp

Abstract

This study proposes a new multimodal neural machine translation (MNMT) model using synthetic images transformed by a latent diffusion model. MNMT translates a source language sentence based on its related image, but the image usually contains noisy information that are not relevant to the source language sentence. Our proposed method first generates a synthetic image corresponding to the content of the source language sentence by using a latent diffusion model and then performs translation based on the synthetic image. The experiments on the English-German translation tasks using the Multi30k dataset demonstrate the effectiveness of the proposed method.

1 Introduction

Recently, multimodal neural machine translation (MNMT) (Specia et al., 2016), which uses images in addition to source language sentences for translation, has attracted attention in the field of machine translation (MT). Images related to source language sentences are considered to improve translation performance by resolving ambiguity during translation and complementing information that is difficult to capture with source language sentences. However, a source language sentence often only describes one aspect of the contents included in its related image.

Figure 1 shows an example from a standard dataset in MNMT, the Multi30k dataset (Elliott et al., 2016). As shown in Figure 1, multiple source language sentences with differing content are associated with a single image in the Multi30k. For example, Source Language Sentence 2 does not mention the house in the related image. Therefore, related images are not necessarily optimal as auxiliary information for MT.

Therefore, in this study, we propose a new MNMT model using a synthetic image generated by image conversion with a latent diffusion model. Specifically, an original related image is converted with a latent diffusion model based on its source language sentence; content unrelated to the source language sentence is eliminated from the original image, and an image conforming with the source language sentence is generated. Subsequently, translation is performed by using the converted synthetic image instead of the original related image. Our aim is to improve translation performance by using related images that better reflect the content of source language sentences as auxiliary information for translation.

We verified the effectiveness of our proposed method on the English-German translation tasks using the Multi30k dataset (Elliott et al., 2016) and the Ambiguous COCO dataset (Elliott et al., 2017). The results confirmed that, compared with a conventional MNMT using the original related images in the Multi30k, our method improved the BLEU score by 0.14 on both the Multi30k Test 2016 and Test 2017, and by 0.39 on the Ambiguous COCO. Additionally, CLIPScore (Hessel et al., 2021), which was used to calculate the similarity between a source language sentence and an image, confirmed that the synthetic images used in our method more closely match the source language sentences than the original related images.

2 Conventional MNMT Models

MNMT models based on Transformer (Vaswani et al., 2017) have recently become mainstream in the field of MNMT. Various attempts have been made to improve their translation performance, including the introduction of visual attention mechanisms (Nishihara et al., 2020), as well as the method of simultaneously learning feature representations of text and images using a shared encoder (Elliott and Kádár, 2017). Li et al. (2022) have proposed a Transformer MNMT model incorporating Selective Attention, an attention mecha-

Proceedings of the 61st Annual Meeting of the
Association for Computational Linguistics - Student Research Workshop, pages 76–82
July 10-12, 2023 ©2023 Association for Computational Linguistics

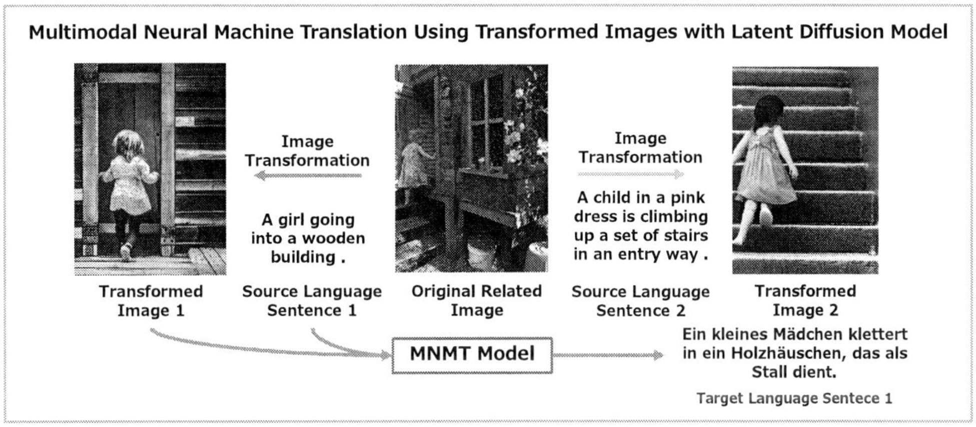

Figure 1: Overview of the Proposed Method

nism that captures relationships between words in a source language sentence and patches of its related image. We outline the Selective Attention MNMT model, which is used as the base MNMT model in this study, below.

The Selective Attention MNMT model first encodes the source language sentence X^{text} and the related image X^{img} into feature expressions H^{text} and H^{img} by Eqs. (1) and (2), respectively.

$$H^{\text{text}} = \text{TextEncoder}(X^{\text{text}}), \quad (1)$$

$$H^{\text{img}} = W\, \text{ImageEncoder}(X^{\text{img}}), \quad (2)$$

where W, TextEncoder, and ImageEncoder are the parameter matrix, Transformer Encoder, and Vision Transformer (Dosovitskiy et al., 2021), respectively.

Then, Selective Attention captures relationships between image patches and source words using an attention mechanism as follows:

$$H^{\text{img}}_{attn} = \text{Softmax}\left(\frac{QK^T}{\sqrt{d_k}}\right) V, \quad (3)$$

where Q, K, and V are H^{text}, H^{img}, and H^{img}, respectively, and d_k is the dimension of H^{text}.

Subsequently, the gated fusion mechanism (Zhang et al., 2020) generates a feature expression H^{out} that represents the source language sentence and the image while controlling the influence of the image by Eqs. (4) and (5).

$$\lambda = \text{Sigmoid}(UH^{\text{text}} + VH^{\text{img}}_{attn}), \quad (4)$$

$$H^{\text{out}} = (1 - \lambda) \cdot H^{\text{text}} + \lambda \cdot H^{\text{img}}_{attn}, \quad (5)$$

where U and V are learnable parameter matrices. Finally, H^{out} is input to the Transformer Decoder to generate a translated sentence.

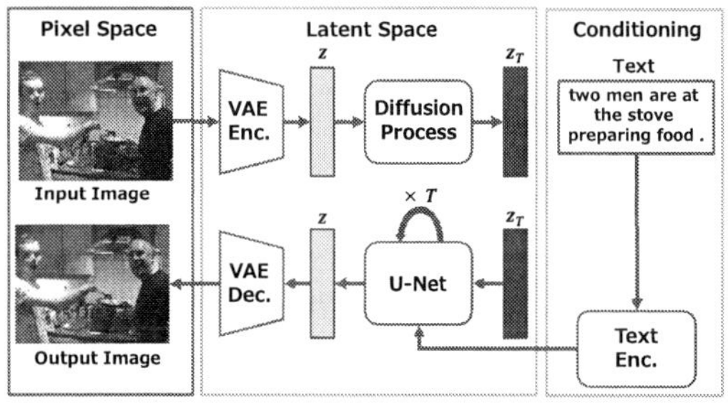

Figure 2: Training Process of a Latent Diffusion Model

3 Proposed Method

In this section, we propose an MNMT model that uses synthetic images transformed from related images based on source language sentences. Figure 1 shows an overview of the proposed method.

The MNMT dataset consists of the triplets of a source language sentence, a target language sentence, and a related image. In typical MNMT datasets, each source language sentence usually only represents one aspect of the content included in the related images; there are many cases where content unrelated to the source language sentence exists in the related image. For example, the image in Figure 1 shows a scene where a girl in a pink dress climbs the stairs to enter a wooden house, but Source Language Sentence 1 does not mention the climbing of stairs. Further, Source Language Sentence 2 does not refer to a house. Therefore, related images are not necessarily the best aids to translation.

Accordingly, our proposed method first uses a latent diffusion model to eliminate content unrelated to the source language sentence from the related image and generate a synthetic image that corresponds to the source language sentence (see Section 3.1). Then, translation is performed with a conventional MNMT model (e.g., the Selective Attention MNMT model in our experiments) using the generated synthetic image and the source language sentence. Because this makes it easier to capture the relationship between the input image and text during translation, we expect the improvement of translation performance.

3.1 Image Transformation: Latent Diffusion Model

This section explains the latent diffusion model (Rombach et al., 2022) used in the image transformation step of our proposed method. The latent diffusion model applies the diffusion model (Sohl-Dickstein et al., 2015) to the latent space of VAE (Kingma and Welling, 2014) and consists mainly of the VAE, U-Net (Ronneberger et al., 2015), and a text encoder (see Figure 2). In the latent diffusion model, an input image is projected from pixel space into a low-dimensional latent space using a VAE Encoder to obtain its latent representation. Then Gaussian noise is continuously added to the latent expression by a diffusion process. Next, in a reverse diffusion process, U-Net is used multiple times to gradually remove noise from the latent expression that contained noise. At this time, the U-Net is conditioned by the feature representation generated from a text by the text encoder. This conditioning is realized by a cross attention mechanism. Finally, the VAE decoder projects the denoised latent representation from latent space to pixel space to obtain the output image.

The loss function for the latent diffusion model is given as follows:

$$L_{\text{LDM}} := \mathbb{E}_{\varepsilon(x),y,\epsilon\sim\mathcal{N}(0,1),t}[\|\epsilon - \epsilon_\theta(z_t, t, \tau_\theta(y))\|_2^2],$$

where ε, ϵ_θ, and τ_θ represent a VAE encoder, an U-Net, and a text encoder, respectively, and x, y, ϵ, t, and z_t are an input image, a text, a Gaussian noise, time, and the latent representation of time t, respectively.

In our proposed method, a source language sentence and its related image are input to the text encoder and the VAE encoder, respectively, to convert the related image into a synthetic image that conforms to the source language sentence.

4 Experiments

4.1 Experimental Setup

We verified the effectiveness of the proposed method on the English-German translation tasks using the Multi30k and the Ambiguous COCO. We used the Multi30k training data (29,000 triplets) and the Multi30k validation data (1,014 triplets) as our training and validation data, and used the Multi30k Test 2016 (1,000 triplets), the Multi30k Test 2017 (1,000 triplets), and the Ambiguous COCO (461 triplets) as our test data.

We compared the translation performance of our proposed method (*MNMT(conv.)*) with the translation performance of 1) an NMT model that does not use related images (*NMT*); 2) an MNMT model that uses original images from the dataset as related images (*MNMT(orig.)*); 3) and an MNMT model that uses images generated only from source language sentences as related images (*MNMT(gen.)*).

Transformer-Tiny[1] was used as the NMT model. This model, with a reduced number of layers, size of hidden layers, number of attention mechanism heads, etc., as compared to typical Transformer models, is suitable for small-scale datasets.[2] According to Wu et al. (2021), we set the number of encoder and decoder layers, the size of the hidden layer, the input size of the feed-forward layer, the number of attention mechanism heads, the dropout, and the label smoothing weight to 4, 128, 256, 5, 0.3, and 0.1, respectively. Adam (Kingma and Ba, 2015) was used as the optimization method, with $\beta_1 = 0.9$ and $\beta_2 = 0.98$. The learning rate was linearly warmed up from $1e^{-7}$ to $5e^{-3}$ over the first 2,000 steps, and then it was decreased proportionally to the number of updates. The vocabulary dictionary was shared between the source language and the target language, and created by Byte Pair Encoding (Sennrich et al., 2016) with 10,000 merge operations.

The Selective Attention MNMT[3] was used as the MNMT model. As for Vision Transformer, vit_base_patch16_384[4] was used for image feature extraction. Stable Diffusion,[5] based on a latent

[1] https://github.com/LividWo/Revisit-MMT

[2] Wu et al. (2021) reported that Transformer-Tiny outperforms Transformer Base/Small on the Multi30k dataset.

[3] https://github.com/libeineu/fairseq_mmt

[4] https://github.com/rwightman/pytorch-image-models

[5] https://github.com/CompVis/

Model	Test 2016	Test 2017	Ambiguous COCO
NMT	40.50	31.31	27.81
MNMT(orig.)	41.06	32.06	27.91
MNMT(gen.)	40.81	31.81	**28.54**
MNMT(conv.)	**41.20**	**32.20**	28.30

Table 1: Translation Performance (BLEU [%])

Model	Test 2016	Test 2017	Ambiguous COCO
MNMT(orig.)	79.59	78.32	78.17
MNMT(conv.)	79.74	79.35	80.08

Table 2: CLIPScore: Similarity between Source Language Sentences and Related Images

diffusion model, was adopted for the generation of related images in *MNMT(gen.)* and the image transformation in *MNMT(conv.)*; the specific model used was stable-diffusion-v1-5.[6] StableDiffusionPipeline and StableDiffusionImg2ImgPipeline from diffusers,[7] were used for implementation. For image generation in *MNMT(conv.)* and *MNMT(gen.)*, we used the default parameters. We set guidance_scale and num_inference_steps to 7.5 and 50 for *MNMT(gen.)*, and guidance_scale and strength to 7.5 and 0.8 for *MNMT(conv.)*. The hyperparameters, optimization methods, and vocabulary dictionary creation methods during training were the same as the settings used for the NMT model.

In decoding for all models, we averaged checkpoints at the last 10 epochs before the end of training, and used beam search with a beam width of 5. BLEU (Papineni et al., 2002) was used as the evaluation measure. We trained the models with five different random seeds, and evaluated the model with the highest BLEU on the validation data.

4.2 Results

Table 1 shows the experimental results. As Table 1 shows, the three MNMT models using image information have higher BLEU scores across all datasets than the NMT model that does not use image information. This confirms that image information helped improve translation performance on the datasets used in our experiments.

Further, a comparison of the three MNMT models shows that our proposed *MNMT(conv.)* achieved the highest translation performance on Test 2016 and Test 2017. *MNMT(gen.)* had a higher translation performance than *MNMT (conv.)* on Ambiguous COCO, but overall, *MNMT (conv.)* had better results, confirming the effectiveness of the proposed method.

5 Discussion

This section analyzes the synthetic images used in the proposed method. Examples of transformed images are shown in Appendix A. In order to investigate how much of the image corresponds to the source language sentence, we computed ClipScore (Hessel et al., 2021), which measures the similarity between the image used and the source language sentence by using $\text{CLIPScore}(\boldsymbol{c}, \boldsymbol{v}) = w \cdot \max(\cos(\boldsymbol{c}, \boldsymbol{v}), 0)$, where $\boldsymbol{c}$ and $\boldsymbol{v}$ are the feature vectors from the text encoder and the image encoder of the CLIP (Radford et al., 2021), respectively. w is used to rescale the output, and following Hessel et al. (2021), we set it to 2.5.

The evaluation results are shown in Table 2. The table shows that the synthetic images converted by our proposed method have a higher similarity to the source language sentences than the original related images across all datasets. In particular, the largest improvement (+1.91 CLIPScore) has been observed on Ambiguous COCO, which includes more ambiguity than the other two test datasets. These results confirm that related images which better reflect the source languages can be used as aids to translation via our proposed method.

6 Conclusion

In this study, we proposed a new MNMT model that uses a latent diffusion model to transform related images into synthetic images that more closely conform to source language sentences and uses the transformed images as auxiliary information for MT. The experiments on the English-German translation tasks using the Multi30k dataset showed that the proposed method can achieve higher translation performance than conventional methods, demonstrating the effectiveness of our proposed method. The evaluation using CLIPScore confirms that the images used in our method possess more similarities to the source language sentences than the original images.

stable-diffusion

[6] https://huggingface.co/runwayml/stable-diffusion-v1-5

[7] https://github.com/huggingface/diffusers

Limitations

In this work, we confirm the effectiveness of the proposed method only on the English-German translation tasks using the Multi30k dataset, the most commonly used dataset in the MNMT reserach area. It is not clear whether the proposed method is effective for translation for language pairs other than English and German or translation when a larger training dataset is used (e.g., when using an existing data augmentation method for MNMT). We will leave these verification experiments for future work.

The proposed method has improved translation performance of MT, but the performance is not perfect and translation results could include translation errors. Accordingly, there still remains a possibility that translation results by the proposed method could convey incorrect information.

The proposed method requires an additional process for transforming images, compared with conventional MNMT models. The experiment, including model training and testing, on the proposed model *MNMT(conv.)* took about 20 hours longer than that on the baseline MNMT model *MNMT(orig.)* when using RTX3090 GPU $\times$ 1.

Acknowledgements

This work was supported by JSPS KAKENHI Grant Number JP22K12177, JP21K12031. These research results were partially obtained from the commissioned research (No. 225) by National Institute of Information and Communications Technology (NICT), JAPAN.

References

Alexey Dosovitskiy, Lucas Beyer, Alexander Kolesnikov, Dirk Weissenborn, Xiaohua Zhai, Thomas Unterthiner, Mostafa Dehghani, Matthias Minderer, Georg Heigold, Sylvain Gelly, Jakob Uszkoreit, and Neil Houlsby. 2021. An image is worth 16x16 words: Transformers for image recognition at scale. In *International Conference on Learning Representations*.

Desmond Elliott, Stella Frank, Loïc Barrault, Fethi Bougares, and Lucia Specia. 2017. Findings of the second shared task on multimodal machine translation and multilingual image description. In *Proceedings of the Second Conference on Machine Translation*, pages 215–233, Copenhagen, Denmark. Association for Computational Linguistics.

Desmond Elliott, Stella Frank, Khalil Sima'an, and Lucia Specia. 2016. Multi30K: Multilingual English-German image descriptions. In *Proceedings of the 5th Workshop on Vision and Language*, pages 70–74, Berlin, Germany. Association for Computational Linguistics.

Desmond Elliott and Ákos Kádár. 2017. Imagination improves multimodal translation. In *Proceedings of the Eighth International Joint Conference on Natural Language Processing (Volume 1: Long Papers)*, pages 130–141, Taipei, Taiwan. Asian Federation of Natural Language Processing.

Jack Hessel, Ari Holtzman, Maxwell Forbes, Ronan Le Bras, and Yejin Choi. 2021. CLIPScore: A reference-free evaluation metric for image captioning. In *Proceedings of the 2021 Conference on Empirical Methods in Natural Language Processing*, pages 7514–7528, Online and Punta Cana, Dominican Republic. Association for Computational Linguistics.

Diederik P. Kingma and Jimmy Ba. 2015. Adam: A method for stochastic optimization. In *International Conference on Learning Representations (Poster)*.

Diederik P. Kingma and Max Welling. 2014. Auto-Encoding Variational Bayes. In *2nd International Conference on Learning Representations*.

Bei Li, Chuanhao Lv, Zefan Zhou, Tao Zhou, Tong Xiao, Anxiang Ma, and JingBo Zhu. 2022. On vision features in multimodal machine translation. In *Proceedings of the 60th Annual Meeting of the Association for Computational Linguistics (Volume 1: Long Papers)*, pages 6327–6337, Dublin, Ireland. Association for Computational Linguistics.

Tetsuro Nishihara, Akihiro Tamura, Takashi Ninomiya, Yutaro Omote, and Hideki Nakayama. 2020. Supervised visual attention for multimodal neural machine translation. In *Proceedings of the 28th International Conference on Computational Linguistics*, pages 4304–4314, Barcelona, Spain (Online). International Committee on Computational Linguistics.

Kishore Papineni, Salim Roukos, Todd Ward, and Wei-Jing Zhu. 2002. Bleu: a method for automatic evaluation of machine translation. In *Proceedings of the 40th Annual Meeting of the Association for Computational Linguistics*, pages 311–318, Philadelphia, Pennsylvania, USA. Association for Computational Linguistics.

Alec Radford, Jong Wook Kim, Chris Hallacy, Aditya Ramesh, Gabriel Goh, Sandhini Agarwal, Girish Sastry, Amanda Askell, Pamela Mishkin, Jack Clark, Gretchen Krueger, and Ilya Sutskever. 2021. Learning transferable visual models from natural language supervision. In *Proceedings of the 38th International Conference on Machine Learning*, volume 139 of *Proceedings of Machine Learning Research*, pages 8748–8763.

Robin Rombach, Andreas Blattmann, Dominik Lorenz, Patrick Esser, and Björn Ommer. 2022. High-resolution image synthesis with latent diffusion models. In *Proceedings of the IEEE/CVF Conference on Computer Vision and Pattern Recognition*, pages 10684–10695.

Olaf Ronneberger, Philipp Fischer, and Thomas Brox. 2015. U-net: Convolutional networks for biomedical image segmentation. In *Medical Image Computing and Computer-Assisted Intervention – MICCAI 2015*, pages 234–241.

Rico Sennrich, Barry Haddow, and Alexandra Birch. 2016. Neural machine translation of rare words with subword units. In *Proceedings of the 54th Annual Meeting of the Association for Computational Linguistics (Volume 1: Long Papers)*, pages 1715–1725, Berlin, Germany. Association for Computational Linguistics.

Jascha Sohl-Dickstein, Eric Weiss, Niru Maheswaranathan, and Surya Ganguli. 2015. Deep unsupervised learning using nonequilibrium thermodynamics. In *Proceedings of the 32nd International Conference on Machine Learning*, volume 37 of *Proceedings of Machine Learning Research*, pages 2256–2265.

Lucia Specia, Stella Frank, Khalil Sima'an, and Desmond Elliott. 2016. A shared task on multimodal machine translation and crosslingual image description. In *Proceedings of the First Conference on Machine Translation: Volume 2, Shared Task Papers*, pages 543–553, Berlin, Germany. Association for Computational Linguistics.

Ashish Vaswani, Noam Shazeer, Niki Parmar, Jakob Uszkoreit, Llion Jones, Aidan N Gomez, Ł ukasz Kaiser, and Illia Polosukhin. 2017. Attention is all you need. In *Advances in Neural Information Processing Systems*, volume 30.

Zhiyong Wu, Lingpeng Kong, Wei Bi, Xiang Li, and Ben Kao. 2021. Good for misconceived reasons: An empirical revisiting on the need for visual context in multimodal machine translation. In *Proceedings of the 59th Annual Meeting of the Association for Computational Linguistics and the 11th International Joint Conference on Natural Language Processing (Volume 1: Long Papers)*, pages 6153–6166, Online. Association for Computational Linguistics.

Zhuosheng Zhang, Kehai Chen, Rui Wang, Masao Utiyama, Eiichiro Sumita, Zuchao Li, and Hai Zhao. 2020. Neural machine translation with universal visual representation. In *International Conference on Learning Representations*.

A Appendix

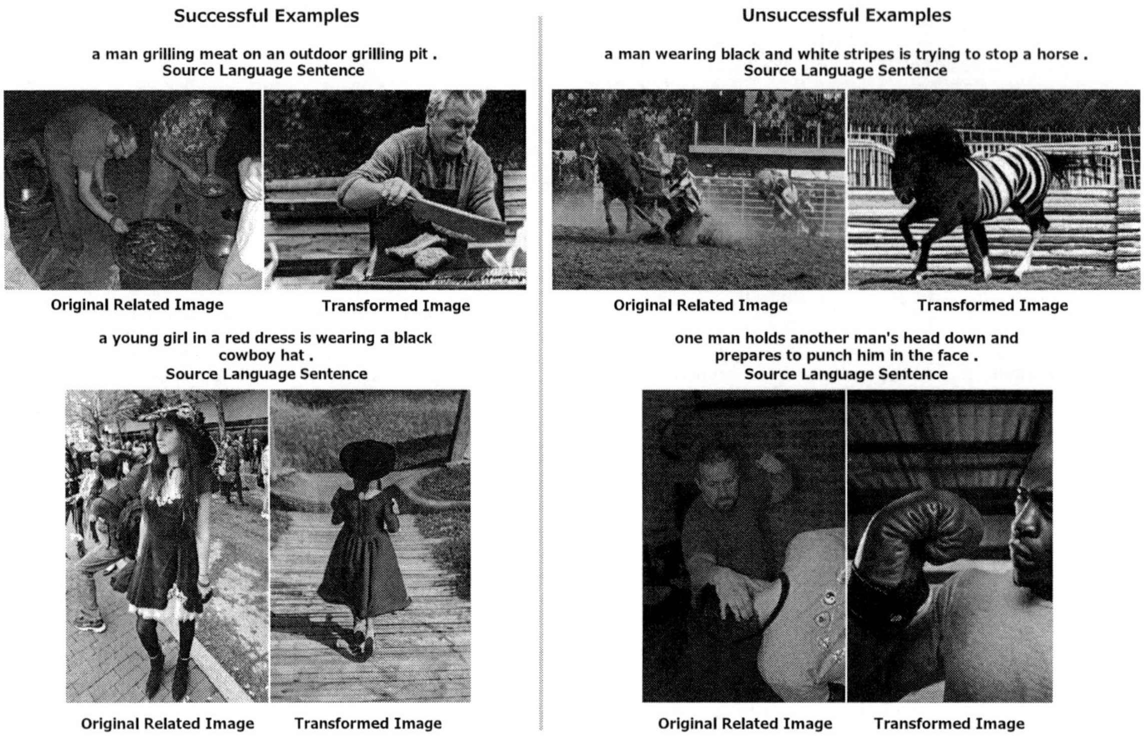

Figure 3: Successful (Left) and Unsuccessful (Right) Examples of our Image Transformation

Enhancing Ancient Chinese Understanding with Derived Noisy Syntax Trees

Shitou Zhang[1,2], **Ping Wang**[1,*], **Zuchao Li**[2,*], **Jingrui Hou**[3]
[1]School of Information Management, Wuhan University
[2]School of Computer Science, Wuhan University
[3]Department of Computer Science, Loughborough University
{shitouzhang,wangping,zcli-charlie}@whu.edu.cn
J.Hou@lboro.ac.uk

Abstract

Despite the rapid development of neural-based models, syntax still plays a crucial role in modern natural language processing. However, few studies have incorporated syntactic information into ancient Chinese understanding tasks due to the lack of syntactic annotation. This paper explores the role of syntax in ancient Chinese understanding based on the noisy syntax trees from unsupervised derivation and modern Chinese syntax parsers. On top of that, we propose a novel syntax encoding component – confidence-based syntax encoding network (cSEN) to alleviate the side effects from the existing noise caused by unsupervised syntax derivation and the incompatibility between ancient and modern Chinese. Experiments on two typical ancient Chinese understanding tasks, ancient poetry theme classification and ancient-modern Chinese translation, demonstrate that syntactic information can effectively enhance the understanding of ancient Chinese over strong baselines, and that the proposed cSEN plays an important role in noisy scenarios.

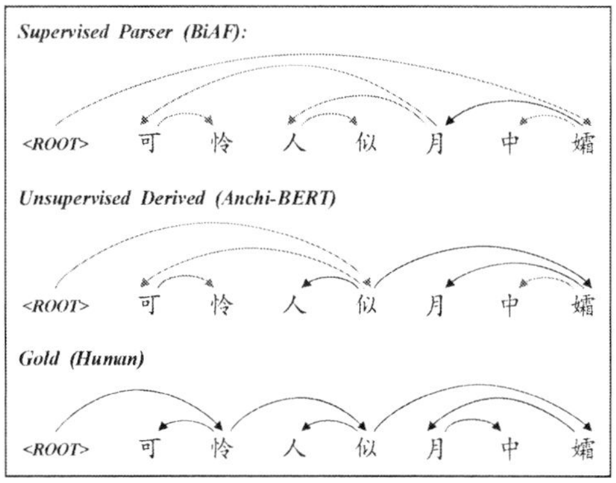

Figure 1: Unlabeled dependency parses from different parsers, where red arcs indicate prediction noises.

1 Introduction

Ancient Chinese literature, such as classical poetry, books, and records, is a highly representative and distinctive cultural heritage that is receiving increasing attention from the NLP academia. However, directly applying modern Chinese processing methods to ancient texts is not appropriate due to the differences in syntax and semantics between ancient and modern Chinese. Chinese is one of the oldest written languages in the world, with a history of at least 6,000 years (Norman, 1988). Over time, the language has undergone many changes, such as the transition from literary to vernacular Chinese in the early 20th century (Weiping, 2017), resulting in a significant gap between ancient and modern Chinese.

Syntactic features has been utilized in a wide range of NLP tasks, including coreference resolution (Fang and Fu, 2019; Trieu et al., 2019; Jiang and Cohn, 2022), machine reading comprehension (Zhang et al., 2020; Guo et al., 2020), and machine translation (Currey and Heafield, 2019; Zhang et al., 2019a; Bugliarello and Okazaki, 2020). Despite the effectiveness of syntax in modern Chinese understanding (Li et al., 2018; Xia et al., 2019; Zhang et al., 2020), few studies have incorporated syntactic information into ancient Chinese processing. Most works only take into account explicit features, such as era (Chang et al., 2021) and imagery (Shen et al., 2019), ignoring implicit syntactic features. The main reason for this lies in two aspects: (1) the linguistic gap between ancient and modern Chinese makes it difficult for supervised modern Chinese syntax parsers to correctly parse ancient Chinese expressions; (2) training a supervised ancient Chinese syntax parser from scratch can be highly costly due to the lack of annotated data.

Unsupervised syntax parsing or directly employing modern Chinese parsers will inevitably cause noise and performance degradation. A unlabeled example and corresponding human annotation on ancient Chinese sentence "可怜人似月中孀(*It is*

* Corresponding authors.

Proceedings of the 61st Annual Meeting of the Association for Computational Linguistics - Student Research Workshop, pages 83–92
July 10-12, 2023 ©2023 Association for Computational Linguistics

pitiful like Chang'e in the moon)" are shown in Figure 1. To address this challenge, we propose a novel syntax encoding structure – confidence-based syntax encoding network (cSEN), which alleviates the negative effect of noise by measuring confidence of arcs in syntax graphs. Specifically, confidence is calculated by performing Biaffine transformation over the sequence representation and the derived syntactic graph adjacency matrix. With this obtained confidence, our model is capable of distinguishing useful syntactic features from noise.

Moreover, compared with modern Chinese, ancient Chinese has more concise expressions and thus more compact structures, each token is highly relative to the preceding and following one. Considering such linguistic characteristic, we incorporate another graph feature – left-right branch (LRB), which captures local features to further improve ancient Chinese understanding. Experiments are conducted on two typical ancient Chinese understanding tasks, thematic classification of ancient poetry and ancient-modern Chinese translation. Results show that our model achieves significant improvements over powerful baselines, and our proposed cSEN can effectively handle the noise in the derived syntax trees. To our best knowledge, our proposed cSEN is the first solution that makes the syntax practical in ancient Chinese processing. The proposed cSEB can serve as a backbone for enriching our understanding of ancient texts, offering a scalable and consistent solution for education, research, and broadening the public's access to these significant cultural treasures.

Overall, the contributions of this paper can be concluded in four folds:

- This study fills the research gap of exploring the role of syntax in ancient Chinese understanding. Our work demonstrates that syntactic information, even noisy parses from unsupervised derivation, can benefit ancient Chinese understanding substantially.

- We propose a novel architecture – confidence-based syntax encoding network (cSEN), which alleviates the negative effect of noise in syntax parses, thus making it practical to utilize derived syntactic information to enhance ancient Chinese understanding.

- The effectiveness of cSEN is evaluated on two typical ancient Chinese understanding tasks, ancient poetry thematic classification and ancient-modern Chinese translation. Results show that our model yields significantly better performance in noisy scenarios over powerful baselines.

- We create a new dataset for the thematic classification of ancient Chinese poetry, with 22,360 poems divided into 10 theme categories. This dataset offers a data foundation for related research and helps to eliminate the lack of available ancient Chinese annotated corpora.

2 Related Work

2.1 Syntax Role in Modern Chinese Understanding

As syntax is highly correlated with semantics, syntactic features, including constituent and dependency structures, have been utilized in many modern Chinese understanding tasks and have been shown to be helpful clues. Li et al. (2018) explored the effect of syntax on semantic role labeling (SRL) and confirmed that high-quality syntactic parsing can effectively enhance syntactically-driven SRL. Xia et al. (2019) designed a syntax-aware multi-task learning framework for Chinese SRL by extracting implicit syntactic representations as external inputs for the SRL model. Jiang et al. (2018) incorporated syntactic features to expand identified triplets for improving Chinese entity relation extraction. Zhang et al. (2020) proposed a syntax-aware approach for solving machine reading comprehension, which incorporates explicit syntactic constraints into the attention mechanism for better linguistically motivated word representations. Sun et al. (2022) utilized syntactic features, which capture depth-level structure information, including non-consecutive words and their relations, to enhance recognition of Chinese implicit inter-sentence relations. Zhu et al. (2022) incorporated syntactic dependency information to determine entity boundaries for improving Chinese named entity recognition. Despite the increasing attention that syntax is receiving in modern Chinese understanding, few studies have attempted to utilize syntactic features for ancient Chinese understanding.

2.2 Ancient-Modern Chinese Translation

Unlike bilingual translation tasks, such as Chinese-English, ancient and modern Chinese are written using the same characters. Despite that, translating between ancient and modern Chinese can still be challenging for native speakers. This is due to two factors: (1) the syntactical structure and grammatical order of ancient Chinese are different from those of modern Chinese, making ancient Chinese expressions more concise yet also more confusing; (2) ancient Chinese frequently employs allusion, metaphor, and symbolic imagery to implicitly evoke sensory and emotional experiences, which increases the complexity of disambiguating the intended message.

In recent years, advancements in deep learning have led to significant progress in neural machine translation. For example, Zhang et al. (2019b) proposed an unsupervised algorithm that constructs sentence-aligned ancient-modern pairs, and an end-to-end neural model with copying mechanism and local attention to translate between ancient and modern Chinese. Liu et al. (2019) applied RNN-based (Bahdanau et al., 2014) and Transformer-based (Vaswani et al., 2017) machine translation models to this task. Considering the monolingual nature of this task, Yang et al. (2021) utilized pre-trained model UNILM (Dong et al., 2019) and an ancient Chinese pre-trained model Guwen-BERT to enhance performance. Over time, the Chinese language has evolved a lot, resulting in different characteristics of ancient Chinese in different eras. To address this, Chang et al. (2021) proposed a time-aware translation method, where the model predicts both the translation results and its particular era, and uses the predicted chronological feature as auxiliary information to bridge the linguistic gap between Chinese language in different eras.

2.3 Classification of Ancient Chinese Poetry

Classification of ancient Chinese poetry provides a basis for higher-level tasks, such as sentiment or style controllable poetry generation (Yang et al., 2018; Chen et al., 2019; Shao et al., 2021). In the past, statistical features and machine learning algorithms were commonly used. For example, Hou and Frank (2015) proposed a weakly supervised sentiment classification approach, which created a sentiment lexicon based on Weighted Personalized PageRank (WPPR). Shen et al. (2019) incorporated imagery features for analyzing the sentiment of Tang Poetry. In recent years, neural classifiers have been introduced to the task and made remarkable progress in performance. For instance, Xuan et al. (2018) designed a poetry style recognition model by stacking a genetic algorithm with CNN, and Tang et al. (2020) combined CNN with a gated GRU for solving poetry sentiment classification.

3 Model

In this section, we describe architecture of the proposed cSEN. We first present a basic GAT encoder, then introduce our cSEN. The overview of cSEN is shown in Figure 2.

3.1 Vanilla GAT

GAT is often applied over a sentence encoder to extract graph-based representations of the input text. Given input token sequence $\mathcal{T} = \{t_1, t_2, \ldots, t_l\}$, l denotes the sequence length. The output of the sentence encoder is denoted as matrix $\mathcal{H} \in \mathbb{R}^{l \times n}$, where each row $h_i \in \mathbb{R}^n$ is the representation of token t_i.

With dependency structure of the input sequence from a syntax parser, we construct a dependency graph $\mathcal{G} = (\mathcal{V}, \mathcal{E})$, where $\mathcal{V}$ is the set of tokens and $\mathcal{E}$ is the set of arcs. In the graph encoding, we employ the form of adjacency matrix to describe the graph, in which the positions with arcs and diagonal are assigned to ones, denoted as $\mathcal{M}^{(\text{dep})}$. Linear transformation is performed by multiplying the sentence representation $\mathcal{H}$ with a matrix $\mathcal{W} \in \mathbb{R}^{n \times n'}$ for feature extraction, where n' denotes the transformed feature dimension:

$$\mathcal{Z} = \mathcal{H}\mathcal{W}.$$

Then, a pair-wise attention operation is performed. For every pair $t_i, t_j \in \mathcal{V}$, it concatenates corresponding representations z_i and z_j, then takes the dot product with vector $a \in \mathbb{R}^{2n'}$ and applies a **LeakyReLU** activation function:

$$\mathcal{S}^{(\text{raw})}[i, j] = \textbf{LeakyReLU}([z_i \oplus z_j]^T a),$$

where $\oplus$ represents the concatenation operation, and $\mathcal{S}^{(\text{raw})}$ is a score matrix with the size of $(l \times l)$ that captures inter-node relations. To integrate the graph structure, the adjacency matrix $\mathcal{M}^{(\text{dep})}$ is used to constrain the function scope before a regular **Softmax** operation is performed. By doing this, each token can only attend to its head tokens and itself. The obtained attention weights matrix then is used for scaling the transformed sentence representation $\mathcal{Z}$ and calculating the final attentional output:

$$\mathcal{W}^{(\text{attn})} = \textbf{Softmax}(\mathcal{S}^{(\text{raw})} \times \mathcal{M}^{(\text{dep})}).$$

$$\mathcal{H}^{(\text{attn})} = \mathcal{W}^{(\text{attn})}\mathcal{Z}.$$

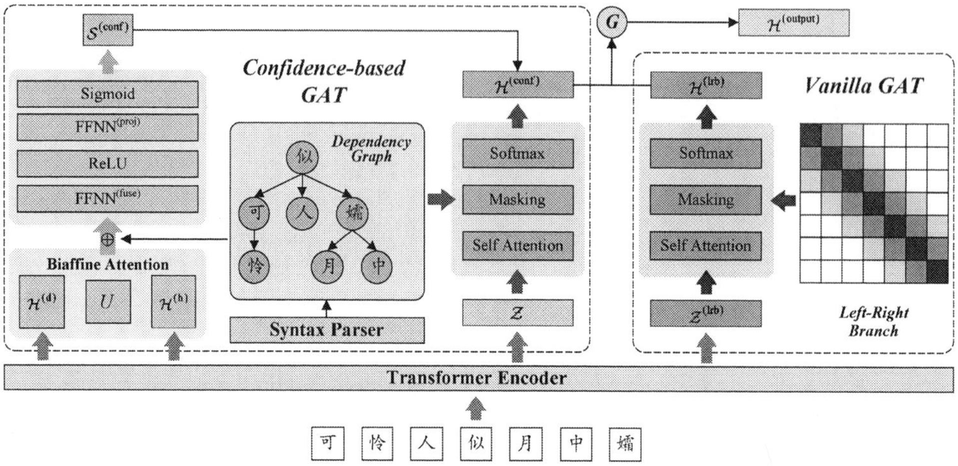

Figure 2: Architecture of the proposed cSEN. ⊕ and Ⓖ represents the concatenation operation and the gated mechanism, respectively. We present $\mathcal{M}^{(\text{dep})}$ in the form of graph where arcs are pointing from heads to dependencies. The cells in $\mathcal{M}^{(\text{lrb})}$ are colored to highlight the local dependencies, and darker color indicates higher correlation.

3.2 Confidence-based GAT

As discussed above, GAT guides the encoding process by constraining the scope of the attention computation. Therefore, the presence of noise in the graph will inevitably impact the encoding output. To alleviate the negative effects of noise on the model's performance, we propose a confidence-based GAT, which measures the confidence of the graph adjacency matrix, helping the model distinguish reliable syntactic information from noise.

Similar to vanilla GAT, we first model the pair-wise relationships. Two separate linear transformations are performed over the sentence representation $\mathcal{H}$ to obtain the role-aware representations. The outputs are denoted as $\mathcal{H}^{(\text{d})}$ and $\mathcal{H}^{(\text{h})}$ respectively, both of which have the size of $(l \times n')$:

$$\mathcal{H}^{(\text{d})} = \mathcal{H}\mathcal{W}^{(\text{d})}; \mathcal{H}^{(\text{h})} = \mathcal{H}\mathcal{W}^{(\text{h})}.$$

Then, Biaffine attention (Dozat and Manning, 2016) are calculated on the role-aware representations for pair-wise relationship scoring:

$$\mathcal{S}^{(\text{bi})} = \mathcal{H}^{(\text{d})} U \mathcal{H}^{(\text{h})T},$$

where U is an intermediate matrix with the size of $(n' \times n')$. Confidence scores are calculated by concatenating the pair-wise relationship scores and the adjacency matrix and passing them through processing as follows,

$$\mathcal{S}^{(\text{fuse})} = \textbf{ReLU}(\textbf{FFNN}^{(\text{fuse})}(\left[\mathcal{S}^{(\text{bi})} \oplus \mathcal{M}^{(\text{dep})}\right])),$$

$$\mathcal{S}^{(\text{conf})} = \textbf{Sigmoid}(\textbf{FFNN}^{(\text{proj})}(\mathcal{S}^{(\text{fuse})})).$$

where $\textbf{FFNN}^{(\text{fuse})}$ performs a linear transformation to fuse the two feature spaces along with an **ReLU** activation, and $\textbf{FFNN}^{(\text{proj})}$ is used to reduce the dimension from $2l$ to l, so that **Sigmoid** can be applied to project the confidence features to the same magnitude as the attention scores. With this obtained confidence scores $\mathcal{S}^{(\text{conf})}$, we can remedy the original attention restrain process:

$$\mathcal{W}^{(\text{conf})} = \textbf{Softmax}(\mathcal{W}^{(\text{attn})} + \mathcal{S}^{(\text{conf})}),$$

$$\mathcal{H}^{(\text{conf})} = \mathcal{W}^{(\text{conf})}\mathcal{Z}.$$

In summary, cSEN alleviates the negative effect of noise in graphs through a two-fold process. First, cSEN measures the confidence of the derived syntax parses. This confidence score is then used to soft-mask noisy arcs and highlight previously undetected ones. Second, considering the linguistic characteristics of ancient Chinese, the Left-Right Branch feature is incorporated to broaden the scope of syntax graph encoding and smooth out noise and incompatibility. The combined effect of these aspects helps alleviate performance degradation caused by noise.

3.3 Left-Right Branch Feature

Inspired by the ubiquity of local dependencies in ancient Chinese, we introduce a novel straightforward and effective feature, left-right branch, to further improve the GAT encoding. To model local inter-token relations, we populate a matrix $\mathcal{M}^{(\text{lrb})}$ of the same size as $\mathcal{M}^{(\text{dep})}$ following

$$\mathcal{M}^{(\text{lrb})}[i,j] = \begin{cases} 1, & \text{if } j \in \{i-1, i+1\} \\ 0, & \text{otherwise.} \end{cases}$$

This indicates that there exist arcs in the graph connecting the node and its close left and right neighbors. The left-right branch features are encoded using another GAT component, yielding a sequence representation $\mathcal{Z}^{(lrb)}$ and a positional-information-introduced attention weight matrix $\mathcal{W}^{(\text{lrb})}$. The outputs from $\mathcal{M}^{(dep)}$ and $\mathcal{M}^{(lrb)}$ are combined with a gated mechanism to produce the final output:

$$\mathcal{H}^{(\text{lrb})} = \mathcal{W}^{(\text{lrb})}\mathcal{Z}^{(\text{lrb})},$$

$$g = \textbf{Sigmoid}(\textbf{FFNN}^{(\text{gate})}(\left[\mathcal{H}^{(\text{conf})} \oplus \mathcal{H}^{(\text{lrb})}\right])),$$

$$\mathcal{H}^{(\text{output})} = g \times \mathcal{H}^{(\text{conf})} + (1-g) \times \mathcal{H}^{(\text{lrb})}.$$

4 Experiments

We evaluate the effectiveness of cSEN module using two typical ancient Chinese understanding tasks: Thematic classification of ancient poetry and ancient-modern Chinese translation. We build our model by incorporating the cSEN module into existing solid baselines. For the classification task, we follow the work of (Vaibhav et al., 2019) which has a BERT-GAT-BiLSTM backbone architecture. And for the translation task, our model is based on (Jin et al., 2020) where dependency graphs are incorporated into neural sequence-to-sequence models with a pointer network.

4.1 Data

To address the scarcity of annotated data for thematic classification, we constructed a novel dataset[1]. Two graduate students specializing in Chinese literature study annotated 22,360 poems, categorizing them into one of ten distinct themes under the guidance of an experienced ancient Chinese linguist. This meticulous process ensured high-quality, reliable annotations. Any conflicted labelling between the two annotators was resolved through consultation with the supervisor, guaranteeing a consistent annotation standard. The dataset is then randomly divided into a training set (20,360), a development set (800), and a test set (1,200). The distribution of themes in the dataset is detailed in Table 1.

For the ancient-modern Chinese translation, we adopt the ancient-modern Chinese parallel corpus contributed by the open source NiuTrans project[2]. The corpus contains 967,255 sentence pairs extracted from ancient Chinese books. We divided the corpus into training, validation, and test sets with corresponding sizes of 900,000, 60,000, and 7,255.

	Train	Dev	Test
#Object-chanting	1129	47	66
#Landscape	1097	44	47
#Persons	2403	91	129
#History	1087	40	76
#Homesickness	9013	357	522
#Mourning	503	18	31
#War	1746	62	115
#Pastoral	1219	47	84
#Farewell	1460	60	83
#Boudoir-plaint	703	34	47
Total	20360	800	1200

Table 1: Data statistics of the ancient Chinese poetry thematic classification dataset

4.2 Syntax Parsing

We experiment with two settings – modern supervised parsers and ancient unsupervised syntax derivation. For modern supervised parsing, we adopt the Biaffine dependency parse (Dozat and Manning, 2016) and train it on CTB7 (Xue et al., 2010). For unsupervised syntax derivation, we follow the work of Wu et al. (2020), which utilizes linguistic knowledge gained from pre-trained language model BERT to infer syntactic dependency structure without direct supervison. We attempt two variants of BERT for syntax derivation and backbone sentence encoder, BERT-wwm-ext (Cui et al., 2021) and Anchi-BERT (Tian et al., 2021). BERT-wwm-ext is trained on the modern Chinese corpus containing 5.4B words, while Anchi-BERT is trained upon a ancient Chinese corpus with the size of 39.5M tokens. In addition, we treat the left-right branch as a special kind of syntax parses. Anchi-BERT is trained on a smaller ancient Chinese corpus (39.5M tokens), while BERT wwm ext is trained on a larger modern Chinese corpus (5.4B tokens). We also treat left-right branch features as a distinct class of syntax parses.

For clarity, the syntactic parses from the Biaffine parser, BERT-wwm derivation, and Anchi-BERT derivation are denoted as *BiAF*, *WWMD*, *ANCD* respectively, in the following part.

4.3 Implementation and Hyper-parameters

For the thematic classification, our model is built by stacking BERT, a graph encoder, and a single-layer LSTM. For the baseline, we do not incorporate syn-

[1]Upon publication of this paper, this dataset will be made available for research purposes.

[2]https://github.com/NiuTrans/Classical-Modern

Methods	Parses	BERT-wwm Micro F1	BERT-wwm Macro F1	Anchi-BERT Micro F1	Anchi-BERT Macro F1
Baseline	None	91.7	89.2	92.4	90.4
GAT	*LRB*	91.5	88.9	93.3	91.4
	BiAF	92.3	89.7	93.3	91.2
	WWMD	91.4	88.8	92.7	90.8
	ANCD	91.8	89.2	93.2	91.0
	BiAF+LRB	92.7	90.4	93.3	91.2
	WWMD+LRB	91.7	89.6	93.2	91.2
	ANCD+LRB	90.8	88.2	92.8	90.7
	BiAF+ANCD+LRB	91.7	88.8	92.6	90.6
cSEN	*BiAF+LRB*	91.4	89.2	93.3	91.6
	WWMD+LRB	92.8	90.7	93.6	**91.9**
	ANCD+LRB	91.3	89.1	93.2	91.3
	BiAF+ANCD+LRB	91.0	89.1	**93.8**	**91.9**

Table 2: Comparison with baseline model and syntax-aware methods on the thematic classification task.

Methods	Parses	BLEU	RG-1 F-score	RG-2 F-score	RG-L F-score
Baseline	None	37.14	69.71	46.24	67.62
GAT	*LRB*	37.42	69.86	46.36	67.72
	BiAF	37.45	70.23	46.93	68.21
	WWMD	37.46	70.20	46.89	68.14
	ANCD	37.55	69.90	46.53	67.85
	BiAF+ANCD+LRB	34.62	69.20	45.15	67.15
cSEN	*BiAF+ANDC+LRB*	**37.73**	**70.27**	**47.09**	**68.23**

Table 3: Experimental Results of the ancient and modern Chinese translation task.

tax parses, rendering the graph encoder ineffective in shaping the attention scope. The graph encoder's node embedding dimension is set to 128, and the hidden size in LSTM is set to 100. We adopt the Adam optimizer with $\rho = 5e-5$ and $\epsilon = 1e-8$, using a batch size of 32. All classifiers are trained for 10 epochs on the train set by default.

We mostly follow the parameter settings from (Jin et al., 2020) for the ancient-modern Chinese translation. The Adam optimizer is configured with $\rho = 1e-4$ and $\epsilon = 1e-8$. And all models are trained for 50 epochs with a batch size of 108.

4.4 Results

4.4.1 Ancient Poetry Thematic Classification

Table 2 presents the results of ancient poetry thematic classification. We report the results in Micro-F1 and Macro-F1 scores. The table is divided into three blocks, showing the results of the baseline model, vanilla GAT, and the proposed cSEN. The baseline model achieves 92.4 in Micro F1 and 90.4 in Macro F1, showing strong performance.

From the results in the first two blocks, it can be found that incorporating syntactic trees with GAT encoder brings substantial improvement, proving the value of syntactic information for enhancing ancient Chinese understanding. Through comparing the results of employing Anchi-Bert as the sentence encoder and those obtained employing Bert-wwm, we can see that Anchi-Bert outperforms BERT-wwm with a significant lead in all cases. Recall that Anchi-Bert was pre-trained on a much smaller corpus. Also, the performance of syntactic trees derived by BERT-wwm is inferior to the other three. This once more indicates the linguistic gap and syntactic incompatibility between ancient and modern Chinese.

Unsupervised syntax trees derived by Anchi-BERT performs roughly the same as those produced by the Biaffine parser. Additionally, LRB is the best-performing syntax parse among all, improving the performance by 0.9 in Micro F1 and 1.0 in Macro F1. It can be partially explained by the fact that ancient poems are comprised by a few brief sentences, which are highly concise and structurally compact. This results in fewer long-range dependencies, and each token is closely dependent on the immediate preceding or succeeding token.

From the third block, it can be seen that when using Anchi-BERT as sentence encoder, cSEN brings

Variants	Micro F1	Macro F1
cSEN	**93.8**	**91.9**
w/o Confidence	92.8	91.1
w/o Gate	93.0	91.0

Table 4: Ablation study results.

Syntax Trees	Micro F1	Macro F1
[*ANCD*] + (*LRB*)	93.2	91.3
[*BiAF*] + (*LRB*)	93.3	91.6
[*BiAF* + *LRB*] + (*ANCD*)	92.8	90.9
[*ANCD* + *LRB*] + (*BiAF*)	92.8	90.5
[*BiAF* + *ANCD*] + (*LRB*)	**93.8**	**91.9**

Table 5: Comparison of different combination configurations on syntactic parses. Parses in square brackets are merged onto a single adjacency matrix and parses in parentheses are incorporated by the gated mechanism

performance gains across all syntax trees setups, raising the top Micro and Macro F1 scores to 93.8 and 91.9, respectively. This demonstrates that: (1) cSEN's denoising capability is effective for utilizing noisy syntactic information to improve ancient Chinese understanding; (2) cSEN can handle noise introduced by different parses, whether it is from a supervised modern Chinese parser or unsupervised derivation.

4.4.2 Ancient-Modern Chinese Translation

Results of the ancient-modern Chinese translation are shown in Table 3. We use BLEU (Papineni et al., 2002) and ROUGE (Lin, 2004) scores for performance evaluation. The baseline model without syntax parses achieves 37.14 in BLEU score and F-scores of 69.71, 46.24, 67.62 in ROUGE-1, ROUGE-2, and ROUGE-L respectively. With single syntactic parses incorporated, all models achieve better performance in all metrics, proving that syntax can effectively improve ancient-modern Chinese translation. LRB is relatively the weakest one, slightly increasing BLEU score by 0.28, and ROUGE f-scores by 0.15, 0.12, 0.10. This might be caused by that sentences from the ancient books have more long-distance dependencies and more complicated syntactic structures that left right branch can not recover. Anchi-BERT derived syntax parses have better performance with an improvement of 0.41 in BLEU score, and 0.19, 0.29, and 0.23 in ROUGE scores. BERT-wwm derived syntax trees and trees generated by Biaffine parser have similar results. In contrast to Anchi-BERT derived trees, their performance are inferior in BLEU scores but better in ROUGE F-scores. Feeding multiple syntactic parses into the GAT-based model simultaneously leads to a significant performance drop. While replacing GAT with the proposed cSEN increases performance in all metrices, with 37.73 in BLEU score and 70.27, 47.09, 68.23 in ROUGE F-scores. From the above results, we conclude that syntax parses from unsupervised derivation or modern Chinese syntax parsers introduce noise and degrade model performance. With our confidence learning, model is able to distinguish and separate informative syntactic information from noise, thus alleviating its negative effect.

Table 6 shows three ancient-to-modern Chinese translation examples produced by different models. From generations for Sent 1, we can see a common error: due to the lack of contextual information, all three models assume the surname of "the father" useing the most common Chinese surnames, such as "Li" and "Zhang". For Sent 2, the generations from the baseline model and vanilla GAT differ significantly from the human-annotated reference. They fail to recognize the relationship between the characters,such as who "其娣" refers to, thus generating tranlations that did not correspond to the facts. In contrast, with stronger denoising capability, cSEN is able to correctly encodes the information in ancient Chinese texts, thus producing higher-quality translations.

5 Exploration

In this section, we investigate the impact of different cSEN components and analyze the nature of different syntax parses.

First, we conduct ablation studies on cSEN. Results are reported in Table 4. Both the removal of the confidence (equivalent to vanilla GAT) and the removal of the gated mechanism lead to significant performance degradation. This indicates that both modules are crucial for effectively utilizing syntactic information from noisy parses.

Second, we experiment with different syntax tree combination setups. Table 5 lists the findings. Combining two syntax parsers onto a single dependency graph can provide richer syntactic information and produce higher performance than using alone syntax parses, no matter it is from unsupervised derivation or a supervised parser. We also explore the incorporation position of LRB features. It can be observed that the model performance suffers significantly if LRB features and graph parses

Sent	Ancient Chinese
1	src: 父岘，少骁勇，事章大宝为帐内部曲。 ref: 父亲陈岘，年轻时骁勇，侍奉章大宝，任帐内部曲。 trl: His father, Chen Xian, was brave when he was young. He served Zhang Dabao, as an in-tent soldier.
2	src: 晋伐骊戎，骊戎男女以骊姬。归生奚齐。其娣生卓子。 ref: 晋国攻打骊戎，骊戎男把骊姬献给晋献公，回国后生了奚齐，她的妹妹生了卓子。 trl: Jin state attacked Li Rong. Li Rong's men presented Li Ji to Jin Xian Gong. After returning the state, Li Ji gave birth to Xi Qi, and her sister gave birth to Zhuo Zi.
3	src: 及竣事，又曰：杨存中之罢，朕不安寝者三夕。 ref: 等到事毕后，又说：杨存中被罢免，我有三天不得安寝。 trl: After the matter was over, he said: "The dismissal of Yang Cunzhong, made me unable to sleep for three days."
Baseline	
1	父亲张岘，少年时骁勇善战，在章大宝帐下当兵，任章大宝的部曲。 His father, Zhang Xian, was brave and good at fighting when he was young. He served as a soldier under the command of Zhang Dabao, and was Zhang Dabao's soldier.
2	晋国讨伐骊戎，骊戎男女献上骊姬，回国后生了奚齐，骊戎的妹妹生了卓子。 Jin state attacked Li Rong, and Li Rong's men and women presented Li Ji, and after returning the state, they gave birth to Xi Qi, and Li Rong's sister gave birth to Zhuo Zi.
3	等到完成任务，又说：杨存中被罢免，朕三夜不安寝。 After completing the task, he said: "The dismissal of Yang Cunzhong, made me unable to sleep for three nights."
Vanilla GAT	
1	父亲李岘，少年时骁勇善战，在章大宝手下做事。 His father, Li Xian, was brave and good at fighting when he was young, and worked under Zhang Dabao.
2	晋国讨伐骊戎，骊戎男娶了骊姬，嫁给了奚齐，奚齐的妹妹生了卓子。 Jin state attacked Li Rong. Li Rong's men married Li Ji, married Xi Qi, and Xi Qi's sister gave birth to Zhuo Zi.
3	等到完工，又说：杨存中被罢免的事，我感到不安宁 的有三个晚上。 After the work was finished, he said: I felt uneasy about Yang Cunzhong's dismissal for three nights.
cSEN	
1	父亲陈岘，年轻时骁勇，事奉章大宝任帐内部曲。 trl: His father, Chen Xian, was brave when he was young. He served Zhang Dabao as an in-tent soldier.
2	晋国攻打骊戎，骊戎男把骊姬送给晋国，回国后生了奚齐，她的妹妹生了卓子。 Jin state attacked Li Rong. Li Rong's men presented Li Ji to Jin State. After returning the state, Li Ji gave birth to Xi Qi, and her sister gave birth to Zhuo Zi.
3	等到事情完毕，又说：杨存中被罢免，我三天不安寝。 trl: After the matter was over, he said: "The dismissal of Yang Cunzhong, made me unable to sleep for three days."

Table 6: Ancient-to-modern Chinese translation examples generated by the baseline model, vanilla GAT, and cSEN. The first block shows the original ancient Chinese sentence (src), human-annotated modern Chinese reference (ref), and corresponding English translations (trl).

are directly merged together. This again indicates the necessity of our gated method for LRB feature integration.

Third, as illustrated in Figure Figure 3, we compare our model and baselines over different input lengths. cSEN performs better in relative longer sentences, according to the results. This supports the hypothesis that syntax helps guide longer sentence understanding as dependency reduces the distance. Because of the incompatibility between modern and ancient Chinese, unsupervised derivation is more effective than supervised parsing when compared to other syntax parsers. In most cases, cSEN yeilding better performance due to its stronger denoising capabilities.

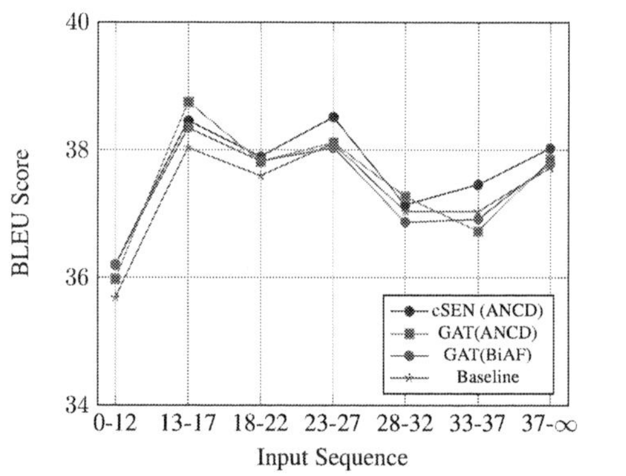

Figure 3: BLEU scores for different input sentence lengths.

6 Conclusions

In this paper, we investigate the role of syntax in improving ancient Chinese understanding. Due to lack of syntax annotation, syntax trees are obtained by unsupervised derivation and supervised modern Chinese parser. To alleviate the negative effect of noise, we propose a confidence-based syntax encoding network (cSEN). Experimental results on two typical ancient Chinese understanding tasks show that our model can effectively distinguish informative syntactic information from noise and achieve better performance. The application of our proposed cSEN can enhance the accessibility of ancient Chinese resources by offering a scalable and consistent solution for mining semantic information of ancient Chinese texts.

Limitations

The main limitation of our study comes from the extra parameters caused by confidence calculation, in which two separate self-attention operations and Biaffine transformation are performed. Incremental parameters results in a more time-consuming training process, and a higher hardware demand for storage. To address this issue, we plan to combine parameters from different attentional transformations into shared weight matrices in our future work to reduce the model size.

Acknowledgements

This paper was partially supported by the National Natural Science Foundation of China [No. 72074171].

References

Dzmitry Bahdanau, Kyunghyun Cho, and Yoshua Bengio. 2014. Neural machine translation by jointly learning to align and translate. *arXiv preprint arXiv:1409.0473*.

Emanuele Bugliarello and Naoaki Okazaki. 2020. Enhancing machine translation with dependency-aware self-attention. In *Proceedings of the 58th Annual Meeting of the Association for Computational Linguistics*, pages 1618–1627.

Ernie Chang, Yow-Ting Shiue, Hui-Syuan Yeh, and Vera Demberg. 2021. Time-aware ancient chinese text translation and inference. *arXiv preprint arXiv:2107.03179*.

Huimin Chen, Xiaoyuan Yi, Maosong Sun, Wenhao Li, Cheng Yang, and Zhipeng Guo. 2019. Sentiment-controllable chinese poetry generation. In *IJCAI*, pages 4925–4931.

Yiming Cui, Wanxiang Che, Ting Liu, Bing Qin, and Ziqing Yang. 2021. Pre-training with whole word masking for chinese bert. *IEEE/ACM Transactions on Audio, Speech, and Language Processing*, 29:3504–3514.

Anna Currey and Kenneth Heafield. 2019. Incorporating source syntax into transformer-based neural machine translation. In *Proceedings of the Fourth Conference on Machine Translation (Volume 1: Research Papers)*, pages 24–33.

Li Dong, Nan Yang, Wenhui Wang, Furu Wei, Xiaodong Liu, Yu Wang, Jianfeng Gao, Ming Zhou, and Hsiao-Wuen Hon. 2019. Unified language model pre-training for natural language understanding and generation. *Advances in Neural Information Processing Systems*, 32.

Timothy Dozat and Christopher D Manning. 2016. Deep biaffine attention for neural dependency parsing. *arXiv preprint arXiv:1611.01734*.

Kong Fang and J Fu. 2019. Incorporating structural information for better coreference resolution. In *Twenty-Eighth International Joint Conference on Artificial Intelligence IJCAI-19*.

Shaoru Guo, Yong Guan, Ru Li, Xiaoli Li, and Hongye Tan. 2020. Incorporating syntax and frame semantics in neural network for machine reading comprehension. In *Proceedings of the 28th International Conference on Computational Linguistics*, pages 2635–2641.

Yufang Hou and Anette Frank. 2015. Analyzing sentiment in classical chinese poetry. In *Proceedings of the 9th SIGHUM workshop on language Technology for Cultural Heritage, social sciences, and humanities (LaTeCH)*, pages 15–24.

Fan Jiang and Trevor Cohn. 2022. Incorporating constituent syntax for coreference resolution. *arXiv preprint arXiv:2202.10710*.

Yishun Jiang, Gongqing Wu, Chenyang Bu, and Xuegang Hu. 2018. Chinese entity relation extraction based on syntactic features. In *2018 IEEE International Conference on Big Knowledge (ICBK)*, pages 99–105. IEEE.

Hanqi Jin, Tianming Wang, and Xiaojun Wan. 2020. Semsum: Semantic dependency guided neural abstractive summarization. In *Proceedings of the AAAI conference on artificial intelligence*, volume 34, pages 8026–8033.

Zuchao Li, Shexia He, Jiaxun Cai, Zhuosheng Zhang, Hai Zhao, Gongshen Liu, Linlin Li, and Luo Si. 2018. A unified syntax-aware framework for semantic role labeling. In *Proceedings of the 2018 Conference on Empirical Methods in Natural Language Processing*, pages 2401–2411.

Chin-Yew Lin. 2004. Rouge: A package for automatic evaluation of summaries. In *Text summarization branches out*, pages 74–81.

Dayiheng Liu, Kexin Yang, Qian Qu, and Jiancheng Lv. 2019. Ancient–modern chinese translation with a new large training dataset. *ACM Transactions on Asian and Low-Resource Language Information Processing (TALLIP)*, 19(1):1–13.

Jerry Norman. 1988. *Chinese*. Cambridge University Press.

Kishore Papineni, Salim Roukos, Todd Ward, and Wei-Jing Zhu. 2002. Bleu: a method for automatic evaluation of machine translation. In *Proceedings of the 40th annual meeting of the Association for Computational Linguistics*, pages 311–318.

Yizhan Shao, Tong Shao, Minghao Wang, Peng Wang, and Jie Gao. 2021. A sentiment and style controllable approach for chinese poetry generation. In *Proceedings of the 30th ACM International Conference on Information & Knowledge Management*, pages 4784–4788.

Yabo Shen, Yong Ma, Chunguo Li, Shidang Li, Mingliang Gu, Chaojin Zhang, Yun Jin, and Yingli Shen. 2019. Sentiment analysis for tang poetry based on imagery aided and classifier fusion. In *International Conference on Artificial Intelligence for Communications and Networks*, pages 283–290. Springer.

Kaili Sun, Yuan Li, Huyin Zhang, Chi Guo, Linfei Yuan, and Quan Hu. 2022. Syntax–aware graph convolutional network for the recognition of chinese implicit inter-sentence relations. *The Journal of Supercomputing*, pages 1–24.

Yongrui Tang, Xumei Wang, Peng Qi, and Yan Sun. 2020. A neural network-based sentiment analysis scheme for tang poetry. In *2020 International Wireless Communications and Mobile Computing (IWCMC)*, pages 1783–1788. IEEE.

Huishuang Tian, Kexin Yang, Dayiheng Liu, and Jiancheng Lv. 2021. Anchibert: a pre-trained model for ancient chinese language understanding and generation. In *2021 International Joint Conference on Neural Networks (IJCNN)*, pages 1–8. IEEE.

Hai Long Trieu, Anh-Khoa Duong Nguyen, Nhung Nguyen, Makoto Miwa, Hiroya Takamura, and Sophia Ananiadou. 2019. Coreference resolution in full text articles with bert and syntax-based mention filtering. In *Proceedings of The 5th Workshop on BioNLP Open Shared Tasks*, pages 196–205.

Vaibhav Vaibhav, Raghuram Mandyam Annasamy, and Eduard Hovy. 2019. Do sentence interactions matter? leveraging sentence level representations for fake news classification. *arXiv preprint arXiv:1910.12203*.

Ashish Vaswani, Noam Shazeer, Niki Parmar, Jakob Uszkoreit, Llion Jones, Aidan N Gomez, Łukasz Kaiser, and Illia Polosukhin. 2017. Attention is all you need. *Advances in neural information processing systems*, 30.

Chen Weiping. 2017. An analysis of anti-traditionalism in the new culture movement. *Social Sciences in China*, 38(2):175–187.

Zhiyong Wu, Yun Chen, Ben Kao, and Qun Liu. 2020. Perturbed masking: Parameter-free probing for analyzing and interpreting bert. In *Proceedings of the 58th Annual Meeting of the Association for Computational Linguistics*, pages 4166–4176.

Qingrong Xia, Zhenghua Li, and Min Zhang. 2019. A syntax-aware multi-task learning framework for chinese semantic role labeling. *arXiv preprint arXiv:1911.04641*.

Jing Xuan, Zhongshi He, Liangyan Li, Weidong He, Fei Guo, Hang Zhang, and Qiong Wu. 2018. Brain-oriented cconvolutional neural network computer style recognition of classical chinese poetry. *NeuroQuantology*, 16(4).

Nianwen Xue, Zixin Jiang, Xiuhong Zhong, Martha Palmer, Fei Xia, Fu-Dong Chiou, and Meiyu Chang. 2010. Chinese treebank 7.0. `https://catalog.ldc.upenn.edu/LDC2010T07`. Accessed: 2022-05-20.

Cheng Yang, Maosong Sun, Xiaoyuan Yi, and Wenhao Li. 2018. Stylistic chinese poetry generation via unsupervised style disentanglement. In *Proceedings of the 2018 conference on empirical methods in natural language processing*, pages 3960–3969.

Zinong Yang, Ke-jia Chen, and Jingqiang Chen. 2021. Guwen-unilm: Machine translation between ancient and modern chinese based on pre-trained models. In *CCF International Conference on Natural Language Processing and Chinese Computing*, pages 116–128. Springer.

Meishan Zhang, Zhenghua Li, Guohong Fu, and Min Zhang. 2019a. Syntax-enhanced neural machine translation with syntax-aware word representations. *arXiv preprint arXiv:1905.02878*.

Zhiyuan Zhang, Wei Li, and Qi Su. 2019b. Automatic translating between ancient chinese and contemporary chinese with limited aligned corpora. In *CCF International Conference on Natural Language Processing and Chinese Computing*, pages 157–167. Springer.

Zhuosheng Zhang, Yuwei Wu, Junru Zhou, Sufeng Duan, Hai Zhao, and Rui Wang. 2020. Sg-net: Syntax-guided machine reading comprehension. In *Proceedings of the AAAI Conference on Artificial Intelligence*, volume 34, pages 9636–9643.

Peng Zhu, Dawei Cheng, Fangzhou Yang, Yifeng Luo, Dingjiang Huang, Weining Qian, and Aoying Zhou. 2022. Improving chinese named entity recognition by large-scale syntactic dependency graph. *IEEE/ACM Transactions on Audio, Speech, and Language Processing*, 30:979–991.

The Turing *Quest*: Can Transformers Make Good NPCs?

Qi chen Gao
Brock University
1812 Sir Isaac Brock Way
St. Catharines, ON, Canada
qgao@brocku.ca

Ali Emami
Brock University
1812 Sir Isaac Brock Way
St. Catharines, ON, Canada
aemami@brocku.ca

Abstract

In this paper, we investigate the potential of using large pre-trained language models to generate non-playable character (NPC) scripts in video games. We introduce a novel pipeline that automatically constructs believable NPC scripts for various game genres and specifications using Transformer-based models. Moreover, we develop a self-diagnosis method, inspired by prior research, that is tailored to essential NPC characteristics such as coherence, believability, and variety in dialogue. To evaluate our approach, we propose a new benchmark, *The Turing Quest*, which demonstrates that our pipeline, when applied to GPT-3, generates NPC scripts across diverse game genres and contexts that can successfully deceive judges into believing they were written by humans. Our findings hold significant implications for the gaming industry and its global community, as the current reliance on manually-curated scripts is resource-intensive and can limit the immersiveness and enjoyment of players.

1 Introduction

Over the past decade, there has been a growing interest in applying deep learning models to Natural Language Generation (NLG) for open-domain dialogue systems and conversational agents. In parallel, the gaming industry has been striving to create more immersive experiences for players by enhancing their interactions with non-playable characters (NPCs). However, the potential of utilizing state-of-the-art deep learning models, such as Transformer-based models, to create NPC scripts remains largely unexplored.

Pre-trained Transformer-based language models (PLMs) like OpenAI's GPT-3 (Brown et al., 2020) and ChatGPT (Schulman et al., 2022) have demonstrated impressive conversational abilities (Milne-Ives et al., 2020). In certain contexts, the text generated by these models can be nearly indistinguishable from human-written text (M Alshater, 2022) without the aid of external tools or watermarks (Gambini et al., 2022). The use of these models in real-world applications has been expanding in areas such as customer service automation (Xu et al., 2017) (Zou et al., 2021), educational conversational agents (Molnár and Szüts, 2018), and mental health dialogue systems (Abd-Alrazaq et al., 2019).

Despite their growing prevalence, the effectiveness and generalization capabilities of PLMs in various contexts remain uncertain. One such uncharted domain is the creation of "non-playable characters" or NPCs in video games.

When comparing chatbots to NPCs, the latter can be considered as a narrative-driven variant of goal-oriented chatbots. However, NPCs and chatbots serve different purposes and operate in distinct environments. Generating NPC scripts presents unique challenges, as the dialogue must be consistent with the game's plot, genre, and the NPC's character to maintain player immersion and suspension of disbelief (Kerr and Szafron, 2009). According to Lee and Heeter (2015), NPC believability hinges on "*the size and nature of the cognitive gap between the [NPC that] players experience and the [NPC] they expect*". Players anticipate NPCs with individualized and possibly dynamic traits, which should be reflected in their dialogue. While incorporating personality into dialogue systems is well-studied (Qian et al., 2017) (Smestad and Volden, 2019) (de Haan et al., 2018), the challenge of generating goal-oriented, believable NPC scripts that align with a game's narrative and thematic elements, while preserving player immersion, remains substantial.

The ability to automatically generate contextually appropriate dialogue for a specified character could have an effect on the design paradigms of future video games. While manually scripted narratives and plot points will continue to hold their value, developers could augment player immersion

Proceedings of the 61st Annual Meeting of the Association for Computational Linguistics - Student Research Workshop, pages 93–103
July 10-12, 2023 ©2023 Association for Computational Linguistics

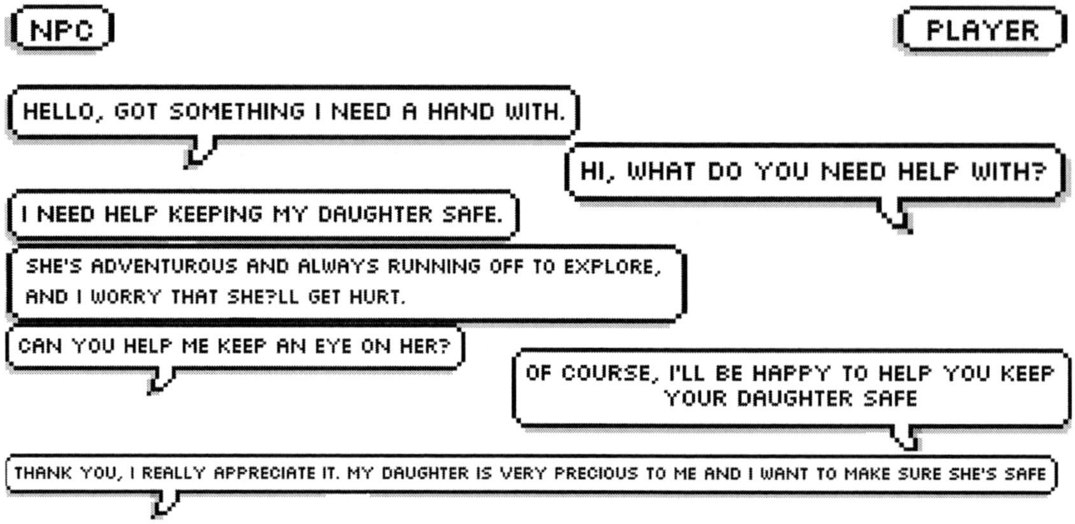

Figure 1: A sample output of our NPC construction pipeline.

by allowing an array of NPCs to dynamically respond to a player's in-game progression.

Traditionally, game design involves scripted dialogues only for NPCs that contribute directly to a quest or story line, thereby limiting the extent of player interaction. It is not often possible for a player to initiate a conversation with a companion about an ongoing quest or solicit their views, creating an impression that, from an NPC's perspective, the player's existence is confined to the quests they undertake.

Simply implementing an interactive companion system necessitates writing dialogues for every quest for all possible companions—a labor-intensive task. Expanding this system to encompass a majority of a game's NPCs would further compound these challenges, increasing the amount of labour to an unreasonable degree. The vast amount of dialogue required for each narrative stage would significantly exceed typical time and resource constraints of most developers. Despite the potential enrichment of the player experience, the practicality of creating such an immersive, dialogue-rich environment using solely human-authored dialogue in game development remains questionable.

In this study, we investigate the application of Transformer-based models like GPT-3 to the task of creating NPCs and generating believable scripts. To this end, we develop an NPC construction pipeline capable of generating dialogue based on the NPC's attributes alone. Our pipeline comprises three key modules: a) a *Feature Characterization Schema* that classifies NPCs based on personality traits and world descriptions, b) an *Automatic Prompt Creation* process that employs the schema to generate tailored prompts for conditioning language models, and c) a *Dialogue Generation* phase that uses the customized prompts to generate scripts with Transformer-based PLMs. Figure 1 provides an example of dialogue generated through this pipeline. We also devise and automate an evaluation metric for NPC dialogue quality, drawing inspiration from related literature (Brown et al., 2020). Lastly, we propose the Turing Quest: a test using human judges to assess the believability and quality of generated NPC scripts.

2 Related Work

In recent years, there has been a growing interest in dialogue systems and conversational agents. However, the exploration of dialogue generation for NPCs in video games, despite their similarities to chatbots, remains limited. Although most video games in the past decade include NPC dialogue, research on automating its creation using Artificial Intelligence (AI) is still in its infancy.

NPC Dialogue generation. In the early 2000s, efforts in NLP to create better NPC dialogue relied on hand-crafted algorithms and manually authored grammars (Schlünder and Klabunde, 2013) (Ryan et al., 2016). Schlünder and Klabunde (2013) succeeded in generating greetings that players perceived as more polite and appropriate than in-game greetings. However, their rule-based method relied on labor-intensive, discrete human-defined steps that were difficult to scale into full branching conversations. With recent advancements in goal-oriented chatbots utilizing machine learning techniques such as reinforcement learning (Liu et al., 2020) and dialogue generation through deep reinforcement learning (Li et al., 2016) (Li, 2020), automating NPC dialogue generation becomes increasingly feasible.

The introduction of AI into games has led to the application of various AI techniques and algorithms to enhance gameplay experiences through improved bots (Nareyek, 2004) and adaptive experiences (Raifer et al., 2022). There has been significant research into using machine learning to create bots that provide challenging and entertaining opponents for players (Håkansson and Fröberg, 2021). However, this trend of applying machine learning to different game design tasks does not extend to dialogue generation for NPCs.

Although pre-trained language models such as GPT-3 continue to expand their applicability, generalization remains an unsolved problem. While PLMs like GPT-3 have shown natural language generation capabilities (Topal et al., 2021), research into NLG with Transformer-based models trained on NPC dialogue has revealed that the generated dialogue "compared rather poorly to human-written [dialogue]" in terms of purpose and coherence (Kalbiyev, 2022). Nevertheless, generalization difficulty for LMs is not unique to NPC dialogue (Ye et al., 2021). We hypothesize that NPC dialogue is not merely another generalization problem but a distinct task. This hypothesis is supported by the inadequacy of chatbot evaluation metrics (Peras, 2018) when applied to NPC dialogue.

NPC Dialogue Metrics. Metrics proposed for chatbots do not directly translate to suitable metrics for NPC dialogue. While chatbot success is often determined by how "human" they sound and their ability to maintain a conversation with a human (Turing, 1950), NPC dialogue is always directed and goal-oriented. Generating dialogue for NPCs presents unique challenges compared to text generation in fictional settings. The generated dialogue must be consistent with the game world and the NPC's specific traits and personality, and it should ensure coherence and contextual relevance in relation to the player's input. No test equivalent to the Turing test or its alternatives, such as the Winograd schema (WSC) (Winograd, 1972; Levesque et al., 2011) exists specifically for NPC dialogue. To our knowledge, there is no standard metric to evaluate the quality of generated NPC dialogue. One suggested metric for NPC dialogue is "coherence, relevance, human-likeness, and fittingness" (Kalbiyev, 2022). While coherence, relevance, and human-likeness can be applied to chatbots, fittingness—defined by Kalbiyev (2022) as how well the response fits the game world—is unique to NPCs.

3 NPC Construction Pipeline

The objective of the NPC construction pipeline is to automatically generate coherent, contextually appropriate, and engaging utterances for an NPC, given the dialogue history between the NPC and a player, as well as the contextual information about the NPC and the game. The pipeline consists of three modules, which serve to a) characterize the NPC according to a generalized representation schema that captures crucial information about the NPC's role, personality, and game context, b) generate short prompts based on the characterization, providing contextually relevant pretexts for the language model (LM), and c) generate utterances based on these prompts using an LM optimized for NPC dialogue generation.

3.1 Module 1: Feature Characterization Schema

The first module in the pipeline involves developing a schema that characterizes a given NPC according to a number of game- and NPC-relevant features. Identifying the most concise set of features needed to define any NPC is a challenging task, as NPCs not only exhibit vastly different personalities but can also serve different purposes for the player and the game world. For example, in the action role-playing game, "The Elder Scrolls V: Skyrim" (Bethesda Game Studios, 2011), the NPC *Balgruuf the Greater* is a Jarl, i.e., a king or ruler who assigns quests to the player to maintain peace. In contrast, a character like *KL-E-0* from "Fallout 4" (Bethesda Game Studios, 2015), a robot arms dealer in a post-nuclear apocalyptic world, has little concern for peace. Based on (Warpefelt, 2016), NPCs should possess both a ludic function and a narrative framing for their actions to be coherent and believable. That is, an NPC should fulfill a gameplay or mechanical purpose—i.e., a ludic function—while advancing the narrative through their actions.

To develop a characterization of NPCs that captures their differences across various games and genres, we should consider several important features, such as their relationship and role with respect to the player (e.g., buying and selling, providing quests, etc.) and their individual personality and values. Taking into account narrative purpose, ludic purposes, and the personality and characteristic differences of NPCs, we propose five game-specific features to characterize and distinguish NPCs:

	Narrative	Ludic function
World Desc.	✓	
NPC Role		✓
NPC Personality	✓	
Game State	✓	✓
NPC Objective	✓	✓

Table 1: The features and their purpose(s).

Each of these five features either fulfills a ludic function or contributes to the game's narrative, and in some cases, a feature serves both purposes. This schema enables us to classify NPCs based on their in-game mechanics (Hunicke et al., 2004) while also capturing their role in the game's story. By incorporating these features into the NPC construction pipeline, we can create NPCs that not only adhere to the context and constraints of the game world but also exhibit distinct and engaging personalities, which can significantly enhance players' immersion and overall gaming experience.

World Description. A world description provides a summary of the story thus far, including information about the game world and its unique characteristics. Without this information, actions, thoughts, and utterances may be incoherent or unfitting, as they lack awareness of the setting and genre. This may result in dialogue or actions that conflict with the player's expectations. For instance, if Balgruuf from the previous example, originating from a fantasy adventure game, were placed in a sci-fi horror set in space, his actions, appearance, and dialogue would clash with the rest of the game. NPCs become "essentially incomprehensible if they are not framed according to the narrative" (Warpefelt, 2016). Ignoring information related to the setting, genre, and themes present in the NPC's world may affect the believability and fittingness of the NPC. More importantly, the narrative dissonance generated could shatter the *willful suspension of disbelief*—coined by Samuel Taylor Coleridge (1971)—and break the player's immersion in the game's world and story.

Role. Each unique NPC is created to fulfill a purpose. Continuing from the previous example, Balgruuf primarily functions as a *quest-giver*—facilitating the player's progression through the main quest line and occasionally offering side quests to enrich the narrative experience. Omitting his role would fail to represent a critical function of his character. Defining the role of an NPC, whether as a vendor, quest giver, or storyteller, etc., is thus crucial. We selected these roles based on the typology of NPCs and the NPC model proposed in (Warpefelt, 2016). We adapted the types of NPCs from (Warpefelt, 2016) and simplified the set of NPC types to those that would feasibly have a conversation with the player while also merging entries that were similar in their roles. This resulted in eight types of NPCs, six neutral or friendly roles, and two non-friendly roles, as shown below, in Table 2.

Metatype	Role
Functional	Vendor Service Provider Questgiver
Providers	Story teller
Friendly	Ally Companion
Adversaries	Enemy Villain

Table 2: Adapted NPC types.

The role an NPC occupies influences their expected dialogue. Although these roles are not mutually exclusive within a single NPC (e.g., some NPCs can be vendors at times while providing a quest at another time), at any given point during a dialogue with a player, the NPC occupies only one of these roles.

Personality. To describe any given NPC, it is necessary to elaborate on their personality and unique characteristics that distinguish them from other characters. These characteristics include physical attributes and appearances, psychological and personality traits such as the strength of the *OCEAN* personality traits proposed in (Digman, 1990), likes and dislikes, etc. This feature focuses on the details of the NPC's character, such as their occupation, beliefs, and other related details. NPCs are characters at their core, making it essential to incorporate these details into their depiction.

Game State. This describes the progression of the game and changes to the NPC's location. The NPC's dialogue may change based on the objectives completed by the player and the current state of the in-game world. The addition of this feature allows us to focus on the NPC during any single time frame during the course of the game. This enables better classification of dynamic NPCs that change over the course of the game and react to the player's actions. This feature also allows specifying details such as the current location of the NPCs and the scope of information the NPC possesses. Game state serves both a narrative and ludic purpose; for example, a shopkeeper may offer more goods depending on the player's actions, and the NPC's location also aids in framing their actions and dialogue, as a vendor may only offer certain goods in specific towns.

Objective. The NPC Objective is the purpose of the NPC apart from the player. According to Dennett Daniel (1981), *personhood* consists of six different themes: Rationality, Intentionality, Stance, Reciprocity, Communication, and Consciousness. Providing an NPC with a *role* satisfies intentionality, as each action should be motivated by what the NPC was designed to achieve. However, giving them goals and aspirations allows the NPC to have a *stance* and perhaps even *consciousness* (Kalbiyev, 2022). If a blacksmith's objective is to raise enough money for their family, they should act and speak accordingly. Their actions and dialogue should not solely reflect their personality but also their objective. This feature allows the schema to capture complex and dynamic NPCs with intricate values and goals not fully represented by their *role* or *personality*. The addition of this feature enables the NPC to have a greater purpose than merely serving as an outlet for exposition or facilitating a game function.

With these features, we propose that each unique NPC can be encapsulated and represented wholly, as shown in figure 2. Each one of these features is independent of one another, allowing for modularity when designing NPCs. However, clashing combinations may still exist regardless of the modular nature of this schema.

World	A fantasy world of Dragons and magic; Skyrim
Role	Questgiver
Personality	Nord, Jarl of Whiterun, Loyal, Noble, Blonde, reasonable
State	Sitting on throne in dragonsreach. Contemplating the war and recent reports of dragons
Goal	The safety and prosperity of the people of whiterun and a solution to the looming dragon threat.

Figure 2: Completed features for "Balgruuf the Greater".

3.2 Module 2: Prompt Creation

Prompt creation was designed with the feature representation schema in mind. Providing the LM with sufficient information about an NPC is crucial to ensure that the generated dialogue remains consistent with the character's identity. These requirements are akin to the challenges faced by the feature representation schema. Consequently, the prompt creation module integrates the various features present in the schema and uses them as a prompt. The first line of each prompt begins with the sentence "You are an NPC in a game", followed by optional details such as a name, some details about the world that the NPC inhabits, the role of the NPC, basic personal characteristics, their current state (e.g., sitting outside thinking about their daughter), and finally their goal(s). Most of these categories are optional, except for the NPC type (i.e., their *role*), which must always be present. By incorporating these features, the prompt creation module empowers users to guide the LM in generating diverse NPCs with individualized personalities, allowing for greater customization without the need for prior fine-tuning or training.

NPC Header. Utilizing this prompt creation method, we created the NPC header, a representative example is depicted in figure 3. This header plays a pivotal role in dialogue generation by providing essential information about the character. For our needs, we also created a player header using the same information used in the NPC header, guiding the LM to mimic a player's behavior and facilitate automated dialogue generation. The generated player dialogue is less creative and more prone to repetition compared to human-written dia-

You are an NPC in a game
Your name is [name]*

*= Exists only if name provided

World: A bustling town full of fresh adventurers and traders. A world with magic and species such as elves, kobolds, and dragons.

Role: Vendor

Personality: Retired adventurer, General store owner, helpful, trustworthy, respected, energetic

State: behind the counter in the general store

Objective: To aid the new generation of adventurers and to live a quiet life

Figure 3: Example of an NPC header.

logue. This issue is beyond the scope of this paper, as our focus lies on NPC dialogue generation.

3.3 Module 3: Dialogue Generation

Dialogue generation was executed automatically and iteratively. The prompt was structured as a combination of the header and the current dialogue history. The header section is continually swapped depending on which agent's dialogue—NPC or player—is currently being generated. By placing the header at the top of the prompt and swapping it for the active agent, PLMs can generate dialogue that is coherent with the current speaker and their traits.

First Sentences. In early development-stage results, GPT-3 demonstrated difficulty in generating effective first sentences. Combined with the inherent challenge of generating human-like responses, this led to a significant drop in the overall quality of dialogue—often resulting in both NPC and player generating blank lines or constantly repeating the same responses. A workaround was developed by employing a small set of hand-written first sentences based on the genre and NPC type. This workaround allowed the conversation to avoid immediate repetition while minimizing interference with dialogue generation.

Repetition. In our preliminary testing, we found that PLMs struggle to avoid repetition when the player dialogue is similar to a past query or sentence. This often caused the NPC's response to be similar or even identical to its previous response. To circumvent this issue, we implemented a dynamic frequency penalty. The dynamic frequency penalty incrementally increases when the NPC or player generates a response that already exists in the conversation. After detecting a repetition and incrementing the frequency penalty, the LM attempts to regenerate with the same prompt, excluding the repeated sentence. This process occurs up to three times or until a new sentence is generated before resetting the frequency penalty to the original value before any increments. This technique significantly reduced overall repetitions and drastically decreased the occurrence of loops appearing early in the conversation.

4 Evaluation

To assess the performance of the NPC construction pipeline and the resulting generated dialogue, we designed a comprehensive evaluation metric that examines dialogue quality based on coherency, believability, degree of repetition, alignment of the NPC's dialogue with their role, and fittingness of the NPC's dialogue within their world. These categories draw from and adapt Kalbiyev (2022)'s metric for evaluating video game dialogue. Each metric is assigned a score between one and five, with the sum of these scores indicating the overall quality of the dialogue.

Self-diagnosis harnesses the capacity of Transformer-based language models to detect patterns within text and their few-shot learning performance to enable rapid, automated evaluation of dialogue without prior fine-tuning. We conducted a human evaluation of 66 different NPC scripts to assess the accuracy and reliability of our self-diagnosis approach. After each conversation was evaluated and scored, we found a correlation between parameters and their average score. By including our full NPC header, we were able to generate dialogue of higher quality. We then conducted a single-blind test where human judges were asked to determine whether an NPC script was generated by AI or written manually by a human.

4.1 Self-Diagnosis

We investigated the ability of pretrained language models, such as GPT-3, to understand, evaluate, and diagnose dialogue when given a specific nontrivial query (e.g., "whether an NPC behaved coherently"). Schick et al. (2021) demonstrate that PLMs can identify socially undesirable attributes in text, such as racism and violence. We propose that this self-diagnosis capability is not only applicable to socially undesirable attributes but also enables PLMs to self-diagnose a broader and more general set of attributes, themes, and behaviors without further fine-tuning. For simple questions, such as if a genre was clearly distinguishable in text, PLMs perform accurately in a zero-shot environment without examples and further guidance. This behavior is supported by Sanh et al. (2022). However, this performance does not hold when dealing with more complicated and potentially subjective questions.

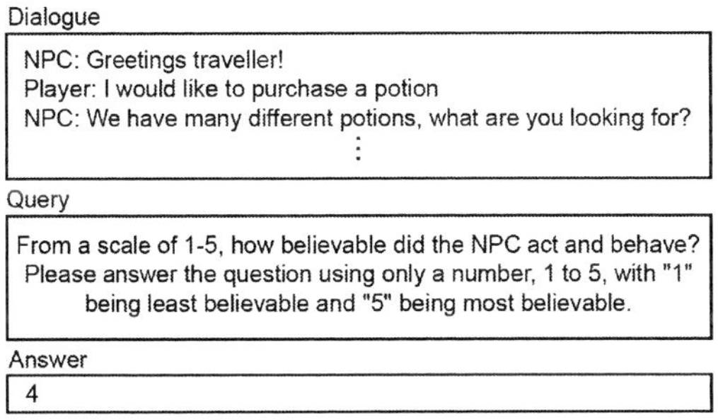

Figure 4: Prompt structure of self-diagnosis.

Our self-diagnosis approach consists of providing examples of different scoring dialogue for each metric that needed further clarification. By scoring dialogue", we mean, for example, giving the LM a prompt like "What a perfect score looks like" or "What a 3 should look like". In preliminary tests, we found that simply inputting a script and posing a question led to relatively reliable results; however, the output occasionally did not align with human responses or logic. By formulating the question more precisely and asking for a numeric response rather than a free-form sentence response, we were able to obtain a numeric answer more accurately. To account for potential variability in the responses, we set the temperature to 0 for each test, yielding a deterministic model devoid of stochastic behavior. We leveraged the PLM's few-shot learning abilities by adding three examples of different scoring sample dialogue before the prompt. This approach aligns scores obtained through self-diagnosis more closely with human scores on queries that a PLM would otherwise have difficulties with.

4.2 The Turing Quest

To evaluate the performance of our NPC Construction pipeline and the degree to which the resulting generated dialogue appears human-written, we propose a test tailored to NPC dialogue—the *Turing Quest*. Inspired by the Turing test (Turing, 1950), the goal of this test is to determine whether a generated NPC script can be distinguished from human-written dialogue by human judges. A script passes the Turing Quest if the judge deems it human-written, and fails if perceived as AI-generated. Conducting this test on multiple NPC script samples helps assess the proficiency of state-of-the-art PLMs in generating convincing NPC dialogue.

The Turing Quest is a self-administered questionnaire. For each script, it asks the judge to determine if the NPC's dialogue is written by a human or an AI. Since the scope of this test is to determine the believability of an NPC's dialogue, the player's dialogue can be manually written by a human.

For our test, six NPC scripts were evaluated by 12 individual judges. Four of the six scripts were generated by GPT-3, one was manually written, and the final script was sampled from the game *Skyrim*. Our test group comprised twelve people familiar with video games and NPCs. From the responses of our judges, we determined the average passing rate was 64.58% for all AI-generated scripts. The best performing generated script had a pass rate of 75%. Interestingly, 75% of judges believed that the dialogue sampled from Skyrim was AI-generated and 50% thought the same for the manually written script. This could highlight the expectations of players regarding the current state and abilities of LMs and conversational agents. These findings provide strong empirical evidence that our pipeline, when applied to PLMs, is capable of producing NPC scripts that resemble and perhaps even surpass human-written NPC dialogue.

5 Experiments and Results

5.1 Parameter Search and Model Selection

We conducted a comprehensive random grid parameter search to identify the optimal model and parameters for generating high-quality NPC dialogue. Three key parameters influenced the quality and score of the generated dialogue: the language model, temperature setting, and the integration of our NPC construction pipeline prompt.

Utilizing different versions of GPT-3 (OpenAI's text-davinci-002, text-curie-001, and text-babbage-001 models) and a range of temperatures (0 to 1, incremented by 0.1), we compared the quality of dialogue generated with our full prompt and a minimal version without the world description, NPC Personality, game state, and NPC objective sections. We repeated the experiment with another NPC role to ensure generalizability[1].

[1]The code to reproduce all of our experimental results are available at https://github.com/FieryAced/-NPC-Dialogue-Generation.

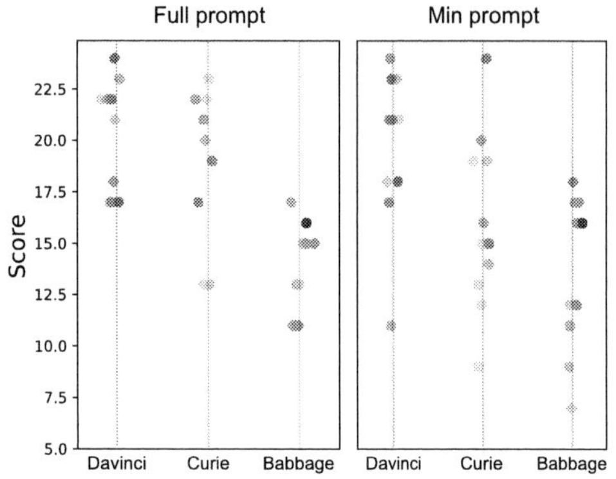

Figure 5: Evaluation Scores of varying models and temperatures.

Our analysis revealed a significant decline in quality from the text-davinci-002 to text-curie-001 models, and an even more pronounced decrease between text-curie-001 and text-babbage-001. This is consistent with recent research which has shown that larger and more complex models, such as GPT-3's text-davinci-002 model, have the ability to learn and generalize more complex patterns from larger and more diverse datasets, resulting in better performance across a wide range of natural language processing tasks (Brown et al., 2020).

Furthermore, the recently proposed InstructGPT framework by Ouyang et al. (2022) allows for targeted fine-tuning of pre-trained language models to better suit the task at hand. This approach involves providing additional instructions during fine-tuning, such as providing task-specific prompts or data augmentation techniques, which results in improved performance for downstream tasks. With the success of InstructGPT, it is becoming increasingly clear that language models can be further optimized for specific use-cases by adjusting their architecture or fine-tuning process. Thus, it is reasonable to assume that newer and more advanced models, such as text-davinci-003, should generally perform better than their predecessors. Finally, our analysis shows that full-prompt models outperformed minimal prompt ones, with an average 4.06 point higher score, demonstrating the effectiveness of our prompting method.

A Pearson correlation test (excluding the atypical data point with a temperature of 0) showed a positive correlation between temperature and score, $r(8) = .7055, p = .022646$. Higher temperature values yielded better results, with the highest average scores at temperatures of 0.9 and 0.8.

Based on these findings, we recommend using advanced Transformer-based LMs like OpenAI's GPT-3 "text-davinci-002" at a temperature around 0.9, along with our NPC construction pipeline, for optimal NPC script generation.

5.2 Results

Self-Diagnosis: To assess the reliability of the self-diagnosis module, we manually evaluated 66 NPC scripts using the same metrics applied in self-diagnosis. A Pearson correlation test showed a strong positive correlation between self-diagnosed and human-evaluated scores, $r(64) = .8092, p < .00001$. This demonstrates the module's consistency and correlation with human evaluation scores.

Turing Quest Results: Our NPC construction pipeline, when using the recommended parameters, generates dialogue that not only passes as human-written but also scores highly on the evaluation metric. On average, our generated dialogue was thought to be hand-written 64.58% of the time with the best performing script passing as human written 75% of the time. The generated NPC scripts exhibit goal-oriented behavior and adherence to the in-game world and genre, maintaining player immersion. The Turing Quest results further confirm the high quality of the generated dialogue.

6 Conclusion

We developed a novel pipeline capable of automatically generating NPC scripts comparable or of superior quality to human-written NPC dialogue using Transformer-based PLMs. We then created a self-diagnosis module which provides a method to evaluate and compare the quality of NPC dialogue quantitatively. Finally, our proposal of the Turing Quest allows us to determine the capabilities of a language model when applied to the task of NPC dialogue generation and whether a script passes as human-written. While the NPC construction pipeline allows for modularity even in between responses, that aspect was not explored in depth in this paper. We will explore dialogue generation for dynamic NPCs with evolving roles or attributes in future research.

Limitations

The dialogue generated for the player exhibits a higher degree of repetition and has a tendency towards looping. This limitation exists as we did not focus on generating player dialogue as that is a different problem of its own. To account for this limitation, both the self-diagnosis and the Turing Quest only evaluate the NPC's dialogue.

Currently, the maximum context window for the dialogue history portion is limited by the max tokens of a given model minus the tokens required for the NPC header. Despite being a rare occurrence, it is possible that the dialogue history becomes so long that the model may not be able to generate any responses as there is no more remaining space. We did not experience this problem; however, a workaround would be to discard the oldest dialogue history entry as needed. This approach however may cause the NPC to lose out on information that it would otherwise be able to leverage in dialogue.

Ethics Statement

The presence of bias within NPC models/systems poses a significant risk particularly as the demographic of young individuals, still in the age of development, who enjoy playing video games continues to expand. In 2006, 92% of children in the ages of 2-17 had played video games (Doğan, 2006). 97% of players under the age of of 18 play more that an hour of games daily (Granic et al., 2014). According to recent statistics, the global demographic of active video game players is projected to increase over 5% year-over-year (Doğan, 2006), reaching over 3 billion active players worldwide in 2023[2]. This means, in the future, video games will reach more young children and adolescents. If the presence of bias is not addressed, it could subconsciously normalize problematic behaviours seen in games in children as humans are a product of both nature and nurture (Plomin and Asbury, 2005). This in turn may lead to more biases being overlooked or ignored by the next generation of researchers, creating a vicious cycle.

Acknowledgements

This work was supported by the Natural Sciences and Engineering Research Council of Canada and by the New Frontiers in Research Fund.

[2]https://www.statista.com/statistics/748044/number-video-gamers-world

References

Alaa A Abd-Alrazaq, Mohannad Alajlani, Ali Abdallah Alalwan, Bridgette M Bewick, Peter Gardner, and Mowafa Househ. 2019. An overview of the features of chatbots in mental health: A scoping review. *International Journal of Medical Informatics*, 132:103978.

Bethesda Game Studios. 2011. The elder scrolls v: Skyrim.

Bethesda Game Studios. 2015. Fallout 4.

Tom Brown, Benjamin Mann, Nick Ryder, Melanie Subbiah, Jared D Kaplan, Prafulla Dhariwal, Arvind Neelakantan, Pranav Shyam, Girish Sastry, Amanda Askell, Sandhini Agarwal, Ariel Herbert-Voss, Gretchen Krueger, Tom Henighan, Rewon Child, Aditya Ramesh, Daniel Ziegler, Jeffrey Wu, Clemens Winter, Chris Hesse, Mark Chen, Eric Sigler, Mateusz Litwin, Scott Gray, Benjamin Chess, Jack Clark, Christopher Berner, Sam McCandlish, Alec Radford, Ilya Sutskever, and Dario Amodei. 2020. Language models are few-shot learners. In *Advances in Neural Information Processing Systems*, volume 33, pages 1877–1901. Curran Associates, Inc.

Hayco de Haan, Joop Snijder, Christof van Nimwegen, and Robbert Jan Beun. 2018. Chatbot personality and customer satisfaction. *Info Support Research*.

C Dennett Daniel. 1981. Conditions of personhood. *The Identities of Persons*, 175.

John M Digman. 1990. Personality structure: Emergence of the five-factor model. *Annual review of psychology*, 41(1):417–440.

Filiz Öztütüncü Doğan. 2006. Video games and children: violence in video games. In *New/Yeni Symposium Journal*, volume 44, pages 161–164.

Margherita Gambini, Tiziano Fagni, Fabrizio Falchi, and Maurizio Tesconi. 2022. On pushing deepfake tweet detection capabilities to the limits. In *14th ACM Web Science Conference 2022*, WebSci '22, page 154–163, New York, NY, USA. Association for Computing Machinery.

Isabela Granic, Adam Lobel, and Rutger CME Engels. 2014. The benefits of playing video games. *American psychologist*, 69(1):66.

Carl Håkansson and Johan Fröberg. 2021. Application of machine learning to construct advanced npc behaviors in unity 3d.

Robin Hunicke, Marc Leblanc, and Robert Zubek. 2004. Mda: A formal approach to game design and game research. *AAAI Workshop - Technical Report*, 1.

A Kalbiyev. 2022. Affective dialogue generation for video games. Master's thesis, University of Twente.

Christopher Kerr and Duane Szafron. 2009. Supporting dialogue generation for story-based games. In *Proceedings of the AAAI Conference on Artificial Intelligence and Interactive Digital Entertainment*, volume 5, pages 154–160.

Michael Sangyeob Lee and Carrie Heeter. 2015. Cognitive intervention and reconciliation: Npc believability in single-player rpgs. *International Journal of Role-Playing*, 5:47–65.

Hector Levesque, Ernest Davis, and Leora Morgenstern. 2011. The winograd schema challenge. In *AAAI Spring Symposium: Logical Formalizations of Commonsense Reasoning*.

Jiwei Li, Will Monroe, Alan Ritter, Michel Galley, Jianfeng Gao, and Dan Jurafsky. 2016. Deep reinforcement learning for dialogue generation. *arXiv preprint arXiv:1606.01541*.

Piji Li. 2020. An empirical investigation of pre-trained transformer language models for open-domain dialogue generation. *CoRR*, abs/2003.04195.

Jianfeng Liu, Feiyang Pan, and Ling Luo. 2020. Gochat: Goal-oriented chatbots with hierarchical reinforcement learning. In *Proceedings of the 43rd International ACM SIGIR Conference on Research and Development in Information Retrieval*, SIGIR '20, page 1793–1796, New York, NY, USA. Association for Computing Machinery.

Muneer M Alshater. 2022. Exploring the role of artificial intelligence in enhancing academic performance: A case study of chatgpt. *Available at SSRN*.

Madison Milne-Ives, Caroline de Cock, Ernest Lim, Melissa Harper Shehadeh, Nick de Pennington, Guy Mole, Eduardo Normando, and Edward Meinert. 2020. The effectiveness of artificial intelligence conversational agents in health care: Systematic review. *J Med Internet Res*, 22(10):e20346.

György Molnár and Zoltán Szüts. 2018. The role of chatbots in formal education. In *2018 IEEE 16th International Symposium on Intelligent Systems and Informatics (SISY)*, pages 000197–000202. IEEE.

Alexander Nareyek. 2004. Ai in computer games: Smarter games are making for a better user experience. what does the future hold? *Queue*, 1(10):58–65.

Long Ouyang, Jeffrey Wu, Xu Jiang, Diogo Almeida, Carroll Wainwright, Pamela Mishkin, Chong Zhang, Sandhini Agarwal, Katarina Slama, Alex Ray, et al. 2022. Training language models to follow instructions with human feedback. *Advances in Neural Information Processing Systems*, 35:27730–27744.

Dijana Peras. 2018. Chatbot evaluation metrics. *Economic and Social Development: Book of Proceedings*, pages 89–97.

Robert Plomin and Kathryn Asbury. 2005. Nature and nurture: Genetic and environmental influences on behavior. *The Annals of the American Academy of Political and Social Science*, 600(1):86–98.

Qiao Qian, Minlie Huang, Haizhou Zhao, Jingfang Xu, and Xiaoyan Zhu. 2017. Assigning personality/identity to a chatting machine for coherent conversation generation. *CoRR*, abs/1706.02861.

Maya Raifer, Guy Rotman, Reut Apel, Moshe Tennenholtz, and Roi Reichart. 2022. Designing an automatic agent for repeated language–based persuasion games. *Transactions of the Association for Computational Linguistics*, 10:307–324.

James Ryan, Michael Mateas, and Noah Wardrip-Fruin. 2016. Characters who speak their minds: Dialogue generation in talk of the town. In *Twelfth Artificial Intelligence and Interactive Digital Entertainment Conference*.

Samuel Taylor Coleridge. 1971. *Biographia Literaria, 1817*.

Victor Sanh, Albert Webson, Colin Raffel, Stephen H. Bach, Lintang Sutawika, Zaid Alyafeai, Antoine Chaffin, Arnaud Stiegler, Teven Le Scao, Arun Raja, Manan Dey, M Saiful Bari, Canwen Xu, Urmish Thakker, Shanya Sharma Sharma, Eliza Szczechla, Taewoon Kim, Gunjan Chhablani, Nihal Nayak, Debajyoti Datta, Jonathan Chang, Mike Tian-Jian Jiang, Han Wang, Matteo Manica, Sheng Shen, Zheng Xin Yong, Harshit Pandey, Rachel Bawden, Thomas Wang, Trishala Neeraj, Jos Rozen, Abheesht Sharma, Andrea Santilli, Thibault Fevry, Jason Alan Fries, Ryan Teehan, Tali Bers, Stella Biderman, Leo Gao, Thomas Wolf, and Alexander M. Rush. 2022. Multitask prompted training enables zero-shot task generalization.

Timo Schick, Sahana Udupa, and Hinrich Schütze. 2021. Self-Diagnosis and Self-Debiasing: A Proposal for Reducing Corpus-Based Bias in NLP. *Transactions of the Association for Computational Linguistics*, 9:1408–1424.

Björn Schlünder and Ralf Klabunde. 2013. Greetings generation in video role playing games. In *Proceedings of the 14th European Workshop on Natural Language Generation*, pages 167–171, Sofia, Bulgaria. Association for Computational Linguistics.

J Schulman, B Zoph, C Kim, J Hilton, J Menick, J Weng, JFC Uribe, L Fedus, L Metz, M Pokorny, et al. 2022. Chatgpt: Optimizing language models for dialogue.

Tuva Lunde Smestad and Frode Volden. 2019. Chatbot personalities matters. In *International conference on internet science*, pages 170–181. Springer.

M. Onat Topal, Anil Bas, and Imke van Heerden. 2021. Exploring transformers in natural language generation: Gpt, bert, and xlnet. *CoRR*, abs/2102.08036.

A. M. Turing. 1950. I.—COMPUTING MACHINERY AND INTELLIGENCE. *Mind*, LIX(236):433–460.

Henrik Warpefelt. 2016. *The Non-Player Character: Exploring the believability of NPC presentation and behavior*. Ph.D. thesis, Stockholm University.

Terry Winograd. 1972. Understanding natural language. *Cognitive Psychology*, 3(1):1–191.

Anbang Xu, Zhe Liu, Yufan Guo, Vibha Sinha, and Rama Akkiraju. 2017. A new chatbot for customer service on social media. In *Proceedings of the 2017 CHI conference on human factors in computing systems*, pages 3506–3510.

Qinyuan Ye, Bill Yuchen Lin, and Xiang Ren. 2021. Crossfit: A few-shot learning challenge for cross-task generalization in nlp.

Yicheng Zou, Lujun Zhao, Yangyang Kang, Jun Lin, Minlong Peng, Zhuoren Jiang, Changlong Sun, Qi Zhang, Xuanjing Huang, and Xiaozhong Liu. 2021. Topic-oriented spoken dialogue summarization for customer service with saliency-aware topic modeling. In *Proceedings of the AAAI Conference on Artificial Intelligence*, volume 35, pages 14665–14673.

Making the Most Out of the Limited Context Length: Predictive Power Varies with Clinical Note Type and Note Section

Hongyi Zheng[1] **Yixin Tracy Zhu**[1] **Lavender Yao Jiang**[1, 2]
Kyunghyun Cho[1] **Eric Karl Oermann**[1, 2]
NYU Center for Data Science[1] NYU Langone Health[2]
{hz2212, yz5880, lyj2002, kyunghyun.cho}@nyu.edu, eric.oermann@nyulangone.org

Abstract

Recent advances in large language models have led to renewed interest in natural language processing in healthcare using the free text of clinical notes. One distinguishing characteristic of clinical notes is their long time span over multiple long documents. The unique structure of clinical notes creates a new design choice: when the context length for a language model predictor is limited, which part of clinical notes should we choose as the input? Existing studies either choose the inputs with domain knowledge or simply truncate them. We propose a framework to analyze the sections with high predictive power. Using MIMIC-III, we show that: 1) predictive power distribution is different between nursing notes and discharge notes and 2) combining different types of notes could improve performance when the context length is large. Our findings suggest that a carefully selected sampling function could enable more efficient information extraction from clinical notes.

1 Introduction

Electronic Health Records (EHR) enable the development of language model based clinical predictor, which takes in clinical notes to predict patient outcomes. Clinical notes in EHR exhibit two unique characteristics. 1) Clinical notes cover a long time span (from a few weeks to over a year), which results in their sparsity of information-rich sections. 2) Clinical notes also tend to be long: many discharge notes could take up to $10,000$ tokens, which makes using the entire note as model input computationally expensive. 3) The strong noise level in the medical notes (usually due to the domain-specific abbreviations and typos) also poses a challenge to extract information effectively.

These distinguishing characteristics of clinical notes lead to a new design choice: when the context length is limited due to the constrained compute or model architecture, what parts of clinical notes should we sample to maximize the model's performance? We propose a framework to subsample text sections with high predictive power.

Empirically, we explore the distribution of predictive power over clinical note types and sections by searching over these variables. We found that 1) the predictive power distribution is different between nursing notes and discharge notes: the predictive power is stronger at the beginning and end of discharge notes, while uniform within nursing notes. 2) The effect of combining sections from different types of notes improves the performance when the context size is large, but harms the performance when the context size is small. More details of task formulation can be found at section 3. Our code is publicly available on GitHub[1].

2 Related Work

Existing methods for subsampling clinical notes for the BERT-based model are mostly based on domain knowledge. For instance, Yang et al. (2022) and Darabi et al. (2020) choose discharge notes as they summarize patients' visits. Thapa et al. (2022) chooses the notes within three days before a cutoff time in consideration of timeliness. While these assumptions are based on domain knowledge, they require human input and may not generalize. Thus, we are interested in exploring a data-driven sampling choice without assumptions of expert inputs.

Another related, but orthogonal approach to the limited context length problem is note aggregation. Instead of subsampling notes, Huang et al. (2019) propose to feed everything to the model, one maximum context length at a time, and aggregate the outputs for the final prediction. In their work, notes of one patient are split into a partition of subsequences, and the patient's re-admission risk is obtained by taking a weighted average of probabilities computed from each subsequence. This method's

[1] https://github.com/nyuolab/EfficientTransformer

Proceedings of the 61st Annual Meeting of the Association for Computational Linguistics - Student Research Workshop, pages 104–108

compute cost scales with the aggregated sequence length, which can be expensive for records with long clinical notes. In contrast, our method aims to find one single information-rich segment as input.

3 Method

We formalize our prediction task as follows: given a set of clinical notes x associated with an admission record, we want to predict the class label y which is our patient outcome of interest. Ideally, we want to train a classifier f_{w^*} to approximate $p(y \mid x)$. The optimal parameter is

$$w^* = \arg\max_w m(f_w(x), y),$$

where m is a metric function of interest. Nevertheless, due to the computational constraint, we need to reduce the input size via a sampling function s_θ so that $s_\theta(x)$ fits the input length limit and preserves information. Empirically, the optimal parameters are

$$w^*, \theta^* = \arg\max_{w,\theta} m(f_w(s_\theta(x), y)).$$

We say a sample function s_θ has a higher predictive power if $m(f_{w^*}(s_\theta(x), y))$ is larger.

While current works chose s_θ based on prior medical knowledge or simply fix it as a truncation function, we propose to explore different sampling functions s_θ to make the most out of the limited context length with the highest predictive power. Notice that in our work, s and θ are searched manually, instead of using learning algorithms.

4 Experimental Setup

We hypothesize that for 30-day all-cause readmission prediction, there exists an alternative sampling function that enables similar or better performance than the commonly used "truncated discharge notes". More formally, we focus on a parameterized sampling function with 2 variables: 1) which section of tokens to include, 2) what type(s) of clinical notes to use.

Model We finetuned two clinical language models in our experiments. The first is Clinical-BERT (Alsentzer et al., 2019), which continued to pretrain BERT using approximately 2 million notes from MIMIC-III and has a maximum sequence length of 512. The second is the ClinicalLongformer (Li et al., 2022), which continued to pretrain Longformer (Beltagy et al., 2020) with MIMIC-III notes and enables input of up to 4096 tokens. Both models are finetuned to predict the probability of 30-day all-cause readmission: that is, whether the patient will be re-admitted to the hospital within 30 days of their discharge dates.

Dataset We use the discharge notes and nursing notes in the `noteevent` table of the MIMIC-III database (Johnson et al., 2016). There are $40,000$ de-identified admission records available to use after filtering out all admission records without nursing notes and discharge notes. The admission records are split into 75% train, 12.5% validation, and 12.5% test sets. Other types of medical notes such as physician notes are excluded from consideration in our experiments due to their scarcity in the database. See Appendix A for data preprocessing.

Sliding Window To extract different sections of the clinical notes, we use a sliding window technique. Let n be the window's width. Let l be the total number of tokens of the text. The window is placed based on an input parameter $p \in [0, 1]$ indicating the location of the midpoint of the window, where the window interval is

$$[lp - n/2, lp + n/2].$$

In case where $lp - n/2 < 0$, we shifted the window backward so that the front of the window aligns with the beginning of the input tokens. In the case where $lp + n/2 > l$ we shifted the window forward to let the back of the window match the end of the tokens. Also, when $l < n$, we ignore the input p and pad the tokens to maximum input length n.

We try 11 different values of p $(0.0, 0.1, \cdots 1.0)$ for ClinicalBERT and 2 values of p (0.0 and 1.0) for ClincialLongformer along with an additional fragmented window trial $p =$ both which looks into the first $n/2$ and last $n/2$ tokens of the input text. Similarly, when $l < n$, we simply pad the sequence to the window's length.

Mixing Notes To control different types of clinical notes, we experimented with the following options: 1) first nursing note, 2) last nursing note, 3) discharge note, 4) first nursing notes + discharge note, 5) last nursing notes + discharge notes. For options with two types of notes, $n/2$ tokens are allocated to each type, and three values for p_1 and p_2 each $(0.0, 1.0$ and both$)$ are used to select $n/2$ tokens from each type of note, resulting in 9 possible input parameter combinations.

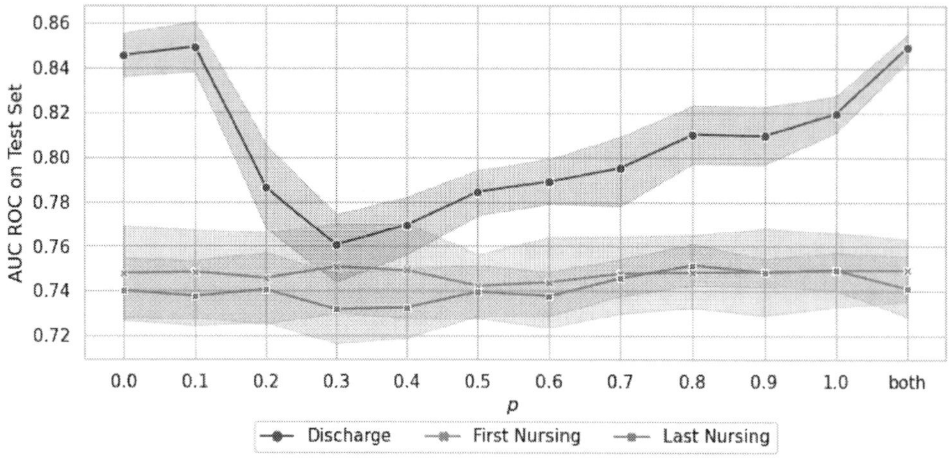

Figure 1: Performance of ClinicalBERT on Different Text Sections and Different Types of Notes, Error Bars Represent 95% Confidence Intervals

5 Results

5.1 Different Sections in Nursing Notes and Discharge Notes

We finetune ClinicalBERT and ClinicalLongformer on different sections of nursing and discharge notes. We used sliding windows to extract a sequence of tokens that meets the model's maximum sequence length. We have three key observations.

Different Types of Clinical Notes Show Disparate Predictive Power Distributions Over Text Sections. As shown in Figure 1, the discharge notes (blue line) show quite uneven predictive power distribution, where the beginning ($p = 0.0$) and end ($p = 1.0$) sections of the text provide strong predictive power while the middle sector ($0.2 \leq p \leq 0.5$) shows a significant dip in predictive power. In contrast, the predictive power of the nursing notes (orange and green line) turns out to be uniformly distributed: using different sections of the nursing notes ($0.0 \leq p \leq 1.0$) does not make a significant difference. We speculate that this discrepancy may stem from the domain knowledge that discharge notes are more structured than nursing notes: they often start with basic descriptions of the patient information and ends with suggestions for the patients, whereas nursing notes often have multiple types of information mixed together throughout the text.

Nursing Notes Provide Modest Predictive Power. Nursing notes produce decent re-admission prediction results: according to Figure 1 and Figure 2, although their predictive power is not as strong as discharge notes (which are typically written right before patients leave the hospital), they consistently achieve AUC ROC scores of over 0.7 which indicates modest predictability (Schneeweiss et al., 2001). Moreover, the first nursing notes (orange line in Figure 1, second group of bars in Figure 2) of each admission provide similar predictive power as compared to the last nursing notes (green line in Figure 1, third group of bars in Figure 2), indicating the possibility of re-admission risk evaluation at the early stage of the admission. This finding is especially valuable from the perspective of intervention, as it is more practical to decide whether the patient should be discharged at the time before the discharge note is written. Also, the abundance of nursing notes makes them a suitable alternative for re-admission risk evaluation tasks when discharge notes are unavailable.

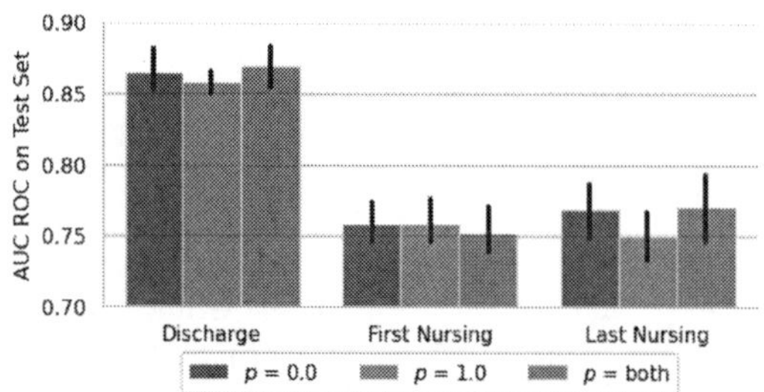

Figure 2: Performance of ClinicalLongformer on Different Text Sections and Different Types of Notes, Error Bars Represent 95% Confidence Intervals

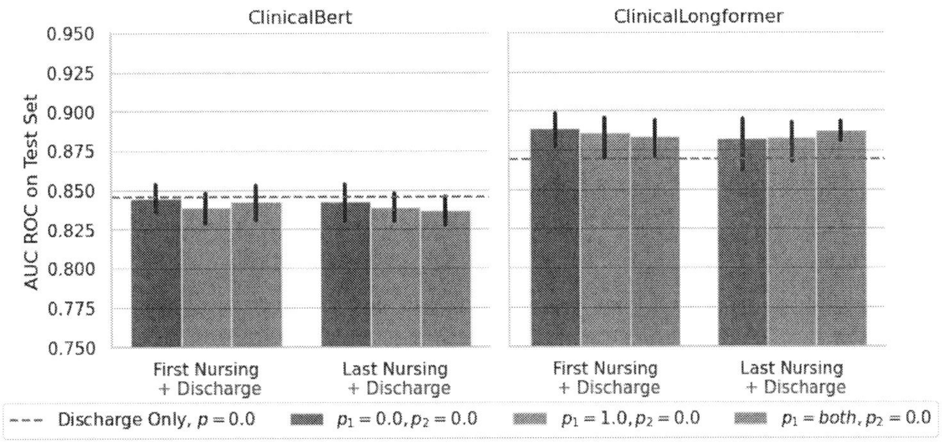

Figure 3: Performance of ClinicalBERT and ClinicalLongformer on Clinical Note Combinations, Error Bars Represent 95% Confidence Intervals

Preserving the Beginning Tokens Is Not the Only Option. It is generally assumed that when the available input tokens are limited, the leading tokens of each clinical note should be used. Nevertheless, our experiments show that for discharge notes, spending half of the available tokens on the beginning section and spending the remaining half on the end section ($p = \mathrm{both}$) achieves slightly better performance (AUC ROC of 0.849 versus 0.845 for ClinicalBERT, 0.869 versus 0.864 for ClinicalLongformer) as compared to using the leading token only ($p = 0.0$). We speculate that this helps as it avoids the weakly predictive middle sector of the clinical notes.

5.2 Combining Sections from Different Types

We combine text sections from two different types of clinical notes and finetune ClinicalBERT and ClinicalLongformer. This experiment helps us investigate the question: when the amount of available tokens is fixed, does combining information from different clinical notes work better than using discharge notes only? Since discharge notes are shown to provide strong predictive power in our prior experiments, we only investigate the note type combinations that include discharge notes (first nursing + discharge, last nursing + discharge).

The Effect of Allocating Tokens to Different Types of Clinical Notes Depends on the Context Size. When the context size is relatively large (ClinicalLongformer, as shown in the right side of figure 3), allocating the available tokens to different types of clinical notes (blue, orange, and green bars) leads to improvements in performance. The baseline (dashed red line) uses discharge notes only and has a lower AUC ROC (0.013 to 0.019) than models finetuned with combined notes. However, when the context is small (Clinical BERT, as shown in the left side of figure 3), distributing the already limited number of tokens to different clinical notes hurts the performance: the AUC ROC of ClinicalBERT finetuned with mixed notes falls below the baseline performance by -0.009 to -0.001. We speculate that this may be related to the uneven predictive power distribution in discharge notes: if there are already a sufficient number of tokens covering the most informative sections of the discharge notes, the rest of the discharge notes might not be as informative as the prior nursing notes.

6 Discussion and Future Works

Our findings suggest that when the input size is constrained, a carefully selected sampling function that chooses the text with high predictive power could benefit model performance. Specifically on the task of readmission prediction from MIMIC-III notes, we show that the predictive power varies across note types and note sections. This insight enables more efficient information extraction from long and noisy clinical notes, which is beneficial when the computing resource is limited and the context length needs to be controlled.

Our findings call for two future directions. First, the performance disparities between ClinicalBERT and ClinicalLongformer (subsection 5.2) indicate that the best strategy to allocate the input context is related to the maximum sequence length, and more work should be done to determine their exact relationship. Another direction is investigating the predictive power pattern based on the authorship of the clinical note. We showed (subsection 5.1) that discharge notes (written by doctors) have a more uneven predictive power pattern as compared to nursing notes (written by nurses). How the domain knowledge of the author would affect the clinical note quality is worth investigating.

Limitations

We acknowledge three limitations in our experiments. First, in our second experiment, we fixed the window size for each type of note to be $n/2$. A more comprehensive investigation could also search for the optimal window size for each note type. Second, although we explored one fragmented window configuration $p = \text{both}$, we did not explore other fragmented window configurations due to resource constraints. Lastly, we did not investigate more types of clinical notes (e.g., physician notes and ECG notes) because MIMIC-III has limited examples for other note types. We expect it to be resolved in future works with MIMIC-IV's publication (Johnson et al., 2023).

References

Emily Alsentzer, John R. Murphy, Willie Boag, Wei-Hung Weng, Di Jin, Tristan Naumann, and Matthew B. A. McDermott. 2019. Publicly available clinical bert embeddings.

Iz Beltagy, Matthew E. Peters, and Arman Cohan. 2020. Longformer: The long-document transformer. *CoRR*, abs/2004.05150.

Sajad Darabi, Mohammad Kachuee, Shayan Fazeli, and Majid Sarrafzadeh. 2020. Taper: Time-aware patient ehr representation. *IEEE Journal of Biomedical and Health Informatics*, 24(11):3268–3275.

Kexin Huang, Jaan Altosaar, and Rajesh Ranganath. 2019. Clinicalbert: Modeling clinical notes and predicting hospital readmission. *arXiv preprint arXiv:1904.05342*.

Alistair Johnson, Lucas Bulgarelli, Lu Shen, Alvin Gayles, Ayad Shammout, Steven Horng, Tom Pollard, Sicheng Hao, Benjamin Moody, Brian Gow, Li-wei Lehman, Leo Celi, and Roger Mark. 2023. Mimic-iv, a freely accessible electronic health record dataset. *Scientific Data*, 10:1.

Alistair E.W. Johnson, Tom J. Pollard, Lu Shen, Li wei H. Lehman, Mengling Feng, Mohammad Ghassemi, Benjamin Moody, Peter Szolovits, Leo Anthony Celi, and Roger G. Mark. 2016. Mimic-iii, a freely accessible critical care database. *Nature*.

Yikuan Li, Ramsey M. Wehbe, Faraz S. Ahmad, Hanyin Wang, and Yuan Luo. 2022. Clinical-longformer and clinical-bigbird: Transformers for long clinical sequences. *CoRR*, abs/2201.11838.

Sebastian Schneeweiss, John D Seeger, Malcolm Maclure, Philip S Wang, Jerry Avorn, and Robert J Glynn. 2001. Performance of comorbidity scores to control for confounding in epidemiologic studies using claims data. *American journal of epidemiology*, 154(9):854–864.

Nischay Bikram Thapa, Sattar Seifollahi, and Sona Taheri. 2022. Hospital readmission prediction using clinical admission notes. In *Australasian Computer Science Week 2022*, pages 193–199.

Grace Yang, Ming Cao, Lavender Y Jiang, Xujin C Liu, Alexander Cheung, Hannah Weiss, Davied Kurland, Kyunghyun Cho, and Eric K Oermann. 2022. Language model classifier aligns better with physician word sensitivity than xgboost on readmission prediction. *arXiv preprint arXiv:2211.07047*.

Appendices

A Preprocessing

We preprocessed the dataset with the following approach: First of all, admission records with missing discharge notes or missing nursing notes are eliminated. Then, for each remaining admission record, the nursing notes associated with that record are sorted according to their timestamp. The first and last created nursing notes for each admission are selected and concatenated with the discharge notes of the same admission record to produce the clinical note set for every admission. Lastly, we clean the datasets by removing the de-identification patterns ('[** de-identified info **]') in the clinical notes, which usually occupy a lot of tokens.

Intriguing Effect of the Correlation Prior on ICD-9 Code Assignment

Zihao Yang[1,2], Chenkang Zhang[1,2], Muru Wu[1,2], Xujin Chris Liu[2,3], Lavender Yao Jiang[1,2], Kyunghyun Cho[1,4,5,6], Eric Karl Oermann[2,7,8,1]

[1]Center for Data Science, New York University
[2]Department of Neurosurgery, NYU Langone Health
[3]Department of Electrical and Computer Engineering, NYU Tandon School of Engineering
[4]Courant Institute of Mathematical Sciences, New York University
[5]Canadian Institute for Advanced Research
[6]Prescient Design
[7]Department of Radiology, NYU Langone Health
[8]Neuroscience Institute, NYU Langone Health
{gavin.yang,stephen.zhang,wm1077,chris.liu,lyj2002,kyunghyun.cho}@nyu.edu,
eric.oermann@nyulangone.org

Abstract

The Ninth Revision of the International Classification of Diseases (ICD-9) is a standardized coding system used to classify health conditions. It is used for billing, tracking individual patient conditions, and for epidemiology. The highly detailed and technical nature of the codes and their associated medical conditions make it difficult for humans to accurately record them. Researchers have explored the use of neural networks, particularly language models, for automated ICD-9 code assignment. However, the imbalanced distribution of ICD-9 codes leads to poor performance. One solution is to use domain knowledge to incorporate a useful prior. This paper evaluates the usefulness of the correlation bias: we hypothesize that correlations between ICD-9 codes and other medical codes could help improve language models' performance. We showed that while the correlation bias worsens the overall performance, the effect on individual class can be negative or positive.[1] Performance on classes that are more imbalanced and less correlated with other codes is more sensitive to incorporating the correlation bias. This suggests that while the correlation bias has potential to improve ICD-9 code assignment in certain cases, the applicability criteria need to be more carefully studied.

1 Introduction

Electronic Health Records (EHRs) contain patient information in the form of clinical notes, structured data tables, and biomedical imaging and time series. For easy tracking and analysis of health data across different healthcare systems, and critically for billing purposes, hospitals and insurance companies assign codes of a standardized coding system to characterize the clinical conditions of patients. Wrong code assignments may result in billing issues that increase patients' expenses substantially, misdiagnosis, and poor tracking of population level health conditions nationally. The Ninth Revision of the International Classification of Diseases (ICD-9) is a system used worldwide to classify and code diseases, injuries, and other health conditions. There were extensive efforts studying the automated assignment of ICD-9 codes to health records and relevant documents (Yan et al., 2022).

With recent developments in NLP, there has been a focus on the use of neural networks (Yu et al., 2019; Mullenbach et al., 2018; Teng et al., 2020). One particularly recent direction is in the use of language models. Originally introduced in BERT (Devlin et al., 2019), the recipe of pretraining and finetuning of language models has shown promising performance in many tasks. Researchers have applied BERT for assigning ICD-9 codes from medical documents (Huang et al., 2022; Pascual et al., 2021; Zhang et al., 2020). However, BERT and other encoder-based language models perform poorly on ICD-9 code assignment (Yan et al., 2022).

One challenge is the extremely imbalanced distribution of ICD-9 codes. Following the distribution of medical conditions in the real world, some codes occur frequently while other codes may appear only once (Yan et al., 2022). It is difficult for models

[1]The implementation code is available on github: https://github.com/nyuolab/text2table

Proceedings of the 61st Annual Meeting of the Association for Computational Linguistics - Student Research Workshop, pages 109–118

to correctly predict minority codes because few samples exist in the dataset (Sun et al., 2009). A proposed solution is to incorporate domain knowledge that provides useful priors for the minority codes (Bai and Vucetic, 2019; Wang et al., 2020; Zeng et al., 2019).

We hypothesize that one useful prior for ICD-9 code assignment is the correlation between ICD-9 codes and other relevant coding systems. We term other relevant coding systems auxiliary tasks because language models in our experiments predict codes from these systems in addition to ICD-9 codes. The auxiliary tasks are Current Procedural Terminology (CPT) codes and Diagnosis-Related Group (DRG) codes. This correlation prior stems from the domain knowledge that labels from other coding systems give information about ICD-9 codes. For example, patients who underwent artery bypass surgeries (CPT code 33533) are likely to have heart failures (ICD-9 code 428.0). To test our hypothesis, we investigate the effect of multitasking on correlated auxiliary tasks and encouraging similar label correlations between training labels and model predictions through regularization. We showed that 1) on average, utilizing correlations hurts language models' performance on predicting ICD-9 codes from discharge summaries, 2) for each ICD-9 code, utilizing correlations might hurt or help, 3) ICD-9 codes that are more imbalanced and less correlated with auxiliary tasks experience larger performance changes (both positive and negative) from incorporating the correlation prior. Our findings suggest that the correlation prior has the potential to improve predictions of certain ICD-9 codes, but this method suffers from instability when the main task has an imbalanced label distribution and a weak correlation with auxiliary tasks.

2 Related Work

Domain knowledge One useful prior for ICD-9 codes is its hierarchical structure. For example, a high-level code (e.g., 428.0 heart failure) encompasses its corresponding low-level codes (e.g., 428.1 left heart failure, 428.2 systolic heart failure). Tsai et al. (2019) incorporated this hierarchical prior and improved models' performance on predicting imbalanced ICD-9 codes.

CorrLoss CorrLoss is a regularization technique (Rieger et al., 2022) that encourages consistent label correlations between ground truth and predictions. Rieger et al. (2022) uses CorrLoss on the facial affect recognition task to integrate the correlation priors for facial movements. Corrloss can be used in any domain where correlation between prediction targets provides a useful signal. Thus, we adopt Corrloss to integrate information of the correlations between different kinds of diagnosis and procedure codes.

3 Methods

Task overview We formulate the task of code assignment into a multilabel text classification task because each patient has multiple codes corresponding to their discharge summaries. Each binary label in the task corresponds to a specific code. Formally, our classifier aims to approximate the probability $p(y_1, \ldots, y_n|x)$, where each y_i is an ICD-9 code and x is a discharge summary.

The Correlation Prior We hypothesize that correlations between ICD-9 and other coding systems are a useful prior for ICD-9 code assignment and choose to incorporate the prior in two ways.

First, we added the auxiliary tasks of predicting other medical codes (e.g., CPT). Formally, we train a classifier to approximate

$$p(y, z|x) = p(y|x)\, p(z|x, y), \qquad (1)$$

where y is a sequence of ICD-9 codes (the main task), z is a sequence of other medical codes (the auxiliary task), and x is a discharge summary. Our domain knowledge assumes that the absolute correlation $\text{abs}(\rho(y, z)|x) > 0$, so y, z are not conditionally independent given x and $p(z|x, y) \neq p(z|x)$. This is desirable because otherwise, we are strictly increasing the difficulty of the task from learning $p(y|x)$ to learning $p(y|x)\, p(z|x)$.

There are benefits and concerns associated with Equation 1, and their trade-off is unclear *a priori*. One benefit is that extra dependency information from $p(z|x, y)$ could potentially simplify learning $p(y, z|x)$. One drawback is that the additional prediction targets z could worsen the curse of dimensionality. Whether the benefit would outweigh the drawback is difficult to determine without running a controlled experiment.

Second, we used CorrLoss to encourage similar label correlation patterns between training and predictions. Formally, we added a regularization term $c = \sum_{i \neq j} c(d_i, d_j)$. Each summation term scales with a correlation difference:

$$c(d_i, d_j) \propto |\rho(d_i, d_j)_{y_{\text{train}}} - \rho(d_i, d_j)_{\hat{y}}|, \qquad (2)$$

		PROC	PROC+CPT	PROC+DRG	PROC+DIAG
ClinicalBERT	original	**0.4528**	0.397	0.3939	0.408
	CorrLoss	0.4037	0.3594	0.3272	0.363
RoBERTa	original	**0.4421**	0.4009	0.3884	0.4116
	CorrLoss	0.3736	0.3236	0.2816	0.3692
Longformer	original	**0.4712**	0.4227	0.3886	0.4219
	CorrLoss	0.4139	0.335	0.212	0.3549

Table 1: Macro F1 scores of experiments, in which procedure ICD-9 is the main task, on MIMIC-III-50 test set. For each model, the best F1 score is in bold. PROC means procedure ICD-9. DIAG means diagnosis ICD-9. PROC+CPT means that procedure ICD-9 is the main task and CPT is the auxiliary task.

where d_i, d_j are different classes, $\rho(d_i, d_j)_v$ is the correlation between class d_i and d_j in a vector v, y_{train} is the training labels, $\hat{y}$ is the predicted labels, and ρ is the Pearson correlation function.

Dataset We built two datasets from the Medical Information Mart for Intensive Care III (MIMIC-III) (Johnson et al., 2016), a database of EHRs. Our first dataset, subsequently referred to as "MIMIC-III", contains examples of each patient's discharge summary, and associated diagnosis and procedure codes (diagnosis ICD-9, procedure ICD-9, CPT, and DRG). Because this dataset is extremely imbalanced, we further select the top 50 most frequently used codes for each kind of coding system to construct a second dataset that represents a more ideal scenario. Following the convention of related literature, we call this dataset "MIMIC-III-50" (Vu et al., 2020; Luo et al., 2021; Li and Yu, 2020). Statistics of the MIMIC-III dataset are in Appendix A.

Models and Evaluation We use ClinicalBERT (Alsentzer et al., 2019), RoBERTa (Liu et al., 2019), Longformer (Beltagy et al., 2020) (justification in Appendix C). We use the macro F1 as our metric for comparison because this metric treats all classes equally, which means minority codes are as important as majority codes in evaluation (Branco et al., 2016; Sun et al., 2009; Ferri et al., 2009). Because it is an imbalanced classification, the default threshold of 0.5 is not suitable (Zhou and Liu, 2006; Zou et al., 2016). Instead, we tune the threshold according to the precision-recall curve to maximize the F1 score for each individual label.

4 Experiments

To test whether the correlation prior is useful for ICD code assignment, we incorporate multitasking (Equation 1) and CorrLoss (Equation 2) into our model and check if they improve performance. Specifically, we studied two main tasks (diagnosis ICD-9 codes and procedure ICD-9 codes). For each main task, we added one of the three auxiliary tasks: DRG codes, CPT codes, and the other ICD-9 codes (for diagnosis ICD-9 code, the auxiliary task can be procedure ICD-9 code, and vice versa). We trained both main-task-only models and multitasking models with and without CorrLoss.

5 Results

Multitasking and CorrLoss hurt performance on MIMIC-III-50 and do not significantly impact performance on MIMIC-III. Table 1 shows the macro-F1 score on procedure ICD-9 of the MIMIC-III-50 dataset. We observe two patterns for each language model. First, adding auxiliary tasks always decreases the performance of models in comparison to predicting main tasks only. Second, regularizing with CorrLoss always decreases the performance of models in comparison to not using CorrLoss. The same pattern exists for predicting diagnosis ICD-9 of the MIMIC-III-50 dataset (Appendix Table 6). However, on the full MIMIC-III dataset, multitasking and CorrLoss do not impact models' performance significantly (Appendix B).

6 Analysis

Since the macro F1 score does not show significant changes from multitasking and CorrLoss on the full MIMIC-III dataset, we investigate whether the performance changes for individual labels. Specifically, we analyzed how label imbalance (measured by Shannon entropy, defined in Appendix D.1) and label correlation (measured by the average absolute Pearson correlation coefficient between each main task label and all auxiliary task labels, as defined in Appendix D.1) affect the model's performance.

For individual ICD-9 code, incorporating the correlation prior may hurt or help. Figure 1 shows that there exist labels with both negative and positive performance changes.

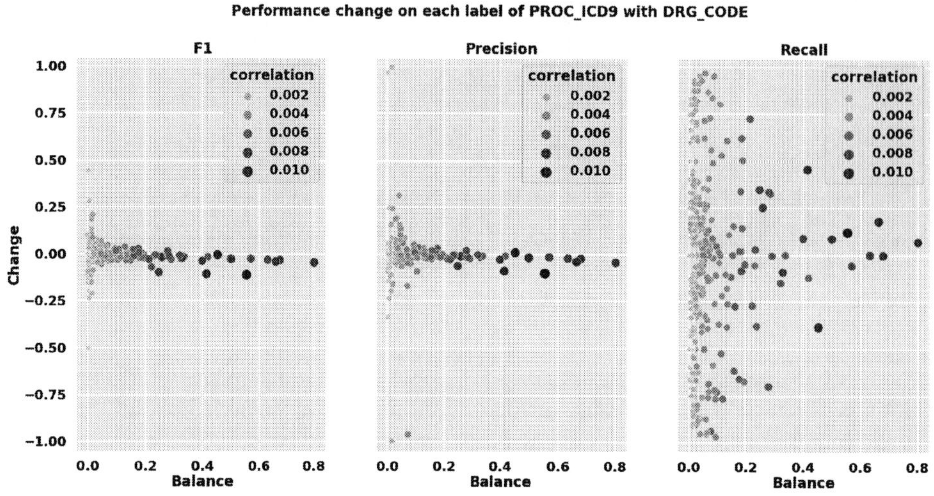

Figure 1: The plot of ClinicalBERT's performance changes (Y axis) on labels of procedure ICD-9, when DRG is added as the auxiliary task, versus the balances (X axis) of the labels, and versus the correlations (sizes and colors of the units) between each label with the whole auxiliary DRG task. CorrLoss is not included.

Labels that are more imbalanced and less correlated to auxiliary labels experience larger changes. Figure 1 shows two relationships: (1) more balanced labels (closer to the right) have less performance changes (spread of dots on the y axis), (2) labels that are more correlated with the auxiliary task (darker dots) have less performance changes (spread along the y axis). All the other plots of different tasks and setups show similar patterns (Appendix D.1).

		top50	bottom50
ClinicalBERT	+CPT	0.333	0.273
	+DRG	0.28	0.413
	+DIAG	0.3	0.387
RoBERTa	+CPT	0.4	0.3
	+DRG	0.393	0.353
	+DIAG	0.313	0.287
Longformer	+CPT	0.34	0.427
	+DRG	0.34	0.28
	+DIAG	0.347	0.307

Table 2: The percentages of positive macro F1 score changes on the top 50 most balanced procedure ICD-9 labels and on the bottom 50 least balanced procedure ICD-9 labels, with different auxiliary tasks and models. CorrLoss is not included.

In both extreme scenarios (imbalanced label, small correlation with auxiliary labels) and ideal scenarios (balanced labels, high correlation with auxiliary labels), **incorporating correlation is more likely to hurt than help.** Table 2 shows that for the top 50 most balanced labels and the bottom 50 least balanced labels, if we utilize correlations (with multitasking and CorrLoss), the percentage of positive F1 score changes is always less than 50%. Table 3 shows that for the top 50 labels that are most correlated with the auxiliary tasks and the bottom 50 labels that are least correlated with the auxiliary tasks, utilizing correlations also leads to $< 50\%$ positive F1 score change.

		top50	bottom50
ClinicalBERT	+CPT	0.333	0.327
	+DRG	0.32	0.327
	+DIAG	0.293	0.247
RoBERTa	+CPT	0.487	0.333
	+DRG	0.373	0.387
	+DIAG	0.267	0.293
Longformer	+CPT	0.433	0.327
	+DRG	0.28	0.273
	+DIAG	0.333	0.24

Table 3: The percentages of positive macro F1 score changes on the top 50 procedure ICD-9 labels that are most correlated with the auxiliary task and on the bottom 50 procedure ICD-9 labels that are least correlated with the auxiliary task, with different auxiliary tasks and models. CorrLoss is included.

7 Discussion

Since multitasking and CorrLoss worsen language models' overall performance, it contradicts our hypothesis that the correlations between ICD-9 codes and other medical codes would be a useful prior. Nevertheless, the performance changes on individual labels are more nuanced and show potential for improving prediction of certain ICD-9 codes. We wonder what characterizes the labels that benefit from incorporating the correlation prior (dots with positive changes in Figure 1). Perhaps for those labels, the additional dependency information gained from the auxiliary tasks outweigh the increased learning complexity from a larger output space. A prerequisite for a rigorous investigation would be quantifying the trade-off between the dependency information and the learning complexity.

We recognize three limitations that may influence the interpretation of our results and call for future works. First, we did not conduct a hyperparameter search for the regularization strength of CorrLoss. Second, since F1 score decreases are substantial and universal across all experiments on MIMIC-III-50, we did not run experiments multiple times with different seeds. Third, we did not provide a rigorous explanation of what caused our empirical findings. Future works can investigate the plausible hypothesis that the trade-off between the dependency information and the learning complexity causes these findings. Besides these limitations, future works can also investigate more scenarios and methods of incorporating the correlation prior.

References

Emily Alsentzer, John Murphy, William Boag, Wei-Hung Weng, Di Jindi, Tristan Naumann, and Matthew McDermott. 2019. Publicly Available Clinical BERT Embeddings. In *Proceedings of the 2nd Clinical Natural Language Processing Workshop*, pages 72–78, Minneapolis, Minnesota, USA. Association for Computational Linguistics.

Tian Bai and Slobodan Vucetic. 2019. Improving Medical Code Prediction from Clinical Text via Incorporating Online Knowledge Sources. In *The World Wide Web Conference*, WWW '19, pages 72–82, New York, NY, USA. Association for Computing Machinery.

Iz Beltagy, Matthew E. Peters, and Arman Cohan. 2020. Longformer: The Long-Document Transformer. ArXiv:2004.05150 [cs].

Paula Branco, Luís Torgo, and Rita P. Ribeiro. 2016. A Survey of Predictive Modeling on Imbalanced Domains. *ACM Computing Surveys*, 49(2):31:1–31:50.

Jacob Devlin, Ming-Wei Chang, Kenton Lee, and Kristina Toutanova. 2019. BERT: Pre-training of Deep Bidirectional Transformers for Language Understanding. In *Proceedings of the 2019 Conference of the North American Chapter of the Association for Computational Linguistics: Human Language Technologies, Volume 1 (Long and Short Papers)*, pages 4171–4186, Minneapolis, Minnesota. Association for Computational Linguistics.

C. Ferri, J. Hernández-Orallo, and R. Modroiu. 2009. An experimental comparison of performance measures for classification. *Pattern Recognition Letters*, 30(1):27–38.

Chao-Wei Huang, Shang-Chi Tsai, and Yun-Nung Chen. 2022. PLM-ICD: Automatic ICD Coding with Pretrained Language Models. In *Proceedings of the 4th Clinical Natural Language Processing Workshop*, pages 10–20, Seattle, WA. Association for Computational Linguistics.

Alistair E. W. Johnson, Tom J. Pollard, Lu Shen, Liwei H. Lehman, Mengling Feng, Mohammad Ghassemi, Benjamin Moody, Peter Szolovits, Leo Anthony Celi, and Roger G. Mark. 2016. MIMIC-III, a freely accessible critical care database. *Scientific Data*, 3(1):160035. Number: 1 Publisher: Nature Publishing Group.

Jinhyuk Lee, Wonjin Yoon, Sungdong Kim, Donghyeon Kim, Sunkyu Kim, Chan Ho So, and Jaewoo Kang. 2020. BioBERT: a pre-trained biomedical language representation model for biomedical text mining. *Bioinformatics*, 36(4):1234–1240.

Fei Li and Hong Yu. 2020. ICD Coding from Clinical Text Using Multi-Filter Residual Convolutional Neural Network. *Proceedings of the AAAI Conference on Artificial Intelligence*, 34(05):8180–8187. Number: 05.

Yinhan Liu, Myle Ott, Naman Goyal, Jingfei Du, Mandar Joshi, Danqi Chen, Omer Levy, Mike Lewis, Luke Zettlemoyer, and Veselin Stoyanov. 2019. RoBERTa: A Robustly Optimized BERT Pretraining Approach. ArXiv:1907.11692 [cs].

Junyu Luo, Cao Xiao, Lucas Glass, Jimeng Sun, and Fenglong Ma. 2021. Fusion: Towards Automated ICD Coding via Feature Compression. In *Findings of the Association for Computational Linguistics: ACL-IJCNLP 2021*, pages 2096–2101, Online. Association for Computational Linguistics.

James Mullenbach, Sarah Wiegreffe, Jon Duke, Jimeng Sun, and Jacob Eisenstein. 2018. Explainable Prediction of Medical Codes from Clinical Text. In *Proceedings of the 2018 Conference of the North American Chapter of the Association for Computational Linguistics: Human Language Technologies, Volume 1 (Long Papers)*, pages 1101–1111, New Orleans, Louisiana. Association for Computational Linguistics.

Damian Pascual, Sandro Luck, and Roger Wattenhofer. 2021. Towards BERT-based Automatic ICD Coding: Limitations and Opportunities. In *Proceedings of the 20th Workshop on Biomedical Language Processing*, pages 54–63, Online. Association for Computational Linguistics.

Ines Rieger, Jaspar Pahl, Bettina Finzel, and Ute Schmid. 2022. CorrLoss: Integrating Co-Occurrence Domain Knowledge for Affect Recognition. In *2022 26th International Conference on Pattern Recognition (ICPR)*, pages 798–804. ISSN: 2831-7475.

Yanmin Sun, Andrew K. C. Wong, and Mohamed S. Kamel. 2009. Classification of imbalanced data: a review. *International Journal of Pattern Recognition and Artificial Intelligence*, 23(04):687–719. Publisher: World Scientific Publishing Co.

Fei Teng, Wei Yang, Li Chen, LuFei Huang, and Qiang Xu. 2020. Explainable Prediction of Medical Codes With Knowledge Graphs. *Frontiers in Bioengineering and Biotechnology*, 8.

Shang-Chi Tsai, Ting-Yun Chang, and Yun-Nung Chen. 2019. Leveraging Hierarchical Category Knowledge for Data-Imbalanced Multi-Label Diagnostic Text Understanding. In *Proceedings of the Tenth International Workshop on Health Text Mining and Information Analysis (LOUHI 2019)*, pages 39–43, Hong Kong. Association for Computational Linguistics.

Thanh Vu, Dat Quoc Nguyen, and Anthony Nguyen. 2020. A Label Attention Model for ICD Coding from Clinical Text. volume 4, pages 3335–3341. ISSN: 1045-0823.

Ke Wang, Xuyan Chen, Ning Chen, and Ting Chen. 2020. Automatic Emergency Diagnosis with Knowledge-Based Tree Decoding. volume 4, pages 3407–3414. ISSN: 1045-0823.

Chenwei Yan, Xiangling Fu, Xien Liu, Yuanqiu Zhang, Yue Gao, Ji Wu, and Qiang Li. 2022. A survey of automated International Classification of Diseases coding: development, challenges, and applications. *Intelligent Medicine*, 2(3):161–173.

Ying Yu, Min Li, Liangliang Liu, Zhihui Fei, Fang-Xiang Wu, and Jianxin Wang. 2019. Automatic ICD code assignment of Chinese clinical notes based on multilayer attention BiRNN. *Journal of Biomedical Informatics*, 91:103114.

Min Zeng, Min Li, Zhihui Fei, Ying Yu, Yi Pan, and Jianxin Wang. 2019. Automatic ICD-9 coding via deep transfer learning. *Neurocomputing*, 324:43–50.

Zachariah Zhang, Jingshu Liu, and Narges Razavian. 2020. BERT-XML: Large Scale Automated ICD Coding Using BERT Pretraining. In *Proceedings of the 3rd Clinical Natural Language Processing Workshop*, pages 24–34, Online. Association for Computational Linguistics.

Zhi-Hua Zhou and Xu-Ying Liu. 2006. Training cost-sensitive neural networks with methods addressing the class imbalance problem. *IEEE Transactions on Knowledge and Data Engineering*, 18(1):63–77. Conference Name: IEEE Transactions on Knowledge and Data Engineering.

Quan Zou, Sifa Xie, Ziyu Lin, Meihong Wu, and Ying Ju. 2016. Finding the Best Classification Threshold in Imbalanced Classification. *Big Data Research*, 5:2–8.

A Dataset Statistics

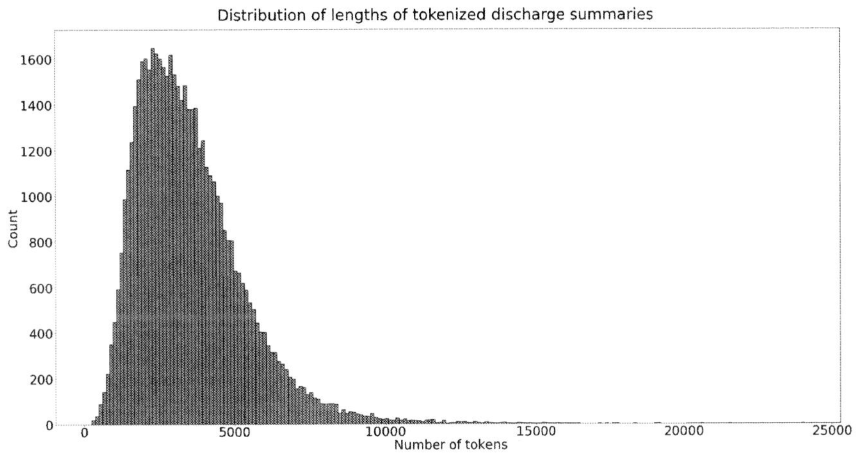

Figure 2: The distribution of lengths of tokenized discharge summaries in MIMIC-III dataset.

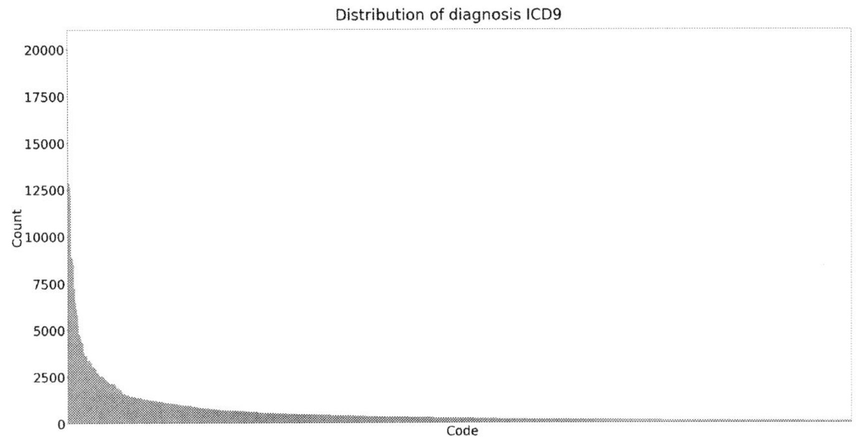

Figure 3: The distribution of diagnosis ICD-9. There are 6918 diagnosis ICD-9 codes. 6062 Codes occur less than or equal to 100 times in MIMIC-III dataset. They are not included for clarity.

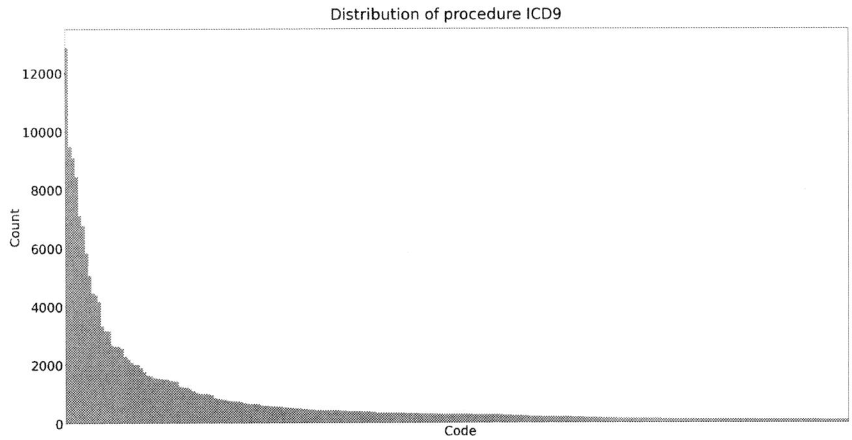

Figure 4: The distribution of procedure ICD-9. There are 2011 procedure ICD-9 codes. 1767 Codes occur less than or equal to 100 times in MIMIC-III dataset. They are not included for clarity.

B Results

		PROC	PROC+CPT	PROC+DRG	PROC+DIAG
ClinicalBERT	original	0.0098	0.0094	0.0091	0.0097
	CorrLoss	0.0102	0.0099	0.0088	0.0087
RoBERTa	original	0.0097	0.0089	0.0087	0.0088
	CorrLoss	0.0095	0.0095	0.0098	0.0089
Longformer	original	0.0088	0.0088	0.0095	0.0085
	CorrLoss	0.0094	0.0085	0.0091	0.0078

Table 4: Macro F1 scores of experiments, in which procedure ICD-9 is the main task, on full MIMIC-III test set.

		DIAG	DIAG+CPT	DIAG+DRG	DIAG+PROC
ClinicalBERT	original	0.0068	0.0066	0.0066	0.0067
	CorrLoss	0.0066	0.0069	0.0069	0.0068
RoBERTa	original	0.0069	0.0065	0.0062	0.0065
	CorrLoss	0.0071	0.0071	0.0066	0.0065
Longformer	original	0.0072	0.0069	0.007	0.0071
	CorrLoss	0.007	0.0068	0.0076	0.0071

Table 5: Macro F1 scores of experiments, in which diagnosis ICD-9 is the main task, on full MIMIC-III test set.

		DIAG	DIAG+CPT	DIAG+DRG	DIAG+PROC
ClinicalBERT	original	0.3755	0.3296	0.3351	0.3351
	CorrLoss	0.3235	0.2966	0.2947	0.2992
RoBERTa	original	0.3851	0.3255	0.3307	0.3341
	CorrLoss	0.3143	0.2822	0.2713	0.2939
Longformer	original	0.4408	0.349	0.3544	0.3552
	CorrLoss	0.3364	0.2963	0.2906	0.3027

Table 6: Macro F1 scores of experiments, in which diagnosis ICD-9 is the main task, on MIMIC-III-50 test set.

C Justifcation of Models

The variant of ClinicalBERT we use is Bio+Discharge Summary BERT model because it was further trained on discharge summaries from MIMIC-III after initialized from BioBERT (Lee et al., 2020).

We use RoBERTa because it is a variant of vanilla BERT that was trained differently to improve its performance on a range of NLP tasks.

We use Longformer because it can handle long text sequences. BERT and many BERT-based models cannnot handle text sequences longer than 512 tokens. Many tokenized discharge summaries are text sequences longer than 512 tokens and Longformer can benefit from more complete understandings of discharge summaries.

Each model represents a different improvement on top of vanilla BERT: ClinicalBERT improves through domain-specific pretraining; RoBERTa improves through tuning training setup; and Longformer improves through incorporating more information from the input. With these models, we cover a significant part of the improvement spectrum, which shows that the pattern we present is generalizable to different models.

D Analysis

D.1 Performance on Each Label

Other figures Since there are 72 experiments that have auxiliary tasks, there are 72 corresponding plots. Thus, it is unreasonable to include all of them in the appendix. You can find all plots in our github repository: `https://github.com/nyuolab/text2table/tree/main/notebooks`.

Shannon Entropy

$$H(X) = -\sum_{i=1}^{n} p(x_i) \log_2 p(x_i) \tag{3}$$

In this equation, $H(X)$ represents the entropy of a label X with possible outcomes x_1, x_2, ..., x_n. In our context, $n = 2$ because a label only has two possible outcomes: 1 (positive) or 0 (negative). The term $p(x_i)$ represents the probability of the i-th outcome, and the logarithm is taken with base 2 to give the result in units of bits. The sum is taken over all possible outcomes of X. With only two possible outcomes, a label's Shannon entropy will be close to 1 if it is balanced, and will be close to 0 if it is imblanced.

Representation of Correlations

$$C(a, B) = \frac{\sum_{b \in B} |P(a, b)|}{card(B)} \tag{4}$$

In this equation, $C(a, B)$ represents the correlations between a label of the main task a and a set containing labels of the auxiliary task. For each label of the auxiliary task $b \in B$, $|P(a, b)|$ represents the absolute value of the Pearson correlation coefficient bettwen a and b. $card(B)$ is the cardinality of B (i.e. the number of labels in B).

D.2 Performance in Different Scenarios

		top50	bottom50
ClinicalBERT	+CPT	0.453	0.32
	+DRG	0.54	0.293
	+PROC	0.48	0.38
RoBERTa	+CPT	0.48	0.313
	+DRG	0.507	0.307
	+PROC	0.48	0.333
Longformer	+CPT	0.5	0.32
	+DRG	0.48	0.393
	+PROC	0.433	0.287

Table 7: The percentages of positive macro F1 score changes on the top 50 most balanced diagnosis ICD-9 labels and on the bottom 50 least balanced diagnosis ICD-9 labels, with different auxiliary tasks and models. CorrLoss is not included in all experiments we examine in this table.

		top50	bottom50
ClinicalBERT	+CPT	0.347	0.36
	+DRG	0.327	0.313
	+DIAG	0.273	0.28
RoBERTa	+CPT	0.32	0.32
	+DRG	0.353	0.36
	+DIAG	0.273	0.22
Longformer	+CPT	0.353	0.367
	+DRG	0.28	0.293
	+DIAG	0.307	0.26

Table 8: The percentages of positive macro F1 score changes on the top 50 most balanced procedure ICD-9 labels and on the bottom 50 least balanced procedure ICD-9 labels, with different auxiliary tasks and models. CorrLoss is included in all experiments we examine in this table.

		top50	bottom50
ClinicalBERT	+CPT	0.413	0.307
	+DRG	0.533	0.28
	+PROC	0.487	0.293
RoBERTa	+CPT	0.46	0.3
	+DRG	0.493	0.373
	+PROC	0.473	0.34
Longformer	+CPT	0.453	0.293
	+DRG	0.487	0.34
	+PROC	0.5	0.307

Table 9: The percentages of positive macro F1 score changes on the top 50 most balanced diagnosis ICD-9 labels and on the bottom 50 least balanced diagnosis ICD-9 labels, with different auxiliary tasks and models. CorrLoss is included in all experiments we examine in this table.

		top50	bottom50
ClinicalBERT	+CPT	0.507	0.333
	+DRG	0.493	0.287
	+PROC	0.473	0.347
RoBERTa	+CPT	0.48	0.247
	+DRG	0.513	0.36
	+PROC	0.46	0.347
Longformer	+CPT	0.487	0.313
	+DRG	0.493	0.34
	+PROC	0.427	0.313

Table 11: The percentages of positive macro F1 score changes on the top 50 diagnosis ICD-9 labels that are most correlated with the auxiliary task and on the bottom 50 diagnosis ICD-9 labels that are least correlated with the auxiliary task, with different auxiliary tasks and models. CorrLoss is not included in all experiments we examine in this table.

		top50	bottom50
ClinicalBERT	+CPT	0.467	0.32
	+DRG	0.307	0.373
	+DIAG	0.367	0.287
RoBERTa	+CPT	0.387	0.267
	+DRG	0.413	0.407
	+DIAG	0.32	0.307
Longformer	+CPT	0.427	0.367
	+DRG	0.34	0.307
	+DIAG	0.42	0.307

Table 10: The percentages of positive macro F1 score changes on the top 50 procedure ICD-9 labels that are most correlated with the auxiliary task and on the bottom 50 procedure ICD-9 labels that are least correlated with the auxiliary task, with different auxiliary tasks and models. CorrLoss is not included in all experiments we examine in this table.

		top50	bottom50
ClinicalBERT	+CPT	0.467	0.373
	+DRG	0.52	0.3
	+PROC	0.46	0.333
RoBERTa	+CPT	0.493	0.32
	+DRG	0.52	0.433
	+PROC	0.473	0.253
Longformer	+CPT	0.46	0.32
	+DRG	0.513	0.467
	+PROC	0.453	0.34

Table 12: The percentages of positive macro F1 score changes on the top 50 diagnosis ICD-9 labels that are most correlated with the auxiliary task and on the bottom 50 diagnosis ICD-9 labels that are least correlated with the auxiliary task, with different auxiliary tasks and models. CorrLoss is included in all experiments we examine in this table.

Classical Out-of-Distribution Detection Methods Benchmark in Text Classification Tasks

Mateusz Baran[1,2] **Joanna Baran**[1] **Mateusz Wójcik**[1,2] **Maciej Zięba**[1,3] **Adam Gonczarek**[2]

[1]Wroclaw University of Science and Technology
{firstname.lastname}@pwr.edu.pl
[2]Alphamoon Ltd., Wrocław
{firstname.lastname}@alphamoon.ai
[3]Tooploox Ltd., Wrocław

Abstract

State-of-the-art models can perform well in controlled environments, but they often struggle when presented with out-of-distribution (OOD) examples, making OOD detection a critical component of NLP systems. In this paper, we focus on highlighting the limitations of existing approaches to OOD detection in NLP. Specifically, we evaluated eight OOD detection methods that are easily integrable into existing NLP systems and require no additional OOD data or model modifications. One of our contributions is providing a well-structured research environment that allows for full reproducibility of the results. Additionally, our analysis shows that existing OOD detection methods for NLP tasks are not yet sufficiently sensitive to capture all samples characterized by various types of distributional shifts. Particularly challenging testing scenarios arise in cases of background shift and randomly shuffled word order within in domain texts. This highlights the need for future work to develop more effective OOD detection approaches for the NLP problems, and our work provides a well-defined foundation for further research in this area.

1 Introduction

Systems based on artificial intelligence (AI) have to be safe and trustworthy (Amodei et al., 2016). Ensuring user reliance on these systems requires a cautious approach in making predictions. AI tools should avoid decisions on examples that significantly deviate from the training data. This is especially risky when the classifier shows excessive confidence in its incorrect decisions, leading to the propagation of errors in the system pipeline (Commission et al., 2019). However, current models are often trained under the closed-world assumption, limited to specific domains (Park et al., 2022). Test sets drawn from the same domain for evaluation may not reflect real-world scenarios accurately (Teney et al., 2020). This poses challenges when deploying such models in production environments (Schrouff et al., 2022).

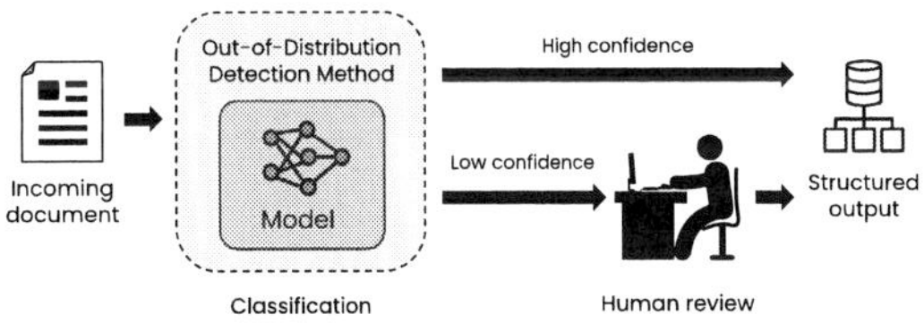

Figure 1: Trustworthy mechanism in document processing platform. Classification models need additional method to detect OOD samples and provide them to human review.

Real-world data is often completely different from training one. The change in data distribution can be caused by several factors such as user behavior, legal regulations, market trends or seasonal changes. In an *open-world* scenario, the AI-based system can be even exposed to inputs that deviate from the trained task. A significant risk that may arise is the possibility of model overconfidence while predicting data of this nature. As a result, there is a business need for detecting examples outside the domain (Hendrycks and Gimpel, 2017). Out-of-distribution (OOD) detection techniques can be well applied in a production system with human-in-the-loop technology (Wu et al., 2022), where it is important to quickly identify whether an input sample is characterized by a distributional shift. Such an example should be handled then by a human expert in order to avoid potential misclassification by the model. The essence of such systems is to find a trade-off between the accuracy and automation (Mosqueira-Rey et al., 2022) (Figure 1). This way, the model can achieve the highest possible performance on in-distribution (ID) data and difficult shifted data can be given to human verification, thus increasing the credibility of the overall system. The bottleneck here is a well-designed OOD detection method, which must be sensitive enough to capture all examples outside the domain.

Proceedings of the 61st Annual Meeting of the Association for Computational Linguistics - Student Research Workshop, pages 119–129

The problem of OOD identification is mainly investigated for vision classification tasks (Yang et al., 2022a; Kuan and Mueller, 2022), whereas in the field of NLP, studies on this topic are limited. We fill the missing gap by proposing a comprehensive analysis of existing OOD approaches for text classification tasks. In this work, we focus on the **post-hoc** techniques which are most suitable for business applications i.e. they have to fulfil the requirement of smooth integration into existing systems, without the need for additional OOD training data or any changes in model architecture. Ultimately, we evaluated eight methods in two different scenarios. The first one includes grouping test data into three splits according to the similarity to the in-distribution set: *Near-OOD*, *Far-OOD* and *Distinct-OOD* (Yang et al., 2021). The AI system is evaluated based on the degree of domain difference between training and test samples. The second scenario considers the division of datasets according to the shift of distribution (Arora et al., 2021). There are many categories of distribution shift (Hupkes et al., 2022), but in this study, we consider two types – semantic and background. **Semantic shift** occurs when new labels appear, which may be due to the lack of a sufficient number of classes representing the training data or the emergence of new classes over time. In distinction, the **background shift** is class independent. It appears when the characteristic features of text change (e.g. source origin, writing style), which can happen even within the same class. The reason may be language evolution, regional conditions, etc. – such factors are difficult to predict and adequately address in the training set. By preparing data separated into different kinds of shift, we gain an in-depth insight into the origin of the data, on which a particular OOD detection method performs better or worse.

We also provide a well-structured research environment that allows the full reproducibility of the achieved outcomes and evaluation of another NLP models. The source code is available on GitHub[1]. To summarize, our contribution is as follows:

- we adjust the existing OOD detection techniques to the text classification problems,
- we comprehensively evaluate the revised methods using two different scenarios tailored to the NLP domain,
- we deliver the complete experimental framework for evaluating the OOD methods.

[1]https://github.com/mateuszbaransanok/TrustworthyAI

2 Related Work

In recent years, there has been a growing interest in developing robust methods that can detect out-of-distribution examples. The work of Hendrycks and Gimpel (2017) has played a significant role in advancing this field. Their Maximum Softmax Probability (MSP) method, which relies on the softmax output of a neural network, has become a reference for subsequent research and still remains as the solid baseline approach (Zhang et al., 2023). The benefit of the MSP was its independence from the specific task domain. Since then, many researchers have extended this method or proposed novel techniques to address the challenge of detecting OOD data.

The first to popularize the interest in the OOD topic were computer vision (CV) researchers (Bengio et al., 2011). The emerged techniques in this field were summarized in a survey by Yang et al. (2021). The authors proposed a unified framework that groups OOD detection methods into categories based on their common underlying mechanisms. Among them, the following ones can be distinguished: (1) **output-based** (Liu et al., 2020; Liang et al., 2018) techniques which detect OOD samples based on output vector obtained by classification model for given input; (2) **gradient-based** (Huang et al., 2021) focus on analyzing the fluctuation of the gradient flow through the model layers to verify that the input is OOD; (3) **density-based** (Zong et al., 2018) methods involve modeling a density function from the training set and then determining whether a new example belongs to the same distribution; (4) **distance-based** (Sun et al., 2022; Ren et al., 2021) measure the dissimilarity between a new input and the training data by computing standard metrics such as cosine similarity, Euclidean or Mahalanobis distance. Another work of Yang et al. (2022a) provides a comprehensive evaluation of 13 methods for OOD detection in CV. Notably, the experimental results show that simple preprocessing techniques can be highly effective, outperforming even more sophisticated methods in identifying OOD examples. In addition, post-hoc methods have demonstrated considerable effectiveness in OOD detection and have made significant impact in this task. The NLP community is also more and more interested in addressing the challenge of OOD detection data, especially after the appearance of text processing automation systems. Despite the expectation that pre-trained language models (PLMs) would generalize well to unseen data, many existing transformer-based architectures perform poorly in an open-world assumption setup. This was proven by the work (Yang et al., 2022b) where the authors created the GLUE-X benchmark to reliably test the robustness of PLMs against OOD samples exposure, without using any of the previously mentioned techniques dedicated to OOD. Their achieved results confirm the necessity of further development of OOD detection methods. Currently, researchers are continuously proposing techniques tailored for the NLP tasks (Rawat et al., 2021; Zhou et al., 2021), revisiting existing ones (Podolskiy et al., 2021) or designing completely novel approaches that can address specific shifts in data distribution (Arora et al., 2021; Chen et al., 2023). The latter two publications particularly highlight the importance of dividing datasets into semantic and background shift sets, as they provide valuable findings and a better understanding of how the model works on different data types.

Evidently, there have been several NLP articles addressing OOD detection, but their comparison to existing methods has been limited. A comprehensive study which evaluates various OOD detection approaches on a larger scale and addressing the specific needs of businesses is still lacking. To fill this gap, we have developed a benchmark that provides a fair comparison of these techniques while testing their performance across different distributional shift scenarios. All the selected methods have been inspired by CV achievements, and we have specifically chosen those that can be easily integrated into an existing AI system with minimal complexity.

3 Benchmark Outline

This section provides an overview of the datasets and the model architecture, with a detailed description of the techniques reimplemented in our benchmark for detecting out-of-domain examples. The metrics used for evaluating the effectiveness of the detection methods are also presented.

3.1 Datasets

News Category Dataset (Misra, 2022) is one of the biggest news dataset. It contains around 210k news headlines from HuffPost published between 2012 and 2022. The dataset comprises of 42 classes that are heavily imbalanced. Therefore, the most similar classes were combined to avoid confusion between similar classes. Ultimately, we obtained 17 representative classes.

Twitter Topic Classification (Antypas et al., 2022) is a topic classification dataset collected from Twitter posts. It consists of 3184 high-quality tweets that have been assigned to one of six classes.

SST-2 (The Stanford Sentiment Treebank) (Socher et al., 2013) is a corpus with fully labeled parse trees that allows for an analysis of the compositional effects in language sentiment. The corpus includes almost 70k sentences extracted from movie reviews. Sentences were annotated with regard to their polarization (positive or negative).

IMDB (Maas et al., 2011) is a large collection of movie reviews from the Internet Movie Database created for the binary sentiment classification task. According to the original 10-point movie rating scale from the website, the dataset samples were filtered to include only highly polarized texts annotated as positive (≥ 7) or negative (≤ 4).

Yelp Polarity Review (Zhang et al., 2015) dataset includes almost 600k customer reviews which are labeled as positive or negative based on the number of stars given by the reviewer. Specifically, texts with ≤ 2 stars are labeled as negative, while those with ≥ 3 are labeled as positive. Due to the large size of the dataset, we created a smaller version by randomly selecting a subset of 75k reviews.

Language Detection Dataset (Saji, 2021) is a small dataset for language detection task. It contains texts in 17 different languages. For benchmark purposes, we filter out languages that do not use Latin alphabet. We've also excluded English texts to create a clear out-of-distribution dataset. Finally, dataset consist around 6k samples and all of them are used for OOD evaluation.

20 Newsgroups (McGraw Hill, 1995) consists of around 18k newsgroups posts on 20 topics. It is divided in two sets for training and evaluation. Moreover, we allocated an additional subset from the training set for validation purposes.

3.2 Model

In all experiments, we used transformer-based (Vaswani et al., 2017) RoBERTa$_{\text{base}}$ (Liu et al., 2019) model as a backbone with a fully connected layer as a classification head. The model was pretrained on English corpora, but it supports multiple languages.

3.3 Methods

We decided to compare **post-hoc** methods that are suitable to apply to trained models. They mainly use information based on model statistics such as intermediate layer values, gradients or non-deterministic properties of dropout regularization, etc. Their implementation is technically straightforward and independent of the type of model used.

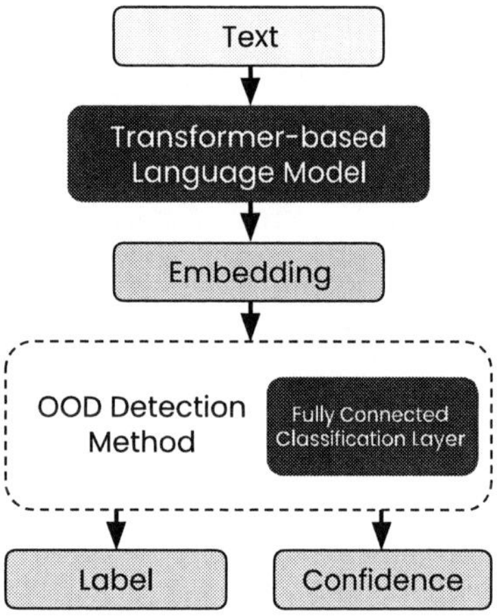

Figure 2: Benchmark schema – fine-tuned PLM-based classifier followed by OOD detection method.

An overview of our benchmark methodology is outlined in Figure 2. In addition to label prediction, we obtain a real-valued *confidence* score that indicates the level of confidence that the model has in whether the given sample belongs to the ID data. We reimplemented eight OOD detection techniques and adapted them to the NLP classification pipeline.

(1) **Maximum Softmax Probability (MSP)** (Hendrycks and Gimpel, 2017) employs the softmax score to check the certainty of whether an example belongs to a domain – we refer to it as the baseline method in our work.

(2) **Energy-based** (Liu et al., 2020) uses an energy score function to indicate model confidence.

(3) **Rectified Activations (ReAct)** (Sun et al., 2021) is a simple technique for reducing model overconfidence on OOD examples by truncating the high activations during evaluation.

(4) **KL-Matching (KLM)** (Hendrycks et al., 2022) calculates the minimum KL-divergence between the softmax probabilities and the mean class-conditional distributions.

(5) **GradNorm** (Huang et al., 2021) utilizes information obtained from the gradient space of model's classification layer. This approach uses the vector norm of gradients to distinguish between ID and OOD samples, with the assumption that higher norm values correspond to in-distribution data.

(6) **Directed Sparisification (DICE)** (Sun and Li, 2022) selectively chooses a subset of weights through sparsification, which helps to eliminate irrelevant information from the output.

(7) **Virtual-logit Matching (ViM)** (Wang et al., 2022a) combines information from feature space (PLM embedding) and output logits, providing both class-agnostic and class-dependent knowledge simultaneously for better separation of OOD data.

(8) **K-nearest neighbors (KNN)** (Sun et al., 2022) computes the distance between the embedding of an input example and the embeddings of the training set, and uses it to determine whether the example belongs to the ID or not.

The first four methods use signals originating from the output layer of the model. GradNorm focuses solely on the gradients that flow through the classification head, while methods from 6 to 8 operate on the embedding of a PLM. Most techniques (specifically no. 3-4, 6-8) need an initial configuration on the training or validation set to estimate the required statistics for ID data. To ensure consistency in the benchmarking process, the hyperparameters for the above methods were set to the values recommended in their original papers.

3.4 Metrics

To compare the chosen methods, we used three the most common metrics for OOD detection.

AUROC calculates the area under the Receiver Operating Characteristic (ROC) curve. The ROC curve plots the true positive rate against the false positive rate, and a larger area under the curve indicates better performance. This was used as our primary evaluation metric.

AUPR-IN measures the area under the Precision-Recall (PR) curve. The PR curve displays how well the method can identify true positives with high precision, and AUPR provides a measure of overall performance. The *"IN"* suffix indicates that this metric pertains to in-distribution data.

FPR@95 is the false positive rate when the true positive rate is set to 95%. Lower scores indicate better performance.

Table 1: Datasets setup for experiments.

Dataset	#Classes	Train / Val / Test	Avg. words
NC/I	7	66223 / 26475 / 39688	9.95
NC/O	10	- / - / 48522	9.77
Twitter	6	- / - / 3184	29.80
IMDB	2	25000 / 5000 / 20000	231.15
SST-2	2	43221 / 5000 / 20000	9.53
Yelp	2	50000 / 5000 / 20000	133.11
Language	9	- / - / 5864	19.08
NCR/I	7	- / - / 39688	9.95
NCR/O	10	- / - / 48522	9.77
Computer	5	2965 / 456 / 1460	218.63
Politics	4	1959 / 315 / 979	406.53
Sports	4	2363 / 432 / 1182	224.43

4 Data Preparation

In our study, we have paid particular attention to provide a complete and unbiased comparison of OOD detection methods. To achieve this goal, we adopted two diverse perspectives: one inspired by the field of computer vision (Yang et al., 2022a) and the other drawn from works dedicated to the NLP domain (Rawat et al., 2021; Arora et al., 2021).

4.1 Scenario 1

The first perspective intends to provide a detailed analysis of considered techniques based on the similarity between OOD examples and the training set. The degree of similarity is defined here in a human-intuitive way, taking into account such factors as thematic proximity, task dissimilarity or the sentence correctness.

As a base in-distribution data, we chose *News Category* dataset using the seven most popular classes (**NC/I**). The remaining classes were considered as out-of-distribution split (**NC/O**) which represents data in close semantic shift. The *Twitter Topic Classification* dataset has categories that are similar to those in the *News Category* dataset, but the sentence construction is significantly different. Both sets create the **Near-OOD** data setup. Another prepared collection, **Far-OOD** includes datasets with reviews of movies, hotels and restaurants that are vastly different from *NC/I* data – it is a connection of *SST-2*, *Yelp* and *IMDB*. Additionally, we prepared one more group named **Distinct-OOD** containing *Language Detection* dataset. With the inclusion of non-English texts there, we obtain a distinct set of tokens that the RoBERTa model has not encountered before, creating a completely separate dataset from the in-distribution data.

Finally, we also designed two collections derived from the *News Category* dataset by randomly shuffling words from all those available within each category. The new dataset, called *News Category Random*, retained the original number of examples and the number of words in each sample. These sets aimed to examine the classification system behavior when presented with input sentences that are completely disrupted from their original context. The previous partition into ID (**NCR/I**) and OOD (**NCR/O**) subsets was maintained.

4.2 Scenario 2

This scenario investigated the performance of detection methods for OOD examples under semantic and background shift. For semantic shift, we utilized the *20 Newsgroups* dataset that is a hierarchical collection of documents. Among the four top-level categories, we selected three - **Computer**, **Sports**, and **Politics** - as training sets for the model, while excluding the *"misc"* category due to potential data leakage issues. Subsequently, we generated various combinations of these categories, treating each one in turn as an in-distribution set, while considering the others as a OOD data. For example, the model could be trained on the samples from Computer class (ID dataset) and evaluated later on Sports and Politics (OOD).

In order to test the impact of background shift, we took three sentiment classification datasets – *IMDB*, *SST-2* and *Yelp*, which are based on user reviews and represent different domains. Although these datasets have similar linguistic properties, the topics they address are distinct. Again, we constructed various combinations of these collections by treating each one as the ID set and the others as OOD sets.

5 Experiments

In this section, we describe the details of a training procedure and present the outcomes from the experiments.

5.1 Training Setup

The PLM fine-tuning duration took maximally 100 epochs with an early stopping mechanism (Raskutti et al., 2011) applied (patience = 10 epochs). By using this technique, we were able to conserve computational resources while still obtaining high-performing models. The learning rate hyperparameter was always set to $2e-5$. To prevent overfitting and enhance the model's generalization capabilities, we used a weight decay $w_d = 0.01$ with

Table 2: AUROC (%) and standard deviations for methods evaluated on datasets from first scenario.

	Near-OOD		Far-OOD			Distinct-OOD		
Method	NC/O	Twitter	IMDB	SST-2	Yelp	Language	NCR/I	NCR/O
MSP	$74.2_{\pm0.3}$	$74.8_{\pm2.4}$	$96.6_{\pm3.1}$	$84.2_{\pm3.3}$	$95.3_{\pm1.5}$	$95.1_{\pm1.9}$	$59.0_{\pm0.8}$	$80.5_{\pm0.6}$
Energy	$77.6_{\pm0.4}$	$84.8_{\pm1.9}$	$99.6_{\pm0.5}$	$92.6_{\pm2.6}$	$98.6_{\pm0.7}$	$98.7_{\pm0.6}$	$60.1_{\pm1.0}$	$84.9_{\pm0.7}$
GradNorm	$77.2_{\pm0.5}$	$81.8_{\pm2.7}$	$99.0_{\pm1.1}$	$90.8_{\pm2.2}$	$97.8_{\pm0.8}$	$97.8_{\pm0.7}$	$60.5_{\pm1.4}$	$85.0_{\pm0.8}$
KLM	$62.9_{\pm0.4}$	$54.0_{\pm3.8}$	$92.5_{\pm6.2}$	$67.7_{\pm4.6}$	$88.9_{\pm3.7}$	$86.7_{\pm3.9}$	$50.6_{\pm0.1}$	$68.5_{\pm0.6}$
ReAct	$77.5_{\pm0.4}$	$84.5_{\pm2.0}$	$99.6_{\pm0.5}$	$92.4_{\pm2.8}$	$98.6_{\pm0.7}$	$98.7_{\pm0.6}$	$60.0_{\pm1.0}$	$84.7_{\pm0.7}$
DICE	$58.2_{\pm0.6}$	$60.9_{\pm3.2}$	$76.6_{\pm5.8}$	$60.9_{\pm1.4}$	$84.4_{\pm2.2}$	$69.3_{\pm2.8}$	$51.2_{\pm0.9}$	$60.4_{\pm1.4}$
KNN	$\mathbf{80.1_{\pm0.2}}$	$\mathbf{92.9_{\pm1.2}}$	$\mathbf{99.8_{\pm0.1}}$	$\mathbf{96.4_{\pm1.1}}$	$\mathbf{99.5_{\pm0.1}}$	$\mathbf{99.6_{\pm0.1}}$	$\mathbf{67.6_{\pm1.3}}$	$\mathbf{88.7_{\pm0.5}}$
ViM	$79.9_{\pm0.2}$	$89.2_{\pm1.5}$	$90.6_{\pm3.1}$	$96.0_{\pm0.9}$	$92.9_{\pm1.6}$	$98.1_{\pm0.8}$	$60.7_{\pm0.8}$	$86.1_{\pm0.4}$

Adam optimizer (Zhang, 2018). The best performing model was selected based on F1-score achieved on the validation set, and the final results were reported on the test set (see Appendix A). To minimize the influence of randomness on the outcomes, we trained PLM five times for each task using different initial seeds.

During each experiment, the PLM was fine-tuned on ID data, which consisted of training and validation splits. The evaluation of the OOD detection methods themselves was performed on predefined test data. A complete overview of the split sizes along with the number of classes in all data collections is presented in Table 1.

5.2 Results

The outcomes from experiments on data prepared in the first scenario (Section 4.1) are shown in Table 2. The *KNN* clearly outperformed the other OOD detection techniques on all three data groups. *Energy-based* method also stands out with its good results as well as *ViM*, except with its results on IMDB and Yelp dataset (worse than baseline *MSP*). As expected, the values of evaluation metrics on the NC/O dataset were the lowest among *Near-OOD* and *Far-OOD* divisions. This dataset was separated from the original dataset used in the training, making it the most difficult to properly identify as OOD due to the distributional closeness. The most challenging among the *Far-OOD* collections appeared to be *SST-2*, probably because of a small average number of words per example. The *Language* turned out to be the easiest dataset to detect OOD samples, and almost all methods performed well on it. The two worst performing approaches on the presented NLP tasks can be distinguished, i.e. *DICE* and *KLM*. Their measures were always worse than *MSP*, sometimes even nearly random (a little above 50%) – *DICE* on NC/O and *KLM* on Twitter.

Interesting results can be seen in the last part of Table 2. Randomization of words in case of NC/O dataset (which created NCR/O) significantly increased the model confidence in detecting OOD examples comparing with initial NC/O samples. However, the OOD methods could not cope well with shuffled in-domain *News category* data (NCR/I), which a human would recognize as the OOD.

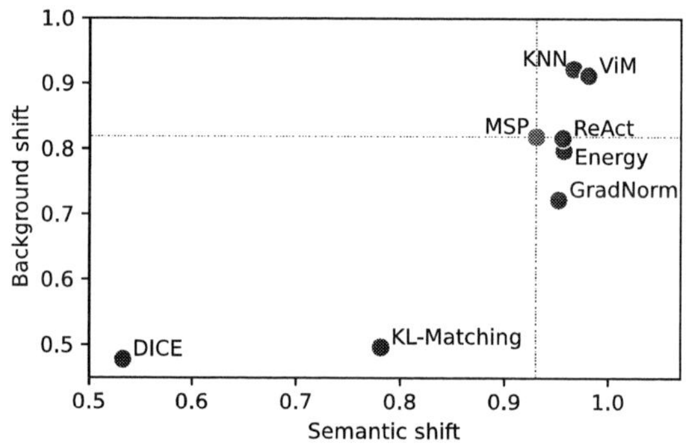

Figure 3: The performance of the methods is presented in AUROC depending on the type of distribution shift. The baseline method and its asymptotes are highlighted in pink color to facilitate comparison with other methods.

Table 3 presents AUROC scores obtained from the second scenario (Section 4.2) evaluation. The results demonstrate that the *ViM* method is more effective in detecting OOD samples with semantic shift to ID data. However, for background shift data, *ViM* is not always the best and is outperformed by *KNN* on IMDB and Yelp datasets. The SST-2 dataset proved to be problematic again, but

Table 3: AUROC (%) and standard deviations for methods evaluated on datasets from second scenario. The first part of the table refers to semantic shift, where the second part refers to background shift.

ID	OOD	MSP	Energy	GradNorm	KLM	ReAct	DICE	KNN	ViM
Computer	Politics	$91.5_{\pm1.9}$	$96.3_{\pm1.1}$	$95.5_{\pm0.9}$	$78.0_{\pm7.3}$	$96.2_{\pm1.2}$	$34.6_{\pm13.2}$	$97.0_{\pm0.5}$	$\mathbf{98.6_{\pm0.3}}$
	Sports	$89.8_{\pm2.7}$	$94.9_{\pm1.6}$	$94.1_{\pm1.6}$	$74.5_{\pm4.6}$	$94.6_{\pm1.7}$	$51.9_{\pm6.9}$	$95.7_{\pm0.9}$	$\mathbf{97.7_{\pm0.6}}$
Politics	Computer	$94.4_{\pm0.8}$	$96.0_{\pm0.6}$	$95.5_{\pm0.7}$	$82.8_{\pm4.6}$	$95.9_{\pm0.6}$	$63.9_{\pm3.2}$	$96.9_{\pm0.2}$	$\mathbf{98.3_{\pm0.2}}$
	Sports	$91.4_{\pm1.1}$	$93.4_{\pm0.9}$	$92.9_{\pm1.0}$	$72.3_{\pm5.6}$	$93.3_{\pm0.9}$	$58.6_{\pm2.4}$	$95.3_{\pm0.4}$	$\mathbf{97.3_{\pm0.3}}$
Sports	Computer	$95.7_{\pm0.6}$	$97.0_{\pm0.9}$	$96.8_{\pm0.5}$	$81.6_{\pm3.9}$	$96.9_{\pm0.9}$	$58.1_{\pm7.6}$	$97.6_{\pm0.4}$	$\mathbf{98.5_{\pm0.2}}$
	Politics	$95.3_{\pm0.2}$	$96.5_{\pm0.6}$	$96.4_{\pm0.5}$	$79.9_{\pm2.5}$	$96.5_{\pm0.7}$	$52.4_{\pm11.5}$	$97.2_{\pm0.3}$	$\mathbf{98.0_{\pm0.1}}$
IMDB	SST-2	$85.3_{\pm0.8}$	$84.3_{\pm1.8}$	$77.8_{\pm3.0}$	$61.2_{\pm1.7}$	$84.5_{\pm1.9}$	$84.6_{\pm3.3}$	$\mathbf{97.8_{\pm1.2}}$	$97.3_{\pm0.7}$
	Yelp	$76.0_{\pm3.3}$	$74.9_{\pm4.1}$	$66.2_{\pm3.6}$	$32.0_{\pm1.0}$	$75.3_{\pm4.3}$	$49.6_{\pm8.6}$	$97.5_{\pm1.1}$	$\mathbf{98.4_{\pm0.8}}$
SST-2	IMDB	$83.2_{\pm1.4}$	$82.7_{\pm2.2}$	$70.3_{\pm2.3}$	$55.0_{\pm2.7}$	$83.3_{\pm2.4}$	$34.5_{\pm10.7}$	$\mathbf{87.2_{\pm1.7}}$	$83.9_{\pm3.3}$
	Yelp	$75.7_{\pm2.2}$	$75.0_{\pm3.1}$	$61.3_{\pm2.7}$	$51.3_{\pm3.0}$	$75.7_{\pm3.4}$	$35.4_{\pm8.4}$	$\mathbf{87.8_{\pm0.4}}$	$80.1_{\pm2.8}$
Yelp	IMDB	$79.5_{\pm0.5}$	$79.2_{\pm1.6}$	$71.7_{\pm1.9}$	$38.6_{\pm1.3}$	$79.5_{\pm1.6}$	$26.8_{\pm5.1}$	$84.7_{\pm0.8}$	$\mathbf{88.6_{\pm0.7}}$
	SST-2	$91.6_{\pm0.5}$	$91.5_{\pm0.9}$	$86.1_{\pm1.0}$	$59.9_{\pm2.5}$	$91.7_{\pm0.9}$	$55.8_{\pm8.5}$	$98.5_{\pm0.3}$	$\mathbf{99.0_{\pm0.1}}$

only when used as a training set. It is worth noting that the average length of texts per SST-2 is considerably different from IMDB and Yelp collections, which mainly contain longer texts. These observations suggest that *KNN* is more stable in terms of different data characteristics. To further emphasize the importance of comparing methods based on the type of shift, we created a visualization in Figure 3. The *ReAct*, *Energy*, and *GradNorm* techniques turned out to be better than the baseline, but only for the semantic shift case.

To summarize, either *KNN* or *ViM* is the preferred choice among all the analyzed OOD detection approaches. Other reported metric values (AUPR-IN and FPR@95) from all experiments are attached in Appendix B.

5.3 Computational Resources

All experiments were conducted on a workstation equipped with a mid-range *Nvidia RTX 3060* GPU with 12GB of memory, a high-end *Intel(R) Core(TM) i9-10900X* CPU with 20 cores and 40 threads, and 256 GB RAM. These resources provided sufficient capacity for running the experiments and training the models used in this work, including analysis and processing of large datasets. In total, we trained 35 models, taking 222 GPU-hours while evaluation alone lasted 124 GPU-hours.

6 Conclusions

The latest advancements in OOD detection techniques have surpassed the conventional *MSP* baseline. In this work, we applied some of them to the NLP classification problems, selecting only post-hoc approaches because of their easy integration to already trained PLM model. Most of the examined techniques achieved better results than the *MSP*, but their performance varied when subjected to different types of data distributional shift. Background shift was particularly challenging for the majority of methods to properly distinguish OOD examples. The *KNN* and *ViM* methods were found to be the most effective, and their performance was also stable. Hence, they are better alternatives to *MSP* for out-of-distribution detection. However, it should be kept in mind that it is likely that the *ViM* method is sensitive to cases where the language model was trained on short texts and later exposed to a long text from outside the domain.

The proposed by us the unique analysis of *Distinct-OOD* scenario, allowed to draw interesting findings. The tested methods were able to identify texts in different languages very easily as a OOD examples, but they had problems detecting OOD on the *News Category Random* with shuffled data. This means that PLM models, despite their ability to detect contextual nuances in text, still tends to behave like Bag-of-Words (Zhang et al., 2010) in text classification tasks. Business-wise, such structurally disturbed examples should not be further processed by AI systems. Therefore, OOD methods employed in NLP should better address semantic disorders in input sentences.

In conclusion, the overall performance of current OOD detection techniques is still low and unsatisfactory, particularly when presented with the *Near-OOD* samples. Further research is necessary for the development of OOD detection methods, especially in the field of NLP, where more and more document processing automation systems are being developed, where ensuring reliability is important for users. Our work addresses the need for a comprehensive framework to evaluate the quality of OOD detection and provides easy extensibility to emerging methods.

7 Limitations

While our study provides valuable insights, it is important to keep in mind its limitations. Firstly, it was confined to text classification and did not include other NLP problems such as Named Entity Recognition (NER) (Wang et al., 2022b), Question Answering (QA) (Pandya and Bhatt, 2021), etc. Expanding this research to a wider range of tasks would provide a better understanding of the methods' performance in diverse data scenarios. Additionally, the inclusion of a task shift can be valuable, where the model is trained on a single task but OOD data come from a totally different prediction problems.

Secondly, we conducted our experiments using only RoBERTa model. We chose a widely used language model for text classification, but there are several other architectures worth testing, especially large language models (LLMs) (Zhao et al., 2023) that now becoming extremely popular. A more comprehensive evaluation of the models and methods could provide more insights into whether the development of transformer-based methods contributes to better detection of OOD data.

Finally, due to restricted computational time, we did not perform a hyperparameter search for either model or methods. We just used recommend values from the original publications. This may have affected the obtained results, and it is certainly an aspect worth investigating in the future.

8 Ethics Statement

The authors believe that their work does not raise any ethical questions of harm or discrimination. Moreover, they acknowledge that the benchmark has a wide range of potential applications and want to make it clear that they are not responsible for any unethical applications of their work.

Acknowledgements

The research was conducted under the Implementation Doctorate programme of Polish Ministry of Science and Higher Education (DWD/6/0322/2022) with cooperation of the Artificial Intelligence Department at Wroclaw University of Science and Technology. It was partially co-funded by the European Regional Development Fund within the Priority Axis 1 "Enterprises and innovation", Measure 1.2. "Innovative enterprises, sub-measure 1.2.1. "Innovative enterprises – horizontal competition" as part of ROP WD 2014-2020, support contract no. RPDS.01.02.01-02-0063/20-00. The work conducted by Maciej Zieba was supported by the National Centre of Science (Poland) Grant No. 2021/43/B/ST6/02853.

References

Dario Amodei, Chris Olah, Jacob Steinhardt, Paul F. Christiano, John Schulman, and Dan Mané. 2016. Concrete problems in AI safety. *CoRR*, abs/1606.06565.

Dimosthenis Antypas, Asahi Ushio, Jose Camacho-Collados, Leonardo Neves, Vitor Silva, and Francesco Barbieri. 2022. Twitter Topic Classification. In *Proceedings of the 29th International Conference on Computational Linguistics*, Gyeongju, Republic of Korea. International Committee on Computational Linguistics.

Udit Arora, William Huang, and He He. 2021. Types of out-of-distribution texts and how to detect them.

Yoshua Bengio, Frédéric Bastien, Arnaud Bergeron, Nicolas Boulanger–Lewandowski, Thomas Breuel, Youssouf Chherawala, Moustapha Cisse, Myriam Côté, Dumitru Erhan, Jeremy Eustache, Xavier Glorot, Xavier Muller, Sylvain Pannetier Lebeuf, Razvan Pascanu, Salah Rifai, François Savard, and Guillaume Sicard. 2011. Deep learners benefit more from out-of-distribution examples. In *Proceedings of the Fourteenth International Conference on Artificial Intelligence and Statistics*, volume 15 of *Proceedings of Machine Learning Research*, pages 164–172, Fort Lauderdale, FL, USA. PMLR.

Sishuo Chen, Wenkai Yang, Xiaohan Bi, and Xu Sun. 2023. Fine-tuning deteriorates general textual out-of-distribution detection by distorting task-agnostic features. *EACL*.

European Commission, Content Directorate-General for Communications Networks, and Technology. 2019. *Ethics guidelines for trustworthy AI*. Publications Office.

Dan Hendrycks, Steven Basart, Mantas Mazeika, Andy Zou, Joe Kwon, Mohammadreza Mostajabi, Jacob Steinhardt, and Dawn Song. 2022. Scaling out-of-distribution detection for real-world settings.

Dan Hendrycks and Kevin Gimpel. 2017. A baseline for detecting misclassified and out-of-distribution examples in neural networks. *Proceedings of International Conference on Learning Representations*.

Rui Huang, Andrew Geng, and Yixuan Li. 2021. On the importance of gradients for detecting distributional shifts in the wild. In *NeurIPS*, volume abs/2110.00218.

Dieuwke Hupkes, Mario Giulianelli, Verna Dankers, Mikel Artetxe, Yanai Elazar, Tiago Pimentel, Christos Christodoulopoulos, Karim Lasri, Naomi Saphra, Arabella Sinclair, Dennis Ulmer, Florian Schottmann, Khuyagbaatar Batsuren, Kaiser Sun, Koustuv Sinha, Leila Khalatbari, Maria Ryskina, Rita Frieske, Ryan Cotterell, and Zhijing Jin. 2022. State-of-the-art generalisation research in nlp: a taxonomy and review. *CoRR*, abs/2210.03050.

Johnson Kuan and Jonas Mueller. 2022. Back to the basics: Revisiting out-of-distribution detection baselines.

Shiyu Liang, Yixuan Li, and R. Srikant. 2018. Enhancing the reliability of out-of-distribution image detection in neural networks. In *International Conference on Learning Representations*.

Weitang Liu, Xiaoyun Wang, John D. Owens, and Yixuan Li. 2020. Energy-based out-of-distribution detection. In *NeurIPS*.

Yinhan Liu, Myle Ott, Naman Goyal, Jingfei Du, Mandar Joshi, Danqi Chen, Omer Levy, Mike Lewis, Luke Zettlemoyer, and Veselin Stoyanov. 2019. Roberta: A robustly optimized BERT pretraining approach. *CoRR*, abs/1907.11692.

Andrew L. Maas, Raymond E. Daly, Peter T. Pham, Dan Huang, Andrew Y. Ng, and Christopher Potts. 2011. Learning word vectors for sentiment analysis. In *Proceedings of the 49th Annual Meeting of the Association for Computational Linguistics: Human Language Technologies*, pages 142–150, Portland, Oregon, USA. Association for Computational Linguistics.

McGraw Hill. 1995. 20 newsgroups dataset.

Rishabh Misra. 2022. News category dataset. *arXiv preprint arXiv:2209.11429*.

Eduardo Mosqueira-Rey, Elena Hernández-Pereira, David Alonso-Ríos, José Bobes-Bascarán, and Ángel Fernández-Leal. 2022. Human-in-the-loop machine learning: A state of the art. *Artif. Intell. Rev.*, 56(4):3005–3054.

Hariom A Pandya and Brijesh S Bhatt. 2021. Question answering survey: Directions, challenges, datasets, evaluation matrices. *arXiv preprint arXiv:2112.03572*.

Hyunji Park, Yogarshi Vyas, and Kashif Shah. 2022. Efficient classification of long documents using transformers. In *Proceedings of the 60th Annual Meeting of the Association for Computational Linguistics (Volume 2: Short Papers)*, pages 702–709, Dublin, Ireland. Association for Computational Linguistics.

A. V. Podolskiy, Dmitry Lipin, A. Bout, E. Artemova, and Irina Piontkovskaya. 2021. Revisiting mahalanobis distance for transformer-based out-of-domain detection. In *AAAI Conference on Artificial Intelligence*.

Garvesh Raskutti, Martin J. Wainwright, and Bin Yu. 2011. Early stopping for non-parametric regression: An optimal data-dependent stopping rule. In *2011 49th Annual Allerton Conference on Communication, Control, and Computing (Allerton)*, pages 1318–1325.

Mrinal Rawat, Ramya Hebbalaguppe, and Lovekesh Vig. 2021. Pnpood : Out-of-distribution detection for text classification via plug andplay data augmentation.

Jie Ren, Stanislav Fort, Jeremiah Liu, Abhijit Guha Roy, Shreyas Padhy, and Balaji Lakshminarayanan. 2021. A simple fix to mahalanobis distance for improving near-ood detection. *CoRR*, abs/2106.09022.

Basil Saji. 2021. A dataset for language detection. https://www.kaggle.com/datasets/basilb2s/language-detection. Accessed: 2023-04-15.

Jessica Schrouff, Natalie Harris, Sanmi Koyejo, Ibrahim M Alabdulmohsin, Eva Schnider, Krista Opsahl-Ong, Alexander Brown, Subhrajit Roy, Diana Mincu, Christina Chen, Awa Dieng, Yuan Liu, Vivek Natarajan, Alan Karthikesalingam, Katherine A Heller, Silvia Chiappa, and Alexander D' Amour. 2022. Diagnosing failures of fairness transfer across distribution shift in real-world medical settings. In *Advances in Neural Information Processing Systems*, volume 35, pages 19304–19318. Curran Associates, Inc.

Richard Socher, Alex Perelygin, Jean Wu, Jason Chuang, Christopher D. Manning, Andrew Ng, and Christopher Potts. 2013. Recursive deep models for semantic compositionality over a sentiment treebank. In *Proceedings of the 2013 Conference on Empirical Methods in Natural Language Processing*, pages 1631–1642, Seattle, Washington, USA. Association for Computational Linguistics.

Yiyou Sun, Chuan Guo, and Yixuan Li. 2021. React: Out-of-distribution detection with rectified activations. In *NeurIPS*, pages 144–157.

Yiyou Sun and Yixuan Li. 2022. Dice: Leveraging sparsification for out-of-distribution detection.

Yiyou Sun, Yifei Ming, Xiaojin Zhu, and Yixuan Li. 2022. Out-of-distribution detection with deep nearest neighbors. In *International Conference on Machine Learning*, pages 20827–20840. PMLR.

Damien Teney, Kushal Kafle, Robik Shrestha, Ehsan Abbasnejad, Christopher Kanan, and Anton van den Hengel. 2020. On the value of out-of-distribution testing: An example of goodhart's law. In *Proceedings of the 34th International Conference on Neural Information Processing Systems*, NIPS'20, Red Hook, NY, USA. Curran Associates Inc.

Ashish Vaswani, Noam Shazeer, Niki Parmar, Jakob Uszkoreit, Llion Jones, Aidan N Gomez, Ł ukasz Kaiser, and Illia Polosukhin. 2017. Attention is all you need. In *Advances in Neural Information Processing Systems*, volume 30. Curran Associates, Inc.

Haoqi Wang, Zhizhong Li, Litong Feng, and Wayne Zhang. 2022a. Vim: Out-of-distribution with virtual-logit matching. In *NeurIPS*, volume abs/2203.10807.

Yu Wang, Hanghang Tong, Ziye Zhu, and Yun Li. 2022b. Nested named entity recognition: A survey. *ACM Trans. Knowl. Discov. Data*, 16(6).

Xingjiao Wu, Luwei Xiao, Yixuan Sun, Junhang Zhang, Tianlong Ma, and Liang He. 2022. A survey of human-in-the-loop for machine learning. *Future Generation Computer Systems*, 135:364–381.

Jingkang Yang, Pengyun Wang, Dejian Zou, Zitang Zhou, Kunyuan Ding, Wenxuan Peng, Haoqi Wang, Guangyao Chen, Bo Li, Yiyou Sun, Xuefeng Du, Kaiyang Zhou, Wayne Zhang, Dan Hendrycks, Yixuan Li, and Ziwei Liu. 2022a. Openood: Benchmarking generalized out-of-distribution detection. *NeurIPS*.

Jingkang Yang, Kaiyang Zhou, Yixuan Li, and Ziwei Liu. 2021. Generalized out-of-distribution detection: A survey. *arXiv preprint arXiv:2110.11334*.

Linyi Yang, Shuibai Zhang, Libo Qin, Yafu Li, Yidong Wang, Hanmeng Liu, Jindong Wang, Xing Xie, and Yue Zhang. 2022b. Glue-x: Evaluating natural language understanding models from an out-of-distribution generalization perspective.

Xiang Zhang, Junbo Zhao, and Yann LeCun. 2015. Character-level Convolutional Networks for Text Classification. *arXiv:1509.01626 [cs]*.

Yin Zhang, Rong Jin, and Zhi-Hua Zhou. 2010. Understanding bag-of-words model: A statistical framework. *International Journal of Machine Learning and Cybernetics*.

Yuhang Zhang, Weihong Deng, and Liang Zheng. 2023. Unsupervised evaluation of out-of-distribution detection: A data-centric perspective.

Zijun Zhang. 2018. Improved adam optimizer for deep neural networks. In *2018 IEEE/ACM 26th International Symposium on Quality of Service (IWQoS)*, pages 1–2.

Wayne Xin Zhao, Kun Zhou, Junyi Li, Tianyi Tang, Xiaolei Wang, Yupeng Hou, Yingqian Min, Beichen Zhang, Junjie Zhang, Zican Dong, Yifan Du, Chen Yang, Yushuo Chen, Zhipeng Chen, Jinhao Jiang, Ruiyang Ren, Yifan Li, Xinyu Tang, Zikang Liu, Peiyu Liu, Jian-Yun Nie, and Ji-Rong Wen. 2023. A survey of large language models. *CoRR*, abs/2303.18223.

Wenxuan Zhou, Fangyu Liu, and Muhao Chen. 2021. Contrastive out-of-distribution detection for pre-trained transformers. In *Proceedings of the 2021 Conference on Empirical Methods in Natural Language Processing*, pages 1100–1111, Online and Punta Cana, Dominican Republic. Association for Computational Linguistics.

Bo Zong, Qi Song, Martin Renqiang Min, Wei Cheng, Cristian Lumezanu, Dae ki Cho, and Haifeng Chen. 2018. Deep autoencoding gaussian mixture model for unsupervised anomaly detection. In *ICLR (Poster)*.

A Training Details

Each model was trained on five different seeds from range $[2021, 2025]$. Table 4 includes averaged classification metrics with standard deviation.

Table 4: Training metrics on test set.

Dataset	Accuracy	F1 Score	Precision	Recall
NC/I	$82.4_{\pm 0.1}$	$81.8_{\pm 0.1}$	$81.7_{\pm 0.2}$	$82.0_{\pm 0.2}$
Computer	$89.2_{\pm 0.3}$	$89.3_{\pm 0.4}$	$89.3_{\pm 0.4}$	$89.3_{\pm 0.3}$
Politics	$94.7_{\pm 0.3}$	$94.6_{\pm 0.3}$	$94.6_{\pm 0.4}$	$94.7_{\pm 0.3}$
Sports	$97.5_{\pm 0.2}$	$97.5_{\pm 0.2}$	$97.5_{\pm 0.2}$	$97.5_{\pm 0.2}$
IMDB	$94.7_{\pm 0.1}$	$94.7_{\pm 0.1}$	$94.7_{\pm 0.1}$	$94.7_{\pm 0.1}$
SST-2	$93.9_{\pm 0.1}$	$93.8_{\pm 0.1}$	$93.7_{\pm 0.1}$	$93.8_{\pm 0.1}$
Yelp	$96.9_{\pm 0.0}$	$96.9_{\pm 0.0}$	$96.9_{\pm 0.0}$	$96.9_{\pm 0.0}$

B Evaluation Details

The values for all metrics that were considered in our experiments are listed below. Tables 5 and 6 refer to the Scenario 1 of OOD data preparation; Tables 7 and 8 report the results from the Scenario 2.

Table 5: AUPR-IN (%) and standard deviations for methods evaluated on datasets from first scenario.

Method	NC/O	Twitter	IMDB	SST-2	Yelp	Language	NCR/I	NCR/O
MSP	71.7$_{\pm0.4}$	97.3$_{\pm0.3}$	98.4$_{\pm1.5}$	91.9$_{\pm1.8}$	97.4$_{\pm0.8}$	99.2$_{\pm0.3}$	59.2$_{\pm1.1}$	80.4$_{\pm0.7}$
Energy	74.5$_{\pm0.6}$	98.5$_{\pm0.2}$	99.8$_{\pm0.2}$	96.3$_{\pm1.3}$	99.2$_{\pm0.4}$	99.8$_{\pm0.1}$	58.8$_{\pm1.3}$	84.0$_{\pm0.9}$
GradNorm	73.9$_{\pm0.7}$	98.2$_{\pm0.3}$	99.5$_{\pm0.6}$	95.4$_{\pm1.1}$	98.8$_{\pm0.4}$	99.7$_{\pm0.1}$	58.5$_{\pm1.9}$	83.8$_{\pm1.0}$
KL-Matching	51.0$_{\pm0.4}$	90.9$_{\pm0.7}$	94.1$_{\pm5.1}$	72.0$_{\pm2.8}$	87.7$_{\pm3.6}$	96.6$_{\pm1.3}$	48.3$_{\pm0.2}$	54.8$_{\pm0.5}$
ReAct	74.3$_{\pm0.5}$	98.4$_{\pm0.2}$	99.8$_{\pm0.2}$	96.1$_{\pm1.4}$	99.2$_{\pm0.4}$	99.8$_{\pm0.1}$	58.9$_{\pm1.4}$	83.7$_{\pm0.9}$
DICE	51.8$_{\pm0.7}$	96.0$_{\pm0.4}$	91.0$_{\pm2.6}$	82.6$_{\pm0.9}$	94.1$_{\pm0.9}$	95.0$_{\pm0.5}$	51.0$_{\pm1.0}$	56.7$_{\pm1.5}$
KNN	**78.5$_{\pm0.1}$**	**99.3$_{\pm0.1}$**	**99.9$_{\pm0.0}$**	**98.3$_{\pm0.5}$**	**99.8$_{\pm0.1}$**	**99.9$_{\pm0.0}$**	**68.9$_{\pm1.3}$**	**88.6$_{\pm0.6}$**
VIM	77.1$_{\pm0.1}$	99.0$_{\pm0.2}$	96.5$_{\pm1.1}$	98.1$_{\pm0.5}$	97.1$_{\pm0.6}$	99.7$_{\pm0.1}$	58.9$_{\pm0.9}$	85.5$_{\pm0.4}$

Table 6: FPR@95 (%) and standard deviations for methods evaluated on datasets from first scenario. Lower scores indicate better performance.

Method	NC/O	Twitter	IMDB	SST-2	Yelp	Language	NCR/I	NCR/O
MSP	82.3$_{\pm0.8}$	77.3$_{\pm4.8}$	19.6$_{\pm18.8}$	61.3$_{\pm7.8}$	21.5$_{\pm6.7}$	29.3$_{\pm10.7}$	91.3$_{\pm0.5}$	75.2$_{\pm1.4}$
Energy	75.2$_{\pm1.0}$	55.7$_{\pm7.3}$	2.4$_{\pm2.7}$	35.8$_{\pm10.5}$	7.1$_{\pm3.5}$	7.6$_{\pm3.5}$	89.0$_{\pm0.6}$	63.8$_{\pm1.9}$
GradNorm	75.9$_{\pm0.8}$	65.1$_{\pm6.9}$	5.7$_{\pm6.3}$	44.0$_{\pm7.9}$	11.2$_{\pm4.0}$	12.9$_{\pm5.0}$	88.8$_{\pm0.7}$	63.7$_{\pm2.1}$
KL-Matching	85.8$_{\pm0.5}$	85.4$_{\pm3.5}$	33.8$_{\pm29.7}$	76.4$_{\pm4.6}$	30.2$_{\pm8.7}$	55.7$_{\pm9.2}$	92.3$_{\pm0.3}$	80.2$_{\pm0.8}$
ReAct	75.3$_{\pm1.1}$	55.3$_{\pm7.2}$	2.2$_{\pm2.5}$	35.6$_{\pm10.6}$	7.0$_{\pm3.4}$	7.6$_{\pm3.6}$	89.2$_{\pm0.6}$	64.2$_{\pm1.9}$
DICE	95.2$_{\pm0.3}$	99.9$_{\pm0.0}$	100.0$_{\pm0.0}$	99.9$_{\pm0.1}$	99.4$_{\pm0.9}$	100.0$_{\pm0.0}$	96.3$_{\pm0.3}$	97.1$_{\pm0.5}$
KNN	73.9$_{\pm0.6}$	**34.4$_{\pm5.4}$**	**0.2$_{\pm0.1}$**	**22.1$_{\pm8.6}$**	**2.2$_{\pm0.7}$**	**1.4$_{\pm0.5}$**	**85.7$_{\pm0.7}$**	**56.1$_{\pm1.6}$**
VIM	**71.5$_{\pm0.5}$**	57.8$_{\pm4.7}$	86.5$_{\pm12.4}$	23.7$_{\pm5.2}$	63.3$_{\pm10.7}$	13.2$_{\pm8.0}$	88.9$_{\pm0.5}$	63.4$_{\pm1.1}$

Table 7: AUPR-IN (%) and standard deviations for methods evaluated on datasets from second scenario. The first part of the table refers to semantic shift, where the second part refers to background shift.

ID	OOD	MSP	Energy	GradNorm	KLM	ReAct	DICE	KNN	VIM
Computer	Politics	95.2$_{\pm1.1}$	97.7$_{\pm0.7}$	97.4$_{\pm0.5}$	77.7$_{\pm8.2}$	97.6$_{\pm0.7}$	56.1$_{\pm11.4}$	98.2$_{\pm0.3}$	**99.1$_{\pm0.2}$**
	Sports	93.3$_{\pm1.9}$	96.4$_{\pm1.1}$	96.0$_{\pm1.0}$	71.3$_{\pm5.5}$	96.2$_{\pm1.2}$	64.3$_{\pm9.0}$	97.1$_{\pm0.6}$	**98.3$_{\pm0.4}$**
Politics	Computer	93.8$_{\pm0.7}$	94.8$_{\pm0.7}$	94.6$_{\pm0.7}$	67.3$_{\pm9.0}$	94.7$_{\pm0.7}$	68.9$_{\pm2.2}$	96.7$_{\pm0.2}$	**97.9$_{\pm0.2}$**
	Sports	91.6$_{\pm1.2}$	92.8$_{\pm1.0}$	92.4$_{\pm1.2}$	60.8$_{\pm9.6}$	92.6$_{\pm1.1}$	67.5$_{\pm1.9}$	95.8$_{\pm0.3}$	**97.1$_{\pm0.3}$**
Sports	Computer	96.3$_{\pm0.7}$	96.9$_{\pm1.1}$	97.1$_{\pm0.5}$	70.1$_{\pm7.4}$	96.8$_{\pm1.1}$	67.2$_{\pm6.4}$	98.0$_{\pm0.3}$	**98.7$_{\pm0.2}$**
	Politics	96.6$_{\pm0.4}$	97.1$_{\pm0.9}$	97.4$_{\pm0.5}$	75.3$_{\pm1.7}$	97.1$_{\pm0.9}$	66.0$_{\pm9.7}$	98.2$_{\pm0.2}$	**98.6$_{\pm0.1}$**
IMDB	SST-2	86.2$_{\pm1.4}$	84.8$_{\pm1.8}$	73.7$_{\pm6.6}$	52.2$_{\pm1.2}$	85.0$_{\pm1.8}$	85.5$_{\pm3.6}$	**98.1$_{\pm1.0}$**	97.6$_{\pm0.6}$
	Yelp	82.1$_{\pm2.8}$	80.8$_{\pm3.6}$	71.5$_{\pm3.3}$	38.8$_{\pm0.6}$	81.2$_{\pm3.9}$	51.4$_{\pm8.0}$	97.9$_{\pm0.8}$	**98.6$_{\pm0.6}$**
SST-2	IMDB	85.7$_{\pm1.5}$	85.1$_{\pm2.0}$	69.4$_{\pm3.0}$	48.6$_{\pm1.4}$	85.7$_{\pm2.2}$	41.1$_{\pm5.0}$	**91.4$_{\pm0.8}$**	86.5$_{\pm2.5}$
	Yelp	76.3$_{\pm2.8}$	75.4$_{\pm3.5}$	60.5$_{\pm3.5}$	47.4$_{\pm1.5}$	76.3$_{\pm3.8}$	40.6$_{\pm3.6}$	**91.4$_{\pm0.4}$**	82.5$_{\pm2.6}$
Yelp	IMDB	83.5$_{\pm0.5}$	82.7$_{\pm2.5}$	76.1$_{\pm2.3}$	41.1$_{\pm0.5}$	83.0$_{\pm2.4}$	36.8$_{\pm1.6}$	88.2$_{\pm0.6}$	**91.2$_{\pm0.5}$**
	SST-2	93.8$_{\pm0.4}$	93.7$_{\pm0.7}$	88.8$_{\pm0.8}$	50.2$_{\pm1.6}$	93.9$_{\pm0.7}$	63.3$_{\pm8.2}$	98.9$_{\pm0.2}$	**99.3$_{\pm0.1}$**

Table 8: FPR@95 (%) and standard deviations for methods evaluated on datasets from second scenario. The first part of the table refers to semantic shift, where the second part refers to background shift. Lower scores indicate better performance.

ID	OOD	MSP	Energy	GradNorm	KLM	ReAct	DICE	KNN	VIM
Computer	Politics	55.9$_{\pm11.7}$	20.9$_{\pm7.4}$	31.0$_{\pm8.4}$	61.6$_{\pm12.6}$	21.3$_{\pm7.5}$	99.9$_{\pm0.1}$	17.3$_{\pm4.6}$	**7.2$_{\pm1.8}$**
	Sports	61.4$_{\pm9.3}$	30.8$_{\pm8.8}$	39.7$_{\pm8.7}$	66.7$_{\pm9.6}$	31.4$_{\pm8.6}$	99.1$_{\pm0.9}$	29.6$_{\pm6.3}$	**14.1$_{\pm5.6}$**
Politics	Computer	38.4$_{\pm8.9}$	22.0$_{\pm4.0}$	28.1$_{\pm8.9}$	42.1$_{\pm9.8}$	22.7$_{\pm4.1}$	98.8$_{\pm0.9}$	22.8$_{\pm4.6}$	**9.4$_{\pm1.6}$**
	Sports	55.8$_{\pm7.4}$	35.6$_{\pm4.7}$	42.5$_{\pm9.4}$	59.4$_{\pm7.8}$	36.5$_{\pm4.7}$	99.4$_{\pm0.5}$	35.8$_{\pm5.0}$	**16.2$_{\pm3.1}$**
Sports	Computer	27.9$_{\pm6.6}$	18.1$_{\pm5.7}$	18.2$_{\pm5.1}$	32.2$_{\pm5.1}$	18.8$_{\pm6.0}$	96.0$_{\pm2.3}$	11.8$_{\pm4.2}$	**6.0$_{\pm1.6}$**
	Politics	30.5$_{\pm3.6}$	21.0$_{\pm2.8}$	21.0$_{\pm2.9}$	33.9$_{\pm2.3}$	21.7$_{\pm3.3}$	95.5$_{\pm7.4}$	17.7$_{\pm2.6}$	**9.1$_{\pm1.2}$**
IMDB	SST-2	65.6$_{\pm0.9}$	68.5$_{\pm9.4}$	67.3$_{\pm1.6}$	65.6$_{\pm0.9}$	69.1$_{\pm10.7}$	54.4$_{\pm9.6}$	**12.5$_{\pm8.2}$**	14.0$_{\pm3.9}$
	Yelp	92.3$_{\pm1.3}$	92.8$_{\pm2.8}$	93.3$_{\pm1.0}$	92.3$_{\pm1.3}$	92.6$_{\pm2.9}$	93.8$_{\pm7.2}$	15.1$_{\pm9.1}$	**8.2$_{\pm6.5}$**
SST-2	IMDB	**77.7$_{\pm2.3}$**	79.6$_{\pm7.3}$	81.8$_{\pm1.5}$	78.0$_{\pm2.3}$	79.1$_{\pm8.9}$	100.0$_{\pm0.0}$	88.3$_{\pm10.9}$	79.0$_{\pm17.8}$
	Yelp	84.5$_{\pm2.4}$	85.8$_{\pm6.2}$	87.6$_{\pm1.2}$	84.8$_{\pm2.3}$	85.2$_{\pm7.0}$	99.7$_{\pm0.2}$	**81.0$_{\pm9.0}$**	82.2$_{\pm13.1}$
Yelp	IMDB	83.7$_{\pm0.6}$	83.5$_{\pm1.4}$	87.1$_{\pm0.7}$	83.6$_{\pm0.6}$	83.2$_{\pm1.4}$	99.7$_{\pm0.1}$	74.9$_{\pm3.8}$	**62.4$_{\pm2.5}$**
	SST-2	58.4$_{\pm2.4}$	58.6$_{\pm4.0}$	66.7$_{\pm2.5}$	58.4$_{\pm2.4}$	57.9$_{\pm4.2}$	96.1$_{\pm4.7}$	3.8$_{\pm1.5}$	**2.4$_{\pm0.8}$**

Can LMs Store and Retrieve 1-to-N Relational Knowledge?

Haruki Nagasawa[1] **Benjamin Heinzerling**[2,1] **Kazuma Kokuta**[1] **Kentaro Inui**[1,2]
[1]Tohoku University [2]RIKEN
{haruki.nagasawa.s8, kokuta.kazuma.r3}@dc.tohoku.ac.jp
benjamin.heinzerling@riken.jp kentaro.inui@tohoku.ac.jp

Abstract

It has been suggested that pretrained language models can be viewed as knowledge bases. One of the prerequisites for using language models as knowledge bases is how accurately they can store and retrieve world knowledge. It is already revealed that language models can store much 1-to-1 relational knowledge, such as "country and its capital," with high memorization accuracy. On the other hand, world knowledge includes not only 1-to-1 but also 1-to-N relational knowledge, such as "parent and children." However, it is not clear how accurately language models can handle 1-to-N relational knowledge. To investigate language models' abilities toward 1-to-N relational knowledge, we start by designing the problem settings. Specifically, we organize the character of 1-to-N relational knowledge and define two essential skills: (i) memorizing multiple objects individually and (ii) retrieving multiple stored objects without excesses or deficiencies at once. We inspect LMs' ability to handle 1-to-N relational knowledge on the controlled synthesized data. As a result, we report that it is possible to memorize multiple objects with high accuracy, but generalizing the retrieval ability (expressly, enumeration) is challenging.

1 Introduction

As a result of their pretraining on large amounts of text, language models (LMs) store certain world knowledge facts, such as "Paris is the capital of France", in their parameters and can retrieve that knowledge when given a suitable prompt. Since the ability to store and retrieve knowledge is also a key functionality of knowledge bases (KBs; Weikum et al., 2021), prior work has proposed to view language models as knowledge bases (Petroni et al., 2019). Quantitative evaluation of world knowledge in LMs has focused on 1-to-1 relational knowledge involving two entities, such as a country and its capital (Petroni et al., 2019; Heinzerling and Inui, 2021; Safavi and Koutra, 2021; Razniewski et al., 2021). However, the question if and how well LMs can handle 1-to-N relations, such as relations between parents and their children, is underexplored so far.

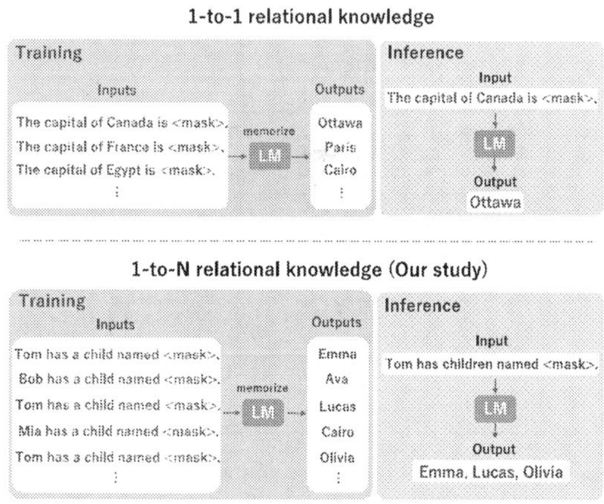

Figure 1: Memorize and enumerate relational knowledge. We are considering a synthetic setting in which the LM is made to memorize a specific set of individual relations and then needs to aggregate those relations into 1-to-N relations.

Here, we conduct a study to assess the capability of LMs to store and retrieve 1-to-N relations in a manner similar to knowledge bases. We consider a setting in which the model first is trained to memorize individual relation instances, such as "Tom has a child named Emma", "Bob has a child named Ava", "Tom has a child named Lucas", and "Tom has a child named Olivia". During inference the model then has to retrieve 1-to-N relation, e.g., "Tom has children named Emma, Lucas, Olivia" (Figure 1).

To investigate the possibility of viewing LMs as KBs more precisely, it is necessary to clarify the basic abilities of LMs, such as how accurately they can store 1-to-N relational knowledge and how flexibly they can retrieve multiple entities they have stored.

Proceedings of the 61st Annual Meeting of the Association for Computational Linguistics - Student Research Workshop, pages 130–138
July 10-12, 2023

Our study represents the first comprehensive investigation of 1-to-N relational knowledge. Our contributions are summarized as follows: (1) We identified the capabilities necessary for LMs to handle 1-to-N relational knowledge, taking into account its unique properties. Specifically, LMs must be able to accurately memorize any object appearing discretely and enumerate multiple objects without over- or under-recall based on memory. (§ 3) (2) Based on the identified capabilities, we formulated two training schemes: element-valued supervision for "memorization" and set-valued supervision for "enumerating." (§ 4) (3) We conducted a quantitative evaluation of LMs' "memorization" abilities from both subject-oriented and object-oriented perspectives and categorized the errors encountered during "enumerating." Our results suggest that LMs are able to store 1-to-N relational knowledge with reasonable accuracy, but generalizing the ability to enumerate proves to be challenging. (§ 6)

2 Related Work

Factual knowledge probing Petroni et al. (2019) investigated how much knowledge LMs had acquired from large corpora by having models such as pretrained BERT (Devlin et al., 2019) solve problems in the "fill-in-the-blank" format. They also pointed out three critical advantages of treating LMs as KBs: "LMs require no schema engineering, do not need human annotations, and support an open set of queries."

Jiang et al. (2020) and Brown et al. (2020) also worked on creating optimal prompts for extracting correct answers from pretrained LMs. These investigations aim to extract knowledge that LMs have acquired implicitly during pretraining. On the other hand, we are interested in the degree to which knowledge can be handled accurately when LMs explicitly learn it. Thus, investigating what and how well pretrained LMs acquire 1-to-N relational knowledge from corpora is beyond our scope.

Storing 1-to-1 relational knowledge Heinzerling and Inui (2021) established two basic requirements for treating LMs as KBs: "(i) the ability to store a lot of facts involving a large number of entities and (ii) the ability to query stored facts." Based on these requirements, they elaborately examined how much and how accurately LMs can store 1-to-1 relational knowledge by comparing various entity representations. However, the behavior of LMs concerning 1-to-N relational knowledge remains unclear.

Set handling This study explores handling multiple objects, which can be achieved by handling a set of objects. Previous works such as Deep Sets (Zaheer et al., 2017) and Set Transformer (Lee et al., 2019) are representative ones that address set handling in neural networks or transformers (Vaswani et al., 2017).

Both focus on sets as inputs, being permutation-invariant and treating sets of arbitrary size. While this study focuses on sets as outputs rather than inputs, the properties such as permutation-invariant are considered to be essential aspects in common.

3 Designing an approach to 1-to-N relational knowledge

In this section, we describe the unique properties of 1-to-N relational knowledge and what capabilities of LMs are needed to handle 1-to-N relational knowledge.

To begin with, we define three significant unique factors that make 1-to-N relational knowledge challenging to deal with: First, when the subject or relation under consideration changes, the number of objects associated with it changes. For example, consider answering the question, "{Subject} has children named <mask>." The difficulty is that the number of correct objects changes depending on the input. Second, considering existing corpora, multiple objects are likely to occur discretely. For example, Barack Obama has two children, Malia and Sasha, but only Malia may appear in some specific contexts, and only Sasha may appear in other contexts.. Finally, third, when we assume a situation where an LM is used practically as a KB, it is necessary to output these discretely appearing objects together to avoid generating an inadequate response to the input query.

Therefore, given the above properties, the two essential LMs' competencies considered necessary to manage 1-to-N relational knowledge are as follows. (i) "the ability to accurately memorize any objects appearing discretely." (ii) "the ability to retrieve multiple objects without over- or under-recall based on memory." In order to consider an end-to-end approach to 1-to-N relational knowledge, this study tackles it as a generative task using the sequence-to-sequence model (Sutskever et al., 2014), which allows for flexible responses based on input.

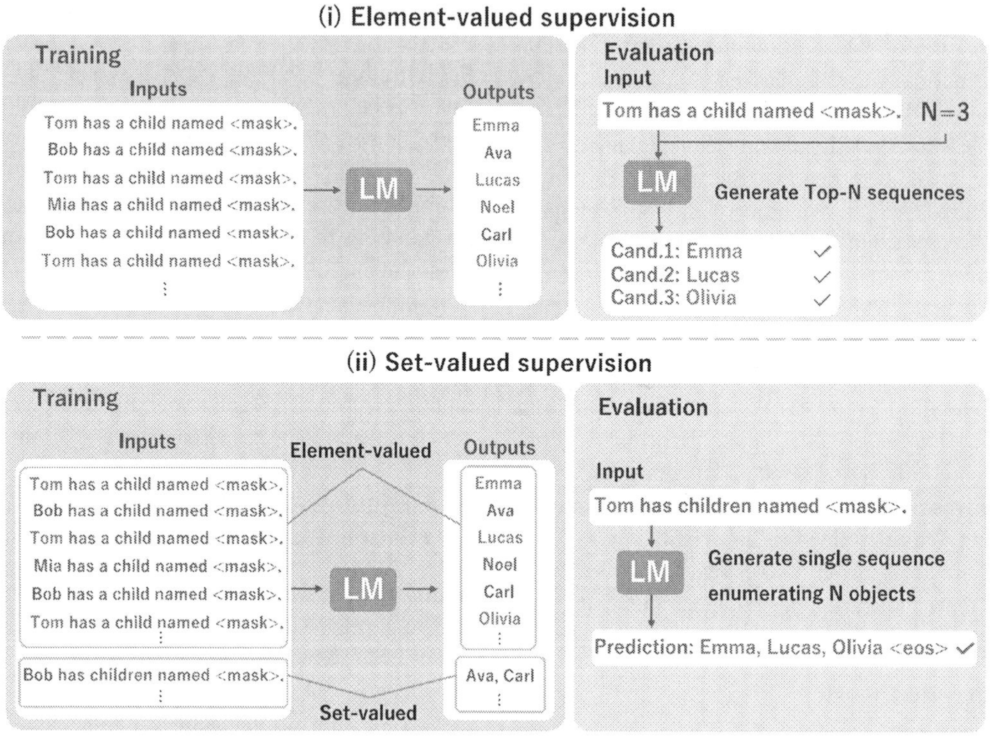

Figure 2: (i) Element-valued supervision and (ii) set-valued supervision. **Element-valued supervision** is intended to have the LM memorize all objects of a 1-to-N relation individually. For a given subject, there are as N relation instances. We train the model to output a single object entity when given an input query about a subject entity. During the evaluation, N sequences are generated using a beam search of size N to verify if all N object entities are stored and retrieved. **Set-valued supervision** is used to train the model to enumerate all objects for a given entity and predicate in one prediction step.

4 Method

4.1 Terminology

In this work, we make use of the following terms:

Relation triple: A triple consisting of a *subject* and an *object* entity, as well as a predicate that describes the relation that holds between the subject and the object, e.g., (Tom, hasChild, Emma).

1-to-N relation: A set of relation triples with the same subject and predicate, but different objects, e.g., (Tom, hasChild, Emma) and (Tom, hasChild, Lucas).

Individual relation instance: A relation triple expressed in text, for example "Tom has a child named Emma."

Element: Viewing a 1-to-N relation as a set, we refer to individual relation instances as *elements* of that set, e.g., "Tom has a child named Emma." is an element of the 1-to-N relation that holds between Tom and his children.

Element-valued supervision: One of the two supervised training schemes we employ. A model is trained on elements, i.e., individual relation instances, of 1-to-N relations. Concretely, the model is given a relation instance with the object masked out, e.g., "Tom has a child named <mask>." and has to predict the masked out object, e.g., "Emma". The goal of this training scheme is to have the model memorize individual objects based on their corresponding subjects.

Set-valued supervision: In the second of our supervised training schemes the model is trained to predict the set of all objects for a given subject and predicate, e.g., given "Tom has children named <mask>.", the model has to generate the text "Emma, Lucas, Olivia".

Table 1: Templates: We used different templates for each model to fit each pretraining setting.

		Parent-children	Director-titles
BART	Element-valued supervision	{Sbj} has a child named <mask>.	{Sbj} directed a film titled <mask>.
	Set-valued supervision	{Sbj} has children named <mask>.	{Sbj} directed following movies: <mask>.
T5	Element-valued supervision	What is the name of {Sbj}'s child?	What movie did {Sbj} direct?
	Set-valued supervision	What are the names of {Sbj}'s children?	What are the titles of movies {Sbj} directed?

4.2 Handling of 1-to-N Relational Knowledge

We investigate the behavior of LMs for 1-to-N relational knowledge when explicitly trained. Specifically, we use the sequence-to-sequence model to generate variable-length responses to inputs.

As described in § 3, the two abilities necessary for LMs to handle 1-to-N relational knowledge are (i)memorizing multiple discretely appearing objects and (ii)enumerating memorized objects without excess or deficiency. In this section, we conduct two experiments, each corresponding to the essential abilities.

(i) Memorization The first experiment is aimed at "memorization" through element-valued supervision. Here, 1-to-N relational knowledge is decomposed into a one-to-one form, and we train LMs to memorize multiple objects individually. In the learning process, one object is output in response to an input for a particular subject, and then all objects will be memorized in this fashion. Therefore, the state in which the LMs memorize all N objects can also be paraphrased as the state in which the LMs can output all N objects.

Therefore, the evaluation of whether LMs memorized multiple objects is checked by generating multiple sequences using beam-search. Specifically, N sequences are generated for a subject using the same query as the training data. By checking how many correct objects are included in the sequences, we evaluate how many objects the LMs memorized.

(ii) Enumeration The second experiment attempts to acquire "the ability to enumerate memorized objects." Here, training by set-valued supervision is performed in conjunction with memorization by element-valued supervision. The reason for using the two supervisory methods together is the premise that to enumerate multiple objects, it is necessary to memorize them in the first place. Although it is possible to perform element-valued supervision and then shift to set-valued supervision, catastrophic forgetting of memorized objects may occur during the training of set-valued supervision. Indeed, we have confirmed that catastrophic forgetting of memorized objects occurs during set-valued supervision, so in this paper, the two supervisory methods are used together. For some subjects in the training data, LMs explicitly learn the behavior of enumerating the objects in response to queries that explicitly ask for multiple objects. We then test whether set-valued supervision allows LMs to enumerate objects for other subjects as well, i.e., whether they can generalize the ability to enumerate.

5 Experimental setup

5.1 Synthetic Data

In the following experiments, we uniquely prepared the 1-to-N dataset to measure how well LMs can accurately store plenty of facts. Specifically, we randomly obtained canonical names of parents and their two to four children from Wikidata (Vrandečić and Krötzsch, 2014). We also randomly obtained the canonical names of directors and their two to four representative films from IMDb Datasets[1]. Therefore, by preparing 1-to-2, 1-to-3, and 1-to-4 relational knowledge, we will observe how LMs performance changes as the number of objects increases. We only collected data that meets the following conditions.

- To ensure that all entities are distinguishable, there is no data with the same canonical name across both subjects and objects.
- Only entities consisting of four or fewer words separated by spaces or hyphens are used to adjust for storing difficulty due to word length.

We only consider memorizing and enumerating entities which appear in the training data.

[1]https://www.imdb.com/interfaces/

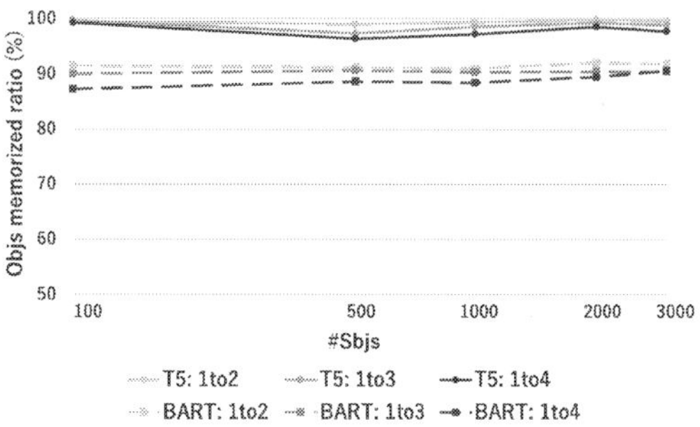

(a) Parent-children dataset

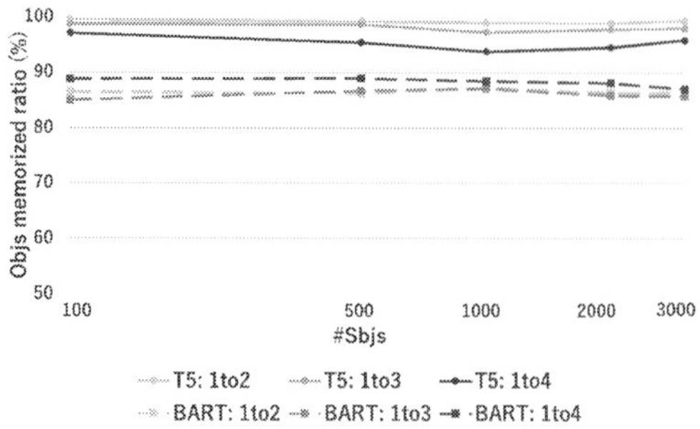

(b) Director-titles dataset

Figure 3: Object-oriented memorization accuracy: showing how many objects LMs memorized

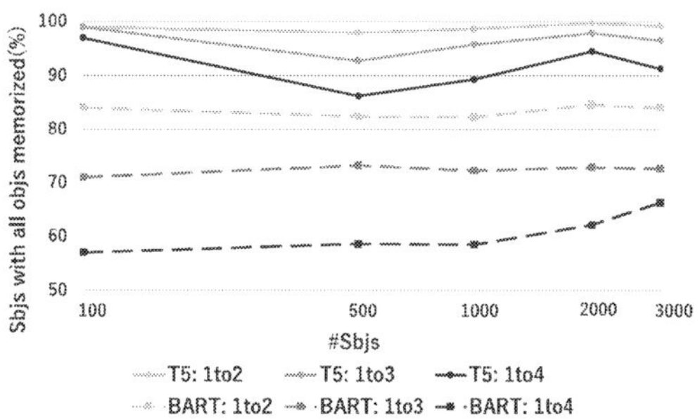

(a) Parent-children dataset

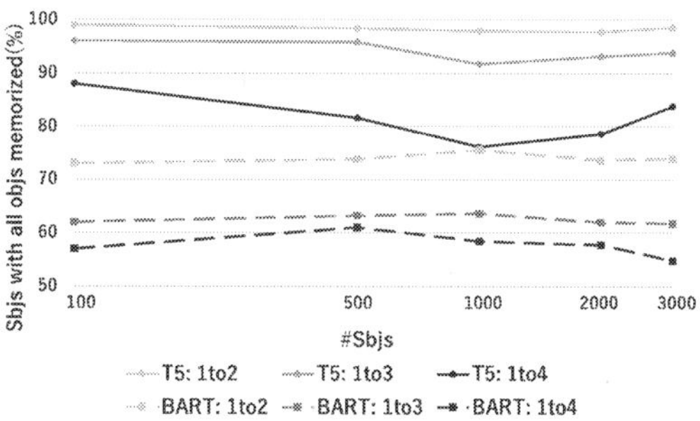

(b) Director-titles dataset

Figure 4: Subjects-oriented memorization accuracy: showing how many subjects are there that LMs memorized their corresponding N objects.

5.2 Models and Training settings

We used the pretrained BART-base (Lewis et al., 2020) and T5-base (Raffel et al., 2019) as the sequence-to-sequence model in the experiments. The training in the two experiments described below (§ 6.1 and § 6.2) was continued until the models strongly overfit the training data. Precisely, we continued training until the accuracy of the training data no longer improved by more than 30 epochs.

The accuracy was calculated as follows: for element-valued supervision, the accuracy was determined by whether the model could generate the correct object for each subject in the input. If the model generated one of the correct N objects for each subject, it was considered correct; otherwise, incorrect. For set-valued supervision, the accuracy was determined by whether the model generated a set of multiple correct objects with no omissions or additions. If the model generated a complete set of correct objects, it was considered correct; otherwise, incorrect.

As detailed training settings, the learning rate was started at 5e-5 in common with BART and T5, and it was reduced by half if the accuracy did not improve by more than three epochs. The batch size was varied according to the model and training data size/domain. AdamW (Loshchilov and Hutter, 2019) was commonly used as the optimizer. In addition, a different template was used for each model so that the input sentence templates were similar to the pretraining settings for each (BART uses <mask> token in pretraining, but T5 does not.) The templates used are listed in Table 1.

6 Experiments

6.1 Element-valued supervision

In the first experiment, we investigated the ability to memorize multiple objects using element-valued supervision. Here, we tested whether the LMs could correctly store N objects associated with a single subject. Specifically, as shown in Figure 2, the learning process of having one object generated for each input sentence, such as "{Subject} has a child named <mask>." or "{Subject} directed a film titled <mask>." was performed for all objects. Thus, the learning setup is such that there are as many target sentences as objects for each input sentence.

Table 2: Accuracy of enumerate operation

	Model	BART-base			T5-base		
	Set-valued supervision ratio	30%	60%	90%	30%	60%	90%
Parent-children	1-to-2	46.7	45.8	49.3	27.0	40.7	**49.5**
	1-to-3	8.33	9.33	9.67	10.7	16.8	**20.7**
	1-to-4	1.00	1.33	2.17	0.500	2.33	**2.67**
Director-titles	1-to-2	42.0	43.3	**44.17**	19.8	24.2	28.7
	1-to-3	22.5	24.2	**26.3**	14.8	15.8	23.7
	1-to-4	6.17	10.7	**11.3**	2.33	3.83	7.00

We then checked the degree to which LMs trained with element-valued supervision could recall multiple objects through the generation of N sequences using beam search. To be precise, N was for the number of objects associated with the input subject, and we analyzed the count of correct objects within those sequences.

In this experiment, we also tested whether the LMs' memorization accuracy changed when the training data size, i.e., the number of entities, was varied. Here, we evaluated this memorization accuracy from two perspectives.

Object-oriented memorization accuracy The first perspective is object-oriented memorization accuracy, shown in Figure 3, which evaluates the degree of recall of objects in the training data. Figure 3a and 3b correspond to the parent-children and director-titles datasets, respectively. The solid blue line corresponds to T5, and the dashed yellow line to BART, with darker colors corresponding to 1toN relational knowledge with more objects. The results show that T5 has better memorization accuracy than BART, although no significant differences by data domain were observed. Also, the larger N, i.e., the greater the number of objects associated with one subject, the more likely N entities could not be memorized.

Subject-oriented memorization accuracy The second perspective, subject-oriented memorization accuracy, evaluated how many subjects were memorized with all related N objects. Specifically, in generating multiple objects by beam search, we show how many subjects existed for which all N objects were generated.

The results are shown in Figure 4, where 4a and 4b correspond to the parent-children and director-title datasets, respectively, as in Figure 3. The results confirmed that, overall, T5 has higher memorization accuracy. Looking at performance by the number of objects, it is clear that, in common with the two data domains and two models, the greater the number of objects, the more difficult it was to remember all of them in conjunction with the subject.

Interestingly, both memorization accuracies in the two perspectives show roughly independent behavior concerning data size. One possible reason for the higher overall memory accuracy of T5 is that the parameter size of the T5-base is about 1.5 times larger than that of BART-base. This may contribute to higher memory accuracy. The fact that 100% memorization accuracy was not achieved for either data size may suggest that memorizing 1-to-N relational knowledge is not easy for LMs. Examples of LMs' predictions are shown in Table 3.

6.2 Element-valued and Set-valued supervision

In this subsequent experiment, the model was trained with element-valued and set-valued supervision to acquire the ability to enumerate all associated objects. More expressly, compared to the first experiment, we additionally employed set-valued supervision, which involved using "{Subject} has children named <mask>." as the input sentence and "{Object1}, {Object2}, ..." as the corresponding target sentence, as an example. This approach aimed to generalize the model's ability to enumerate all accurately memorized objects in response to queries requesting multiple objects.

We conducted both element-valued and set-valued supervision during training. Specifically, we trained LMs using element-valued supervision on all subjects to memorize all associated objects. We fixed the training data size at 3000 subjects for each. Simultaneously, we randomly selected 20% of the subjects, i.e, 600 subjects, as a test set for set-valued supervision. For the remaining 80% of

Table 3: Examples of generated N sequences for element-valued supervision. Showing 1-to-3 relational knowledge, which includes leakage of memorization. Objects with green background color are correct and those with red are incorrect.

Data Domain	1-to-N	Subject	Gold objects	Top-N sequences
Parent-children	1-to-3	Dr. Dre	Hood Surgeon La Tanya Danielle Young Truice Young	BART 1: Hood Surgeon 2: Truice Young 3: Young Hood Surgeon T5 1: Hood Surgeon 2: Truice Young 3: La Tanya Danielle Young
Director-titles	1-to-3	Jack Holton	A Dream for Christmas Escape to Witch Mountain The Wild Country	BART 1: Escape to Witch Mountain 2: A Dream for Christmas 3: The Wild Country T5 1: Escape to Witch Mountain 2: A Dream for Christmas 3: Adventures in Dinosaur City

the subjects, we varied the proportion of subjects for which set-valued supervision was applied (i.e., 30%, 60%, or 90%) to examine whether the generalization ability would change depending on the number of instances that the LMs learned how to enumerate their corresponding objects.

The goal was to investigate how well the model could generalize to subjects in the test set when using set-valued supervision and to determine the impact of varying the proportion of subjects with set-valued supervision on model performance.

The results (Table 2) show that the enumerating accuracy is highest when the supervision ratio is 90% for all, indicating that it is important to have many training instances to generalize the enumerating capability.

Although there are differences in the enumerating accuracy scores across data domains and models, we found a tendency for the enumeration performance to decrease significantly as the number of target words increases.

Error analysis Quantitative error distributions are shown in Table 4, and specific examples of incorrect answers are shown in Table 5. Table 4 shows that for small numbers of objects (e.g., 1-to-2), BART tended to generate incorrect objects (labeled "Incorrect"), while T5 often duplicated the same object (labeled "Duplication"), highlighting a noticeable difference between the two models. As the number of objects increased (e.g., 1-to-3, 1-to-4), both models were more likely to produce wrong answers due to missing objects (labeled "Missing"). The distribution of errors across different datasets was generally similar, but both models were more prone to missing objects in the parent-children dataset, suggesting that the type of entity names might have an impact on the error patterns.

7 Conclusion

We addressed handling 1-to-N relational knowledge by a generative approach using the sequence-to-sequence model. Since little work has been done on 1-to-N relational knowledge in previous studies, we started by organizing the properties of 1-to-N relational knowledge and setting up the capabilities considered necessary for LMs based on these properties.

Specifically, we defined two essential capabilities: "memory of discretely appearing multiple objects" and "enumeration of objects based on memory." Then, we developed training schemes based on these perspectives. We used element-valued supervision and beam search for the former to memorize and evaluate multiple objects. We found that nearly 90% of the objects could be memorized, although we observed a tendency for memory omissions to occur as the number of objects increased. However, we also confirmed that it is challenging to achieve 100% perfect memory.

For the latter, we attempted to generalize "enu-

Table 4: Quantitative error analysis on 90% set-valued supervision: showing the number of incorrect responses generated by the model, categorized into three types of errors. "Incorrect" denotes model-generated sequences that contain one or more incorrect objects. Responses that lack objects are classified as "Missing" (omission of objects), while those with duplicate instances of the same object are labeled as "Duplication."

	Model	BART-base			T5-base		
	Error Type	Incorrect	Missing	Duplication	Incorrect	Missing	Duplication
Parent-children	1-to-2	280	0	18	154	2	147
	1-to-3	229	306	7	93	287	96
	1-to-4	175	406	6	105	380	99
Director-titles	1-to-2	298	0	37	156	1	271
	1-to-3	70	352	20	41	287	130
	1-to-4	25	481	25	37	441	80

Table 5: Examples of enumerating error for the parent-children dataset. The error part is colored in red. These errors are for 1-to-3 relational knowledge and were generated by the T5, which is trained with 90% set-valued supervision.

Error	Subject	Gold and Prediction
Missing	Jeb Bush	Gold: George P. Bush, Noelle Bush, John Bush Jr. Pred: John Bush Jr., Noelle Bush (missing)
Incorrect	Shimon Peres	Gold: Tsvia Walden, Hemi Peres, Yoni Peres Pred: Tsvia Walden, Yoni Peres, Leo Peres
Duplication	Alice Meynell	Gold: Viola Meynell, Everard Meynell, Madeline Lucas Pred: Viola Meynell , Madeline Lucas, Viola Meynell
Excess(Incorrect)	Alan Alda	Gold: Beatrice Alda, Elizabeth Alda, Eve Alda Pred: Elizabeth Alda, Beatrice Alda, Eve Alda, Nanna Alda

meration ability" by set-valued supervision in conjunction with memorization by element-valued supervision. The results showed that learning more data improved the generalization performance for acquiring enumeration ability. However, we also observed the LM's behavior, which aligns with human intuition: the more objects increase, the more difficult it becomes to enumerate all of them correctly. Notably, the generalization performance for 1-to-2 relational knowledge was only about 50% for the test set, and for 1-to-4 relational knowledge, only about 10% generalization performance at most.

For our next steps, we are considering the following approach. The training setup of the current element-valued supervision is characterized by multiple target sentences for one input sentence, which is incompatible with the model's learning algorithm. Therefore, we would like to test a memorizing method using ordinal numerals such as first and second to distinguish each template for N objects. We would also like to investigate this memorization method's effect on the generalization performance of enumeration.

As for enumeration, which has been difficult to generalize, we would like to examine effective means of improving performance for a small number of objects. Specifically, we are considering adjusting the hyperparameters for text generation and verifying whether errors in enumerating will be reduced. After that, we would like to explore learning methods to enumerate N objects without needing hyperparameters adjustment in stages.

Introducing our 1-to-N problem setting into the LMs-as-KBs paradigm opens up many more intriguing challenges. While we investigated this setting under a controlled condition with a uniform frequency of object appearance, the frequency of each of the N objects in a corpus is likely to vary in reality. Furthermore, there may be multiple paraphrases expressing the same relation.

For example, in our study, we only considered the phrase "{Subject} has a child named {Object}." but there are other phrases such as "{Subject}'s child is {Object}." or "{Object} is a daughter of {Subject}." As a primary avenue for future research, we will explore whether LMs can handle 1-to-N relational knowledge effectively under these more complex conditions.

Acknowledgements

This work was supported by JSPS KAKENHI Grant Number 21K17814 and JST CREST Grant Number JPMJCR20D2, Japan.

References

Tom B. Brown, Benjamin Mann, Nick Ryder, Melanie Subbiah, Jared Kaplan, Prafulla Dhariwal, Arvind Neelakantan, Pranav Shyam, Girish Sastry, Amanda Askell, Sandhini Agarwal, Ariel Herbert-Voss, Gretchen Krueger, Tom Henighan, Rewon Child, Aditya Ramesh, Daniel M. Ziegler, Jeffrey Wu, Clemens Winter, Christopher Hesse, Mark Chen, Eric Sigler, Mateusz Litwin, Scott Gray, Benjamin Chess, Jack Clark, Christopher Berner, Sam McCandlish, Alec Radford, Ilya Sutskever, and Dario Amodei. 2020. Language models are few-shot learners. In *Advances in Neural Information Processing Systems 33: Annual Conference on Neural Information Processing Systems 2020, NeurIPS 2020, December 6-12, 2020, virtual.*

Jacob Devlin, Ming-Wei Chang, Kenton Lee, and Kristina Toutanova. 2019. BERT: pre-training of deep bidirectional transformers for language understanding. In *Proceedings of the 2019 Conference of the North American Chapter of the Association for Computational Linguistics: Human Language Technologies, NAACL-HLT 2019, Minneapolis, MN, USA, June 2-7, 2019, Volume 1 (Long and Short Papers)*, pages 4171–4186. Association for Computational Linguistics.

Benjamin Heinzerling and Kentaro Inui. 2021. Language models as knowledge bases: On entity representations, storage capacity, and paraphrased queries. In *Proceedings of the 16th Conference of the European Chapter of the Association for Computational Linguistics: Main Volume, EACL 2021, Online, April 19 - 23, 2021*, pages 1772–1791. Association for Computational Linguistics.

Zhengbao Jiang, Frank F. Xu, Jun Araki, and Graham Neubig. 2020. How can we know what language models know. *Trans. Assoc. Comput. Linguistics*, 8:423–438.

Juho Lee, Yoonho Lee, Jungtaek Kim, Adam R. Kosiorek, Seungjin Choi, and Yee Whye Teh. 2019. Set transformer: A framework for attention-based permutation-invariant neural networks. In *Proceedings of the 36th International Conference on Machine Learning, ICML 2019, 9-15 June 2019, Long Beach, California, USA*, volume 97 of *Proceedings of Machine Learning Research*, pages 3744–3753. PMLR.

Mike Lewis, Yinhan Liu, Naman Goyal, Marjan Ghazvininejad, Abdelrahman Mohamed, Omer Levy, Veselin Stoyanov, and Luke Zettlemoyer. 2020. BART: denoising sequence-to-sequence pre-training for natural language generation, translation, and comprehension. In *Proceedings of the 58th Annual Meeting of the Association for Computational Linguistics, ACL 2020, Online, July 5-10, 2020*, pages 7871–7880. Association for Computational Linguistics.

Ilya Loshchilov and Frank Hutter. 2019. Decoupled weight decay regularization. In *7th International Conference on Learning Representations, ICLR 2019, New Orleans, LA, USA, May 6-9, 2019*. OpenReview.net.

Fabio Petroni, Tim Rocktäschel, Sebastian Riedel, Patrick S. H. Lewis, Anton Bakhtin, Yuxiang Wu, and Alexander H. Miller. 2019. Language models as knowledge bases? In *Proceedings of the 2019 Conference on Empirical Methods in Natural Language Processing and the 9th International Joint Conference on Natural Language Processing, EMNLP-IJCNLP 2019, Hong Kong, China, November 3-7, 2019*, pages 2463–2473. Association for Computational Linguistics.

Colin Raffel, Noam Shazeer, Adam Roberts, Katherine Lee, Sharan Narang, Michael Matena, Yanqi Zhou, Wei Li, and Peter J. Liu. 2019. Exploring the limits of transfer learning with a unified text-to-text transformer. *CoRR*, abs/1910.10683.

Simon Razniewski, Andrew Yates, Nora Kassner, and Gerhard Weikum. 2021. Language models as or for knowledge bases. *CoRR*, abs/2110.04888.

Tara Safavi and Danai Koutra. 2021. Relational world knowledge representation in contextual language models: A review. *CoRR*, abs/2104.05837.

Ilya Sutskever, Oriol Vinyals, and Quoc V. Le. 2014. Sequence to sequence learning with neural networks. In *Advances in Neural Information Processing Systems 27: Annual Conference on Neural Information Processing Systems 2014, December 8-13 2014, Montreal, Quebec, Canada*, pages 3104–3112.

Ashish Vaswani, Noam Shazeer, Niki Parmar, Jakob Uszkoreit, Llion Jones, Aidan N. Gomez, Lukasz Kaiser, and Illia Polosukhin. 2017. Attention is all you need. In *Advances in Neural Information Processing Systems 30: Annual Conference on Neural Information Processing Systems 2017, December 4-9, 2017, Long Beach, CA, USA*, pages 5998–6008.

Denny Vrandečić and Markus Krötzsch. 2014. Wikidata: a free collaborative knowledgebase. *Communications of the ACM*, 57(10):78–85.

Gerhard Weikum, Xin Luna Dong, Simon Razniewski, and Fabian M. Suchanek. 2021. Machine knowledge: Creation and curation of comprehensive knowledge bases. *Found. Trends Databases*, 10(2-4):108–490.

Manzil Zaheer, Satwik Kottur, Siamak Ravanbakhsh, Barnabás Póczos, Ruslan Salakhutdinov, and Alexander J. Smola. 2017. Deep sets. *CoRR*, abs/1703.06114.

Theoretical Linguistics Rivals Embeddings in Language Clustering for Multilingual Named Entity Recognition

Sakura Imai[1], **Daisuke Kawahara**[1], **Naho Orita**[1], **Hiromune Oda**[2]
[1]Waseda University [2]The University of Tokyo
sakura_imai@toki.waseda.jp, {dkw, orita}@waseda.jp
hiromuneoda@g.ecc.u-tokyo.ac.jp

Abstract

While embedding-based methods have been dominant in language clustering for multilingual tasks, clustering based on linguistic features has not yet been explored much, as it remains baselines (Tan et al., 2019; Shaffer, 2021). This study investigates whether and how theoretical linguistics improves language clustering for multilingual named entity recognition (NER). We propose two types of language groupings: one based on morpho-syntactic features in a nominal domain and one based on a head parameter. Our NER experiments show that the proposed methods largely outperform a state-of-the-art embedding-based model, suggesting that theoretical linguistics plays a significant role in multilingual learning tasks.

1 Introduction

Language clustering has been used to facilitate an effective cross-lingual transfer for low-resource languages in various tasks, such as machine translation (Tan et al., 2019). While the majority of recent clustering approaches depend on embeddings from language models, linguistic knowledge has not yet been exploited enough. Previous studies have merely used descriptive typological features (Oncevay et al., 2020) and a coarse language family classification as baselines (Shaffer, 2021). We argue that there is large room for improvement in language clustering using linguistics knowledge.

This study examines two language classifications based on theoretical linguistics and tests their effectiveness in multilingual NER. Multilingual NER is selected because comparison models are available from Shaffer (2021), namely an embedding-based classification and a language family classification. Although there are datasets available for NER in various languages (Tedeschi et al., 2021; Adelani et al., 2021; Rahimi et al., 2019), our study focuses on Indo-European languages because there is a rich body of research in theoretical linguistics.

Our classification approaches draw on morpho-syntactic parameters proposed primarily in theoretical syntax. The first classification is based on a language tree created by Ceolin et al. (2021), which reflects various morpho-syntactic parameters in a nominal domain. The second classification uses the head parameter (Chomsky, 1981), which indicates the "head" of a phrase in relation to its complements. We select these parameters because NER is a task that identifies mentions and types of named entities that are mostly nouns.

We show that clustering languages based on such parameters results in more effective language groupings beyond the state-of-the-art embedding-based method. Moreover, our clustering approaches demonstrate comparable or better performance than a model trained with all Indo-European languages (hence regardless of a substantial difference in the data size). These results suggest that theoretical linguistics has a promising potential in multilingual NLP tasks.

2 Related Work

In the current age of globalization, collecting information using various languages is getting more important than ever. Multilingual models have gained increasing attention for this purpose. Recently, pre-trained large-scale multilingual models using neural networks, such as Multilingual BERT (mBERT) (Devlin et al., 2019) and XLM-RoBERTa (Conneau et al., 2020), have provided competitive results. However, the amount of labeled data available for fine-tuning these multilingual models is highly skewed toward "major" languages. In fact, there are more than 2,000 low-resource languages with little or no labeled data (Joshi et al., 2020).

To alleviate the problem with low-resource languages, cross-lingual transfer learning has been proposed (Artetxe and Schwenk, 2019). The aim of this method is to adapt a language model trained

Proceedings of the 61st Annual Meeting of the Association for Computational Linguistics - Student Research Workshop, pages 139–151
July 10-12, 2023

with high-resource languages to low-resource languages. Various transfer learning methods have been proposed. For example, Patil et al. (2022) proposed a technique using subword units (byte pair encoding (Sennrich et al., 2016)). Ri and Tsuruoka (2022) investigated which conditions make cross-lingual transfer learning possible by conducting artificial language experiments.

Language clustering is another kind of transfer learning method mainly used in machine translation. Tan et al. (2019) compared clustering by language family and by embeddings and reported that the embedding-based clustering better improved translation accuracy. Oncevay et al. (2020) proposed a language clustering method that integrates syntactic features of WALS (Dryer and Haspelmath, 2013) and embeddings from machine translation models. As for NER, Shaffer (2021) compared clustering by language family and by embeddings and reported that the embedding-based clustering outperformed language family clustering. In sum, clustering by linguistic prior was used as baselines, and these baselines did not attain better results than the ones with embeddings.

Other than language clustering, linguistic knowledge has been widely used in various NLP tasks (O'Horan et al., 2016; Gerz et al., 2018; Ponti et al., 2019). For example, some approaches use typological or phylogenetic features in multilingual fine-tuning for cross-lingual transfer (Lin et al., 2019; Pires et al., 2019; Dhamecha et al., 2021; de Vries et al., 2022). Likewise, language family information or typological features, such as word order, have been used in various kinds of multilingual tasks, such as machine translation (Saleh et al., 2021; Chronopoulou et al., 2022), dependency parsing (Ammar et al., 2016), and pre-training (Fujinuma et al., 2022).

Crucially, however, the linguistic information used in all these studies is limited to the extent of language family and typological features which are directly observable. No studies using more profound linguistic knowledge have been conducted. Therefore, it remains to be seen whether and to what extent linguistic knowledge other than linguistic family and typological features could help improve clustering for multilingual tasks.

3 Language Clustering using Parameters of Theoretical Linguistics

3.1 Linguistic Parameters

As shown in Section 2, multiple studies have attempted to use linguistic priors for multilingual NLP tasks. However, the knowledge used in these studies remains descriptive and unable to represent the internal nature of language.

Thus, we use "linguistic parameters" proposed by Chomsky (1981) in theoretical linguistics for our clustering to capture the characteristics of language that cannot be seen superficially and cannot be captured by phylogenetic comparison of languages. As seen in Sections 3.3 and 3.4, linguistic parameters are morpho-syntactically more detailed and abstract than typological features in WALS that have been used in the previous studies. We apply these parameters to our clustering methods and conduct experiments on multilingual NER.

3.2 Selection of Tasks and Languages

This study selects NER as the target task for comparison with Shaffer's (2021) study, which tried to improve the performance of multilingual NER by clustering languages based on embeddings and language family.

We use 25 languages that belong to the Indo-European language family because there is a sufficient amount of annotated data available for NER, and there is a rich body of literature in theoretical linguistics.

Table 1 lists the languages used in this study. Each language is represented by its ISO 639-1 language code[1], which is summarized in Appendix (Table 10). In the previous study (Shaffer, 2021), sub-families such as Celtic were not used, despite that their NER data are available. To conduct more comprehensive experiments, we select languages from a broader range of sub-families.

3.3 Clustering based on Nominal Parameters

NER is a task that identifies and classifies entities in texts. Since the named entities are mostly represented as noun phrases, clustering languages by features related to a noun phrase would be effective for training. Thus, we focus on morpho-syntactic parameters that capture cross-linguistic similarities and differences in a nominal domain.

[1] http://www.infoterm.info/standardization/iso_639_1_2002.php

Sub-family	Languages	Shaffer (2021)
Romance	ro, fr, es, pt, it, scn	fr, es, it
Germanic	af, nl, de, is, en, da, no, fo	de, en, da
Greek	el	-
Slavic	bg, pl, ru, sl, hr	ru
Indo-Iranian	ps, mr, hi	hi
Celtic	cy, ga	-

Table 1: The languages used in this study and Shaffer (2021).

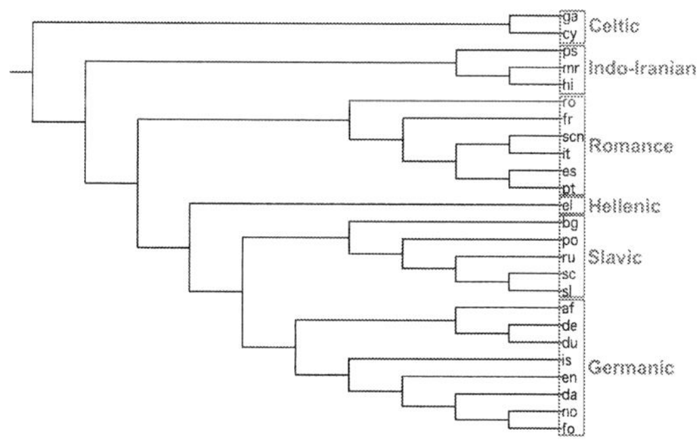

Figure 1: Language tree by Ceolin et al. (2021).

To cluster languages by nominal parameters, we use a language tree proposed by Ceolin et al. (2021). They classified Indo-European languages based on 94 morpho-syntactic parameters in a nominal domain. An example of nominal parameters, "grammaticalized gender" is shown in (1).

(1) a. il libro
the.MASC book.MASC

b. la macchina
the.FEM car.FEM

In languages such as Italian, the gender of definite articles varies depending on the gender of nouns as seen in (1a, 1b).

This parameter is just one example and many other types of parameters are considered in (Ceolin et al., 2021): e.g., the presence/absence of the definite article added to the relative clause and the presence/absence of genitive markings using an adposition. These parameters have often been discussed in theoretical syntax, but many of them are not included in descriptive studies, such as WALS. The relevant language tree is shown in Figure 1, which was created by Ceolin et al. (2021) based on the inter-lingual distances.[2]

To make clusters, we incrementally combine sub-families close to each other in the language tree. For example, to create 3 clusters, we first combine

#	Sub-family
1	Germanic, Slavic, Hellenic, Romance
2	Indo-Iranian
3	Celtic

Table 2: Clustering by Figure 1 (number of clusters: 3).

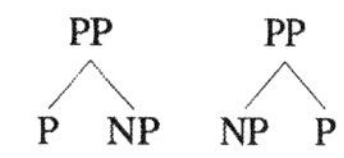

Figure 2: Head-initial (left) and head-final (right) of pre/postpositional phrase (PP).

Germanic and Slavic because they are close to each other in the tree (Figure 1). Hellenic and then Romance are merged into the German-Slavic group. Celtic and Indo-Iranian remain as independent clusters. Table 2 summarizes these 3 clusters. For our experiments, the number of clusters is determined by the elbow method described in Section 4.2.

3.4 Clustering based on the Head Parameter

To identify named entities in text, a language model may use contextual information surrounding the noun phrases. Since a noun phrase is often a part of a verb phrase as an object or a part of an adpositional phrase (i.e., a pre/postpositional phrase) that represents location, clustering languages by this kind of structural information may lead to a more effective clustering.

Based on this hypothesis, the same 25 Indo-European languages are clustered by the head parameter. The head parameter determines where the head (the "core" element) of a phrase is placed in the phrase structure. For example, in the case of a pre/postpositional phrase (PP), if it is head-initial, the head, i.e., the preposition (P), precedes the noun phrase (NP), and vice versa (see Figure 2).

The crucial difference from previous descriptive work such as WALS is that the word order of modifiers (e.g., adverbs for verbs and adjectives for nouns) is irrelevant, but the order of the head (e.g., V in VP) and its complement (e.g., NP for V in VP) is crucial under the head parameter. This is different from the word order classifications in WALS, where the order of the head is no more or less significant than that of modifiers and the notion of head is much less clear. Thus, the head parameter offers a simpler and more abstract framing of word order in a phrase, which crucially focuses on the position of the head and its complement in a phrase. Table 3 shows the classification based on the head

[2] https://github.com/AndreaCeolin/Boundaries

Head Parameter	Sub-Family
Mainly Head-Initial	Romance, Slavic, Germanic, Greek, Celtic
Mainly Head-Final	Indo-Iranian

Table 3: Clustering based on the head parameter (number of clusters: 2).

parameter.

4 NER Experiments

We conduct experiments on NER using the two clustering methods described in Section 3.

4.1 Experimental Setup

There are several datasets available for NER experiments, such as WikiNEuRal (Tedeschi et al., 2021) and MasakhaNER (Adelani et al., 2021). Among them, we select the WikiAnn dataset[3] (Rahimi et al., 2019) because it has an extensive coverage of Indo-European languages, where these languages have been well-documented in theoretical linguistics. The WikiAnn dataset consists of Wikipedia articles for 176 languages that are automatically annotated with three types of named entities: LOC (location), PER (person), and ORG (organization).

An overview of our experiments is shown in Figure 3. First, the training sets of all languages in a cluster are concatenated and fed into a pre-trained language model for fine-tuning. We use XLM-RoBERTa-base[4] (Conneau et al., 2020) as the pre-trained language model. This model has 270M parameters and was trained on 2.5TB of CommonCrawl data in 100 languages. Then, the evaluation set of each language in the cluster is used to evaluate and calculate an F1 score. We perform this evaluation for each cluster using the seqeval framework (Nakayama, 2018) three times and calculate the mean F1 score and standard deviation. For all experiments, we set the batch size to 32, the maximum length of the input to 512, and the learning rate to 5e-5 and conduct three epochs of fine-tuning. We use NVIDIA V100 SXM2 on ABCI[5] as our computing resource, and the average time cost for fine-tuning is approximately one hour.

In our experiments, we select three classifications as baselines. The first is monolingual in which each language is taken as a single cluster. The second is a clustering based on embeddings, and the last is Indo-European all languages (IE-all). Since all the target languages shown in Table 1 are phylogenetically classified into the Indo-European family, using "language family" for clustering corresponds to using a single cluster consisting of all languages in this study.

4.2 Clustering based on Embeddings

We use the embedding-based clustering method proposed by Shaffer (2021) for comparison. An overview of embedding-based clustering is shown in Figure 4.

First, a pre-trained language model is fine-tuned with a language identification task using the WikiAnn training sets. We trained XLM-RoBERTa-base for 3 epochs, setting the batch size to 32, the random seed to 42, and the learning rate to 5e-5. Following Shaffer (2021), we tried a single seed for this preliminary experiment. Language identification is the task of predicting which language the input text is written. We use all 25 languages in Table 1.

Next, each sentence in the WikiAnn validation sets is given to the fine-tuned XLM-RoBERTa model to obtain embeddings from the [CLS] tokens. Based on the obtained embeddings, clustering is performed recursively by agglomerative clustering. We then label the cluster for each input sentence and choose the most frequent cluster for each language among its sentences.

Table 4 shows the resulting clusters using 1,000 and 10,000 samples from the validation set for each language in the WikiAnn dataset. 1,000 and 10,000 are the maximum number of inputs from the validation sets, respectively. For languages that have the validation samples for less than the limits, all samples are used to obtain embeddings.

The optimal number of clusters is determined to be 3 by the elbow method (Thorndike, 1953) when comparing with the clustering method using the nominal parameters described in Section 3 (see Section 5.1 for the experimental results with other numbers of clusters {2, 4, 5}). The elbow method is used to align our embedding-based method with Shaffer's (2021) study, to make a comparison with the clusterings by the nominal parameters. The number of clusters is aligned to 2 to generate clusters when compared with the clustering method using the head parameter.

[3]https://huggingface.co/datasets/wikiann
[4]https://huggingface.co/xlm-roberta-base
[5]https://abci.ai/

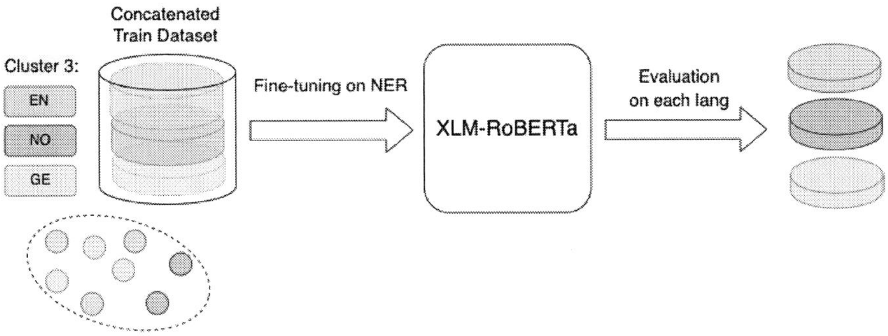

Figure 3: Outline of our experiments on named entity recognition.

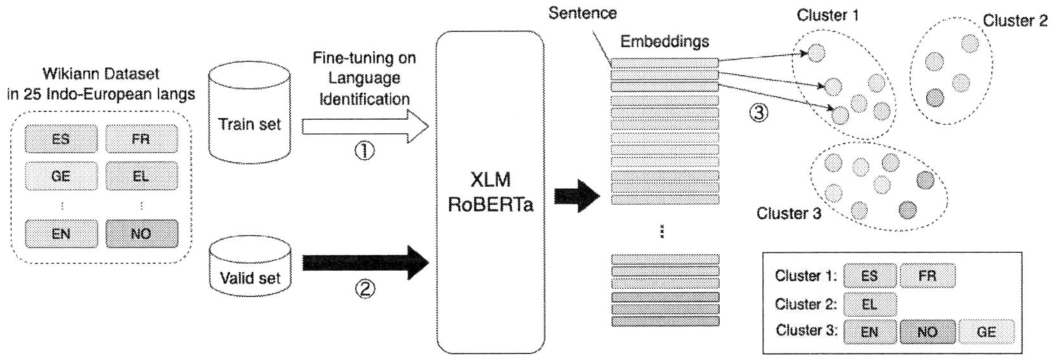

Figure 4: Overview of embedding-based clustering a la Shaffer (2021): The details of this method are described in Section 4.2.

#	Languages 1,000 samples	 10,000 samples
1	cy, ga, ps, mr, hi, ro, fr, bg, pl, ru, sl, hr, af, nl, de, is, en, da, no, fo	ga, ro, fr, es, pt, it, scn, pl, sl, hr, de, en
2	es, pt, it, scn	mr, hi, ru, af, nl, is, da, no, fo
3	el	cy, ps, el, bg

Table 4: Embedding-based clustering results when using 1,000 and 10,000 samples from validation sets from the WikiAnn dataset (number of clusters: 3).

4.3 Results

Table 5 shows the comparisons in the NER evaluations of monolinguals and the clusterings using the nominal parameters, embeddings (1,000 and 10,000 samples), and all languages in Indo-European family (IE-all). Table 6 shows the results with the head parameter.

We first compare the NER evaluations of the clusterings based on the morpho-syntactic parameters and embeddings. The NER evaluations using the nominal parameters (Table 5) show that the clustering by the nominal parameters is superior to that of by embeddings. More than 70% of all the target languages attained the better scores. The clustering based on the head parameter (Table 6) outperformed the embedding-based clusterings as well, achieving the best scores in 80% of the target languages.

We then compare our methods using morpho-syntactic parameters with a model using all the Indo-European languages (IE-all). As for the number of languages that achieved the best score, 11 languages attained better scores with the clustering by the nominal parameters. This is slightly lower than the scores with the IE-all, which was 14 languages (Table 5). The clustering based on the head parameter scored the best in that approximately 70% of all the target languages outperformed the model with the IE-all (Table 6).

5 Analysis

5.1 Quantitative Analysis

Our parameter-based methods significantly outperformed the embedding-based method as in Section

lang	#train	mono	3 clusters			IE-all
			noun	#1000	#10000	
cy	10,000	91.09	91.57	91.73	92.42	**92.95**
ga	1,000	76.51	**85.72**	84.11	84.43	84.90
ps	100	0.00	**55.92**	54.68	53.32	52.22
mr	5,000	85.50	86.96	87.93	**88.58**	88.34
hi	5,000	86.06	86.89	89.18	**89.90**	89.47
ro	20,000	92.64	**94.32**	94.04	93.98	94.18
fr	20,000	88.99	91.04	90.74	90.53	**91.05**
es	20,000	89.19	91.51	91.34	90.52	**91.63**
pt	20,000	90.24	92.11	91.79	91.43	**92.15**
it	20,000	90.79	**92.22**	91.93	91.52	92.06
scn	100	1.18	80.08	75.58	77.12	**81.04**
el	20,000	90.07	**91.21**	90.40	90.07	91.04
bg	20,000	92.48	93.25	92.64	93.34	**93.42**
pl	20,000	89.86	91.34	91.12	91.22	**91.43**
ru	20,000	88.52	89.96	89.32	**90.02**	89.88
sl	15,000	93.02	**93.89**	93.65	93.88	93.86
hr	20,000	90.90	92.05	91.88	**92.06**	92.02
af	5,000	89.06	91.19	91.51	90.75	**91.80**
nl	20,000	90.64	**92.59**	91.74	92.17	92.49
de	20,000	87.47	88.59	88.13	88.31	**88.70**
is	1,000	73.98	87.54	86.75	87.44	**88.29**
en	20,000	82.27	84.12	**84.22**	83.97	84.01
da	20,000	91.73	**93.15**	92.59	93.03	93.04
no	20,000	91.98	93.32	93.14	93.24	**93.49**
fo	100	0.00	86.61	86.35	87.44	**87.69**

Table 5: Nominal parameters clustering evaluations (F1). Each score is the mean over 3 training runs. The highest score for each language is indicated in **bold**.

lang	#train	mono	2 clusters			IE-all
			head	#1000	#10000	
cy	10,000	91.09	**93.15**	92.22	91.88	92.95
ga	1,000	76.51	**85.37**	84.11	84.38	84.90
ps	100	0.00	**55.92**	55.31	55.02	52.22
mr	5,000	85.50	86.96	**88.71**	88.29	88.34
hi	5,000	86.06	86.89	**89.48**	89.42	89.47
ro	20,000	92.64	**94.43**	94.04	94.17	94.18
fr	20,000	88.99	**91.10**	90.74	90.56	91.05
es	20,000	89.19	**91.66**	91.34	90.52	91.63
pt	20,000	90.24	92.00	91.79	91.43	**92.15**
it	20,000	90.79	92.03	91.93	91.52	**92.06**
scn	100	1.18	77.04	75.58	77.12	**81.04**
el	20,000	90.07	**91.49**	90.91	91.28	91.04
bg	20,000	92.48	**93.60**	93.22	93.34	93.42
pl	20,000	89.86	91.38	91.12	91.33	**91.43**
ru	20,000	88.52	89.86	89.77	**89.98**	89.88
sl	15,000	93.02	**93.97**	93.65	93.95	93.86
hr	20,000	90.90	**92.27**	91.88	92.07	92.02
af	5,000	89.06	91.70	91.30	91.73	**91.80**
nl	20,000	90.64	**92.56**	91.90	92.23	92.49
de	20,000	87.47	**89.06**	88.13	88.61	88.70
is	1,000	73.98	88.04	87.28	87.63	**88.29**
en	20,000	82.27	**84.37**	84.22	84.02	84.01
da	20,000	91.73	**93.39**	92.76	92.91	93.04
no	20,000	91.98	93.46	93.05	93.34	**93.49**
fo	100	0.00	88.21	87.58	**88.70**	87.69

Table 6: Head parameter clustering evaluations (F1). Each score is the mean over 3 training runs. The highest score for each language is indicated in **bold**.

4.3. This suggests that the parameters in theoretical linguistics have a yet-to-be-explored potential in multilingual NLP. This section provides some more detailed analysis that supports this claim.

Clustering results First, we observe some unstable results in the embedding-based clustering. Table 4 shows that the resulting clusters greatly differ depending on the number of samples used to obtain embeddings. Thus, the embedding-based clustering could lead to inconsistent results and may not always be the most effective method.

The elbow method Moreover, we found that the optimal number of clusters determined by the elbow method did not result in the best performance in the embedding-based approach. For example, while the elbow method identified 3 clusters as optimal, the best scores were obtained when the number of clusters was 5 with 10,000 samples. This indicates that the optimal number of clusters obtained by the elbow method may not always be the most effective one, at least in NER.[6] Thus, we examine the results with different numbers of clusters. In particular, we compare clustering by embeddings and by the nominal parameters.[7] Tables 7 and 8 show the resulting clusters obtained by the embedding-based clustering when $k = 2, 3, 4, 5$ and Table 9 shows the NER results using these clusters and the results using the nominal parameters.

Sample size In the results of embedding-based clustering, the clustering with 10,000 samples always outperforms the clustering with 1,000 samples, regardless of the number of clusters. Thus, the following compares clustering by the nominal parameters and by the embeddings with 10,000 samples. Overall, clustering by the nominal parameters achieved better scores than by embeddings, except in the case of 5 clusters. When the number of the clusters is 5, 11 languages achieved better scores in the nominal parameters while 13 languages did so in the embedding-based clustering. We think this difference is due to the biased distribution in Cluster #1 of the embedding-based clustering (Table 8), i.e., 18 languages out of 25 languages are clustered together, while the clusters obtained by the nom-

[6] Shaffer (2021) also used the elbow method to determine the number of clusters (which was 4) but their experiments did not test other numbers of clusters.

[7] While there are only 2 clusters available in the head-parameter classification (i.e., either head-initial or head-final), we could test different numbers of clusters using the nominal parameters.

#	The number of clusters 2	3	4	5
1	cy, ps, mr, hi, el, bg, ru, af, nl, is, da, no, fo	cy, ps, el, bg	cy, ps, el, bg	cy, ps, bg
2	ga, ro, fr, es, pt, it, scn, pl, sl, hr, de, en	ga, ro, fr, es, pt, it, scn, pl, sl, hr, de, en	ga, ro, fr, es, pt, it, scn, pl, sl, hr, de, en	ga, ro, fr, es, pt, it, scn, pl, sl, hr, de, en
3	-	mr, hi, ru, af, nl, is, da, no, fo	mr, hi, af, nl	mr, hi, af, nl
4	-	-	ru, is, da, no, fo	ru, is, da, no, fo
5	-	-	-	el

Table 7: Embedding-based clustering with different cluster numbers (using 1,000 samples).

#	The number of clusters 2	3	4	5
1	cy, ga, ps, mr, hi, ro, fr, el, bg, pl, ru, sl, hr, af, nl, de, is, en, da, no, fo	cy, ga, ps, mr, hi, ro, fr, bg, pl, ru, sl, hr, af, nl, de, is, en, da, no, fo	cy, ga, ps, mr, hi, ro, fr, pl, ru, sl, hr, af, nl, de, is, en, da, no, fo	cy, ga, ps, mr, hi, ro, fr, pl, sl, hr, af, nl, de, is, en, da, no, fo
2	es, pt, it, scn	es, pt, it, scn	es, pt, it, scn	es, pt, it, scn
3	-	el	el	el
4	-	-	bg	bg
5	-	-	-	ru

Table 8: Embedding-based clustering with different cluster numbers (using 10,000 samples).

inal parameters distribute relatively evenly (Cluster #1{Germanic, Slavic}, #2{Hellenic}, #3{Romance}, #4{Indo-Iranian}, #5{Celtic}). Despite of this difference in the training data, clustering by nominal parameters achieved comparable results.

NER results with IE-all We have also run the NER experiments using all the Indo-European languages (see IE-all in Tables 5 and 6). Since this contains the largest training samples in our experiments, the performance would have been better than the other methods using clusters that normally contain the smaller training data. However, the nominal parameters showed comparable results, and the head parameter outperformed better than the IE-all. Together with the comparison results from the embedding-based method above, we argue that the parameters from theoretical linguistics have a potential to mitigate the data sparsity problem that has been present in the multilingual NLP tasks.

Methodological compatibility Another point to note is that some languages seem to be more compatible with a particular method than others. For example, one of low-resource languages, Pashto (ps) and some high-resource languages, such as Romanian (ro) and Danish (da), showed the best scores when using the clusters obtained by our parameter-based approach. On the other hand, Siciliano (scn) with the IE-all and relatively low-resource languages such as Marathi (mr) and Hindi (hi) with the embedding-based clustering demonstrated the best scores. These results indicate that different methods might have captured different aspects of languages regardless of the amount of data and that linguistic properties effective in clustering may differ depending on language.

5.2 Qualitative Analysis

This section attempts to provide some qualitative analysis based on the predictions obtained in the NER evaluations. We use the prediction data in English from our results of the head parameter clustering (Table 3) and the embedding-based clustering with 10,000 samples (Table 4). In the following examples, **h** indicates a prediction result from the head parameter clustering, which is correct. The notation **e** indicates a prediction from the embedding-based clustering, which is incorrect.

In (2h), the named entity representing an organization (ORG) "Allen Fieldhouse" appears after the preposition "at". It is clearly predictable to English speakers that words representing location (LOC) or ORG appear after "at", while it is less likely with words describing person (PER). However, the type of entity was not correctly predicted with the embedding-based clustering (2e). The correct prediction in (2h) seems reasonable if identification of the head along with its complement could facilitate inferring the contexts where a named entity occurs.

lang	#train	2 clusters			3 clusters			4 clusters			5 clusters		
		noun	#1000	#10000	noun	#1000	#10000	noun	#1000	#10000	noun	#1000	#10000
cy	10,000	91.57	**92.22**	91.88	91.57	91.73	**92.42**	91.57	91.73	**91.98**	91.57	91.27	**92.64**
ga	1,000	**85.72**	84.11	84.38	**85.72**	84.11	84.43	**85.72**	84.11	84.53	**85.72**	84.11	85.13
ps	100	53.97	**55.31**	55.02	**55.92**	54.68	53.32	**55.92**	54.68	55.37	**55.92**	52.97	53.54
mr	5,000	88.34	**88.71**	88.29	86.96	87.93	**88.58**	86.96	87.38	**88.09**	86.96	87.38	**88.13**
hi	5,000	**90.09**	89.48	89.42	86.89	89.18	**89.90**	86.89	88.66	**89.70**	86.89	88.66	**88.98**
ro	20,000	**94.32**	94.04	94.17	**94.32**	94.04	93.98	93.69	**94.04**	94.02	93.69	94.04	**94.06**
fr	20,000	**91.01**	90.74	90.56	**91.04**	90.74	90.53	90.39	**90.74**	90.52	90.39	**90.74**	90.32
es	20,000	**91.38**	91.34	90.52	**91.51**	91.34	90.52	90.96	**91.34**	90.52	90.96	**91.34**	90.52
pt	20,000	**92.14**	91.79	91.43	**92.11**	91.79	91.43	91.57	**91.79**	91.43	91.57	**91.79**	91.43
it	20,000	**92.16**	91.93	91.52	**92.22**	91.93	91.52	91.54	**91.93**	91.52	91.54	**91.93**	91.52
scn	100	76.54	75.58	**77.12**	**80.08**	75.58	77.12	76.77	75.58	**77.12**	76.77	75.58	**77.12**
el	20,000	91.18	90.91	**91.28**	**91.21**	90.40	90.07	**91.18**	90.40	90.07	**90.07**	90.07	**90.07**
bg	20,000	**93.44**	93.22	93.34	93.25	92.64	**93.34**	**93.18**	92.64	92.48	**93.19**	92.58	92.48
pl	20,000	**91.45**	91.12	91.33	**91.34**	91.12	91.22	91.19	91.12	**91.23**	91.18	91.12	**91.24**
ru	20,000	**90.01**	89.77	89.98	89.96	89.32	**90.02**	**89.97**	89.18	89.66	**89.81**	89.18	88.52
sl	15,000	93.79	93.65	**93.95**	93.89	93.65	**93.88**	**93.93**	93.65	93.61	93.78	93.65	**93.81**
hr	20,000	**92.12**	91.88	92.07	92.05	91.88	**92.06**	91.91	91.88	**92.14**	**91.97**	91.88	91.91
af	5,000	91.16	91.30	**91.73**	91.19	**91.51**	90.75	**91.46**	90.73	91.18	**91.37**	90.73	91.14
nl	20,000	**92.62**	91.90	92.23	**92.59**	91.74	92.17	**92.26**	90.86	92.14	92.14	90.86	**92.20**
de	20,000	88.51	88.13	**88.61**	**88.59**	88.13	88.31	88.25	88.13	**88.33**	88.25	88.13	**88.38**
is	1,000	**87.65**	87.28	87.63	**87.54**	86.75	87.44	**87.92**	86.51	87.77	87.51	86.51	**87.71**
en	20,000	84.11	**84.22**	84.02	84.12	**84.22**	83.97	83.75	**84.22**	83.89	83.83	**84.22**	83.89
da	20,000	**93.10**	92.76	92.91	**93.15**	92.59	93.03	**93.00**	92.43	92.78	92.92	92.43	**92.99**
no	20,000	**93.48**	93.05	93.34	**93.32**	93.14	93.24	**93.31**	92.79	93.27	**93.24**	92.79	93.17
fo	100	87.01	87.58	**88.70**	86.61	86.35	**87.44**	**88.70**	87.72	87.76	86.78	87.72	**88.33**

Table 9: Nominal parameter clustering evaluations for the number of clusters {2, 3, 4, 5} (F1). Each score is the mean over 3 training runs. In each number of clusters, the highest score for each language is indicated in **bold**.

(2) h. His 46 points tied the record for most points scored by an opponent at **Allen Fieldhouse**.
ORG

e. ... an opponent at **Allen Fieldhouse**.
PER

In (3e), a named entity consisted of three words "Arlington National Cemetery" was wrongly predicted to be split into ORG and LOC. This indicates that the named entity is not correctly identified as the complement of "in." Given this, we conjecture that clustering by the head parameter can be helpful in correctly predicting the position of the head in the phrase. Specifically, learning from the sequences of a P-head followed by its NP complement may have facilitated identifying the span of the named entity.

(3) h. He died in 1887 and was buried in **Arlington National Cemetery**.
ORG

e. ... in **Arlington** **National Cemetery**.
ORG **LOC**

5.3 Annotation Errors in the WikiAnn Dataset

When examining the incorrect predictions in English data, we found that the WikiAnn dataset contains some non-negligible annotation errors. From our sampling-based examination, we estimate that approximately 1% of annotation errors could be included in the WikiAnn dataset. Examples of the annotation errors found in the WikiAnn dataset are shown in (4) and (5). In (4), *Cleveland, Ohio* is not an organization name. In (5), although *Sanremo* is a named entity indicating location, the unnecessary brackets "[[" could have caused an error in its annotation.

(4) He was born in **Cleveland , Ohio**.
ORG

(5) Washhouse in [[Sanremo, **Italy**, ...
LOC

Since the annotations of the WikiAnn dataset were machine-generated, some errors could have occurred in its process. However, these annotation errors need to be revised to improve the reliability of NER evaluations.

6 Conclusion

We have proposed two language clustering methods based on the morpho-syntactic parameters proposed in theoretical linguistics. We showed that these clustering methods outperformed the embedding-based clustering in multilingual NER with Indo-European languages. We have also compared the model using all the Indo-European languages as the training data. Despite the large difference in the data size, our approach outperformed this model as well. These results suggest that parameters in theoretical linguistics have a potential utility in multilingual NLP tasks and that this direction is worth exploring.

Future work will extend this approach to other language families as well as different multilingual tasks, such as machine translation. Another direction would be to probe the clusters derived from the embedding-based method to explore features that might not have been captured by our approach or any approaches that make use of explicit linguistic features.

Limitations

The morpho-syntactic parameters used in this study are just a fraction of various other linguistic parameters that have been proposed in theoretical syntax (e.g., Roberts 2019). A set of optimal language parameters for language clustering may vary depending on the target task. It remains to be seen whether and how various parameters in theoretical linguistics could improve different NLP tasks. For example, cross-lingual transfer learning may be performed more effectively by carefully tailoring the linguistic parameters to a particular task, like what we have done for NER.

Related to the above point, one limitation of our approach would be the fact that some languages have not yet been investigated well in theoretical linguistics, particularly some underdocumented or endangered languages. Even as for well-documented languages in theoretical linguistics, some parameters still remain controversial, such as the so-called NP/DP parameter (e.g., Bošković 2012). Thus, our approach proceeds in tandem with the advancement of theoretical linguistics.

Ethics Statement

We used a freely available dataset and a pre-trained model from the Hugging Face Hub for our experiments. We selected a pre-trained model with an appropriate size (XLM-RoBERTa-base) given our purpose of use. We needed to perform many rounds of clustering and fine-tuning for the pre-trained model. Therefore, we set preliminary experiments beforehand with a smaller sample size for each step to ensure that the experiments could be performed effectively.

Acknowledgements

This work was supported by JSPS KAKENHI Grant Number JP21H04901.

References

David Ifeoluwa Adelani, Jade Abbott, Graham Neubig, Daniel D'souza, Julia Kreutzer, Constantine Lignos, Chester Palen-Michel, Happy Buzaaba, Shruti Rijhwani, Sebastian Ruder, Stephen Mayhew, Israel Abebe Azime, Shamsuddeen H. Muhammad, Chris Chinenye Emezue, Joyce Nakatumba-Nabende, Perez Ogayo, Aremu Anuoluwapo, Catherine Gitau, Derguene Mbaye, Jesujoba Alabi, Seid Muhie Yimam, Tajuddeen Rabiu Gwadabe, Ignatius Ezeani, Rubungo Andre Niyongabo, Jonathan Mukiibi, Verrah Otiende, Iroro Orife, Davis David, Samba Ngom, Tosin Adewumi, Paul Rayson, Mofetoluwa Adeyemi, Gerald Muriuki, Emmanuel Anebi, Chiamaka Chukwuneke, Nkiruka Odu, Eric Peter Wairagala, Samuel Oyerinde, Clemencia Siro, Tobius Saul Bateesa, Temilola Oloyede, Yvonne Wambui, Victor Akinode, Deborah Nabagereka, Maurice Katusiime, Ayodele Awokoya, Mouhamadane MBOUP, Dibora Gebreyohannes, Henok Tilaye, Kelechi Nwaike, Degaga Wolde, Abdoulaye Faye, Blessing Sibanda, Orevaoghene Ahia, Bonaventure F. P. Dossou, Kelechi Ogueji, Thierno Ibrahima DIOP, Abdoulaye Diallo, Adewale Akinfaderin, Tendai Marengereke, and Salomey Osei. 2021. MasakhaNER: Named entity recognition for African languages. *Transactions of the Association for Computational Linguistics*, 9:1116–1131.

Waleed Ammar, George Mulcaire, Miguel Ballesteros, Chris Dyer, and Noah A. Smith. 2016. Many languages, one parser. *Transactions of the Association for Computational Linguistics*, 4:431–444.

Mikel Artetxe and Holger Schwenk. 2019. Massively multilingual sentence embeddings for zero-shot cross-lingual transfer and beyond. *Transactions of the Association for Computational Linguistics*, 7:597–610.

Željko Bošković. 2012. *On NPs and Clauses*, page 179–246. De Gruyter Mouton, Berlin, Boston.

Andrea Ceolin, Cristina Guardiano, Giuseppe Longobardi, Monica Alexandrina Irimia, Luca Bortolussi, and Andrea Sgarro. 2021. At the boundaries of syntactic prehistory. *Philosophical Transactions of the Royal Society B*, 376.

Noam Chomsky. 1981. *Lectures on Government and Binding*. De Gruyter, Berlin, Germany.

Alexandra Chronopoulou, Dario Stojanovski, and Alexander Fraser. 2022. Language-family adapters for multilingual neural machine translation. *ArXiv*, abs/2209.15236.

Alexis Conneau, Kartikay Khandelwal, Naman Goyal, Vishrav Chaudhary, Guillaume Wenzek, Francisco Guzmán, Edouard Grave, Myle Ott, Luke Zettlemoyer, and Veselin Stoyanov. 2020. Unsupervised cross-lingual representation learning at scale. In *Proceedings of the 58th Annual Meeting of the Association for Computational Linguistics*, pages 8440–8451, Online. Association for Computational Linguistics.

Wietse de Vries, Martijn Wieling, and Malvina Nissim. 2022. Make the best of cross-lingual transfer: Evidence from POS tagging with over 100 languages. In *Proceedings of the 60th Annual Meeting of the Association for Computational Linguistics (Volume 1: Long Papers)*, pages 7676–7685, Dublin, Ireland. Association for Computational Linguistics.

Jacob Devlin, Ming-Wei Chang, Kenton Lee, and Kristina Toutanova. 2019. BERT: Pre-training of deep bidirectional transformers for language understanding. In *Proceedings of the 2019 Conference of the North American Chapter of the Association for Computational Linguistics: Human Language Technologies, Volume 1 (Long and Short Papers)*, pages 4171–4186, Minneapolis, Minnesota. Association for Computational Linguistics.

Tejas Dhamecha, Rudra Murthy, Samarth Bharadwaj, Karthik Sankaranarayanan, and Pushpak Bhattacharyya. 2021. Role of Language Relatedness in Multilingual Fine-tuning of Language Models: A Case Study in Indo-Aryan Languages. In *Proceedings of the 2021 Conference on Empirical Methods in Natural Language Processing*, pages 8584–8595, Online and Punta Cana, Dominican Republic. Association for Computational Linguistics.

Matthew S. Dryer and Martin Haspelmath, editors. 2013. *WALS Online*. Max Planck Institute for Evolutionary Anthropology, Leipzig.

Yoshinari Fujinuma, Jordan Boyd-Graber, and Katharina Kann. 2022. Match the script, adapt if multilingual: Analyzing the effect of multilingual pretraining on cross-lingual transferability. In *Proceedings of the 60th Annual Meeting of the Association for Computational Linguistics (Volume 1: Long Papers)*, pages 1500–1512, Dublin, Ireland. Association for Computational Linguistics.

Daniela Gerz, Ivan Vulić, Edoardo Maria Ponti, Roi Reichart, and Anna Korhonen. 2018. On the relation between linguistic typology and (limitations of) multilingual language modeling. In *Proceedings of the 2018 Conference on Empirical Methods in Natural Language Processing*, pages 316–327, Brussels, Belgium. Association for Computational Linguistics.

Pratik Joshi, Sebastin Santy, Amar Budhiraja, Kalika Bali, and Monojit Choudhury. 2020. The state and fate of linguistic diversity and inclusion in the NLP world. In *Proceedings of the 58th Annual Meeting of the Association for Computational Linguistics*, pages 6282–6293, Online. Association for Computational Linguistics.

Yu-Hsiang Lin, Chian-Yu Chen, Jean Lee, Zirui Li, Yuyan Zhang, Mengzhou Xia, Shruti Rijhwani, Junxian He, Zhisong Zhang, Xuezhe Ma, Antonios Anastasopoulos, Patrick Littell, and Graham Neubig. 2019. Choosing transfer languages for cross-lingual learning. In *Proceedings of the 57th Annual Meeting of the Association for Computational Linguistics*, pages 3125–3135, Florence, Italy. Association for Computational Linguistics.

Hiroki Nakayama. 2018. seqeval: A python framework for sequence labeling evaluation. Software available from https://github.com/chakki-works/seqeval.

Helen O'Horan, Yevgeni Berzak, Ivan Vulić, Roi Reichart, and Anna Korhonen. 2016. Survey on the use of typological information in natural language processing. In *Proceedings of COLING 2016, the 26th International Conference on Computational Linguistics: Technical Papers*, pages 1297–1308, Osaka, Japan. The COLING 2016 Organizing Committee.

Arturo Oncevay, Barry Haddow, and Alexandra Birch. 2020. Bridging linguistic typology and multilingual machine translation with multi-view language representations. In *Proceedings of the 2020 Conference on Empirical Methods in Natural Language Processing (EMNLP)*, pages 2391–2406, Online. Association for Computational Linguistics.

Vaidehi Patil, Partha Talukdar, and Sunita Sarawagi. 2022. Overlap-based vocabulary generation improves cross-lingual transfer among related languages. In *Proceedings of the 60th Annual Meeting of the Association for Computational Linguistics (Volume 1: Long Papers)*, pages 219–233, Dublin, Ireland. Association for Computational Linguistics.

Telmo Pires, Eva Schlinger, and Dan Garrette. 2019. How multilingual is multilingual BERT? In *Proceedings of the 57th Annual Meeting of the Association for Computational Linguistics*, pages 4996–5001, Florence, Italy. Association for Computational Linguistics.

Edoardo Maria Ponti, Helen O'Horan, Yevgeni Berzak, Ivan Vulić, Roi Reichart, Thierry Poibeau, Ekaterina Shutova, and Anna Korhonen. 2019. Modeling language variation and universals: A survey on typological linguistics for natural language processing. *Computational Linguistics*, 45(3):559–601.

Afshin Rahimi, Yuan Li, and Trevor Cohn. 2019. Massively multilingual transfer for NER. In *Proceedings of the 57th Annual Meeting of the Association for Computational Linguistics*, pages 151–164, Florence, Italy. Association for Computational Linguistics.

Ryokan Ri and Yoshimasa Tsuruoka. 2022. Pretraining with artificial language: Studying transferable knowledge in language models. In *Proceedings of the 60th Annual Meeting of the Association for Computational Linguistics (Volume 1: Long Papers)*, pages 7302–7315, Dublin, Ireland. Association for Computational Linguistics.

Ian Roberts. 2019. *Parameter Hierarchies and Universal Grammar*. Oxford University Press.

Fahimeh Saleh, Wray Buntine, Gholamreza Haffari, and Lan Du. 2021. Multilingual neural machine translation: Can linguistic hierarchies help? In *Findings of the Association for Computational Linguistics: EMNLP 2021*, pages 1313–1330, Punta Cana, Dominican Republic. Association for Computational Linguistics.

Rico Sennrich, Barry Haddow, and Alexandra Birch. 2016. Neural machine translation of rare words with subword units. In *Proceedings of the 54th Annual Meeting of the Association for Computational Linguistics (Volume 1: Long Papers)*, pages 1715–1725, Berlin, Germany. Association for Computational Linguistics.

Kyle Shaffer. 2021. Language clustering for multilingual named entity recognition. In *Findings of the Association for Computational Linguistics: EMNLP 2021*, pages 40–45, Punta Cana, Dominican Republic. Association for Computational Linguistics.

Xu Tan, Jiale Chen, Di He, Yingce Xia, Tao Qin, and Tie-Yan Liu. 2019. Multilingual neural machine translation with language clustering. In *Proceedings of the 2019 Conference on Empirical Methods in Natural Language Processing and the 9th International Joint Conference on Natural Language Processing (EMNLP-IJCNLP)*, pages 963–973, Hong Kong, China. Association for Computational Linguistics.

Simone Tedeschi, Valentino Maiorca, Niccolò Campolungo, Francesco Cecconi, and Roberto Navigli. 2021. WikiNEuRal: Combined neural and knowledge-based silver data creation for multilingual NER. In *Findings of the Association for Computational Linguistics: EMNLP 2021*, pages 2521–2533, Punta Cana, Dominican Republic. Association for Computational Linguistics.

Robert L. Thorndike. 1953. Who belongs in the family? *Psychometrika*, 18:267–276.

A Appendix

The summary of the languages used in our experiments is shown in Table 10.

Table 11 shows the NER evaluations of head parameter-based clustering with standard deviation scores in parentheses.

Tables 12 and 13 represent the NER evaluations when we set the number of clusters to {2, 3} and {4, 5}, respectively, with standard deviations in parentheses (see Section 5.1 for the details).

ISO 639-1 Code	Language	Sub-family
cy ga	Welsh Irish	Celtic
ps mr hi	Pashto Marathi Hindi	Indo-Iranian
ro fr es pt it scn	Romanian French Spanish Portuguese Italian Siciliano	Romance
el	Greek	Hellenic
bg pl ru sl hr	Bulgarian Polish Russian Slovenian Serbo-Croatian	Slavic
af nl de is en da no fo	Afrikaans Dutch German Icelandic English Danish Norwegian Faroese	Germanic

Table 10: The summary of language codes mentioned in this paper, along with the sub-families they belong to.

lang	#train	mono	head	2 clusters #1000	2 clusters #10000	family
cy	10,000	91.09 (0.30)	**93.15 (0.03)**	92.22 (0.37)	91.88 (0.37)	92.95 (0.45)
ga	1,000	76.51 (1.18)	**85.37 (0.54)**	84.11 (0.61)	84.38 (0.21)	84.90 (0.45)
ps	100	0.00 (0.00)	**55.92 (2.84)**	55.31 (1.40)	55.02 (0.76)	52.22 (1.31)
mr	5,000	85.5 (0.03)	86.96 (0.39)	**88.71 (0.66)**	88.29 (0.40)	88.34 (0.37)
hi	5,000	86.06 (0.54)	86.89 (0.30)	**89.48 (0.42)**	89.42 (0.80)	89.47 (0.45)
ro	20,000	92.64 (0.11)	**94.43 (0.27)**	94.04 (0.12)	94.17 (0.11)	94.18 (0.03)
fr	20,000	88.99 (0.14)	**91.10 (0.09)**	90.74 (0.09)	90.56 (0.13)	91.05 (0.15)
es	20,000	89.19 (0.12)	**91.66 (0.31)**	91.34 (0.10)	90.52 (0.19)	91.63 (0.02)
pt	20,000	90.24 (0.06)	92.00 (0.22)	91.79 (0.07)	91.43 (0.06)	**92.15 (0.06)**
it	20,000	90.79 (0.21)	92.03 (0.12)	91.93 (0.11)	91.52 (0.07)	**92.06 (0.10)**
scn	100	1.18 (1.67)	77.04 (1.46)	75.58 (1.20)	77.12 (1.63)	**81.04 (2.88)**
el	20,000	90.07 (0.15)	**91.49 (0.05)**	90.91 (0.08)	91.28 (0.17)	91.04 (0.09)
bg	20,000	92.48 (0.07)	**93.60 (0.17)**	93.22 (0.11)	93.34 (0.03)	93.42 (0.11)
pl	20,000	89.86 (0.08)	91.38 (0.11)	91.12 (0.04)	91.33 (0.10)	**91.43 (0.17)**
ru	20,000	88.52 (0.14)	89.86 (0.16)	89.77 (0.07)	**89.98 (0.12)**	89.88 (0.02)
sl	15,000	93.02 (0.04)	**93.97 (0.27)**	93.65 (0.19)	93.95 (0.10)	93.86 (0.16)
hr	20,000	90.90 (0.22)	**92.27 (0.03)**	91.88 (0.12)	92.07 (0.13)	92.02 (0.04)
af	5,000	89.06 (0.09)	91.70 (0.31)	91.30 (0.57)	91.73 (0.31)	**91.80 (0.20)**
nl	20,000	90.64 (0.15)	**92.56 (0.23)**	91.90 (0.10)	92.23 (0.07)	92.49 (0.07)
de	20,000	87.47 (0.10)	**89.06 (0.32)**	88.13 (0.05)	88.61 (0.06)	88.70 (0.01)
is	1,000	73.98 (2.36)	88.04 (0.40)	87.28 (0.39)	87.63 (0.56)	**88.29 (0.77)**
en	20,000	82.27 (0.14)	**84.37 (0.15)**	84.22 (0.23)	84.02 (0.06)	84.01 (0.09)
da	20,000	91.73 (0.11)	**93.39 (0.27)**	92.76 (0.09)	92.91 (0.15)	93.04 (0.03)
no	20,000	91.98 (0.13)	93.46 (0.16)	93.05 (0.07)	93.34 (0.20)	**93.49 (0.09)**
fo	100	0.00 (0.00)	88.21 (1.52)	87.58 (1.09)	**88.70 (1.22)**	87.69 (0.75)

Table 11: Head parameter clustering evaluations (F1): Each score is the mean over 3 training runs, with a standard deviation in parentheses. The highest score for each language is indicated in **bold**.

lang	#train	2 clusters noun	2 clusters #1000	2 clusters #10000	3 clusters noun	3 clusters #1000	3 clusters #10000
cy	10,000	91.57 (0.12)	**92.22 (0.37)**	91.88 (0.37)	91.57 (0.12)	91.73 (0.03)	**92.42 (0.59)**
ga	1,000	**85.72 (0.04)**	84.11 (0.61)	84.38 (0.21)	**85.72 (0.04)**	84.11 (0.61)	84.43 (0.60)
ps	100	53.97 (3.36)	**55.31 (1.40)**	55.02 (0.76)	**55.92 (2.84)**	54.68 (1.07)	53.32 (2.06)
mr	5,000	88.34 (0.35)	**88.71 (0.66)**	88.29 (0.40)	86.96 (0.39)	87.93 (0.31)	**88.58 (0.44)**
hi	5,000	**90.09 (0.29)**	89.48 (0.42)	89.42 (0.80)	86.89 (0.30)	89.18 (0.54)	**89.90 (0.29)**
ro	20,000	**94.32 (0.10)**	94.04 (0.12)	94.17 (0.11)	**94.32 (0.05)**	94.04 (0.12)	93.98 (0.12)
fr	20,000	**91.01 (0.04)**	90.74 (0.09)	90.56 (0.13)	**91.04 (0.03)**	90.74 (0.09)	90.53 (0.02)
es	20,000	**91.38 (0.18)**	91.34 (0.10)	90.52 (0.19)	**91.51 (0.08)**	91.34 (0.10)	90.52 (0.19)
pt	20,000	**92.14 (0.12)**	91.79 (0.07)	91.43 (0.06)	**92.11 (0.10)**	91.79 (0.07)	91.43 (0.06)
it	20,000	**92.16 (0.15)**	91.93 (0.11)	91.52 (0.07)	**92.22 (0.12)**	91.93 (0.11)	91.52 (0.07)
scn	100	76.54 (0.92)	75.58 (1.20)	**77.12 (1.63)**	**80.08 (2.69)**	75.58 (1.20)	77.12 (1.63)
el	20,000	91.18 (0.21)	90.91 (0.08)	**91.28 (0.17)**	**91.21 (0.01)**	90.40 (0.11)	90.07 (0.15)
bg	20,000	**93.44 (0.07)**	93.22 (0.11)	93.34 (0.03)	93.25 (0.02)	92.64 (0.07)	**93.34 (0.15)**
pl	20,000	**91.45 (0.09)**	91.12 (0.04)	91.33 (0.10)	**91.34 (0.02)**	91.12 (0.04)	91.22 (0.05)
ru	20,000	**90.01 (0.08)**	89.77 (0.07)	89.98 (0.12)	89.96 (0.18)	89.32 (0.06)	**90.02 (0.04)**
sl	15,000	93.79 (0.10)	93.65 (0.19)	**93.95 (0.10)**	93.89 (0.22)	93.65 (0.19)	**93.88 (0.09)**
hr	20,000	**92.12 (0.11)**	91.88 (0.12)	92.07 (0.13)	92.05 (0.07)	91.88 (0.12)	**92.06 (0.11)**
af	5,000	91.16 (0.16)	91.30 (0.57)	**91.73 (0.31)**	91.19 (0.37)	**91.51 (0.40)**	90.75 (0.17)
nl	20,000	**92.62 (0.02)**	91.90 (0.10)	92.23 (0.07)	**92.59 (0.17)**	91.74 (0.12)	92.17 (0.16)
de	20,000	88.51 (0.04)	88.13 (0.05)	**88.61 (0.06)**	**88.59 (0.13)**	88.13 (0.05)	88.31 (0.13)
is	1,000	**87.65 (0.23)**	87.28 (0.39)	87.63 (0.56)	**87.54 (0.24)**	86.75 (0.39)	87.44 (0.16)
en	20,000	84.11 (0.29)	**84.22 (0.23)**	84.02 (0.06)	84.12 (0.09)	**84.22 (0.23)**	83.97 (0.05)
da	20,000	**93.10 (0.11)**	92.76 (0.09)	92.91 (0.15)	**93.15 (0.18)**	92.59 (0.15)	93.03 (0.10)
no	20,000	**93.48 (0.06)**	93.05 (0.07)	93.34 (0.20)	**93.32 (0.13)**	93.14 (0.02)	93.24 (0.06)
fo	100	87.01 (0.90)	87.58 (1.09)	**88.70 (1.22)**	86.61 (0.59)	86.35 (1.26)	**87.44 (0.66)**

Table 12: Nominal parameter clustering evaluations with the number of clusters {2, 3} (F1): Each score is the mean over 3 training runs, with a standard deviation in parentheses. The highest score for each language is indicated in **bold**.

lang	#train	4 clusters noun	4 clusters #1000	4 clusters #10000	5 clusters noun	5 clusters #1000	5 clusters #10000
cy	10,000	91.57 (0.12)	91.73 (0.03)	**91.98 (0.42)**	91.57 (0.12)	91.27 (0.34)	**92.64 (0.13)**
ga	1,000	**85.72 (0.04)**	84.11 (0.61)	84.53 (0.27)	**85.72 (0.04)**	84.11 (0.61)	85.13 (0.81)
ps	100	**55.92 (2.84)**	54.68 (1.07)	55.37 (0.69)	**55.92 (2.84)**	52.97 (2.53)	53.54 (2.79)
mr	5,000	86.96 (0.39)	87.38 (0.86)	**88.09 (0.19)**	86.96 (0.39)	87.38 (0.86)	**88.13 (0.52)**
hi	5,000	86.89 (0.30)	88.66 (0.37)	**89.70 (0.09)**	86.89 (0.30)	88.66 (0.37)	**88.98 (0.38)**
ro	20,000	93.69 (0.04)	**94.04 (0.12)**	94.02 (0.08)	93.69 (0.04)	94.04 (0.12)	**94.06 (0.13)**
fr	20,000	90.39 (0.03)	**90.74 (0.09)**	90.52 (0.21)	90.39 (0.03)	**90.74 (0.09)**	90.32 (0.14)
es	20,000	90.96 (0.13)	**91.34 (0.10)**	90.52 (0.19)	90.96 (0.13)	**91.34 (0.10)**	90.52 (0.19)
pt	20,000	91.57 (0.06)	**91.79 (0.07)**	91.43 (0.06)	91.57 (0.06)	**91.79 (0.07)**	91.43 (0.06)
it	20,000	91.54 (0.06)	**91.93 (0.11)**	91.52 (0.07)	91.54 (0.06)	**91.93 (0.11)**	91.52 (0.07)
scn	100	76.77 (1.32)	75.58 (1.20)	**77.12 (1.63)**	76.77 (1.32)	75.58 (1.20)	**77.12 (1.63)**
el	20,000	**91.18 (0.13)**	90.4 (0.11)	90.07 (0.15)	**90.07 (0.15)**	90.07 (0.15)	**90.07 (0.15)**
bg	20,000	**93.18 (0.10)**	92.64 (0.07)	92.48 (0.07)	**93.19 (0.10)**	92.58 (0.03)	92.48 (0.07)
pl	20,000	91.19 (0.02)	91.12 (0.04)	**91.23 (0.09)**	91.18 (0.10)	91.12 (0.04)	**91.24 (0.05)**
ru	20,000	**89.97 (0.15)**	89.18 (0.18)	89.66 (0.02)	**89.81 (0.20)**	89.18 (0.18)	88.52 (0.14)
sl	15,000	**93.93 (0.18)**	93.65 (0.19)	93.61 (0.02)	93.78 (0.06)	93.65 (0.19)	**93.81 (0.06)**
hr	20,000	91.91 (0.06)	91.88 (0.12)	**92.14 (0.10)**	**91.97 (0.09)**	91.88 (0.12)	91.91 (0.17)
af	5,000	**91.46 (0.70)**	90.73 (0.05)	91.18 (0.12)	**91.37 (0.31)**	90.73 (0.05)	91.14 (0.34)
nl	20,000	**92.26 (0.11)**	90.86 (0.17)	92.14 (0.04)	92.14 (0.14)	90.86 (0.17)	**92.20 (0.15)**
de	20,000	88.25 (0.09)	88.13 (0.05)	**88.33 (0.07)**	88.25 (0.21)	88.13 (0.05)	**88.38 (0.06)**
is	1,000	**87.92 (0.83)**	86.51 (0.09)	87.77 (0.40)	87.51 (0.37)	86.51 (0.09)	**87.71 (0.25)**
en	20,000	83.75 (0.19)	**84.22 (0.23)**	83.89 (0.14)	83.83 (0.03)	**84.22 (0.23)**	83.89 (0.03)
da	20,000	**93.00 (0.05)**	92.43 (0.08)	92.78 (0.09)	92.92 (0.10)	92.43 (0.08)	**92.99 (0.04)**
no	20,000	**93.31 (0.11)**	92.79 (0.00)	93.27 (0.06)	**93.24 (0.07)**	92.79 (0.00)	93.17 (0.13)
fo	100	**88.70 (1.58)**	87.72 (0.82)	87.76 (1.06)	86.78 (2.33)	87.72 (0.82)	**88.33 (0.28)**

Table 13: Nominal parameter clustering evaluations for the number of clusters {4, 5} (F1): Each score is the mean over 3 training runs, with a standard deviation in parentheses. The highest score for each language is indicated in **bold**.

Native Language Prediction from Gaze: a Reproducibility Study

Lina Skerath
IT University of Copenhagen

Paulina Toborek
IT University of Copenhagen

Anita Zielińska
IT University of Copenhagen

Maria Barrett
IT University of Copenhagen
mbarrett@itu.dk

Rob van der Goot
IT University of Copenhagen
robv@itu.dk

Abstract

Numerous studies found that the linguistic properties of a person's native language affect the cognitive processing of other languages. However, only one study has shown that it was possible to identify the native language based on eye-tracking records of natural L2 reading using machine learning. A new corpus allows us to replicate these results on a more interrelated and larger set of native languages. Our results show that comparable classification performance is maintained despite using less data. However, analysis shows that the correlation between L2 eye movements and native language similarity may be more complex than the original study found.

1 Introduction

Research has shown that a speaker's native language can affect their learning and performance in a foreign language (Berkes and Flynn, 2012; Alonso, 2016; Cop et al., 2017). The eye movements of a reader, namely fixations and saccades, are a window to the online cognitive processing of text with milliseconds accurateness (Rayner, 1998). Native speakers of different languages may exhibit different eye movement patterns when reading a foreign language, with those reading in their native language making shorter and more frequent fixations while making longer fixations due to the increased cognitive load when reading in other languages (Hopp, 2010; Rayner et al., 2012; Berzak et al., 2022).

Several researchers have examined eye-movement patterns across different nationalities, exploring various aspects such as sentence reading times, fixation count, and saccade duration (Cop et al., 2015). Roberts and Siyanova-Chanturia (2013) showed that gaze data could be used for examining, e.g., reading processes, second language acquisition, and discourse processing, as well as give relevant insights into fields of second language acquisition and processing. Early research in Native Language Identification (Tsur and Rappoport, 2007) focused on the relationship between a person's native language and their writing in a second language, while Berzak et al. (2017) for the first time predicted a reader's native language using machine learning across four languages (Chinese, Japanese, Portuguese, and Spanish) using only eye-tracking features from natural reading in their second language (L2), English. The study leveraged the knowledge that different languages have unique features, such as word order, grammatical rules, and phonological features, that affect language processing in other languages.

Despite a general interest in eye-tracking corpora for L2 reading, e.g., (Cop et al., 2017), until recently, there has not been a publicly available dataset with enough languages to reproduce the results of Berzak et al. (2017). Berzak et al. (2017) used a subset of the licensed CELER dataset (Berzak et al., 2022) which is the largest eye-tracking corpus by the number of L2 readers encompassing five different native language backgrounds. The Multilingual Eye-movement COrpus (MECO) L2 dataset (Kuperman et al., 2022)[1] comprises English L2 reading by 12 different language backgrounds and allows replication of the findings by Berzak et al. (2017) on a different and larger set of languages which is why we employ the MECO dataset for this study.

In this study, we replicate the study by Berzak et al. (2017) and classify the native language of the reader from eye-tracking records of them reading English from another corpus.[2] We include readers from seven different language backgrounds that are more interrelated than the original study; the

[1] Publicly available at https://osf.io/q9h43/

[2] The code and data used in the project is publicly available at https://github.com/linaskerath/ANLP_project

Proceedings of the 61st Annual Meeting of the Association for Computational Linguistics - Student Research Workshop, pages 152–159
July 10-12, 2023

LANGUAGE	ISO	n PARTICIPANTS
Estonian	et	23
English	en	21
Finnish	fi	23
German	de	23
Hebrew	he	18
Italian	it	20
Spanish	es	21

Table 1: Number of participants by native language and language ISO code in the data set.

linguistic similarity of the languages used in this study is in the range of 0.64–0.89[3]. The original study did not explore languages in this range but only less similar languages (linguistic similarity <.5) plus one very similar language pair (linguistic similarity >.95).

2 Data

The MECO data was collected in 12 eye-tracking laboratories around the world. Participants were young adults ranging from 18 to 39 years old with high levels of L2 proficiency, which was ensured through English instruction in higher education. For more comprehensive information about the dataset, we refer to the authors' paper (Kuperman et al., 2022).

The MECO data set includes eye-tracking input gathered from native speakers of 12 languages recorded during reading an English encyclopedic text. Due to an insufficient number of participants in some of the cohorts, we used the subset of seven languages with the most participants. To avoid overfitting, we randomly undersampled 23 participants for the two largest cohorts, equivalent in size to the third largest group within the dataset as shown in Table 1. Berzak et al. (2017) used 36 to 37 readers for each language.

We only use the texts read by all the participants (also named "shared regime" in Berzak et al. (2017)). The total amount of words read per participant is 595 words, while the original study used 900 words. The feature set employed comprises three word-based measurements: First Fixation duration (FF), First Pass duration (FP) which is the sum of all fixations during the first pass reading of the word, and Total fixation duration (TF).

[3]The calculation is explained in §3.3.1

3 Methods

In this section, we describe the methods employed to replicate Berzak et al. (2017), giving a detailed description of the steps deviating from the setup of the original study.

3.1 Features

All data gaps encountered in the MECO dataset related to words marked as skipped by participants during reading, so it is legitimized to replace such shortages with zeros. Additionally, following the approach of the original research, we normalize all fixation times with the reading time of the entire sentence. The final data set consists of three fixation measures columns per word or cluster, where each row represents data collected from one person.

Words in Fixed Context (WFC) The WFC feature set considers the fixation times for specific words, and no aggregation is performed on the unigram level. The bigrams and trigrams fixation times are then obtained by simply summing values of unigrams that are a part of the interest area. Columns of the dataset consist of the 3 features for every n-gram in the corpus - 5364 features in total.

Syntactic Clusters (SC) In Berzak et al. (2017), syntactic features were obtained from the original Penn Treebank. As no manually annotated syntactic features are available for our data we use predicted syntactic information instead (described in detail in Appendix B). Following Berzak et al. (2017) we use the average FF, FP and TF over n-grams (n=1-3) of the UPOS labels, PTB POS tags, and UD dependency labels as features. For example: the average fixation time of a participant on the UPOS sequence ADV ADJ is a single feature.

Information Clusters (IC) Next to grouping the features by syntactic labels, the average fixation times were calculated for clusters created by the length of the words, measured as a number of characters. For bi- and trigrams, lengths of words were summed and thus clusters were created based on this sum.

3.2 Model

For interpretation, we compare to a majority class baseline. Following the original paper, we use a log-linear model to obtain the Native Language Identification from Reading (NLIR) performance as well as the model-based language similarity (3.3.2). We implement the model using scikit-learn (Pedregosa

	Shared regime		
Majority Class	15.44		
	unigrams	+bigrams	+trigrams
IC	47.52	48.19	48.86
SC	57.62	73.29	76.57
SC+IC	52.29	73.29	77.95
WFC	**81.29**	79.29	77.95

Table 2: NLIR results for log-linear model and majority class baseline.

et al., 2011) and use the 'lbfgs' solver in accordance with the original paper. A reader's native language encoded as a categorical variable is used as the model's target variable. We report our results based on 10-fold cross-validation. To preserve a similar distribution of languages in train and test data, we employ a stratified K-Folds split. We train the same model on the three feature sets described in the previous section and an additional combination of SC and IC feature sets.

To ensure comparability with the original paper despite the different amounts of languages, we analyze model performance with different amounts of languages. We train the model on each possible combination of languages and group them by the number of languages. We take the mean accuracy score of each group size and plot the results (figure 1). We note that our classes are slightly imbalanced, so arguably F1 could be a better metric but to compare to previous work and because the classes are almost balanced, we choose to use accuracy.

3.3 Similarity metrics

Berzak et al. (2014, 2017) suggest a link between English as a second language (ESL) production and linguistic similarities. To recreate the language similarity plots from the original study, we derive the same model-based metric and a cosine similarity based on syntactic and geographical features of a language.

3.3.1 Linguistic-based similarity

We use the same procedure and data as the original study to derive this similarity metric.The data is obtained from URIEL Typological Compendium (Littell et al., 2017a). Information selected is data derived from the World Atlas of Language Structures, features from Syntactic Structures of the World's Languages, and data from parsing the prose topological descriptions in Ethnologue. This information is supplemented by data on the languages belonging to different families, retrieved from Glottolog's world language tree. We use lang2vec (Littell et al., 2017b) for obtaining the complete feature vectors (with KNN completion). After truncating features with the same values among all languages,[4] we get a total of 189 features. The similarity scores between languages are then calculated as a cosine similarity of their feature vectors.

3.3.2 Model-based similarity

The model-based similarity captures native language similarities paralleled in reading patterns. In the same way as Berzak et al. (2017), we define "the classification uncertainty for a pair of native languages y and y' in our data collection D, as the average probability assigned by the NLIR classifier to one language given the other being the true native language." It is called English Reading Similarity (ERS) and is defined as:

$$ERS_{y,y'} = \frac{\sum\limits_{(x,y)\in D_y} p(y'|x;\theta) + \sum\limits_{(x,y')\in D'_y} p(y|x;\theta)}{|D_y| + |D'_y|}$$

The model, trained on all seven languages to perform NLIR, is used to extract language similarity. We separately feed test data sets for a single language y at a time and extract prediction probabilities for each other language y'. Then a mean of the two language probabilities is calculated.

It is suggested that a higher classification uncertainty indicates greater language similarity. In figure 2 we plot the similarity metrics against each other to test this in the original study implied link.

4 Results

Table 2 presents the results for the baseline and the log-linear model when using 10-fold cross-validation. The model is trained and evaluated on all seven languages.

All variants of the model perform substantially better than the majority class baseline. Similarly to the results by Berzak et al. (2017), the model trained on the WFC feature set achieves the highest cross-validation accuracy (81.29%). While the model trained on syntactic and information cluster features improves with additional bi- and tri-grams, the words in the fixed context feature set do not follow this trend which differs from the original paper's results.

[4]Note that this can be considered non-standard, as the features of a language might impact the similarity between two other languages. We mainly used this strategy to follow the previous setup

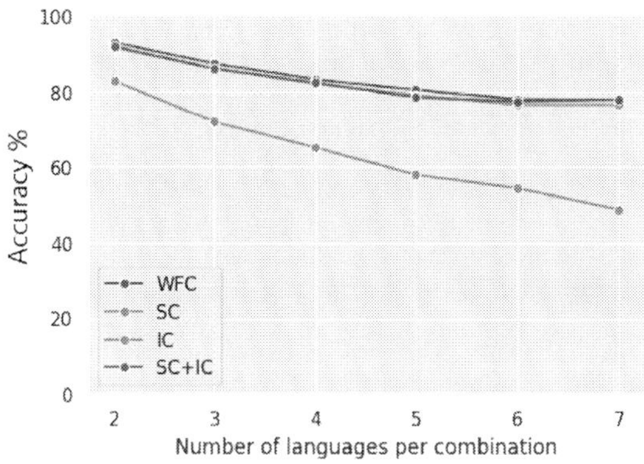

Figure 1: Mean performance of all combinations of languages using uni+bi+trigram features.

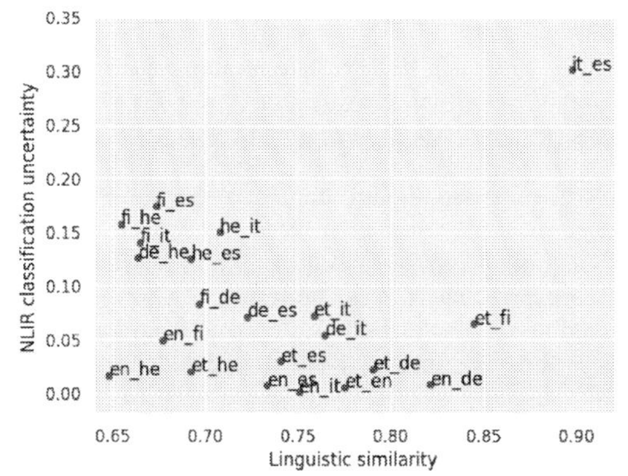

Figure 2: Linguistic similarities from URIEL against mean NLIR classification uncertainty of the unigram SC+IC model.

Since the original study was done with a different number of languages, we investigate how the performance changes depending on the number of target classes. Figure 1 shows the changes in model performance depending on how many target classes it has. E.g., 3 on the x axis corresponds to a group of all combinations (C_7^3) of any three languages in the train set. The y-axis shows the mean performance of all classifiers in that group. The results of each classifier in a group vary, thus, we plot the mean performance. As expected, we see that for all feature sets the performance drops when the number of language increase.

5 Discussion

As evident from Table 2, our model seems to perform similarly to the original paper's results (Table 3, Appendix A). We can not compare these results directly due to the difference in languages, yet, for all combinations of four languages in our data set,

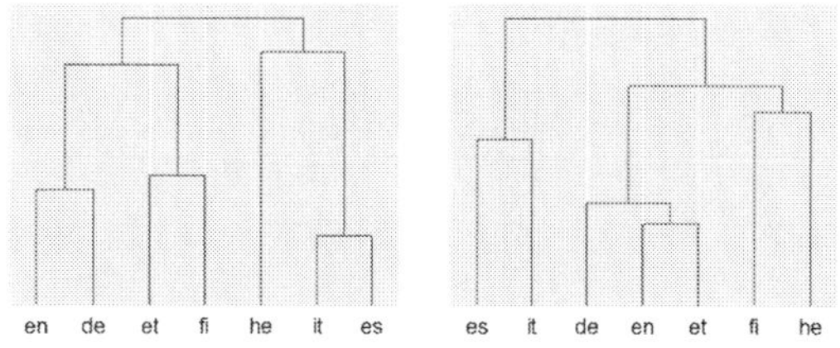

(a) Linguistic similarities (b) Class uncertainty

Figure 3: Ward hierarchical clustering. Based on the unigrams SC+IC model.

we observe in Figure 1) that the average performance is 81 % (compared to 71% in Berzak et al. (2017). However, since we train our model with 3 more languages than the original study and still get similar results, we can confirm that machine learning models can pick up the differences in reading patterns of different native language readers. Contrary to the original paper, we do not see large improvements in performance with additional bigram and trigram features.

We also explore language similarity by looking at the suggested positive correlation between classification uncertainty and linguistic similarities. Results from Berzak et al. (2017) are included in Figure 5, Appendix A for convenience. The plot reproduced in Figure 2 does not seem to confirm this hypothesis as no clear trend is visible. We observe that the uncertainty when classifying native speakers vs. L2 reading is substantially lower (mean 0.01) than when distinguishing two groups of L2 readers from those of different native languages (mean 0.11). We also compute a correlation coefficient of 0.06 which does not indicate a significant correlation found by Berzak et al. Similarly, Ward hierarchical clustering for linguistic similarities and classification uncertainty, presented in Figure 3, does not present a closeness between grouping using either of these metrics. The plots have little overlaps on the set of languages we used, contrary to the original finding, see Figure 4, and share a little similarity both in terms of languages in each cluster and the general shape of the tree. This suggests that the relation between the English reading patterns and language similarities of the native language found by Berzak et al. (2017) may be more nuanced than the original plot (Figure 4, Appendix A) initially suggests.

6 Conclusion

We replicate the finding of Berzak et al. (2017) and are the first to confirm their finding that a reader's native language can be predicted from gaze patterns when reading English text. Having a larger set of more interrelated languages than the original study, we achieve comparable classification results supporting the suggested cross-linguistic influence from the native language to L2. Despite the satisfactory performance of the NLIR model, the results of investigating the relationship between reading patterns and linguistic similarity are not as straightforward. We believe the relation to be more nuanced than suggested as we are not able to replicate the same outcomes.

Acknowledgements

Maria Barrett is supported by a research grant (34437) from VILLUM FONDEN.

References

R.A. Alonso. 2016. *Crosslinguistic Influence in Second Language Acquisition*. G - Reference,Information and Interdisciplinary Subjects Series. Multilingual Matters.

Eva Berkes and Suzanne Flynn. 2012. Multilingualism: New perspectives on syntactic development.

Yevgeni Berzak, Chie Nakamura, Suzanne Flynn, and Boris Katz. 2017. Predicting native language from gaze. In *Proceedings of the 55th Annual Meeting of the Association for Computational Linguistics (Volume 1: Long Papers)*, pages 541–551, Vancouver, Canada. Association for Computational Linguistics.

Yevgeni Berzak, Chie Nakamura, Amelia Smith, Emily Weng, Boris Katz, Suzanne Flynn, and Roger Levy. 2022. Celer: A 365-participant corpus of eye movements in l1 and l2 english reading. *Open Mind*, 6:41–50.

Yevgeni Berzak, Roi Reichart, and Boris Katz. 2014. Reconstructing native language typology from foreign language usage. In *Proceedings of the Eighteenth Conference on Computational Natural Language Learning*, pages 21–29, Ann Arbor, Michigan. Association for Computational Linguistics.

Alexis Conneau, Kartikay Khandelwal, Naman Goyal, Vishrav Chaudhary, Guillaume Wenzek, Francisco Guzmán, Edouard Grave, Myle Ott, Luke Zettlemoyer, and Veselin Stoyanov. 2020. Unsupervised cross-lingual representation learning at scale. In *Proceedings of the 58th Annual Meeting of the Association for Computational Linguistics*, pages 8440–8451, Online. Association for Computational Linguistics.

Uschi Cop, Nicolas Dirix, Denis Drieghe, and Wouter Duyck. 2017. Presenting geco: An eyetracking corpus of monolingual and bilingual sentence reading. *Behavior research methods*, 49:602–615.

Uschi Cop, Denis Drieghe, and Wouter Duyck. 2015. Eye movement patterns in natural reading: A comparison of monolingual and bilingual reading of a novel. *PLOS ONE*, 10(8):1–38.

Jacob Devlin, Ming-Wei Chang, Kenton Lee, and Kristina Toutanova. 2019. BERT: Pre-training of deep bidirectional transformers for language understanding. In *Proceedings of the 2019 Conference of the North American Chapter of the Association for Computational Linguistics: Human Language Technologies, Volume 1 (Long and Short Papers)*, pages 4171–4186, Minneapolis, Minnesota. Association for Computational Linguistics.

Holger Hopp. 2010. Ultimate attainment in l2 inflection: Performance similarities between non-native and native speakers. *Lingua*, 120:901–931.

Victor Kuperman, Noam Siegelman, Sascha Schroeder, Cengiz Acarturk, Svetlana Alexeeva, Simona Amenta, Raymond Bertram, Rolando Bonandrini, Marc Brysbaert, Daria Chernova, Sara Fonseca, Nicolas Dirix, Wouter Duyck, Argyro Fella, Ram Frost, Carolina Gattei, Areti Kalaitzi, Kaidi Lõo, Marco Marelli, and Kerem Usal. 2022. Text reading in english as a second language: Evidence from the multilingual eye-movements corpus. *Studies in Second Language Acquisition*, pages 1–35.

Patrick Littell, David R. Mortensen, Ke Lin, Katherine Kairis, Carlisle Turner, and Lori Levin. 2017a. Uriel and lang2vec: Representing languages as typological, geographical, and phylogenetic vectors. In *Proceedings of the 15th Conference of the European Chapter of the Association for Computational Linguistics: Volume 2, Short Papers*, pages 8–14. Association for Computational Linguistics.

Patrick Littell, David R. Mortensen, Ke Lin, Katherine Kairis, Carlisle Turner, and Lori Levin. 2017b. URIEL and lang2vec: Representing languages as typological, geographical, and phylogenetic vectors. In *Proceedings of the 15th Conference of the European Chapter of the Association for Computational Linguistics: Volume 2, Short Papers*, pages 8–14, Valencia, Spain. Association for Computational Linguistics.

F. Pedregosa, G. Varoquaux, A. Gramfort, V. Michel, B. Thirion, O. Grisel, M. Blondel, P. Prettenhofer, R. Weiss, V. Dubourg, J. Vanderplas, A. Passos, D. Cournapeau, M. Brucher, M. Perrot, and E. Duchesnay. 2011. Scikit-learn: Machine learning in Python. *Journal of Machine Learning Research*, 12:2825–2830.

Keith Rayner. 1998. Eye movements in reading and information processing: 20 years of research. *Psychological bulletin*, 124(3):372.

Keith Rayner, Alexander Pollatsek, Jane Ashby, and Charles Clifton Jr. 2012. *Psychology of reading*. Psychology Press.

Ryokan Ri, Ikuya Yamada, and Yoshimasa Tsuruoka. 2022. mLUKE: The power of entity representations in multilingual pretrained language models. In *Proceedings of the 60th Annual Meeting of the Association for Computational Linguistics (Volume 1: Long Papers)*, pages 7316–7330, Dublin, Ireland. Association for Computational Linguistics.

Leah Roberts and Anna Siyanova-Chanturia. 2013. Using eye-tracking to investigate topics in l2 acquisition and l2 processing. *Studies in Second Language Acquisition*, 35.

Oren Tsur and Ari Rappoport. 2007. Using classifier features for studying the effect of native language on the choice of written second language words. In *Proceedings of the Workshop on Cognitive Aspects of Computational Language Acquisition*, pages 9–16, Prague, Czech Republic. Association for Computational Linguistics.

Rob van der Goot, Ahmet Üstün, Alan Ramponi, Ibrahim Sharaf, and Barbara Plank. 2021. Massive choice, ample tasks (MaChAmp): A toolkit for multitask learning in NLP. In *Proceedings of the 16th Conference of the European Chapter of the Association for Computational Linguistics: System Demonstrations*, pages 176–197, Online. Association for Computational Linguistics.

A Results by Berzak et al. (2017)

	Shared regime		
Majority Class	25.52		
Random Clusters	22.76		
	unigrams	+bigrams	+trigrams
Information Clusters (IC)	41.38	44.14	46.21
Syntactic Clusters (SC)	45.52	57.24	58.62
Information Clusters (IC)	51.72	57.24	60.0
Words in Fixed Context (WFC)	64.14	68.28	**71.03**

Table 3: Native Language Identification from Reading results by Berzak et al. (2017)

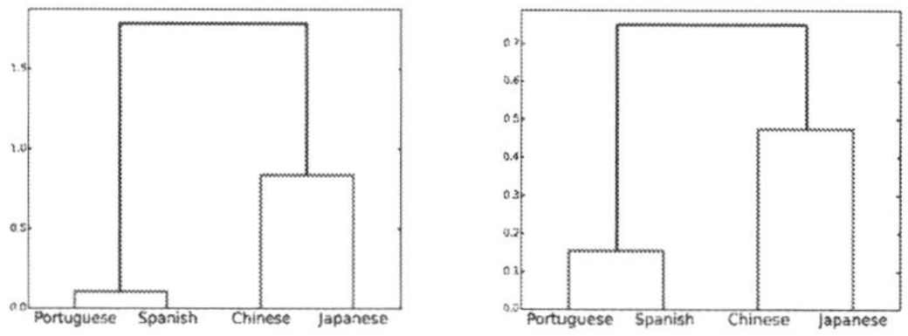

(b) Linguistic tree (c) English reading tree

Figure 4: Ward hierarchical clustering of linguistic similarities between languages and NLIR average pairwise classification uncertainties by Berzak et al. (2017)

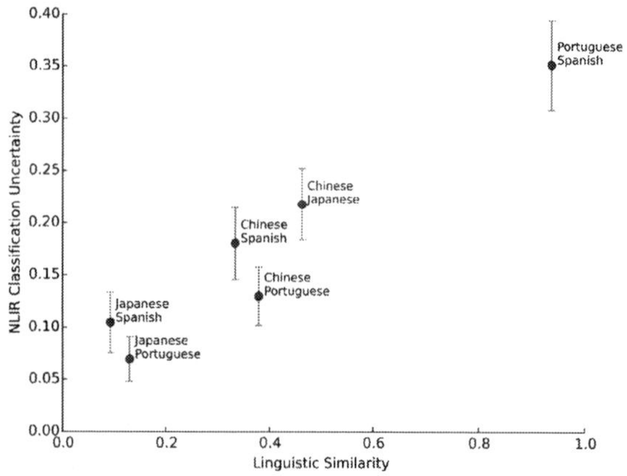

Figure 5: Linguistic similarities against mean NLIR classification uncertainty from Berzak et al. (2017)

B Obtaining Syntactic Annotations

We trained a multi-task MaChAmp model (van der Goot et al., 2021), including UPOS, PTB POS, lemmatization, morphological tagging, and dependency parsing. We used MaChAmp v0.4 with default settings, trained on the English Web Treebank v2.11 (because it has PTB tags and is English). It uses the combined (summed cross-entropy) loss of all tasks. We do not use the morphological tags and lemmas but include them for future work. All default hyperparameters are used and the default dev-split is used for model picking. We first ran the parser on the untokenized input but noticed that it quite commonly outputs the PUNCT label and corresponding relations to (end-of-sentence) words that have punctuation attached. So we pre-split using the BasicTokenizer from huggingface (which only separates punctuations) and use the labels of the words for the combined string. We compared mBERT (Devlin et al., 2019) with XLM-R Large (Conneau et al., 2020) and MLUKE (Ri et al., 2022). We compared their outputs on the MECO dataset manually and found the best performance with the XLM-R Large model (although MLUKE gets higher accuracies on EWT-dev).

C Limitations

The MECO dataset (Kuperman et al., 2022) is recorded at different labs following the same strict protocol. Nevertheless, location and experimenter effects may be confounding factors for the NLIR task. The CELER data (Berzak et al., 2022), used by (Berzak et al., 2017), seems to all be recorded at the same lab. Since we confirm their hypothesis, we do not see this as a fatal flaw in our study. There is no other available dataset that would allow us to replicate their finding.

MedTem2.0: Prompt-based Temporal Classification of Treatment Events from Discharge Summaries

Yang Cui, Lifeng Han, and **Goran Nenadic**
Department of Computer Science
The University of Manchester
Oxford Rd, Manchester M13 9PL, UK
yang.cui-2@student.manchester.ac.uk
lifeng.han, g.nenadic@manchester.ac.uk

Abstract

Discharge summaries are comprehensive medical records that encompass vital information about a patient's hospital stay. A crucial aspect of discharge summaries is the temporal information of treatments administered throughout the patient's illness. With an extensive volume of clinical documents, manually extracting and compiling a patient's medication list can be laborious, time-consuming, and susceptible to errors. The objective of this paper is to build upon the recent development on clinical NLP by temporally classifying treatments in clinical texts, specifically determining whether a treatment was administered between the time of admission and discharge from the hospital. State-of-the-art NLP methods including prompt-based learning on Generative Pre-trained Transformers (GPTs) models and fine-tuning on pre-trained language models (PLMs) such as BERT were used to classify temporal relations between treatments and hospitalisation periods in discharge summaries. Fine-tuning with the BERT model achieved an F1 score of 92.45% and a balanced accuracy of 77.56%, while prompt learning using the T5 model and mixed templates resulted in an F1 score of 90.89% and a balanced accuracy of 72.07%. Our codes and data are available at `https://github.com/HECTA-UoM/MedTem`.

1 Introduction

Clinical texts contain important temporal information, such as medication start and end dates, appointment dates, and diagnosis dates. Extracting this information can provide insights into a patient's medical history and allow doctors to make more informed decisions about their treatment. However, this process requires a significant amount of time and effort. To help healthcare professionals make informed decisions more efficiently, leading to better patient outcomes, we designed the project **MedTem**, medication and treatment event extraction and their relation modelling with temporal information. By using natural language processing (NLP) methods to extract temporal information from clinical texts, doctors can spend less time deciphering medical records and more time focusing on providing the best care possible to their patients. This study reports findings from MedTem2.0, a follow-up work from our previous investigation MedTem (Tu, 2022).

Clinical texts can be challenging to process due to their unstructured nature and the use of medical jargon. Thus, developing effective NLP techniques for extracting temporal information from clinical texts is crucial for improving healthcare outcomes. The primary goal of this work is to classify temporal information related to medication, surgeries, and other treatments within Electronic Health Records (EHRs) to determine if these treatments occurred during the hospitalisation period. This work aims to develop a system capable of classifying temporal information using prompt-based learning (PBL) from texts, which could aid healthcare professionals in understanding patients' medical histories and facilitate research in clinical text mining.

As an example, in Table 1, given the admission and discharge dates, we aim to determine if the *a left carotid endarterectomy* and *vein patch angioplasty* were used during the hospitalisation period. The note indicates that those treatments were administered on 3/3/92, which is during the admission and discharge dates, suggesting that it was used during hospitalisation. We assume that all treatment information is provided and only need to analyse the temporal information.

To the best of our knowledge, this is the first attempt at using prompt-based learning for the temporal classification of treatments in the clinical domain, with the following outcomes: 1) we established a high baseline score with 90.89% F1 measurement and 72.07% balanced accuracy by using prompt-based learning, demonstrating the

Proceedings of the 61st Annual Meeting of the
Association for Computational Linguistics - Student Research Workshop, pages 160–183
July 10-12, 2023

clinical free text		
Admission Date	**Discharge Date**	**Doctor's Note**
02/22/92	*03/08/92*	*She was, therefore, cleared for the operating room, and on 3/3/92, she underwent* ***a left carotid endarterectomy****, with continuous electroencephalogram monitoring and* ***vein patch angioplasty****, which was uneventful .*

Table 1: Task Example

effectiveness of the developed system for classifying temporal relationships between treatments and hospitalisation times; 2) we achieved improved performance using fine-tuning with the BERT model, resulting in a 92.45% F1 score and 77.56% balanced accuracy.

2 Methodologies

2.1 Task Overview

The pipeline shown in Figure 1 presents the methodology. The key approaches entail deriving gold labels from annotated datasets, following several pre-processing steps such as few-shot learning and sentence segmentation, among others. To evaluate the efficacy of prompt-based learning in temporally classifying treatment entities, two widely-adopted paradigms were used for comparison: pre-trained fine-tuning and prompt-based learning. Within these paradigms, three state-of-the-art pre-trained language models were used to perform the task: the Masked Language Model BERT, Seq2seq model T5 and Auto-regressive Language Model GPT-2 (Devlin et al., 2018; Raffel et al., 2020; Radford et al., 2019). All these models are based on Transformer structures but with different architecture/components, BERT for the encoder, GPT for the decoder, and T5 for both the encoder and decoder. We used BERT-base instead of BERT-large because the latter one costs too much power that the Colab platform we used could not afford.

2.2 Data Pre-processing

Step I: Generation of Gold Standard The i2b2 temporal relations corpus we used contains pre-existing layers of gold standard annotations, such as clinical concepts (problems, tests, treatments) and coreference relations (Uzuner et al., 2012, 2011), which can facilitate temporal reasoning.

In each discharge note, there are three types of annotations: events, temporal expressions, and temporal relations. Event annotations (EVENTs) encompass three distinct clinical concepts (i.e. PROBLEMs, TESTs, and TREATMENTs), clinical departments, EVIDENTIALs (words or phrases patients use to describe their symptoms), and OCCURRENCEs (other events, such as admission, that indicate the patient's timeline). Each EVENT possesses three attributes: TYPE, MODALITY, and POLARITY. For this specific task, we only need to identify the TYPE of EVENT as TREATMENT and OCCURRENCE among all the TYPE attributes (PROBLEM, TEST, TREATMENT, CLINICAL_DEPT, EVIDENTIAL, or OCCURRENCE). Figure 2 shows the discharge summary paragraph; the EVENTs in this record are shown in Table 2.

In clinical records, the temporal expression annotations use the TIMEX3 tag, which includes four categories: time, date, duration, and frequency. Each TIMEX3 value (VAL) is standardised to a unified format, such as time and date being represented as [YYYY-MM-DD]T[HH:MM]. Additionally, the MOD attribute indicates the characteristics of the temporal expression. Table 3 shows the TIMEX3 in the sample clinical record snippet. Once we have acquired all the EVENT and TIMEX3 information, we can map the temporal relations (TLINKs) between time and events, or between events themselves (Table 4). The TLINK categories include BEFORE, AFTER, BEGUN_BY, ENDED_BY, DURING, SIMULTANEOUS, OVERLAP, and BEFORE_OVERLAP.

Upon identifying all the treatment EVENTs and their relationships with admission and discharge times, we assign a label of "ON" to those entities where treatment occurs after or overlaps with the admission time and is also before or overlaps with the discharge time, indicating that the treatment was administered during hospitalisation. Conversely, we assign a label of "OFF" to the remaining treatments, signifying that they were not used during hospitalisation. Figure 3 illustrates the application of this rule-based approach for generating

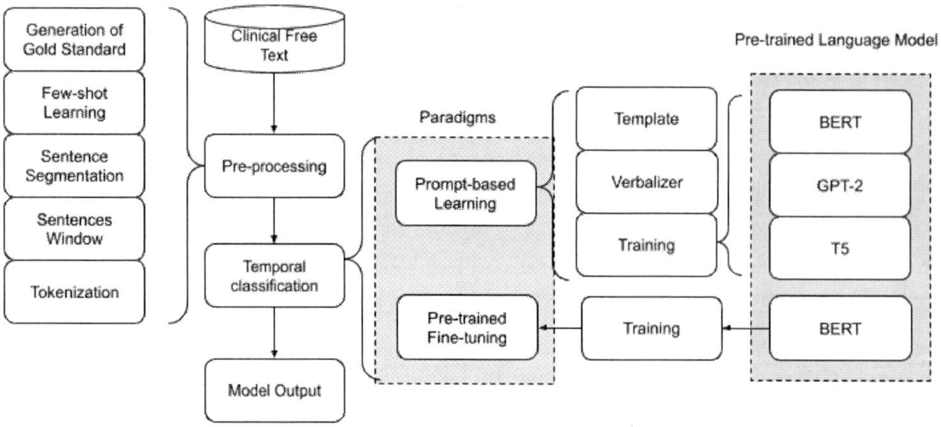

Figure 1: System Pipeline

Admission Date :
06/11/1991
Discharge Date :
06/22/1991
HISTORY OF PRESENT ILLNESS :
Patient is a 28 year old gravida IV , para 2 with metastatic cervical cancer admitted with a question of malignant pericardial effusion . Patient underwent a total abdominal hysterectomy in 02/90 for a 4x3.6x2 cm cervical mass felt to be a fibroid at Vanor .

Figure 2: Sample Clinical Record Snippet (Underscored: EVENTs, Italics: TIMEX3s)

the necessary gold labels. These gold labels comprise the document name, discharge note, treatment entity, and the label. In this study, the provided dataset consists of a training dataset and a testing dataset. After processing the data using the gold label generator as above, we obtained 3,075 ON-labelled training samples (indicating treatments used during hospital stays) and 762 OFF-labelled samples (indicating treatments not used during hospital stays). This results in an imbalanced label set on the dataset.

Step II: Few-shot Learning to Balance Labels To address the label-imbalance issue, we used a few-shot learning approach to create a balanced training dataset. This involved randomly selecting an equal number of samples from each label and combining them to form the few-shot training dataset.

Furthermore, most notes contain numerous abbreviations, such as "mcg subq q.d.", which stands for "micrograms subcutaneously once daily". However, since our objective is to analyse temporal information related to treatments, addressing dosage and frequency abbreviations is not necessary.

Step III: Sentence Segmentation Due to the nature of the dataset, which consists of clinical discharge notes, doctors frequently use brief sentences or even short phrases to describe various treatments, tests, or other patient-related information. This characteristic simplifies the process of *Sentence Segmentation*, which can be achieved by splitting the text based on newline characters ("/n") and periods ("."). The rationale behind sentence segmentation is to preserve and enhance the extraction of contextual information within the text, as distinct sentences often address different topics or aspects.

Step IV: Sentence Window An interesting aspect is that a single treatment may be mentioned multiple times in one clinical note, each referring to different events with distinct time sequences. Providing the entire text as input data would be imprecise and inaccurate. Additionally, clinical notes predominantly consist of factual statements and clinical declarations, with sentences generally

Event	Type	Modality	Polarity
[Admission]	OCCURRENCE	FACTUAL	POS
[Discharge]	OCCURRENCE	FACTUAL	POS
[gravida IV]	OCCURRENCE	FACTUAL	POS
[metastatic cervical cancer]	PROBLEM	FACTUAL	POS
[malignant pericardial effusion]	PROBLEM	POSSIBLE	POS
[a total abdominal hysterectomy]	TREATMENT	FACTUAL	POS
[a fibroid]	PROBLEM	POSSIBLE	POS
[Vanor]	CLINICAL_DEPT	FACTUAL	POS

Table 2: EVENT Annotation Examples

	document name	discharge note	treatment entity	label(1-ON,0-OFF)
0	472.xml.tlink	Admission Date : 2017-06-16 Discharge Date : 2...	specific interventions	1
1	626.xml.tlink	Admission Date : 06/25/1990 Discharge Date : 0...	crutches	1
2	167.xml.tlink	Admission Date : 2019-06-25 Discharge Date : 2...	extubated	1
3	236.xml.tlink	ADMISSION DATE : 08/15/1998 DISCHARGE DATE : 0...	a left internal mammary artery graft to the le...	0
4	387.xml.tlink	Admission Date : 2013-08-24 Discharge Date : 2...	monitored very closely	1

Figure 3: Example of Generated Gold Label

TIMEX3	Type	VAL	Mod
[06/11/1991]	DATE	1991-06-11	NA
[06/22/1991]	DATE	1991-06-22	NA

Table 3: TIMEX3 Annotation Examples

being independent. As a result, we used a **Sentence Window** approach to extract valuable information. For instance, if the target treatment entity is in the target sentence, and the sentence window size is set to 4, the model selects two sentences before and after the target sentence. The input data consists of the target sentence, its surrounding sentences, and the key temporal information of admission and discharge times, which appear at the beginning of every clinical note. Thus, this approach ensures that the model incorporates relevant temporal information and context.

Step V: Tokenization Tokenization is a crucial step in the natural language processing pipeline, wherein paragraphs are segmented into sentences, and sentences are further broken down into individual tokens or words (Koehn, 2009). This process enables the conversion of unstructured textual data into a structured, word-based data format, facilitating subsequent processing and analysis. By transforming unstructured data into structured data, we can represent textual information as vectors, and tokenization serves as the foundational step in this transformation.

In prompt-based learning, designing a template that includes an input sequence and prompting sentence is essential. However, creating a tokenizer for this purpose can be time-consuming and prone to errors. This is due to the presence of specific information, such as masked tokens or auto-generated tokens, embedded in the template, which requires careful handling during tokenization. Any mismatches in masked tokens can result in serious consequences. Furthermore, different PLMs may have distinct architectures, leading to varying tokenization strategies, necessitating consistency in context processing.

2.3 Prompt-based Learning vs Fine-Tuning

In conventional supervised learning for NLP, the objective is to predict an **output y** based on an **input x** utilising the model $P(y|x;\theta)$ (Manning and Schutze, 1999). In classification tasks, **y** denotes the class label corresponding to **input x**. To train the model's parameters θ, a dataset consisting of input-output pairs is required for predicting this conditional probability (Goodfellow et al., 2016). However, obtaining adequately annotated (labelled) data for certain domains can be challenging. Prompt learning methods address this limitation by learning a language model (LM) that estimates the probability $P(x;\theta)$ of the text **x** itself. Consequently, this probability is used to predict **y**, thereby bypassing the need for extensive labelled datasets (Liu et al., 2023; Ding et al., 2021). There

From extent	Type	To extent
[Admission]	SIMULTANEOUS	[06/11/1991]
[Discharge]	SIMULTANEOUS	[06/22/1991]
[gravida IV]	BEFORE	[SECTIME: 06/11/1991]
[para 2]	BEFORE	[SECTIME: 06/11/1991]
[para 2]	OVERLAP	[gravida IV]
[...]	...	[...]
[a total abdominal hysterectomy]	BEFORE	[SECTIME: 06/11/1991]

Table 4: TLINK Annotation Examples

will be three main steps of doing that including prompt construction, answer selection, and answer mapping (refer to Appendix C.1).

We used **OpenPrompt**, a toolkit for implementing prompt learning in downstream tasks (Ding et al., 2021). It offers a function for loading PLMs, tokenizers, and other required configurations, which function accommodates the choice of PLMs (MLM, LM, and Seq2seq) and conducts tokenization accordingly. Designed with encapsulated data processing APIs, users can apply a human-readable style to create templates and conveniently operate on both the input and template simultaneously.

To identify the optimal prompt format for this task, we examine various components in the prompt-based construction. We explore different large langauge model (LLM) architectures, and adjust the template's structure and format within the prompt construction. We modify the answer's form in answer selection to correspond with the chosen template.

In this context, we will first define the templates and verbalizers used within the framework and our experiments. We refer to the traditional prompt-based learning approach that uses human designed templates and verbalizers as *manual templates* and *manual verbalizers* respectively. This strategy was initially introduced as Pattern-Exploiting Training (PET) by Schick and Schütze (Schick and Schütze, 2020).

Manual Template Creating manual components in prompt learning can be quite intricate, as slight modifications to the tokens can lead to significant changes in performance. Domain expertise is typically required for effective engineering of these components. Examples of manual template can be a statement or question-answering format.

The **Soft Template** (Example 1) approach shares similarities with the manual method but replaces fixed manual components with soft (trainable) tokens or embeddings, denoted as <[soft]>. Combining some fixed manual components with soft tokens leads to the **Mixed Template** approach (Example 2), which uses both fixed and trainable elements in the template construction.

Listing 1: Example of Soft Template

```
text = '<[clinical_record]> <[soft]>
    <[treatment]> <[soft]> <[soft]>
    <[mask]> <[soft]>.'
```

Listing 2: Example of Mixed Template

```
text = '<[clinical_record]> Question:
    <[treatment]> <[soft]> <[soft]>
    <[soft]> <[soft]> <[soft]>. Is it
    correct? <[mask]>'
```

Leveraging the T5 model's encoder-decoder architecture, we can generate variable-length output sequences based on the input sequence. With this advantage, the PLM can generate part of the prompt within the manual template. Choosing to sacrifice human interpretability, one can create soft prompt components instead. A typical mixed template takes the form $x_0 = [P_0, P_1, \dots, P_j], x, [P_{j+1}, P_{j+2}, \dots, P_k]$, [MASK], where for $i \in 0, 1, \dots, k$, P_i represents the token of the template.

Verbalizer The verbalizer functions as a mechanism that maps single or multiple distinct tokens to well-defined class labels. The embedding or hidden state associated with the $<$ [MASK] $>$ position, generated by the PLM, is subsequently processed through a standard language model head or classifier. This step computes the probabilities connected to the class label tokens derived from the verbalizer. In this task, a **Manual Verbalizer** was used, which entailed manually constructing a list of answers. These answers can be either token-based or span-based, depending on the specific template

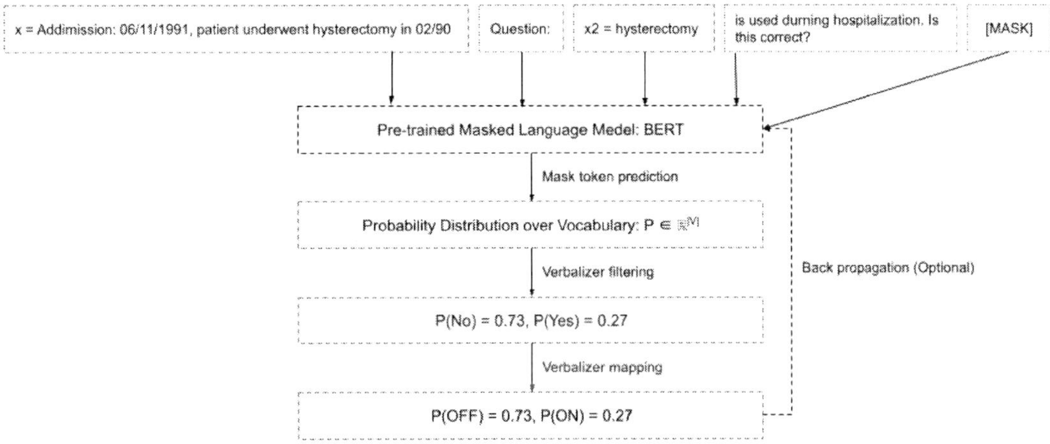

Figure 4: Illustration of Manual Template and Verbalizer in Prompt Learning

used.

In a similar fashion to the soft template, a **Soft Verbalizer** can be conceptualised as replaced words in the verbalizer with trainable embeddings for each class. As a result, when useing a soft verbalizer, there is no necessary to establish a mapping from vocabulary V to class C, as the trainable vectors lack semantic meaning.

2.4 Traditional Fine-tuning

In traditional fine-tuning methodology, the downstream task uses a multilayer perceptron (MLP) denoted as $f_{MLP}(\cdot)$. This MLP takes the pooled sequence embedding generated by the PLM as input and delivers an n-dimensional vector, where n represents the numeral of classes (Kowsari et al., 2019). Given an input text x, the PLM first processes the raw input to obtain the m-dimensional embedding for each token. Next, a pooling process, such as the mean, is involved in all the token's embeddings to generate a single sequence embedding $h(x)$ with the same m-dimensional size. The sentence embedding $h(x)$ is then fed into the MLP block through a typical feed-forward process to obtain the likelihood distribution across n classes using a softmax operator.

Figure 4, 5, and 6 illustrate the examples of PBL and PLM fine-tuning on our task, adapted from (Taylor et al., 2022).

2.5 Evaluation Methods

We take the label "ON" as the positive class and label "OFF" as the negative class. In addition to F1 score, we used balanced accuracy as a performance measure for our model, which calculates the average recall across all classes. The decision to use balanced accuracy instead of overall accuracy stems from the imbalanced distribution of class labels in the test dataset, with 3164 instances of label "ON" and 921 instances of the label "OFF". Balanced accuracy considers the performance of the model on each class individually, thus avoiding potential misinterpretations that can arise from using overall accuracy when one class is substantially more prevalent than the other.

3 Experimental Work

3.1 Dataset

In this project, we use electronic health records (EHRs) from the National NLP Clinical Challenges (n2c2, formerly known as i2b2) dataset, which is part of an annual challenge workshop [1]. We primarily focus on the 2012 n2c2 challenge (Sun et al., 2013b), which is centred around temporal relations. The dataset consists of 310 patient clinical history records and hospital course sections from Partners Healthcare and Beth Israel Deaconess Medical Center, along with clinical events, time expressions, and temporal relationship annotations (Sun et al., 2013a). For ethical reasons and to protect patient privacy, the data has been de-identified and abstracted, including the obfuscation or alteration of names, addresses, and other personal information. Additionally, accurate time information has been randomly shifted.

[1] https://n2c2.dbmi.hms.harvard.edu/about-n2c2

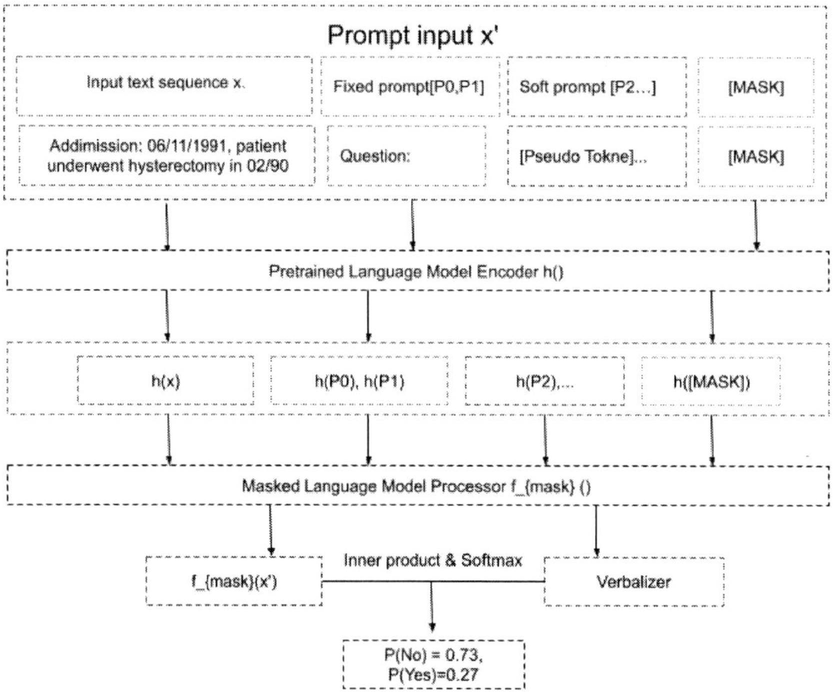

Figure 5: Illustration of Mixed Template and Verbalizer in Prompt Learning.

3.2 Output from Prompt-based Learning

We adopt a systematic approach to optimise the performance of different PLMs. Initially, we use various PLMs by the full training dataset, basic manual templates, and verbalizers, while fixing the sentence window for input text and adjusting the learning rate to identify the optimal performance for each model. Comparing the results, we will determine the best-performing PLM at this stage.

Next, with the best PLM and fixed sentence window, we will train the model using the full dataset while varying templates and verbalizers to identify the most effective template. Furthermore, we will maintain the best PLM and template while altering the sentence window to assess the impact of input text on performance.

Upon completing the hyperparameter selection for prompt-based learning, we will obtain the best-performing model. Finally, we will use few-shot learning to compare this model with the fine-tuning paradigm.

3.2.1 Different Language Models

To evaluate the performance of various models, we use a combination of admission and discharge information along with three sentences that include the target sentence and the sentences immediately preceding and following it, where the target sentence contains the target treatment entity. Moreover, we use manual templates and verbalizers, with the template following a question-answering format. The verbalizer is set to a collection of words, specifically "Yes", "No". The entire training process spans 5 epochs.

	L.R.	F1.on	B.Accy.
BERT	1E-4	87.29	50
	2E-4	**90.75**	**69.72**
	5E-6	90.14	69.57
GPT-2	6E-5	90.57	70.24
	2E-5	**90.79**	**71.19**
	5E-6	90.28	65.58
T5	6E-5	90.69	70.43
	4E-5	**91.24**	**71.43**
	2E-5	90.12	68.36

Table 5: Performance of Different PLM. L.R.: learning rate; F1.on: score of ON class; B.A.:Balanced Accuracy

Upon adjusting the learning rate for the various PLMs, several examples of results were obtained in table 5. The bold font indicates the highest score for each PLM. In fact, there was not a big difference between them. T5 is 1.71 and 0.24 higher than BERT and GPT-2 under balanced accuracy

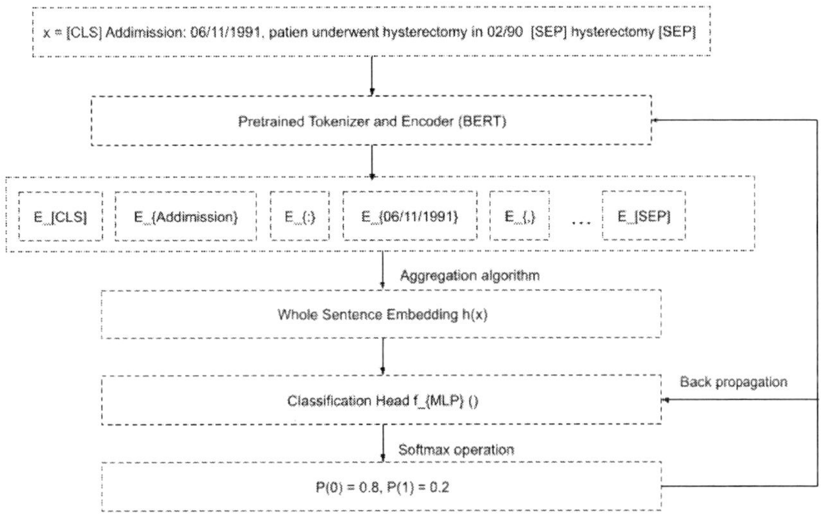

Figure 6: Illustration of Conventional Fine-tuning Method. (Here [CLS] and [SEP] tokens are special tokens for BERT-based models that are added to the beginning and end of sequences.)

respectively and held a 0.49 and 0.45 advantage in F1 score.

During the training process, we observed that all the results demonstrated a higher recall than precision, indicating that the model correctly identifies most of the true positive cases (with few false negatives). This situation can be attributed to the training data having a significantly larger number of positive examples compared to negative ones, which is also reflected in the testing dataset. Additionally, when examining the negative class accuracy, the models only achieve approximately 50%. This suggests that they are not proficient in detecting negative classes. However, when using a balanced training dataset, the negative class accuracy increases to 61%.

3.2.2 Different Prompt Learning Setups

In order to assess the effectiveness of different combinations of templates and verbalizers, we used a variety of templates in conjunction with both manual and soft verbalizers. For the manual template, we used a question-answering format, combined with a yes, no manual verbalizer and a soft verbalizer. Additionally, the soft template used Example 1 for prompting, with fixed and predefined positions and lengths for the soft tokens, and was combined with the same manual and soft verbalizers as the manual template. For the mixed template, we used Example 2 along with the same verbalizers as before. During the comparison of different prompt engineering approaches, we also experimented with various text lengths for each template category.

Template	Verbalizer	F1.on	B.Accy.
Manual	Manual	**91.24**	**71.43**
	Soft	90.85	70.52
Soft	Manual	**90.68**	68.33
	Soft	89.8	**72.48**
Mixed	Manual	**90.89**	**72.07**
	Soft	90.7	69.01

Table 6: Performance of Different Prompt Learning. F1.on: score of ON class; B.Accy.: Balanced Accuracy

The evaluation results presented in Table 6 reveal that the (Manual, Manual) combination, with the format (Template, Verbalizer), achieves the highest F1 score of 91.24. This indicates its strong capability to classify "ON" class samples. Additionally, the (Soft, Soft) setup demonstrates the best balanced accuracy of 72.42, which is more suitable when the "OFF" class is as important as the positive class. We list error analysis examples and comparisons of different input text in Appendix (F). The (Mixed, Manual) configuration showcases comparatively good results for both evaluation metrics and will be used as the standard for the next section of comparisons.

3.3 PBL vs Traditional Fine-Tuning

The Hyperparameters-optimised outputs from PBL and traditional fine-tuning are displayed in Table

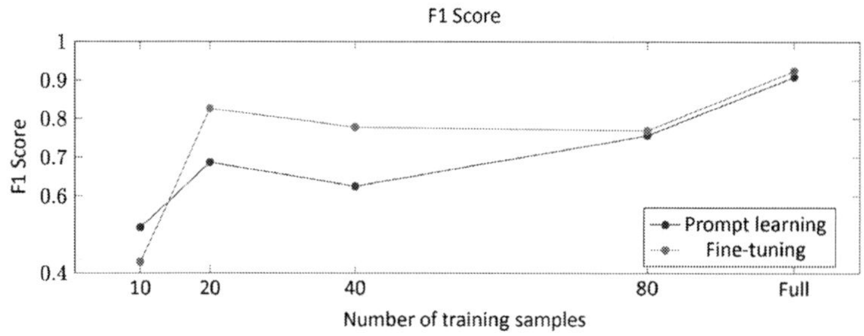

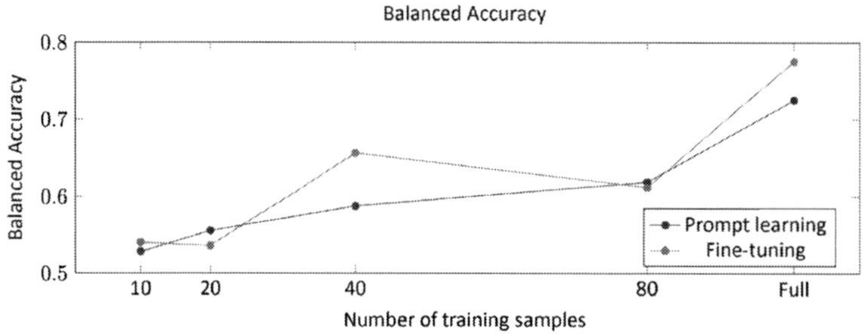

Figure 7: Balanced Accuracy and F1 Score for Prompt Learning and Traditional Fine-tuning Frameworks Across the Temporal Classification Task. ("Full" refers to a full training dataset size.)

7 and Figure 7, with the hyper-parameter sets in Appendix (G).

Paradigm	F1 score	B.Accy.
Traditional fine-tuning	92.45	77.56
Prompt-based learning	91.79	75.08

Table 7: Hyperparameter Optimised Model for Temporal Classification. B.Accy.: Balanced accuracy

4 Related Work

Early research in temporal relation classification focused on extracting and representing temporal information from clinical text. Hripcsak et al. (2002) proposed a method for representing clinical events and their temporal relationships using an interval-based temporal model, laying the groundwork for understanding temporal dependencies in clinical text.

Inspired by the TimeML standard (Pustejovsky et al., 2003) for annotating temporal expressions and relations in text, the THYME (Temporal Histories of Your Medical Events) annotation guidelines were developed by Styler IV et al. (2014) to adapt TimeML for clinical narratives. These guidelines provided a foundation for temporal relation classification research in the clinical domain. However, achieving temporal understanding in clinical narratives is challenging due to the complexity of determining implicit temporal relations, handling temporal granularity, and dealing with diverse temporal expressions.

5 Conclusion and Future Work

In this work, two state-of-the-art approaches were developed to classify the relative timing of treatments in hospital discharge summaries, focusing on determining whether a treatment was administered during hospitalisation or not. These approaches used cutting-edge pre-trained language models, BERT, GPT-2, and T5, in conjunction with prompt-based learning and fine-tuning paradigms. Both approaches achieved F1 scores of 91.79% and 92.45%, and balanced accuracy of 75.08% and 77.56%, respectively, on the n2c2 2012 Temporal Relations dataset. The primary challenge was accurately classifying the "OFF" class due to data imbalance and complex semantic meanings that made it difficult for the models to make correct decisions. Future work could investigate the impact of fixed tokens on mixed template performance or the role of longer sequence lengths in soft templates for improved understanding. Additionally, a more comprehensive comparison of prompt learning and traditional fine-tuning can be conducted across various clinical domain tasks, using frozen PLMs in conjunction with few-shot learning methods.

Limitations

There are several limitations to the experiments conducted in this project that should be acknowledged:

- Selection of the best pre-trained language model (PLM) for prompt-based learning: The evaluation method used to compare the performance of BERT, GPT-2, and T5 in the context of manual templates and manual verbalizers may not be entirely accurate. The performance of these models did not show significant differences, making it difficult to determine the best model for prompt-based learning. Furthermore, other domain-specific PLMs, such as Bio-BERT, which may be better suited for handling clinical data, were not considered in this project.

- Limited exploration of templates: The experiments utilized a limited number of templates, particularly for soft and mixed templates. These templates were primarily based on prompts derived from manual templates. Further experimentation is needed to explore different patterns, such as varying the position and length of soft token sequences or using soft tokens in mixed templates to replace manual tokens (e.g., "Question:").

- Comparison with frozen PLMs: The experiments did not include a comparison between fine-tuned and frozen PLMs, as done in Taylor's study (Taylor et al., 2022). This comparison could provide valuable insights into the performance trade-offs between these two approaches.

- Addressing the effects of imbalanced datasets, several strategies have gained popularity. 1) Re-sampling techniques, for example, Monte Carlo Simulation Analysis, can be used to balance class distribution by oversampling the minority class, undersampling the majority class, or the combination of these two (Gladkoff et al., 2021). 2) Data augmentation techniques, such as the use of Generative Adversarial Networks (GANs), can generate new examples for the minority class by applying transformations to existing data. 3) Furthermore, machine learning approaches like bagging and bootstrapping can reduce variances by implementing a "voting system" that enables models to make better decisions.

- Finally, it would be advantageous to develop a post-processing step that generates a table displaying all treatments along with their corresponding temporal information. This would create an end-to-end system that physicians could use as a practical tool.

Future research should address these limitations by exploring a broader range of PLMs, templates, and experimental setups to provide a more comprehensive understanding of the performance characteristics of prompt-based learning methods in the clinical domain. Application to some more powerful computational resources will also extend this work.

Ethical Discussion

The n2b2 (formerly i2b2) 2012 Temporal Relations dataset was used for the development of the approach in this project. This dataset comprises patient-level data in the form of discharge summaries. These documents have been de-identified in accordance with the Health Insurance Portability and Accountability Act of 1996 privacy regulations by the organizers of the n2c2 2012 NLP challenge (Act, 1996). The dataset was obtained with permission for academic use only after signing a Data Use and Confidentiality Agreement with the n2c2 National Center for Biomedical Computing. So no further ethical approval forms were required to gain access to the dataset.

Acknowledgements

We thank the reviewers for their precious comments on making our paper better. The work was partially supported by Grant EP/V047949/1 "Integrating hospital outpatient letters into the healthcare data space" (funder: UKRI/EPSRC).

References

Accountability Act. 1996. Health insurance portability and accountability act of 1996. *Public law*, 104:191.

Akiko Aizawa. 2003. An information-theoretic perspective of tf–idf measures. *Information Processing & Management*, 39(1):45–65.

Tom Brown, Benjamin Mann, Nick Ryder, Melanie Subbiah, Jared D Kaplan, Prafulla Dhariwal, Arvind Neelakantan, Pranav Shyam, Girish Sastry, Amanda

Askell, et al. 2020. Language models are few-shot learners. *Advances in neural information processing systems*, 33:1877–1901.

Wendy W Chapman, Will Bridewell, Paul Hanbury, Gregory F Cooper, and Bruce G Buchanan. 2001. A simple algorithm for identifying negated findings and diseases in discharge summaries. *Journal of biomedical informatics*, 34(5):301–310.

William A Chren. 1998. One-hot residue coding for low delay-power product cmos design. *IEEE Transactions on circuits and systems II: Analog and Digital Signal Processing*, 45(3):303–313.

Ronan Collobert and Jason Weston. 2008. A unified architecture for natural language processing: Deep neural networks with multitask learning. In *Proceedings of the 25th international conference on Machine learning*, pages 160–167.

Jacob Devlin, Ming-Wei Chang, Kenton Lee, and Kristina Toutanova. 2018. Bert: Pre-training of deep bidirectional transformers for language understanding. *arXiv preprint arXiv:1810.04805*.

Richard S Dick, Elaine B Steen, Don E Detmer, et al. 1997. The computer-based patient record: an essential technology for health care.

Ning Ding, Shengding Hu, Weilin Zhao, Yulin Chen, Zhiyuan Liu, Hai-Tao Zheng, and Maosong Sun. 2021. Openprompt: An open-source framework for prompt-learning. *arXiv preprint arXiv:2111.01998*.

Chelsea Finn, Pieter Abbeel, and Sergey Levine. 2017. Model-agnostic meta-learning for fast adaptation of deep networks. In *International conference on machine learning*, pages 1126–1135. PMLR.

Serge Gladkoff, Irina Sorokina, Lifeng Han, and Alexandra Alekseeva. 2021. Measuring uncertainty in translation quality evaluation (tqe). *arXiv preprint arXiv:2111.07699*.

Yoav Goldberg and Omer Levy. 2014. word2vec explained: deriving mikolov et al.'s negative-sampling word-embedding method. *arXiv preprint arXiv:1402.3722*.

Ian Goodfellow, Yoshua Bengio, and Aaron Courville. 2016. *Deep learning*. MIT press.

Yuxian Gu, Xu Han, Zhiyuan Liu, and Minlie Huang. 2021. Ppt: Pre-trained prompt tuning for few-shot learning. *arXiv preprint arXiv:2109.04332*.

Aaron Li-Feng Han, Xiaodong Zeng, Derek F Wong, and Lidia S Chao. 2015. Chinese named entity recognition with graph-based semi-supervised learning model. In *Proceedings of the Eighth SIGHAN Workshop on Chinese Language Processing*, pages 15–20.

Lifeng Han, Gleb Erofeev, Irina Sorokina, Serge Gladkoff, and Goran Nenadic. 2022. Examining large pre-trained language models for machine translation: What you don't know about it. In *Proceedings of the Seventh Conference on Machine Translation (WMT)*, pages 908–919, Abu Dhabi, United Arab Emirates (Hybrid). Association for Computational Linguistics.

Jerry R Hobbs, Douglas Appelt, David Is Bear, and Mabry Tyson. 1997. Extracting information from natural-language text. *Finite-state language processing*, page 383.

Sepp Hochreiter and Jürgen Schmidhuber. 1997. Long short-term memory. *Neural computation*, 9(8):1735–1780.

George Hripcsak, John HM Austin, Philip O Alderson, and Carol Friedman. 2002. Use of natural language processing to translate clinical information from a database of 889,921 chest radiographic reports. *Radiology*, 224(1):157–163.

Philipp Koehn. 2009. *Statistical machine translation*. Cambridge University Press.

Kamran Kowsari, Kiana Jafari Meimandi, Mojtaba Heidarysafa, Sanjana Mendu, Laura Barnes, and Donald Brown. 2019. Text classification algorithms: A survey. *Information*, 10(4):150.

Jinhyuk Lee, Wonjin Yoon, Sungdong Kim, Donghyeon Kim, Sunkyu Kim, Chan Ho So, and Jaewoo Kang. 2020. Biobert: a pre-trained biomedical language representation model for biomedical text mining. *Bioinformatics*, 36(4):1234–1240.

Pengfei Liu, Weizhe Yuan, Jinlan Fu, Zhengbao Jiang, Hiroaki Hayashi, and Graham Neubig. 2023. Pre-train, prompt, and predict: A systematic survey of prompting methods in natural language processing. *ACM Computing Surveys*, 55(9):1–35.

Christopher Manning and Hinrich Schutze. 1999. *Foundations of statistical natural language processing*. MIT press.

Bryan McCann, Nitish Shirish Keskar, Caiming Xiong, and Richard Socher. 2018. The natural language decathlon: Multitask learning as question answering. *arXiv preprint arXiv:1806.08730*.

Erwan Moreau, Ashjan Alsulaimani, Alfredo Maldonado, Lifeng Han, Carl Vogel, and Koel Dutta Chowdhury. 2018. Semantic reranking of crf label sequences for verbal multiword expression identification.

James Pustejovsky, José M Castano, Robert Ingria, Roser Sauri, Robert J Gaizauskas, Andrea Setzer, Graham Katz, and Dragomir R Radev. 2003. Timeml: Robust specification of event and temporal expressions in text. *New directions in question answering*, 3:28–34.

Xipeng Qiu, Tianxiang Sun, Yige Xu, Yunfan Shao, Ning Dai, and Xuanjing Huang. 2020. Pre-trained models for natural language processing: A survey. *Science China Technological Sciences*, 63(10):1872–1897.

Alec Radford, Karthik Narasimhan, Tim Salimans, Ilya Sutskever, et al. 2018. Improving language understanding by generative pre-training.

Alec Radford, Jeff Wu, Rewon Child, David Luan, Dario Amodei, and Ilya Sutskever. 2019. Language models are unsupervised multitask learners.

Colin Raffel, Noam Shazeer, Adam Roberts, Katherine Lee, Sharan Narang, Michael Matena, Yanqi Zhou, Wei Li, and Peter J Liu. 2020. Exploring the limits of transfer learning with a unified text-to-text transformer. *The Journal of Machine Learning Research*, 21(1):5485–5551.

Ellen Riloff. 1996. Automatically generating extraction patterns from untagged text. In *Proceedings of the national conference on artificial intelligence*, pages 1044–1049.

Timo Schick and Hinrich Schütze. 2020. Exploiting cloze questions for few shot text classification and natural language inference. *arXiv preprint arXiv:2001.07676*.

Chaitanya Shivade, Preethi Raghavan, Eric Fosler-Lussier, Peter J Embi, Noemie Elhadad, Stephen B Johnson, and Albert M Lai. 2014. A review of approaches to identifying patient phenotype cohorts using electronic health records. *Journal of the American Medical Informatics Association*, 21(2):221–230.

Mohammad Shoeybi, Mostofa Patwary, Raul Puri, Patrick LeGresley, Jared Casper, and Bryan Catanzaro. 2019. Megatron-lm: Training multi-billion parameter language models using model parallelism. *arXiv preprint arXiv:1909.08053*.

Richard Socher, Alex Perelygin, Jean Wu, Jason Chuang, Christopher D Manning, Andrew Y Ng, and Christopher Potts. 2013. Recursive deep models for semantic compositionality over a sentiment treebank. In *Proceedings of the 2013 conference on empirical methods in natural language processing*, pages 1631–1642.

William F Styler IV, Steven Bethard, Sean Finan, Martha Palmer, Sameer Pradhan, Piet C De Groen, Brad Erickson, Timothy Miller, Chen Lin, Guergana Savova, et al. 2014. Temporal annotation in the clinical domain. *Transactions of the association for computational linguistics*, 2:143–154.

Weiyi Sun, Anna Rumshisky, and Özlem Uzuner. 2013a. Annotating temporal information in clinical narratives. *Journal of biomedical informatics*, 46:S5–S12.

Weiyi Sun, Anna Rumshisky, and Ozlem Uzuner. 2013b. Evaluating temporal relations in clinical text: 2012 i2b2 challenge. *Journal of the American Medical Informatics Association*, 20(5):806–813.

Niall Taylor, Yi Zhang, Dan Joyce, Alejo Nevado-Holgado, and Andrey Kormilitzin. 2022. Clinical prompt learning with frozen language models. *arXiv preprint arXiv:2205.05535*.

Hangyu Tu. 2022. *Extraction of Temporal Information from Clinical Free Text*. MSc. Thesis, The University of Manchester.

Özlem Uzuner, Andreea Bodnari, Shuying Shen, Tyler Forbush, John Pestian, and Brett R South. 2012. Evaluating the state of the art in coreference resolution for electronic medical records. *Journal of the American Medical Informatics Association*, 19(5):786–791.

Özlem Uzuner, Brett R South, Shuying Shen, and Scott L DuVall. 2011. 2010 i2b2/va challenge on concepts, assertions, and relations in clinical text. *Journal of the American Medical Informatics Association*, 18(5):552–556.

Ashish Vaswani, Samy Bengio, Eugene Brevdo, Francois Chollet, Aidan N Gomez, Stephan Gouws, Llion Jones, Łukasz Kaiser, Nal Kalchbrenner, Niki Parmar, et al. 2018. Tensor2tensor for neural machine translation. *arXiv preprint arXiv:1803.07416*.

Ashish Vaswani, Noam Shazeer, Niki Parmar, Jakob Uszkoreit, Llion Jones, Aidan N Gomez, Łukasz Kaiser, and Illia Polosukhin. 2017. Attention is all you need. *Advances in neural information processing systems*, 30.

David Wadden, Ulme Wennberg, Yi Luan, and Hannaneh Hajishirzi. 2019. Entity, relation, and event extraction with contextualized span representations. *arXiv preprint arXiv:1909.03546*.

Yuping Wu, Lifeng Han, Valerio Antonini, and Goran Nenadic. 2022. On cross-domain pre-trained language models for clinical text mining: How do they perform on data-constrained fine-tuning? *arXiv preprint arXiv:2210.12770*.

Jingqing Zhang, Yao Zhao, Mohammad Saleh, and Peter Liu. 2020. Pegasus: Pre-training with extracted gap-sentences for abstractive summarization. In *International Conference on Machine Learning*, pages 11328–11339. PMLR.

A Background and More Literature

In this section, We introduce some key concepts and then explore the methods and techniques used in clinical text mining, with a particular focus on temporal classification (Tu, 2022). We will begin by examining the fundamentals of clinical text mining and its applications in healthcare, followed by an in-depth discussion on the challenges associated with temporal event extraction and classification. Next, we will delve into the recent developments in prompt-based learning and its potential to revolutionise the field of clinical text mining, including its ability to handle diverse NLP tasks with a unified framework.

Our objective is to provide a comprehensive overview of the current landscape of clinical text mining in the context of temporal classification, emphasising the emerging role of prompt-based learning and its potential to drive further innovation and improvement in healthcare research and practice.

A.1 Temporal Classification from EHRs

Electronic Health Records (EHRs) have evolved from the concept of Computer Patient Records (CPR) proposed by the Institute of Medicine in 1991 (Dick et al., 1997). Temporal relation classification of clinical events is crucial in understanding the chronological sequence and dependencies of events within electronic health records (EHRs). Extracting and analysing temporal information from EHRs can enhance our comprehension of disease progression, treatment efficacy, and patient risk factors, ultimately leading to improved healthcare outcomes.

A.2 Related NLP Applications

Rule-based methods in NLP involve using a predefined set of linguistic rules, patterns, or heuristics to process and analyse text. These rules are often developed by domain experts or linguists, reflecting the inherent structure and patterns present in the language. For instance, in Named Entity Recognition (NER) tasks, rule-based approaches can identify proper names, organisations, and locations using regular expressions (Hobbs et al., 1997), which often target words starting with a capital letter. And Chapman (Chapman et al., 2001) proposes a rule-based algorithm designed for detecting negated concepts in clinical text. The advantages of rule-based methods include their speed and the lack of requirement for extensive computational resources.

However, rule-based methods have many limitations such as low recall (Riloff, 1996). In certain domains, only experts can develop effective rules. Changes in the data source might render existing rules ineffective. Moreover, rule-based methods can be challenging to apply in temporal classification tasks involving free text, due to the absence of a standard format and the diverse and varied language expressions.

Statistical sequence models are particularly well-suited for language processing tasks due to their ability to handle variable-length sequences, such as sentences. CRFs have been widely used in sequence labelling tasks such as part-of-speech tagging, information extraction, and named entity recognition (NER) (Moreau et al., 2018; Han et al., 2015). In clinical domain, Shivade et al. (2014) used a combination of HMMs and CRFs for clinical named entity recognition (NER) tasks. They used these methods to identify medical concepts such as medications, dosages, and durations from clinical text. Their results demonstrated that HMMs and CRFs could effectively recognize medical concepts, with CRFs outperforming HMMs in most cases.

Before the advent of word embeddings, researchers primarily used statistical techniques like one-hot encoding (Chren, 1998) and TF-IDF (Aizawa, 2003) to represent words based on their frequency of occurrence in the text. This led to the creation of large, sparse vectors for word representation. The introduction of Word2Vec (Goldberg and Levy, 2014) offered several advantages, including lower-dimensional, dense, and continuous vectors that captured semantic similarity between words based on their co-occurrence with other words.

With the development of hardware capabilities, large neural networks have become feasible, which allows the exploration of deep learning architectures that can discover hidden features and automatically learn representations from the input in an end-to-end structure, mostly via the encoder-decoder style (Goodfellow et al., 2016). Collobert and Weston (2008) first introduced temporal convolutional neural networks (CNNs) for named entity recognition (NER) tasks. To model long sequences, Hochreiter and Schmidhuber (1997) proposed the long short-term memory (LSTM) model based on the architecture of recurrent neural networks (RNNs), addressing the challenge of capturing long-distance historical information and mitigating the vanishing gradient problem faced by RNNs.

Tu (2022) used a combination of Bidirectional Long Short-Term Memory (BiLSTM) and Conditional Random Fields (CRF) to perform Named Entity Recognition (NER) tasks on a clinical dataset. The model achieved a weighted average accuracy of 0.98 and a macro-averaging score of 0.69. Additionally, they explored the use of a Convolutional Neural Network (CNN) with BiLSTM, resulting in improved performance compared to the BiLSTM+CRF model. This hybrid model demonstrated a precision of 85.67%, recall of 87.83%, and an F1-score of 88.17%.

A.3 Recent Large Language Models

A.3.1 Pre-trained Language Models

The development of the Transformer architecture by Vaswani et al. (2017) brought NLP to a new stage with its self-attention mechanism, which enhances the model's ability to capture long-range dependencies among words in the input sequence. Pre-trained language models like BERT, GPT, and T5, which are based on the Transformer architecture, have achieved state-of-the-art performance on numerous tasks. These models learn contextualised word representations, different from traditional word representations (e.g., Word2Vec, GloVe), which map words to fixed-length vectors and assume words in similar contexts have similar meanings. In contrast, pre-trained models learn context-dependent representations, capturing contextual information more effectively (Qiu et al., 2020). This process allows models to better "understand" language, context, and words.

A.3.2 Fine-tuning Paradigm

Fine-tuning has been the traditional approach for adopting pre-trained language models (PLMs) to specific tasks. This is usually done by task-specific layers or heads on top of the pre-trained model and adjusting the model's weights through back-propagation (Wu et al., 2022). It has achieved state-of-the-art results in many NLP tasks, such as sentiment analysis (Socher et al., 2013), named entity recognition (Wadden et al., 2019) and machine translation (Vaswani et al., 2018; Han et al., 2022). However, it requires lots of training data, which may not be available in certain scenarios, and to fine-tuning a model can be computationally expensive.

Fine-tuning From 2017 to 2019, there was a paradigm shift in NLP model learning, with researchers moving away from fully supervised methods and increasingly adopting the pre-training and fine-tuning paradigm. This approach uses a fixed architecture pre-trained language model (PLM) to predict the probability of observed textual data. The PLM is adapted to different downstream tasks by fine-tuning additional parameters using objective functions specific to each task. For instance, Zhang et al. (Zhang et al., 2020) introduced a loss function for predicting salient sentences, and when combined with PLMs and fine-tuning, it resulted in state-of-the-art performance on various popular datasets and tasks (Devlin et al., 2018). However, the fine-tuning approach is most suitable when large-scale text data is available for optimising the objective function, which is not always feasible in certain domains. In the case of clinical records, data privacy issues and the need for clinical experts to annotate data for training make it difficult to produce large open clinical datasets. For example, BERT models trained on non-medical text tend to perform poorly when applied to medical domain tasks (Lee et al., 2020; Wu et al., 2022). Additionally, each specific task requires its own fine-tuning process, and as the NLP field continues to increase model sizes to improve performance (e.g., Microsoft's Megatron (Shoeybi et al., 2019) with 530 billion parameters), full or partial fine-tuning of these massive models demands considerable computational, financial resources, and time (Han et al., 2022). These concerns have led to the emergence of a new paradigm called prompt-based learning, which aims to achieve strong performance across a wide range of applications without the need for extensive fine-tuning.

A.3.3 Few-shot Learning

Few-shot learning is an area of machine learning that focuses on training models to recognize or generalize new concepts with very limited labelled examples. This approach aims to alleviate the need for large amounts of labelled data, which can be costly and time-consuming to obtain. The few-shot learning problem is typically framed in terms of episodes, where each episode consists of a small support set and a query set. The support set contains a few labelled examples of each class, while the query set comprises unlabelled examples from the same classes. The goal is to learn a model that can accurately classify the query set instances based on the limited information provided in the support set. Finn et al. (Finn et al., 2017) proposed MAML, a meta-learning algorithm that learns an optimal initialisation of model parameters, enabling rapid adaptation to new tasks with few gradient updates.

A.3.4 Prompt-based Learning Paradigm

Prompt-based learning is a recent paradigm in NLP that leverages pre-trained language models (PLMs) like GPT-3 (Brown et al., 2020) to perform various tasks without the need for fine-tuning. This approach involves using carefully designed prompts or templates that guide the PLM to generate desired outputs based on the input context. Moreover, this approach is especially useful in situations with limited task-specific training data, as it does not require retraining the entire model, however, crafting effective prompts for specific tasks can be challenging and may require manual engineering or iterative search procedures. It gives me the inspiration to construct a fine prompt learning and challenge with more traditional fine-tuning methods.

Prompt-based learning emerged with the advent of models like T5 and GPT-3, as researchers discovered that pre-trained language models (PLMs) could be effectively guided by textual prompts in low-data scenarios. The T5 model innovation suggested that PLMs possess strong language understanding capabilities, and by providing appropriate instructions or prompts, they can adapt to various tasks (Liu et al., 2023). This approach, dubbed "pre-train, prompt, and predict" or prompt-based learning, revolves around prompt engineering, which tailors prompts to suit different downstream tasks.

For instance, given the sentence "Patient is complaining of a stomachache" an emotion recognition task can be framed by adding a prompt like "Patient felt so ___", prompting the language model to fill in the blank with an emotion-laden word. Similarly, for translation tasks, a prompt like "English: Patient is complaining of a stomachache, Chinese: ___" can be used. ChatGPT's ability to understand and answer questions in natural language can also be considered a form of prompting, influencing the quality of responses.

OpenPrompt Ding et al. (Ding et al., 2021) introduced a unified, user-friendly toolkit called OpenPrompt to facilitate prompt-based learning with PLMs. OpenPrompt's modular and combinable research-friendly framework enables the integration of various tasks, prompting techniques, and PLMs while accommodating different template formats, verbalizer formats, and initialization strategies. Taylor et al. (Taylor et al., 2022) applied prompt learning to the clinical domain using frozen language models by using the OpenPrompt framework. Their research compared prompt-based learning and fine-tuning in clinical classification tasks, finding that prompt learning typically matched traditional fine-tuning performance on full datasets and outperformed it in few-shot settings which means prompt learning is more adopted training with smaller datasets. Additionally, prompt learning excelled when working with frozen PLMs, showcasing its potential with fewer trainable parameters.

A.4 Summary

In this section, we delve into prior work concerning temporal classification and examine the fundamental concepts and methods used in constructing our model. Given the absence of previous studies utilising prompt-based learning for temporal classification in the clinical domain, there are no established guidelines or approaches for this task. In the following section, we will provide a detailed explanation of the methodology used to develop our model, outlining each step of the process.

B On Dataset Used

Figure 8 presents the format used for training the model, where the discharge note column contains clinical text information, and the treatment entity column comprises treatment entities. The training dataset consists of 3,836 samples, with 3,075 having the label "ON" (treatment used during hospitalisation) and 762 having the label "OFF" (treatment not used during hospitalisation), resulting in an imbalanced distribution with label "ON" being four times more prevalent than label "OFF".

To gain a deeper understanding of the dataset, various statistical analyses were conducted. As depicted in Figure 9, the word count distribution for clinical notes, excluding the first five lines, is displayed. The first five lines of each note, which contain admission and discharge dates, are not considered beneficial for statistical analysis. The figure illustrates that most sentences have fewer than 20 words, and no sentences in the training dataset exceed 80 words. Based on this information, the maximum input sequence length can be determined.

C Learning Models

C.0.1 State-of-the-Art PLMs

A pre-trained language model is a neural network model that has already been trained on a large corpus of text data before being fine-tuned for specific tasks (Han et al., 2022). These models are designed to learn the structure and nuances of a language by predicting the next word in a sentence or reconstructing a sentence with masked words. By learning the complex patterns and relationships

	document name	discharge note	treatment entity	label
0	422.xml.tlink	Admission Date : 2017-07-12 Discharge Date : 2...	oxycodone	1
1	631.xml.tlink	ADMISSION DATE : 10/10/97 DISCHARGE DATE : 10/...	diabetes control	1
2	272.xml.tlink	Admission Date : 2011-09-24 Discharge Date : 2...	extubated	1
3	96.xml.tlink	Admission Date : 11/17/2003 Discharge Date : 1...	pain control	0
4	422.xml.tlink	Admission Date : 2017-07-12 Discharge Date : 2...	a standing IVF order	1
...	...	...	...	...
3832	422.xml.tlink	Admission Date : 2017-07-12 Discharge Date : 2...	repletion	1
3833	736.xml.tlink	Admission Date : 03/17/1998 Discharge Date : 0...	Gentamicin	1
3834	577.xml.tlink	Admission Date : 2009-06-23 Discharge Date : 2...	levofloxacin	1
3835	177.xml.tlink	Admission Date : 2012-11-21 Discharge Date : 2...	CellCept	1
3836	26.xml.tlink	Admission Date : 12/11/2005 Discharge Date : 1...	oral analgesics	0

Figure 8: Training Dataset Format

within the language, these models can generate contextually relevant embeddings or representations of words and phrases.

Masked Language Model: BERT BERT (Bidirectional Encoder Representations from Transformers) is a pre-trained language model developed by Google researchers in 2018 (Devlin et al., 2018). As its name suggests, it uses the encoder architecture from the Transformer model but with a deeper structure, as shown in Figure 14. The BERT-base language model comprises 12 encoder blocks, which is twice the size of a standard Transformer Encoder.

In contrast to OpenAI's GPT (Generative Pre-trained Transformer), BERT uses a bidirectional Transformer block connection layer (Figure 15), allowing it to access information from both preceding and following content, while GPT only considers the preceding content during training. Although the concept of "bi-directionality" is not new. For example, ELMo uses two individual objective functions $P(w_i|w_1, ...w_{i-1})$,$P(w_i|w_{i+1}, ..., w_n)$ to train the language model. However, BERT uses a single objective function:

$$P(w_i|w_1, ...w_{i-1}, w_{i+1}, ..., w_n) \tag{1}$$

to train the language model, integrating both preceding and following context.

The Masked Language Model (MLM) serves as one of BERT's pre-training tasks, wherein it randomly masks certain words in a sentence with the [mask] token. By leveraging the bidirectional Encoder Representations, BERT predicts the masked words based on both preceding and following context, resulting in a more comprehensive understanding of word meanings. Additionally, the Next Sentence Prediction (NSP) pre-training task trains the model to discern the relationship between sentences by determining whether sentence B follows sentence A in the original text (Devlin et al., 2018).

The input for BERT consists of Token Embeddings, Segment Embeddings, and Position Embeddings, as illustrated in Figure 16. Each input sentence is treated as a sequence of tokens, with every sequence starting with a special classification token, [CLS]. BERT uses another special token, [SEP], to separate sentences and assigns segment embeddings to each token to indicate whether it belongs to sentence A or B. This enables BERT to handle various downstream tasks, such as separating question and answer sequences (Devlin et al., 2018). By incorporating position embeddings, the model generates distinct word vector outputs for the same word based on its contextual environment, thereby enhancing the model's accuracy.

Fine-tuning enables BERT to accommodate various downstream tasks by adjusting the corresponding inputs and outputs (Figure 17). The same pre-trained model parameters are used to initialise models for different downstream tasks, and all parameters are fine-tuned end-to-end to adapt the model to the specific task. In comparison to pre-training, fine-tuning is relatively cost-effective and computationally efficient.

Auto-regressive Language Model: GPT-2 The Generative Pre-trained Transformer 2 (GPT-2) is

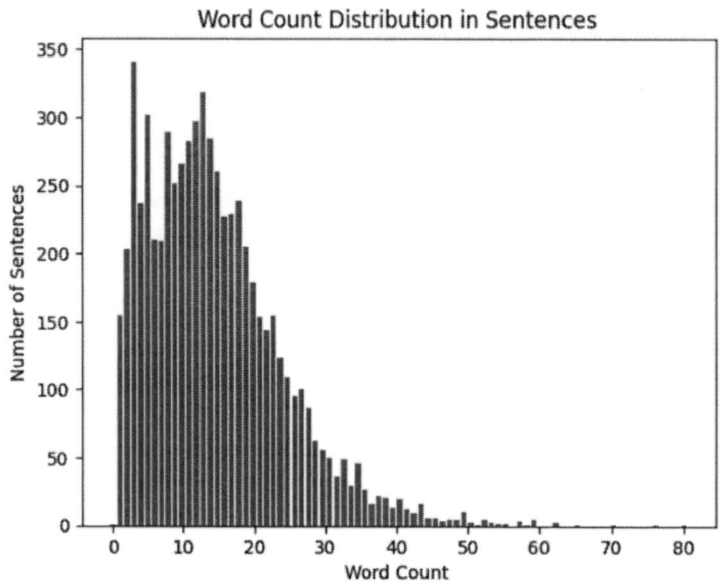

Figure 9: Word Count Distribution in Sentences

an advanced language model introduced by OpenAI in 2019, building upon the foundation of the original GPT (Radford et al., 2019). GPT-2 uses a transformer-based decoder architecture with multi-layer, multi-head self-attention mechanisms, as shown in Figure 18. This design allows GPT-2 to generate sequences of arbitrary length, making it particularly adept at producing highly coherent and contextually relevant text, often used for question-answering and summarization tasks.

GPT-2 differs from BERT in several ways. As an autoregressive model, GPT-2 predicts one token at a time, using previously generated tokens as context for subsequent predictions based on the equation of $p(s_{s-k}, ..., s_n|s_1, ..., s_{n-k-1})$. This process continues until the desired output length is achieved or an end-of-sequence token is generated. By modelling a sequence of outputs as a product of conditional probabilities, GPT-2 leverages the natural sequence of symbols inherent in language. Unlike BERT's bidirectional approach, GPT-2 uses masked self-attention, processing input sequences in a unidirectional manner, resulting in more contextually relevant text generation (Radford et al., 2018).

One innovative aspect of GPT-2 is its ability to perform supervised learning tasks using an unsupervised pre-training model. While traditional supervised learning aims to estimate $p(output|input)$, GPT-2 seeks to model $p(output|input, task)$, allowing for a more generalised model across various tasks. This approach has been used in multitask and meta-learning settings. For instance, a translation training example could be presented as a sequence (translate to French, English text, French text), enabling the model to understand the translation task and the relationship between input and output (McCann et al., 2018).

Seq2Seq: T5 T5, an abbreviation for Text-To-Text Transfer Transformer, proposes the idea that fine-tuning models for specific tasks may no longer be necessary (Raffel et al., 2020). Instead, a large pre-trained model can be used for any task, with the main focus on adapting the task into appropriate textual inputs and outputs (Raffel et al., 2020). For example, refer to Figure 19, in translation tasks, inputting "translate English to German" followed by a [sequence] results in the model producing the translated [sequence]. Similarly, for summarization tasks, inputting "summarise" along with the [sequence] generates a summary of the [sequence]. This method establishes a unified Text-to-Text format for NLP tasks, expressed as $[Prefix + SequenceA] \rightarrow [SequenceB]$, enabling the use of the same model, loss function, training process, and decoding process across all NLP tasks with different prefix information.

To accomplish this, a powerful language model that genuinely comprehends language is required.

The Google team developed a strategy to determine the optimal model architecture and parameters, ultimately creating a robust baseline. First, they examined three popular model architectures. The encoder-decoder Transformer (Vaswani et al., 2017), also known as a seq2seq model (left panel of Figure 20), comprises two layer stacks: the encoder processes the input sequence and encodes each token, while the decoder generates a new output sequence with each token based on the decoding input and previous output sequences. The language model architecture (middle one of Figure 20), akin to the decoder in an encoder-decoder Transformer, predicts output at each time-step based on previous time-step predictions, with GPT-2 being a typical Example The Prefix LM (language model) incorporates fully-visible masking applied to the prefix, rendering the architecture more effective for a wide range of text-to-text tasks shown in the left panel of Figure 20. Following experimentation, the Google team determined that the encoder-decoder architecture is the most suitable for the text-to-text framework, thus adopting it for T5 (Raffel et al., 2020).

Subsequently, they used masked language modelling (BERT-style) as an unsupervised pre-training method. Similar to BERT, but using masks to replace spans surrounding the original masked tokens as corruption strategies, with a 15% corruption rate and 3 corrupted span length according to experimental results.

After utilising multi-task learning to train with the C4 (Colossal Clean Crawled Corpus) dataset, which comprises hundreds of gigabytes of clean English text extracted from the web, the Google team acquired the best pre-trained language model, T5, among numerous combinations of model architecture, training methods, and various parameters.

C.1 Prompt-Based Learning

Prompt Construction The first step involves creating a *prompting function* $f_{prompt}(\cdot)$, which transforms the input **x** into a prompted $x' = f_{prompt}(x)$ (Liu et al., 2023). This function entails two stages: (1) Designing a *template*, a string containing an *input slot* [X] for the input **x** and an *answer slot* [Z] for the generated answer, which is mapped to the output **y**. (2) Filling the slot [X] with the input **x**.

In the case of temporal classification for treatment "a total abdominal hysterectomy," the template could be structured as "[Input] Here is the clinical record, treatment a total abdominal hysterectomy [Z] during the hospitalisation." Additionally, templates can be categorised based on the position of the empty slot, such as close (prompts with slots in the middle of the text) or prefix prompts (slots appearing before the entity) z (Liu et al., 2023).

Answer Selection Subsequently, the language model (LM) is used to identify the highest-probability text $\hat{z}$. Liu et al. (Liu et al., 2023) characterises Z as a collection of acceptable values for z, indicating that the LM determines the most probable answer z from the set of answers Z. This process is also referred to as answer engineering or verbalisation (we will consistently use the terms verbalizer[2] and verbalization).

The verbalizer can be regarded as a mapping between one or many distinct tokens and unique class labels. The embedding generated at the <[MASK]> position by using PLM is through a large language model head or classifier, and prediction of the tokens from verbalizer class labeled are obtained. In the previous temporal classification example, Z = "is", "is not" corresponds to class labels Y = ON, OFF.

The function $f_{fill}(x', z)$ fills the slot [Z] in prompt x' with a potential answer z. Lastly, the probability of the corresponding filled prompt is calculated using a PLM $P(\cdot;\theta)$, as shown in Eq. 2:

$$\hat{z} = search_{z \in Z} P(f_{fill}(x', z); \theta) \qquad (2)$$

The search function could use argmax for the highest-scoring output or sampling to randomly generate outputs according to the LM's probability distribution (Liu et al., 2023).

Answer Mapping The final step maps the highest-scoring answer $\hat{z}$ to the highest-scored output $\hat{y}$. While this step might not be crucial in binary classification, it is necessary for tasks like translation or sentiment analysis with multiple words (e.g., "good", "wonderful", "perfect") mapped to the same class (e.g., "++"). Thus, a mapping process between the answer and the true output value is required (Ding et al., 2021).

D Parameters and Settings

The code below shows how to load the PLM of T5 and tokenizer in OpenPrompt: " plm, tokenizer, model_config, WrapperClass = load_plm ("t5", "t5-base") "

2

E More Discussion on PLM Outputs

The dataset we used is derived from clinical notes, implying that in real life, there are indeed more positive labels than negative ones. In some cases, having a high recall may be more important than having high precision. For instance, in medical diagnosis, it could be crucial to identify all patients with a specific disease (high recall) to ensure they receive appropriate treatment, even if some healthy patients are misclassified as having the disease (low precision). It is unclear whether recall is more important than precision in the context of temporal information of treatment. However, doctors can adjust the model's preference based on their specific situations.

It is not surprising that T5 outperforms the other models in the comparison. Firstly, T5 is the most recent model among the three and has been extensively tested by Raffel et al. (Raffel et al., 2020) to evaluate its advantages and disadvantages relative to the other architectures. Their results suggest that T5's encoder-decoder architecture performs better than BERT and GPT-2 in certain tasks. our experiment also demonstrates that T5 has a slight advantage over BERT and, more notably, GPT-2, which exhibit comparable performance.

Secondly, although it is not universally true that "bigger models are better" in the NLP field, OpenAI has made significant strides in showcasing the effectiveness of larger models in recent years. The development of models such as GPT-2, GPT-3, and, more recently, Megatron-Turing, has demonstrated that models with more parameters can improve performance on a variety of natural language processing tasks, as illustrated in Figure 10. In our experiment, we used *bert-base-uncased*, which has 110M parameters, and the *gpt-2* model with 117M parameters. However, *T5-base* model has 220M parameters, twice as many as *bert-base-uncased*. Therefore, T5 is the best model for temporal classification in the clinical domain when compared to the other two models.

F PBL with Differed Input Text

One intuitive method to create prompts is to manually craft templates based on human understanding. For instance, we can create a cloze-style manual template using Code 3, where the $<$ [MASK] $>$ token appears in the middle of the template. According to the code example, the $<$ [MASK] $>$ token can be filled with "is" or "is not".

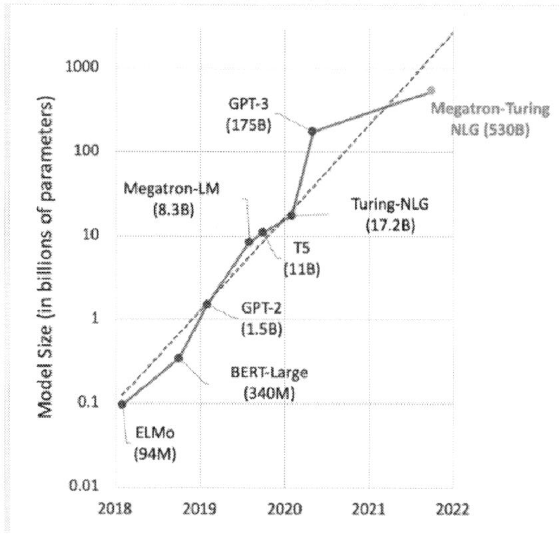

Figure 10: Development of Model in NLP Recently (from COMP34312 week5 slides)

Listing 3: Example of cloze manual template

```
text = '<[clinical_record]> In this
    paragraph of the note,
    <[treatment]> <[mask]> used between
    admission and discharge time.'
```

Another popular manual template approach is the question prompt shown in Figure 4, in which the $<$ [MASK] $>$ token is placed at the end. In this template, a discriminative statement or question is presented, such as "Question: this treatment was used between admission and discharge time. Is it correct?" Combined with the clinical context input, the PLM decides whether the statement is correct. Therefore, the possible answers for $<$ [MASK] $>$ can be "yes" or "no".

Listing 4: Example of manual template with question

```
text = '<[clinical_record]> Question:
    <[treatment]> were used between
    admission and discharge time. Is it
    correct? <[mask]>'
```

In the previous work, Gu et al. (2021) report a mixed template tokens and soft tokens in some yields better than manual and soft template, and Taylor et al. (Taylor et al., 2022) propose that soft template working with soft verbalizer perform the best on ICD9 Triage task in clinical domain.

During manual template engineering, some interesting findings were made. Initially, the manual template was designed as "<clinical note>. Question: <treatment> was used during hospitalisation. Is it correct?". While this appeared sufficient, upon analysing errors in the testing data, a particular example revealed that the treatment in question was used during the patient's last hospitalisation but not the current one. Consequently, the template was modified to specify "between admission and discharge time", which better emphasised the temporal aspect.

Furthermore, certain errors were identified due to complex language logic. During this period, chatGPT was a popular topic in NLP domain, and the GPT-3.5 model demonstrated remarkable question-answering abilities. we input a template (shown in Figure 11) to the chatGPT and the chatGPT model provided an incorrect response, despite giving an accurate explanation, which is not self coherent. This indicates that GPT-3.5 and the T5 model have difficulty capturing information from words such as "attempt" and "but".

By comparing the results of the cloze (Example 3) and question prompt (Example 4) in the manual template, it was found that the question prompt performed better. This suggests that the PLM may be more proficient in judging discriminative statements or providing answers after processing the entire input sentence. The (Mixed, Manual) pair also performed well, possibly because the generated soft tokens, based on the input sentence and fixed template tokens, provided guidance for the model to better select an answer from the set of possible responses.

F.0.1 Different Input Text

Experiments of Different Input Text In this experiment, the input length for clinical records was modified by controlling the number of sentences in the input text using a sentence window size, as well as the number of sentences before and after the target sentence.

Discussion and Summary of Different Input Text The results displayed in Table.8 indicate that as the number of input sentences increases, both the F1 score and balanced accuracy improve. However, when the input text becomes too long, such as the entire clinical text, the performance slightly declines. It was found that a window size of 6, comprising 3 sentences before the target sentence, the target sentence itself, and 2 sentences after, yielded the best F1 score and balanced accuracy of 91.79 and 75.08, respectively.

G PBL vs Traditional Fine-tuning

G.0.1 Summary of Prompt-based Learning Evaluation

In conclusion, the prompt-based learning paradigm experiments led to the establishment of a benchmark for the best-performing prompt model. The hyperparameter details are provided in Table.9. In the following section, this model will be compared to the traditional fine-tuning paradigm using a few-shot learning approach.

G.1 Prompt Learning versus Traditional Fine-tuning

In this section, we present a benchmark comparison between Prompt-based Learning (PBL) and Traditional Fine-tuning (FT) under few-shot settings. Table 10 displays the selected hyperparameters for Fine-tuning. we chose to focus on a mixed template approach, which combines a manually designed template for the task with soft and trainable tokens. Since few-shot scenarios can introduce bias and variance that significantly affect performance, we aggregated the results from 10 trials and averaged them, providing a more accurate assessment.

The results (Table 7 and Figure 7) indicate that in the temporal classification task, the traditional fine-tuning model outperforms the prompt learning model. The prompt learning model performs better than the fine-tuning model only when the training set size is 10 in terms of F1 score, and when the dataset size is 20, the prompt learning model's balanced accuracy is slightly higher. This finding is consistent with Taylor's work (Taylor et al., 2022), which showed that prompt learning did not outperform fine-tuning in various clinical domain classification tasks, such as ICD-9 50, ICD-9 Triage, and In-hospital mortality. However, in specific classification tasks under Frozen PLM conditions, prompt learning exhibited better performance. In this context, "frozen" refers to the absence of updates to the model's weights and parameters during the fine-tuning process.

These results were surprising, as prompt learning has been frequently reported to be more effective in few-shot settings in numerous publications. There could be several reasons for this discrepancy. First, the soft and trainable tokens in the mixed template were not trained using a separate optimizer, which may have resulted in suboptimal tokens for the given task. Second, the benchmark for prompt learning might not be accurate due to computa-

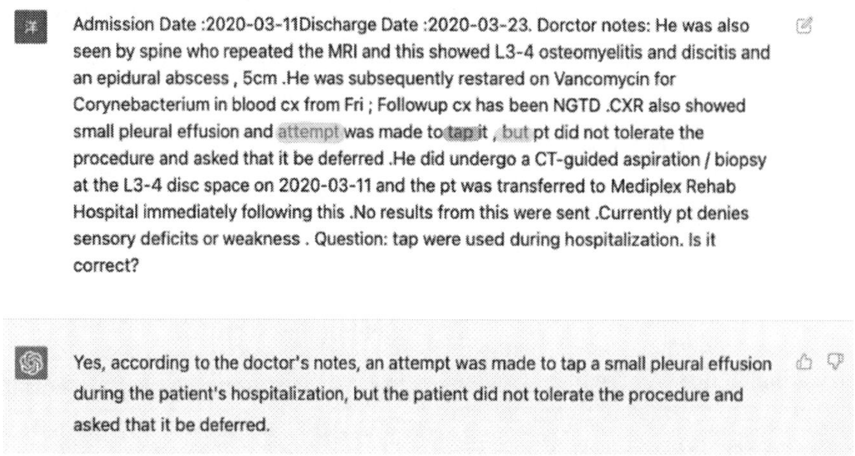

Figure 11: Example of error analysis with ChatGPT.("tap" is the treatment)

Sentences window size	(sentences before, sentences after)	F1 score of ON class	B.Accy.
1	(0,0)	88.13	64.24
2	(0,1)	89.58	65.89
3	(1,1)	90.89	72.07
4	(1,2)	91.60	73.29
5	(2,2)	91.93	73.00
6	(3,2)	**91.79**	**75.08**
7	(3,3)	91.44	71.71
Whole text		84.86	63.95

Table 8: Performance of Different Input Text (B.Accy.: Balanced Accuracy)

Parameter	Value
PLM	T5
learning rate	4E-5
batch size	4
epochs	5
optimizer	AdamW
template	mixed template
verbalizer	manual verbalizer
input sentences window size	6 (3,2)

Table 9: Hyperparameter Selection for Prompt-based Learning

Parameter	Value
PLM	BERT
learning rate	2E-5
batch size	4
epochs	5
optimizer	AdamW
input sentences window size	6 (3,2)

Table 10: Hyperparameter Selection for Fine-tuning

tional resource and time limitations. For instance, the best PLM and learning rate were determined based on a manual template and manual verbalizer, but these selections may not be ideal for mixed and soft templates. Third, potential biases in the training process could have impacted the results, as no validation set was used for prompt learning, possibly preventing the selection of the best model during training. Furthermore, averaging the results of 10 trials might not provide a sufficiently accurate assessment, and more trials could be necessary. Fourth, in a few-shot learning scenario, useing a language model pre-trained on medication and clinical domain data might be more beneficial for clinical classification tasks. Finally, prompt-based learning is a relatively new paradigm with much-untapped potential, whereas traditional fine-tuning has a well-developed training and tuning process.

Upon examining errors from the test dataset of prompt-based learning, specifically for both "ON"

```
  "label": "OFF",
  "meta": "727.xml.tlink",
  "clinical_record": "Admission Date: 2014-03-31 Discharge Date :
2014-04-01 . Dorctor notes: No maternal fever . No prolonged rupture of
membranes . Clear amniotic fluid . Anesthesia by epidural . Vaginal
delivery . Apgars were 8 and 9 . ",
  "treatment": "Anesthesia",
```


Figure 12: Example of an error in OFF class


```
  "label": "ON",
  "meta": "208.xml.tlink",
  "clinical record": "Admission Date : 2018-05-26 Discharge Date :
2018-05-31 . Dorctor notes: WBC s since admission were as high as
14,000 but normalized . She also had 2 echocardiograms which revealed
persistent pericardial effusions . She has been gently diuresed but has
worsening ARF . Her O2 requirement has increased despite diuresis . She
denies any CP / cough / fever , abdominal pain / diarrhea , black or
bloody stools or headache . Her urine output decreased to nearly zero .
",
  "treatment": "diuresis",
```


Figure 13: Example of an error in ON class

and "OFF" classes as shown in Figures 12 and 13, it becomes evident that determining whether a treatment was administered during hospitalisation can be challenging. The input content often lacks sufficient temporal information to clearly indicate the treatment status. Furthermore, there are instances of ambiguity in the dataset annotations, which complicates the classification task. The sentence tense and specific temporal expressions might be the only cues for understanding the event timeline, even for human readers, without considering the broader context of the document. It is also worth noting that discharge summaries are typically prepared at the end of a patient's hospital stay, and as such, they do not describe the hospitalisation period as the present. These observations highlight the complexities involved in classifying temporal relationships in clinical texts and the need for further improvements in methods to effectively address such challenges.

H Learning Structures

Figure 21 illustrates the general architecture of OpenPrompt, which allows for modifications to the PLM-related class (purple block) and the prompt-related class (blue block).

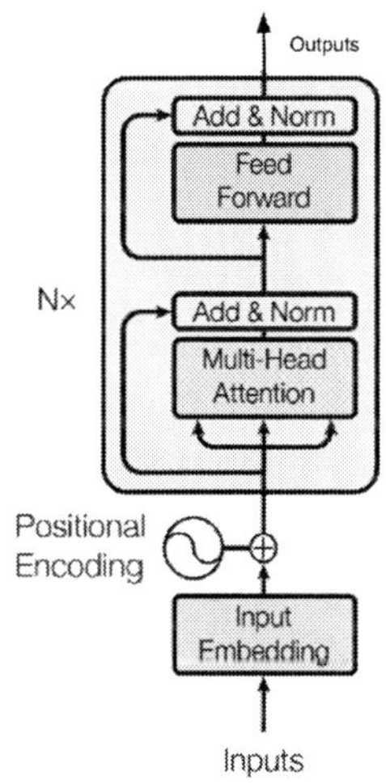

Figure 14: BERT Architecture (Vaswani et al., 2017)

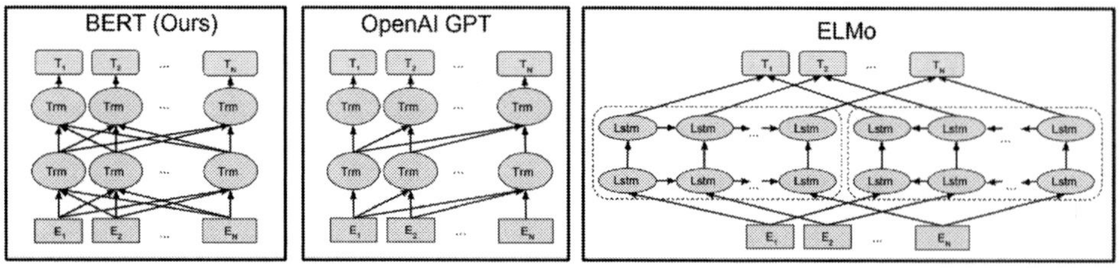

Figure 15: Differences in Rre-training Model Architectures (Devlin et al., 2018)

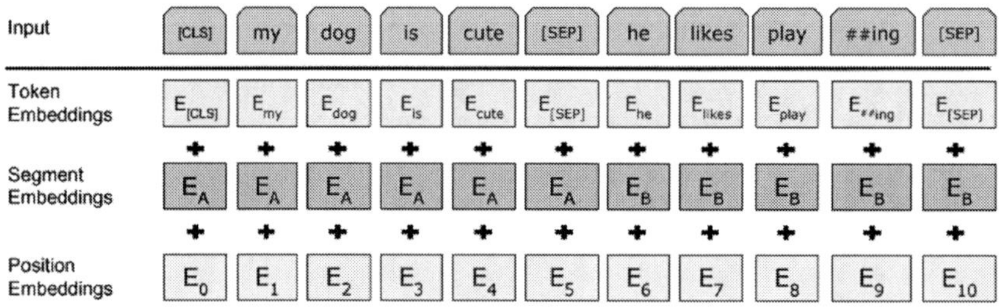

Figure 16: BERT Input Representation (Devlin et al., 2018)

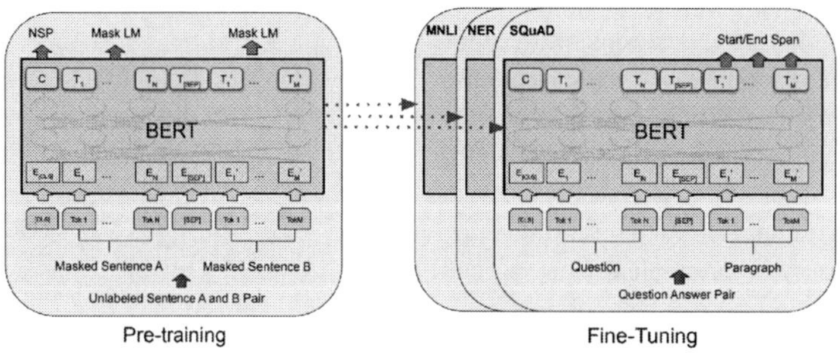

Figure 17: Overall Pre-training and Fine-tuning Procedures for BERT (Devlin et al., 2018)

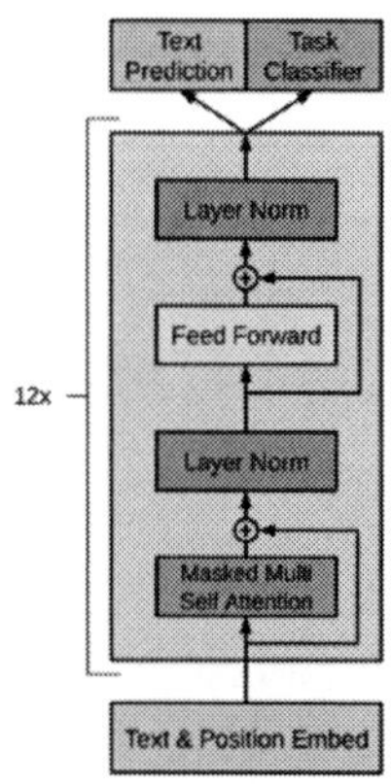

Figure 18: Architecture of GPT2 (Radford et al., 2018)

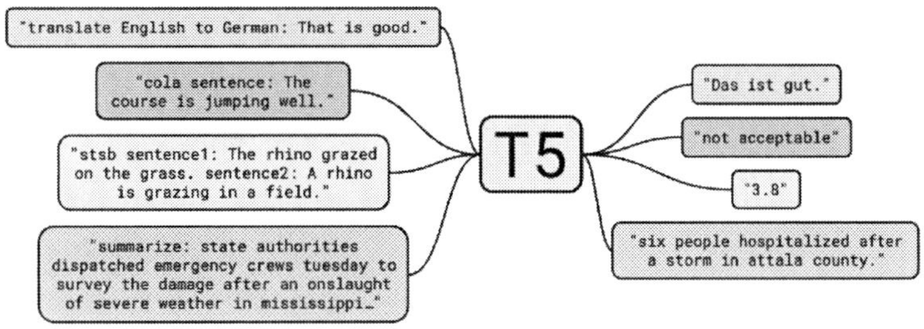

Figure 19: Text-to-text Framework (Raffel et al., 2020)

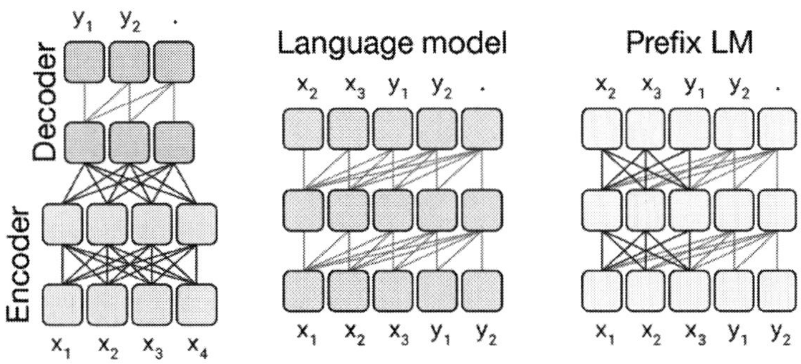

Figure 20: Different Transformer Architecture (Raffel et al., 2020)

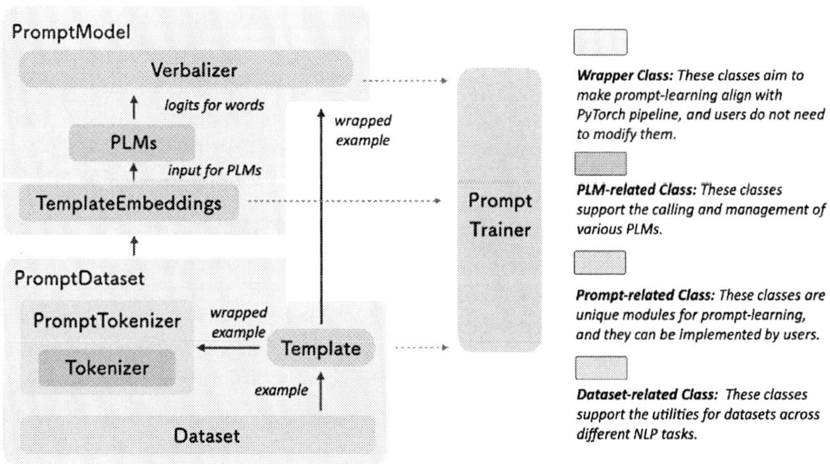

Figure 21: OpenPrompt Overall Architecutre (Ding et al., 2021)

Sudden Semantic Shifts in Swedish NATO Discourse

Brian Bonafilia, Bastiaan Bruinsma, Denitsa Saynova, and Moa Johansson

Chalmers University of Technology

bbonafilia@gmail.com, {sebastianus.bruinsma, saynova, moa.johansson}@chalmers.se

Abstract

In this paper, we investigate a type of semantic shift that occurs when a sudden event radically changes public opinion on a topic. Looking at Sweden's decision to apply for NATO membership in 2022, we use word embeddings to study how the associations users on Twitter have regarding NATO evolve. We identify several changes that we successfully validate against real-world events. However, the low engagement of the public with the issue often made it challenging to distinguish true signals from noise. We thus find that domain knowledge and data selection are of prime importance when using word embeddings to study semantic shifts.

1 Introduction

A well-known adage in Natural Language Processing is that one knows a word by the company it keeps (Firth, 1957). Yet, this company does not need to be stable and can change in either the long or short term. When this happens, the word undergoes a *semantic shift*. One common way to study these semantic shifts is by using temporal – or diachronic – word embeddings.

Most semantic shifts are slow and happen over many years or decades. Examples are words such as "nice", "broadcast" and "gay" which today have a different meaning than they would have had in the nineteenth century. Yet, while such shifts occur over various decennia, other shifts are more rapid. For example, the word "hero" changed its context from "veteran" and " superman" to "frontliner" and "covidwarrior" during the COVID-19 pandemic in a matter of months (Guo et al., 2022).

The speed of semantic change depends on various factors, such as whether the word has more than one meaning or how common it is in use (Hamilton et al., 2016). Also, *sudden* semantic change can occur during high-impact events, such as abrupt political, social, or cultural changes. For example, Tahmasebi et al. (2012) notes that the meaning of the word "terrorism" changed rapidly after the events of September 11, 2001. This, combined with the knowledge that a change in the meaning of a word also changes the opinions people associate with that word (Pérez and Tavits, 2023), makes understanding such sudden shifts relevant if we wish to understand people's changing opinions during real-world events.

Here, we use word embeddings to focus on an abrupt event in the case of Sweden: the country's decision to apply for NATO membership in 2022, following the Russian invasion of Ukraine. This decision was a sudden shift and a marked change in the country's stance on foreign affairs and defense.

To study this shift, we focus on the time from September 11, 2021, to September 11, 2022, the day of the 2022 Swedish general election. We chose this period as we wished to examine how the language used around NATO changed under the assumption that NATO would be a major election issue in Sweden. To measure the semantic shifts, we use the word embeddings from a Word2Vec (Mikolov et al., 2013) model to estimate the semantic context of a set of words of interest. We then track these words over time to see if and how they changed by comparing the rank sorting of the most similar words between various periods.

From here on, this paper will proceed as follows. First, we will introduce the background to the Swedish application for NATO membership, and how it can serve as a marked and sudden change. We then introduce our data and the procedure we used for pre-processing. Following this, we discuss our methods and the findings that result from them. We end with some brief conclusions and several suggestions for further research.

2 Background

For over two hundred years, Sweden followed a self-proclaimed policy of non-alignment ("alliansfrihet") (Brommesson et al., 2022). As a result,

Proceedings of the 61st Annual Meeting of the Association for Computational Linguistics - Student Research Workshop, pages 184–193
July 10-12, 2023 ©2023 Association for Computational Linguistics

it did not take part in most major wars, nor became part of any military alliance during the Cold War. And while it often participated in NATO exercises (Wieslander, 2022), full membership was rarely considered. Thus, Minister for Defense Peter Hultqvist could describe a Swedish membership of NATO as unthinkable as late as November 2021 (Bolin, 2023, p.307). After the invasion of Ukraine in February 2022 though, the government changed its position. This sudden change was possible due to the support of the opposition for membership and the disengagement of most citizens on the issue (Hinnfors, 2022). As a result, the government announced its plans to join NATO on April 13 and formally applied for NATO membership on May 16, 2022.

Within this timeframe, three events are of note. First, there was the Turkish opposition to Swedish membership, rooted in that country's opposition to Sweden's support for Kurdish parties and activists (Henley and Michaelson, 2022). Second, there was a "No Confidence" vote in the Swedish House of Representatives on the future of Minister for Justice Morgan Johansson. While he survived this vote thanks to the support of Kurdish-Iranian MP Amineh Kakabaveh, in return the government had to affirm an earlier agreement made in 2021 that stated that "people from those [Kurdish] organizations coming to Sweden are not terrorists" – a line of reasoning that went straight against Turkish demands (Duxbury, 2022). Third, there was the NATO Summit that took place between 28 – 30 June, where all NATO members (Turkey included) extended a formal invitation to both Finland and Sweden to join NATO.

A final point of note is that over this period, the application to NATO membership was what Berglez (2022) calls a "hidden issue". That is, both the government and opposition aimed to - and succeeded - in drawing attention away from it and were thereby followed by most of the media. An illustration of this is that the words "alliansfrihet" and "NATO" only occurred respectively 471 and 7936 times in the main Swedish media over the period of a year around the application. Moreover, the use of both words peaks around May, after which their number drops to almost zero until the elections in September.

3 Related Work

We base our decision to use global word embeddings to capture sudden semantic shifts on a well-founded body of work. Not only are they able to capture the semantic similarity and alignment between words, but they are also able to track the shifts in the meaning of political concepts. For example, Guo et al. (2022) show that the meaning of medical words changed before and after the first outbreak of Covid-19, while Rodman (2020); Rheault and Cochrane (2020) does the same for parliamentary data, and Durrheim et al. (2023) successfully use global embeddings to measure sociological concepts such as bias.

Of note is that all these papers opt to use *global* word embeddings instead of *contextual* word embeddings (e.g. ELMo (Peters et al., 2018), BERT (Devlin et al., 2019)). While *global* word embeddings associate a single embedding vector with a word, *contextual* word embeddings assign a different vector for the same word depending on the sentence in which it appears. While this has the advantage of being able to take the context of the specific occurrence of a word into account, it does not provide a way to represent the position of a single word in the embedding space. That is, when we care about the global shift of words (as we do here), we need a global and not a contextual embedding. As such, most authors in the social sciences, and we here as well, opt to use global embeddings.

4 Data

To measure our semantic shifts, we rely on Swedish-language Twitter posts ("tweets") that focus on NATO. We do so as Twitter's broad user base touches all segments of society, allowing us to get a complete picture of the debate around NATO. Besides, as tweets have a limit of 280 characters, their length is very similar. This has the advantage that it improves data consistency while reducing computational complexity.

Within our year-long period, we collected $1,188,556$ tweets, made by a total of $64,315$ users participating in $507,359$ conversations. Of these, $329,336$ are retweets, leaving $859,220$ original tweets. We collected a tweet if it contained any one of a set of search terms relating to NATO. To generate these terms, we drew on both theoretical expectations (deductive) as well as first results (inductive). As such, we ended up with seventy-five unique search terms covering NATO, alliances, and the war in Ukraine (see Bonafilia (2023) for a complete list). Many of these words were either compound words that contain "nato" or relate to NATO and are specific enough to only occur in that context. Thus, we did not include general terms such as "allians" (alliance), unless they were part of the phrase "militär allians" (military alliance) or "allians med turkiet" (alliance with Turkey). In the end, we included a tweet when: a) it contained any of the search terms, b) the tweet is a response to another tweet that contained a search term, or c) the tweet has a response containing a search term.

Based on the background of the NATO issue as sketched above, we divide our tweets into four periods. First, there is the pre-invasion period, ranging from September 11, 2021, to 24 February 2022 (the date of the Russian military invasion of Ukraine). Second, there is the post-invasion period running from February 24 to April 13, the date of the joint press conference of the Swedish PM Andersson and her Finnish colleague Marin, where both announced the possibility of their countries joining NATO. Third, there is the pre-application period, running between April 13 and the formal application on May 16. Finally, there is the post-application period, running between May 16 and the elections on September 11. Table 1 shows the number of tweets for each of the periods.

	Tweets	Words
Pre-Invasion	131 889	2.3 M
Post-Invasion	413 517	6.8 M
Pre-Application	294 453	5.1 M
Post-Application	346 948	5.4 M

Table 1: Sizes of the Twitter dataset for each period.

To support our choice for these four periods, we look at the daily number of tweets we gathered (see Figure 1). Here, we see that at the boundaries of the four periods (indicated by arrows 2, 3, and 5) there are clear peaks in the number of tweets. Besides, we find smaller peaks between January 15 – 19 (during the Russian military build-up near the Ukrainian border), on May 13 (the first Turkish signal of opposition to Sweden's entry into NATO), on June 7 (during the "No Confidence" vote against Morgan Johansson), and on June 28 (the NATO summit in Madrid).

5 Pre-Processing

Given that the choice – and order of – preprocessing steps will influence our analysis, we discuss each of these steps in turn (Denny and Spirling, 2018). First, we remove any URLs and mentions to other users as well as some minor punctuation. Second, we split our tweets into individual tokens. For this, we use the NLTK library's *nltk.TweetTokenizer*, as it splits hashtags and emojis better than other tokenizers (Bird et al., 2009). Third, we lowercase all tokens, create n-grams (with no limit, so 3-grams can occur), and remove all remaining punctuation. Finally, we normalize the spelling of our tokens to address the various spellings of the same word (e.g. "grey" and "gray"). For a more detailed overview of the pre-processing see Bonafilia (2023).

We did not perform the common steps of removing stop words or lemmatizing the tokens, as we found that these steps weakened the relationship between related words. Singletons and low-frequency words were filtered out by the Gensim library (Řehůřek and Sojka, 2010), which was used for the analysis.

6 Method

The model we chose to find our word embeddings is *Word2Vec* (Mikolov et al., 2013). This is a single-layer neural network that is trained to predict a word from its context – Continuous Bag-of-Words (CBOW) – or context from a given word – Skip-gram (SG). We opted to use both architectures given that they are different in the associations they capture, their computational efficiency, and their sensitivity to less-frequent words (Mikolov et al., 2013).

6.1 Training of the Model

As with all other embedding models, *Word2Vec* needs a large amount of text to be able to capture word associations. As the tweets from each period contained insufficient data to train a new model, we used Twitter data for each period to *fine-tune* an already trained model representing general Swedish. This initial model was trained on Swedish media text (Göteborgs-Posten, SVT, and Wikipedia) from 2003 until 2014, made available by Språkbanken's Korp language resource (Borin et al., 2012). The total number of tokens in this corpus is 759 million, with about 1.04 million unique tokens which appear at least ten times. We chose the cut-off dates

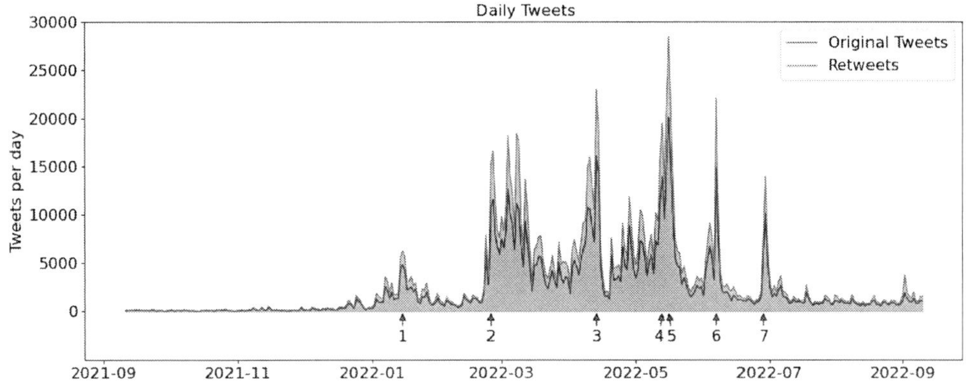

Figure 1: Tweets found by the search criteria from 2021-09-11 until 2022-09-11. The timeline of tweets with key dates: (1) January 2022, build-up of Russian forces near the Ukrainian border, (2) February 24th, the Russian Federation invades Ukraine, (3) April 13th, Swedish and Finnish PMs hold a joint press conference about the decision to join NATO, (4) Turkey expresses opposition to Sweden joining NATO on May 13th, and (5) May 16th, Sweden and Finland formally apply to join NATO. (6) A vote of No Confidence is held for Justice Minister Morgan Johansson on June 7th, and (7) the NATO Summit in Madrid on June 28th.

of 2003 and 2014 to avoid biasing the model with inputs from after the Maidan uprisings in Ukraine in 2014. This control over the input period and model parameters was our main motivation to train and validate a new model rather than use a publicly available set of pre-trained vectors.

We then trained two base models – one for the Skip-gram and one for the Continuous Bag-of-Words architecture. For both, we used Negative Sampling, a window size of 5, a minimum number of word occurrences of 10, and 160 training iterations. To validate our base model, we used the word similarities and relatedness from SuperSim by Hengchen and Tahmasebi (2021) and a QVEC-CCA scoring as introduced by Tsvetkov et al. (2016) using a Swedish pack available from Språkbanken's Korp (Borin et al., 2013). In all cases, the results indicated that the base models were well trained (Bonafilia, 2023).

We then fine-tuned both the SG and CBOW architectures on the tweets made within each period, using our pre-trained models as a base. Because the Word2Vec model training is a stochastic process, and as we have to account for instability due to data variability, we trained 10 models for each case on a different uniform random sample of 90% of the text data from that period when we perform our bootstrapping. We then ranked the most similar words based on the average cosine similarity across all 10 models.

6.2 Analysis Approach

Once we have our model, we have to formalize a search method to decide which words we want to select to look at. While we are aware that we could use the embeddings themselves to find the most similar and most different words – we opt here for a *subjective* approach. The reason for this is that we know our topic of interest (NATO) and can draw on prior knowledge not included in the model.

For the core selection of words, we take those that have either a direct relation to NATO or are synonymous with it (e.g. "försvarsalliansen" (defense alliance)), have a link to states or persons involved in Sweden's application (e.g. "erdogan", "putin", "finland"), have an association with the topics raised in the NATO discussion (e.g. "suveränitet" (sovereignty)), or words for which one subset of users in the polarization study had a markedly different use as indicated by word embeddings than another subset of users (e.g. "inkompetent" (incompetent), "dotters" (daughter's)). Besides this, we also draw on a study of words linked to polarized opinions on the issue of Sweden's entry into NATO (Bonafilia, 2023). In the end, this results in a list of 8000 words.

We then use these 8000 words and compare the averaged most similar words across the different time steps to find novel associations. While doing so, we ignore words that appeared in similar placements in all periods, such as synonyms or inflections of the word of interest. As not all the 8000 show interesting behavior, we then perform a second selection of words.

For refining the selection of words, we take all those words that fall under any one of the following criteria:

- Words which domain knowledge suggested are relevant.
- Words seen to be polarizing by Bonafilia (2023).
- Words which markedly changed their most similar words from the pre-trained model or between periods as determined by Rank-Biased Overlap (RBO) (Webber et al., 2010) of the sorted list of most similar words.
- Words for which unique words appeared among the most similar words in one of the periods but not among the most similar words in any other period.

After this second selection, we perform a last, manual review to look at general trends and to drop noisy findings. We did so as we wanted to drop those words which had very different embedding only because they were too infrequent to have a meaningful embedding at all.

7 Results

As both architectures lead to different results, we will look at both the results of the Continuous Bag-of-Words (CBOW) and the Skip-gram (SG) in turn. For each of the two, select four words that we deemed showed interesting patterns. These are "natoansökan" (NATO application) and "försvaret" (defense), as well as two unique ones for each – "nato" (NATO) and "säkerhet" (security) for COBW and "förskolor" (preschools) and "putin" (Putin) for SG. For each word, we give the top four words associated with it based on their cosine similarity. Besides these, we will also reflect on several other words that we found showed interesting behavior.

7.1 Continuous Bag-of-Words

Table 2 shows the words with the highest cosine similarity for each of the four words for the CBOW model. Also, in Figure 2, we show, for each of these four words, the comparison of the Rank-Biased Overlap between the list of the most similar words for each period and the list from the pre-trained CBOW model. Words such as "natoansökan", "nato" and "säkerhet" have a consistently low agreement in all periods, indicating a substantial shift from the base model. While "försvaret" drops to zero in the Pre-Application period as the agreement is lost completely, however, from Table 2 it is hard to determine the meaning of the shift, illustrating the difficulty in isolating the signal from noise and interpreting the results. In the pre-training data, "natoansökan" (NATO application) is so infrequently used that the word embeddings are meaningless. In the period leading up to the application, the subject of Sweden's NATO application becomes topical enough that a hashtag (#natoansökan) starts to be used. Also, for the topic of "säkerhet" (security), we find that it becomes related to the concepts of "suveränitet" (sovereignty) as the discussion of Sweden giving up neutrality to join a defensive alliance takes shape.

The word "nato" itself, becomes closely associated with the word "sverige" (Sweden), as both have a higher frequency (11×10^{-3}) and (6×10^{-3}) when compared with the pre-trained data (1×10^{-5} and 8×10^{-4} respectively). Leading to the word "nato" having a more meaningful word embedding in the base model. The reason for this is that "nato", being one of the search words, is so frequent in our data, that it has a high association with all other words. This makes the embedding relatively uninteresting to look at, as the embedding of the word is more related to other words of high frequency - such as "sverige" (Sweden) and "vi" (we) - than with words of similar meaning. This underscores the limitation of using word embeddings to find meaningful shifts for words that are deliberately sought out to generate the dataset.

7.2 Skip-gram

Table 3 shows the words with the highest cosine similarity for the Skip-gram architecture and Figure 3 shows the RBO results. Here, it can be seen that during the period after the Russian invasion of Ukraine and before the application, there is an association between "natoansökan" (NATO application) and "destabiliserande" (destabilizing). References to destabilization appeared almost exclusively during this period. This also fits well with the political consensus at the time, i.e. that a Swedish application to NATO would destabilize the country by jeopardizing its relationship with Russia. After the press conference on April 13, this changed and an association with "eventuell" (possible) and other words relating to the (likeliness of the) process of

	natoansökan	försvaret	nato	säkerhet
Base	sverigesregering	försvarsmakten	försvarsalliansen	rättssäkerhet
	regeringsbildandet	flygvapnet	fn	trovärdighet
Pre-Invasion	osansökan	försvarsmakten	sverige	säkerhetspolitik
	emuomröstning	underhållet	ukraina	natoansökning
	natooption	rättsväsendet	usa	konkurrenskraft
	intresseanmälan	välfärdssystemet	vi	stabilitet
Post-Invasion	medlemskapsansökan	försvarsmakten	sverige	säkerhetspolitik
	natoanslutning	totalförsvaret	vi	natoansökning
	dispensansökan	försvarsanslaget	ukraina	suveränitet
	osansökan	försvarsförmågan	finland	frihet
Pre-Application	#natoansökan	underhållet	sverige	suveränitet
	natomedlamskap	försvarsförmågan	#nato	rättssäkerhet
	ansökningsprocess	bnp	finland	försvarskapacitet
	medlemskapsansökan	insatsförsvaret	vi	säkerhetspolitik
Post-Application	natoanslutningen	luftsförsvaret	sverige	säkerhetspolitik
	natoprocess(en)	totalförsvaret	finland	överlevnad
	natomedlemskap	välfärdssystemet	turkiet	oljeförsörjning
	natoansökningen	insatsförsvaret	#nato	suveränitet

Table 2: Words with top cosine similarity in Continuous Bag-of-Words models grouped by period, for "natoansökan" (NATO application), "försvaret" (defense), "nato" (NATO), and "säkerhet" (security)

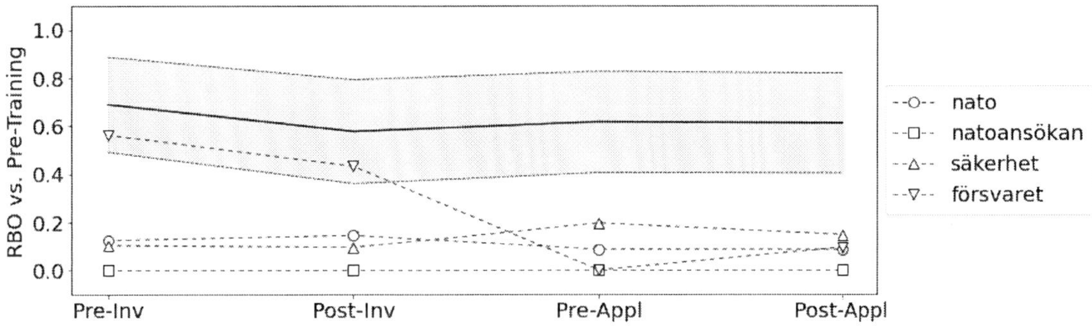

Figure 2: Comparison of the Rank-Biased Overlap between a list of the most similar words in each period and the pre-trained CBOW model for a small selection of words. A higher RBO value signifies more agreement with the base model and therefore a smaller semantic shift. The Average (solid line) and one standard deviation (shading) for 1000 randomly chosen words are also shown.

application, began to appear. We can see a similar change for "försvaret" (defense) from where the association shifts from words relating to maintenance and juridical matters before the application to a connection to the spending goal of 2% of GDP (the words "2%" and "bnp") for NATO members afterward.

Furthermore, we see a neutral word such as "förskolor" (preschool) has a strong cosine similarity to "kärnvapen" (nuclear weapons) in the period leading up to the application. While seemingly contradictory, the reason behind this is that during this time, Left Party leader Nooshi Dadgostar made a public statement regarding not wanting NATO's nuclear weapons to be housed within Sweden, alluding to a possibility of nuclear weapon silos near her daughter's preschool. This generated conversation among Twitter users discussing the pros and cons of the NATO application, resulting in the SG model finding the similarity in the contexts in which these words appeared in. Also, we see the emergence of novel words related to Vladimir Putin. For ex-

	natoansökan	försvaret	förskolor	putin
Base	sverigesregering ratificera	försvarsmakten flygvapnet	skolor äldreboenden	vladimirputin medvedev
Pre-Invasion	medlemsansökan byggförhandlingarna omvärldsutveckling drömregering	försvarsmakten invasionförsvaret förbandsverksamhet fm	gymnasieskolor äldreboenden fritidshem vårdcentraler	ryssland biden nato xi
Post-Invasion	medlemsansökan natomedlemskap destabilisera(nde) natoanslutning	försvarsmakten bnp rusta anslagen	polisstationer äldreboenden gymnasieskolor fritidshem	ryssland han ukraina nato
Pre-Application	natoanslutning eventuell natomedlemskap svensk	bnp 2% rusta försvarskostnaderna	dotters dagis kärnvapen kärnvapenbaser	ryssland putler erdogan ryssen
Post-Application	sveriges finlands natoprocessen inlämnad	bnp 2% försvarsanslaget materielanskaffning	skolbibliotek förskoleverksamhet fritidshem gymnasieskolor	erdogan ryssland biden putler

Table 3: Words with top cosine similarity in Skip-gram models grouped by period, for "natoansökan" (NATO application), "försvaret" (defense), "förskolor" (preschools) and "putin" (Putin)

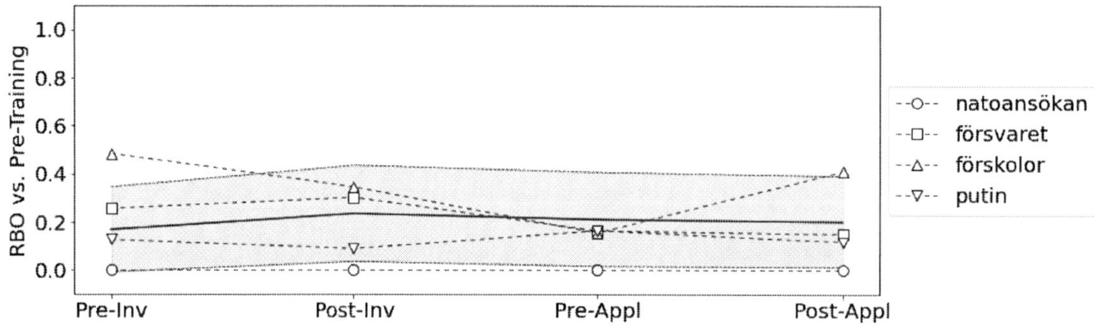

Figure 3: Comparison of the Rank-Biased Overlap between a list of the most similar words in each period and the pre-trained SG model for a small selection of words. A higher RBO value signifies more agreement with the base model and therefore a smaller semantic shift. The Average (solid line) and one standard deviation (shading) for 1000 randomly chosen words are also shown.

ample, the word "putler" is meant to draw a connection between Russia's invasion of Ukraine and the aggression of Nazi Germany during the Second World War. Finally, when looking at the RBO results, in contrast to CBOW, SG shows a larger average shift from the baseline model for all periods. This results in the approach yielding less clear results and the need for more noise words to be filtered to find useful examples, making it harder to detect a true signal. For example, even when "förskolor" becomes a relevant word, the dip in the rank order similarity is small since the similarity was low across the board.

7.3 Further Examples

Other words (not shown here), also exhibit a strong relationship with certain events during the period. Thus, the word "inkompetent" (incompetent) first had associations with words like "korrumperad" (corrupted) and "felprioriteringar" (misplaced priorities), but later switched those to words such as "minister" (Minister), and "morganjohansson"

(Morgan Johansson) at the time of the vote of no-confidence against Minister for Justice Morgan Johansson. Besides, the word "natomotståndare" (NATO opponent), while first being associated with the Left Party (a traditional opponent of Swedish NATO membership), became associated with the Green Party and individual Social Democrats (such as former Minister for Defense Peter Hultqvist) instead. Finally, as expected, we observe that the word "kiev" is first associated with other cities, such as Tbilisi, while Post-Invasion it gains an association with the Ukrainian "kyiv" spelling, presumably by Twitter users who wished to express solidarity with Ukraine. Finally, while the word "azov" in the pre-training data referred to the Sea of Azov or any of a number of Ukrainian and Russian locations, the most similar words were other places in the area. Later, during the Post-Invasion period, this changed. First, the use of "azov" centered around the alleged neo-Nazi ties of the Azov Battalion, a Ukrainian militia, and then later became associated with the Siege of Mariupol, where defenders had occupied the "Azovstal" Steel Plant.

8 Conclusion

Our aim with this study was to look at the sudden semantic shift that we expected to occur when Sweden decided to apply for NATO membership in 2022. Looking at various words related to this application process, we find that word embeddings are a powerful tool to capture some of those shifts. Moreover, when validating them against real-world events, we find that those shifts are both accurate and meaningful. Yet, the sparsity of the dataset often makes it difficult to separate signal from noise when looking at the model results alone.

The misalignment between the signals that each of the two model architectures – SG and CBOW – manage to capture, as well as the difficulty of validating and interpreting the results exemplifies the challenges in using word embeddings for automatically detecting and measuring semantic shifts. Thus, there is a need for extensive human interpretation and validation based on domain knowledge together with a broad range of statistics that can reveal different aspects of the patterns captured by the models. Despite this though, word embeddings are still a powerful method that can aid the discovery process. As we showed, they are efficient enough to process large amounts of data and capture several underlying word relationships and sudden semantic shifts.

9 Suggestions for Further Research

We see two suggestions for further research, two methodological and one practical. On the methodological side, we saw that selecting Tweets by their relationship to NATO resulted in a skewed frequency of NATO-related words when compared with those in the pre-trained model. Such a sparse dataset with non-representative word distributions makes the study of the search words hard. To allay this, one could extend the criteria to capture a broader and more diverse representation of the language used during the period.

Another methodological option is the consideration of a different model. Two alternatives to the model we used here are FastText (Joulin et al., 2017) and GloVe (Pennington et al., 2014). Both offer a different perspective on word embeddings and might address some of the issues we faced here.

From the practical side, we assumed that Swedish NATO membership would be a major electoral issue and that a single year was enough to capture this debate. Both proved to be wrong. NATO membership was rarely discussed in the period leading up to the elections, and at the time of writing, Sweden's NATO aspirations are still unfulfilled. Thus, further research could extend the data collection period to gain a better view of any shifts in the word embeddings.

Acknowledgments

This work was supported by the Wallenberg AI, Autonomous Systems and Software Program – Humanities and Society (WASP-HS) funded by the Marianne and Marcus Wallenberg Foundation and the Marcus and Amalia Wallenberg Foundation.

References

Peter Berglez. 2022. Hur påverkades valrörelsen 2022 av omvärlden? In Niklas Bolin, Kajsa Falasca, Marie Grusell, and Lars Nord, editors, *Snabbtänkt 2.0 22*, page 111. Mittuniversitetet, Demicom, Sundsvall.

Steven Bird, Edward Loper, and Ewan Klein. 2009. *Natural Language Processing with Python*. O'Reilly Media, Sebastopol, CA.

Niklas Bolin. 2023. The Repercussions of the Russian Invasion of Ukraine on the Populist Radical Right in Sweden. In Gilles Ivaldi and Emilia Zankina, editors, *The Impacts of the Russian Invasion of Ukraine on Right-Wing Populism in Europe*, pages 302–313. European Center for Populism Studies (ECPS), Brussels.

Brian Bonafilia. 2023. Methods for Detecting Echo Chambers in Social Media Networks. Master's thesis, Chalmers University of Technology.

Lars Borin, Markus Forsberg, and Lennart Lönngren. 2013. SALDO: A Touch of Yin to WordNet's Yang. *Language Resources and Evaluation*, 47(4):1191–1211.

Lars Borin, Markus Forsberg, and Johan Roxendal. 2012. Korp – the corpus infrastructure of Språkbanken. In *Proceedings of the Eight International Conference on Language Resources and Evaluation (LREC'12)*, Paris. European Language Resources Association (ELRA).

Douglas Brommesson, Ann-Marie Ekengren, and Anna Michalski. 2022. Sweden's Policy of Neutrality: Success Through Flexibility? In Caroline de la Porte, Guðný Björk Eydal, Jaakko Kauko, Daniel Nohrstedt, Paul 't Hart, and Bent Sofus Tranøy, editors, *Successful Public Policy in the Nordic Countries: Cases, Lessons, Challenges*, pages 284–305. Oxford University Press, Oxford.

Matthew J. Denny and Arthur Spirling. 2018. Text Preprocessing For Unsupervised Learning: Why It Matters, When It Misleads, And What To Do About It. *Political Analysis*, 26(2):168–189.

Jacob Devlin, Ming-Wei Chang, Kenton Lee, and Kristina Toutanova. 2019. BERT: Pre-training of deep bidirectional transformers for language understanding. In *Proceedings of the 2019 Conference of the North American Chapter of the Association for Computational Linguistics: Human Language Technologies, Volume 1 (Long and Short Papers)*, pages 4171–4186, Minneapolis, MN. Association for Computational Linguistics.

Kevin Durrheim, Maria Schuld, Martin Mafunda, and Sindisiwe Mazibuko. 2023. Using Word Embeddings to Investigate Cultural Biases. *British Journal of Social Psychology*, 62(1):617–629.

Charles Duxbury. 2022. Swedish Government Narrowly Survives No-Confidence Vote. Politico (EU), 06-07-2022.

J. R. Firth. 1957. Applications of General Linguistics. *Transactions of the Philological Society*, 56(1):1–14.

Yanzhu Guo, Christos Xypolopoulos, and Michalis Vazirgiannis. 2022. How COVID-19 is Changing Our Language: Detecting Semantic Shift in Twitter Word Embeddings. In *Conférence Nationale en Intelligence Artificielle 2022 (CNIA 2022)*, Saint-Etienne, France.

William L. Hamilton, Jure Leskovec, and Dan Jurafsky. 2016. Diachronic Word Embeddings Reveal Statistical Laws of Semantic Change. In *The 54th Annual Meeting of the Association for Computational Linguistics – Proceedings of the Conference, Vol. 1 (Long Papers)*, pages 1489–1501, Stroudsburg, PA. Association for Computational Linguistics.

Simon Hengchen and Nina Tahmasebi. 2021. SuperSim: A Test Set for Word Similarity and Relatedness in Swedish. In *Proceedings of the 23rd Nordic Conference on Computational Linguistics (NoDaLiDa)*, pages 268–275, Linköping. Linköping University Electronic Press.

Jon Henley and Ruth Michaelson. 2022. Erdoğan: Turkey 'not positive' about Sweden and Finland joining Nato. The Guardian, 13-05-2022.

Jonas Hinnfors. 2022. Socialdemokraterna: högervridning och hot utifrån. In Niklas Bolin, Kajsa Falasca, Marie Grusell, and Lars Nord, editors, *Snabbtänkt 2.0 22*, page 39. Mittuniversitetet, Demicom, Sundsvall.

Armand Joulin, Edouard Grave, Piotr Bojanowski, and Tomas Mikolov. 2017. Bag of tricks for efficient text classification. In *Proceedings of the 15th Conference of the European Chapter of the Association for Computational Linguistics: Volume 2, Short Papers*, pages 427–431. Association for Computational Linguistics.

Tomas Mikolov, Kai Chen, Greg Corrado, and Jeffrey Dean. 2013. Efficient Estimation of Word Representations in Vector Space.

Jeffrey Pennington, Richard Socher, and Christopher D. Manning. 2014. GloVe: Global Vectors for Word Representation. In *Proceedings of the 2014 Conference on Empirical Methods in Natural Language Processing (EMNLP)*, pages 1532–1543, Stroudsburg, PA. Association for Computational Linguistics.

Efrén Pérez and Margit Tavits. 2023. *Voicing Politics: How Language Shapes Public Opinion*. Princeton University Press, Princeton, NJ.

Matthew E. Peters, Mark Neumann, Mohit Iyyer, Matt Gardner, Christopher Clark, Kenton Lee, and Luke Zettlemoyer. 2018. Deep contextualized word representations. In *Proceedings of the 2018 Conference of the North American Chapter of the Association for Computational Linguistics: Human Language Technologies, Volume 1 (Long Papers)*, pages 2227–2237, Stroudsburg, PA. Association for Computational Linguistics.

Radim Řehůřek and Petr Sojka. 2010. Software Framework for Topic Modelling with Large Corpora. In *Proceedings of the LREC 2010 Workshop on New Challenges for NLP Frameworks*, pages 45–50, Valletta. ELRA.

Ludovic Rheault and Christopher Cochrane. 2020. Word Embeddings for the Analysis of Ideological Placement in Parliamentary Corpora. *Political Analysis*, 28(1):112–133.

Emma Rodman. 2020. A Timely Intervention: Tracking the Changing Meanings of Political Concepts with Word Vectors. *Political Analysis*, 28(1):87–111.

Nina Tahmasebi, Gerhard Gossen, Nattiya Kanhabua, Helge Holzmann, and Thomas Risse. 2012. NEER: An Unsupervised Method for Named Entity Evolution Recognition. In *Proceedings of COLING 2012: Technical Papers*, pages 2553–2568, Mumbai. The COLING 2012 Organizing Committee.

Yulia Tsvetkov, Manaal Faruqui, and Chris Dyer. 2016. Correlation-based Intrinsic Evaluation of Word Vector Representations. In *Proceedings of the 1st Workshop on Evaluating Vector-Space Representations for NLP*, pages 111–115, Stroudsberg, PA. Association for Computational Linguistics.

William Webber, Alistair Moffat, and Justin Zobel. 2010. A Similarity Measure for Indefinite Rankings. *ACM Transactions on Information Systems*, 28(4):1–38.

Anna Wieslander. 2022. "The Hultqvist doctrine" – Swedish Security and Defence Policy after the Russian Annexation of Crimea. *Defence Studies*, 22(1):35–59.

Building a Buzzer-Quiz Answering System

Naoya Sugiura **Kosuke Yamada** **Ryohei Sasano**
Koichi Takeda **Katsuhiko Toyama**
Graduate School of Informatics, Nagoya University, Japan
{sugiura.naoya.e7,yamada.kosuke.v1}@s.mail.nagoya-u.ac.jp
{sasano,takedasu,toyama}@i.nagoya-u.ac.jp

Abstract

A buzzer quiz is a genre of quiz in which multiple players simultaneously listen to a quiz being read aloud and respond it by buzzing in as soon as they can predict the answer. Because incorrect answers often result in penalties, a buzzer-quiz answering system must not only predict the answer from only part of a question but also estimate the predicted answer's accuracy. In this paper, we introduce two types of buzzer-quiz answering systems: (1) a system that directly generates an answer from part of a question by using an autoregressive language model; and (2) a system that first reconstructs the entire question by using an autoregressive language model and then determines the answer according to the reconstructed question. We then propose a method to estimate the accuracy of the answers for each system by using the internal scores of each model.

1 Introduction

We use the term "buzzer quiz" to refer to a genre of quiz in which questioner reads quiz questions aloud and players answer by buzzing in as soon as they can predict the answer. A well-known example of a similar format to what we call a buzzer quiz here is the U.S. TV program *Jeopady!*, in which contestants must buzz in with a lock-out device before trying to answer a question. However, in *Jeopady!*, answers are only allowed after all the questions have been read aloud, whereas we assume a format in which answers are allowed while the questions are being read out. Because of the importance of buzzing in quickly, players normally answer incomplete questions in buzzer quiz.

Quizzes have been studied as open-domain question answering (QA) tasks because they do not limit the scope of knowledge. However, the major datasets for open-domain QA tasks, like Natural Questions (Kwiatkowski et al., 2019) and TriviaQA (Joshi et al., 2017) cointain complete questions. Consequently, systems built using those datasets (Karpukhin et al., 2020; Yamada et al., 2021; Izacard and Grave, 2021) are not designed to answer incomplete questions. Furthermore, it is certainly crucial in buzzer quizzes to give correct answers, but it is also essential to consider the plausibility of a predicted answer based on the given question at that moment and to decide whether to actually respond. For example, consider the question listed in Table 1 if it has not been read past the phrase "200-hit." At that point, because other baseball players also hold records comparable to that of Pete Rose, it is difficult to narrow the answer down to a single candidate. This makes the predicted answer at that moment more likely to be incorrect, so it would be better not to answer at that point. On the other hand, once the question has been read further, the predicted answer converges to the correct answer, "Ichiro Suzuki." Hence, to construct a more effective buzzer-quiz answering system, we need an indicator of a predicted answer's likelihood of being correct, which call a "confidence score."

We believe that the capability to respond to buzzer quizzes by answering incomplete questions could help replicate the human capacity to smoothly generate responses in a conversation by

Q (75% completeness): Pete Rose and this player are tied with ten 200-hit seasons each. This Japanese outfielder played most of his career with the Mariners, and currently plays for the Marlins.
Confidence score: 0.991 **A:** Ichiro Suzuki *correct*
Q (25% completeness): Pete Rose and this player are tied with ten 200-hit seasons each. This Japanese outfielder played most of his career with the Mariners, and currently plays for the Marlins.
Confidence score: 0.125 **A:** Ty Cobb *incorrect*

Table 1: Examples of quiz question text and output of answering system. Gray texts indicate the unread portions of the question text. "Completeness" denotes the percentage of the question text that has been read, and the "confidence score" refers to a value indicating the likelihood of the predicted answer being correct.

Proceedings of the 61st Annual Meeting of the Association for Computational Linguistics - Student Research Workshop, pages 194–199
July 10-12, 2023 ©2023 Association for Computational Linguistics

sequentially predicting the content of the dialogue. In this study, we first constructed a buzzer-quiz answering system that produces appropriate answers for incomplete questions, and we propose the methods for calculating the confidence scores for two different models. Specifically, we constructed two systems: the **GPT-only** system, which directly generates answers in response to a question by using GPT (Radford et al., 2018); and the **GPT+DPR** system, which generates answers through a retriever-reader approach using Dense Passage Retrieval (DPR) (Karpukhin et al., 2020), after completing the question via GPT. For the former system, we calculate a confidence score by using token output probabilities during answer generation, while for the latter system, we use scores that are used in the output of the model.

2 Proposed Method

We propose two types of buzzer-quiz answering systems based on open-domain QA systems. We also propose methods to estimate the accuracy of the answers in each system by using the internal scores in each model.

2.1 Open-Domain QA System

In open-domain QA, there are two mainstream approaches. The first is a generation-based approach that generates answers directly in response to input questions. A representative model is GPT (Radford et al., 2018), which is a pre-trained language model that is based on the Transformer decoder (Vaswani et al., 2017) and is trained to predict word sequences from a context by using a large text corpus. Because of this property, GPT can be used in language generation tasks that involve generating text in response to input text. In the case of QA, GPT can generate answers by formatting the input in such a way as to infer only the answer to a question. Furthermore, because GPT often achieves higher performance through fine-tuning with datasets from downstream tasks, such fine-tuning can be applied to build QA models.

The second major open-domain QA approach is a retriever-reader approach that searches for documents related to a question and extracts the answer from the documents. A representative model is the retriever-reader model, which uses DPR as the retriever. DPR uses a dual encoder network with different BERT models (Devlin et al., 2019) for questions and documents. When sentences are input to BERT, a special token `[CLS]` is inserted at the beginning of a document, and the embedding representations for the question text and each document are obtained. Then, documents are selected according to the semantic similarity calculated as the inner product of the obtained representations (Karpukhin et al., 2020). In the reader, BERT predicts the relevant documents containing the correct answer and extracts the answer portion within a document. Specifically, it predicts the document that is most likely to contain the answer at the position of the token `[CLS]`. Then, it performs the answer-portion extraction from the predicted document and determines the start and end points of the token sequence that forms the answer.

2.2 Buzzer-Quiz Answering Systems

The effectiveness of the open-domain QA systems that answer complete questions has been confirmed, but their effectiveness for a buzzer-quiz answering system remains unclear because such a system requires to answer incomplete questions. Generally, when only part of a question is given, the nature of the problem differs significantly from the case of a complete question, because there may be multiple possible answers, or the necessary information to determine the answer might not be available yet.

In this study, we constructed two buzzer-quiz answering systems: one that relies solely on inference via GPT, called the GPT-only system, and another that uses GPT for question completion and applies the retriever-reader approach with DPR, called the GPT+DPR system. For the GPT-only system, the designed input format is "[question text] + '/the answer is'," which prompts the model to generate the answer within the single quotation marks, which is then used as the predicted answer. The purpose of inserting a slash '/' between the question text and "the answer is" is to make the model recognize the boundary of the question text, which prevents the completion of incomplete questions. For the GPT+DPR system, an incomplete question is input to the GPT to complete the question text, and the resulting complete question is then used as input for the DPR-based retriever-reader model to generate the answer.

2.3 Confidence Scores

Next, we propose to calculate the confidence scores for predicted answers by using the internal scores that each model uses when it generates the outputs for the buzzer-quiz answering system. Here, the confidence score means an indicator for judging whether a predicted answer is correct. For higher values of our proposed confidence scores, we expect a higher percentage of correct answers.

For the GPT-only model, we use the generation probability of the first token in the predicted answer (referred to as the **generation score**) as the confidence score. When given a sentence's first n tokens during sentence completion, GPT outputs the $(n+1)$-th token from the vocabulary with the highest generation score. The first token largely determines the direction of the answer in the buzzer quiz, because the answer often comprises a small number of tokens. Hence, we adopt only the first token's generation score as the confidence score.

As for the GPT+DPR model, three internal scores can be used as confidence scores: the **document score** and the **extraction score** calculated by the reader, as well as their arithmetic mean, the **average score**. In the reader, each `[CLS]` token in a document is scored through a learned linear layer, and the document with the highest score is selected; this is the document score. Then, the model extracts the span containing the answer from the selected document by calculating a span score, which comprises a start score and an end score. The extraction score is the sum of these start and end scores.

3 Experiments

We conducted two experiments: an evaluation of the proposed buzzer-quiz answering system's accuracy, and an investigation of the effectiveness of the confidence scores for each model. We define question completeness as $x\%$ when a question is truncated after the first $x\%$ of the text in terms of the character count. For the accuracy verification, we applied the GPT-only and the GPT+DPR models to questions with completeness levels of 25%, 50%, 75%, and 100%. For investigation of the confidence scores' effectiveness, we evaluated the confidence scores for each model by examining the relationship between the confidence scores and the accuracy at each level of question completeness.

3.1 Settings

Datasets We used the 2nd AIO Official Dataset (AIO),[1] which contains past questions from Japanese quiz competitions. The AIO dataset is officially divided into a training set, a development set, and a test set. In addition, we collected past questions from the Japanese quiz application "Minna de Hayaoshi Quiz" (Minhaya)[2] as additional training data. Table 2 shows the number of quiz-answer pairs and the average number of characters in the questions for the datasets. Note that the training of DPR required positive and negative documents in addition to quiz-answer pairs. Accordingly, DPR was trained using only the AIO dataset, whereas the Minhaya dataset was used only for training GPT.

Subset	Source	Size	Length
Train	AIO	17,735	48.2
	Minhaya	35,149	64.8
Dev	AIO	1,000	46.9
Test	AIO	2,000	51.6

Table 2: Overview of the datasets. "Length" means the average number of characters for the questions.

Comparison Models We compared both models, GPT-only and GPT+DPR, in the accuracy verification. In the investigation of confidence score effectiveness, for GPT-only, we used the generation score; in contrast, for GPT+DPR, we used all three scores, i.e., the document score, extraction score, and average score.

We used the Japanese GPT model[3] on Hugging Face Hub (Wolf et al., 2020) and a DPR model[4] based on Japanese BERT-large,[5] which is pre-trained the Japanese Wikipedia corpus. For GPT-only, we fine-tuned the model on the training set with the input format "[question text] + '/ the answer is' [answer]." For GPT+DPR, GPT was fine-tuned using only the questions from the training set. In both cases, the training was conducted for 5 epochs. DPR was based on Japanese BERT-large for both the retriever and reader components. The retriever was trained for 5 epochs with a batch size of 128 and a learning rate of 1e-5, and the reader was trained for 3 epochs with a batch size of 8 and a learning rate of 2e-5.

Metrics In the accuracy verification, the correctness of the predicted answer was assessed in terms

[1]https://sites.google.com/view/project-aio/dataset

[2]https://livequiz.work/minhaya1/

[3]https://huggingface.co/rinna/japanese-gpt-1b

[4]https://github.com/cl-tohoku/AIO2_DPR_baseline

[5]https://huggingface.co/cl-tohoku/bert-large-japanese

Model	25%	50%	75%	100%
GPT-only	11.9	27.9	45.6	56.2
GPT+DPR	11.9	28.8	45.9	62.0

Table 3: Results of accuracy verification. The x% represents the question completeness.

of exact matching. In the investigation of confidence score effectiveness, we created curves of the correct answer rate with respect to the answer generation rate, and we evaluated the effectiveness in terms of the area under the curve (AUC). Here, the answer generation rate was the proportion of times that the system actually provided an answer. If the models only answered questions for which the confidence score exceeded a threshold α, we can control the answer rate by changing α. On the other hand, the correct answer rate was the proportion of correct answers among the answers output by the models. If α is set to a value below 0, the answer rate will coincide with the overall correct answer rate of the system. As α increases, only questions with high confidence scores will be answered, so the correct answer rate will be expected to increase.

3.2 Accuracy Verification

Table 3 lists the accuracies for the GPT-only and GPT+DPR models for each level of question completeness. As the question completeness decreased, the correct answer rate also decreased, but the rate of decrease was not proportional. From 100% to 75%, the decline was relatively gentle. This was likely because many important words that determine the answer appear in the first half of a question, whereas cases with information-rich words appearing in the latter half of a question are relatively rare. Comparing the scores of the two models, we see that GPT+DPR performed better when the question completeness was 100%. When the questions were incomplete, however, there was no significant difference in performance between the two models was observed.

3.3 Confidence Score Effectiveness

Table 4 lists the AUC values for each level of question completeness. Among the three confidence scores for GPT+DPR, using the document score yielded the highest AUC. Furthermore, among all the results, the generation score for GPT-only achieved the highest AUC.

Next, because the document score had the highest AUC for GPT+DPR, we used it to compare

Model	Score	25%	50%	75%	100%
GPT-only	generation score	**41.4**	**63.6**	**81.2**	**85.9**
	document score	31.8	58.1	77.3	84.8
GPT+DPR	extraction score	25.0	51.3	70.0	84.1
	average score	29.1	56.1	75.8	84.0

Table 4: AUC values for each level of question completeness. "Score" means the internal scores we used.

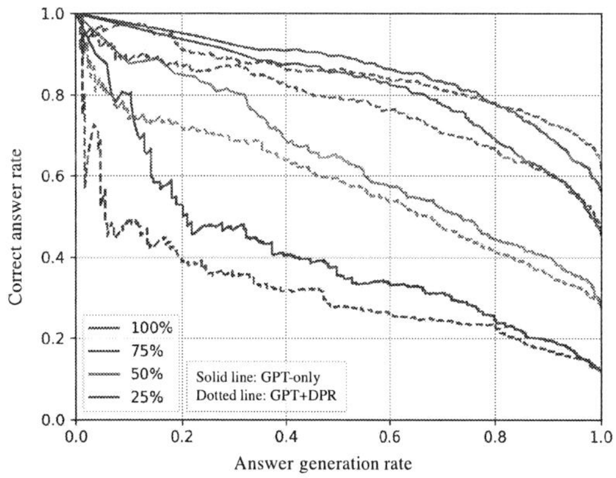

Figure 1: Curves of the correct answer rate vs. the answer generation rate. The x% represents the question completeness.

the correct answer rate vs. answer generation rate curves of the GPT-only model and the GPT+DPR models. Figure 1 shows the results. For all settings, we can observe that the accuracy was increased by limiting the questions to be answered to only those with high confidence scores, thus confirming the effectiveness of the confidence scores. Comparing GPT-only and GPT+DPR, as listed in Table 3, the accuracy at an answer rate of 1.0 was higher for GPT+DPR when the question completeness was 100%, and equivalent in for less-complete questions. When the answer rate was less than 0.8, however, GPT-only had higher accuracy in all cases. This difference was more obvious when both the question completeness and the answer rate were low. For example, in the case of 25% question completeness and an answer rate of 0.1, the accuracy of GPT+DPR is around 0.5, whereas that of GPT-only was around 0.8, thus showing a significant difference. Accordingly, we can conclude that the GPT-only model is more suitable for buzzer quizzes.

Table 5 shows examples of quiz question text and output from the GPT-only system. Examples (a) and (b) are cases with 25% question completeness, while Examples (c) and (d) are cases with 75% question completeness. In Examples (a) and

	Examples
(a)	**Q (25% completeness):** ごはんの上にハンバーグと目玉焼きを乗せ、グレービーソースをかけたハワイの名物料理は何でしょう? (This is a rice dish topped with a hamburger steak and a fried egg, which is covered with gravy sauce and originated in Hawaii. What is this?) **Confidence score:** 0.996 **A:** ロコモコ (loco moco) *correct*
(b)	**Q (25% completeness):** オーストリアの首都はウィーンですが、オーストラリアの首都はどこでしょう? (The capital of Austria is Vienna, but what is the capital of Australia?) **Confidence score:** 0.982 **A:** キャンベラ (Canberra) *incorrect*
(c)	**Q (75% completeness):** 約5年の歳月をかけてシスティーナ礼拝堂の祭壇に描かれた、ミケランジェロの代表作である絵画は何でしょう? (This painting was created over the span of about five years in the Sistine Chapel. Now, this is known as one of Michelangelo's masterpieces. What is this?) **Confidence score:** 0.991 **A:** 最後の審判 (The Last Judgment) *correct*
(d)	**Q (75% completeness):** 1985年に発売され、全世界で4000万本以上を売り上げたという任天堂ファミリーコンピュータのゲームで、「スーマリ」などと略されるものは何? (This game was launched for the Nintendo Family Computer in 1985 and has sold 40 million copies, which is often referred to by the abbreviation "Su-Mari." What is this?) **Confidence score:** 0.955 **A:** ドンキーコング (Donkey Kong) *incorrect*

Table 5: Examples of quiz question text and output from the GPT-only system. Since the actual data are in Japanese, English translations are given in parentheses.

(c), the system predicted correct answers with high confidence scores because sufficient information was provided to narrow down the answer. In contrast, in Examples (b) and (d), the system predicts the answers with high confidence scores, but the answers are incorrect. Example (b) is a question text with contrasting first and second halves, which would be difficult to answer in a situation where only the first half of the question is given. Example (d) is incorrect because the question text is mostly clear, but does not contain the key information that determines one answer.

4 Conclusion

In this study, we constructed two models for answering buzzer quiz questions, which have not been considered in previous research: GPT-only and GPT+DPR. Then, we evaluated the accuracy for various levels of question completeness. Furthermore, we investigated the relationship between the model's internal scores, which were treated as confidence scores, and the accuracy; as a result, the validity of using the internal scores of the models as confidence scores was confirmed.

In the future, we consider the use of more powerful models like FiD (Izacard and Grave, 2021) or GPT-4 (OpenAI, 2023) to improve the correct answer rate for quizzes. We also would like to validate the differences in performance between our systems and humans.

Limitations

We built buzzer quiz answering systems. However, they do not take into account the time required to respond, and these systems do not have the ability to generate real-time responses, which is essential in actual buzzer quizzes. Additionally, the experiments in this study were conducted only in Japanese, and it remains unclear whether similar results would be obtained in other languages. Particularly, English has a significantly different sentence structure compared to Japanese, hence further investigation is necessary to confirm whether appropriate results can be achieved.

Acknowledgements

This work was partly supported by JSPS KAKENHI Grant Number 21H04901.

References

Jacob Devlin, Ming-Wei Chang, Kenton Lee, and Kristina Toutanova. 2019. BERT: Pre-training of deep bidirectional transformers for language understanding. In *Proceedings of the 2019 Conference of the North American Chapter of the Association for Computational Linguistics: Human Language Technologies (NAACL 2019)*, pages 4171–4186.

Gautier Izacard and Edouard Grave. 2021. Leveraging passage retrieval with generative models for open domain question answering. In *Proceedings of the 16th*

Conference of the European Chapter of the Association for Computational Linguistics: Main Volume (EACL 2021), pages 874–880.

Mandar Joshi, Eunsol Choi, Daniel Weld, and Luke Zettlemoyer. 2017. TriviaQA: A large scale distantly supervised challenge dataset for reading comprehension. In *Proceedings of the 55th Annual Meeting of the Association for Computational Linguistics (ACL 2017)*.

Vladimir Karpukhin, Barlas Oguz, Sewon Min, Patrick Lewis, Ledell Wu, Sergey Edunov, Danqi Chen, and Wen-tau Yih. 2020. Dense passage retrieval for open-domain question answering. In *Proceedings of the 2020 Conference on Empirical Methods in Natural Language Processing (EMNLP 2020)*, pages 6769–6781.

Tom Kwiatkowski, Jennimaria Palomaki, Olivia Redfield, Michael Collins, Ankur Parikh, Chris Alberti, Danielle Epstein, Illia Polosukhin, Jacob Devlin, Kenton Lee, Kristina Toutanova, Llion Jones, Matthew Kelcey, Ming-Wei Chang, Andrew M. Dai, Jakob Uszkoreit, Quoc Le, and Slav Petrov. 2019. Natural questions: A benchmark for question answering research. *Transactions of the Association for Computational Linguistics (TACL)*, 7.

OpenAI. 2023. Gpt-4 technical report.

Alec Radford, Karthik Narasimhan, Tim Salimans, and Ilya Sutskever. 2018. Improving language understanding by generative pre-training. Open AI Technical Report.

Ashish Vaswani, Noam Shazeer, Niki Parmar, Jakob Uszkoreit, Llion Jones, Aidan N Gomez, Łukasz Kaiser, and Illia Polosukhin. 2017. Attention is all you need. In *Advances in Neural Information Processing Systems 30 (NIPS 2017)*, pages 5998–6008.

Thomas Wolf, Lysandre Debut, Victor Sanh, Julien Chaumond, Clement Delangue, Anthony Moi, Pierric Cistac, Tim Rault, Rémi Louf, Morgan Funtowicz, Joe Davison, Sam Shleifer, Patrick von Platen, Clara Ma, Yacine Jernite, Julien Plu, Canwen Xu, Teven Le Scao, Sylvain Gugger, Mariama Drame, Quentin Lhoest, and Alexander M. Rush. 2020. Transformers: State-of-the-art natural language processing. In *Proceedings of the 2020 Conference on Empirical Methods in Natural Language Processing: System Demonstrations (EMNLP 2020)*, pages 38–45.

Ikuya Yamada, Akari Asai, and Hannaneh Hajishirzi. 2021. Efficient passage retrieval with hashing for open-domain question answering. In *Proceedings of the 59th Annual Meeting of the Association for Computational Linguistics and the 11th International Joint Conference on Natural Language Processing (Volume 2: Short Papers) (ACL-IJCNLP 2021)*, pages 979–986.

Probing for Hyperbole in Pre-Trained Language Models

Nina Skovgaard Schneidermann[1], **Daniel Hershcovich**[2] and
Bolette Sandford Pedersen[1]
[1]Center for Language Technology,
[2]Department of Computer Science
University of Copenhagen
ninasc@hum.ku.dk, dh@di.ku.dk, bspedersen@hum.ku.dk

Abstract

Hyperbole is a common figure of speech, which is under-explored in NLP research. In this study, we conduct edge and minimal description length (MDL) probing experiments for three pre-trained language models (PLMs) in an attempt to explore the extent to which hyperbolic information is encoded in these models. We use both word-in-context and sentence-level representations as model inputs as a basis for comparison. We also annotate 63 hyperbole sentences from the HYPO dataset according to an operational taxonomy to conduct an error analysis to explore the encoding of different hyperbole categories. Our results show that hyperbole is to a limited extent encoded in PLMs, and mostly in the final layers. They also indicate that hyperbolic information may be better encoded by the sentence-level representations, which, due to the pragmatic nature of hyperbole, may therefore provide a more accurate and informative representation in PLMs. Finally, the inter-annotator agreement for our annotations, a Cohen's Kappa of 0.339, suggest that the taxonomy categories may not be intuitive and need revision or simplification.

1 Introduction

Hyperbole is a common figure of speech that involves the use of exaggerated language for emphasis or effect (Claridge, 2010). Humans exaggerate in a variety of registers and contexts, spanning from the colouring of informal, everyday speech to a literary trope or a rhetorical means of persuasion. Hyperboles intentionally augment or diminish a feature of some referent of discourse, presenting this feature on some more or less abstract scale of magnitude. The task of hyperbole identification poses a challenge to natural language processing in that it is highly pragmatic and utilizes context and background knowledge to distinguish between literal and exaggerated usage of a given lexical unit. As an illustration of the pragmatic nature of hyperbole, we can inspect the following two example sentences, wherein (1A) is hyperbolic and (1B) is literal:

(1A) I've seen this movie *at least eighty thousand times.*

(1B) These products are tested *at least eighty thousand times.*

In (1A), it is reasonable to assume that the speaker is exaggerating the number of times they have seen this particular movie to emphasize their enjoyment or familiarity with it because this would otherwise be a significant and unrealistic time investment. However, when it comes to a particular product, it has likely gone through rigorous testing and quality control measures, which means that the statement in (1B) can reasonably be interpreted literally.

Hyperbole identification has recently attracted the interest of NLP researchers who have collected datasets manually or semi-automatically and shown that computational modelling of hyperbole is indeed plausible (Troiano et al., 2018). However, it remains an under-explored area of research in figurative language processing (FLP), primarily because its subjective and contextual nature complicates computational modelling of the phenomenon and makes it challenging to apply a standard for collecting high-quality annotated data (Biddle et al., 2021).

This paper seeks to contribute to the growing research on hyperbole identification in two ways: Firstly, we perform probing tasks to investigate whether pre-trained language models (PLMs) encode hyperbolic information in its representation without fine-tuning on task-specific data.[1] In recent years, probing tasks

[1]By "hyperbolic", we consistently refer to the figure of speech, not the mathematical space.

Proceedings of the 61st Annual Meeting of the Association for Computational Linguistics - Student Research Workshop, pages 200–211

have emerged as a popular approach in NLP for interpreting and analyzing model representations, and it has previously been shown that PLMs do encode both simile and metaphorical knowledge (Chen et al., 2022). However, to our knowledge, hyperbole probing remains so far unexplored. Therefore, we replicate edge and minimal description length (MDL) probing experiments for metaphor described by Aghazadeh et al. (2022) on a small hyperbole dataset constructed by Troiano et al. (2018). We expect that encoding hyperbole may present a larger challenge to PLMs than metaphor because hyperbole knowledge is primarily pragmatic rather than semantic (McCarthy and Carter, 2004).

Secondly, we build an operational taxonomy based on a meta-analysis of the linguistic treatment of hyperbole, and annotate an existing dataset according to said taxonomy (McCarthy and Carter, 2004; Mora, 2009; Claridge, 2010; Burgers et al., 2016; Troiano et al., 2018). We then use these annotations to analyze errors in model predictions to further shed light on the types of hyperboles that may pose a particular challenge to PLMs, as well as when constructing training corpora for the phenomenon. Our work will hopefully provide insight into the challenges of PLMs in identifying hyperbole, as well as contribute to developing an operational annotation standard for computational modelling of hyperbole.[2]

The remainder of this paper is structured as follows: Section 2 contains an overview of related work in hyperbole research, as well as probing experiments on other figures of speech. Section 3 provides a background on the linguistic research that is the framework for our operational taxonomy and annotation. Section 4 is a short explanation of probing tasks for PLMs, which we relate to the aim of our experiments. Section 5 outlines our experimental setup and describes the modifications made to the HYPO dataset. Section 6 provides our results and preliminary error analysis, and section 7 is a discussion of said results, as well as ideas for future research. Section 8 contains a summary and conclusions.

2 Related Work

In this section, we outline previous research related to both hyperbole and probing experiments on other figures of speech.

Hyperbole in NLP. While tropes such as metaphor and sarcasm have received considerable attention within figurative language processing research (Abulaish et al., 2020; Rai and Chakraverty, 2020; Moores and Mago, 2022), the automatic modelling of hyperbole is still at a relatively early stage. Research within this area can be roughly split into two objectives, hyperbole identification (HI) and hyperbole generation (HG).

Within the first, and for our purposes most interesting, category, Troiano et al. (2018) introduce the task of hyperbole detection by showing that classical machine learning pipelines can identify hyperboles with beyond-chance accuracy. For this purpose, they collect HYPO, the only manually constructed corpus of 709 English hyperboles, and include with the hyperbolic sentence s two contrasting corpora: One consisting of the manually constructed literal paraphrases to each of the sentences, and another consisting of a contrastive non-hyperbolic example using the same minimal lexical unit. They then identify a set of hand-crafted features targeting qualitative and quantitative aspects of exaggeration and report the best-performing classifier to be logistic regression using the literal paraphrases as negative examples, which achieves a 76% F1 score. In the same realm, Kong et al. (2020) address hyperbole detection using deep learning techniques on a constructed Chinese corpus and find that an LSTM with hand-crafted and embedding features produced superior results (85.4% accuracy). Biddle et al. (2021) construct a multitask learning classification architecture for hyperbole detection using a multitask BERT-based approach, wherein the model is fine-tuned on the HYPO dataset and takes the literal paraphrases as privileged information using triplet sampling. The authors find

[2]Our code for the probing tasks is available at `https://github.com/NiSc91/HyperboleProbe`

that their model improves the logistic regression baseline described by Troiano et al. (2018) by 10%. The authors also devise a series of test sentences to linguistically probe their model for extreme case formulations (ECFs), quantitative, and qualitative hyperboles, as described by Mora (2009), and find that their model particularly excels at hyperboles containing ECFs, which may be due to the lexical substitution between the hyperbole and the literal paraphrase being minimal.

Recent frameworks have also leveraged pre-trained language models to generate hyperbole and expand on existing hyperbole data in a semi-supervised way. Specifically, Tian et al. (2021) construct a sentence-level hyperbole generation model by fine-tuning it on sentences from a Reddit corpus using the syntactic pattern known as the "so ... that" pattern, which is said to be a productive strategy for hyperbole (McCarthy and Carter, 2004). The authors annotate the data with semantic relationships within the sentence and feed the annotations to COMeT models (Bosselut et al., 2019) trained to generate commonsense and counterfactual inference. They then train a classifier to rank hyperbole candidates and use a paraphrase model to generalize to more syntactic patterns. An HG approach by Zhang and Wan (2021) involves constructing a large-scale hyperbole corpus, HypoXL, and proposes an unsupervised approach to hyperbole generation wherein a fine-tuned BART model is used to fill in masked hyperbolic spans.

While these efforts point towards the possibility of successfully training computational models for the task of identifying hyperbole, the research so far also has significant gaps: Firstly, hyperbole in NLP lacks a unifying definition or linguistically motivated formal theory to describe the phenomenon. This is reflected in a lack of a consistent annotation scheme and procedure for hyperbole identification in the available data, which makes hyperbole studies relatively far behind investigations of metaphor, where most annotated data use either the Metaphor Identification Procedure and its extensions (MIP/MIPVU; Group, 2007; Steen et al., 2019), or Conceptual Metaphor Theory (CMT; Lakoff and Johnson, 1980) as a procedure for annotation. This consistency of theoretical framework and annotation procedure makes it easier to perform experiments generalizing across languages and datasets. Secondly, limited attempts have been made to probe pre-trained language models on how well they encode hyperbole without any fine-tuning. This makes it unclear whether models simply reconstruct the hyperboles found in the fine-tuning objective, and how well the model is able to learn hyperbolic information in a zero-shot or few-shot setting.

Our experiment is, to our knowledge, the first one to not utilize a fine-tuned model on hyperbolic sentences and to instead use probing methods to test for the encoding of hyperbolic information in PLMs.

Probing PLMs for Figurative Language Information. Probing techniques provide ways to understand and interpret the internal representations learned by deep neural networks (Belinkov, 2022). They typically involve extracting particular features or representations from a model's intermediate layers to gain insights into its structure or decision-making process. Several recent experiments have been designed to probe PLMs for information on figurative language. Namely, Chen et al. (2022) tackle similarity interpretation (SI) and generation (SG) tasks by probing simile knowledge from PLMs by testing it on similarity triple completion, i.e. sentences that take the form *[NP1] is as [ADJ] as [NP2]*. Their approach is to manually construct masked sentences with this syntactic pattern and predict the candidate words in the masked position. To that end, they adopt an auxiliary training process with the MLM loss to enhance the prediction diversity of candidate words. While this kind of probing works well to generate particular syntactic constructions, it would be ineffective for hyperbole due to its relatively limited dependence on syntax.

Instead, we choose to adapt several experiments conducted for metaphor probing by Aghazadeh et al. (2022) for hyperbole. The

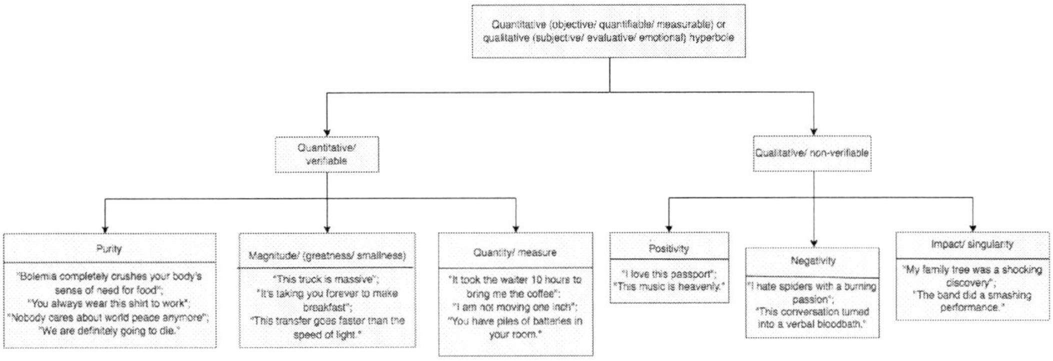

(a) Subtree and examples for the Dimension category.

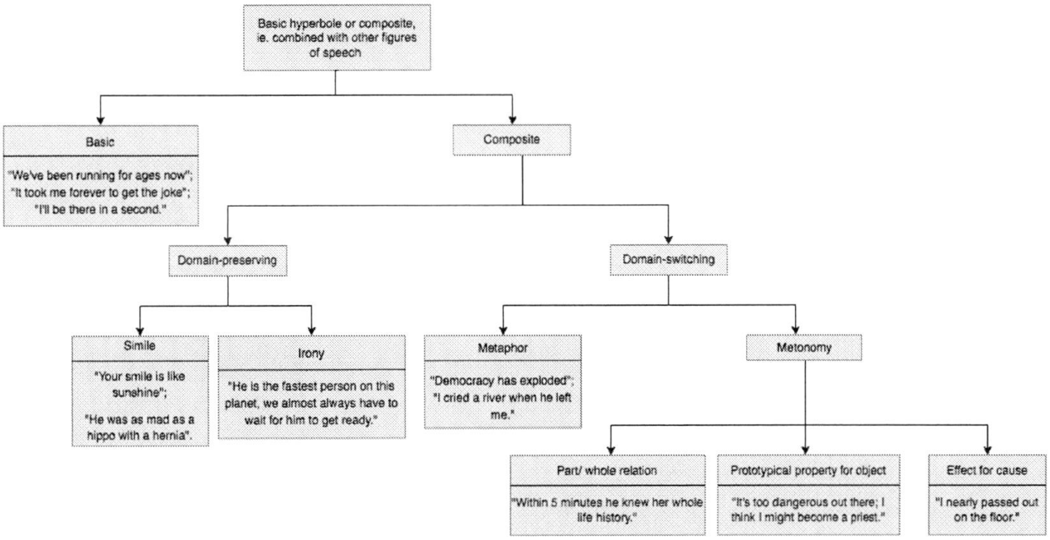

(b) Subtree and examples for the Type category.

Figure 1: The first two categories in the proposed taxonomy for hyperbole with examples for each.

authors conduct probing in two ways: First, they train a linear probing classifier on 3 different PLMs to evaluate the accuracies and extractabilities with which they encode metaphorical knowledge. Secondly, they use MDL probing to analyze the depth of the encoding of metaphorical information in multi-layer representations. The authors further extend their experiment by generalizing across four datasets and four languages. The results suggest that contextual representations in PLMs do encode metaphorical knowledge, mostly in their middle layers, and that it is possible to transfer this information across languages and datasets provided the annotation is consistent across training and testing sets.

While we can replicate the basic probing experiments, we cannot test the model's generalizability given the scarce hyperbole data. However, we do expect that it is possible via these techniques to learn something about the internal representations of hyperbole.

3 A Taxonomy for Hyperbole

In simple terms, hyperbole involves exaggerating a feature's property X beyond what is justified by the literal state of affairs (Claridge, 2010; Troiano et al., 2018). Stated in a more discourse-centred way, hyperbole occurs when an expression is more extreme than justified given the ontological referent, i.e. the entity in the world referenced by the text (Burgers et al.,

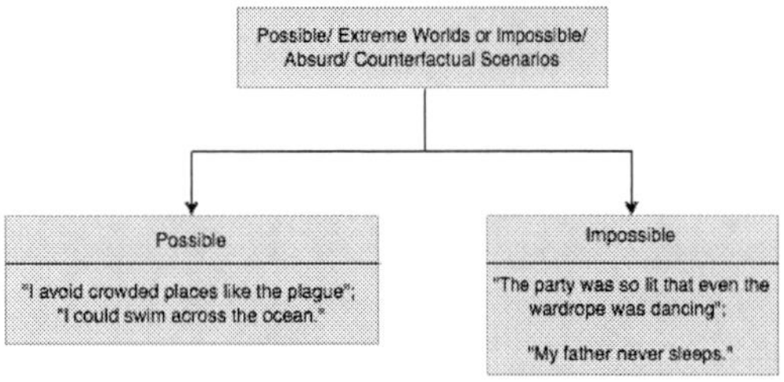

(a) Subtree and examples for the Possibility category.

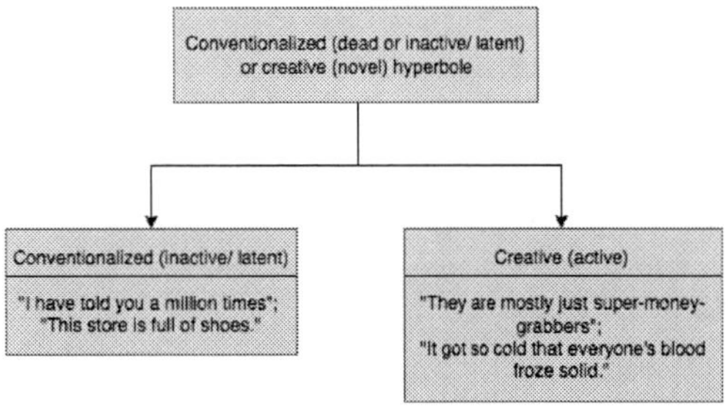

(b) Subtree and examples for the Conventionality category.

Figure 2: The last two categories in the taxonomy.

2016). While much of the work on hyperbole has previously been subsumed under studies of metaphor, humour, and verbal irony, recent corpus linguistic analyses have shed light on more fine-grained characteristics. Namely, the consensus in the treatment of hyperbole in literature is that the phenomenon is, among others, characterized by the presence of extreme case formulations (ECF), the ability of hyperbole to create either extreme possible worlds or downright counterfactual and absurd scenarios, and its augmentation of some property along a qualitative or quantitative scale (McCarthy and Carter, 2004; Mora, 2009; Claridge, 2010).

In the following, we outline some of the key characteristics and visualize them in an operational taxonomy (see Figures 1 and 2).

Dimension. There is widespread agreement that hyperbole occurs on a scale of magnitude along two main dimensions: a quantitative scale and a qualitative scale (Mora, 2009; Claridge, 2010; Troiano et al., 2018). The distinction between these scales refers to whether a hyperbole primarily concerns objective and measurable aspects or subjective and evaluative emotional states of affairs. According to Mora (2009), who conducted a corpus analysis of natural conversation on a 52000 word subset of the British National Corpus (BNC), quantitative hyperboles comprise 61% of the analyzed hyperboles and include the semantic fields of completeness, universality, measure, and magnitude. Qualitative (evaluative) hyperboles concern positive or negative sentiments, as well as impact or singularity; e.g. 'shocking', 'smashing' etc. However, an important point to make here is that there is a significant overlap between these dimensions, as hyperboles will generally have an evaluative function: For instance, the expression that somebody has "piles of batteries in their room" could be said to be a negative evaluation of the state of the room, but we choose to annotate such expressions as primarily quantitative, as the exaggerated property is one of measure. Another potentially relevant distinction is that quantitative hyperboles have a verifiable element, whereas purely qualitative hyperboles often serve to convey an internal subjective mental or emotional state (Claridge, 2010): For instance, in the statement, *It was the worst meal I have ever had*, the speaker could either be conveying their honest opinion of the meal, or they could be using exaggeration as a figure of speech to emphasize their disappointment with the meal.

Type. We use the term "type" to refer to whether the hyperbole is basic or composite, i.e., whether it stands alone or is combined with another figure of speech. According to Claridge (2010), hyperboles are basic if they preserve the semantic domain of the corresponding literal paraphrase, and composite if it involves a domain transfer where elements of a source domain is mapped onto a target domain. The latter is primarily the case with metaphor and, to a lesser extent, metonymy <citeclaridge2010hyperbole. In our annotations, we analyze simile as domain-preserving, even though we recognize that simile can be analyzed as an explicit metaphor (Burgers et al., 2018).

Degree of possibility. This distinction is one of degree and refers to the extent to which hyperboles generate impossible, absurd, or counterfactual scenarios. This is purely pragmatic and influences the degree to which a statement may be perceived as hyperbolic (McCarthy and Carter, 2004; Troiano et al., 2018).

Level of conventionality. This last dichotomy refers to the fact that hyperboles can use either more conventional or more novel and creative language to express exaggeration. This also impacts the extent to which a statement is perceived as a hyperbole: For instance, to say that one has not seen a person *for ages* is so frequent that it could be considered a latent or dead hyperbole, in the sense that it might not be viewed as intentional exaggeration for a specific purpose (McCarthy and Carter, 2004). However, in our annotation, we do label such frequent sentences as hyperbolic, although a conventionalized one.

4 Probing PLMs for Hyperbole

Probing language models aims to answer questions related to the model's internal representation, such as the location and depth of the encoding of a linguistic property in the multi-layer representation, or which input features contributed to a particular behaviour of the PLM (Belinkov, 2022). Standard probing methods involve training a linear classifier on top of a PLM to predict a linguistic property of interest, where a high probing performance on the task is associated with the model encoding said property. It is common practice to freeze the parameters of the PLM, which serves to prevent the gradients of the probing classifier from back-propagating into the model and thereby altering its pre-trained representation (Tenney et al., 2019). Following Aghazadeh et al. (2022), our experiments are not aimed at improving the accuracy of hyperbole identification tasks; we simply want to check the extent to which hyperbole knowledge may be encoded in the base representations. To that end, we employ edge probing, in which the classifier receives span-level representations from the PLM as inputs after they have been projected to a fixed-dimensional layer, 250 in this case. Thus, we define the span input to the PLM as the minimal lexical unit conveying hyperbolic information as given by the HYPO dataset (Troiano et al., 2018).

One common criticism of edge probing is that it may not be explanatory in the sense that it does not provide insight into whether a model is learning a linguistic property or simply memorizing the task (Belinkov, 2022). An information-theoretic perspective on addressing this limitation is to combine the probing quality of the classifier with some metric of the effort needed to extract the linguistic knowledge. This approach is known as MDL probing (Voita and Titov, 2020), wherein effort intuitively refers to the number of steps required by the PLM to encode a compressed representation of the input sequence. Following Aghazadeh et al. (2022), we use the online coding implementation of MDL, which measures a representation's ability to learn from various portions of the data. We report the compression, which is given by $N \cdot \log_2(K)$. In the context of language modelling, N refers to the size of the dataset, and K is the set of unique sequences being compressed. A random classifier will have a compression of 1, and increased data compression is associated with a better encoding of the given property.

5 Experiments

Here we describe our data and setup.

Dataset and annotation. We utilize HYPO, a manually constructed English hyperbole dataset (Troiano et al., 2018) of 709 hyperboles with corresponding literal paraphrases, as well as a *minimal units corpus* that provides the contrastive negative (literal) examples for each hyperbole (see examples (1A) and (1B) in §1).

For the purpose of our experiment, we first discard the corpus of literal paraphrases as we are interested in contrasting the hyperbolic usage of a particular word or phrase with a literal usage of the same word or phrase. It would otherwise not be possible to construct spans. To obtain span labels for each hyperbole and its negative contrast sentence, we programmatically extract the positions of each minimal

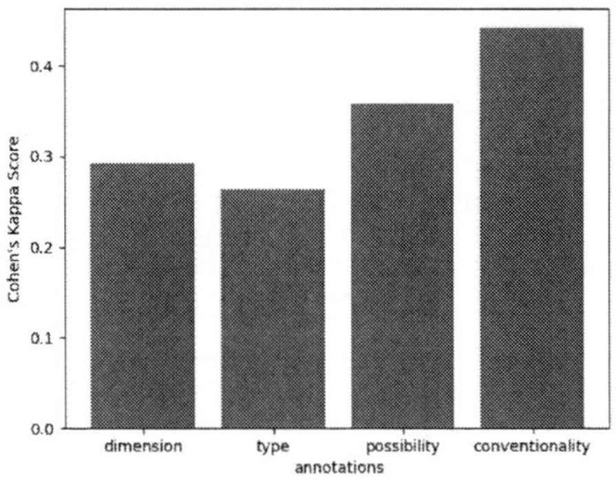

Figure 3: Inter-annotator agreement for the four aspects.

lexical unit and manually adapt the labels as needed; namely, we exclude examples with multiple spans and those without minimal unit contrasts.[3] Our final dataset contains 1396 span-labelled hyperbolic and literal sentences, which we split into training (70%), test (20%), and development (10%) sets.

We meticulously annotate the 63 hyperbolic sentences in the development sample using the operative taxonomy outlined in §3.[4] In order to obtain inter-annotator agreement, we enliste the help of additionally 5 annotators, assigning 12-13 sentences to each. As a result, each sentence is annotated twice. We observe a mean Cohen's Kappa of 0.339 (see Figure 3), suggesting only fair agreement, with particular difficulties on the dimension and type spectra on the taxonomy.

Experimental setup. We conduct edge- and MDL probing experiments for three models, BERT (Devlin et al., 2018), RoBERTa (Liu et al., 2019), and Electra (Clark et al., 2020). Following Aghazadeh et al. (2022), all the models are initiated from the base versions of the Huggingface Transformer library (Wolf et al., 2020), with 12 layers, 768 hidden size, and 110m parameters. In line with the procedure described in detail by by Tenney et al. (2019), we use the contextual vector representation for each span as inputs to the model, followed by a projection-layer and self-attention pooling to collapse the span vectors down to a fix-length 256-dimensional representation. The edge probing classifier, which in this case is a single linear layer, is then trained on top of the PLM. We do not change the original hyperparameters; we keep the batch size of 32 and the learning rate of $5e-5$, and train over 5 epochs for each experiment. During model training, the development set is used to monitor the model's performance and as a stopping criterion at each epoch. The MDL probe is based on the same structure as the edge probing experiment (Aghazadeh et al., 2022). One minor change we make to accommodate the small size of our data is to delete the smallest fraction trained on by the MDL probe, as it would otherwise amount to a single example. We run our experiments in two configurations: One in which we use the manually labelled hyperbole spans as inputs to the PLM, which follows the classic edge probing procedure. We call this the word-in-context (WiC) representation to emphasize that the model only has access to the rest of the sentence through the context embeddings (Tenney et al., 2019). In the other configuration, which is used as basis for comparison, we feed the entire sentence span to the model - the so-called sentence-level configuration.

[3]See examples in Appendix A.

[4]Similar fine-grained annotations were conducted by citettroiano2018computational, although they weren't included in the HYPO dataset, and inter-annotator agreement were not measured due to expected degree of difficulty.

Experiment	Word-in-Context Accuracy	Word-in-Context μ-F1	Sentence Level Accuracy	Sentence Level μ-F1
BERT	0.69	0.6895	0.72	0.7184
RoBERTa	0.72	0.7220	0.78	0.7762
ELECTRA	0.73	0.7256	0.78	0.7761

Table 1: Edge probing classification results.

6 Results

All our results are reported on the test set.

Edge probing results. The edge probing classification results are in Table 1 and the classification scores for the hyperboles and the literal sentences are in Table 2. We only report last layer scores, as we just evaluate the base representations.

Experiment	Class	Precision	Recall	F1
Word-in-Context				
BERT	literal	0.70	0.66	0.68
	nonliteral	0.68	0.72	0.70
RoBERTa	literal	0.73	0.71	0.72
	nonliteral	0.71	0.73	0.72
Electra	literal	0.74	0.71	0.72
	nonliteral	0.72	0.74	0.73
Sentence Level				
BERT	literal	0.78	0.61	0.69
	nonliteral	0.68	0.82	0.74
RoBERTa	literal	0.80	0.74	0.77
	nonliteral	0.75	0.82	0.78
ELECTRA	literal	0.84	0.69	0.76
	nonliteral	0.73	0.87	0.79

Table 2: Performance metrics for each of the models.

Annotation	WiC	Sentence	Total
QUAL	0.784	0.865	37
QUANT	0.692	0.731	26
PDOM	0.676	0.765	34
SDOM	0.828	0.862	29
NPOSS	0.769	0.821	39
POSS	0.708	0.792	24
CONV	0.806	0.806	36
NCONV	0.667	0.815	27

Table 3: Recall for word-in-context and sentence-level annotations for each category.

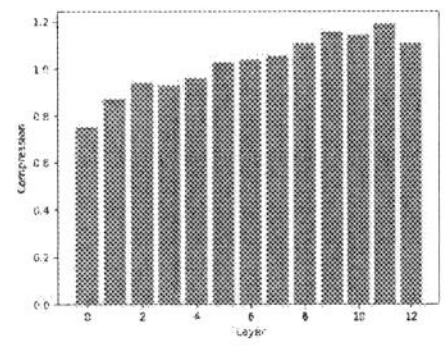

BERT WiC.

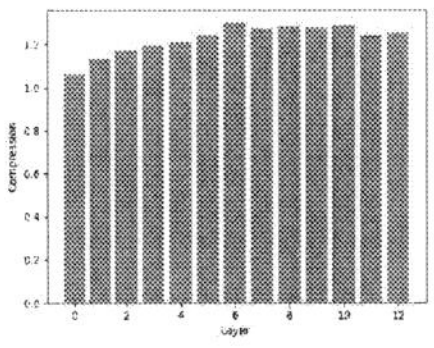

BERT sentence-level.

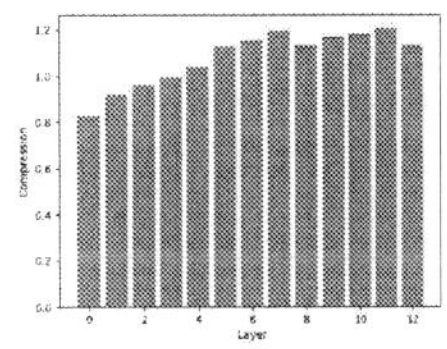

RoBERTa WiC.

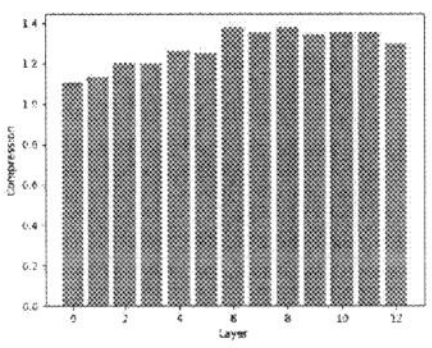

RoBERTa Sentence-level.

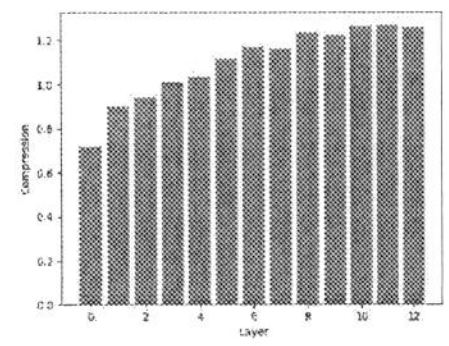

ELECTRA WiC.

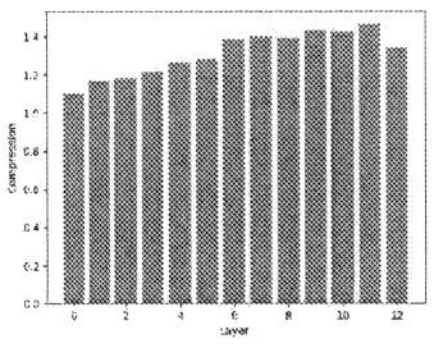

ELECTRA sentence-level.

Figure 4: Compression for each of the models.

MDL probing results. We report the compression for each of the experiments in Figure 4. The best layer is consistently near the top layer, but not the top layer itself.

Error analysis. Our error analysis is conducted for the model with the best recall, RoBERTa, and is only conducted for the hyperbolic examples, i.e. the 63 annotated hyperboles in the development set. We choose the best layer based on the compression displayed in Figure 4; i.e. layer 11 for the WiC representation and layer 8 for the sentence-level representation.

Table 3 report the recalls, i.e. the percentages of correctly predicted hyperboles, for each of the annotated categories, for both of our experiments, along with the distributions of each of the annotations on the 63 samples.

7 Discussion

We observe notably lower scores than for the metaphor probing experiments across the board: Based on the compression reported for the MDL probes, only reaching up to 1.4 in the best configuration, we can conclude that hyperbolic information does appear to a minor extent to be encoded in PLM representations. This is in line with our expected hypothesis that encoding hyperbole may pose a bigger challenge given its primarily pragmatic nature, and also fits with the fact that PLMs have been reported to struggle with pragmatic inference and commonsense knowledge (Rogers et al., 2020). Perhaps more interestingly, we can inspect the compression for each of the 12 layers reported in Figure 4 to understand where hyperbole is best encoded by the representation, which appears to mostly be in the final layers. This is different from metaphor and may lend further credence to the idea that pragmatics is typically encoded deeper into the PLM. However, since we are employing a very small dataset, the extent to which we can draw definite conclusions is limited. In the future, we would like to extend our experiments to more data and languages to measure generalizability.

Upon analyzing the MDL compressions of the two model representations, we make an intriguing observation that the sentence-level representation consistently outperforms the WiC representation, with compressions reaching up to 1.4 for the top layer. This discovery raises thought-provoking questions about the amount of hyperbole information inferred by the contextual embeddings, as hyperbole often surpasses the token or phrase level. For example, consider the sentence, "The temperature was so low, I saw polar bears wearing jackets." In this case, the entire complement sentence creates the hyperbole. This leads to discussions about defining the lexical unit of hyperboles for corpus collection and annotation purposes (Burgers et al., 2016). As for the model representations themselves, while PLMs theoretically encode context in their representation, it is worth exploring how much information is contained within and between subwords in the WiC representation. Employing interpretability metrics could provide further insights into this matter.

Considering the low inter-annotator agreement and that recall seems to generally increase with the frequency of the subcategory in the sample, it is challenging to draw insights from the model error analysis (see Table 3). However, we may tentatively conclude that the models have an easier time with conventional hyperboles, which is the opposite finding to that of Troiano et al. (2018) for traditional machine learning pipelines. Similarly surprisingly is it that the PLMs have better recall for domain-switching hyperboles than domain-preserving ones, which may also be confounded by a strength variable. Furthermore, when manually expecting the false positives, we observe that some sentences predicted to be hyperbolic do indeed contain words and phrases with a potential hyperbolic interpretation, e.g. *paradise* in the sentence "He thought a place awaited him in paradise",, suggesting that analyzing hyperbole in a larger context might provide further insights.

Finally, the low inter-annotator agreement, particularly on the dimension and type dichotomies, suggests that the hyperbole categories are not intuitively well-understood or discriminated. During discussions with annotators upon completion of the task, we had several instances where overlap of the dimension subcategories was so large that annotators could argue for either one, and it also wasn't clear to annotators when a semantic domain-switch was present. The latter suggests that more linguistic training may be necessary to identify combined figures of speech in context, for instance, through application of the hyperbole identification procedure (HIP) (Burgers et al., 2016). As a consequence, we would like to change our approach to hyperbole annotation in future corpus construction and investigate to which extent these categories are indeed computationally relevant. Our negative findings lend credence to the claim by Biddle et al. (2021) that annotation schemes may present a bottleneck for further development of of the task. We would also like to explore approaches for model evaluation of hyperbole types using conceptual knowledge bases and linguistic resources; namely leveraging framenets to explore their utility for metaphorical hyperboles, as well as investigating templates using particular syntactic patterns for evaluating quantitative hyperboles.

8 Conclusions

This study has attempted to probe three pre-trained language models (PLMs) for hyperbolic knowledge to better inspect how this information is encoded in their representations. We find, predictably, that knowledge of hyperbole is only to a limited extend encoded by PLMs, and, somewhat more surprisingly, that sentence-level representations appear to be supperior to word-in-context (WiC) representations, which may further highlight that most hyperbolic information does in fact exist beyond the token or phrase level. In the future, we would like to contribute with more hyperbole data with an operational annotation procedure, extend to cross-lingual experiments, as well as investigate the role of linguistic resources for hyperbole identification.

References

Muhammad Abulaish, Ashraf Kamal, and Mohammed J Zaki. 2020. A survey of figurative language and its computational detection in online social networks. *ACM Transactions on the Web (TWEB)*, 14(1):1–52.

Ehsan Aghazadeh, Mohsen Fayyaz, and Yadollah Yaghoobzadeh. 2022. Metaphors in Pre-Trained Language Models: Probing and Generalization Across Datasets and Languages. In *Proceedings of the 60th Annual Meeting of the Association for Computational Linguistics (Volume 1: Long Papers)*, pages 2037–2050, Dublin, Ireland. Association for Computational Linguistics.

Yonatan Belinkov. 2022. Probing Classifiers: Promises, Shortcomings, and Advances. *Computational Linguistics*, 48(1):207–219.

Rhys Biddle, Maciek Rybinski, Qian Li, Cecile Paris, and Guandong Xu. 2021. Harnessing privileged information for hyperbole detection. In *Proceedings of the the 19th Annual Workshop of the Australasian Language Technology Association*, pages 58–67.

Antoine Bosselut, Hannah Rashkin, Maarten Sap, Chaitanya Malaviya, Asli Celikyilmaz, and Yejin Choi. 2019. COMET: Commonsense transformers for automatic knowledge graph construction. In *Proceedings of the 57th Annual Meeting of the Association for Computational Linguistics*, pages 4762–4779, Florence, Italy. Association for Computational Linguistics.

Christian Burgers, Britta C Brugman, Kiki Y Renardel de Lavalette, and Gerard J Steen. 2016. HIP: A method for linguistic hyperbole identification in discourse. *Metaphor and Symbol*, 31(3):163–178.

Christian Burgers, Kiki Y Renardel de Lavalette, and Gerard J Steen. 2018. Metaphor, hyperbole, and irony: Uses in isolation and in combination in written discourse. *Journal of Pragmatics*, 127:71–83.

Weijie Chen, Yongzhu Chang, Rongsheng Zhang, Jiashu Pu, Guandan Chen, Le Zhang, Yadong Xi, Yijiang Chen, and Chang Su. 2022. Probing Simile Knowledge from Pre-trained Language Models. In *Proceedings of the 60th Annual Meeting of the Association for Computational Linguistics (Volume 1: Long Papers)*, pages 5875–5887, Dublin, Ireland. Association for Computational Linguistics.

Claudia Claridge. 2010. *Hyperbole in English: A Corpus-Based Study of Exaggeration*. Cambridge University Press.

Kevin Clark, Minh-Thang Luong, Quoc V Le, and Christopher D Manning. 2020. Electra: Pre-training text encoders as discriminators rather than generators. *arXiv preprint arXiv:2003.10555*.

Jacob Devlin, Ming-Wei Chang, Kenton Lee, and Kristina Toutanova. 2018. Bert: Pre-Training of deep bidirectional transformers for language understanding. *arXiv preprint arXiv:1810.04805*.

Pragglejaz Group. 2007. MIP: A Method for Identifying Metaphorically Used Words in Discourse. *Metaphor and Symbol*, 22(1):1–39.

Li Kong, Chuanyi Li, Jidong Ge, Bin Luo, and Vincent Ng. 2020. Identifying Exaggerated Language. In *Proceedings of the 2020 Conference on Empirical Methods in Natural Language Processing (EMNLP)*, pages 7024–7034, Online. Association for Computational Linguistics.

George Lakoff and Mark Johnson. 1980. Conceptual metaphor in everyday language. *The journal of Philosophy*, 77(8):453–486.

Yinhan Liu, Myle Ott, Naman Goyal, Jingfei Du, Mandar Joshi, Danqi Chen, Omer Levy, Mike Lewis, Luke Zettlemoyer, and Veselin Stoyanov. 2019. RoBERTa: A Robustly Optimized BERT Pretraining Approach.

Michael McCarthy and Ronald Carter. 2004. "There's millions of them": Hyperbole in everyday conversation. *Journal of Pragmatics*, 36(2):149–184.

Bleau Moores and Vijay Mago. 2022. A survey on automated sarcasm detection on twitter. *arXiv preprint arXiv:2202.02516*.

Laura Cano Mora. 2009. All or nothing: A semantic analysis of hyperbole. *Revista de Lingüística y Lenguas Aplicadas*, 4(1):25–35.

Sunny Rai and Shampa Chakraverty. 2020. A survey on computational metaphor processing. *ACM Computing Surveys (CSUR)*, 53(2):1–37.

Anna Rogers, Olga Kovaleva, and Anna Rumshisky. 2020. A primer in BERTology: What we know about how BERT works. *Transactions of the Association for Computational Linguistics*, 8:842–866.

Gerard Steen, Aletta G Dorst, J Berenike Herrmann, Anna Kaal, Tina Krennmayr, and Tryntje Pasma. 2019. Mipvu: A manual for identifying metaphor-related words. *Metaphor identification in multiple languages: MIPVU around the world*, pages 24–40.

Ian Tenney, Patrick Xia, Berlin Chen, Alex Wang, Adam Poliak, R Thomas McCoy, Najoung Kim, Benjamin Van Durme, Sam Bowman, Dipanjan Das, and Ellie Pavlick. 2019. What do you learn from context? probing for sentence structure in contextualized word representations. In *International Conference on Learning Representations*.

Yufei Tian, Arvind krishna Sridhar, and Nanyun Peng. 2021. HypoGen: Hyperbole Generation with Commonsense and Counterfactual Knowledge.

Enrica Troiano, Carlo Strapparava, Gözde Özbal, and Serra Sinem Tekiroğlu. 2018. A computational exploration of exaggeration.

Elena Voita and Ivan Titov. 2020. Information-Theoretic Probing with Minimum Description Length.

Thomas Wolf, Lysandre Debut, Victor Sanh, Julien Chaumond, Clement Delangue, Anthony Moi, Pierric Cistac, Tim Rault, Remi Louf, Morgan Funtowicz, Joe Davison, Sam Shleifer, Patrick von Platen, Clara Ma, Yacine Jernite, Julien Plu, Canwen Xu, Teven Le Scao, Sylvain Gugger, Mariama Drame, Quentin Lhoest, and Alexander Rush. 2020. Transformers: State-of-the-art natural language processing. In *Proceedings of the 2020 Conference on Empirical Methods in Natural Language Processing: System Demonstrations*, pages 38–45, Online. Association for Computational Linguistics.

Yunxiang Zhang and Xiaojun Wan. 2021. MOVER: Mask, over-generate and rank for hyperbole generation. *arXiv preprint arXiv:2109.07726*.

A Fine-grained Annotation Examples

Table 4 shows example data, along with the spans and annotations (taken from the development set of the data). The annotations are constructed along dimension (QUANT/QUAL), type (PDOM/SDOM), possibility (POSS/NPOSS), and conventionality (CONV/NCONV).

Hyperbole	Literal	Dim.	Type	Poss.	Conv.
Marriage is the *grave* of love.	I have gone to visit the grave of a friend.	QUAL	SDOM	NPOSS	CONV
So much snow that it is like walking in the *firmament*.	Some stars in the firmament have a name.	QUANT	PDOM	NPOSS	NCONV
The ancient castle was so big that it took *a week* to walk from one end to the other.	It took a week to walk from one end of the region to the other.	QUANT	PDOM	POSS	CONV
His feet are *colder than the arctic*.	The Antarctic is colder than the Arctic.	QUANT	PDOM	NPOSS	NCONV

Table 4: Sample data with annotations. Token spans are marked by italics around the word or phrase.

Towards Efficient Dialogue Processing in the Emergency Response Domain

Tatiana Anikina
DFKI / Saarland Informatics Campus,
Saarbrücken, Germany
tatiana.anikina@dfki.de

Abstract

In this paper we describe the task of adapting NLP models to dialogue processing in the emergency response domain. Our goal is to provide a recipe for building a system that performs dialogue act classification and domain-specific slot tagging while being efficient, flexible and robust. We show that adapter models (Pfeiffer et al., 2020) perform well in the emergency response domain and benefit from additional dialogue context and speaker information. Comparing adapters to standard fine-tuned Transformer models we show that they achieve competitive results and can easily accommodate new tasks without significant memory increase since the base model can be shared between the adapters specializing on different tasks. We also address the problem of scarce annotations in the emergency response domain and evaluate different data augmentation techniques in a low-resource setting.

1 Introduction

Emergency response is a very challenging domain for NLP for a variety of reasons. First, this domain has strict requirements regarding memory and computational efficiency. Often it is not feasible to load several large NLP models because of the limitations in the available infrastructure (e.g., memory of the machine where the models are running). Second, the environment is often noisy and the speakers communicate using domain-specific lexicon and abbreviations. Third, emergency situation environment is very changeable and the domain may vary from a rescue operation in a car accident to explosions or building collapse. Hence, the ideal dialogue processing system for the emergency response domain should be memory efficient, robust and flexible at the same time.

To address the efficiency aspect we use adapters[1] (Pfeiffer et al., 2020) that were tested on a variety of NLP tasks and have shown a comparable performance with the full fine-tuning while using only 1% of the parameters of the fully fine-tuned models. Adapters are small in size, can be easily shared and combined with different models. This is especially interesting in our use case since we deploy the same base model (`bert-base-german-cased`) for several tasks[2].

To tackle the problem of noisy, incomplete and domain-specific communication we investigate whether it is possible to boost the performance by integrating additional context and experiment with different ways of encoding it (e.g., by adding speaker, previous turn and dialogue summary information). We also experiment with various linguistic features and test how they affect the performance (e.g., by embedding the POS tags or including the ISO-style dialogue act annotations).

Finally, to simulate the low-resource scenario which is very common for the emergency response domain we reduce the amount of the training and development data to 12% of the original dataset and apply different ways of data augmentation including backtranslation, LM-based word replacements and random edit operations.

Figure 1 provides an overview of different experimental settings addressed in this work. To our knowledge, this is the first work that explores dialogue processing in the emergency response domain with adapters and performs a comprehensive study of the context integration and data augmentation in this setting.

2 Related Work

Adapters (Houlsby et al., 2019; Rebuffi et al., 2017) seem like a natural choice for lightweight and ef-

[1]The code and the pre-trained models are available at https://github.com/tanikina/emergency_response_dialogue

[2]We also tried multilingual BERT but it resulted in worse performance in our pilot experiments. Hence, we decided to focus on the model that was trained on German only and has a reasonably small size (436 MB).

Proceedings of the 61st Annual Meeting of the Association for Computational Linguistics - Student Research Workshop, pages 212–225

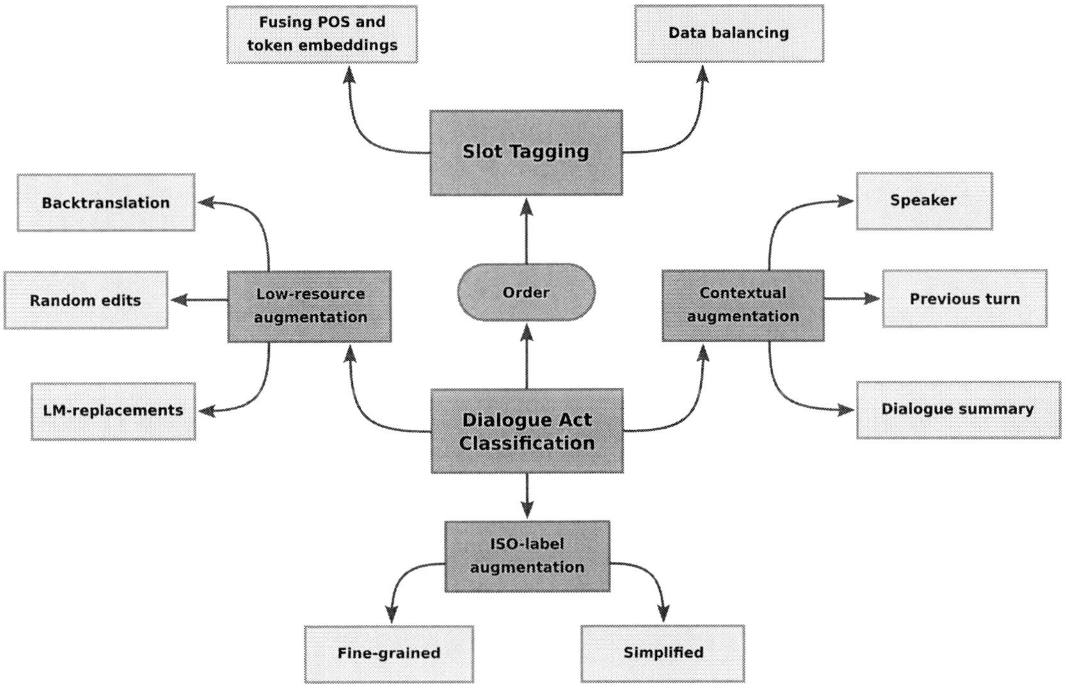

Figure 1: Overview of the Experiments

ficient NLP models. Adapters implement a fine-tuning strategy that involves only a small amount of trainable parameters per task. Each adapter adds a small set of newly initialized and trainable weights at each layer of the transformer architecture (Vaswani et al., 2017). Hence, the original network has mostly fixed parameters and can be efficiently transferred between the tasks. Adapters have shown good performance comparable to the fully fine-tuned models on a variety of tasks including, e.g., sentiment analysis, commonsense reasoning, paraphrase detection and entailment (Pfeiffer et al., 2021) and further modifications and improvements to the original idea were proposed in the recent work by Rücklé et al. (2020); Fu et al. (2022). Adapters have been successfully used for low-resource speech recognition (Hou et al., 2021), cross-lingual transfer (Parovic et al., 2022) and tested on the named entity recognition and classification tasks (Lee et al., 2022).

Also, in the field of dialogue processing there is a growing body of work involving adapter models. For example Xu et al. (2021) inject knowledge into pre-trained language models using adapters and explore grounded dialogue response generation with adapters. Another work by Madotto et al. (2020) proposes a simple and efficient method based on residual adapters in the continual learning setting for task-oriented dialogue systems. Wang et al. (2021) design a GPT-Adapter-CopyNet system that combines adapters and CopyNet modules into GPT-2 in order to perform transfer learning and dialogue entity generation. Their system significantly outperforms the baselines models on both DSTC8 and MultiWOZ data.

Efficiency and robustness are crucial in the low-resource setting when we have a limited amount of data. The main objective of data augmentation is to generate new data points by modifying the existing ones through a variety of transformations and while some of these transformations can be very simple such as random token deletion or insertion (Wei and Zou, 2019; Miao et al., 2020), others might require more computation and processing power, e.g., backtranslation (Edunov et al., 2018) or LM-based substitutions (Kobayashi, 2018; Kumar et al., 2020). Feng et al. (2021) and Chen et al. (2021) provide comprehensive surveys of the techniques and methods for data augmentation in NLP that served as a motivation for our work.

3 Data

The dataset used in our experiments is based on the dialogues collected during several robot-assisted disaster response training sessions (Kruijff-

Korbayova et al., 2015; Willms et al., 2019). All dialogues are in German and they represent team communication between a team leader or mission commander and several operators who remotely operate robots in order to explore some area, find hazardous materials, locate fires, damage or victims. Figure 2 shows a part of one dialogue translated into English.

speaker	original turn	translation
TL:	*UGV2 von Teamleader.*	*UGV2 for team leader.*
UGV:	*UGV2, kommen.*	*UGV2, coming.*
TL:	*Ja, UGV2, wir brauchen nochmal schärfere Bilder von dem Fass und der Kennzeichnung.*	*Yes, UGV2, we need again sharper pictures of the barrel and the sign.*
UGV:	*Ich habe Sie nicht verstanden, können Sie wiederholen?*	*I didn't understand you, could you repeat?*
TL:	*Ja, von dem Fass brauchen wir nochmal bessere Bilder, und auch von der Kennzeichnung.*	*Yes, we need better pictures of the barrel, and also of the sign.*

Figure 2: Example of communication between the Team Leader (TL) and the Unmanned Ground Vehicle operator (UGV).

The complete dataset contains 2,542 dialogue turns annotated with dialogue acts and domain-specific slots. For the dialogue act classification we reserve 2,261 turns for training, 281 turns for development and 283 for testing. In the low-resource setting we leave the test set unchanged but reduce the amount of the training samples to 310 (240 in training and 70 in development).

Figure 3 shows the overall distribution of different dialogue act labels in the data and Figure 6 in the appendix provides an example for each label. There are seven main labels: Call, CallResponse, InfoRequest, InfoProvide, Confirm, Disconfirm, Order and the additional label Other for the cases that do not fit in any of the main categories. The labels are derived based on the domain expertise and represent categories that are important for the emergency response domain. Part of the dataset is also annotated according to the ISO standard for dialogue act classification by Bunt et al. (2020)

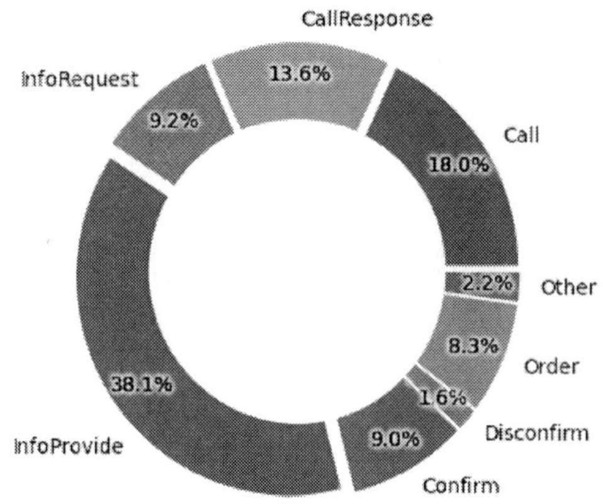

Figure 3: Dialogue Act Distribution

and we use these fine-grained labels in some of the experiments described in Section 4.

In the emergency response domain it is very important to correctly recognize and annotate all deployment orders (*Einsatzbefehl* in German). Note that not every utterance classified as request according to the ISO standard would qualify as Order in our domain. E.g., the request *"Could you repeat, please?"* is not a deployment order since it does not require performing a domain-specific action and should be classified as information request (InfoRequest).

For each turn annotated as Order we also perform the slot tagging. The slots are based on the regulation document of the emergency responders Feuerwehr-Dienstvorschrift (1999). We show an example containing all relevant Order slots in Figure 4. Note that the distribution of slots is quite uneven (see Figure 5). Some slots are present in almost every dialogue turn classified as Order (e.g., Unit is present in 67% of the turns and Task appears in 99% of them) while other slots are annotated only in 8% of the turns (Way). Also, the slots can be nested and the same token may belong to several slots. E.g., in *"Schickst du mir noch ein Foto?"* (Will you send me also the photo?), *"du"* (you) is part of the slot Task and also the slot Unit. This is the reason why we train separate models for each slot and then combine the results to provide final annotations.

For the slot tagging task we experiment with the full data as well as with the sampled data since the distribution of the negative versus positive instances per label varies a lot (see Figure 5 for the details). For the sampled data we limit the amount of negative samples (turns without the slot annota-

A-Trupp zur Brandbekämpfung mit Schaumstrahlrohr zum Pkw über die Wiese vor!
Einheit Auftrag Mittel Ziel Weg
A-Squad to extinguish the fire with a foam jet nozzle to the car across the meadow !
Unit Task Means Goal Way

Figure 4: Slot Tags for Deployment Order

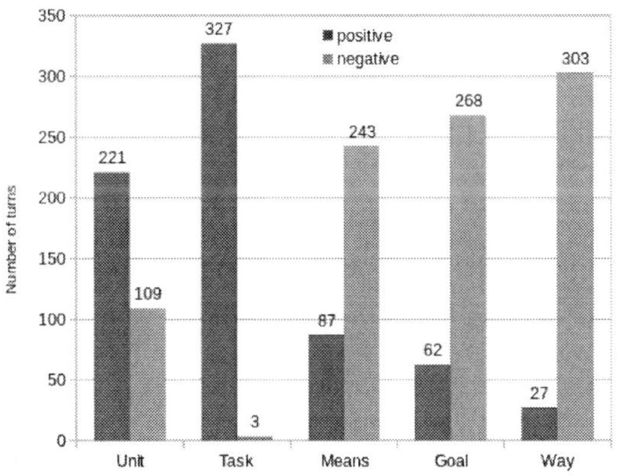

Figure 5: Slot Distribution

tion) to maximum 80% of the corresponding positive samples. Our intuition is that having uneven distribution with too many negative samples may hinder the model's performance and it might be easier for the adapter model to learn the tagging task on more balanced data. We test this idea and describe our results in the next section.

4 Experiments

Our experiments aim to answer the following research questions:

- Can we replace fully tuned BERT models with adapter models for dialogue act classification and slot tagging in the emergency response domain?
- Does integrating context and linguistic features in the model result in better performance?
- Does data augmentation in the low-resource setting help to improve the performance and what are the best ways to augment the data?

4.1 Vanilla BERT vs. Adapters

In order to check whether adapter models work well for dialogue act classification we compare their performance to vanilla BERT fine-tuned on the same data. Both models use the same base `bert-base-german-cased` model as a backbone and are trained for 20 epochs. The best performing checkpoint is selected based on the loss on the development set. When only the current turn embeddings are used as input we obtain 0.82 F1 score with the fine-tuned BERT and 0.80 F1 with the adapter model (Table 1). Adding speaker to the input results in 0.80 F1 for BERT and 0.79 F1 score for adapter.

We also compare the performance of the fully tuned BERT vs. adapters on the slot tagging task. Since the slots can be nested we train a separate model for each slot type (i.e., 5 adapters or 5 fine-tuned BERT models per setting). We use BIO notation for each slot type and compute F1 scores based on the token-level annotations. The results are summarized in Table 2. Since the distribution among the slots is uneven we also experiment with the setting where we reduce the amount of negative samples and balance the data.

It is clear from the evaluation results presented in Table 2 that adapters consistently outperform BERT on the slot tagging task and also benefit from the sampling of negative examples. Reducing the amount of negative samples gives us 9% increase in the macro F1 score for adapters while it does not bring any improvement for the vanilla BERT and effectively hurts the model's performance in terms of micro F1 (0.86 vs. 0.99). It turns out that we can use fewer parameters of the adapter model to achieve better results with the balanced classes.

Interestingly, the fully fine-tuned BERT model trained on the full data achieves the same macro F1 as the model trained on the sampled data but their micro F1 scores differ (0.99 vs. 0.86). One possible explanation is that since tuning of the BERT model involves more parameters that need to be updated in each iteration the training process becomes less stable. The difference in training stability between the adapters and the fully fledged fine-tuning in the low-resource setting is an interesting research question that needs further investigation.

Setting	Fine-tuned BERT	Adapter
OnlyTurn	0.82	0.80
Speaker+Turn	0.80	0.79
Context+Speaker+Turn	**0.91**	0.84
Context+AllSpeakers+Turn	0.90	**0.85**
Summary+Speaker+Turn	0.80	0.73

Table 1: Macro F1 scores on the dialogue act classification task (BERT vs. adapters).

Slot Label	Adapt+full	Adapt+sampled	BERT+full	BERT+sampled
Unit	0.93	0.92	0.82	0.80
Task	0.75	0.82	0.77	0.41
Means	0.86	0.89	0.82	0.88
Goal	0.57	0.81	0.59	0.67
Way	0.70	0.80	0.57	0.77
Macro F1	0.76	**0.85**	0.71	0.71
Micro F1	0.99	0.99	0.99	0.86

Table 2: Adapters (Adapt) vs. fine-tuned BERT (BERT) on the slot tagging task.

4.2 Contextual Augmentation

In the next set of experiments we look into the impact of context on the dialogue act classification (Table 1). First, we train both vanilla BERT and adapter model using only the current turn text as an input (OnlyTurn). This results in 0.82 F1 score for BERT and 0.80 F1 for the adapter. Next, we add the speaker information (Speaker+Turn) and obtain 0.80 for BERT and 0.79 for the adapter model. Moreover, adding the previous dialogue turn as additional context (Context+Speaker+Turn) results in a big improvement for both fine-tuned BERT (0.91 F1) and adapter (0.84 F1).

To integrate more context into the model input we also experiment with extractive summarization of the dialogue using the `Summarizer` model introduced in Miller (2019). We limit dialogue context to 10 previous turns and set the number of summary sentences to 3 (Summary+Speaker+Turn). However, this additional information seems to confuse the model which is especially striking in the case of adapters. Compared to the baseline Speaker+Turn (0.79 F1) the average score drops by 6 point (0.73 F1). The BERT model performance does not decrease in this setting compared to the baseline but it also does not show any improvement.

As a baseline for further experiments we use the version that encodes only the speaker information and the current turn text (Speaker+Turn). The main reason to select this setting as a baseline instead of OnlyTurn with a slightly higher macro F1 score is the fact that there is an important difference in how these two models annotate instances of the class Order. Speaker+Turn model has a better F1 score for the class Order (0.86) compared to the OnlyTurn version (0.77) and since correct processing of orders is crucial for our domain we choose this setting for the baseline. Another reason to pick Speaker+Turn and not the best-performing version that includes additional context (Context+AllSpeakers+Turn) is the fact that it is simpler and quicker to compute.

4.3 Adding Linguistic Information

Dialogue Act Classification

The subset of our dataset also provides the ISO-based annotations of dialogue acts according to Bunt et al. (2020) which we use to train a separate classifier that generates fine-grained ISO labels. These labels are added to the input of our main classifier that performs the domain-specific dialogue act classification. The distribution of the labels according to the ISO standard is shown in Table 7 in the appendix. We split the data into 1,224 samples for training and 170 for development. Although the overall accuracy of this classifier is only 62% it performs differently on different labels. The categories that have many instances in the training set (e.g., AutoPositive and TurnAccept) achieve F1 score around 0.81 and 0.82 but most of the rare labels are being misclassified.

After training the adapter-based classifier on the

ISO labels we run it on our training, development and test data to annotate the turns with additional ISO labels. Here we do not use the gold labels to simulate a realistic scenario when gold annotations are not available. The generated labels are then translated into German and added to the turn text with a special `[SEP]` token as a separator. The evaluation results are summarized in Table 3. The first column shows the scores for each of the dialogue acts when the baseline model (Speaker+Turn) is used. The second column shows the performance when additional (generated) labels are added to the input. We obtain an overall 3% improvement in the F1 scores with the additional ISO labels. We also consider a simplified version of the labels when we automatically map the original ISO taxonomy to the closest equivalents in the domain-specific taxonomy (see Table 8 in the appendix). The performance of the adapter model with such simplified dialogue act annotations is slightly worse than the ISO version (0.81 vs. 0.82).

Slot Tagging

To investigate whether linguistic annotations are also useful for the slot tagging task we annotate each word with its part of speech tag using the `SpaCy` library and 7 coarse categories including noun, pronoun, verb, preposition, adverb, adjective and other. For each tag we generate an embedding and combine it with the BERT embedding of the corresponding token. To process the combined embeddings we use a custom adapter head that adds two linear layers on top of the Transformer model, the tanh activation function and the final fully connected layer that outputs scores for the slot labels (BIO tags). The evaluation results of the adapter models with and without embedded POS information are presented in Table 4. Although the overall F1 score does not change we can see an improvement for almost every category (Task, Means and Way) except for the category Goal[3]. It is possible that for the class Goal the over-reliance on the POS information leads to some misclassifications.

4.4 Data Augmentation in the Low-Resource Setting

In order to simulate a low-resource scenario for the dialogue act classification we reduce the amount of the training and development data. The test set is left unchanged but the training set is reduced from 2,261 to 240 instances and the development set from 281 to 70 instances. As shown in Table 5 the performance drops to 0.47 F1 score on the test set when the model is trained on the reduced data.

First, we experiment with backtranslations using the `NLPAug` library. We translate between German and English and then back to German with `Helsinki-NLP/opus-mt` models and add these additional data as new instances with the same labels to the training data. This gives us an average improvement of 9 points in the F1 score. We also test whether adding more backtranslated samples helps to improve the performance and add the samples translated from German to French and back. However, doubling the amount of backtransalted data does not bring any further improvements (see Table 5). When looking at the generated backtranlations we notice that many instances are correct and represent good paraphrases. E.g., *"Und guck mal ob du ein genaues Bild von diesen Samples kriegen kannst"* (And see if you can get a clear picture of these samples) was backtranslated into *"Und sehen Sie, ob Sie ein genaues Bild von diesen Proben bekommen können"* which is semantically equivalent. However, sometimes the generated samples contain repetitions, hallucinations or incorrect translations. For example, *"Einsatzleiter"* (group leader) was translated into *"Operations Managers"* which is not a valid term in the emergency response domain.

Although backtranslation brings a substantial boost in performance, it also involves computationally heavy translation models, requires some extra processing time[4] and may not be feasible for some language pairs. Hence, we also experiment with cheaper and less time- and resource-consuming methods for data augmentation. First, we apply random masking to different proportions of the original tokens and generate substitutions using `bert-base-german-cased` language model. Table 6 shows in each row the proportion of the replaced tokens and each column shows the number of augmentation rounds. When selecting a new word for the masked token we set the parameter topk to 10 and iterate over all generated tokens to select the one that is different from the original word and does not represent a subtoken starting with ##, we also ignore all `[unused punctuation]` tokens. Some of the LM-

[3]Here we report the results of a single run but the trend was consistent among several runs of the model.

[4]It takes around 7 minutes to backtranslate 240 instances.

Dialogue Act	Adapter Baseline	Adapter+ISO DA	Adapter+simple ISO DA
Call	0.88	0.85	0.84
CallResponse	0.84	0.81	0.80
InfoRequest	0.98	0.83	0.97
InfoProvide	0.87	0.88	0.88
Confirm	0.44	0.52	0.49
Disconfirm	0.44	0.73	0.73
Order	0.86	0.83	0.79
Other	1.00	1.00	1.00
Macro F1	0.79	**0.82**	0.81

Table 3: Performance of the adapter model with and without additional ISO dialogue act labels (F1 scores).

Slot Label	Adapter Baseline	Adapter+POS
Unit	0.92	0.92
Task	0.82	0.85
Means	0.89	0.91
Goal	0.81	0.76
Way	0.80	0.82
Macro F1	**0.85**	**0.85**

Table 4: Performance of the adapters models with and without part-of-speech information on the slot tagging task.

based replacements are near-synonyms and match the context quite well (e.g., substituting *"Realbild"* (real picture) with *"Gesamtbild"* (overall picture)). However, sometimes the substituted token changes the meaning significantly. For instance, when replacing *"ja"* in *"ja kommt sofort"* (yes, coming immediately) with *"Geld"* (money) we generate a nonsensical in our domain sentence *"Geld kommt sofort"* (money comes immediately). We believe that this might be the reason why the performance of this approach is not consistently better as in case of backtranslations, although some settings (e.g., 60% LM replacements 5x) achieve similar performance. Also, we observe that replacing more than 60% tokens or augmenting more than 10 times is not beneficial for the model and leads to decreased performance.

The simplest and cheapest way of augmenting the data in terms of both time and computational resources is random editing. We add new instances by applying three different operations to randomly selected tokens: insert, delete or swap and similarly to the case of LM substitutions we experiment with different settings w.r.t. the number of edited tokens as well as the amount of the augmented data. As shown in Table 6 we get an overall improvement over the baseline model with 0.47 F1 score but there is no clear pattern regarding how many times or how many tokens should be changed. The experimental results show that the gains from adding new edited data are diminishing after 5 rounds of augmentation and the best performance can be achieved with 5 augmentation rounds and 40% edited tokens (Macro F1 0.57).

Training Details

All the experiments reported in this paper were performed on a a single GPU NVIDIA GeForce RTX 2080. We use `adapter-transformers` library to train the adapter models and `transformers` library for tuning the standard BERT models. As a base model we use `bert-base-german-cased`. We run the `SpaCy` library for the POS tag annotation with `de_core_news_sm` model for German and `Summarizer` for generating dialogue summaries. Baktranslations are performed with the data augmentation library `NLPAug`. Further details about exact versions of the software and training hyperparameters can be found in the appendix (Figures 9 and 10).

5 Discussion

Our experiments show that adapter models can be successfully applied in a very specific and challenging domain such as emergency response. Although fine-tuning BERT gives a slightly better performance (0.80 vs. 0.79 F1 for the baseline), adapters are much more efficient in terms of memory and

Dialogue Act	Baseline (full)	Baseline (low-resource)	Backtranslated 1x	Backtranslated 2x
Call	0.88	0.32	0.68	0.63
CallResponse	0.84	0.35	0.78	0.69
InfoRequest	0.98	0.87	0.70	0.79
InfoProvide	0.87	0.59	0.65	0.71
Confirm	0.44	0.56	0.66	0.65
Disconfirm	0.44	0.29	0.35	0.35
Order	0.86	0.76	0.64	0.67
Other	1.00	0.05	0.00	0.00
Macro F1	0.79	0.47	**0.56**	0.56

Table 5: Performance of the adapter model on the full and low-resource dialogue act classification with and without backtranslations (F1 scores).

LM-based word replacements				
%	**1x**	**2x**	**5x**	**10x**
0.1	0.50	0.50	0.49	0.51
0.2	0.45	0.49	0.48	0.52
0.4	0.54	0.53	0.55	0.54
0.6	0.52	0.53	**0.56**	0.54
Random edits: insert, delete, swap				
%	**1x**	**2x**	**5x**	**10x**
0.1	0.48	0.52	0.55	0.53
0.2	0.54	0.51	0.56	0.55
0.4	0.52	0.52	**0.57**	0.54
0.6	0.56	0.54	0.53	0.54

Table 6: Dialogue act classification performance (macro F1) on the augmented data. The baseline macro F1 is 0.47.

computational resources. As shown in Table 10 in the appendix an average size of an adapter model is 3.6MB compared to 436.4MB of the fully tuned BERT model. Also, adapters are very flexible and can be easily combined and stacked in different ways to perform a variety of annotations on top of the same base model.

We found that contextual augmentation (Context+AllSpeakers+Turn setting) is very beneficial for adapters and helps to increase F1 score up to 6 points compared to the baseline version. However, including longer context and dialogue summary actually confuses the model and hurts the performance. Hence, we conclude that for the dialogue act classification task the best way of integrating context is to combine the current and the previous turn with the speaker information. Adding linguistic features such as ISO dialogue acts and POS tags also helps to boost the performance but to a smaller extent (e.g. adding an ISO label increases F1 score by up to 3 points). The slot tagging task with adapters outperforms vanilla BERT in all settings and greatly benefits from the data balancing and negative sampling.

In the low-resource setting with 12% of the original data we find that adding backtranslated samples helps to improve the performance by up to 9 F1 points. However, multiple backtranslations are not necessarily useful and performance plateaus after one round of augmentation. LM-base word replacements and random edits can achieve similar performance but have a greater variance across the settings with different number of edits and augmentation rounds.

The dialogue turn tokens have different relevance to the task in the emergency response domain and replacing words blindly may result in unrealistic or simply wrong instances. E.g., *"kommen"* (coming) has a specific meaning according to the communication protocol used by the responders and represents an instance of the CallResponse class. Replacing *"kommen"* with *"gehen"* (going) or another similar verb results in the wrong interpretation and should not be labeled as CallResponse. In the future we would like to explore various constraints on the token substitutions and include more domain knowledge and ontology information to perform targeted replacements and edits.

Active learning for text classification (Schröder and Niekler, 2020; Zhang et al., 2022) is another approach that may work well in our domain. We have already shown that adapters benefit from balancing the data and it would be interesting to see whether they further improve by learning in stages when the model starts with he balanced dataset with easy-to-classify labels and the difficulty level gradually increases with each epoch. Also, in the future we would like to explore conditional text generation with the models like BART (Lewis et al., 2019) or T5 (Raffel et al., 2020) which can be trained to generate text given the corresponding label.

6 Limitations

The main limitation of our work is the focus on the specific domain and the dataset that is not yet publicly available. However, we should note that the dataset can be requested for further research and replication studies and it will be released in the future.We believe that testing adapters with different settings in the emergency response domain is a valuable contribution but we are also aware of the fact that the dataset used in our experiments is not large or exhaustive enough to cover all the variety of topics relevant for the emergency response. For example, our data cover cases of explosions, leakages of hazardous materials and building collapse but do not include any dialogues for open field rescue operations or car accidents.

Another issue that is worth mentioning is the fact that all recordings were collected during the training sessions and not the actual missions. Hence, the responders might be under less pressure than in a real life-threatening situation and their communication might be more of a textbook case. However, all simulations had a realistic setting that includes several operators, robots and points of interest (objects or locations) and we believe that the recorded communication is representative for the domain in question.

7 Conclusion

In this work we evaluate the performance of several adapter models in the emergency response domain. We demonstrate that adapters show similar performance to the vanilla fine-tuned BERT in the baseline setting (0.79 vs. 0.80 F1 score) while using only 1% of the parameters of the fully tuned model. Our experiments show that including additional context such as previous turn and speaker can improve the performance by up to 6 points in F1 score. Also adding linguistic annotations such as ISO dialogue acts boosts the performance in dialogue act classification. The slot tagging task mostly benefits from the balanced data. As for the low-resource setting, it shows a substantial improvement over the baseline (9 F1 points) when a single round of backtranslated turns is added to the training set.

Acknowledgements

The author was supported by the German Ministry of Education and Research (BMBF) in the project CORA4NLP (grant Nr. 01IW20010).

We also thank the anonymous reviewers for their valuable feedback as well as Prof. Josef van Genabith, Dr. Simon Ostermann and Bernd Kiefer for their advice and support of this project.

References

Harry Bunt, Volha Petukhova, Emer Gilmartin, Catherine Pelachaud, Alex Chengyu Fang, Simon Keizer, and Laurent Prévot. 2020. The ISO standard for dialogue act annotation, second edition. In *Proceedings ofThe 12th Language Resources and Evaluation Conference, LREC 2020, Marseille, France, May 11-16, 2020*, pages 549–558.

Jiaao Chen, Derek Tam, Colin Raffel, Mohit Bansal, and Diyi Yang. 2021. An empirical survey of data augmentation for limited data learning in nlp. *Transactions of the Association for Computational Linguistics*, 11:191–211.

Sergey Edunov, Myle Ott, Michael Auli, and David Grangier. 2018. Understanding back-translation at scale. In *Proceedings of the 2018 Conference on Empirical Methods in Natural Language Processing*, pages 489–500, Brussels, Belgium. Association for Computational Linguistics.

Steven Y. Feng, Varun Gangal, Jason Wei, Sarath Chandar, Soroush Vosoughi, Teruko Mitamura, and Eduard Hovy. 2021. A survey of data augmentation approaches for NLP. In *Findings of the Association for Computational Linguistics: ACL-IJCNLP 2021*, pages 968–988, Online. Association for Computational Linguistics.

Feuerwehr-Dienstvorschrift. 1999. Feuerwehrdienstvorschrift 100 führung und leitung im einsatz: Führungssystem, bundesamt für bevölkerungsschutz und katastrophenhilfe.

Chin-Lun Fu, Zih-Ching Chen, Yun-Ru Lee, and Hung-yi Lee. 2022. AdapterBias: Parameter-efficient token-dependent representation shift for adapters in

NLP tasks. In *Findings of the Association for Computational Linguistics: NAACL 2022*, pages 2608–2621, Seattle, United States. Association for Computational Linguistics.

Wenxin Hou, Hanlin Zhu, Yidong Wang, Jindong Wang, Tao Qin, Renjun Xu, and Takahiro Shinozaki. 2021. Exploiting adapters for cross-lingual low-resource speech recognition. *IEEE/ACM Transactions on Audio, Speech, and Language Processing*, 30:317–329.

Neil Houlsby, Andrei Giurgiu, Stanislaw Jastrzebski, Bruna Morrone, Quentin de Laroussilhe, Andrea Gesmundo, Mona Attariyan, and Sylvain Gelly. 2019. Parameter-efficient transfer learning for nlp. In *International Conference on Machine Learning*.

Sosuke Kobayashi. 2018. Contextual augmentation: Data augmentation by words with paradigmatic relations. In *Proceedings of the 2018 Conference of the North American Chapter of the Association for Computational Linguistics: Human Language Technologies, Volume 2 (Short Papers)*, pages 452–457, New Orleans, Louisiana. Association for Computational Linguistics.

Ivana Kruijff-Korbayova, Francis Colas, Mario Gianni, Fiora Pirri, Joachim Greeff, Koen Hindriks, Mark Neerincx, Petter Ogren, Tomáš Svoboda, and Rainer Worst. 2015. Tradr project: Long-term human-robot teaming for robot assisted disaster response. *KI - Künstliche Intelligenz*, 29.

Varun Kumar, Ashutosh Choudhary, and Eunah Cho. 2020. Data augmentation using pre-trained transformer models. In *Proceedings of the 2nd Workshop on Life-long Learning for Spoken Language Systems*, pages 18–26, Suzhou, China. Association for Computational Linguistics.

Jaeseong Lee, Seung-won Hwang, and Taesup Kim. 2022. FAD-X: Fusing adapters for cross-lingual transfer to low-resource languages. In *Proceedings of the 2nd Conference of the Asia-Pacific Chapter of the Association for Computational Linguistics and the 12th International Joint Conference on Natural Language Processing (Volume 2: Short Papers)*, pages 57–64, Online only. Association for Computational Linguistics.

Mike Lewis, Yinhan Liu, Naman Goyal, Marjan Ghazvininejad, Abdelrahman Mohamed, Omer Levy, Veselin Stoyanov, and Luke Zettlemoyer. 2019. Bart: Denoising sequence-to-sequence pre-training for natural language generation, translation, and comprehension. In *Annual Meeting of the Association for Computational Linguistics*.

Edward Ma. 2019. Nlp augmentation.

Andrea Madotto, Zhaojiang Lin, Zhenpeng Zhou, Seungwhan Moon, Paul A. Crook, Bing Liu, Zhou Yu, Eunjoon Cho, and Zhiguang Wang. 2020. Continual learning in task-oriented dialogue systems. In *Conference on Empirical Methods in Natural Language Processing*.

Zhengjie Miao, Yuliang Li, Xiaolan Wang, and Wang Chiew Tan. 2020. Snippext: Semi-supervised opinion mining with augmented data. *Proceedings of The Web Conference 2020*.

Derek Miller. 2019. Leveraging BERT for extractive text summarization on lectures. *CoRR*, abs/1906.04165.

Marinela Parovic, Goran Glavas, Ivan Vulic, and Anna Korhonen. 2022. Bad-x: Bilingual adapters improve zero-shot cross-lingual transfer. In *North American Chapter of the Association for Computational Linguistics*.

Jonas Pfeiffer, Aishwarya Kamath, Andreas Rücklé, Kyunghyun Cho, and Iryna Gurevych. 2021. AdapterFusion: Non-destructive task composition for transfer learning. In *Proceedings of the 16th Conference of the European Chapter of the Association for Computational Linguistics: Main Volume*, pages 487–503, Online. Association for Computational Linguistics.

Jonas Pfeiffer, Andreas Rücklé, Clifton Poth, Aishwarya Kamath, Ivan Vulić, Sebastian Ruder, Kyunghyun Cho, and Iryna Gurevych. 2020. Adapterhub: A framework for adapting transformers. In *Proceedings of the 2020 Conference on Empirical Methods in Natural Language Processing: System Demonstrations*, pages 46–54.

Colin Raffel, Noam Shazeer, Adam Roberts, Katherine Lee, Sharan Narang, Michael Matena, Yanqi Zhou, Wei Li, and Peter J. Liu. 2020. Exploring the limits of transfer learning with a unified text-to-text transformer. *J. Mach. Learn. Res.*, 21:140:1–140:67.

Sylvestre-Alvise Rebuffi, Hakan Bilen, and Andrea Vedaldi. 2017. Learning multiple visual domains with residual adapters. In *NIPS*.

Andreas Rücklé, Gregor Geigle, Max Glockner, Tilman Beck, Jonas Pfeiffer, Nils Reimers, and Iryna Gurevych. 2020. Adapterdrop: On the efficiency of adapters in transformers. In *Conference on Empirical Methods in Natural Language Processing*.

Christopher Schröder and Andreas Niekler. 2020. A survey of active learning for text classification using deep neural networks. *ArXiv*, abs/2008.07267.

Ashish Vaswani, Noam M. Shazeer, Niki Parmar, Jakob Uszkoreit, Llion Jones, Aidan N. Gomez, Lukasz Kaiser, and Illia Polosukhin. 2017. Attention is all you need. In *NIPS*.

Weizhi Wang, Zhirui Zhang, Junliang Guo, Yinpei Dai, Boxing Chen, and Weihua Luo. 2021. Task-oriented dialogue system as natural language generation. *Proceedings of the 45th International ACM SIGIR Conference on Research and Development in Information Retrieval*.

Jason Wei and Kai Zou. 2019. Eda: Easy data augmentation techniques for boosting performance on text classification tasks. In *Conference on Empirical Methods in Natural Language Processing*.

Christian Willms, Constantin Houy, Jana-Rebecca Rehse, Peter Fettke, and Ivana Kruijff-Korbayová. 2019. Team communication processing and process analytics for supporting robot-assisted emergency response. In *IEEE International Symposium on Safety, Security, and Rescue Robotics, SSRR 2019, Würzburg, Germany, September 2-4, 2019*, pages 216–221.

Thomas Wolf, Lysandre Debut, Victor Sanh, Julien Chaumond, Clement Delangue, Anthony Moi, Pierric Cistac, Tim Rault, Remi Louf, Morgan Funtowicz, Joe Davison, Sam Shleifer, Patrick von Platen, Clara Ma, Yacine Jernite, Julien Plu, Canwen Xu, Teven Le Scao, Sylvain Gugger, Mariama Drame, Quentin Lhoest, and Alexander Rush. 2020. Transformers: State-of-the-art natural language processing. In *Proceedings of the 2020 Conference on Empirical Methods in Natural Language Processing: System Demonstrations*, pages 38–45, Online. Association for Computational Linguistics.

Yan Xu, Etsuko Ishii, Zihan Liu, Genta Indra Winata, Dan Su, Andrea Madotto, and Pascale Fung. 2021. Retrieval-free knowledge-grounded dialogue response generation with adapters. In *Workshop on Document-grounded Dialogue and Conversational Question Answering*.

Zhisong Zhang, Emma Strubell, and Eduard Hovy. 2022. A survey of active learning for natural language processing. In *Proceedings of the 2022 Conference on Empirical Methods in Natural Language Processing*, pages 6166–6190, Abu Dhabi, United Arab Emirates. Association for Computational Linguistics.

A Appendix

label	original	translation
Call	*UGV 2 von Teamleader.*	*UGV 2 for team leader.*
CallResponse	*UGV 2, kommen.*	*UGV 2, coming.*
InfoRequest	*Du sprachst eben von einer anderen Ebene, habt ihr die schon erreicht?*	*You were talking about another floor, have you already reached it?*
InfoProvide	*Foto ist erstellt und geteilt.*	*Photo was made and shared.*
Confirm	*Ja, mache ich.*	*Yes, I will do this.*
Disconfirm	*Wir haben aktuell immer noch Probleme mit der Steuerung.*	*We are currently still having problems with the controls.*
Order	*Schickst du mir noch mal ein aktuelles Foto euren Standortes?*	*Will you send me again the current photo of you position?*

Figure 6: Dialogue Act Examples

ISO Dialogue Act	Samples	ISO Dialogue Act	Samples
Allo-positive	4	Agreement	5
Auto-negative	5	DeclineOffer	5
AddressRequest	10	ChoiceQuestion	10
Instruct	10	SetQuestion	11
Pausing	17	Promise	18
AcceptOffer	19	CheckQuestion	20
TurnTake	20	Disconfirm	24
Other	29	Question	36
Confirm	37	PropositionalQuestion	38
Offer	39	Answer	45
AcceptRequest	47	Request	107
Auto-positive	159	TurnAccept	207
TurnAssign	217	Inform	255

Table 7: Distribution of the ISO dialogue acts.

Simplified Dialogue Act	Original ISO Labels
Call	TurnTake, TurnAssign
CallResponse	TurnAccept
InfoRequest	Question, ChoiceQuestion, SetQuestion, CheckQuestion, PropositionalQuestion
InfoProvide	Answer, Inform, Offer, Promise, AddressRequest, Instruct
Confirm	Confirm, Agreement, AcceptOffer, AcceptRequest
Disconfirm	Disconfirm, Auto-negative
Order	Request
Other	All other labels

Table 8: Mapping between the ISO labels and the domain-specific dialogue acts.

Library	Version	URL	Reference
Adapter-transformers	3.1.0	`https://github.com/adapter-hub/adapter-transformers`	Pfeiffer et al. (2020)
Transformers	4.18.0	`https://github.com/huggingface/transformers/`	Wolf et al. (2020)
Summarizer	0.10.1	`https://github.com/dmmiller612/bert-extractive-summarizer`	Miller (2019)
NLPAug	1.1.10	`https://github.com/makcedward/nlpaug`	Ma (2019)
SpaCy	3.2.4	`https://spacy.io/`	NA

Table 9: External libraries used in the experiments.

Parameters	**Adapt Dialogue Acts**	**BERT Dialogue Acts**	**Adapt Slots**	**BERT Slots**
Base Model	bert-base-german-cased		bert-base-german-cased	
Learning Rate	1e-4	1e-4	1e-3	1e-5
Number of Epochs	20	20	12	12
Batch Size	32	16	16	16
Optimizer	AdamW	AdamW	AdamW	AdamW
Avg. Training Time	6 min	22 min	4 min	4 min
Avg. Model Size	3.6MB	436.4MB	3.6MB	434.1MB

Table 10: Training parameters for different model types. The best performing model was selected based on the loss on the development set.

I already said that! Degenerating redundant questions in open-domain dialogue systems

Long Mai, Julie Carson-Berndsen

ML-Labs, School of Computer Science, University College Dublin, Ireland

long.mai@ucdconnect.ie, julie.berndsen@ucd.ie

Abstract

Neural text generation models have achieved remarkable success in carrying on short open-domain conversations. However, their performance degrades significantly in the long term, especially in their ability to ask coherent questions. A significant issue is the generation of redundant questions where the answer has already been provided by the user. We adapt and evaluate different methods, including negative training, decoding, and classification, to mitigate the redundancy problem. We also propose a simple yet effective method for generating training data without the need for crowdsourcing human-human or human-bot conversations. Experiments with the BlenderBot model show that our combined method significantly reduces the rate of redundant questions from 27.2% to 8.7%, while improving the quality of the original model. The code, dataset, and trained models can be found at our repository[1].

1 Introduction

Despite recent significant improvements in text generation techniques, open-domain dialogue generation is nowhere near perfect. Large-scale neural-based models, such as GPT-3 (Brown et al., 2020) and BlenderBot (Roller et al., 2020b; Chen et al., 2021; Shuster et al., 2022), still present many issues including but not limited to contradiction (Li et al., 2021a), "hallucinations" (Shuster et al., 2021), offensive and toxic responses (Roller et al., 2020a; Dinan et al., 2022), which undermine their use in real-world applications. As a result, many social chatbots (Hakkani-Tur, 2021) still rely heavily on hand-designed dialogue managers and scripted responses. End-to-end neural-based models are only used for handling unexpected inputs, but only for a few turns, before giving back control to the hand-designed dialogue manager (Konrád et al., 2021). Although neural-based models have shown superior performance in generating statement responses,

[1]https://github.com/mailong25/redundancy-dialogue

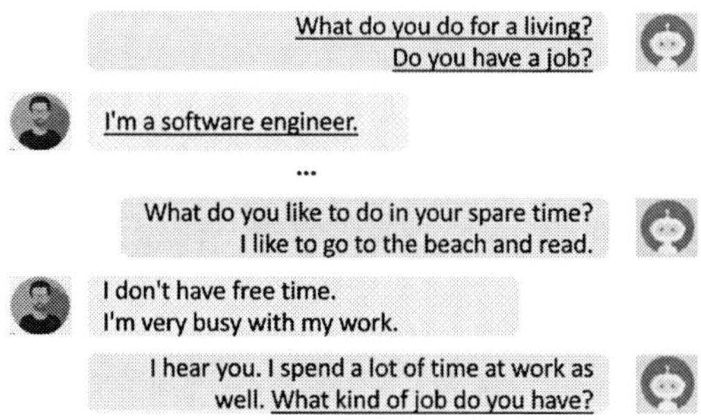

Figure 1: Examples of redundant questions generated by the BB3 model.

they are also reported to ask undesirable questions such as redundant, irrelevant, and topic-changing questions (Konrád et al., 2021; Paranjape et al., 2020). This is because the models are often trained on short conversations, which results in generating questions that prioritize local appropriateness over global cohesiveness. This is why the quality of generated questions often degrades rapidly when the conversation is carried on over multiple turns.

To address difficulties of long-term dialogue generation, a multi-session dialogue dataset (MSC) (Xu et al., 2021) has been proposed with an average conversation turn of 53; this is significantly higher than any of the previous datasets, of 2-15 turns. The authors also proposed a memory-augmented model that makes use of summary of the conversation for generating global-coherent responses. However, the issue of redundant questions is still present. Figure 1 shows examples of redundant questions generated by the recent Blenderbot 3.0 (BB3) chatbot (Shuster et al., 2022), partly trained on MSC with memory-augmentation. Redundant questions can be categorized into explicit and implicit. Explicit are questions that have been asked previously in the dialogue context while implicit are the ones in which the answers are already given or can be inferred but was not previously asked.

Proceedings of the 61st Annual Meeting of the Association for Computational Linguistics - Student Research Workshop, pages 226–236

The problem of redundant questions can also be attributed to the maximum likelihood training objective that does not explicitly teach the model what kinds of questions it should *not* ask. Although several techniques, such as unlikelihood training (Welleck et al., 2019), negative training (He and Glass, 2019), and contrastive learning (Su et al., 2022; Su and Collier, 2022) have been proposed to mitigate undesirable behaviors of maximum likelihood training, none of them have been focused on preventing bad questions from being generated.

This study is the first to address the problem of redundant questions in open-domain dialogue systems. We adapt and evaluate different methods, including unlikelihood training, contrastive training, contrastive decoding, and classification to mitigate the redundancy problem. Whether a question is redundant or not is determined based on the previous speaker's personas, which are input to the model alongside the truncated dialogue history. As there are no relevant datasets for this task, we created the first one, called the Non-Redundant Questions (NRQ) dataset, to facilitate training. To demonstrate the effectiveness of the proposed method, we apply it to improve the question-asking ability of the Blenderbot 2.0 model (BB2) (Chen et al., 2021) - a simpler version, but comparable to the recent BB3 model. Experimental results show that our proposed methods reduce the redundant question rate of the original BB2 model from 27.2% to 8.7%, which results in better overall performance.

2 Related work

2.1 Decoding methods

The generation of redundant questions is highly related to repetition problems in neural-based dialogue models in which the model tends to copy words and phrases from the preceding context (Xu et al., 2022). Prior studies often tackled this issue by controlling the decoding stage. Several beam search variants and stochastic decoding methods, such as top-k (Fan et al., 2018) or nucleus sampling (Holtzman et al., 2019), have been proposed to reduce the level of repetition by favoring less likely but non-repetitive candidates. Contrastive decoding (Su and Collier, 2022) is also proposed to mitigate the repetition issue. Another simple yet effective approach is N-gram blocking (Kulikov et al., 2018) in which N-gram presented in the preceding context are blocked during candidate expansion. However, the solution is not suitable for dealing with implicit or explicit redundant questions with no N-gram in common.

2.2 Training methods

Although improved decoding algorithms can reduce redundant question rates, the underlying issue has not been resolved: the model still assigns a high probability for undesirable response candidates. Several training methods have been proposed to address this problem. For dialogue response generation, (He and Glass, 2019) proposed a negative training framework to resolve the problem of malicious and generic responses. (Welleck et al., 2019) stated that the standard likelihood training objective for text generation is a flawed approach, which contributes significantly to the generation of undesirable behaviors. They then proposed an unlikelihood training objective that forces unlikely generations to be assigned a lower probability by the model. The method is then applied to reduce not only dull and repetitive sentences but also inconsistent and contradictory responses (Li et al., 2021b). Another approach to discourage the model from generating undesirable texts is contrastive training (Cao and Wang, 2021; Li et al., 2022), which aims to differentiate the embedding representations of positive and negative responses.

3 Methodology

3.1 Dialogue generation

The goal of open-domain dialogue generation is to predict the target response $y = (y_1, y_2, .., y_n)$, given the dialogue context $x = (x_1, x_2.., x_m)$ and augmented information $s = (s_1, s_2, .., s_k)$. The dialogue context $x_{1:m}$ is the concatenated history utterances from both speakers while the augmented information $s_{1:k}$ can be scenarios, external knowledge, speaker personas, etc.

Since using the full dialogue context is computationally expensive, prior studies often use a truncated one, e.g. last 128 tokens, alongside personas from both speakers. The introduction of personas is to make sure the newly generated response is consistent with what has been said in the dialogue history. In this study, we propose another utility of speaker personas: to avoid asking redundant questions. For example, if one of the partner's personas is *I am a vegan*, then the chatbot should not ask a question like *What is your favorite kind of meat?*.

To augment the generation with personas, we use the Fusion-in-Decoder (Izacard and Grave, 2020)

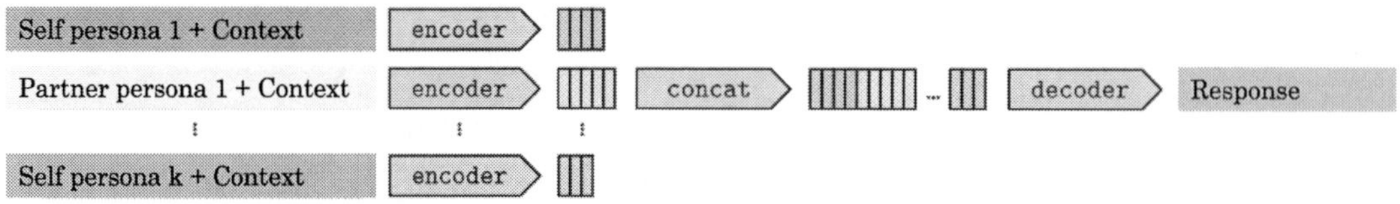

Figure 2: Response generation with augmented speaker personas using Fusion-in-Decoder method.

as shown in Figure 2. We prepend each of the top N personas to the dialogue context and encode them independently using an encoder. The decoder then attends to the concatenated encoding outputs to produce a final response. To extract speaker personas from conversation history, we use a pre-trained BB2 Memory Decoder from ParlAI[2]. All partner personas are used to produce the responses.

3.2 Likelihood training

Given a dataset $D^+ = \{(x^+, s^+, y^+)\}$ collected from real human conversations, we train a response generation model using standard maximum likelihood estimation (MLE)

$$\mathcal{L}_{MLE}(p_\theta, x^+, s^+, y^+) = -\sum_{t=0}^{|y^+|} log\ p_\theta(y_t^+|x^+, s^+, y_{<t}^+)$$

where x^+ is the truncated dialogue context, s^+ is the speaker personas, y^+ is the next target response, and y_t^+ is the t-th token of y^+.

4 Redundancy mitigation methods

4.1 Unlikelihood training

We apply the unlikelihood loss (UL) (Welleck et al., 2019) to discourage the model from generating undesirable responses. Given an incoherent dataset $D^- = \{(x^-, s^-, y^-)\}$, the loss is computed as:

$$\mathcal{L}_{UL}(p_\theta, x^-, s^-, y^-) = -\sum_{t=0}^{|y^-|} \beta(y_t^-)\ log(1 - p_\theta(y_t^-|x^-, s^-, y_{<t}^-))$$

where y^- is the undesirable response, and s^- contains partner's persona that make y^- a redundant question. $\beta(y_t^-)$ is a candidate-dependent scale that controls how much the token t-th should be penalized. We set $\beta = 0$ for the first two tokens of the question and for tokens that do not belong to the question. The β values for the remaining tokens are set to 1.

We train the model with a mixture of likelihood and unlikelihood losses to avoid degradation. The likelihood is performed on D^+ to push up the probability of tokens in the positive response y^+ while unlikelihood is performed on D^- to push down the probability of tokens in the undesirable response y^-. It should be noted that samples from D^+ and D^- can overlap or differ. In this study, we generate D^- using the same samples from D^+.

For each positive sample (x^+, s^+, y^+) in D^+, we generate the corresponding negative one (x^-, s^-, y^-) by keeping x and y: $x^- = x^+$; $y^- = y^+$. We then append an additional partner persona s_{neg} to the existing personas: $s^- = s^+ + s_{neg}$. The negative persona s_{neg} is chosen so that its presence will turn the positive response y^+ into a negative one. For example, if the positive response is *What is your favourite kind of meat?*, then an example of s_{neg} should be *I am a vegan.* A simple strategy to generate s_{neg} is to extract the partner persona from the next response in the dialogue. Figure 3 illustrates how a positive and a negative training sample are generated.

As the samples from D^+ and D^- overlap, the total loss can be now written as follow:

$$\mathcal{L} = \mathcal{L}_{MLE}(p_\theta, x, s^+, y) + \mathcal{L}_{UL}(p_\theta, x, s^-, y)$$

4.2 Classification

As the model can produce multiple responses given the input, we can filter out candidates containing redundant questions. Hence, we can build a binary classification model that can detect whether a generated response contains such questions. The model takes three inputs: the truncated dialogue context, partner speaker persona, and the generated response. Rather than inputting all speaker personas at once for a single prediction, we split them into multiple one-sentence personas and perform multiple predictions. If any of the predictions indicate redundancy in the generated response, we classify it as containing redundant questions.

To generate training data for the classification model, we use the same D^+ and D^- sets discussed

[2] https://parl.ai/docs/zoo.html

in Section 4.1. For the redundant class, we pair up the negative partner persona s_{neg} with the target response y and dialogue context x. Meanwhile, we replace s_{neg} with a partner persona presented in s^+ to form the non-redundant class.

We fine-tune three pre-trained language models, namely XLnet (Yang et al., 2019), RoBERTa (Liu et al., 2019), and DeBERTa (He et al., 2020), for classification task. Each training sample is formed by concatenating the dialogue context, partner speaker persona, and generated response with a separator token in between.

4.3 Contrastive decoding

To address the repetition problem in text generation, (Su et al., 2022) has proposed a new approach called contrastive decoding. Since the method was originally designed for decoder-only language models (e.g., GPT2), we made some modifications to adapt it to encoder-decoder models.

Given the context x and prefix decoded text $y_{<t}$, the selection of the output token y_t follows:

$$y_t = \arg\max_{v \in V^{(k)}} \{(1-\alpha) \times \overbrace{p_\theta(v \mid y_{<t}, x)}^{\text{model confidence}} - \alpha \times \underbrace{\max\{sim\left(h_v, h_{x_j^n}\right)\}}_{\text{degeneration penalty}}\}$$

Where $V^{(k)}$ is the set of top-k predictions from the model's probability distribution $p_\theta(\cdot \mid y_{<t})$. The representation of token v, denoted as h_v, refers to the decoder output (i.e., the hidden state of the final layer) given the concatenation of the prefix $y_{<t}$ and v, as well as the encoder outputs of the dialogue context x. Similarly, the representation $h_{x_j^n}$ is the decoder output of the j-th token of the n-th turn in the dialogue context. $h_{x_j^n}$ is computed based on the concatenation of the prefix $x_{\leq j}^n$ and x_j^n, as well as the encoder outputs of dialogue context $x^{<n}$. $sim(\cdot, \cdot)$ computes the cosine similarity between token representations while $\alpha \in [0, 1]$ controls the importance of model confidence and degeneration penalty. Model confidence refers to the probability assigned by the model to the candidate v, while the degeneration penalty measures the similarity between the candidate v and all tokens presented in the dialogue context. We set $\alpha = 0.4$ based on the results presented in (Su et al., 2022).

4.4 Contrastive training

Contrastive learning can be used to discourage model from generating undesirable responses (Cao and Wang, 2021). We propose a contrastive training objective that drives the model to favour the generation of non-redundant questions over redundant ones. Given a positive sample $q^+ = (x, s^+, y)$ from D^+ and its corresponding negative sample $q^- = (x, s^-, y)$ from D^-, the objective is to differentiate the question representations between the two samples. Assume that we have a positive set $P = \{q_1^+ = q^+, q_2^+, .., q_m^+\}$ generated from q^+ and a negative set $N = \{q_1^- = q^-, q_2^-, .., q_m^-\}$ generated from q^-, the contrastive loss for q can be written as follow:

$$l = \frac{-1}{\binom{|P|}{2}} \sum_{\substack{q_i^+, q_j^+ \in P \\ q_i^+ \neq q_j^+}} \log \frac{\exp(\text{sim}(\boldsymbol{h}_i^+, \boldsymbol{h}_j^+))}{\sum_{\substack{q_k \in P \cup N \\ q_k \neq q_i^+}} \exp(\text{sim}(\boldsymbol{h}_i^+, \boldsymbol{h}_k))}$$

Where h_i^+ and h_j^+ are representations of q_i^+ and q_j^+, while h_k is representation of q_k, which can be either a sample of the positive or negative set.

Sample construction. Given a positive sample $q^+ = (x, s^+, y)$, we generate its sibling positive/negative samples by keeping x and y but appending an additional partner persona s_{add} to the existing personas s^+. s_{add} is chosen from a persona pool S, which is a collection of all speaker personas extracted from the training set. First, we rank personas in S based on their similarity scores to the context x and then pick the top-k personas as s_{add}. After that, we use the redundant classifier from Section 4.2 to classify the each input (x, s_{add}, y). If the prediction is redundant, we use s_{add} to generate a negative sample, otherwise we use it to construct a positive one.

Sample representation (h_*). We use the outputs of the decoder's last layer to form the representation h for each positive and negative sample. More specifically, we only average over tokens that belong to the question in the target response y.

Training. To avoid model degradation, we combine contrastive loss with the original MLE loss $\mathcal{L} = \mathcal{L}_{MLE} + \mathcal{L}_{CL}$.

4.5 Unlikelihood training with augmented loss

We reuse the sample construction method from Section 4.4 to increase the coverage of the training set and boost the performance of unlikelihood training.

More specifically, we augment the original unlikelihood loss with loss computed from sibling positive and negative samples as follow:

$$\mathcal{L}_{aug} = \frac{1}{|P|}\sum_{i=1}^{|P|}\mathcal{L}_{MLE}(p_\theta, x, s_i^+, y) + \frac{1}{|N|}\sum_{j=1}^{|N|}\mathcal{L}_{UL}(p_\theta, x, s_j^-, y)$$

Where P and N are the positive and negative sets. s_i^+ is the speaker persona of i-th sample from P and s_j^- is the speaker persona of j-th sample from N. Samples from P and N are included in the same batch of training. Using augmented loss helps the model better distinguish between negative and positive samples, which reduces the number of redundant questions while maintaining quality of the original model.

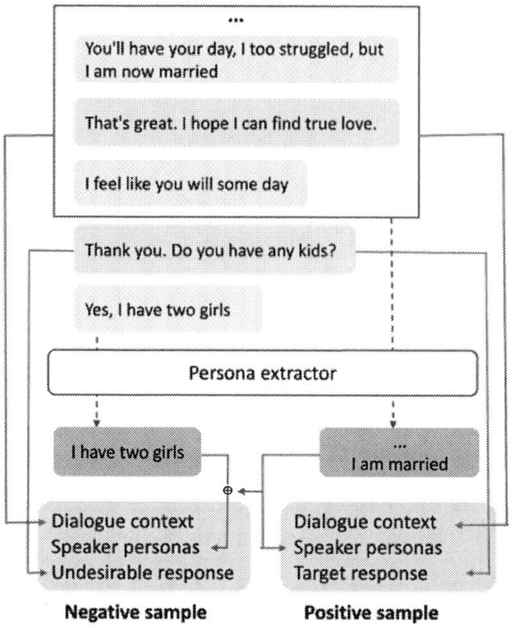

Figure 3: A training sample of NRQ dataset

5 Experiments setup

5.1 NRQ dataset

As there is no available dataset addressing the problem of redundant questions, we create a new non-redundant question set called NRQ, which consists of positive training samples for D^+ and negative samples for D^-. To form our D^+, we gather training samples from Wizard of Wikipedia (WoW) (Dinan et al., 2018), Empathetic Dialogues (ED) (Rashkin et al., 2018), Blended Skill Talk (BST) (Smith et al., 2020), Multi-Session Chat (MSC) (Xu et al., 2021), and Wizard of Internet (WOI) (Komeili et al., 2021) datasets. Note that we only select samples with questions presented in the target response. To extract speaker personas from conversation history, we use a pre-trained Dialogue Summarization Model from ParlAI.

To create negative samples for the NRQ dataset, we use the approach outlined in Section 4.1, illustrated in Figure 3. Specifically, we convert each positive sample (x, s^+, y) into a negative one by augmenting the speaker personas s^+ with a negative partner persona s_{neg} (e.g. *I have two girls*), which we obtain from the partner personas of the next dialogue turn (e.g. *Yes, I have two girls*), denoted as s_{next}. However, this procedure poses two challenges: (i) s_{next} may contain multiple personas, some may not be relevant to the questions posed in the target response y, (ii) s_{next} may be entirely irrelevant, for instance if the next dialogue turn is off-topic or the persona extractor model fails to identify the correct personas. As a result, we rely on human annotators to select only the relevant s_{neg} from s_{next} and discard samples where no relevant s_{neg} can be found. The number of samples in NRQ is 100,181 before filtering, and 50,178 after filtering. We split the final dataset into 46,286 for training, 2,000 for validation, and 1,892 for testing.

Redundant question classification. As described in Section 4.2, we use D^+ and D^- to generate training data for our the redundant question classifier, resulting a total of 48,297 and 45,494 samples for redundant and non-redundant class respectively. In addition, we incorporate human annotation results mentioned above where the negative persona s_{neg} is deemed irrelevant to the question. This provides an additional 39,271 non-redundant samples.

5.2 BB2 Baseline

As training an end-to-end generation model from scratch is computationally expensive, we choose to use the pre-trained BB2 model (3 billion parameters) as baseline. Our goal is to reduce the number of redundant questions generated by the model. The BB2 model is fine-tuned from the Blenderbot1 model (Roller et al., 2020b) on BST, MSC, and WOI datasets. For decoding, we use beam search with 4-gram blocking to prevent repetitive questions from generating. The maximum number of tokens in the dialog context is set to 128.

5.3 Evaluation

Perplexity (PPL) is a metric to measure how well a generation model predicts a response. We want the model to output low perplexity scores for good and coherent responses while producing high perplexity scores for undesirable responses such as redundant questions in our case.

Diversity measures lexical diversity of generated texts, which is computed based on corpus-level repetition at different n-gram levels as follow: **diversity** $= \prod_{n=2}^{4}(1.0 - \frac{rep-n}{100})$, where **rep-n** $= 1.0 - \frac{|unique\ n-grams(C)|}{|total\ n-grams(C)|}$; C is a collections of generated responses by the model.

Coherence measures the semantic similarity between dialogue context and generated response. We use SimCSE following (Su et al., 2022) to compute the similarity in the embedding space.

Redundant question rate is the percentage of generated questions that are redundant. For automatic evaluation, we use the classifier presented in Section 4.2 to check if a question is redundant.

Automatic evaluation is essential for hyperparameter tuning and model selection. To automatically estimate quality of generated texts, we first perform self-chat, i.e two chatbots chatting with each other, to generate 50 bot-bot dialogues using BB2 Baseline. To make sure each dialogue is different, we seed each one with a human-human conversation (25 turns) from the MSC Session1&2 and then generate 40 more turns. After that, we calculate diversity, coherence, and redundant rate scores based on the generated questions.

Human evaluation. We recruited human annotators from Amazon Mechanical Turk to conduct 50 human-bot conversations for evaluation. We seed each human-bot conversation with 25 turns from MSC Session1&2. The human and the bot, i.e BB2 Baseline, are asked to continue each seeded conversation for 40 turns. After that, we asked another group of annotators to manually check if each generated question is a redundant question based on the entire conversation.

Method comparison. We propose a method for a fair comparison between the BB2 Baseline and other approaches mentioned in Section 4. Instead of having each model conduct its own conversations, we use responses generated by the BB2 Baseline as a ground for comparison. For each of the BB2-generated questions, we regenerate it with the compared models and then recompute the evaluation scores. In cases where a model does not generate any questions at the end, we replace the end-of-sentence token with the most probable question-words token (e.g. what, how, when, etc) and continue the decoding process.

Models	Acc	F1-score	
		Redundant	Non-redundant
XLNet	88.3%	85.9	90.0
RoBERTa	88.6%	86.3	90.1
DeBERTa	88.2%	86.5	89.5

Table 1: Redundant question classification results on the test set. *Acc* stands for accuracy.

5.4 Training configuration

We fine-tune the BB2 Baseline using one A100 GPU with an Adam optimizer. The learning rate and batch size are set to 5e-6 and 8. The model is fine-tuned in a multi-task fashion using samples from BST, MSC, WOI, and NRQ datasets. We draw samples from each task equally in a round-robin fashion. We use early stopping based on the combined score of test set perplexity and redundant question rate of bot-bot conversations.

6 Experiment results

Redundant question classification. We first report performances of our redundant question classifier in Table 1. As can be seen, all three models perform similarly well, with RoBERTa achieving the highest accuracy of 88.6%. Therefore, we choose RoBERTa to automatically calculate the redundant question rate of the generation models in subsequent analyses.

Conversation length vs redundant rate. As shown in Figure 4, the redundant question rate increases significantly with respect to the length of the conversation. For BB2 Baseline, the rate is 18.4% at turn 30. The number further increases by another 8.1% when the conversation reaches 65 turns. However, this issue is not a concern in previous studies as most evaluate the chatbots on a short conversation setting (less than 10 turns). The increase in redundant rate can be attributed to the limited number of topics the chatbot can initiate. When the conversation is prolonged, it often revisit topics that have already been discussed.

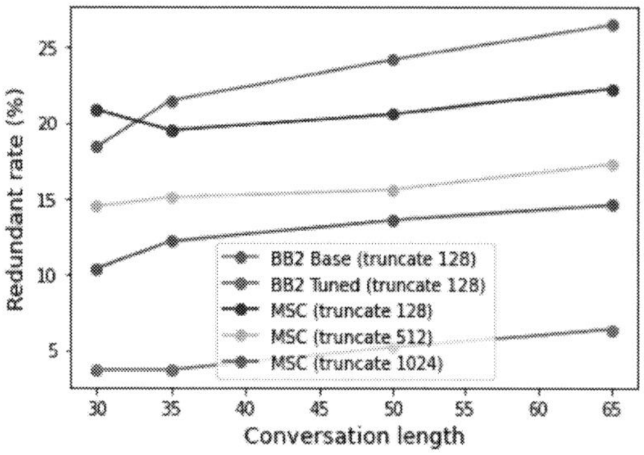

Figure 4: The impact of conversation length and truncated context length on redundant question rate.

Truncated context length vs redundant rate. The limitation of 128 tokens for truncated dialogue in the BB2 Baseline could be the cause of higher redundant question rate. Increasing the truncation length could be considered as a possible solution to address this issue. To investigate this hypothesis, we utilized the MSC model (Xu et al., 2021), which was specifically trained on the MSC dataset to effectively handle long conversations. In Figure 4, the results demonstrate a significant reduction in redundancy rates by extending the truncation length. For conversations with a length of 30, the redundancy rate decreased from 18.4% (truncated at 128) to 10.4% (truncated at 1024). However, it is important to note that despite these improvements, they still fall short compared to the BB2 Tuned model using our proposed methods, while also incurring increased training and inference costs.

Bias in training data. Another contributing factor to the redundant issue is the bias of the BB2 Baseline towards common topics, such as pets, hobbies, and careers, which increases the likelihood of repeating the same topics over again. An explanation can be seen in Table 2, which shows the most frequent redundant questions generated by the BB2 Baseline. Obviously, these questions strongly overlap with the most frequent questions in the training data of BB2 Baseline, demonstrating the model's tendency to generate the most probable questions as a downside of maximum likelihood estimation.

Mitigation methods comparison. We apply mitigation methods to improve the performance of BB2 Baseline. As can be seen in Table 3, our proposed methods are able to not only reduce the redundancy rate but also increase the diversity score. Discussions for each method is provided as below:

Most common redundant questions
Do you have any pets?
What kind of dog do you have?
What do you do for a living?
What are you studying in school?
What kind of music do you like?
Most common questions in training data
What do you do for a living?
Do you have any pets?
Do you have any hobbies?
Where are you from?
What music do you like?

Table 2: Most common redundant questions generated by the BB2 Baseline and most frequent questions presented in the training data of the model.

BB2 Baseline does not perform well in most metrics. The negative perplexity is significantly lower than the positive one, indicating that the model is more likely to generate redundant questions instead of target questions. Additionally, the low measure of lexical diversity suggests that the model tends to produce common but repetitive questions, resulting in a high redundant rate of 26.5%.

Contrastive decoding can significantly reduce the redundant question rate to 17% without the need to retrain the model. This improvement can be explained by the significant increase in diversity score, indicating that the model favors less repetitive questions. We also observe an improvement in coherence score, which is consistent with prior studies (Su et al., 2022).

Unlikelihood training obtains the best redundant rate at 7.5%, thanks to significant increases in negative PPL and diversity score. The slight increase in positive PPL suggests a tiny degradation in the quality of the generated questions, which demonstrates by a lower coherence score. However, using augmented loss and further combining with contrastive decoding bring considerable improvements across all metrics, especially in diversity score.

Contrastive training reduces the redundant rate to 11.4% but it is still pales in comparison to unlikelihood training. Also, using contrastive training comes at the cost of question degeneration, as demonstrated by the increase in both negative and positive PPL. It can be seen that the model is confused between the task of degenerating redundant questions versus degenerating all questions.

Methods	Positive PPL	Negative PPL	Coherence	Diversity	Redundant rate
BB2 Baseline	12.2	7.9	0.34	0.02	26.5%
Contrastive decoding	-	-	0.36	0.07	17.0%
Contrastive training	14.4	69.6	0.34	0.11	11.4%
Unlikelihood training	12.5	37.5	0.32	0.09	7.50%
+ Augmented loss	12.7	38.0	0.33	0.12	6.44%
+ Contrastive decoding	-	-	0.33	0.15	6.66%

Table 3: Performances of different redundancy mitigation methods. Positive PPL refers to the perplexity of target questions from positive samples, while negative PPL refers to the perplexity of redundant questions from negative samples. We compute the positive PPL on the combined test set of BST, MSC, WOI, and NRQ. Negative PPL is computed on the NRQ test set. Coherence, diversity, and redundant rate are computed on the generated questions from 50 bot-bot conversations.

Methods	Redundant
BB2 Baseline	27.2%
Classification	15.4%
Unlikelihood	11.4%
Unlikelihood + Classification	8.7%

Table 4: Evaluation results on 50 human-bot dialogues

BB2 Baseline	BB2 Tuned
37.8%	62.1%

Table 5: Win rate of the BB2 Baseline and our proposed approach.

Human evaluation. Table 4 reports human evaluation results on 50 human-bot dialogues. The results indicate that the BB2 Baseline still has a high redundant question rate of 27.2%, highlighting the need for effective solutions. While using a redundant classifier alone can reduce the rate significantly to 15.4%, this is still much higher than the 11.4% rate achieved with unlikelihood training. The failure of the redundant classifier can be attributed to two reasons: (1) Since the problem of assigning high probabilities to redundant questions remains unaddressed, it is not uncommon that the model generates all candidate responses with redundant questions (2) With an accuracy of 88.6%, the redundant classifier can misclassify some redundant questions as non-redundant. Nevertheless, using classification on top of unlikelihood training can reduce the redundant rate further to 8.7%.

We can see that the improvements in human-bot conversations are considerably lower compared to bot-bot conversations. This is due to the fact that human-bot conversations are typically more varied and less predictable than bot-bot conversations. In contrast, bot-bot conversations tend to revolve around common topics and employ a shared vocabulary that is well-represented in the training data of the NRQ dataset.

Finally, we asked human annotators to compare the overall question-asking ability of the original BB2 Baseline with our proposed method combing unlikelihood training with redundant classifier. For each pair of comparisons, two annotators were asked to choose which of the two generated responses was better, or if they were both equally good or bad. In cases where the annotators disagreed, we manually reviewed the case and determined the correct annotation. When calculating the win rate, we excluded comparison cases where both responses were equal in quality. According to the results presented in Table 5, our approach significantly outperforms the original model.

7 Predictions analysis

We present several successful and failed cases of the proposed approach. Table 6 compares perplexities of the BB2 Baseline and BB2 tuned with unlikelihood training in generating the target questions based on different partners' personas. On the one hand, if the partner's persona, i.e *I have a dog*, has nothing to do with the target question, i.e *What do you do for a living*, then there is not much difference in perplexity between BB2 Baseline and BB2 Tuned. This suggests that the proposed negative training method does not badly affect the question-asking ability of the original BB2 Baseline. On the other hand, if the presence of the partner's persona, i.e *I'm a software engineer*, turns the target question into a redundant question, then the perplexity of the BB2 Tuned model increases significantly to 68.5 while the number for BB2 Baseline remains

Questions	Partner's persona	Question perplexity	
		Baseline	Tuned
What do you do for a living?	I have a dog.	2.04	2.42
	I'm a software engineer.	2.06	68.5
	I'm still in high school.	2.07	3.41
Do you have any pets?	I like to read books.	2.56	2.49
	I have a cat and a dog.	2.52	50.0
	My apartment doesn't allow pets.	2.48	2.93

Table 6: Example perplexities of the BB2 Baseline and BB2 Tuned with NRQ when predicting the target questions.

very low, at 2.06. We also note that one of the weaknesses of the BB2 Tuned model is that it is still unable to spot redundant questions if they are not clearly related to the partner's persona. For instance, the partner's persona *I'm still in high school* can be interpreted as *I don't have a job* but the BB2 Tuned model still assigns a very low perplexity for the redundant question *What do you do for a living*.

8 Conclusion

Asking good questions is an important skill for a chatbot to engage in a long-term conversation. This study first introduces the problem of redundant questions in neural text generation models. Several methods, including negative training, decoding, and classification have been proposed to lower the probabilities of these undesirable questions. We also create the first-of-its-kind dataset named NRQ dataset containing training samples with a redundant question assigned to each dialogue context and speaker personas. We validate our methods with the BB2 model and observed a significant reduction of the redundant rate, which results in a higher rating for the questioning skills of the chatbot. We believe the proposed approaches and datasets will be beneficial for building future dialogue systems.

9 Acknowledgement

This work was funded by Science Foundation Ireland through the SFI Centre for Research Training in Machine Learning (18/CRT/6183).

Limitations

Resource hungry. One of the difficulties in deploying large-scale neural text generation models is resource allocation and latency problems. For example, the BB2 Baseline 3B requires at least a 16GB GPU and a couple of seconds to generate the response using one Tesla V100. As our approach requires inputting all of the partner's persona alongside dialog context, it almost doubles the inference time and increases the use of GPU memory significantly. As a result, it is not resource-friendly when the conversation is prolonged. A possible solution to this is to use the RAG retriever model to select a few relevant partner personas and incorporate only these into the input. However, this may be difficult to do so as we might not know what questions are going to be generated during decoding. A redundant question might be generated because a partner's persona is missing.

The redundant rate is still high. Although the proposed approach significantly reduces the redundant question rate, the number still remained relatively high, at 8.7%. We believe this is a much more serious issue compared to other challenges, such as contradiction or "hallucinations", as it is very uncomfortable for the user to repeat the same information or discuss a topic multiple times during the conversation. As mentioned in the previous sections, one of the main weaknesses of the fine-tuned model is the failure in recognizing the indirect relations between a speaker persona and a redundant question. We believe the problem can be addressed by scaling up the size of the NRQ dataset to cover more of these difficult cases. Better data augmentation techniques can also be used to diversify redundant questions and negative partner personas.

References

Tom Brown, Benjamin Mann, Nick Ryder, Melanie Subbiah, Jared D Kaplan, Prafulla Dhariwal, Arvind Neelakantan, Pranav Shyam, Girish Sastry, Amanda Askell, et al. 2020. Language models are few-shot learners. *Advances in neural information processing systems*, 33:1877–1901.

Shuyang Cao and Lu Wang. 2021. CLIFF: Contrastive learning for improving faithfulness and factuality in abstractive summarization. In *Proceedings of the 2021 Conference on Empirical Methods in Natural Language Processing*, pages 6633–6649, Online and Punta Cana, Dominican Republic. Association for Computational Linguistics.

Moya Chen, Douwe Kiela, Mojtaba Komeili, Spencer Poff, Stephen Roller, Kurt Shuster, Arthur Szlam, Jason Weston, and Jing Xu. 2021. Blender bot 2.0: An open source chatbot that builds long-term memory and searches the internet. https://parl.ai/projects/blenderbot2/.

Emily Dinan, Gavin Abercrombie, Stevie A Bergman, Shannon Spruit, Dirk Hovy, Y-Lan Boureau, Verena Rieser, et al. 2022. Safetykit: First aid for measuring safety in open-domain conversational systems. In *Proceedings of the 60th Annual Meeting of the Association for Computational Linguistics (Volume 1: Long Papers)*. Association for Computational Linguistics.

Emily Dinan, Stephen Roller, Kurt Shuster, Angela Fan, Michael Auli, and Jason Weston. 2018. Wizard of wikipedia: Knowledge-powered conversational agents. *arXiv preprint arXiv:1811.01241*.

Angela Fan, Mike Lewis, and Yann Dauphin. 2018. Hierarchical neural story generation. *arXiv preprint arXiv:1805.04833*.

Dilek Hakkani-Tur. 2021. Alexa prize socialbot grand challenge year iv. In *Alexa Prize SocialBot Grand Challenge 4 Proceedings*.

Pengcheng He, Xiaodong Liu, Jianfeng Gao, and Weizhu Chen. 2020. Deberta: Decoding-enhanced bert with disentangled attention. *arXiv preprint arXiv:2006.03654*.

Tianxing He and James Glass. 2019. Negative training for neural dialogue response generation. *arXiv preprint arXiv:1903.02134*.

Ari Holtzman, Jan Buys, Li Du, Maxwell Forbes, and Yejin Choi. 2019. The curious case of neural text degeneration. *arXiv preprint arXiv:1904.09751*.

Gautier Izacard and Edouard Grave. 2020. Leveraging passage retrieval with generative models for open domain question answering. *arXiv preprint arXiv:2007.01282*.

Mojtaba Komeili, Kurt Shuster, and Jason Weston. 2021. Internet-augmented dialogue generation. *arXiv preprint arXiv:2107.07566*.

Jakub Konrád, Jan Pichl, Petr Marek, Petr Lorenc, Van Duy Ta, Ondřej Kobza, Lenka Hýlová, and Jan Šedivý. 2021. Alquist 4.0: Towards social intelligence using generative models and dialogue personalization. *arXiv preprint arXiv:2109.07968*.

Ilya Kulikov, Alexander H Miller, Kyunghyun Cho, and Jason Weston. 2018. Importance of a search strategy in neural dialogue modelling. *arXiv preprint arXiv:1811.00907*.

Weizhao Li, Junsheng Kong, Ben Liao, and Yi Cai. 2022. Mitigating contradictions in dialogue based on contrastive learning. In *Findings of the Association for Computational Linguistics: ACL 2022*, pages 2781–2788.

Zekang Li, Jinchao Zhang, Zhengcong Fei, Yang Feng, and Jie Zhou. 2021a. Addressing inquiries about history: An efficient and practical framework for evaluating open-domain chatbot consistency. *arXiv preprint arXiv:2106.02228*.

Zekang Li, Jinchao Zhang, Zhengcong Fei, Yang Feng, and Jie Zhou. 2021b. Addressing inquiries about history: An efficient and practical framework for evaluating open-domain chatbot consistency. *arXiv preprint arXiv:2106.02228*.

Yinhan Liu, Myle Ott, Naman Goyal, Jingfei Du, Mandar Joshi, Danqi Chen, Omer Levy, Mike Lewis, Luke Zettlemoyer, and Veselin Stoyanov. 2019. Roberta: A robustly optimized bert pretraining approach. *arXiv preprint arXiv:1907.11692*.

Ashwin Paranjape, Abigail See, Kathleen Kenealy, Haojun Li, Amelia Hardy, Peng Qi, Kaushik Ram Sadagopan, Nguyet Minh Phu, Dilara Soylu, and Christopher D Manning. 2020. Neural generation meets real people: Towards emotionally engaging mixed-initiative conversations. *arXiv preprint arXiv:2008.12348*.

Hannah Rashkin, Eric Michael Smith, Margaret Li, and Y-Lan Boureau. 2018. Towards empathetic open-domain conversation models: A new benchmark and dataset. *arXiv preprint arXiv:1811.00207*.

Stephen Roller, Y-Lan Boureau, Jason Weston, Antoine Bordes, Emily Dinan, Angela Fan, David Gunning, Da Ju, Margaret Li, Spencer Poff, et al. 2020a. Open-domain conversational agents: Current progress, open problems, and future directions. *arXiv preprint arXiv:2006.12442*.

Stephen Roller, Emily Dinan, Naman Goyal, Da Ju, Mary Williamson, Yinhan Liu, Jing Xu, Myle Ott, Kurt Shuster, Eric M Smith, et al. 2020b. Recipes for building an open-domain chatbot. *arXiv preprint arXiv:2004.13637*.

Kurt Shuster, Spencer Poff, Moya Chen, Douwe Kiela, and Jason Weston. 2021. Retrieval augmentation reduces hallucination in conversation. *arXiv preprint arXiv:2104.07567*.

Kurt Shuster, Jing Xu, Mojtaba Komeili, Da Ju, Eric Michael Smith, Stephen Roller, Megan Ung, Moya Chen, Kushal Arora, Joshua Lane, et al. 2022. Blenderbot 3: a deployed conversational agent that continually learns to responsibly engage. *arXiv preprint arXiv:2208.03188*.

Eric Michael Smith, Mary Williamson, Kurt Shuster, Jason Weston, and Y-Lan Boureau. 2020. Can you put it all together: Evaluating conversational agents' ability to blend skills. *arXiv preprint arXiv:2004.08449*.

Yixuan Su and Nigel Collier. 2022. Contrastive search is what you need for neural text generation. *arXiv preprint arXiv:2210.14140.*

Yixuan Su, Tian Lan, Yan Wang, Dani Yogatama, Lingpeng Kong, and Nigel Collier. 2022. A contrastive framework for neural text generation. *arXiv preprint arXiv:2202.06417.*

Sean Welleck, Ilia Kulikov, Stephen Roller, Emily Dinan, Kyunghyun Cho, and Jason Weston. 2019. Neural text generation with unlikelihood training. *arXiv preprint arXiv:1908.04319.*

Jin Xu, Xiaojiang Liu, Jianhao Yan, Deng Cai, Huayang Li, and Jian Li. 2022. Learning to break the loop: Analyzing and mitigating repetitions for neural text generation. *arXiv preprint arXiv:2206.02369.*

Jing Xu, Arthur Szlam, and Jason Weston. 2021. Beyond goldfish memory: Long-term open-domain conversation. *arXiv preprint arXiv:2107.07567.*

Zhilin Yang, Zihang Dai, Yiming Yang, Jaime Carbonell, Russ R Salakhutdinov, and Quoc V Le. 2019. Xlnet: Generalized autoregressive pretraining for language understanding. *Advances in neural information processing systems*, 32.

Is a Knowledge-based Response Engaging?: An Analysis on Knowledge-Grounded Dialogue with Information Source Annotation

Takashi Kodama[1], Hirokazu Kiyomaru[1]
Yin Jou Huang[1], Taro Okahisa[2], Sadao Kurohashi[1,3]
[1]Kyoto University, [2]Shizuoka University, [3]National Institute of Informatics
{kodama, kiyomaru, huang, kuro}@nlp.ist.i.kyoto-u.ac.jp
okahisa-taro@inf.shizuoka.ac.jp

Abstract

Currently, most knowledge-grounded dialogue response generation models focus on reflecting given external knowledge. However, even when conveying external knowledge, humans integrate their own knowledge, experiences, and opinions with external knowledge to make their utterances engaging. In this study, we analyze such human behavior by annotating the utterances in an existing knowledge-grounded dialogue corpus. Each entity in the corpus is annotated with its information source, either derived from external knowledge (database-derived) or the speaker's own knowledge, experiences, and opinions (speaker-derived). Our analysis shows that the presence of speaker-derived information in the utterance improves dialogue engagingness. We also confirm that responses generated by an existing model, which is trained to reflect the given knowledge, cannot include speaker-derived information in responses as often as humans do.

1 Introduction

More and more dialogue research has utilized external knowledge to enable dialogue systems to generate rich and informative responses (Ghazvininejad et al., 2018; Zhou et al., 2018; Moghe et al., 2018; Dinan et al., 2019; Zhao et al., 2020). The major focus of such research is in how to select appropriate external knowledge and reflect it accurately in the response (Kim et al., 2020; Zhan et al., 2021; Rashkin et al., 2021; Li et al., 2022).

However, as shown in Figure 1[1], a good speaker not only informs the dialogue partner of external knowledge but also incorporates his or her own knowledge, experiences, and opinions effectively, which makes the dialogue more engaging. The extent to which models specializing in reflecting given external knowledge can achieve such an engaging behavior has not yet been explored quantitatively.

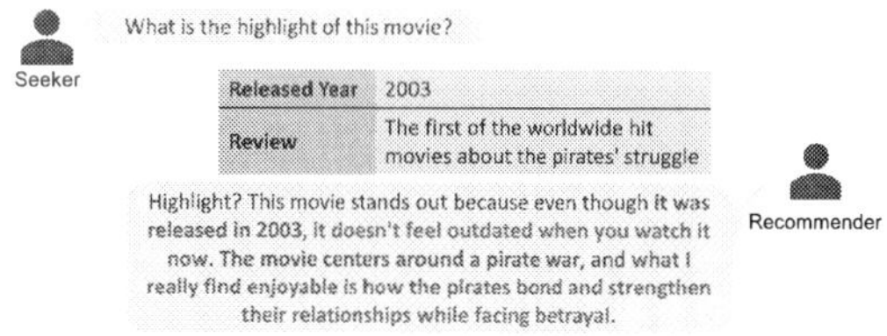

Figure 1: An example of Japanese Movie Recommendation Dialogue (Kodama et al., 2022). The table above the recommender's utterance indicates the external knowledge used in that utterance. The recommender incorporates not only database-derived information but also speaker-derived information.

In this study, we first analyze how humans incorporate speaker-derived information by annotating the utterances in an existing knowledge-grounded dialogue corpus. Each entity in the utterances is annotated with its information source, either derived from external knowledge (database-derived) or the speaker's own knowledge, experiences, and opinions (speaker-derived). The analysis of the annotated dataset showed that engaging utterances contained more speaker-derived information.

In addition, we train a BART-based response generation model in a standard way, i.e., by minimizing perplexity, and investigate the extent to which it incorporates speaker-derived information. The result showed that the response generation model did not incorporate speaker-derived information into their utterances as often as humans do. This result implies that minimizing perplexity is insufficient to increase engagingness in knowledge-grounded response generation and suggests room for improvement in the training framework.

[1]Examples of dialogues presented in this paper are originally in Japanese and were translated by the authors.

Proceedings of the 61st Annual Meeting of the Association for Computational Linguistics - Student Research Workshop, pages 237–243

2 Information Source Annotation

This section describes the annotation scheme for information sources and the annotation results.

2.1 Scheme

We annotate Japanese Movie Recommendation Dialogue (JMRD) (Kodama et al., 2022) with information sources[2]. JMRD is a human-to-human knowledge-grounded dialogue corpus in Japanese. A recommender recommends a movie to a seeker. Each utterance of the recommender is associated with movie information as external knowledge. Each piece of knowledge consists of a knowledge type (e.g., title) and the corresponding knowledge contents (e.g., "Marvel's The Avengers").

In this study, we extract entities from the recommender's utterances and annotate them with their information source. Entities are nouns, verbs, and adjectives and are extracted together with their modifiers to make it easier to grasp their meanings. Entities are extracted using Juman++ (Tolmachev et al., 2020), a widely-used Japanese morphological analyzer. Annotators classify the extracted entities into the following information source types:

Database-derived: The entity is based on the external knowledge used in that utterance.

Speaker-derived: The entity is based on the knowledge, experiences, and opinions that the recommender originally has about the recommended movie.

Other: The entity does not fall under the above two types (e.g., greetings).

An annotation example is shown below.

(1) Utterance: The action scenes$_{\text{(database)}}$ are spectacular$_{\text{(speaker)}}$!
Used knowledge: Genre, Action

We recruited professional annotators, who are native Japanese speakers, to annotate these information source types. One annotator was assigned to each dialogue. After the annotation, another annotator double-checked the contents.

2.2 Result

Table 1 shows the annotation statistics. While JMRD is a knowledge-grounded dialogue corpus and thus inherently contains many database-derived entities, it also contains about 60,000 speaker-derived entities. This result verifies that humans incorporate their own knowledge, experiences, and opinions into their utterances, even in dialogues to convey external knowledge.

	Train	Dev	Test	Total
# dialogues	4,575	200	300	5,075
# utterances (R)	51,080	2,244	3,347	56,671
# entities	235,771	10,320	15,734	261,825
# database-derived	166,958	7,223	10,476	184,657
# speaker-derived	51,170	2,303	4,095	57,568
# other	17,643	794	1,163	19,600

Table 1: Statistics of the information source annotation. R indicates recommender.

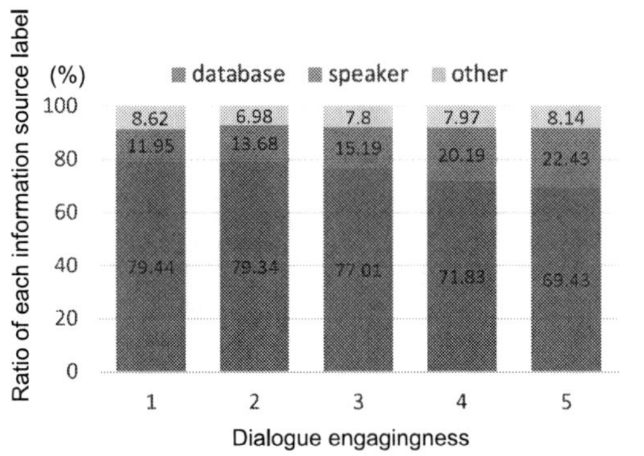

Figure 2: Relationship between dialogue engagingness and ratio of each information source label.

3 Analysis of Human Utterances

We analyze human utterances at the dialogue level and utterance level.

3.1 Dialogue-level Analysis

4,328 dialogues in JMRD have post-task questionnaires on 5-point Likert scale (5 is the best.) We regard the rating of the question to the seekers (i.e., Did you enjoy the dialogue?) as dialogue engagingness and analyze the relationship between this and the ratio of each information source label.

Figure 2 shows that dialogues with high engagingness scores tend to have more speaker-derived entities (or less database-derived) than those with low engagingness scores. When constructing JMRD, recommenders were given a certain amount of external knowledge and asked to use that knowledge to respond. However, recommenders highly rated by their dialogue partners incorporated not only the given external knowledge but also speaker-derived information to some extent in their dialogues.

[2]Examples of dialogue and knowledge in JMRD can be found in Appendix A.1.

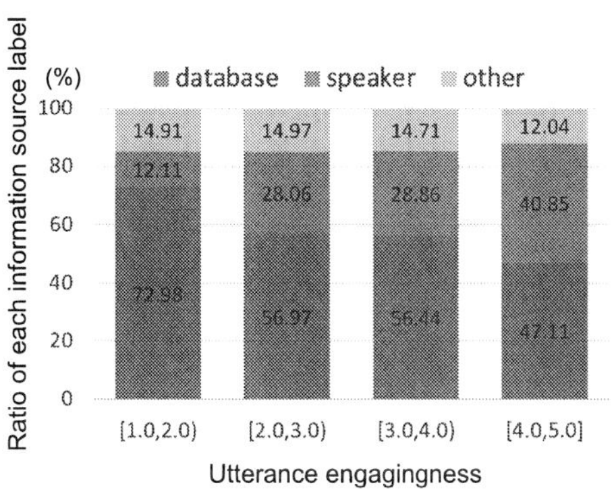

Figure 3: Relationship between utterance engagingness and ratio of each information source label.

3.2 Utterance-level Analysis

We conduct the utterance-level evaluation via crowdsourcing. We randomly extract 500 responses along with their contexts (= 4 previous utterances) from the test set. For each utterance, workers rate utterance engagingness (i.e., Would you like to talk to the person who made this response?) on a 5-point Likert scale, with 5 being the best. Three workers evaluate each utterance, and the scores are averaged.

The average score for utterances with speaker-derived entities was 3.31, while those without speaker-derived entities was 3.07. Student's t-test with p = 0.05 revealed a statistically significant difference between these scores.

Furthermore, Figure 3 shows the relationship between utterance engagingness and the ratio of each information source label. This figure shows that utterances with high scores tend to have more speaker-derived entities. This trend is consistent with that of the dialogue engagingness.

Does subjective knowledge contribute to engagingness? The knowledge type used in JMRD can be divided into subjective knowledge (review) and objective knowledge (title, etc.). Reviews are the opinions of individuals who have watched movies and have similar characteristics to speaker-derived information. We then examine whether there is a difference in engagingness between utterances using subjective and objective knowledge. The average engagingness scores were 3.32 and 3.16[3], respectively, and Student's t-test with p = 0.05 revealed no statistically significant difference. The above analysis demonstrates that information obtained from the speaker's own experience is an important factor in utterance engagingness.

4 Analysis of System Utterances

We investigate the distribution of information source labels in the responses of the model trained on the knowledge-grounded dialogue dataset. First, we train a Response Generator (§4.1) with the dialogue contexts and external knowledge as input and responses as output. Next, an Information Source Classifier (§4.2) is trained with responses and external knowledge as input and information source labels as output. Then, the Information Source Classifier infers the information source labels for the system responses generated by the Response Generator. Finally, we analyze the distribution of inferred information source labels.

4.1 Response Generator

We use a BART$_{large}$ (Lewis et al., 2020) model as a backbone.[4] The input to the model is formed as follows:

$$[CLS]u_{t-4}[SEP]u_{t-3}[SEP]u_{t-2}[SEP] \\ u_{t-1}[SEP][CLS_K]kt^1[SEP]kc^1[SEP]... \\ [CLS_K]kt^M[SEP]kc^M[SEP], \quad (1)$$

where t is the dialogue turn, u_t is the t-th response, and kt^i and kc^i $(1 <= i <= M)$ are the knowledge type and knowledge content associated with the target response, respectively (M is the maximum number of knowledge associated with u_t.) $[CLS_K]$ is a special token. We feed the gold knowledge into the model to focus on how knowledge is reflected in the responses. The model learns to minimize perplexity in generating u_t.

We evaluated the quality of response generation with the SacreBLEU (Post, 2018). BLEU-1/2/3/4 scored high, 81.1/73.5/71.0/69.9. This result is reasonable because the gold knowledge was given.

4.2 Information Source Classifier

We fine-tune a RoBERTa$_{large}$ (Liu et al., 2019) model.[5] The Information Source Classifier performs a sequence labeling task to estimate BIO[6]

[3]We exclude utterances referring to both of subjective and objective knowledge from this result.

[4]https://nlp.ist.i.kyoto-u.ac.jp/?BART%E6%97%A5%E6%9C%AC%E8%AA%9EPretrained%E3%83%A2%E3%83%87%E3%83%AB

[5]https://huggingface.co/nlp-waseda/roberta-large-japanese-seq512

[6]B, I and O stand for Begin, Inside and Outside, respectively.

		engagingness
Context	... Recommender: This movie is an animation movie released in 2015. Seeker: I see.	
Knowledge	{director, Takahiko Kyogoku}, {cast, Emi Nitta}, {cast, Yoshino Nanjo}	
Response	Human: The director is Takahiko Kyogoku, and the voice actors are Emi Nitta and Yoshino Nanjo. These two are also singers.	4.00
	System: The director is Takahiko Kyogoku. The voice actors are Emi Nitta and Yoshino Nanjo.	2.33

Table 2: An example of the human and system response. The blue and red parts refer to database-derived and speaker-derived information, respectively.

	Prec.	Rec.	F1
database-derived	94.92	95.61	95.27
speaker-derived	80.88	84.39	82.60
other	82.93	64.15	72.34
micro avg.	90.52	90.48	90.50

Table 3: Results of the sequence labeling by Information Source Classifier.

Dist. (%)	Human (gold)	Human (pred)	System (pred)
database-derived	66.22	66.75	85.48
speaker-derived	26.33	27.49	10.66
other	7.45	5.77	3.86

Table 4: Distributions of information source labels for human and system responses.

labels of the information source. The input to the model is formed as follows:

$$[CLS]u_t[SEP][CLS_K]kt^1[SEP]kc^1[SEP]... \\ [CLS_K]kt^M[SEP]kc^M[SEP] \quad (2)$$

Table 3 shows precision, recall, and F1 scores for each label and micro average scores across all labels. The micro average F1 score was 90.50, which is accurate enough for the further analysis.

4.3 Analysis for Inferred Labels

The information source labels for system responses are inferred using the classifier trained in Section 4.2. Table 4 shows distributions of information source labels for human and system responses. For a fair comparison, the human responses are also given labels inferred by the classifier (denoted as **Human (pred)**), although they have gold labels (denoted as **Human (gold)**). **Human (gold)** and **Human (pred)** have similar distributions, indicating that the accuracy of the classifier is sufficiently high. For **System (pred)**, the percentage of database-derived labels increased significantly (66.75%→85.48%) and that of speaker-derived information decreased significantly (27.49%→10.66%). This result shows that the response generation model, trained in a standard way, was not able to use speaker-derived information as often as humans do.

Ratio (%)	Human (gold)	Human (pred)	System (pred)
Title	30.21	34.12	27.09
Released Year	16.41	22.31	6.56
Director	13.94	11.96	4.50
Cast	36.11	45.34	23.45
Genre	10.47	15.14	5.49
Review	27.72	31.42	6.32
Plot	13.98	13.68	2.32
No knowledge	57.49	63.08	55.99

Table 5: Average ratios of speaker-derived labels per knowledge type used.

Table 2 shows an example of human and system responses along with the engagingness scores. The system was able to reflect given knowledge in the response appropriately but did not incorporate additional speaker-derived information, such as the information two voice actors also work as singers.

For further analysis, we investigated the average ratios of speaker-derived information by knowledge type used. Table 5 shows the result. Significant drops were observed for reviews (31.42%→6.32%) and plots (13.68%→2.32%). This is probably because reviews and plots are relatively long and informative external knowledge, so the system judged there was no need to incorporate additional speaker-derived information.

Combined with our observation that speaker-derived information improves engagingness, the current model is likely to have lower engagingness due to its inability to effectively incorporate speaker-derived information. Such an ability is hardly learned by simply optimizing a model to reduce the perplexity of response generation, suggesting the need for a novel learning framework.

5 Conclusion

We analyzed the distribution of speaker-derived information in human and system responses in the knowledge-grounded dialogue. The analysis showed that the use of speaker-derived information, as well as external knowledge, made responses more engaging. We also confirmed that the response generation model trained in a standard way generated less speaker-derived information than humans.

It is difficult to make good use of speaker-derived information by simply minimizing the perplexity of the model because a wide variety of speaker-derived information appears in each dialogue. We hope our published annotated corpus becomes a good launch pad for tackling this issue.

Acknowledgements

We would like to thank anonymous reviewers for their insightful comments. This work was supported by NII CRIS collaborative research program operated by NII CRIS and LINE Corporation. This work was also supported by JST, CREST Grant Number JPMJCR20D2, Japan and JSPS KAKENHI Grant Number JP22J15317.

References

Emily Dinan, Stephen Roller, Kurt Shuster, Angela Fan, Michael Auli, and Jason Weston. 2019. Wizard of wikipedia: Knowledge-powered conversational agents. In International Conference on Learning Representations.

Marjan Ghazvininejad, Chris Brockett, Ming-Wei Chang, William B. Dolan, Jianfeng Gao, Wen tau Yih, and Michel Galley. 2018. A knowledge-grounded neural conversation model.

Byeongchang Kim, Jaewoo Ahn, and Gunhee Kim. 2020. Sequential latent knowledge selection for knowledge-grounded dialogue. In International Conference on Learning Representations.

Takashi Kodama, Ribeka Tanaka, and Sadao Kurohashi. 2022. Construction of hierarchical structured knowledge-based recommendation dialogue dataset and dialogue system. In Proceedings of the Second DialDoc Workshop on Document-grounded Dialogue and Conversational Question Answering, pages 83–92, Dublin, Ireland. Association for Computational Linguistics.

Mike Lewis, Yinhan Liu, Naman Goyal, Marjan Ghazvininejad, Abdelrahman Mohamed, Omer Levy, Veselin Stoyanov, and Luke Zettlemoyer. 2020. BART: Denoising sequence-to-sequence pre-training for natural language generation, translation, and comprehension. In Proceedings of the 58th Annual Meeting of the Association for Computational Linguistics, pages 7871–7880, Online. Association for Computational Linguistics.

Sha Li, Mahdi Namazifar, Di Jin, Mohit Bansal, Heng Ji, Yang Liu, and Dilek Hakkani-Tur. 2022. Enhancing knowledge selection for grounded dialogues via document semantic graphs. In Proceedings of the 2022 Conference of the North American Chapter of the Association for Computational Linguistics: Human Language Technologies, pages 2810–2823, Seattle, United States. Association for Computational Linguistics.

Yinhan Liu, Myle Ott, Naman Goyal, Jingfei Du, Mandar Joshi, Danqi Chen, Omer Levy, Mike Lewis, Luke Zettlemoyer, and Veselin Stoyanov. 2019. Roberta: A robustly optimized BERT pretraining approach. abs/1907.11692.

Ilya Loshchilov and Frank Hutter. 2019. Decoupled weight decay regularization. In International Conference on Learning Representations.

Nikita Moghe, Siddhartha Arora, Suman Banerjee, and Mitesh M. Khapra. 2018. Towards exploiting background knowledge for building conversation systems. In Proceedings of the 2018 Conference on Empirical Methods in Natural Language Processing, pages 2322–2332, Brussels, Belgium. Association for Computational Linguistics.

Matt Post. 2018. A call for clarity in reporting BLEU scores. In Proceedings of the Third Conference on Machine Translation: Research Papers, pages 186–191, Brussels, Belgium. Association for Computational Linguistics.

Hannah Rashkin, David Reitter, Gaurav Singh Tomar, and Dipanjan Das. 2021. Increasing faithfulness in knowledge-grounded dialogue with controllable features. In Proceedings of the 59th Annual Meeting of the Association for Computational Linguistics and the 11th International Joint Conference on Natural Language Processing (Volume 1: Long Papers), pages 704–718, Online. Association for Computational Linguistics.

Arseny Tolmachev, Daisuke Kawahara, and Sadao Kurohashi. 2020. Design and structure of the Juman++ morphological analyzer toolkit. Journal of Natural Language Processing, 27(1):89–132.

Haolan Zhan, Hainan Zhang, Hongshen Chen, Zhuoye Ding, Yongjun Bao, and Yanyan Lan. 2021. Augmenting knowledge-grounded conversations with sequential knowledge transition. In Proceedings of the 2021 Conference of the North American Chapter of the Association for Computational Linguistics: Human Language Technologies, pages 5621–5630, Online. Association for Computational Linguistics.

Xueliang Zhao, Wei Wu, Can Xu, Chongyang Tao, Dongyan Zhao, and Rui Yan. 2020. Knowledge-grounded dialogue generation with pre-trained language models. In Proceedings of the 2020 Conference on Empirical Methods in Natural Language Processing (EMNLP), pages 3377–3390, Online. Association for Computational Linguistics.

Kangyan Zhou, Shrimai Prabhumoye, and Alan W Black. 2018. A dataset for document grounded conversations. In Proceedings of the 2018 Conference on Empirical Methods in Natural Language Processing, pages 708–713, Brussels, Belgium. Association for Computational Linguistics.

A Appendices

A.1 Example of JMRD

Table 6 and 7 show examples of the dialogue and knowledge in JMRD.

A.2 Implementation Details

A.2.1 Response Generator

Dialogue contexts, knowledge (knowledge types and contents), and target responses are truncated to the maximum input length of 256, 256, and 128, respectively. The model is trained for up to 50 epochs with a batch size of 512 and 0.5 gradient clipping. We apply early stopping if no improvement of the loss for the development set is observed for three consecutive epochs. We use AdamW optimizer (Loshchilov and Hutter, 2019) with $\beta_1 = 0.9$, $\beta_2 = 0.999$, $\epsilon = 1e-8$ and an initial learning rate $= 1e-5$. We use an inverse square root learning rate scheduler with the first 1,000 steps allocated for warmup. During decoding, we use the beam search with a beam size of 3.

A.2.2 Information Source Classifier

Target responses and knowledge (knowledge types and contents) are truncated to the maximum input length of 128 and 384, respectively. The model is trained for up to 20 epochs with a batch size of 64 and 0.5 gradient clipping. We apply early stopping if no improvement of the f1 score for the development set is observed for three consecutive epochs. We use AdamW optimizer (Loshchilov and Hutter, 2019) with $\beta_1 = 0.9$, $\beta_2 = 0.999$, $\epsilon = 1e-8$ and an initial learning rate $= 1e-5$. We use an inverse square root learning rate scheduler with the first 1,000 steps allocated for warmup.

Turn	Dialogue	Knowledge type	Knowledge content
R_1	Hello.	No knowledge	-
S_1	Hello. Nice to meet you!		
R_2	Do you know "Avengers: Endgame"?	Title	Avengers: Endgame
S_2	I have only heard of the title...		
R_3	This movie was released in 2019.	Released Year	2019
S_3	Got it. Is it an American movie?		
R_4	Yes, It's an American action movie.	Genre	Action
S_4	What are some of the highlights?		
R_5	The highlight is when the heroes gather to confront Thanos, who is an alien villain!	Review	Heroes gather to confront Thanos
S_5	I see! Is this a story of battles in space?		
R_6	No, it takes place on Earth.	No knowledge	-
S_6	Then, the villain will attack the earth...		
R_7	Yes, there are some scary moments.	No knowledge	-
S_7	Is it scary...? I don't really like horror movies, but I like action ones. Would I be able to enjoy watching it?		
R_8	It is not scary like horror movies, so I think you will enjoy watching it!	No knowledge	-
S_8	Good! The fight between Thanos and the heroes sounds exciting!		
R_9	Please watch it!	No knowledge	-
S_9	Yes! I'll have a chance to go to the video store soon and rent "Avengers: Endgame"!		
R_{10}	Thank you!	No knowledge	-
S_{10}	Thank you, too, for this valuable information!		

Table 6: A full dialogue example in JMRD. R and S in Turn column denote recommender and seeker, respectively. Subscript numbers indicate the number of turns in the dialogue. "No knowledge" means that the recommender did not use the given knowledge information.

Knowledge type		Knowledge content
Title		Avengers: Endgame
Released Year		2019
Director	name	Anthony Russo, Joe Russo
	description	Director, producer, screenwriter, actor, and editor for television and film in the United States.
Cast	$cast_1$ name	Robert Downey Jr.
	$cast_1$ description	an American actor, voice actor, musician, and producer.
	$cast_2$ name	Chris Evans
	$cast_2$ description	an American actor. He was born in Sudbury, Massachusetts.
Genre		Action, Adventure
Review		5 sentences, such as "Heroes gather to confront Samus."
Plot		10 sentences, such as "In 2018, three weeks after half of all life in the entire universe was erased by decimation (genocide using the power of the Infinity Stone) by Thanos the Titan."

Table 7: An example of knowledge used in JMRD. The director and the casts have two attributes: name and description, respectively.

Choosing What to Mask: More Informed Masking for Multimodal Machine Translation

Júlia Sato*, **Helena Caseli***, **Lucia Specia**†
*Federal University of São Carlos (UFSCar), São Carlos, Brazil
†Imperial College London, London, United Kingdom
juliasato@estudante.ufscar.br
helenacaseli@ufscar.br
l.specia@ic.ac.uk

Abstract

Pre-trained language models have achieved remarkable results on several NLP tasks. Most of them adopt masked language modeling to learn representations by randomly masking tokens and predicting them based on their context. However, this random selection of tokens to be masked is inefficient to learn some language patterns as it may not consider linguistic information that can be helpful for many NLP tasks, such as multimodal machine translation (MMT). Hence, we propose three novel masking strategies for cross-lingual visual pre-training – more informed visual masking, more informed textual masking, and more informed visual and textual masking – each one focusing on learning different linguistic patterns. We apply them to Vision Translation Language Modelling for video subtitles (Sato et al., 2022) and conduct extensive experiments on the Portuguese-English MMT task. The results show that our masking approaches yield significant improvements over the original random masking strategy for downstream MMT performance. Our models outperform the MMT baseline and we achieve state-of-the-art accuracy (52.70 in terms of BLEU score) on the How2 dataset, indicating that more informed masking helps in acquiring an understanding of specific language structures and has great potential for language understanding[1].

1 Introduction

Pre-trained language models have achieved remarkable results on several Natural Language Processing (NLP) tasks (Devlin et al., 2019; Liu et al., 2019; Baevski et al., 2019; Yang et al., 2019; Joshi et al., 2020; Clark et al., 2020; Lan et al., 2020; Zhuang et al., 2021). One of these tasks is multimodal machine translation (MMT), which has attracted considerable attention from both Computer Vision and NLP communities as it not only considers text information but also uses other modal information – mostly visual information – to improve translation outputs (Specia et al., 2016; Elliott et al., 2017; Barrault et al., 2018). Recent advances in this field have achieved significant success and highlighted the efficiency of both multimodal and multilingual pre-training for MMT (Caglayan et al., 2021; Sato et al., 2022).

Nonetheless, most pre-trained models follow BERT's pre-training paradigm (Devlin et al., 2019) and adopt masked language modeling (MLM) and its variants to learn representations by masking tokens and making predictions based on their context. The conventional MLM relies on randomly selecting tokens to be masked and therefore may not consider linguistic information that can be helpful for some NLP tasks, such as MMT.

In this paper, we address this problem through a systematic study of new masking approaches for cross-lingual visual pre-training. We propose *more informed* masking strategies to learn particular language patterns for downstream multimodal machine translation performance. These strategies consist of selectively masking linguistic and visual tokens instead of randomly masking them, focusing on situations that can be favored by a better understanding of specific visual or textual information.

For instance, since most pre-trained language models are based on English, they fail to understand some linguistic patterns that are common in many other languages, such as the grammatical gender of words. The English language treats the grammatical gender of words differently from languages such as French, Spanish, Portuguese, or Italian. While some languages have different words with the same meaning that are found in the feminine and masculine forms, this does not happen in the English language. For example, considering the English-Portuguese translation, the pronoun

[1]The source codes have been released at https://github.com/LALIC-UFSCar/more-informed-masking

Proceedings of the 61st Annual Meeting of the Association for Computational Linguistics - Student Research Workshop, pages 244–253

"they" can be translated to "elas" (feminine) or "eles" (masculine). Another example is the adjective "beautiful", which can be translated to "bonita" (feminine) or "bonito" (masculine) depending on who or what it is referring to.

In this context, we propose three selective masking strategies – more informed visual masking, more informed textual masking, and more informed visual and textual masking – each one focusing on masking specific linguistic and visual tokens that can contribute to better understanding some of these different linguistic patterns. We apply them to Vision Translation Language Modelling for video subtitles (Sato et al., 2022) and run an extensive set of experiments on the Portuguese-English MMT task.

We find that predicting particular masked elements can be a powerful objective for cross-lingual visual pre-training as the pre-trained model can acquire a better understanding of specific language structures. Experimental results show that our masking approaches yield significant improvements over the original random masking strategy for downstream MMT performance. Our models outperform the MMT baseline and achieve state-of-the-art accuracy (52.70 in terms of BLEU score) on the How2 dataset (Sanabria et al., 2018), indicating that more informed masking helps in capturing domain-specific language patterns and has great potential for language understanding.

2 Method

In this section, we present the detailed implementation of three masking strategies: more informed visual masking (Section 2.2.1), more informed textual masking (Section 2.2.2), and more informed visual and textual masking (Section 2.2.3), as well as the VTLM for video subtitles pre-training objective in Section 2.1.

2.1 Visual translation language modelling for video subtitles

The VTLM objective (Caglayan et al., 2021) joins the translation language modelling (TLM) (Conneau and Lample, 2019), which employs the masked language modelling objective, with masked region classification (MRC) (Chen et al., 2020; Su et al., 2020) to generate cross-lingual and multimodal representations. VTLM defines the input x as the concatenation of m-length source language sentence $s^{(1)}_{1:m}$, n-length target language sentence $s^{(2)}_{1:n}$, and $\{v_1, \cdots, v_o\}$ corresponding image features:

$$x = [s^{(1)}_1, \cdots, s^{(1)}_m, s^{(2)}_1, \cdots, s^{(2)}_n, v_1, \cdots, v_o]$$

The final model combines the TLM loss with the MRC loss according to the following equation:

$$\mathcal{L} = \frac{1}{|X|} \sum_{x \in \mathcal{X}} \log Pr(\{\hat{y}, \hat{v}\} | \tilde{x}; \theta)$$

where $\tilde{x}$ is the masked input sequence, $\hat{y}$ denotes the ground-truth targets for masked positions, $\hat{v}$ represents the detection labels and θ denotes the model parameters.

VTLM for video subtitles (Sato et al., 2022) corresponds to VTLM adapted to the Brazilian Portuguese-English language pair and to more challenging circumstances regarding the image-text relationship. Its pre-training has visual and cross-lingual resources and performs MLM and MRC on a three-way parallel multimodal and multilingual corpus, How2 (Sanabria et al., 2018).

Masking. VTLM selects a random set of linguistic and visual input tokens for masking. The masking proportion is 15% and it is applied separately to visual and language flows. For textual masking, 80% of the 15% chosen tokens are replaced with the `[MASK]` token, 10% are replaced with random tokens from the vocabulary, and 10% are kept unchanged. And visual masking follows a similar approach: VTLM replaces its vector of projected features by the `[MASK]` token embedding, with 10% of the masking being equivalent to using region features randomly selected from all images in the batch, and the remaining 10% of the regions are left intact.

2.2 More informed masking strategies

Unlike the original approach, we do not randomly select tokens for masking. Instead, we focus on masking specific tokens in order to learn particular language patterns efficiently. Thus, we propose three new masking strategies that explore more informed ways of masking linguistic and visual tokens.

These approaches are based on the hypothesis that by performing more informed masking (e.g., masking tokens that reveal the grammatical gender of words) the model could come to a better understanding of these concepts, obtaining better performance in the translation of pronouns and words assigned as masculine, feminine, or neuter.

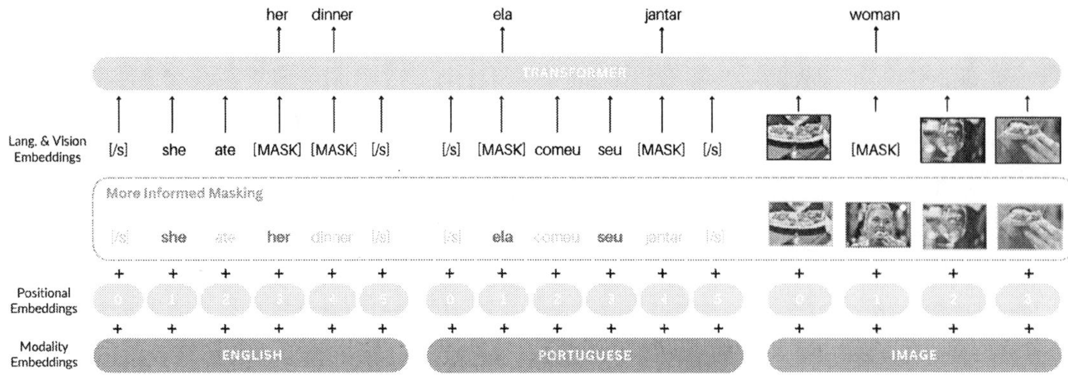

Figure 1: VTLM architecture, highlighting the *more informed visual and textual masking* strategy.

The overall architecture of the model is depicted in Figure 1.

2.2.1 More informed visual masking

This approach consists of changing the visual masking so that the initial selection of tokens for masking is no longer random, and a greater proportion of tokens related to elements categorized as *people* are selected for masking, such as objects in the image categorized as "man", "woman", "boy", or "girl". For convenience, we denote these tokens as T_{People}.

To accomplish this, we changed the visual masking stage to retrieve detection information necessary to perform the identification of class labels during training. Specifically, we used object features that were previously extracted using the Faster R-CNN model (Ren et al., 2015) pre-trained on the Open Images Dataset V4 (Kuznetsova et al., 2020) to retrieve the information needed to identify the categories of visual tokens during training.

At the beginning of the visual masking stage, we obtain the category index from the label map of the Open Images Dataset, as well as the variables containing the class predictions and confidence scores for each image from the batch. We then identify the index associated with each image and the position of each visual token in relation to the set of images from the batch. As a result, we are able to obtain the class label and confidence score for each token candidate to be masked and selectively choose the tokens that will be masked.

We apply this strategy to increase the proportion of T_{People} among masked tokens, with a percentage of 33.34%, 50.0%, and 66.67%. In all cases, the remaining candidate tokens for making do not have the same category as T_{People} and are randomly chosen. We maintained the visual masking ratio: 15% of inputs are selected for masking, from which 80% are replaced with the `[MASK]` token, 10% are replaced with random tokens, and 10% are left intact.

2.2.2 More informed textual masking

Similar to the previous approach, this masking strategy aims to mask a greater amount of tokens that reveal the grammatical gender of words in a given sentence. Thus, the initial selection of tokens for masking was changed to no longer be random and to favor more pronouns – such as "he"/"she", "him"/"her", and "his"/"hers" – among the tokens that will be masked, maintaining the 15% textual masking ratio. For convenience, we denote these tokens as T_{Pronouns}.

As VTLM stores the input textual stream as integer-type *Tensors*, we changed the VTLM architecture to convert this numerical stream to words at the beginning of the textual masking stage and then ascertain each sentence from the batch to identify subject pronouns, object pronouns, and possessive adjectives and pronouns. After identifying these words, they are marked and associated with their original numerical form so that they can be identified later in the selection of tokens for masking. At this stage, T_{Pronouns} are identified and tokens are selectively chosen to be masked, with a higher proportion of T_{Pronouns} being masked.

We performed three experiments with the following percentages of T_{Pronouns}: 33.34%, 50.0%, and 66.67%. In all cases, the remaining masked tokens did not have the same category as T_{Pronouns} and were randomly chosen following the standard approach.

Model	T_{People}	Test		Valid	
		BLEU	METEOR	BLEU	METEOR
VTLM: random masking		51.80	78.04	52.44	78.25
VTLM: more informed visual masking	33.34%	**52.70**	**79.63**	**53.25**	**79.83**
	50.00%	51.92	79.10	52.51	79.41
	66.67%	51.65	78.64	52.26	79.09

Table 1: BLEU and METEOR scores for random masking VTLM (baseline) and more informed visual masking VTLM (our model) for the MMT task.

2.2.3 More informed visual and textual masking

The more informed visual and textual masking strategy is a combination of the two previous approaches, i.e., we mask a greater proportion of T_{People} tokens at the visual masking stage, as well as T_{Pronouns} tokens at the textual masking stage.

This approach aimed to analyze the model behavior when applying more informed visual masking and more informed textual masking simultaneously.

3 Experiments

Pre-training data. We use the How2 corpus (Sanabria et al., 2018) in all stages of experimentation. How2 is a multimodal and multilingual collection of approximately 80,000 instructional videos accompanied by English subtitles and around 300 hours of collected crowdsourced Portuguese translations. For pre-training, we used a set from the How2 corpus that contains 155k features and their corresponding text in English and Portuguese[2]. We applied Moses tokenization[3] and used byte pair encoding (Sennrich et al., 2016) to split words into subword units.

Pre-training. We followed Caglayan et al.'s (2021) work to conduct the experiments. We set the model dimension to 512, the feed-forward layer dimension to 2048, the number of layers to 6 and the number of attention heads to 8. We randomly initialize model parameters rather than using pre-trained LM checkpoints. We use Adam (Kingma and Ba, 2014) with the mini-batch size set to 32 and the learning rate set to 0.0001. We set the dropout (Srivastava et al., 2014) rate to 0.1 in all layers. The pre-training was conducted on a single NVIDIA GeForce GTX 1070 GPU for 1.5M steps, and best checkpoints were selected with respect to validation set accuracy.

Fine-tuning. The encoder and the decoder of Transformer-based (Vaswani et al., 2017) MMT models are initialized with weights from VTLM, and fine-tuned with a smaller learning rate. We use the same hyperparameters as the pre-training phase, but we follow Sato et al.'s (2022) work and decrease the batch size to 16 and the learning rate to 1e-5. For evaluation, we use the models with the lowest validation set perplexity to decode translations with beam size of 8.

Evaluation Metrics. We report the automatic evaluation using BLEU (Papineni et al., 2002) and METEOR (Banerjee and Lavie, 2005). We also conduct qualitative analyzes to better show the effects of the proposed masking strategies.

4 Results

The trained models were evaluated on valid and test sets of How2 for the multimodal machine translation (MMT) task. We compare our models with the original VTLM for video subtitles model (Sato et al., 2022), which has the same architecture but uses the popular random masking strategy instead of ours.

4.1 More informed visual masking

Table 1 shows BLEU and METEOR scores across valid and test sets of How2. The results show that this new masking strategy affects the final performance of the model. For T_{People} = 33.34%, our model achieved 52.70 BLEU and 79.63 METEOR on the test set and 53.25 BLEU and 79.83 METEOR on the valid set for the MMT task, outperforming the baseline by approximately 1 BLEU and 1.6 METEOR. When T_{People} = 50.0%, our model also outperformed the baseline in terms of both BLEU and METEOR, but its performance was slightly inferior to the performance of the first experiment. Finally, when T_{People} = 66.67%, the

[2]The dataset used in this work is publicly available under the Creative Commons BY-SA 4.0 License and BSD-2-Clause License.

[3]https://github.com/moses-smt/mosesdecoder

	Source:	Então ele ou ela não carrega todo o peso do SCBA, na área do ombro ou região ao redor do pescoço.
	Reference:	So he or she is not carrying all the weight of the SCBA, in the shoulder area, or region around the neck.
	Baseline:	So it or it doesn't carry all the weight of the SCBA, in the shoulder area, or region around the neck.
	Our model:	So he or she won't carry all the weight of the SCBA, in the shoulder area, or region around the neck.
	Source:	Então, há algumas maneiras diferentes de levá-lo pra fora.
	Reference:	So there's a couple of different ways to take him out.
	Baseline:	So there's a couple of different ways to take it out.
	Our model:	So there's a couple of different ways to get him out.
	Source:	E nós vamos fazer isso em seu cabelo hoje.
	Reference:	And we're going to be cornrowing that into her hair today.
	Baseline:	And we're going to do that on your hair today.
	Our model:	And we're going to do that on her hair today.
	Source:	Ela pegará neve e a empurrará para o lado da estrada ou ela pegará a sujeira de um ponto alto e a moverá para o lado.
	Reference:	It will catch snow and push it over to the side of the road or it will catch dirt out of a high spot and move it over to the side.
	Baseline:	She will take snow and push it to the side of the road or she will take the dirt from a high point and move it to the side.
	Our model:	It will take snow and push it to the side of the road or it will take the dirt from a high spot and move it to the side.

Table 2: Translation examples of random masking VTLM (baseline) and more informed visual masking VTLM (our model).

performance of our model was superior to the baseline by approximately 0.7 METEOR. However, in terms of BLEU, the performance was inferior to the baseline by approximately 0.16 BLEU, presenting a behavior different from that observed in the last two experiments.

Therefore, the results indicate that more informed visual masking benefits the final performance of the model to a certain extent. By increasing the proportion of T_{People} tokens being masked, there is an improvement in the performance of the model compared to the baseline. Nevertheless, when this proportion becomes greater than 50%, this improvement tends to decrease. This behavior may be explained by the decrease in tokens related to other categories being masked since the visual masking ratio did not change, i.e., it remained at 15%. Thus, excessively increasing the proportion of T_{People} tokens being masked can jeopardize the learning of elements from other categories.

Qualitative Analysis. To better understand the effect of our proposed pre-training masking approach, we compare some examples of texts translated by random masking VTLM (baseline) and more informed visual masking VTLM (our model). The examples are presented in Table 2. In the first example, the baseline mistranslates the subject pronouns "he" and "she", translating both to "it", while our model translates them correctly, achieving better performance. In the second example, the baseline mistranslates the object pronoun "him", translating it to "it", while our model translates it correctly. The third example illustrates the correct translation of the possessive adjective "her" by our model, while the baseline mistranslates it to "your". Finally, the baseline references an object using the subject pronoun "she" instead of "it". In contrast, our model does not make the same mistake and uses the pronoun correctly.

4.2 More informed textual masking

We run the same experiment using three different ratios of T_{Pronouns} – 33.34%, 50.0%, and 66.67% – and the results are shown in Table 3. The results show that this masking strategy also affects the final performance of the model. For T_{Pronouns} = 33.34%, our model scored 52.64 BLEU and 79.45 METEOR on the test set and 52.96 BLEU and 79.53 METEOR on the valid set, outperforming the baseline by approximately 0.7 BLEU and 1.3

Model	T_{Pronouns}	Test		Valid	
		BLEU	METEOR	BLEU	METEOR
VTLM: random masking		51.80	78.04	52.44	78.25
VTLM: more informed textual masking	33.34%	**52.64**	**79.45**	**52.96**	**79.53**
	50.00%	52.39	79.35	52.94	79.51
	66.67%	52.21	79.27	52.82	79.42

Table 3: BLEU and METEOR scores for random masking VTLM (baseline) and more informed textual masking VTLM (our model) for the MMT task.

	Source:	Se você andar seu cachorro do seu lado esquerdo, você quer que ele se sente do lado, porque o que ele faz é apertar, então, se você estiver por aqui, o cachorro deveria tê-lo aqui.
	Reference:	If you walk your dog on your left side you want it to sit on the side because what it does is tighten up so if you're over here the dog should have it over here.
	Baseline:	If you walk your dog on your left side you want him to sit on the side because what he does is squeeze, then if you're standing over here the dog should have him here.
	Our model:	If you walk your dog on your left side you want it to sit on the side because what it does is tighten, then if you're over here the dog should have it here.
	Source:	Ela entra em cena depois que a cena começa entre o policial e Stanley.
	Reference:	She walks into the scene after the scene begins between the police officer and Stanley.
	Baseline:	It goes into scene after the scene starts between the police officer and Stanley.
	Our model:	She goes into scene after the scene starts between the police officer and Stanley.
	Source:	E eu só trabalhei uma noite com ela.
	Reference:	And I only worked one night with her.
	Baseline:	And I just worked a night with it.
	Our model:	And I just worked a night with her.
	Source:	Mas, eu vou tentar de qualquer maneira e você pode ter uma ideia do que você pode querer fazer.
	Reference:	But, I'm going to try it anyway and you can get an idea of what you might want to do.
	Baseline:	But, I'm going to try anyway and you might have an idea of what you might want to do.
	Our model:	But, I'm going to try it anyway and you might get an idea of what you might want to do.

Table 4: Translation examples of random masking VTLM (baseline) and more informed textual masking VTLM (our model).

METEOR. As for T_{Pronouns} = 50.0%, our model also surpassed the baseline, but its performance was worse than in the previous experiment. Finally, for T_{Pronouns} = 66.67%, our model performed better than the baseline in terms of BLEU and METEOR, but its performance was inferior than in the last two experiments, when the chosen proportions were 33.34% and 50.0%.

Therefore, the results indicate that masking more T_{Pronouns} tokens leads to an improvement in the final performance of the model. However, even though our model surpassed the baseline in all experiments, this performance improvement is limited, as the best performance was observed when T_{Pronouns} proportion was 33.34%, followed by 50.0% and 66.67%, respectively.

Qualitative Analysis. Some examples of texts translated by each model are presented in Table 4. In the first example, the random masking VTLM uses the pronouns "he" and "him" to refer to the word "dog" instead of using the pronoun "it", which should have been used in this case. On the other hand, our model does not make the same mistake and uses the correct pronoun in all cases, achieving better translation performance. In the second example, the random masking VTLM mistranslates the subject pronoun "she" and translates it to "it", which is a serious translation error since the pronoun "it" cannot be used to refer to a person. In contrast, our model uses the correct pronoun and achieves better performance. The next example illustrates the incorrect translation of the object pronoun "her" by the baseline, which again uses the pronoun "it" to refer to a person. However, this error is not made by our model, which makes the correct use of the pronoun in the translation.

The three previous examples illustrate situations similar to those observed with the application of more informed visual masking. However, the last example shows a further improvement in translation. This improvement is related to the use of the pronoun "it" as the direct object of a verb. While the baseline omits this pronoun in the translation, our model correctly uses it after the verb "try".

4.3 More informed visual and textual masking

Table 5 shows BLEU and METEOR scores across valid and test sets of How2. The obtained results show that the more informed visual and textual masking strategy also affects the performance of the MMT model. Our model achieved 52.34 BLEU and 78.77 METEOR on the test set and 53.28 BLEU and 79.44 METEOR on the valid set, outperforming the baseline by approximately 0.7 BLEU and 0.9 METEOR.

Although the performance improvement was not very high in terms of BLEU and METEOR, the results indicate that applying more informed visual and textual masking benefits the final performance of the model.

Qualitative Analysis. To further understand the effectiveness of our approach, we compared some examples of texts translated by random masking VTLM (baseline) and more informed visual and textual masking VTLM (our model). The examples are presented in Table 6. In the first example, the random masking VTLM references the word "website" using the subject pronoun "he" instead of the pronoun "it". In contrast, our model does not make the same mistake and uses this pronoun correctly. In the second example, the object pronoun "him" is used incorrectly by the baseline. In this case, the pronoun "it" should have been used and our model makes the correct use of this pronoun. The third case illustrates the correct translation of the possessive adjective "your" by our model, while the baseline mistranslates it to "their". In the fourth example, our model correctly uses the pronoun "it" as the direct object of the verb "take", while the baseline omits this pronoun in the translation.

Finally, the last situation illustrates a new improvement not seen when applying more informed visual masking or more informed textual masking separately. Although visual information improves the overall performance of the standard multimodal model, we observed that it can lead to the incorrect use of certain pronouns. For instance, when the video frame associated with the text has an element categorized as "man", the pronouns used in the translation tend to be "he" or "him". Likewise, when there is an element categorized as "woman" in the video frame, the pronouns tend to be "she" or "her". On the other hand, our more informed masking approach tends to better deal with this bad tendency of multimodal models. In the last example, the two elements categorized as "man" in the image possibly influenced the incorrect choice of the pronoun "him" after the verb "bring" by the baseline model. However, our model did not make the same mistake and used the pronoun "it" correctly.

5 Related Work

Pre-trained language models have become essential in the natural language processing field. One pre-trained model that has attracted considerable attention in this field is BERT (Devlin et al., 2019). BERT introduces masked language modeling (MLM) to efficiently learn bidirectional representations by masking a set of input tokens at random and predicting them afterward. In this approach, 15% of input tokens are randomly selected for masking, from which 80% are replaced with the `[MASK]` token, 10% are replaced with a random token, and 10% are left intact.

Following BERT, several approaches have been proposed to optimize pre-trained language models. Devlin et al. (2019) later propose whole word masking (wwm) in an attempt to address the drawbacks of random token masking in the MLM task. In this approach, input tokens are segmented into units corresponding to whole words, and instead of selecting tokens to mask at random, they mask all of the tokens corresponding to a whole word at once. Zhang et al. (2019) introduce ERNIE to optimize the masking process of BERT by applying entity/phrase masking. Instead of randomly selecting input words, phrase-level masking masks consecutive words and entity-level masking masks the named entities. Clark et al. (2020) present ELECTRA, which uses a generator-discriminator framework. While the generator learns to predict the original words of the masked tokens, the discriminator uses Replaced Token Detection to discriminate whether the input token is replaced by the generator. Levine et al. (2021) propose a principled masking strategy based on the concept of Pointwise Mutual Information (PMI). PMI-masking jointly

Model	Test		Valid	
	BLEU	METEOR	BLEU	METEOR
VTLM: random masking	51.80	78.04	52.44	78.25
VTLM: more informed visual and textual masking	**52.34**	**78.77**	**53.28**	**79.44**

Table 5: BLEU and METEOR scores for random masking VTLM (baseline) and more informed visual and textual masking VTLM (our model) for the MMT task.

	Source:	Isso é o que dá ao meu site as opções de cores que ele tem.
	Reference:	That is what gives my site the color options that it has.
	Baseline:	That's what gives my website to the color options that he has.
	Our model:	That's what gives my website to the color options that it has.
	Source:	E eu vou empurrá-lo de volta.
	Reference:	And I'm going to push it back down.
	Baseline:	And I'm going to push him back.
	Our model:	And I'm going to push it back down.
	Source:	Eles mantêm seus dedos juntos e são bons para muitas atividades.
	Reference:	They keep your fingers kind of together and are good for a lot of activities.
	Baseline:	They keep their fingers together and they're good for many activities.
	Our model:	They keep your fingers together and they're good for a lot of activities.
	Source:	Agora pegue, coloque a marca do oleiro lá.
	Reference:	Now take it, put the potter's mark in there.
	Baseline:	Now take, put your potter's mark on there.
	Our model:	Now take it, put the potter's mark in there.
	Source:	Ele quer trazê-lo de volta naturalmente.
	Reference:	He wants to bring it back naturally.
	Baseline:	He wants to bring him back naturally.
	Our model:	He wants to bring it back naturally.

Table 6: Translation examples of random masking VTLM (baseline) and more informed visual and textual masking VTLM (our model).

masks a token n-gram if it exhibits high collocation over the corpus.

Combining cross-lingual and visual pre-training, Caglayan et al. (2021) propose Visual Translation Language Modelling (VTLM), which extends the TLM framework (Conneau and Lample, 2019) with regional features and performs masked language modeling and masked region classification on a three-way parallel language and vision dataset. The standard masking ratio is maintained (i.e. 15%) and it is applied separately to visual and language flows. VTLM achieved a 44.0 BLEU and 61.3 METEOR on the English-German 2016 test set of Multi30k (Elliott et al., 2016) for the MMT task. Following this approach, Sato et al. (2022) propose VTLM for video subtitles, which extends VTLM to a new language pair and to more challenging circumstances concerning the image-text relationship by using video frames with subtitles instead of images with their corresponding description. They use the same random masking approach for both visual and textual masking and achieved a 51.8 BLEU and 78.0 METEOR on the Portuguese-English test set of How2 (Sanabria et al., 2018) for the MMT task. In this paper, we propose three novel masking strategies for cross-lingual visual pre-training and we apply them to VTLM for video subtitles to test their efficacy for downstream MMT performance.

6 Conclusions

In this work, we show that predicting particular masked elements can benefit cross-lingual visual pre-training as the pre-trained model can acquire a better understanding of specific language structures, which improves downstream tasks such as multimodal machine translation. We present three selective masking strategies that focus on masking specific linguistic and visual tokens that can contribute to understanding some language patterns.

We achieve state-of-the-art accuracy on the How2 dataset and show that our masking approaches yield significant improvements over the original random masking strategy for downstream MMT performance. Even though we only conduct experiments on the MMT task using VTLM as the base model, our method can easily generalize to other models and other NLP tasks. We hope that our work here will further accelerate future research on Brazilian Portuguese and other low-resource languages. For future work, we will investigate the impact of visual and textual masking probability and further explore more effective masking approaches for downstream MMT performance.

Limitations

Although our research led to improvements in the translation of subject pronouns, object pronouns, and possessive adjectives and pronouns, these improvements did not cover non-binary-associated pronouns, such as *they/them/theirs*, *xe/xem/xyr* and *ze/hir/hirs*. The large underrepresentation of non-binary genders in textual and visual data contributes to propagating the misrepresentation of non-binary people by language models. In this paper, we were unable to work against this issue, thus we hope to contribute to a fairer representation of these disadvantaged groups in the future.

Ethics Statement

We acknowledge that all co-authors of this paper are aware of the *ACM Code of Ethics* and honor the code of conduct. We collected our data from a public dataset that permits academic use. As our experiments are limited to the binary linguistic forms represented in the used data, we cannot guarantee that our models will always generate unbiased content.

References

Alexei Baevski, Sergey Edunov, Yinhan Liu, Luke Zettlemoyer, and Michael Auli. 2019. Cloze-driven pretraining of self-attention networks. In *Proceedings of the 2019 Conference on Empirical Methods in Natural Language Processing and the 9th International Joint Conference on Natural Language Processing (EMNLP-IJCNLP)*, pages 5360–5369, Hong Kong, China. Association for Computational Linguistics.

Satanjeev Banerjee and Alon Lavie. 2005. METEOR: An automatic metric for MT evaluation with improved correlation with human judgments. In *Proceedings of the ACL Workshop on Intrinsic and Extrinsic Evaluation Measures for Machine Translation and/or Summarization*, pages 65–72, Ann Arbor, Michigan. Association for Computational Linguistics.

Loïc Barrault, Fethi Bougares, Lucia Specia, Chiraag Lala, Desmond Elliott, and Stella Frank. 2018. Findings of the third shared task on multimodal machine translation. In *Proceedings of the Third Conference on Machine Translation: Shared Task Papers*, pages 304–323, Belgium, Brussels. Association for Computational Linguistics.

Ozan Caglayan, Menekse Kuyu, Mustafa Sercan Amac, Pranava Madhyastha, Erkut Erdem, Aykut Erdem, and Lucia Specia. 2021. Cross-lingual Visual Pre-training for Multimodal Machine Translation. In *Proceedings of the 16th Conference of the European Chapter of the Association for Computational Linguistics: Short Papers*, online. Association for Computational Linguistics.

Yen-Chun Chen, Linjie Li, Licheng Yu, Ahmed El Kholy, Faisal Ahmed, Zhe Gan, Yu Cheng, and Jingjing Liu. 2020. UNITER: Universal image-text representation learning.

Kevin Clark, Minh-Thang Luong, Quoc V. Le, and Christopher D. Manning. 2020. ELECTRA: Pre-training text encoders as discriminators rather than generators. In *ICLR*.

Alexis Conneau and Guillaume Lample. 2019. Cross-lingual language model pretraining. In *Advances in Neural Information Processing Systems*, volume 32. Curran Associates, Inc.

Jacob Devlin, Ming-Wei Chang, Kenton Lee, and Kristina Toutanova. 2019. BERT: Pre-training of deep bidirectional transformers for language understanding. In *Proceedings of the 2019 Conference of the North American Chapter of the Association for Computational Linguistics: Human Language Technologies, Volume 1 (Long and Short Papers)*, pages 4171–4186, Minneapolis, Minnesota. Association for Computational Linguistics.

Desmond Elliott, Stella Frank, Loïc Barrault, Fethi Bougares, and Lucia Specia. 2017. Findings of the second shared task on multimodal machine translation and multilingual image description. In *Proceedings of the Second Conference on Machine Translation*, pages 215–233, Copenhagen, Denmark. Association for Computational Linguistics.

Desmond Elliott, Stella Frank, Khalil Sima'an, and Lucia Specia. 2016. Multi30K: Multilingual English-German image descriptions. In *Proceedings of the 5th Workshop on Vision and Language*, pages 70–74, Berlin, Germany. Association for Computational Linguistics.

Mandar Joshi, Danqi Chen, Yinhan Liu, Daniel S. Weld, Luke Zettlemoyer, and Omer Levy. 2020. SpanBERT: Improving pre-training by representing and predicting spans. *Transactions of the Association for Computational Linguistics*, 8:64–77.

Diederik Kingma and Jimmy Ba. 2014. Adam: A method for stochastic optimization. *International Conference on Learning Representations*.

Alina Kuznetsova, Hassan Rom, Neil Alldrin, Jasper Uijlings, Ivan Krasin, Jordi Pont-Tuset, Shahab Kamali, Stefan Popov, Matteo Malloci, Alexander Kolesnikov, and et al. 2020. The open images dataset v4. *International Journal of Computer Vision*, 128(7):1956–1981.

Zhenzhong Lan, Mingda Chen, Sebastian Goodman, Kevin Gimpel, Piyush Sharma, and Radu Soricut. 2020. ALBERT: A lite BERT for self-supervised learning of language representations. In *8th International Conference on Learning Representations, ICLR 2020, Addis Ababa, Ethiopia, April 26-30, 2020*. OpenReview.net.

Yoav Levine, Barak Lenz, Opher Lieber, Omri Abend, Kevin Leyton-Brown, Moshe Tennenholtz, and Yoav Shoham. 2021. {PMI}-masking: Principled masking of correlated spans. In *International Conference on Learning Representations*.

Yinhan Liu, Myle Ott, Naman Goyal, Jingfei Du, Mandar Joshi, Danqi Chen, Omer Levy, Mike Lewis, Luke Zettlemoyer, and Veselin Stoyanov. 2019. Roberta: A robustly optimized BERT pretraining approach. *CoRR*, abs/1907.11692.

Kishore Papineni, Salim Roukos, Todd Ward, and Wei-Jing Zhu. 2002. Bleu: a method for automatic evaluation of machine translation. In *Proceedings of the 40th Annual Meeting of the Association for Computational Linguistics*, pages 311–318, Philadelphia, Pennsylvania, USA. Association for Computational Linguistics.

Shaoqing Ren, Kaiming He, Ross Girshick, and Jian Sun. 2015. Faster R-CNN: Towards real-time object detection with region proposal networks. In *Advances in Neural Information Processing Systems*, volume 28. Curran Associates, Inc.

Ramon Sanabria, Ozan Caglayan, Shruti Palaskar, Desmond Elliott, Loic Barrault, Lucia Specia, and Florian Metze. 2018. How2: A large-scale dataset for multimodal language understanding. In *Visually Grounded Interaction and Language (ViGIL), Montreal; Canada, December 2018. Neural Information Processing Society (NeurIPS).*, arXiv. arxiv.org. 32nd Annual Conference on Neural Information Processing Systems, NeurIPS ; Conference date: 02-12-2018 Through 08-12-2018.

Júlia Sato, Helena Caseli, and Lucia Specia. 2022. Multilingual and multimodal learning for Brazilian Portuguese. In *Proceedings of the Thirteenth Language Resources and Evaluation Conference*, pages 919–927, Marseille, France. European Language Resources Association.

Rico Sennrich, Barry Haddow, and Alexandra Birch. 2016. Neural machine translation of rare words with subword units. In *Proceedings of the 54th Annual Meeting of the Association for Computational Linguistics (Volume 1: Long Papers)*, pages 1715–1725, Berlin, Germany. Association for Computational Linguistics.

Lucia Specia, Stella Frank, Khalil Sima'an, and Desmond Elliott. 2016. A shared task on multimodal machine translation and crosslingual image description. In *Proceedings of the First Conference on Machine Translation: Volume 2, Shared Task Papers*, pages 543–553, Berlin, Germany. Association for Computational Linguistics.

Nitish Srivastava, Geoffrey Hinton, Alex Krizhevsky, Ilya Sutskever, and Ruslan Salakhutdinov. 2014. Dropout: A simple way to prevent neural networks from overfitting. *Journal of Machine Learning Research*, 15(56):1929–1958.

Weijie Su, Xizhou Zhu, Yue Cao, Bin Li, Lewei Lu, Furu Wei, and Jifeng Dai. 2020. VL-BERT: Pre-training of generic visual-linguistic representations.

Ashish Vaswani, Noam Shazeer, Niki Parmar, Jakob Uszkoreit, Llion Jones, Aidan N Gomez, Ł ukasz Kaiser, and Illia Polosukhin. 2017. Attention is all you need. In *Advances in Neural Information Processing Systems*, volume 30. Curran Associates, Inc.

Zhilin Yang, Zihang Dai, Yiming Yang, Jaime G. Carbonell, Ruslan Salakhutdinov, and Quoc V. Le. 2019. Xlnet: Generalized autoregressive pretraining for language understanding. In *Neural Information Processing Systems*.

Zhengyan Zhang, Xu Han, Zhiyuan Liu, Xin Jiang, Maosong Sun, and Qun Liu. 2019. ERNIE: Enhanced language representation with informative entities. In *Proceedings of the 57th Annual Meeting of the Association for Computational Linguistics*, pages 1441–1451, Florence, Italy. Association for Computational Linguistics.

Liu Zhuang, Lin Wayne, Shi Ya, and Zhao Jun. 2021. A robustly optimized BERT pre-training approach with post-training. In *Proceedings of the 20th Chinese National Conference on Computational Linguistics*, pages 1218–1227, Huhhot, China. Chinese Information Processing Society of China.

Combining Tradition with Modernness: Exploring Event Representations in Vision-and-Language Models for Visual Goal–Step Inference

Chong Shen and **Carina Silberer**
Institute for Natural Language Processing, University of Stuttgart, Germany
{chong.shen,carina.silberer}
@ims.uni-stuttgart.de

Abstract

Procedural knowledge understanding underlies the ability to infer goal–step relations. The task of Visual Goal–Step Inference addresses this ability in the multimodal domain. It requires the identification of images that depict the steps necessary to accomplish a textually expressed goal. The best existing methods encode texts and images either with independent encoders, or with object-level multimodal encoders using blackbox transformers. This stands in contrast to early, linguistically inspired methods for event representations, which focus on capturing the most crucial information, namely actions and participants, to learn stereotypical event sequences and hence procedural knowledge. In this work, we study various methods and their effects on procedural knowledge understanding of injecting the early shallow event representations to nowadays multimodal deep learning-based models. We find that the early, linguistically inspired methods for representing event knowledge do contribute to understand procedures in combination with modern vision-and-language models. This supports further exploration of more complex event structures in combination with large language models.[1]

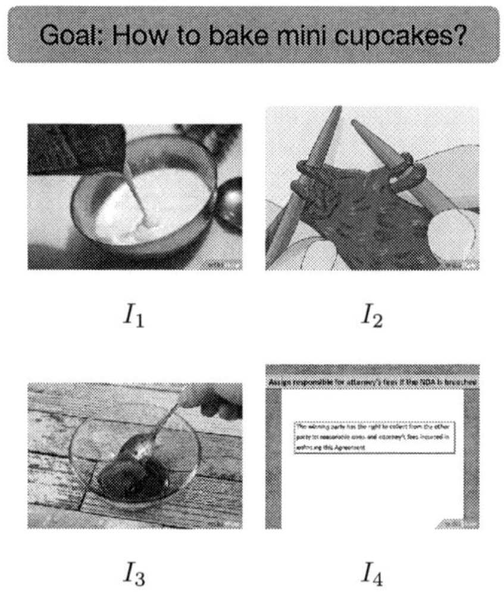

Figure 1: An example of the VGSI task. For the given goal G, image I_1 (*Combine the milk and cream before adding everything to the large bowl*) should be selected since it depicts a step S that leads to accomplishing G.

1 Introduction

Procedural Knowledge Understanding (PKU) implies reasoning about how to complete a task or achieve a goal (Mujtaba and Mahapatra, 2019). While previous works focus on plain texts (Yang and Nyberg, 2015; Zhou et al., 2019; Zhang et al., 2020a,b; Lyu et al., 2021; Sun et al., 2022), recent studies extend the task to the visual–linguistic domain. They ground procedural everyday tasks in the visual world, as a step towards situated procedural understanding in the real world.

Yang et al. (2021) propose a novel PKU task that utilizes both textual and visual information by selecting an image conditioned on a sentence which describes a high-level goal (illustrated in Figure 1, cf. Section 2.2). Their experimental results show that there is still a large gap to human performance on this task. While Yang et al. (2021) represent goal descriptions by their neural embeddings, earlier approaches to representing procedural knowledge or stereotypical event sequences (i.e., goals and steps; cf. scripts, Shank and Abelson, 1977), in contrast, focus on capturing the most essential information of events, namely the actions and their main participants (Balasubramanian et al., 2013; Pichotta and Mooney, 2014, inter alia).

In this work, we explore different ways to inject these linguistically inspired representations to the recent powerful deep learning approaches, and study their contribution to multimodal PKU. Specifically, we investigate the relational event representation (Balasubramanian et al., 2013) and the multi-argument event representation (Pichotta

[1]The code is available at `https://github.com/st143575/Exploring-Event-In-VGSI`.

Proceedings of the 61st Annual Meeting of the Association for Computational Linguistics - Student Research Workshop, pages 254–265
July 10-12, 2023 ©2023 Association for Computational Linguistics

and Mooney, 2014, 2016) due to their simple but condensed structure holding the most crucial information such as the action and the main participants in the main clause. We also evaluate different approaches to encode and inject such event knowledge to the model used by Yang et al. (2021), while also taking the contextual information into account. We conduct our experiments from three perspectives. First, we explore two approaches for event knowledge injection: (1) EVENT replaces the sentence describing the event by the two aforementioned event representations; (2) SENTENCE+EVENT appends the two types of event representations to the sentence describing that event. Second, we compare the embeddings extracted from different layers of the text encoder based on the finding of Jawahar et al. (2019) and Vulić et al. (2020), namely that lexical, syntactic and semantic information tend to be captured by the first, middle and last couple of layers, respectively. And third, we study the contribution of contextualised embeddings to represent the event and its participants compared to local embeddings.

The main contributions of this paper are: (1) comparison between two approaches for linguistically-inspired event knowledge injection for the task of multimodal procedural knowledge learning; (2) comparison of three levels of linguistic information in the text embedding; (3) investigation of local and contextualised event embeddings; (4) assessment of different abstract representations for the implicit subject of instructional texts.

We find that appending the multi-argument event representation to the input sentence with the *<|startoftext|>* token as the implicit subject, and taking the average of the last 4 hidden layers of CLIP's text encoder is the best way to encode and inject event knowledge to a deep learning model. Specifically, first encoding the full sentence and then extracting and averaging the word-level embeddings of the components of the event representation can use the contextual information in the sentence outside the event itself.

2 Related Work

2.1 Event Definitions and Representations

The concept *event* can be defined in various ways. In early works, an event is either defined as a verb (Katz and Arosio, 2001), or an expression that have implicit time dimension and is either a verb or a noun phrase (Schilder and Habel, 2001), or a proposition consisting of the subject and the predicate (Filatova and Hovy, 2001). Pustejovsky et al. (2005) define an event as a predicate describing a state or a circumstance in which something holds true. Li et al. (2021) define an event as the occurrence of an action causing a state change, which is performed by some participant(s) in a particular manner. For instance, image I_3 in Figure 1 illustrates the event of *A person beating together butter and sugar with a mixer.*

Later studies on *script learning* (Zhang, 2022) extend the definition of the event by its surrounding components in the text. Chambers and Jurafsky (2008) represent an event as a *(verb, dependency)*-pair extracted from narrative texts using a dependency parser. Balasubramanian et al. (2013) generate event schemata from news articles using *(subject, verb, object)*-pairs as the event representation. Pichotta and Mooney (2014, 2016) represent events as *(subject, verb, object, preposition)* tuples that model the interactions between entities in a script.

In contrast, recent works focus on extracting events with more complex structures and richer information from contexts. Yu et al. (2022) design a BERT-based framework for building event extractors in a weak supervised manner. Chen et al. (2021) train a multimodal Transformer (Vaswani et al., 2017) to jointly extract events from videos and texts. Wei et al. (2023) propose a framework for zero-shot event extraction using a sibling model to InstructGPT (Ouyang et al., 2022). Knowledge graphs (Hogan et al., 2021) have been widely used to extract events from multimodal data and represent events in a more complex structure (Li et al., 2020, 2022). We adopt the relational event representation of Balasubramanian et al. (2013) and the multi-argument event representation of Pichotta and Mooney (2014) for our experiments due to the low performance of recent event extractors on the dataset used for our experiments.

2.2 Procedural Knowledge Understanding

A *procedure* is a compound event that can be broken down into multiple events (Zhang, 2022). It consists of a goal and a sequence of steps towards accomplishing that goal. Procedural knowledge understanding (PKU) is the task of learning the relations between the goal and the steps. Various approaches have been proposed to understanding procedures using event knowledge. Tandon et al.

(2020) use entity tracking to generate state changes from procedural text. Zhang et al. (2020b) learn goal–step relations and step–step temporal relations in procedural texts and introduce a 4-way multiple choice task for goal–step inference. Yang et al. (2021) extend it to the multimodal domain and learn goal–step relations from texts and images. Lyu et al. (2021) generate the sequence of steps conditioned on a given goal. Zhou et al. (2022) discover the hierarchical structure in procedural knowledge using action linking. Based on the work of Yang et al. (2021), we investigate different ways to encode and inject classical event knowledge to recent deep learning models.

Goal–Step–Inference (Zhang et al., 2020b) is the task of reasoning about goal–step relations from instructional texts. Given a goal sentence and four candidate step descriptions, a model should choose the step that leads to the goal. The main challenge of this task is that it requires to understand both, the actions of goals and steps and their relations. Yang et al. (2021) extend the task to the multimodal domain through the *Visual Goal–Step Inference* task, in which steps are described by images. They attempt to overcome the challenge by matching the goal sentence and the step image. However, they still observe a significant gap between model and human performance. Our work seeks to bridge this gap with multiple approaches by combining state-of-the-art neural models with early linguistically motivated event representations (see above).

2.3 Vision-and-Language Models

In recent years, Vision-and-Language (V&L) models have made tremendous progress on a wide range of multimodal tasks, such as visual commonsense reasoning (Lu et al., 2019), image–text retrieval (Chen et al., 2020), text-to-image and image-to-text generation (Rombach et al., 2022; Li et al., 2023). One strand of models are *fusion encoders* which learn a fused representation of images and texts. For example, LXMERT (Tan and Bansal, 2019) uses attention (Vaswani et al., 2017) to learn intra-modal and cross-modal relationships while training a language encoder, an object relationship encoder and a cross-modality encoder. Although the model learns the alignment between images, objects and words in sentences via the object-level pretraining objectives, it does not understand the relations between the objects and the action. Another line of works propose *dual encoders* which learn separate encodings of images and language. A prominent example is CLIP (Radford et al., 2021), which uses a contrastive objective to train a text encoder (GPT-2, Radford et al., 2019) and an image encoder (e.g., ViT Dosovitskiy et al., 2020). CLIP achieves state-of-the-art performance across multiple tasks. Different from LXMERT, CLIP is trained to match an image as a whole to a text description. We use this advantage and extract image-grounded sentence embeddings using CLIP's text encoder. Since CLIP applies a subtoken-level tokenization, the outputs of its text encoder are embeddings for the subtokens in the input sentence. Although it is a common practice to use the embedding of the classification token as the overall sentence embedding, this approach has been shown to be suboptimal (Vulić et al., 2020). We conduct experiments to find the optimal sentence representation.

3 VGSI: Visual Goal–Step Inference Task

Task Definition. Yang et al. (2021) define VGSI as a 4-way multiple choice problem. As shown in the example in Figure 1, given a textual *goal* G and four images I_i, $i \in \{1, 2, 3, 4\}$ representing four candidate *steps*, the task is to select the image that represents a correct step towards accomplishing G.

In this paper, we additionally explore a stricter definition of VGSI, where the task is to select the respective correct image of *all* steps that are necessary to reach the goal G.

3.1 Methods

3.1.1 Event Representations

To obtain event representations from goal and step sentences, we first extract the *subject*, *verbal predicate*, *direct object* and *prepositional phrase* from the sentences using a dependency parser (Dozat and Manning, 2016)[2].

Implicit Subject Representation. Due to the nature of the dataset of procedural instructions, textual goals and steps are usually imperative sentences, and as a consequence, the subject is left off. To encode the subject, we conduct experiments to compare event representations with no explicitly mentioned subject to those which express the subject (1) by the token *person*, or (2) by the special *<|startoftext|>* token of the CLIP tokenizer. Since the *<|startoftext|>* token added by

[2]We use SuPar available at https://github.com/yzhangcs/parser

us is always between the <|startoftext|> token of the CLIP tokenizer and the verbal predicate, its embedding is supposed to capture syntactic information from these two surrounding tokens via the attention mechanism (i.e. the information about the position of the subject of a sentence). To verify this hypothesis, we conduct two groups of probing experiments using the most common and the least common token in the input text as the pseudo-subject, respectively (see Section 5.1). We find that sentences with the <|startoftext|> token as the pseudo-subject lead to the best result.

Event Representations. The event representation is an essential component of our task. As introduced in Section 2, we represent events in the goal and step sentences using two types of representations: (1) the relational event representation (Balasubramanian et al., 2013) which is a *(subject, verb, object)* tuple, and (2) the multi-argument event representation (Pichotta and Mooney, 2014) which is a *(subject, verb, object, prepositional phrase)* tuple. Table 1 shows examples of all representations we explore. In the case that the object or prepositional phrase is absent, we represent it by a *[PAD]* token, e.g., (<|*startoftext*|>, pour, sauce, *[PAD]*).

Local vs. Contextualised Event. To assess the effectiveness of event representations, we deliberately use non-contextualised embeddings to disentangle the *subj–pred–obj(–pp)* information from the overall sentence. In detail, the components of the event representations are concatenated to form a sentence, which is then encoded by the CLIP text encoder (i.e. GPT-2). For instance, the event (<|*startoftext*|>, pour, sauce) is turned into the input <|*startoftext*|> *pour sauce*. We compare this encoding method to one that uses contextualised embeddings: We first encode the whole sentence and extract all word embeddings. If the tokenizer split a word into subtokens, we mean-pool their corresponding embeddings. Then, we mean-pool the word embeddings which are part of the components of the event representations. For example, the word embeddings in the object phrase *into container or jug* are averaged to a single vector. Note that for both local and contextualised approaches, the CLIP tokenizer automatically adds a <|startoftext|> and an <|endoftext|> token to the start and the end of the input, respectively. We remove these two special tokens after the encoding, such that only the embedding of the <|startoftext|> as the implicit subject is averaged with other words. We evaluate the text embeddings obtained from three groups of layers of CLIP.[3] The visual embeddings, in turn, are the last hidden state of the CLIP image encoder (i.e. ViT).[4]

text	Pour the soy or tamari sauce into a suitable small mixing container or jug.
event$_{rel}$	(<|startoftext|>, pour, sauce)
event$_{mult}$	(<|startoftext|>, pour, sauce, into container or jug)

Table 1: Example of the relational and multi-argument event representation.

3.1.2 Triplet Network for Goal–Step Inference

We use Triplet Network (Hoffer and Ailon, 2015) in all our experiments and use the cosine similarity as the similarity metric.

Training. The triplet network for training is implemented as a three-branch network with a text module and an image module, where the two branches of the image module share the same parameters. The input is a triplet *(G+S,* I_{pos}, I_{neg}*)*, where *G+S* is the embedding of the concatenated goal–step sentence, I_{pos} is the embedding of the positive image, I_{neg} is the embedding of a negative image (see Section 4.3). The model learns a cross-modal embedding space by minimizing the distance between *G+S* and I_{pos}, while maximizing the distance between *G+S* and I_{neg}. Different from Yang et al. (2021) which use *G* as the textual input for training, we use *G+S* because *S* share common information with *I* and serves as a bridge between *G* and *I*. Thus, *G+S* could help the model to better understand the relation between *G* and *I*.

Inference. During inference, we follow the input format of Yang et al. (2021), i.e. the textual input is the goal alone. The model takes each pair (G, I_i), $i \in \{1,2,3,4\}$ from a test data point $(G, [I_1, I_2, I_3, I_4])$ as input. By computing the similarity between G and I_i, the model predicts the correct step image $\hat{I}$ as that with the highest simi-

[3]Based on (Vulić et al., 2020)'s findings, we do not use the embedding of the classification token, cf. Sect. 2.

[4]We use `clip-vit-large-patch14` from HuggingFace available at `https://huggingface.co/openai/clip-vit-large-patch14`

Experiment group	Embed size	#params	Input format	Event injection
SENTENCE	768 (text) 1024 (image)	3,936,256	goal+step (train) goal (test)	s
EVENT	768 (text) 1024 (image)	3,936,256	goal+step (train) goal (test)	e
SENTENCE+EVENT	1536 (text) 1024 (image)	4,722,688	goal+step (train) goal (test)	s+e

Table 2: Embedding size, number of parameters, input formats to the text encoder and event injection approaches of different experiment groups: concatenation of goal and step headline (goal+step), goal only (goal); sentence only (s), event only (e), sentence+event (s+e).

larity as follows:

$$\hat{I} = \arg\max_{I_i} cos(G, I_i) \tag{1}$$

4 Experiments

4.1 Data

We conduct our experiments on **wikiHow-VGSI** (Yang et al., 2021),[5] a dataset for multimodal goal-oriented PKU collected from the English wikiHow[6]. The dataset contains articles of instructions to complete tasks across a wide range of daily-life topics, including health, home and garden, education, recipes etc. Each article contains a *goal G* in the form of a "How to"-sentence and a set of *methods* (e.g., "How to bake mini cupcakes", Figure 1). Each method comprises a list of *steps*. Each step has a *step headline S* which is an imperative sentence describing that step, and an image *I* corresponding to that step (e.g., I_1 and S in Fig. 1). To describe a goal and its steps, we use the *goal G* and the *step headline S* and its associated image *I*, respectively.

We lowercase all the texts in the dataset, and use the special token <|*startoftext*|> to represent the subject in all sentences (i.e., *pseudo-subject*). Specifically, <|*startoftext*|> substitutes *How to* in all goals and is prepended to all step headlines. Since we found some issues in the dataset, such as duplicates or non-English text, we removed 3 goals and 56 step headlines. Details to our filtering procedure are given in Appendix 9.1. As a result, the dataset used for our experiments contains 53,186 goals, 772,221 step headlines and 772,277 step images.

[5]https://github.com/YueYANG1996/wikiHow-VGSI

[6]https://www.wikihow.com/Main-Page

4.2 Models

We assess the benefit of the two approaches for the event knowledge injection (relational and multi-argument representations, see Sect. 3.1.1) when being used as the only representation of the goal *G* and step *S* during training (EVENT), or when being used as additional information to the full sentences (SENTENCE+EVENT). We compare them against only using the full sentence (SENTENCE), which is also employed by Yang et al. (2021). Table 2 gives an overview of the different inputs and the corresponding hyperparameters of the models.

Jawahar et al. (2019) observed that the embeddings obtained from different layers of BERT tend to be dominated by different levels of linguistic information: surface (i.e. lexical) information in bottom layers, syntactic information in middle layers and semantic information in top layers. Thus, we examine sentence embeddings of three linguistic levels in each of these experiment groups: (1) FIRST4 averages the outputs of the first 4 layers of CLIP's text encoder; (2) MIDDLE4 averages the outputs of the 5-th to the 8-th layers of the encoder; (3) LAST4 averages the outputs of the last 4 layers.

4.2.1 EVENT

In this group of experiments, the goal and step sentences are replaced by the event representations extracted from them. For example, the sentence in Table 1 is replaced by <|*startoftext*|> *pour sauce* for the relational event representation and by <|*startoftext*|> *pour sauce into container or jug* for the multi-argument event representation.

4.2.2 SENTENCE+EVENT

In this group of experiments, the event representations are appended to the goal and step sentences. For example, the aforementioned sentence is converted to <|*startoftext*|> *pour the soy or tamari* *sauce into a suitable small mixing container or jug. <|startoftext|> pour sauce.* for the relational event representation, and *<|startoftext|> pour the soy or tamari sauce into a suitable small mixing container or jug. <|startoftext|> pour sauce into container or jug.* for the multi-argument event representation.

4.2.3 SENTENCE

While event representations have been found valuable in earlier, linguistically motivated research on procedural texts (see Section 2), it stands the question whether they fully provide the crucial information for learning procedural knowledge. Hence, we also compare against a model that takes the encoded full sentence describing the goal or the goal+step as textual input, i.e. the model learns the task-relevant features from the full goal sentence or the step headline.

4.3 Training Procedure

We apply the random sampling strategy of Yang et al. (2021) to select negative step images. For each data point, we randomly select three different articles and take a random image from each article as the negative step image. We leave the experiments with other sampling methods used in Yang et al. (2021) to future work.

We initialize the weights using He-uniform with ReLU non-linearity. All models are trained for 200 epochs with batch size 1024 and a learning rate of 1e-5 with early stopping. In each experiment group, the model is trained and evaluated five times. We implemented the models in Keras with Tensorflow 2.0 and trained them on a single RTX A6000.

4.4 Evaluation Measures

We evaluate our models with two settings. The first one, which we call **weak**, follows the original task definition by Yang et al. (2021), where a data point in the test set is considered correctly predicted, if one step towards the goal given by that data point is correctly selected. To better fit the concept of procedural knowledge, we also apply a **strict** setting, in which a data point is correctly predicted, if all the steps required to achieve the goal given by the data point are correctly selected. We report the mean accuracy obtained by the five individual training and testing runs, as well as the corresponding standard deviation.

5 Results

Tables 3 and 5 give the most important results. The full results can be found in Appendix 9.2.

5.1 Event-based Representations

Table 3 shows the performance of the models with the *<|startoftext|>* token as pseudo-subject, using different event representations containing different levels of linguistic knowledge. The last two rows list the results of the best model and the human evaluation in Yang et al. (2021).

As expected, by comparing the EVENT$_{rel,*}$ and EVENT$_{mult,*}$ groups (i.e., <[2],[3]>, <[7],[8]>, <[12],[13]>), we observe that the multi-argument event representation outperforms the relational event representation.

Linguistic Level Embedding. To find out which level of linguistic knowledge is most suitable for the task, we compare the following three groups of results in Table 3: <[2],[7],[12]>, <[3],[8],[13]> and <[5],[10],[15]>. On average, the LAST4 groups achieve the highest accuracy, while the FIRST4 groups perform the worst. The performance gap between FIRST4 and the other two groups is considerably larger than that between MIDDLE4 and LAST4. This indicates that both semantic and syntactic information play important roles in the task, while lexical information is far less important than syntactic and semantic information.

Event Knowledge Injection. The results of <[3],[5]>, <[8],[10]>, and <[13],[15]> in Table 3 show that SENTENCE+EVENT results in higher accuracy than EVENT. This reveals the advantage of attaching event knowledge to the sentence over using only the event knowledge. It also implies that the sentence could provide additional information to the event, which could help models better understand procedural knowledge.

Local vs. Contextualised Embeddings. By comparing the results of local and contextualised event embeddings in Table 3, we observe a significant improvement of the performance in the latter group. On average, the accuracy with contextualised embeddings is 3.71% and 13.73% higher than that with the local ones in the **weak** setting and in the **strict** setting, respectively. This verifies the observation in the last paragraph that sentences provide additional, useful information.

Models	Local Event		Contextualised Event	
	weak	**strict**	**weak**	**strict**
[2] EVENT$_{rel,first4}$	68.9±0.3	9.9±0.3	71.6±0.4	12.2±0.3
[3] EVENT$_{mult,first4}$	75.8±0.4	15.3±0.5	77.0±0.1	15.9±0.2
[5] SENTENCE+EVENT$_{mult,first4}$	80.9±0.8	19.3±1.3	81.0±0.1	19.6±0.3
[7] EVENT$_{rel,middle4}$	70.3±0.2	11.1±0.2	74.9±0	14.9±0.1
[8] EVENT$_{mult,middle4}$	76.9±0.6	16.9±0.9	79.9±0	19.1±0.4
[10] SENTENCE+EVENT$_{mult,middle4}$	82.4±0.1	22.1±0.3	82.8±0.9	22.4±1.5
[12] EVENT$_{rel,last4}$	69.1±0.3	11.5±0.4	75.9±0	16.7±0.1
[13] EVENT$_{mult,last4}$	77.3±0.4	18.8±0.4	80.8±0	21.2±0.2
[15] SENTENCE+EVENT$_{mult,last4}$	81.1±0.7	21.5±0.8	**84.7±0**	**26.4±0.2**
[16] EVENT$_{mult,last4,+1layer}$	76.6±0.3	17.9±0.2	80.5±0	20.7±0
Triplet Net (BERT) (Yang et al., 2021)†	72.8	-	72.8	-
Human (Yang et al., 2021)	84.5	-	84.5	-

Table 3: Accuracy (%) of experiments using different event representations encoded by different layers of the CLIP text encoder. The implicit subject is represented by *<|startoftext|>* (**sot+sent**). †Results adopted from the authors, they are not directly comparable.

Implicit(/Pseudo-)Subject	weak	strict
sot+sent	**82.7**	**22.3**
person+sent	80.3	19.9
-+sent	79.4	19.4
sot	24.2	0.11
most-frequent+sent	79.8	20.3
least-frequent+sent	68.6	10.4

Table 4: Accuracy (%) of SENTENCE experiments using different implicit (top) / pseudo (bottom) subjects: *<|startoftext|>*+sentence (sot+sent), *person*+sentence (person+sent), sentence without subject (-+sent), *<|startoftext|>* only (sot).

Implicit Subject Abstract Representation. The sentences in the dataset either begin with *How to*, or they do not have an explicit subject. Thus, we assess the contribution of different abstract representations for the implicit subject of the sentences. Table 4 (top) shows the performance of the SENTENCE$_{middle4}$ models with four abstract representations as the subject. The results show that *<|startoftext|>* is the most powerful abstract representation for the subject. However, we observe a significant performance degradation when using this token separately as the representation of the whole sentence (i.e. *sot* in Table 4). In this case, the embedding of *<|startoftext|>* is derived from the last hidden state of CLIP's text encoder. A possible reason could be that the *<|startoftext|>* token is always located between the verbal predicate and the *<|startoftext|>* token added by CLIP's tokenizer which indicates the start of the sentence. Hence, its embedding may capture syntactic information about the subject's position in the sentence from these contextual tokens via the attention mechanism. To verify this hypothesis, we conduct two groups of probing experiments for the syntactic information in the *<|startoftext|>* token. We evaluate the SENTENCE$_{middle4}$ model by taking the most and the least frequent token in the dataset (“.” and “50.0”, respectively) as a pseudo-subject of the input text, as we assume them to be generally less informative for the sentences. We observe a considerable performance drop with the least frequent token (see Table 4, bottom), indicating that *<|startoftext|>* indeed gives the model valuable cues about the subject position in a sentence.

5.2 Event-Enhanced Sentences

Table 5 compares the performance of using sentence-only embeddings with using event-enhanced sentence embeddings. As a result, SENTENCE+EVENT outperforms SENTENCE with contextualised event embeddings when using the average of the last 4 hidden layers of the CLIP text encoder. The groups using the first 4 and middle 4 layers achieve comparable performance. Moreover, the best model (i.e., [15]) reaches the human upper

Models	Local Event		Contextualised Event	
	weak	**strict**	**weak**	**strict**
[1] SENTENCE$_{first4}$	81.6±0.1	20.1±0.1	81.2±0.0	19.7±0.2
[5] SENTENCE+EVENT$_{mult,first4}$	80.9±0.8	19.3±1.3	81.0±0.1	19.6±0.3
[6] SENTENCE$_{middle4}$	82.7±0.4	22.3±0.5	82.7±1.1	22.2±1.7
[10] SENTENCE+EVENT$_{mult,middle4}$	82.4±0.1	22.1±0.3	82.8±0.9	22.4±1.5
[11] SENTENCE$_{last4}$	82.1±0.4	22.3±0.7	84.6±0.1	26.0±0.2
[15] SENTENCE+EVENT$_{mult,last4}$	81.1±0.7	21.5±0.8	**84.7±0.0**	**26.4±0.2**
Triplet Net (BERT) (Yang et al., 2021)†	72.8	-	72.8	-
Human (Yang et al., 2021)	84.5	-	84.5	-

Table 5: Accuracy (%) and standard deviation of the experiments using different event representations encoded by different layers of the CLIP text encoder.

bound, demonstrating the necessity of applying the strict evaluation setting.

5.3 Disentangle the Influence of Model Sizes and Embeddings

Since the models in the SENTENCE+EVENT group have more trainable parameters due to the concatenation of sentence- and event embeddings, the performance gain could attribute either to the number of parameters or to the embeddings. To disentangle the influence of these two factors, we conduct an experiment based on EVENT$_{mult,last4}$, with the text module of the triplet network being extended by an additional dense layer. This increases the number of trainable parameters of the model to $4,750,973$, which is comparable with the most effective SENTENCE+EVENT$_{mult,last4}$ models. The results of [16] in Table 3 show that there is no considerable change in performance from [13] and [15], indicating that the performance gain is due to attaching the event representation to the sentence.

6 Qualitative Analysis

We provide a qualitative analysis on the semantic gap between the ground-truth and the predicted images. Figure 2 shows part of an example of the model's predictions for the goal *How to stop twitching in your sleep?* In this example, four out of ten steps are incorrectly predicted.

For Step 5, the textual input for training is *<|startoftext|> stop twitching in your sleep. <|startoftext|> exercise every day.* The model selects Image (e) which depicts a hand holding a heart. The model may associate "twitching" with the heart in the image, but fails to infer the relation between "twitching" and the jogging people in the correct image (a). Thus, the model may not learn causal relationships between the goal and the step image, such as "Jogging can improve people's health condition and thus stop twitching in the sleep".

For Step 7 with the textual input *<|startoftext|> stop twitching in your sleep. <|startoftext|> eat plenty of magnesium.*, the model selects Image (f) illustrating a person sitting at a laptop. Possible reasons could be: (1) The action "eat" is usually performed by humans, but the correct image only describes some food, which the model misses to associate with "eat"; and (2) The phrase "plenty of magnesium" may mislead the model to select the wrong image with a laptop, which is associated more with magnesium than vegetables. Hence, the model may only learn knowledge about simple, superficial properties of the objects in images, and may lack more complex commonsense knowledge about the relations between objects, such as "Laptop is not edible" or "Human cannot take magnesium by eating laptops".

For Step 8, the input is *<|startoftext|> stop twitching in your sleep. <|startoftext|> adjust what you consume before bed.* The model selects the image showing a lady with a hat being pointed to by an arrow. This again indicated that the model's decision heavily relies on the verb. Furthermore, it also suggests that the model has limited capability of identifying the affordances of the objects in the image and associating them with the goal.

For Step 10 with the input *<|startoftext|> stop twitching in your sleep. <|startoftext|> address potential vitamin deficiencies.*, the model again

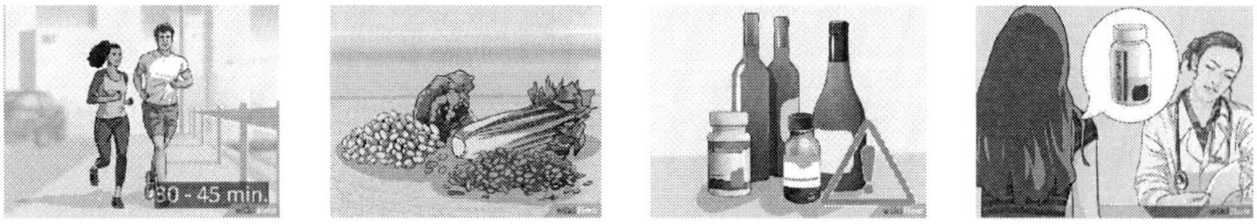

(a) Step 5: <|startoftext|> exercise every day.

(b) Step 7: <|startoftext|> eat plenty of magnesium.

(c) Step 8: <|startoftext|> adjust what you consume before bed.

(d) Step 10: <|startoftext|> address potential vitamin deficiencies.

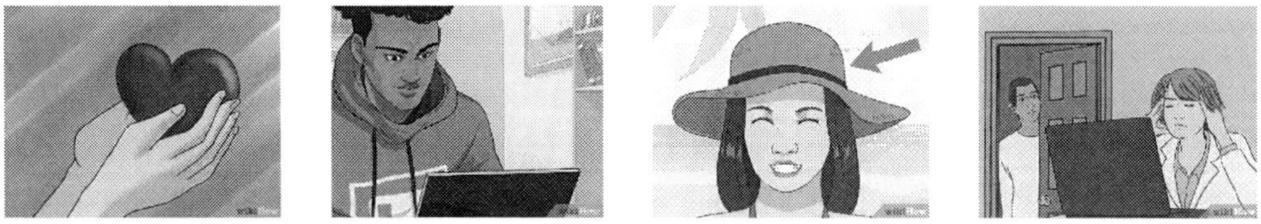

(e) Step 5: <|startoftext|> be gentle.

(f) Step 7: <|startoftext|> search online for job postings.

(g) Step 8: <|startoftext|> put on a sun hat to protect your hair and keep you cool.

(h) Step 10: <|startoftext|> start to learn about and change any patterns in your daily life that may act as triggers or contribute to your loved one's destructive behavior.

Figure 2: Ground-truth (top) and model's false predictions (bottom) for Steps 5, 7, 8, 10. Goal: *How to stop twitching in your sleep?*

seems to not capture causal relationships such as "Vitamin deficiency can lead to twitching in sleep", but to base its inference on shallow object features such as "A man opens the door and wakes the sleeping woman up".

In conclusion, our observations indicate that the model's decision highly depends on shallow features in the image and their alignment to the verbs and nouns in the text, while its effectiveness is impaired by its limited understanding of deeper semantics and causal relationships between the goal and the step images.

7 Conclusions

In this paper, we investigate two linguistically-inspired event knowledge injection approaches for the Visual Goal–Step Inference (VGSI) task. We experimentally compare three levels of linguistic information in the text embedding produced by state-of-the-art neural deep learning models. Furthermore, we also compare event embeddings which encode only the information of the event components themselves with contextualised event embeddings which include information about the overall sentence syntactically not belonging to the arguments forming an event representation itself. Last but not least, we assess different representations for the implicit subject of instructional sentences. We find that the early, linguistically inspired methods for representing event knowledge do contribute to understand procedures in combination with modern V&L models.

8 Limitations

We explore early, very simple structured event representations. Recent works in visual–linguistic semantic representations which use richer representations comprising predicate–argument structures and event types and argument roles, the general graph-based approaches, as well as scene graphs, are left for future work. Furthermore, the wikiHow articles may reflect the bias of their human authors.

Acknowledgements

We would like to thank Professor Parisa Kordjamshidi for her valuable feedback in the Pre-Submission Mentorship Program. We are also grateful to the anonymous reviewers for their detailed comments on our work. We would further like to thank Yue Yang for meaningful discussions about the VGSI task.

References

Niranjan Balasubramanian, Stephen Soderland, Oren Etzioni, et al. 2013. Generating coherent event schemas at scale. In *Proceedings of the 2013 Conference on Empirical Methods in Natural Language Processing*, pages 1721–1731.

Nathanael Chambers and Dan Jurafsky. 2008. Unsupervised learning of narrative event chains. In *Proceedings of ACL-08: HLT*, pages 789–797.

Brian Chen, Xudong Lin, Christopher Thomas, Manling Li, Shoya Yoshida, Lovish Chum, Heng Ji, and Shih-Fu Chang. 2021. Joint multimedia event extraction from video and article. *arXiv preprint arXiv:2109.12776*.

Yen-Chun Chen, Linjie Li, Licheng Yu, Ahmed El Kholy, Faisal Ahmed, Zhe Gan, Yu Cheng, and Jingjing Liu. 2020. Uniter: Universal image-text representation learning. In *Computer Vision–ECCV 2020: 16th European Conference, Glasgow, UK, August 23–28, 2020, Proceedings, Part XXX*, pages 104–120. Springer.

Alexey Dosovitskiy, Lucas Beyer, Alexander Kolesnikov, Dirk Weissenborn, Xiaohua Zhai, Thomas Unterthiner, Mostafa Dehghani, Matthias Minderer, Georg Heigold, Sylvain Gelly, et al. 2020. An image is worth 16x16 words: Transformers for image recognition at scale. *arXiv preprint arXiv:2010.11929*.

Timothy Dozat and Christopher D Manning. 2016. Deep biaffine attention for neural dependency parsing. *arXiv preprint arXiv:1611.01734*.

Elena Filatova and Eduard Hovy. 2001. Assigning timestamps to event-clauses. In *Proceedings of the ACL 2001 Workshop on Temporal and Spatial Information Processing*.

Elad Hoffer and Nir Ailon. 2015. Deep metric learning using triplet network. In *Similarity-Based Pattern Recognition: Third International Workshop, SIMBAD 2015, Copenhagen, Denmark, October 12-14, 2015. Proceedings 3*, pages 84–92. Springer.

Aidan Hogan, Eva Blomqvist, Michael Cochez, Claudia d'Amato, Gerard de Melo, Claudio Gutierrez, Sabrina Kirrane, José Emilio Labra Gayo, Roberto Navigli, Sebastian Neumaier, et al. 2021. Knowledge graphs. *ACM Computing Surveys (CSUR)*, 54(4):1–37.

Ganesh Jawahar, Benoît Sagot, and Djamé Seddah. 2019. What does bert learn about the structure of language? In *ACL 2019-57th Annual Meeting of the Association for Computational Linguistics*.

Graham Katz and Fabrizio Arosio. 2001. The annotation of temporal information in natural language sentences. In *Proceedings of the ACL 2001 Workshop on Temporal and Spatial Information Processing*.

Junnan Li, Dongxu Li, Silvio Savarese, and Steven Hoi. 2023. Blip-2: Bootstrapping language-image pretraining with frozen image encoders and large language models. *arXiv preprint arXiv:2301.12597*.

Manling Li, Ruochen Xu, Shuohang Wang, Luowei Zhou, Xudong Lin, Chenguang Zhu, Michael Zeng, Heng Ji, and Shih-Fu Chang. 2022. Clip-event: Connecting text and images with event structures. In *Proceedings of the IEEE/CVF Conference on Computer Vision and Pattern Recognition*, pages 16420–16429.

Manling Li, Alireza Zareian, Ying Lin, Xiaoman Pan, Spencer Whitehead, Brian Chen, Bo Wu, Heng Ji, Shih-Fu Chang, Clare Voss, et al. 2020. Gaia: A fine-grained multimedia knowledge extraction system. In *Proceedings of the 58th Annual Meeting of the Association for Computational Linguistics: System Demonstrations*, pages 77–86.

Qian Li, Jianxin Li, Jiawei Sheng, Shiyao Cui, Jia Wu, Yiming Hei, Hao Peng, Shu Guo, Lihong Wang, Amin Beheshti, et al. 2021. A compact survey on event extraction: Approaches and applications. *arXiv preprint arXiv:2107.02126*.

Jiasen Lu, Dhruv Batra, Devi Parikh, and Stefan Lee. 2019. Vilbert: Pretraining task-agnostic visiolinguistic representations for vision-and-language tasks. *Advances in neural information processing systems*, 32.

Qing Lyu, Li Zhang, and Chris Callison-Burch. 2021. Goal-oriented script construction. *arXiv preprint arXiv:2107.13189*.

Dena Mujtaba and Nihar Mahapatra. 2019. Recent trends in natural language understanding for procedural knowledge. In *2019 International Conference on Computational Science and Computational Intelligence (CSCI)*, pages 420–424. IEEE.

Long Ouyang, Jeff Wu, Xu Jiang, Diogo Almeida, Carroll L Wainwright, Pamela Mishkin, Chong Zhang, Sandhini Agarwal, Katarina Slama, Alex Ray, et al. 2022. Training language models to follow instructions with human feedback. *arXiv preprint arXiv:2203.02155*.

Karl Pichotta and Raymond Mooney. 2014. Statistical script learning with multi-argument events. In *Proceedings of the 14th Conference of the European Chapter of the Association for Computational Linguistics*, pages 220–229.

Karl Pichotta and Raymond Mooney. 2016. Learning statistical scripts with lstm recurrent neural networks. In *Proceedings of the AAAI Conference on Artificial Intelligence*, volume 30.

James Pustejovsky, Robert Ingria, Roser Sauri, José M Castaño, Jessica Littman, Robert J Gaizauskas, Andrea Setzer, Graham Katz, and Inderjeet Mani. 2005. The specification language timeml.

Alec Radford, Jong Wook Kim, Chris Hallacy, Aditya Ramesh, Gabriel Goh, Sandhini Agarwal, Girish Sastry, Amanda Askell, Pamela Mishkin, Jack Clark, et al. 2021. Learning transferable visual models from natural language supervision. In *International conference on machine learning*, pages 8748–8763. PMLR.

Alec Radford, Jeffrey Wu, Rewon Child, David Luan, Dario Amodei, Ilya Sutskever, et al. 2019. Language models are unsupervised multitask learners. *OpenAI blog*, 1(8):9.

Robin Rombach, Andreas Blattmann, Dominik Lorenz, Patrick Esser, and Björn Ommer. 2022. High-resolution image synthesis with latent diffusion models. In *Proceedings of the IEEE/CVF Conference on Computer Vision and Pattern Recognition*, pages 10684–10695.

Frank Schilder and Christopher Habel. 2001. From temporal expressions to temporal information: Semantic tagging of news messages. In *Proceedings of the ACL 2001 workshop on temporal and spatial information processing*.

Roger Shank and Robert Abelson. 1977. Scripts, plans, goals and understanding.

Chenkai Sun, Tie Xu, ChengXiang Zhai, and Heng ji. 2022. Incorporating task-specific concept knowledge into script learning.

Hao Tan and Mohit Bansal. 2019. Lxmert: Learning cross-modality encoder representations from transformers. *arXiv preprint arXiv:1908.07490*.

Niket Tandon, Keisuke Sakaguchi, Bhavana Dalvi Mishra, Dheeraj Rajagopal, Peter Clark, Michal Guerquin, Kyle Richardson, and Eduard Hovy. 2020. A dataset for tracking entities in open domain procedural text. *arXiv preprint arXiv:2011.08092*.

Ashish Vaswani, Noam Shazeer, Niki Parmar, Jakob Uszkoreit, Llion Jones, Aidan N Gomez, Łukasz Kaiser, and Illia Polosukhin. 2017. Attention is all you need. *Advances in neural information processing systems*, 30.

Ivan Vulić, Edoardo Maria Ponti, Robert Litschko, Goran Glavaš, and Anna Korhonen. 2020. Probing pretrained language models for lexical semantics. *arXiv preprint arXiv:2010.05731*.

Xiang Wei, Xingyu Cui, Ning Cheng, Xiaobin Wang, Xin Zhang, Shen Huang, Pengjun Xie, Jinan Xu, Yufeng Chen, Meishan Zhang, et al. 2023. Zero-shot information extraction via chatting with chatgpt. *arXiv preprint arXiv:2302.10205*.

Yue Yang, Artemis Panagopoulou, Qing Lyu, Li Zhang, Mark Yatskar, and Chris Callison-Burch. 2021. Visual goal-step inference using wikihow. *arXiv preprint arXiv:2104.05845*.

Zi Yang and Eric Nyberg. 2015. Leveraging procedural knowledge for task-oriented search. In *Proceedings of the 38th International ACM SIGIR Conference on Research and Development in Information Retrieval*, pages 513–522.

Pengfei Yu, Zixuan Zhang, Clare Voss, Jonathan May, and Heng Ji. 2022. Building an event extractor with only a few examples. In *Proceedings of the Third Workshop on Deep Learning for Low-Resource Natural Language Processing*, pages 102–109.

Li Zhang. 2022. Reasoning about procedures with natural language processing: A tutorial. *arXiv preprint arXiv:2205.07455*.

Li Zhang, Qing Lyu, and Chris Callison-Burch. 2020a. Intent detection with wikihow. *arXiv preprint arXiv:2009.05781*.

Li Zhang, Qing Lyu, and Chris Callison-Burch. 2020b. Reasoning about goals, steps, and temporal ordering with wikihow. *arXiv preprint arXiv:2009.07690*.

Shuyan Zhou, Li Zhang, Yue Yang, Qing Lyu, Pengcheng Yin, Chris Callison-Burch, and Graham Neubig. 2022. Show me more details: Discovering hierarchies of procedures from semi-structured web data. *arXiv preprint arXiv:2203.07264*.

Yilun Zhou, Julie A Shah, and Steven Schockaert. 2019. Learning household task knowledge from wikihow descriptions. *arXiv preprint arXiv:1909.06414*.

9 Appendix

9.1 Data Preprocessing and Cleaning

1. We remove the goals with file-ID *385799* and *5323060*, as they contain non-English words.

2. Two data points share the same file-ID *411540*, each refers to the goal *How to keep healthy family relationships* and *How to keep relationships healthy within your family*. The first data point is automatically removed when building a mapping from file-IDs to goals.

3. We remove the step headlines with step-IDs *1926747_3_0*, *2191502_0_0* and *985548_2_0*, since they contain only a dot (.) and cannot be parsed by the dependency parser.

9.2 Full Table of the Results

As a supplement to Table 3 and Table 5, Table 6 shows the results of all experiment groups.

Experiments	Local Event weak	Local Event strict	Contextualised Event weak	Contextualised Event strict
[1] SENTENCE$_{first4}$	81.6±0.1	20.1±0.1	81.2±0	19.7±0.2
[2] EVENT$_{rel,first4}$	68.9±0.3	9.9±0.3	71.6±0.4	12.2±0.3
[3] EVENT$_{mult,first4}$	75.8±0.4	15.3±0.5	77.0±0.1	15.9±0.2
[4] SENTENCE+EVENT$_{rel,first4}$	79.9±0.3	17.9±0.7	80.4±0.1	18.6±0.1
[5] SENTENCE+EVENT$_{mult,first4}$	80.9±0.8	19.3±1.3	81.0±0.1	19.6±0.3
[6] SENTENCE$_{middle4}$	82.7±0.4	22.3±0.5	82.7±1.1	22.2±1.7
[7] EVENT$_{rel,middle4}$	70.3±0.2	11.1±0.2	74.9±0	14.9±0.1
[8] EVENT$_{mult,middle4}$	76.9±0.6	16.9±0.9	79.9±0	19.1±0.4
[9] SENTENCE+EVENT$_{rel,middle4}$	81.8±0.3	21.2±0.3	81.8±1.1	20.4±1.8
[10] SENTENCE+EVENT$_{mult,middle4}$	82.4±0.1	22.1±0.3	82.8±0.9	22.4±1.5
[11] SENTENCE$_{last4}$	82.1±0.4	22.3±0.7	84.6±0.1	26.0±0.2
[12] EVENT$_{rel,last4}$	69.1±0.3	11.5±0.4	75.9±0	16.7±0.1
[13] EVENT$_{mult,last4}$	77.3±0.4	18.8±0.4	80.8±0	21.2±0.2
[14] SENTENCE+EVENT$_{rel,last4}$	80.3±0.6	20.2±1.0	84.1±0.4	25.2±1.1
[15] SENTENCE+EVENT$_{mult,last4}$	81.1±0.7	21.5±0.8	**84.7±0**	**26.4±0.2**
[16] EVENT$_{mult,last4,+1layer}$	76.6±0.3	17.9±0.2	80.5±0	20.7±0
Triplet Net (BERT) (Yang et al., 2021)†	72.8	-	72.8	-
Human (Yang et al., 2021)	84.5	-	84.5	-

Table 6: Accuracy (%) of experiments using different event representations encoded by different layers of the CLIP text encoder (full table).

Data Selection for Fine-tuning Large Language Models Using Transferred Shapley Values

Stephanie Schoch Ritwick Mishra Yangfeng Ji
Department of Computer Science
University of Virginia
Charlottesville, VA 22904
{sns2gr,mbc7bu,yangfeng}@virginia.edu

Abstract

Although Shapley values have been shown to be highly effective for identifying harmful training instances, dataset size and model complexity constraints limit the ability to apply Shapley-based data valuation to fine-tuning large pre-trained language models. To address this, we propose TS-DSHAPLEY, an algorithm that reduces computational cost of Shapley-based data valuation through: 1) an efficient sampling-based method that aggregates Shapley values computed from subsets for valuation of the entire training set, and 2) a value transfer method that leverages value information extracted from a simple classifier trained using representations from the target language model. Our experiments applying TS-DSHAPLEY to select data for fine-tuning BERT-based language models on benchmark natural language understanding (NLU) datasets show that TS-DSHAPLEY outperforms existing data selection methods. Further, TS-DSHAPLEY can filter fine-tuning data to increase language model performance compared to training with the full fine-tuning dataset.

1 Introduction

Large language models (LMs) have achieved state-of-the-art performance on many natural language processing (NLP) tasks (Radford et al., 2019; Brown et al., 2020; Sanh et al., 2022). To adapt these models to new datasets and tasks, the standard approach is to fine-tune a pre-trained LM on a targeted downstream task. This allows the pre-trained general linguistic knowledge to be leveraged while fine-tuning to learn the task-specific information. However, during fine-tuning, pre-trained LMs are prone to significant performance degradation in the presence of noisy data (Srivastava et al., 2020). This effect may be further amplified when noisy or otherwise harmful instances are highly influential to the model parameters (Koh and Liang, 2017). As a result, it is important to identify harmful in-

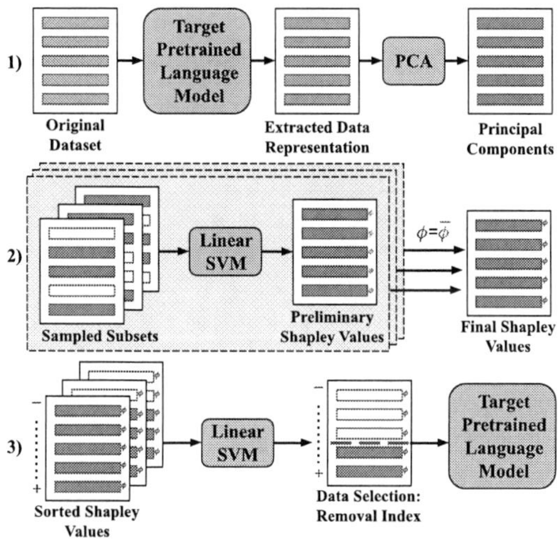

Figure 1: An overview of TS-DSHAPLEY: 1) Process the data using the target LM; 2) Compute *sampling* chains using a subset of the training set and aggregate the resulting Shapley values; and 3) *Transfer* the estimated data value information for use with the target LM by estimating the optimal low value data removal index.

stances in the fine-tuning data that may obfuscate the task information and degrade performance.

To automatically identify harmful data, prior works have used training dynamics (Swayamdipta et al., 2020) and estimation of marginal contributions via leave-one-out retraining (Cook, 1977) or influence functions (Koh and Liang, 2017). Shapley values, which satisfy certain desirable fairness guarantees, have also recently been adopted from cooperative game theory to measure datum contributions, where a data point's Shapley value is the average marginal contribution to every possible data subset (Ghorbani and Zou, 2019).

In practice, Shapley-based data values are approximated using various techniques (Ghorbani and Zou, 2019; Jia et al., 2019b, 2021; Kwon and Zou, 2022; Schoch et al., 2022), as exact Shapley value computation over a dataset would require *exhaustively retraining the model* for every datum on

Proceedings of the 61st Annual Meeting of the Association for Computational Linguistics - Student Research Workshop, pages 266–275
July 10-12, 2023 ©2023 Association for Computational Linguistics

every possible subset (i.e. *exponential complexity with respect to the number of data points*). However, many of the existing approximation methods still exhibit a computational bottleneck when considering datasets and models at scale (e.g. datasets larger than 5K instances). This, in turn, directly limits the application of Shapley-based data valuation to state-of-the-art LMs and many NLP datasets.

To address the challenges posed by 1) the *model constraint* (the model retraining requirement) and 2) the *dataset constraint* (the time-complexity/dataset size relation), we propose Transferred Sampling Data Shapley (TS-DSHAPLEY), an algorithm that utilizes two novel components that directly address each constraint. Specifically, to address the model constraint, we propose to compute Shapley-based data values using a simple, linear model that is trained on the learned representation from the target LM. Additionally, to address the dataset constraint, we propose a sampling-based method that computes Shapley values on data subsets and aggregates them for valuation of the entire training set.

Our contributions are as follows: 1) we propose a sampling-based data Shapley computation method and demonstrate its efficacy empirically using as little as 2% of the original training data; 2) we propose the use of a simple linear classifier with a target model's pre-trained representation and demonstrate empirically the performance gains achieved over alternate pre-trained embeddings; and 3) we show the efficacy of Shapley-based data valuation and selection methods on benchmark NLU tasks using fine-tuned large LMs.[1]

2 Related Work

While Shapley values are often applied in a post hoc manner following model training (Ghorbani and Zou, 2019; Kwon and Zou, 2022; Jia et al., 2019a,b, 2021; Schoch et al., 2022), the demonstrated efficacy makes it a natural extension to apply such methods for data selection *prior to* training. To this end, Shapley values have been used for evaluating data for transfer learning (Parvez and Chang, 2021) and in active learning (Ghorbani et al., 2021).

Further, although Shapley-based data values have primarily been considered model-specific, in practice, a subset of training instances that may harm performance may be mislabeled (Koh and Liang, 2017; Swayamdipta et al., 2020; Ghorbani and Zou, 2019) or exhibit spelling mistakes or grammatical errors (Sun et al., 2020; Srivastava et al., 2020), which should be intrinsic to the dataset. Prior works have demonstrated the transferability of Shapley-based data values across various classifier architectures (Schoch et al., 2022) and have demonstrated the efficacy of surrogate KNN classifiers using pre-trained embeddings (Jia et al., 2021). Notably, our work differs in that we utilize the pre-trained embeddings extracted from the target LM and avoid the k-nearest neighbor assumption that training data far from a test datum do not contribute to its prediction (Jia et al., 2019a).

3 Method

Let $D = \{(x_i, y_i)\}_{i=1}^n$ denote a training set containing n training instances. For each training instance i, the Shapley value ϕ_i is defined as the average marginal contribution of i to every possible subset $S \subseteq D$ that contains this instance (Ghorbani and Zou, 2019): $\phi_i = \sum_{S \subseteq D; i \in S} \frac{1}{\binom{n-1}{|S \setminus \{i\}|}} \{v_{\mathcal{A}}(S) - v_{\mathcal{A}}(S \setminus \{i\})\}$ where $v_{\mathcal{A}}(S)$ is a value function, typically defined as the development accuracy of model $\mathcal{A}$ trained on S. The challenge of calculating ϕ_i is two-fold: the exponential complexity of all possible subsets $S \subseteq D$ and the computational cost of training $\mathcal{A}$ on each S and $S \setminus \{i\}$. While Shapley-based data values are approximated in practice, most existing approximation methods are not efficient enough for large scale learning problems.

3.1 TS-DSHAPLEY

Let $\mathcal{A}_{tgt}$ be the target classifier (i.e. large LM) that we want to fine-tune on a subset of D. To reduce computational cost, we propose to (1) use a linear classifier $\mathcal{A}_{src}$ as the proxy of $\mathcal{A}_{tgt}$ for data valuation; (2) use multi-chain Monte Carlo sampling to compute Shapley values on different subsets of D. For faithful data valuation, we further propose to train $\mathcal{A}_{src}$ on the data representations extracted from $\mathcal{A}_{tgt}$.

Representation Extraction. We extract the representations from the penultimate layer of the pre-trained LM $\mathcal{A}_{tgt}$ as the inputs for training $\mathcal{A}_{src}$. Note that training $\mathcal{A}_{src}$ in this way is equivalent to fixing the LM and only fine-tuning the last classification layer. To further remove the redundancy in

[1] Code is available at `https://github.com/stephanieschoch/ts-dshapley`

the representations and reduce computational cost, we follow prior work by performing PCA on the collection of representations and selecting the first 32 principal components (Ghorbani and Zou, 2019; Kwon and Zou, 2022; Schoch et al., 2022).

Sampling Data Shapley. Instead of directly estimating Shapley-based data values via Monte Carlo sampling on the whole training set, our approach performs Monte Carlo sampling on subsets of the data, which we refer to as *sampling chains*. Within a single sampling chain c, we sample a subset of training instances S_t, estimate their contributions, and repeat T times. The contribution of each instance in S_t is calculated by removing one instance at a time in a random order. For example, the contribution of the first randomly removed instance i is $c_{S_t}(i) = v_{\mathcal{A}_{src}}(S_t) - v_{\mathcal{A}_{src}}(S_t \backslash \{i\})$, the contribution of the second randomly removed instance k is $c_{S_t}(k) = v_{\mathcal{A}_{src}}(S_t \backslash \{i\}) - v_{\mathcal{A}_{src}}(S_t \backslash \{i, k\})$, and so on. On the other hand, if an instance i is not in S_t, $c_{S_t}(i) = 0$.

After T times, the Shapley value of instance i is approximated as $\phi_i \approx \frac{1}{T} \sum_{S_t} c_{S_t}(i)$. To balance the computational efficiency and approximation, we empirically define a range of the size $|S_t| \in [\frac{s}{2}, s]$, with subset size s as the sampling upper bound.

Computation can be further sped up with multiple Monte Carlo sampling chains $S_t^{(c)}, c \in \{1, \ldots, J\}$. The corresponding value approximation is defined as $\phi_i = \frac{1}{J} \sum_c \frac{1}{T} \sum_{S_t^{(c)}} c_{S_t^{(c)}}(i)$. As each chain can be computed independently, the efficiency can be boosted with parallel computing. This novel idea of multi-chain sampling serves as the core of TS-DSHAPLEY and significantly speeds up computation, in practice working with a simple model $\mathcal{A}_{src}$.

Data Selection with TS-DSHAPLEY Values. To identify harmful data points, we use the data removal strategy of Ghorbani and Zou (2019) on $\mathcal{A}_{src}$ and transfer the selection outcome to the target model $\mathcal{A}_{tgt}$. Specifically, we gradually remove training instances from the lowest estimated contribution value to the highest estimated contribution value. Following each removal, we retrain A_{src} and evaluate predictive performance on the held-out development data. As a result, this removal procedure will identify a optimal subset S_{opt} that gives the best predictive performance on A_{src}. With the assumption of data value transferability (Schoch et al., 2022), we expect that $\mathcal{A}_{tgt}$ trained on S_{opt} will give no worse, and likely better performance, than $\mathcal{A}_{tgt}$ trained on D. While this data removal strategy is proposed in prior work (Ghorbani and Zou, 2019), the data selection use case is novel in NLP.

4 Experiments

4.1 Experiment Setup

Pre-trained Large Language Models. We utilize two transformer-based large LMs for which traditional Shapley-based data value computation would be intractable: RoBERTa-base (Liu et al., 2019, 125M parameters) and DistilBERT (Sanh et al., 2019, 66M parameters).

Datasets. We select one GLUE benchmark (Wang et al., 2019) dataset from each task category: SST-2 (Socher et al., 2013), QQP (Iyer et al., 2017), and RTE (Dagan et al., 2006), representing Single-Sentence Tasks, Similarity and Paraphrase Tasks, and Inference Tasks, respectively. Additional dataset details are reported in Appendix A. Notably, we select datasets of varied sizes to reflect diverse sampling subset to training set size ratios.

Data Selection Baselines. We compare against performance when training on the full data subset as well as three selection baselines: leave-one-out (LOO) (Cook, 1977), KNN-shapley (KNN) (Jia et al., 2019a, 2021), and random sampling. For LOO, we use the same classifier architecture as with TS-DSHAPLEY to compute value estimates. For both LOO and KNN, we reduce the dataset using the data removal procedure defined in section 3. Finally, for random sampling, we remove a random sample of data points equal to the number of points removed via TS-DSHAPLEY.

4.2 Data Selection Experiment

To test the efficacy of using TS-DSHAPLEY to select data for fine-tuning large LMs, we compute data values using each method and perform the data removal procedure described in section 3. Specifically, we remove the lowest value data points preceding the data removal step that achieved the highest development accuracy using A_{src}. For TS-DSHAPLEY, we vary the subset size and number of chains based on dataset size, using subset size $= 6.7k(10\%), 7.28k(2\%), 374(15\%)$ and number of chains $= 25, 10, 25$ for SST-2, QQP, and RTE,

Method Category	Method	RoBERTa			DistilBERT		
		SST-2	QQP	RTE	SST-2	QQP	RTE
Full Training Set	Liu et al. (2019)	0.948	0.919	0.787	–	–	–
	Sanh et al. (2019)	–	–	–	0.913	0.885	0.599
	Full Dataset	0.950	0.917	0.788	0.908	0.905	0.618
Data Selection Baselines	Leave-One-Out	0.947	–	0.784	0.912	–	0.614
	KNN Shapley	0.946	0.916	0.781	0.911	0.905	0.622
	Random	0.947	0.917	0.684	0.911	0.905	0.589
Our Method	TS-DSHAPLEY	**0.953**	**0.919**	**0.801**	**0.915**	**0.907**	**0.652**

Table 1: Predictive accuracy when selecting data using each valuation method. Results reflect the mean of five trials. We do not report LOO as a baseline for QQP due to computational intractability.

respectively. Additional training and hyperparameter details, including details of a limited hyperparameter sweep, can be found in Appendix A.

Results Results are shown in Table 1. TS-DSHAPLEY consistently outperforms baseline selection methods as well as performance using the full fine-tuning dataset. Notably, data selection using TS-DSHAPLEY resulted in performance improvements of up to 1.3% and 3.4% for RoBERTa and DistilBERT, respectively, over the predictive performance when training using the full fine-tuning dataset. These results indicate TS-DSHAPLEY successfully identifies data points that harm model performance. As an additional analysis, for the RTE dataset we show the location of harmful points identified by TS-DSHAPLEY on a data map (Swayamdipta et al., 2020) in Appendix B.

4.3 Sampling Hyperparameter Analysis

TS-DSHAPLEY exhibited good performance for data selection across various subset sizes and numbers of chains. For example, on QQP TS-DSHAPLEY outperformed the full dataset and baseline methods when using a subset of just 2% of the training set. To better understand the impact of different parameter values, we utilize a parameter value grid on the RTE dataset and re-compute TS-DSHAPLEY. Specifically, using the best hyperparameters from subsection 4.2 (see Appendix A), we evaluate performance of RoBERTa and DistilBERT using a parameter sweep of subset size as a percentage of the total training set size, subset size $\in \{1, 2, 5, 10, 15\}\%$, and number of chains $\in \{2, 5, 10, 15\}$ and report the Pearson's correlation between each parameter and performance.

Results. All correlations are reported in Appendix B and summarized here. When subset size $> 2\%$, both models demonstrate a high positive correlation between number of chains and performance. For example, when using 15% of the training data, RoBERTa on RTE had a correlation of 0.94. Across the different number of chains, however, there was no consistent pattern of correlation between subset size and performance. This indicates that increasing number of chains (which can be computed in-parallel) may be of more benefit compared to increasing sampling subset size.

Model	Embeddings	SST-2	QQP	RTE
RoBERTa	RoBERTa	**0.953**	**0.919**	**0.801**
	DistilBERT	0.951	0.906	0.762
	GloVe	0.948	0.908	0.767
DistilBERT	DistilBERT	**0.915**	**0.907**	**0.652**
	RoBERTa	0.906	0.903	0.623
	GloVe	0.909	0.903	0.632

Table 2: Predictive accuracy using TS-DSHAPLEY with different word embeddings.

4.4 Effect of Different Embeddings

To test the efficacy of computing TS-DSHAPLEY using the extracted representations from the target LM, we perform an experiment where we use the removal indices computed with 1) the representation from a different language model (e.g. removing indices for fine-tuning RoBERTa using the optimal removal index identified using DistilBERT data representations), and 2) GloVe pre-trained word embeddings (Pennington et al., 2014), as a third-party representation repository.

Results. As shown in Table 2, while alternate embeddings can still lead to improvements over the full data, using the representation from the target LM is beneficial and consistently outperforms other embeddings. The results suggest that low value data is likely a combination of (i) inherently noisy data (e.g. mislabeled instances) and (ii) instances that are harmful to specific models due to different model architectures and pre-training strategies.

5 Conclusion

In this work, we propose TS-DSHAPLEY to address the model and dataset constraints that currently contribute to a computational bottleneck when computing Shapley-based data value estimates.

Limitations

While we demonstrate the efficacy of TS-DSHAPLEY empirically, the current work is limited in terms of theoretical analysis. For example, while we have good empirical performance with a linear SVM, additional analysis could determine if there are optimal ways to select an alternative simple model architecture for the source classifier depending on the target classifier or dataset. Additionally, while we found a strong correlation between number of sampling chains and performance when the subset size was $> 2\%$ of the training data size, the lower subset size threshold to observe this correlation may be dataset dependent, which additional analysis could address.

References

Tom Brown, Benjamin Mann, Nick Ryder, Melanie Subbiah, Jared D Kaplan, Prafulla Dhariwal, Arvind Neelakantan, Pranav Shyam, Girish Sastry, Amanda Askell, et al. 2020. Language models are few-shot learners. *Advances in neural information processing systems*, 33:1877–1901.

R Dennis Cook. 1977. Detection of influential observation in linear regression. *Technometrics*, 19(1):15–18.

Ido Dagan, Oren Glickman, and Bernardo Magnini. 2006. The PASCAL recognising textual entailment challenge. In *Machine learning challenges. evaluating predictive uncertainty, visual object classification, and recognising tectual entailment*, pages 177–190. Springer.

Amirata Ghorbani and James Zou. 2019. Data shapley: Equitable valuation of data for machine learning. In *International Conference on Machine Learning*, pages 2242–2251. PMLR.

Amirata Ghorbani, James Zou, and Andre Esteva. 2021. Data shapley valuation for efficient batch active learning. *arXiv preprint arXiv:2104.08312*.

Shankar Iyer, Nikhil Dandekar, and Kornel Csernai. 2017. First quora dataset release: Question pairs.

Ruoxi Jia, David Dao, Boxin Wang, Frances Ann Hubis, Nezihe Merve Gurel, Bo Li, Ce Zhang, Costas Spanos, and Dawn Song. 2019a. Efficient task-specific data valuation for nearest neighbor algorithms. *Proceedings of the VLDB Endowment*, 12(11):1610–1623.

Ruoxi Jia, David Dao, Boxin Wang, Frances Ann Hubis, Nick Hynes, Nezihe Merve Gürel, Bo Li, Ce Zhang, Dawn Song, and Costas J Spanos. 2019b. Towards efficient data valuation based on the shapley value. In *The 22nd International Conference on Artificial Intelligence and Statistics*, pages 1167–1176. PMLR.

Ruoxi Jia, Fan Wu, Xuehui Sun, Jiacen Xu, David Dao, Bhavya Kailkhura, Ce Zhang, Bo Li, and Dawn Song. 2021. Scalability vs. utility: Do we have to sacrifice one for the other in data importance quantification? In *Proceedings of the IEEE/CVF Conference on Computer Vision and Pattern Recognition*, pages 8239–8247.

Pang Wei Koh and Percy Liang. 2017. Understanding black-box predictions via influence functions. In *International conference on machine learning*, pages 1885–1894. PMLR.

Yongchan Kwon and James Zou. 2022. Beta shapley: a unified and noise-reduced data valuation framework for machine learning. *Proceedings of the 25th International Conference on Artificial Intelligence and Statistics (AISTATS) 2022.*

Yinhan Liu, Myle Ott, Naman Goyal, Jingfei Du, Mandar Joshi, Danqi Chen, Omer Levy, Mike Lewis, Luke Zettlemoyer, and Veselin Stoyanov. 2019. Roberta: A robustly optimized bert pretraining approach. *arXiv preprint arXiv:1907.11692*.

Md Rizwan Parvez and Kai-Wei Chang. 2021. Evaluating the values of sources in transfer learning. In *Proceedings of the 2021 Conference of the North American Chapter of the Association for Computational Linguistics: Human Language Technologies*, pages 5084–5116.

Jeffrey Pennington, Richard Socher, and Christopher Manning. 2014. GloVe: Global vectors for word representation. In *Proceedings of the 2014 Conference on Empirical Methods in Natural Language Processing (EMNLP)*, pages 1532–1543, Doha, Qatar. Association for Computational Linguistics.

Alec Radford, Jeffrey Wu, Rewon Child, David Luan, Dario Amodei, Ilya Sutskever, et al. 2019. Language models are unsupervised multitask learners. *OpenAI blog*, 1(8):9.

Victor Sanh, Lysandre Debut, Julien Chaumond, and Thomas Wolf. 2019. Distilbert, a distilled version of bert: smaller, faster, cheaper and lighter. *arXiv preprint arXiv:1910.01108*.

Victor Sanh, Albert Webson, Colin Raffel, Stephen Bach, Lintang Sutawika, Zaid Alyafeai, Antoine Chaffin, Arnaud Stiegler, Teven Le Scao, Arun Raja, et al. 2022. Multitask prompted training enables zero-shot task generalization. In *The Tenth International Conference on Learning Representations*.

Stephanie Schoch, Haifeng Xu, and Yangfeng Ji. 2022. Cs-shapley: Class-wise shapley values for data valuation in classification. In *Advances in Neural Information Processing Systems*.

Richard Socher, Alex Perelygin, Jean Wu, Jason Chuang, Christopher D Manning, Andrew Y Ng, and Christopher Potts. 2013. Recursive deep models for semantic compositionality over a sentiment treebank. In *Proceedings of the 2013 conference on empirical methods in natural language processing*, pages 1631–1642.

Ankit Srivastava, Piyush Makhija, and Anuj Gupta. 2020. Noisy text data: Achilles' heel of bert. In *Proceedings of the Sixth Workshop on Noisy User-generated Text (W-NUT 2020)*, pages 16–21.

Lichao Sun, Kazuma Hashimoto, Wenpeng Yin, Akari Asai, Jia Li, Philip Yu, and Caiming Xiong. 2020. Adv-bert: Bert is not robust on misspellings! generating nature adversarial samples on bert. *arXiv preprint arXiv:2003.04985*.

Swabha Swayamdipta, Roy Schwartz, Nicholas Lourie, Yizhong Wang, Hannaneh Hajishirzi, Noah A Smith, and Yejin Choi. 2020. Dataset cartography: Mapping and diagnosing datasets with training dynamics. In *Proceedings of the 2020 Conference on Empirical Methods in Natural Language Processing (EMNLP)*, pages 9275–9293.

Alex Wang, Amanpreet Singh, Julian Michael, Felix Hill, Omer Levy, and Samuel R. Bowman. 2019. GLUE: A multi-task benchmark and analysis platform for natural language understanding. In the Proceedings of ICLR.

A Additional Experiment Details

In this section, we include additional experiment setup details.

A.1 Datasets

Dataset statistics are provided in Table 3, with further description provided below.

SST-2: Stanford Sentiment Treebank (Socher et al., 2013) is a collection of English movie reviews with human annotations of their sentiment. The model is tasked with predicting a review's sentiment as positive or negative.

QQP: Quora Question Pairs (Iyer et al., 2017) is a collection of English question pairs from the website Quora where the task is to determine if a pair of questions are similar in meaning.

RTE: Recognizing Textual Entailment (Dagan et al., 2006) combines several English datasets from annual textual entailment challenges, where the task is to predict if the *text* entails the *hypothesis* or not.

A.2 Hyperparameters

For each experiment, we consider a limited hyperparameter sweep for each model, selection method, and task, with batch size $\in \{16, 32\}$ and learning rate $\in \{10^{-5}, 3 \times 10^{-5}\}$. The rest of the hyperparameters are kept consistent across experiment conditions. We report the mean development set accuracy from five random initializations for which we fine-tune for 10 epochs and select the model checkpoint with the highest development set accuracy. Results from each hyperparameter sweep are reported in Table 4 and Table 5.

B Additional Results

B.1 Additional Data Selection Analysis

While we compare directly with baseline selection methods that directly measure estimated data contribution, we perform an additional analysis by comparing the indices removed with TS-DSHAPLEY with the mapped training dynamics using data maps (Swayamdipta et al., 2020). Specifically, we first plot the data map for RoBERTa trained on RTE using the same hyperparameters as in subsection 4.2. Then, we plot the same data map showing only the data points that were identified by TS-DSHAPLEY to be harmful, i.e. removed from the fine-tuning training data. These are shown in Figure 2 and Figure 3, respectively.

We observe that a handful of instances in the hard-to-learn region (identified by Swayamdipta et al. (2020) to contain some mislabeled examples) were removed, as well as a small number of instances in the ambiguous region. Interestingly though, we observe that 1) most of the data points in RTE belonged to the easy-to-learn region, and 2) a cluster of easy-to-learn points were removed. Swayamdipta et al. (2020) found that too many easy-to-learn instances could decrease both in-distribution and out-of-distribution performance and noted that determining how to select an optimal balance of easy-to-learn and ambiguous examples, particularly in low data settings, was an open problem. As TS-DSHAPLEY achieved a performance gain over the full dataset performance, these results suggest that TS-DSHAPLEY may be effective to potentially determine an optimal balance and address this problem. We leave further analysis of this to future work.

B.2 Sampling Hyperparameter Analysis.

Pearson's correlation coefficients for the sampling parameter analysis in section 4 are reported in Table 6 and Table 7, where each result represents the mean of five sampling and chain computation trials.

Dataset	GLUE Task Category	Task	Metric	Data Split	
				Train	Dev
SST-2	Single Sentence Tasks	Sentiment	Acc.	67k	1.8k
QQP	Similarity and Paraphrase Tasks	Paraphrase	Acc./F1	364k	40.4k
RTE	Inference Tasks	NLI	Acc.	2.5k	277

Table 3: Statistics for each dataset. We use the train and development data splits as GLUE tasks have held out test set labels.

Model	Method	SST-2		QQP		RTE	
		BS	LR	BS	LR	BS	LR
RoBERTa	Full Dataset	16	10^{-5}	32	3×10^{-5}	16	3×10^{-5}
	Leave-One-Out	32	10^{-5}	–	–	16	3×10^{-5}
	KNN Shapley	16	10^{-5}	32	3×10^{-5}	16	3×10^{-5}
	Random	32	3×10^{-5}	32	3×10^{-5}	16	3×10^{-5}
	TS-DSHAPLEY	32	10^{-5}	32	3×10^{-5}	16	3×10^{-5}
DistilBERT	Full Dataset	16	10^{-5}	32	3×10^{-5}	32	3×10^{-5}
	Leave-One-Out	32	10^{-5}	–	–	16	10^{-5}
	KNN Shapley	16	10^{-5}	32	3×10^{-5}	16	10^{-5}
	Random	32	3×10^{-5}	16	3×10^{-5}	16	3×10^{-5}
	TS-DSHAPLEY	16	3×10^{-5}	16	10^{-5}	16	3×10^{-5}

Table 4: Batch size (BS) and learning rate (LR) for the data selection experiment based on the hyperparameter sweep defined in section 4.

Model	Embeddings	SST-2		QQP		RTE	
		BS	LR	BS	LR	BS	LR
RoBERTa	RoBERTa	32	10^{-5}	32	3×10^{-5}	16	3×10^{-5}
	DistilBERT	16	10^{-5}	32	10^{-5}	16	3×10^{-5}
	GloVe	16	3×10^{-5}	32	3×10^{-5}	32	3×10^{-5}
DistilBERT	DistilBERT	16	10^{-5}	16	10^{-5}	16	3×10^{-5}
	RoBERTa	32	10^{-5}	32	10^{-5}	32	10^{-5}
	GloVe	32	10^{-5}	32	3×10^{-5}	32	3×10^{-5}

Table 5: Batch size (BS) and learning rate (LR) for the embeddings switch experiment based on the hyperparameter sweep defined in section 4.

Model	Subset Size (%, #)				
	1 (25)	2 (50)	5 (125)	10 (249)	15 (374)
RoBERTa	0.119	0.013	0.892	0.929	0.942
DistilBERT	0.240	0.104	0.613	0.776	0.714

Table 6: Correlations between number of chains and performance for each subset size on the RTE dataset.

Model	Number of Sampling Chains					
	2	5	10	15	20	25
RoBERTa	-0.463	0.127	-0.474	0.013	0.472	0.763
DistilBERT	0.027	-0.034	0.530	0.447	0.737	0.692

Table 7: Correlations between subset size and performance for each number of sampling chains on the RTE dataset.

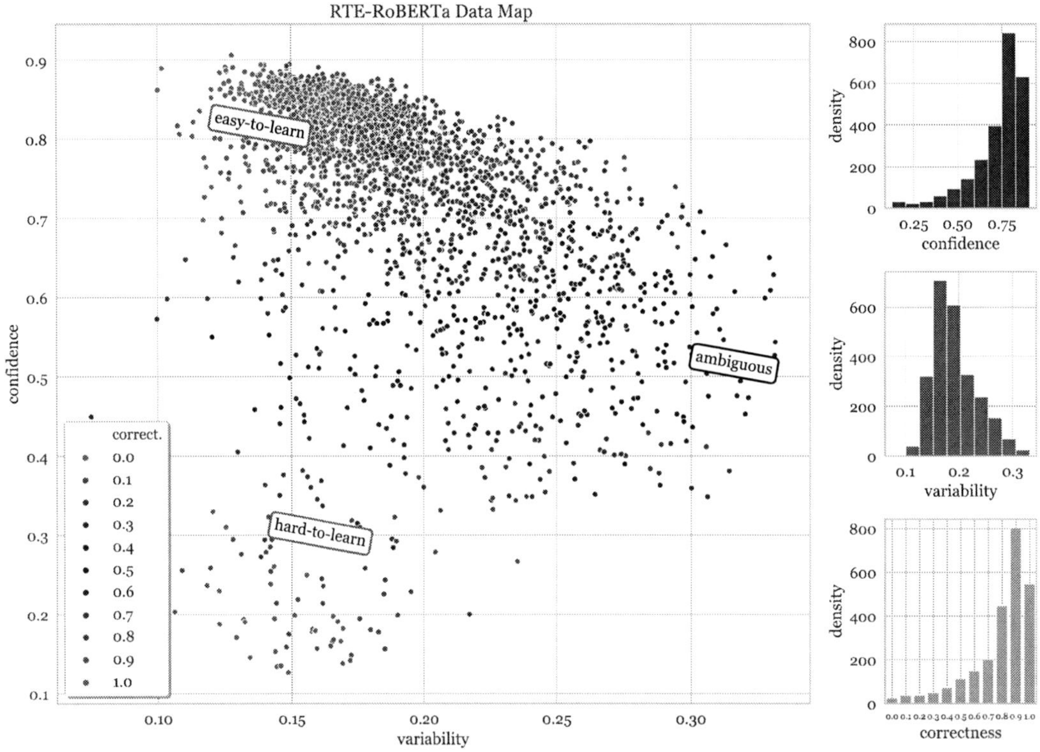

Figure 2: Data map for RoBERTa trained on the RTE dataset.

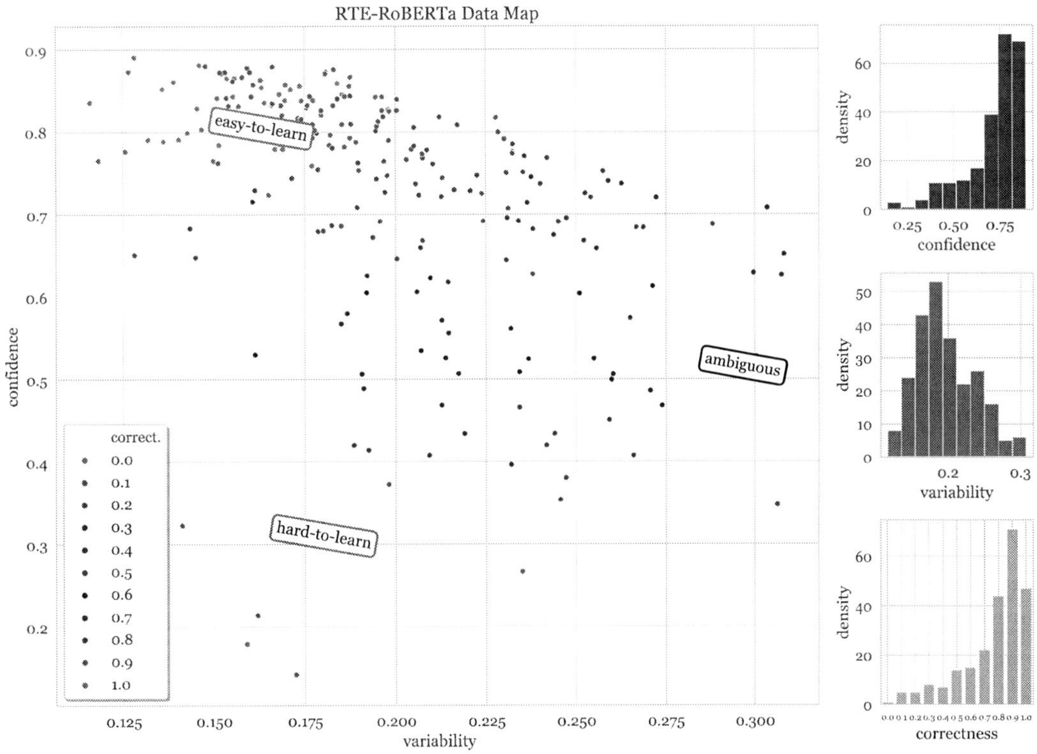

Figure 3: Data map showing location of training instances that were removed by TS-DSHAPLEY for RoBERTa on RTE.

Distractor Generation for Fill-in-the-Blank Exercises by Question Type

Nana Yoshimi[1], **Tomoyuki Kajiwara**[1], **Satoru Uchida**[2], **Yuki Arase**[3], **Takashi Ninomiya**[1]
[1]Ehime University, [2]Kyushu University, [3]Osaka University
{yoshimi@ai., kajiwara@, ninomiya@}cs.ehime-u.ac.jp
uchida@flc.kyushu-u.ac.jp, arase@ist.osaka-u.ac.jp

Abstract

This study addresses the automatic generation of distractors for English fill-in-the-blank exercises in the entrance examinations for Japanese universities. While previous studies applied the same method to all questions, actual entrance examinations have multiple question types that reflect the purpose of the questions. Therefore, we define three types of questions (grammar, function word, and context) and propose a method to generate distractors according to the characteristics of each question type. Experimental results on 500 actual questions show the effectiveness of the proposed method for both automatic and manual evaluation.

1 Introduction

Fill-in-the-blank questions, also known as cloze tests (Taylor, 1953), are one way to assess learners' English proficiency and are widely used in examinations such as TOEIC[1] and in school education. As shown in Figure 1, the question format generally consists of a four-choice option with one correct answer and three distractors. These require substantial costs because they are manually created by question writers with extensive language teaching experience. This study automatically generates distractors to reduce workload.

Most of the previous studies on the automatic generation of cloze tests (Mitkov and Ha, 2003; Sumita et al., 2005; Zesch and Melamud, 2014; Jiang and Lee, 2017; Susanti et al., 2018; Panda et al., 2022) have generated words that are semantically similar to the correct words as distractors. Other methods have been proposed, such as those based on co-occurrence with words in the carrier sentence (Liu et al., 2005; Hill and Simha, 2016), considering the whole context (Yeung et al., 2019), and considering the learner's error tendencies (Sakaguchi et al., 2013). However, these previous studies apply the same method to all questions, which leads to bias in the characteristics of the generated distractors. Actual entrance examinations have multiple question types reflecting the purpose of the questions, such as grammatical knowledge and idiomatic expressions. Existing methods have difficulty in flexibly changing the characteristics of distractors for each question type.

Jeff didn't accept the job offer because of the ____ salary.
(a) low (b) weak (c) cheap (d) inexpensive

Figure 1: Example of English fill-in-the-blank question. (National Center Test for University Admissions, 2018)[2]

In this study, we first manually classify English fill-in-the-blank questions in the entrance examinations for Japanese universities[2] by an expert. Next, we propose a method for automatic distractor generation according to the characteristics of each question type. Experimental results on 500 actual questions show the effectiveness of the proposed method for both automatic and manual evaluation.

2 Related Work

Previous studies have generated distractors in the following three steps: (1) candidate generation, (2) reranking, and (3) filtering.

Jiang and Lee (2017) utilized cosine similarity with word embeddings (Mikolov et al., 2013) to identify candidate words that are semantically similar to the correct word. These candidate words were ranked by similarity and filtered by word 3-gram. That is, if a 3-gram containing a candidate word appears in Wikipedia, that candidate is excluded. It filters out expressions that are actually used in a large-scale corpus to exclude appropriate examples from the distractor candidates.

Yeung et al. (2019) reranked the candidates generated from word embeddings by the mask-filling

[1]https://www.ets.org/toeic.html

[2]https://jcshop.jp/SHOP/18149/list.html

Proceedings of the 61st Annual Meeting of the Association for Computational Linguistics - Student Research Workshop, pages 276–281
July 10-12, 2023 ©2023 Association for Computational Linguistics

Carrier sentence	Correct	Distractors			Type
I hear that one of his three sisters __ four movies a week.	sees	seeing	seen	see	grammar
My mother was surprised __ the news that I passed the test.	at	to	for	in	function word
When you exercise, you should wear __ and loose clothing.	comfortable	delicate	serious	flat	context

Table 1: Examples of question types. From top to bottom, the sources[2] are (Toyo University, 2018), (Meijo University, 2017), (Nakamura Gakuen University, 2018).

probability with BERT (Devlin et al., 2019). They also utilize BERT for filtering, eliminating candidates with too high and too low probabilities.

Panda et al. (2022) proposed candidate generation based on round-trip machine translation. That is, the carrier sentence was first translated into a pivot language and back-translated into English. Then, word alignment was used to obtain a candidate for the correct word and its corresponding word. These candidates were reranked using word embeddings and filtered by WordNet (Miller, 1995). Specifically, synonyms of the correct word in WordNet and words with a different part of speech from the correct word were excluded from the candidates.

These existing methods have been evaluated in different ways on different datasets, making it difficult to compare their performance. We have comprehensively evaluated them and propose further improvements on top of their combinations.

3 Definition of Question Types

An experienced English teacher specializing in English education has categorized the question types for English fill-in-the-blank questions. The analysis covers 500 randomly selected questions from the entrance examinations for Japanese universities in the five-year period from 2017 to 2021. As shown in Table 1, the following three question types were defined:

- **Grammar**: Questions that mainly use the conjugated form of the same word as choices.
- **Function word**: Questions that are choices from a prescribed list of function words.
- **Context**: Questions with choices determined by context or idiomatic expressions.

Table 2 shows the number of occurrences for each question type. Approximately half of the questions were on context, 40% were on function word, and 10% were on grammar. In the next section, we propose how to generate distractors according to the characteristics of each question type.

Question type	Number of questions
Grammar	66 (13.2%)
Function word	195 (39.0%)
Context	239 (47.8%)

Table 2: Statistics of question types.

4 Generating Distractors

Following previous studies (Jiang and Lee, 2017; Yeung et al., 2019; Panda et al., 2022), we also generate distractors through three steps. For candidate generation and reranking, we selected combinations of the existing methods described in Section 2 that maximize performance on the validation dataset[3] for each question type. For filtering, we propose methods according to the characteristics of each question type, which are described below.

4.1 Filtering for Questions on Grammar

For questions on grammar, the conjugated forms of the correct word should be obtained as candidates. Therefore, we apply POS filtering. That is, we exclude candidates that have the same part of speech or the same conjugation as the correct word.

Furthermore, to avoid unreliable distractors that could be the correct answer, we exclude candidates with a high mask-filling probability by BERT (Devlin et al., 2019). Unlike Yeung et al. (2019), called BERT (static), which used two fixed thresholds to select the top θ_H to θ_L, our filter, called BERT (dynamic), dynamically changes the thresholds. Specifically, we exclude candidates that have a higher probability than the correct word. The example of the first sentence in Table 1 shows that "thinks" is eliminated as a candidate for the same

[3]For the validation dataset, 500 questions were randomly selected in addition to the evaluation dataset annotated in Section 3. These questions were automatically annotated with question types by BERT (Devlin et al., 2019). The accuracy of BERT was 84.8% in the 10-fold cross-validation.

Type	Method	Candidate	Reranking	Filtering	$k=3$	$k=5$	$k=10$	$k=20$
Grammar	Jiang-2017	fastText	fastText	Word 3-gram	24.7	21.6	**17.7**	**11.2**
	Yeung-2019	fastText	BERT	BERT (static)	1.5	1.9	3.0	3.4
	Panda-2022	Round-trip	fastText	WordNet	8.6	8.3	5.6	3.6
	Ours	fastText	fastText	POS+BERT (dynamic)	**27.8**	**25.0**	17.0	10.4
Function word	Jiang-2017	fastText	fastText	Word 3-gram	10.3	12.1	11.8	9.3
	Yeung-2019	fastText	BERT	BERT (static)	6.3	7.1	7.3	5.7
	Panda-2022	Round-trip	fastText	WordNet	15.9	16.7	13.1	7.8
	Ours	Round-trip	BERT	List of function words	**19.1**	**22.2**	**21.1**	**13.2**
Context	Jiang-2017	fastText	fastText	Word 3-gram	2.2	2.9	3.7	3.2
	Yeung-2019	fastText	BERT	BERT (static)	1.8	2.0	2.3	2.7
	Panda-2022	Round-trip	fastText	WordNet	**4.2**	5.1	4.6	3.2
	Ours	Round-trip	fastText	BERT (dynamic)	3.8	**5.3**	**5.8**	**4.4**

Table 3: Results of automatic evaluation of generated distractors by F1-score.

part of speech, and "watches" is eliminated as a high probability candidate.

4.2 Filtering for Questions on Function Word

For questions on function words, only function words such as prepositions and conjunctions are basically used as choices. Therefore, we utilize the list of function words[4] for entrance examinations for Japanese universities to exclude candidates not included in this list. The example of the second sentence in Table 1 shows that "time" and "taken" are eliminated.

4.3 Filtering for Questions on Context

Since the questions on context are designed to test knowledge of collocations or idioms, candidates should be obtained for words that often co-occur with surrounding words in the carrier sentence. However, as with questions on grammar, to avoid unreliable distractors, candidates with a high mask-filling probability by BERT are excluded. The example of the third sentence in Table 1 shows that "comfy" and "cosy" are eliminated.

5 Experiments

We evaluate the method of distractor generation on the 500 questions constructed in Section 3.

5.1 Setting

Implementation Details For candidate generation, we implemented methods based on word embeddings (Jiang and Lee, 2017) and round-trip machine translation (Panda et al., 2022). We utilized fastText (Bojanowski et al., 2017) as word embeddings and Transformer (Vaswani et al., 2017), trained on English-German language pairs[5] (Ng et al., 2019; Ott et al., 2019) according to the previous study (Panda et al., 2022), as machine translators. For word alignment, we used Hungarian matching (Kuhn, 1955) based on word embeddings (Song and Roth, 2015).

For reranking, we implemented methods based on word embeddings (Jiang and Lee, 2017) and BERT (Yeung et al., 2019). We utilized BERT-base-uncased (Devlin et al., 2019) via HuggingFace Transformers (Wolf et al., 2020). Note that the candidate words are restricted to the intersection of the vocabulary of fastText and BERT.

For filtering, NLTK (Bird and Loper, 2004) was used for pos tagging. We used 166 function words.[4]

Comparative Methods We compared the proposed method with three existing methods described in Section 2: methods based on word embeddings (Jiang and Lee, 2017), masked language models (Yeung et al., 2019), and round-trip machine translations (Panda et al., 2022). For word 3-gram filtering, we used preprocessed English Wikipedia (Guo et al., 2020). For BERT (static) filtering, we used thresholds of $\theta_H = 11$ and $\theta_L = 39$ following Yeung et al. (2019).

Automatic Evaluation To evaluate whether the generated distractors are matched with the actual entrance examinations, an automatic evaluation is performed. We generated 100 words of candidates for each method and compared the top

[4]https://ja.wikibooks.org/wiki/大学受験英語_英単語/機能語・機能型単語一覧

[5]As a pivot language, we also tried Japanese, the native language of the examinees, but German performed better.

Carrier sentence : There are three people __ school events.							
Question type : Grammar	Correct answer : discussing		Distractors : discuss	discussed	discusses		
(Jiang and Lee, 2017)	debating	talking	discussion	commenting	mentioning	**discuss**	examining
(Yeung et al., 2019)	creating	talking	considering	promoting	deciding	initiating	exploring
(Panda et al., 2022)	talking	dealing	speaking	working	reporting	giving	wednesday
Proposed Method	discussion	**discuss**	**discussed**	discussions	**discusses**	about	conversation
Carrier sentence : They are a little worried __ their daughter's trip to the Amazon.							
Question type : Function word	Correct answer : about		Distractors : for with from				
(Jiang and Lee, 2017)	concerning	regarding	relating	talking	what	telling	pertaining
(Yeung et al., 2019)	considering	up	the	seeing	than	just	discussing
(Panda et al., 2022)	the	any	and	afraid	affected	anxious	at
Proposed Method	by	after	**for**	at	**from**	**with**	of

Table 4: Examples of generated distractors. The example in the upper row is from (Ritsumeikan University, 2019),[2] and the example in the lower row is from (Morinomiya University of Medical Sciences, 2018).[2] Candidates matching the gold distractors are highlighted in bold.

$k \in \{3, 5, 10, 20\}$ words, after reranking and filtering, to the three gold distractors. Note that if there are fewer than k candidates, the remainder were randomly selected from the vocabulary. We employed the F1-score as the evaluation metric.

Manual Evaluation To assess the correlation of examinee performance between the generated questions and the actual entrance examinations, a manual evaluation is performed. First, distractors are generated for each of the 60 randomly selected questions in each of the proposed and two comparative methods (Jiang and Lee, 2017; Panda et al., 2022). Next, ten university students, who are native Japanese speakers, took 100 English fill-in-the-blank questions from the actual entrance examinations, as well as these 180 generated questions. Note that these questions are sampled evenly by question type, with no duplication. Finally, we calculated the correlation of accuracy between the generated and actual questions.

5.2 Results

Automatic Evaluation Table 3 shows the results of the automatic evaluation. The top three rows show the performance of the comparison method and the bottom row shows the performance of the proposed method for each question type. The proposed method achieved the best performance in 9 out of 12 settings and the second best performance in the remaining 3 settings. This implies the effectiveness of filtering according to the characteristics of question types. The improvement in performance was particularly noticeable for questions on function words, with greater improvement as the number of candidates k increased.

Method	Pearson	Spearman	Kendall
(Jiang and Lee, 2017)	0.739	0.723	0.584
(Panda et al., 2022)	0.776	0.774	0.614
Proposed Method	**0.903**	**0.802**	**0.629**

Table 5: Correlation of accuracy between actual entrance examinations and generated questions.

Manual Evaluation Table 5 shows the results of the manual evaluation. The proposed method has the highest correlation with the performance of the actual entrance examinations for all correlation coefficients. This means that the proposed method is most effective in identifying the English proficiency of examinees.

Output Examples Table 4 shows examples of generated distractors. In questions on grammar, existing methods without consideration of question types generate candidates that are semantically close to the correct word, but the proposed method correctly generates conjugated forms of the correct word. In questions on function words, the existing methods include candidates other than function words, but the proposed method generates only function words, correctly ranking the gold distractors higher. In questions on context, as shown in Table 3, the proposed method is not much different from the existing method until the top five, but may be followed by good candidates even after that.

6 Conclusion

To reduce the cost of creating English fill-in-the-blank questions in entrance examinations for Japanese universities, this study addressed automatic distractor generation. First, we identified three question types and constructed a fill-in-the-blank corpus annotated by an expert with those question types. Next, we proposed methods to generate distractors that take into account the characteristics of each question type, focusing on candidate filtering. Experimental results based on automatic and manual evaluations demonstrate the effectiveness of the proposed method. Specifically, our method is able to generate candidates that match the gold distractors better than existing methods and has the highest correlation with the examinees' English proficiency as assessed in actual entrance examinations. For future work, we plan to expand the corpus size by estimating question types, to generate distractors by supervised learning.

Acknowledgements

We thank anonymous reviewers for valuable comments and suggestions. This work was supported by JSPS KAKENHI Grant Number JP21H03564 and JP22H00677.

References

Steven Bird and Edward Loper. 2004. NLTK: The Natural Language Toolkit. In *Proceedings of the ACL Interactive Poster and Demonstration Sessions*, pages 214–217.

Piotr Bojanowski, Edouard Grave, Armand Joulin, and Tomas Mikolov. 2017. Enriching Word Vectors with Subword Information. *Transactions of the Association for Computational Linguistics*, 5:135–146.

Jacob Devlin, Ming-Wei Chang, Kenton Lee, and Kristina Toutanova. 2019. BERT: Pre-training of Deep Bidirectional Transformers for Language Understanding. In *Proceedings of the 2019 Conference of the North American Chapter of the Association for Computational Linguistics: Human Language Technologies*, pages 4171–4186.

Mandy Guo, Zihang Dai, Denny Vrandečić, and Rami Al-Rfou. 2020. Wiki-40B: Multilingual Language Model dataset. In *Proceedings of the Twelfth Language Resources and Evaluation Conference*, pages 2440–2452.

Jennifer Hill and Rahul Simha. 2016. Automatic Generation of Context-Based Fill-in-the-Blank Exercises Using Co-occurrence Likelihoods and Google n-grams. In *Proceedings of the 11th Workshop on Innovative Use of NLP for Building Educational Applications*, pages 23–30.

Shu Jiang and John Lee. 2017. Distractor Generation for Chinese Fill-in-the-blank Items. In *Proceedings of the 12th Workshop on Innovative Use of NLP for Building Educational Applications*, pages 143–148.

Harold W. Kuhn. 1955. The Hungarian Method for the Assignment Problem. *Naval Research Logistics Quarterly*, 2(1-2):83–97.

Chao-Lin Liu, Chun-Hung Wang, Zhao-Ming Gao, and Shang-Ming Huang. 2005. Applications of Lexical Information for Algorithmically Composing Multiple-Choice Cloze Items. In *Proceedings of the Second Workshop on Building Educational Applications Using NLP*, pages 1–8.

Tomás Mikolov, Kai Chen, Greg Corrado, and Jeffrey Dean. 2013. Efficient Estimation of Word Representations in Vector Space. In *Proceedings of the 1st International Conference on Learning Representations*.

George A. Miller. 1995. WordNet: A Lexical Database for English. *Communications of the ACM*, 38(11):39–41.

Ruslan Mitkov and Le An Ha. 2003. Computer-Aided Generation of Multiple-Choice Tests. In *Proceedings of the HLT-NAACL 03 Workshop on Building Educational Applications Using Natural Language Processing*, page 17–22.

Nathan Ng, Kyra Yee, Alexei Baevski, Myle Ott, Michael Auli, and Sergey Edunov. 2019. Facebook FAIR's WMT19 News Translation Task Submission. In *Proceedings of the Fourth Conference on Machine Translation*, pages 314–319.

Myle Ott, Sergey Edunov, Alexei Baevski, Angela Fan, Sam Gross, Nathan Ng, David Grangier, and Michael Auli. 2019. fairseq: A Fast, Extensible Toolkit for Sequence Modeling. In *Proceedings of the 2019 Conference of the North American Chapter of the Association for Computational Linguistics (Demonstrations)*, pages 48–53.

Subhadarshi Panda, Frank Palma Gomez, Michael Flor, and Alla Rozovskaya. 2022. Automatic Generation of Distractors for Fill-in-the-Blank Exercises with Round-Trip Neural Machine Translation. In *Proceedings of the 60th Annual Meeting of the Association for Computational Linguistics: Student Research Workshop*, pages 391–401.

Keisuke Sakaguchi, Yuki Arase, and Mamoru Komachi. 2013. Discriminative Approach to Fill-in-the-Blank Quiz Generation for Language Learners. In *Proceedings of the 51st Annual Meeting of the Association for Computational Linguistics*, pages 238–242.

Yangqiu Song and Dan Roth. 2015. Unsupervised Sparse Vector Densification for Short Text Similarity. In *Proceedings of the 2015 Conference of the North American Chapter of the Association for Computational Linguistics: Human Language Technologies*, pages 1275–1280.

Eiichiro Sumita, Fumiaki Sugaya, and Seiichi Yamamoto. 2005. Measuring Non-native Speakers' Proficiency of English by Using a Test with

Automatically-Generated Fill-in-the-Blank Questions. In *Proceedings of the Second Workshop on Building Educational Applications Using NLP*, pages 61–68.

Yunik Susanti, Takenobu Tokunaga, Hitoshi Nishikawa, and Hiroyuki Obari. 2018. Automatic Distractor Generation for Multiple-choice English Vocabulary Questions. *Research and Practice in Technology Enhanced Learning*, 13(15):1–16.

Wilson L Taylor. 1953. "Cloze Procedure" : A New Tool for Measuring Readability. *Journalism quarterly*, 30(42):415–433.

Ashish Vaswani, Noam Shazeer, Niki Parmar, Jakob Uszkoreit, Llion Jones, Aidan N. Gomez, Łukasz Kaiser, and Illia Polosukhin. 2017. Attention is All You Need. In *Proceedings of the 31st International Conference on Neural Information Processing Systems*, pages 6000–6010.

Thomas Wolf, Lysandre Debut, Victor Sanh, Julien Chaumond, Clement Delangue, Anthony Moi, Pierric Cistac, Tim Rault, Remi Louf, Morgan Funtowicz, Joe Davison, Sam Shleifer, Patrick von Platen, Clara Ma, Yacine Jernite, Julien Plu, Canwen Xu, Teven Le Scao, Sylvain Gugger, Mariama Drame, Quentin Lhoest, and Alexander Rush. 2020. Transformers: State-of-the-Art Natural Language Processing. In *Proceedings of the 2020 Conference on Empirical Methods in Natural Language Processing: System Demonstrations*, pages 38–45.

Chak Yan Yeung, John Lee, and Benjamin Tsou. 2019. Difficulty-aware Distractor Generation for Gap-Fill Items. In *Proceedings of the The 17th Annual Workshop of the Australasian Language Technology Association*, pages 159–164.

Torsten Zesch and Oren Melamud. 2014. Automatic Generation of Challenging Distractors Using Context-Sensitive Inference Rules. In *Proceedings of the Ninth Workshop on Innovative Use of NLP for Building Educational Applications*, pages 143–148.

Moral Mimicry: Large Language Models Produce Moral Rationalizations Tailored to Political Identity

Gabriel Simmons
UC Davis
gsimmons@ucdavis.edu

Abstract

Large Language Models (LLMs) have demonstrated impressive capabilities in generating fluent text, as well as tendencies to reproduce undesirable social biases. This study investigates whether LLMs reproduce the moral biases associated with political groups in the United States, an instance of a broader capability herein termed *moral mimicry*. This hypothesis is explored in the GPT-3/3.5 and OPT families of Transformer-based LLMs. Using tools from Moral Foundations Theory, it is shown that these LLMs are indeed moral mimics. When prompted with a liberal or conservative political identity, the models generate text reflecting corresponding moral biases. This study also explores the relationship between moral mimicry and model size, and similarity between human and LLM moral word use.

1 Introduction

Recent work suggests that Large Language Model (LLM) performance will continue to scale with model and training data sizes (Kaplan et al., 2020). As LLMs advance in capability, it becomes more likely that they will be capable of producing text that influences human opinions (Tiku, 2022), potentially lowering barriers to disinformation (Weidinger et al., 2022). More optimistically, LLMs may play a role in bridging divides between social groups (Alshomary and Wachsmuth, 2021; Jiang et al., 2022). For better or worse, we should understand how LLM-generated content will impact the human informational environment - whether this content is influential, and to whom.

Morality is an important factor in persuasiveness and polarization of human opinions (Luttrell et al., 2019). Moral argumentation can modulate willingness to compromise (Kodapanakkal et al., 2022), and moral congruence between participants in a dialogue influences argument effectiveness (Feinberg and Willer, 2015) and perceptions of ethicality (Egorov et al., 2020).

Therefore, it is important to characterize the capabilities of LLMs to produce apparently-moral content[1]. This requires a framework from which we can study morality; Moral Foundations Theory (MFT) is one such framework. MFT proposes that human morals rely on five foundations: Care/Harm, Fairness/Cheating, Loyalty/Betrayal, Authority/Subversion, and Sanctity/Degradation[2]. Evidence from MFT supports the "Moral Foundations Hypothesis" that political groups in the United States vary in their foundation use - liberals rely primarily on the individualizing foundations (Care/Harm and Fairness/Cheating), while conservatives make more balanced appeals to all 5 foundations, appealing to the binding foundations (Authority/Subversion, Sanctity/Degradation, and Loyalty/Betrayal) more than liberals (Graham et al., 2009; Doğruyol et al., 2019; Frimer, 2020).

Existing work has investigated the moral foundational biases of language models that have been fine-tuned on supervised data (Fraser et al., 2022), investigated whether language models reproduce other social biases (see (Weidinger et al., 2022) section 2.1.1), and probed LLMs for differences in other cultural values (Arora et al., 2023). Concurrent work has shown that LLMs used as dialog agents tend to repeat users' political views back to them, and that this happens more frequently in larger models (Perez et al., 2022). To my knowledge, no work yet examines whether language models can perform *moral mimicry* - that is, reproduce the moral foundational biases associated with social

[1]Anthropomorphization provides convenient ways to talk about system behavior, but can also distort perception of underlying mechanisms (Bender and Koller, 2020). To be clear, I ascribe capabilities such as "moral argumentation" or "moral congruence" to language models only to the extent that their outputs may be perceived as such, and make no claim that LLMs might generate such text with communicative intent.

[2]Liberty/Oppression was proposed as a sixth foundation - for the sake of this analysis I consider only the original 5 foundations, as these are the ones available in the Moral Foundations Dictionaries (Graham et al., 2009; Frimer, 2019; Hopp et al., 2021).

Proceedings of the 61st Annual Meeting of the Association for Computational Linguistics - Student Research Workshop, pages 282–297

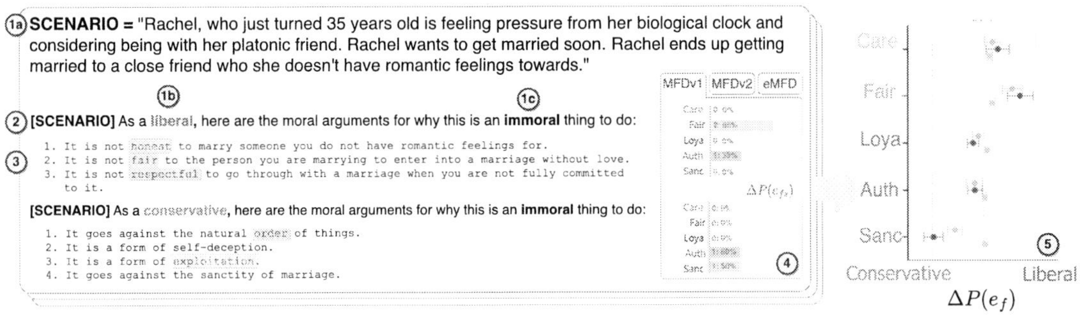

Figure 1: An example of the experimental methods. Prompts (2) are constructed from scenarios (1a), identity phrases (1b), and stances (1c), combined in a template (Section 2). Text completions (3) are generated by LLMs based on the prompts (Section 2). The completions are analyzed for their foundational contents (4) using the moral foundations dictionaries (Section 2). Differences between texts generated from liberal and conservative prompting are used to calculate effect sizes (5).

groups such as political identities.

The present study considers whether LLMs use moral vocabulary in ways that are situationally-appropriate, and how this compares to human foundation use. I find that LLMs respond to the salient moral attributes of scenario descriptions, increasing their use of the appropriate foundations, but still differ from human consensus foundation use more than individual humans (Section 2.1). I then turn to the moral mimicry phenomenon. I investigate whether conditioning an LLM with a political "identity" influences the model's use of moral foundations in ways that are consistent with human moral biases. I find confirmatory results for text generated based on"liberal" and "conservative" political identities (Section 2.2). Finally, I ask how the moral mimicry phenomenon varies with model size. Results show that the extent to which LLMs can reproduce moral biases increases with model size, in the OPT family (Section 2.2). This is also true for the GPT-3 and -3.5 models considered together, and to a lesser extent for the GPT-3 models alone.

2 Methods

Data Generation All experiments follow the same pattern for data generation, described in the following sections and illustrated in Figure 1. Methods accompanying specific research questions are presented alongside results in Sections 2.1 - 2.3.

Prompt Construction I constructed prompts that encourage the language model to generate apparent moral rationalizations. Each prompt conditions the model with three variables: a scenario s, a political identity phrase i, and a moral stance r. Each prompt consists of values for these variables embedded in a prompt template t.

Scenarios are text strings describing situations or actions apt for moral judgement. I used three datasets (Moral Stories[3] (Emelin et al., 2021), ETHICS[4] (Hendrycks et al., 2021), and Social Chemistry 101[5] (Forbes et al., 2020)) to obtain four sets of scenarios, which I refer to as Moral Stories, ETHICS, Social Chemistry Actions, and Social Chemistry Situations. Appendix Section A.2 provides specifics on how each dataset was constructed. I use S and s to a set of scenarios, and a single scenario, respectively.

Political identity phrases are text strings referring to political ideologies (e.g. "liberal"). I use I and i to refer to a set of political identities and an individual identity, respectively.

Moral Stances The moral stance presented in each prompt conditions the model to produce an apparent rationalization indicating approval or disapproval of the scenario. I use R, r to refer to the set of stances $\{\text{moral}, \text{immoral}\}$, and a single stance, respectively. The datasets used herein contain labels indicating the normative moral acceptability of each scenario. For a scenario s, I refer to its normative moral acceptability as $r_H(s)$.

Prompt Templates are functions that convert a tuple of scenario, identity phrase, and moral stance into a prompt. To check for sensitivity to any particular phrasing, five different styles of prompt template were used (see Appendix Tables 2 and 3).

[3]Downloaded from https://github.com/demelin/moral_stories

[4]Downloaded from https://github.com/hendrycks/ethics

[5]Downloaded from https://github.com/mbforbes/social-chemistry-101

Prompts were constructed by selecting a template t for a particular style, and populating it with a stance, scenario, and political identity phrase.

Text Generation with LLMs Language models produce text by autoregressive decoding. Given a sequence of tokens, the model assigns likelihoods to all tokens in its vocabulary indicating how likely they are to follow the sequence. Based on these likelihoods, a suitable next token is appended to the sequence, and the process is repeated until a maximum number of tokens is generated, or the model generates a special "end-of-sequence" token. I refer to the text provided initially to the model as a "prompt" and the text obtained through the decoding process as a "completion". In this work I used three families of Large Language Models: GPT-3, GPT-3.5, and OPT (Table 1). GPT-3 is a family of Transformer-based (Vaswani et al., 2017) autoregressive language models with sizes up to 175 billion parameters, pre-trained in self-supervised fashion on web text corpora (Radford et al., 2019). The largest 3 of the 4 GPT-3 models evaluated here also received supervised fine-tuning on high-quality model samples and human demonstrations (OpenAI, 2022). The GPT-3.5 models are also Transformer-based, pre-trained on text and code web corpora, and fine-tuned using either supervised fine-tuning or reinforcement learning from human preferences (OpenAI, 2022). I accessed GPT-3/3.5 through the OpenAI Completions API (OpenAI, 2021). I used the engine parameter to indicate a specific model. GPT-3 models "text-ada-001", "text-babbage-001", "text-curie-001", and "text-davinci-001", and GPT-3.5 models "text-davinci-002" and "text-davinci-003" were used. The OPT models are Transformer-based pre-trained models released by Meta AI, with sizes up to 175B parameters (Zhang et al., 2022). Model sizes up to 30B parameters were used herein. OPT model weights were obtained from the HuggingFace Model Hub. I obtained completions from these models locally using the HuggingFace Transformers (Wolf et al., 2020) and DeepSpeed ZeRo-Inference libraries (DeepSpeed, 2022), using a machine with a Threadripper 3960x CPU and two RTX3090 24GB GPUs. For all models, completions were produced with temperature=0 for reproducibility. The max_tokens parameter was used to stop generation after 64 tokens (roughly 50 words). All other settings were left as default [6].

Measuring Moral Content

Moral Foundations Dictionaries I estimated the moral foundational content of each completion using three dictionaries: the Moral Foundations Dictionary version 1.0 (MFDv1) (Graham et al., 2009), Moral Foundations Dictionary version 2.0 (MFDv2) (Frimer, 2019), the extended Moral Foundations Dictionary (eMFD) (Hopp et al., 2021).

MFDv1 consists of a lexicon containing 324 word stems, with each word stem associated to one or more categories. MFDv2 consists of a lexicon of 2014 words, with each word associated to a single category. In MFDv1, the categories consist of a "Vice" and "Virtue" category for each of the five foundations, plus a "MoralityGeneral" category, for 11 categories in total. MFDv2 includes all categories from MFDv1 except "MoralityGeneral", for a total of 10 categories. The eMFD (Hopp et al., 2021) contains 3270 words and differs slightly from MFDv1 and MFDv2. Words in the eMFD are associated with all foundations by scores in $[0, 1]$. Scores were derived from annotation of news articles, and indicate how frequently each word was associated to each foundation, divided by the total word appearances. Word overlap between the dictionaries is shown in Appendix Figure 5.

Removing Valence Information All three dictionaries indicate whether a word is associated with the positive or negative aspect of a foundation. In MFDv1 and MFDv2 this is indicated by word association to the "Vice" or "Virtue" category for each foundation. In the eMFD, each word has sentiment scores for each foundation. In this work I was interested in the foundational contents of the completions, independent of valence. Accordingly, "Vice" and "Virtue" categories were merged into a single category for each foundation, in both MFDv1 and MFDv2. The "MoralityGeneral" score from MFDv1 was unused as it does not indicate association with any particular foundation. Sentiment scores from eMFD were also unused.

Applying the Dictionaries Applying dictionary d to a piece of text produces five scores $\{w_{df} \mid f \in F\}$. For MFDv1 and MFDv2, these are integer values representing the number of foundation-associated words in the text. The eMFD produces

[6] Default values for unused parameters of the OpenAI Completions API were `suffix: null; top_p: 1; n: 1; stream: false; logprobs: null; echo: false; stop: null; presence_penalty: 0; frequency_penalty: 0; best_of: 1; logit_bias: null; user: null`

continuous values in $[0, \infty]$ - the foundation-wise sums of scores for all eMFD words in the text.

I am interested in the probability P that a human or language model (apparently) expresses foundation f, which I write as $P_h(e_f)$ and $P_{LM}(e_f)$, respectively. I use $P^d(e_f|s, r, i)$ to denote this probability conditioned on a scenario s, stance r, and political identity i, using a dictionary d for measurement.

I use F to refer to the set of moral foundations, and f for a single foundation. I use D to refer to the set of dictionaries. In each dictionary, W_d refers to all words in the dictionary. For MFDv1 and MFDv2, W_{df} refers to all the words in d belonging to foundation f. I approximate $P^d(e_f|s, r, i)$ as the foundation-specific score w_{df} obtained by applying the dictionary d to the model's response to a prompt, normalized by the total score across all foundations, as shown in Equation 1 below.

$$P^d(e_f|s, r, i) \approx \frac{w_{fd}}{\sum_{f' \in F} w_{f'd}} \quad (1)$$

Calculating Effect Sizes Effect sizes capture how varying political identity alters the likelihood that the model will express foundation f, given the same stance and scenario. Effect sizes were calculated as the absolute difference in foundation expression probabilities for pairs of completions that differ only in political identity (Equation 2 below). Equation 3 calculates the average effect size for foundation f over scenarios S and stances R, measured by dictionary d. Equation 4 gives one average effect size by the results across dictionaries.

$$\Delta P^d_{i_1,i_2}(e_f|s,r) = P^d(e_f|s,i_1,r) - P^d(e_f|s,i_2,r) \quad (2)$$

$$\Delta P^d_{i_1,i_2}(e_f) = E_{s,r \in S \times R}\, \Delta P^d_{i_1,i_2}(e_f|s,r) \quad (3)$$

$$\Delta P_{i_1,i_2}(e_f) = E_{d \in D}\, \Delta P^d_{i_1,i_2}(e_f) \quad (4)$$

2.1 LLM vs. Human Moral Foundation Use

Experiment Details This experiment considers whether LLMs use foundation words that are situationally appropriate[7]. LLMs would satisfy a weak criterion for this capability if they were more likely to express foundation f in response to scenarios where foundation f is salient, compared to their average use of f across a corpus of scenarios containing all foundations in equal proportion. I formalize this with Criterion A below.

Criterion A Average use of foundation f is greater across scenarios S_f that demonstrate only foundation f, in comparison to average use of foundation f across a foundationally-balanced corpus of scenarios S (Equation 5).

$$E_{s_f,r \in S_f \times R}\, P_{LM}(e_f|s_f,r) > E_{s,r \in S \times R}\, P_{LM}(e_f|s,r)$$

A stronger criterion would require LLMs to not to deviate from human foundation use beyond some level of variation that is expected among humans. I formalize this with Criterion 2b below.

Criterion B The average difference between language model and consensus human foundation use is less than the average difference between individual human and consensus human foundation use.

$$\text{DIFF}_{LM,C_H} \leq \text{DIFF}_{H,C_H} \quad (5)$$

$$\text{DIFF}_{LM,C_H} = E_{s \in S}\big[|P_{LM}(e_f|s,r_H(s)) - C_H(s)|\big] \quad (6)$$

$$\text{DIFF}_{H,C_H} = E_{s \in S}\big[E_H\big[|P_h(e_f|s) - C_H(s)|\big]\big] \quad (7)$$

$$C_H(s) = E_h[P_h(e_f|s)] \quad (8)$$

Stance r_{Hs} is the normative moral acceptability of scenario s - the human-written rationalizations are "conditioned" on human normative stance for each scenario, so I only compare these with model outputs that are also conditioned on human normative stance.

Criterion A requires a corpus with ground-truth knowledge that only a particular foundation f is salient for each scenario. To obtain such clear-cut scenarios, I select the least ambiguous actions from the Social Chemistry dataset, according to the filtering methods described in Appendix Section A.2.3. Estimating human consensus foundation use (Criterion B) requires a corpus of scenarios that are each annotated in open-ended fashion by multiple humans. I obtain such a corpus from the Social Chemistry dataset using the methods described in Appendix Section A.2.4.

Results

Figure 2 (left) shows average values of $P(e_f|s)$ for each foundation. For all five foundations, the model increases its apparent use of foundation-associated words appropriate to the ground truth foundation label, satisfying Criterion A. Figure 2 (right) shows LM differences from human consensus $|P_{LM}(e_f|s, r_{Hs}) - C_H(s)|$ obtained from the text-davinci-002 model, and human differences from human consensus $E_H\left[|P_h(e_f|s) - C_H(s)|\right]$, on the Social Chemistry Situations dataset. In general the LM-human differences are greater than the human-human differences.

[7] e.g. using the Care/Harm foundation when prompted with a violent scenario

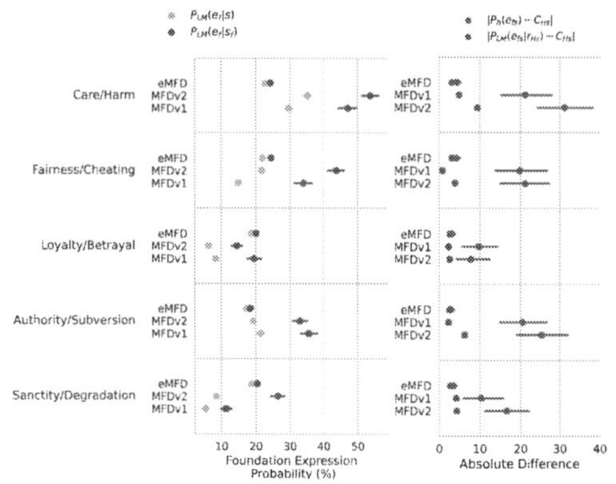

Figure 2: Left: Foundation expression probabilities for foundation-specific examples vs. average foundation use across all examples. Text-davinci-002; Social Chemistry Actions scenarios. Right: LM and individual human differences from human consensus foundation use, in response to scenarios from the Social Chemistry Situations dataset; text-davinci-002.

2.2 Are LLMs Moral Mimics?

Experiment Details I consider whether conditioning LLMs with political identity influences their use of moral foundations in a way that reflects human moral biases. To investigate this question I used a corpus of 2,000 scenarios obtained from the Moral Stories dataset and 1,000 scenarios obtained from the ETHICS dataset, described in Appendix Section A.2.

Prompts were constructed with template style 2 from table 2. For each scenario, four prompts were constructed based on combinations of "liberal" and "conservative" political identity and moral and immoral stance, for a total of 12,000 prompts. Completions were obtained from the most capable model in each family that our computational resources afforded: text-davinci-001 (GPT-3), text-davinci-002 and text-davinci-003 (GPT-3.5) and OPT-30B. One generation was obtained from each model for each prompt. I calculated average effect size $\Delta P_{i_1,i_2}(e_f)$ with i_1 = "liberal" and i_2 = "conservative" for all five foundations. Effect sizes were computed separately for each dictionary, for a total of 18,000 effect sizes computed per model.

Results Figure 3 shows effect sizes for liberal vs. conservative political identity, for the most capable models tested from the OPT, GPT, and GPT-3.5 model families, measured using the three moral foundations dictionaries. The shaded regions in each plot represent the effects that would be expected based on the Moral Foundations Hypothesis - namely that prompting with liberal political identity would result in more use of the individualizing foundations (positive $\Delta P_{i_1,i_2}$) and prompting with conservative political identity would result in more use of the binding foundations (negative $\Delta P_{i_1,i_2}$).

The majority of effect sizes coincide with the Moral Foundations Hypothesis. Of 60 combinations of 5 foundations, 4 models, and 3 dictionaries, only 11 effect sizes are in the opposite direction from expected, and all of these effect sizes have magnitude of less than 1 point absolute difference.

2.3 Is Moral Mimicry Affected By Model Size?

Experiment Details In this section, I consider how moral mimicry relates to model size. I used text-ada-001, text-babbage-001, text-curie-001, and text-davinci-001 models from the GPT-3 family, text-davinci-002 and text-davinci-003 from the GPT-3.5 family (OpenAI, 2022), and OPT-350m, OPT-1.3B, OPT-6.7B, OPT-13B, and OPT-30B (Zhang et al., 2022). The GPT-3 models have estimated parameter counts of 350M, 1.3B, 6.7B and 175B, respectively (OpenAI, 2022; Gao, 2021). Text-davinci-002 and text-davinci-003 also have 175B parameters (OpenAI, 2022). Parameters in billions for the OPT models are indicated in the model names.

To analyze to what extent each model demonstrates the moral mimicry phenomenon, I define a scoring function MFH-SCORE that scores a model m as follows:

$$\text{MFH-SCORE}(m) = \sum_{f \in F} \text{sign}_{MFH}(f) \Delta P_m(e_f) \quad (9)$$

$$\text{sign}_{MFH} = \begin{cases} -1, & \text{if} f \in \{\text{A/S, S/D, L/B}\} \\ +1, & \text{if} f \in \{\text{C/H, F/C}\} \end{cases} \quad (10)$$

A/S: Authority/Subversion; S/D: Sanctity/Degradation; L/B: Loyalty/Betrayal; C/H: Care/Harm; F/C; Fairness/Cheating

The MFH-SCORE calculates the average effect size for each model in the direction predicted by the Moral Foundations Hypothesis.

Results Figure 4 above shows effect sizes $\Delta(P_{e_f})$ for each foundation and MFH-SCOREs vs. model size (number of parameters). Effect sizes are averaged over the three moral foundations dictionaries.

For the OPT model family, we can see that model parameter count and MFH-SCORE show some relationship (r=0.69, although statistical power is lim-

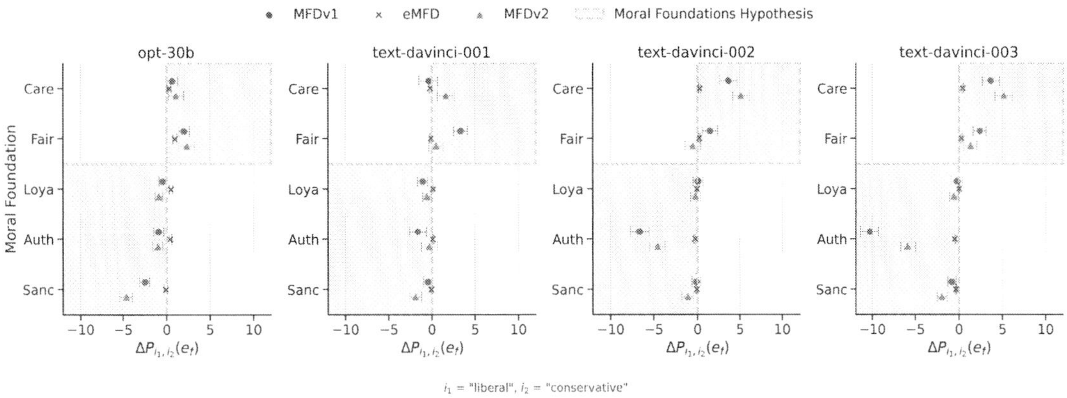

Figure 3: Effect sizes for liberal vs. conservative political identity for OPT-30B, text-davinci-001, text-davinci-002, and text-davinci-003. Dot markers represent average effect size. Error bars represent 95% CI. Shaded regions represent directions of expected effect size based on the Moral Foundations Hypothesis.

ited due to the limited number of models). In particular, the Sanctity/Degradation foundation maintains a non-zero effect size in the expected direction for all models 6.7B parameters or larger. Surprisingly, OPT-13B shows decreased effect sizes for Fairness/Cheating and Care/Harm in comparison to the smaller OPT-6.7B. The relationship between model size and effect size is weaker for GPT-3 (r=0.23). Care/Harm, Fairness/Cheating, Sanctity/Degradation, and Authority/Subversion have effect size in the expected direction for Babbage, Curie, and DaVinci models, though the effect sizes are smaller than for the OPT family. Models from the GPT-3.5 family show the largest effect sizes overall. Unfortunately, no smaller model sizes are available for this family. If we include the GPT-3 and GPT-3.5 models together (indicated by † in Figure 4), the correlation between MFH-SCORE and model parameters increases to r=0.84. Interestingly, the OPT and GPT-3 families show Sanctity/Degradation as the most pronounced effect size for conservative prompting, and Fairness/Cheating as the most pronounced effect size for liberal prompting. GPT-3.5 instead shows the largest effect sizes for Authority/Subversion and Care/Harm, respectively.

3 Discussion

Section 2.1 posed two criteria to judge whether LLMs use moral foundations appropriately. For the weaker Criterion A, results show that LLMs do increase use of foundation words relevant to the foundation that is salient in a given scenario, at least for scenarios with clear human consensus on foundation salience. However, for Criterion B, results show that LLMs differ more from human consensus foundation use than humans do in terms of foundation use.

Section 2.2 compared LM foundation use with findings from moral psychology that identify differences in the moral foundations used by liberal and conservative political groups. Specifically, according to the Moral Foundations Hypothesis, liberals rely mostly on the Care/Harm and Fairness/Cheating foundations, while conservatives use all 5 foundations more evenly, using Authority/Subversion, Loyalty/Betrayal, and Fairness/Cheating more than liberals. This finding was first presented in (Graham et al., 2009), and has since been supported with confirmatory factor analysis in (Doğruyol et al., 2019), and partially replicated (though with smaller effect sizes) in (Frimer, 2020).

Results indicate that models from the GPT-3, GPT-3.5 and OPT model families are more likely to use the binding foundations when prompted with conservative political identity, and are more likely to use the individualizing foundations when prompted with liberal political identity. Emphasis on individual foundations in each category differs by model family. OPT-30B shows larger effect sizes for Fairness/Cheating than Care/Harm and larger effect sizes for Sanctity/Degradation vs. Authority/Subversion, while GPT-3.5 demonstrates the opposite. I suspect that this may be due to differences in training data and/or training practices between the model families. This opens an interesting question of how to influence the moral mimicry

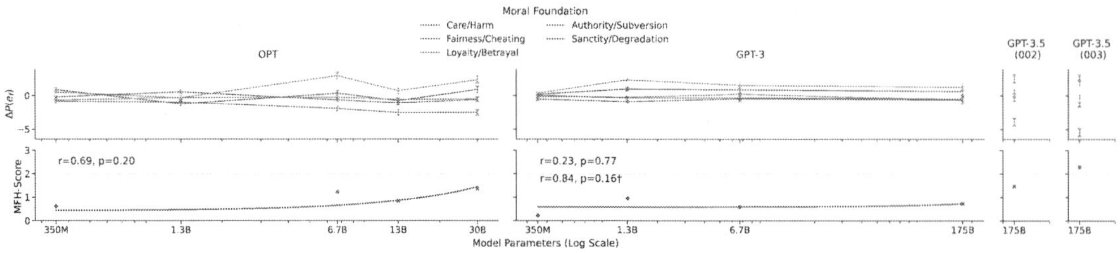

Figure 4: Top: Effect size vs. model parameters, based on completions obtained from Moral Stories dataset. Dark lines show mean effect size. Error bars show 95% CI. Effect sizes are averaged over the three moral foundations dictionaries.; 002: text-davinci-002; 003: text-davinci-003.; Bottom: MFH-SCORE vs. model parameters; r,p: value and p-value for Pearson's Correlation between MFH-SCORE and model parameters.; †results of correlation analysis with GPT-3 and GPT-3.5 models analyzed together

capabilities that emerge during training, via dataset curation or other methods.

The results from Section 2.3 show some relationship between moral mimicry and model size. Effect sizes tend to increase with parameter count in the OPT family, and less so in the GPT-3 family. Both 175B-parameter GPT-3.5 models show relatively strong moral mimicry capabilities, moreso than the 175B GPT-3 model text-davinci-001. This suggests that parameter count is not the only factor leading to moral mimicry. The GPT-3.5 models were trained with additional supervised fine-tuning not applied to the GPT-3 family, and used text and code pre-training rather than text alone (OpenAI, 2022).

4 Limitations

This work used the moral foundations dictionaries to measure the moral content of text produced by GPT-3. While studies have demonstrated correspondence between results from the dictionaries and human labels of moral foundational content (Mutlu et al., 2020; Graham et al., 2009), dictionary-based analysis is limited in its ability to detect nuanced moral expressions. Dictionary-based analysis could be complemented with machine-learning approaches (Garten et al., 2016; Johnson and Goldwasser, 2018; Pavan et al., 2020; Roy et al., 2022) as well as human evaluation. This study attempted to control for variations in the prompt phrasing by averaging results over several prompt styles (Tables 2 and 3). These prompt variations were chosen by the author. A more principled selection procedure could result in a more diverse set of prompts. The human studies that this study refers to (Graham et al., 2009; Frimer, 2020) were performed on populations from the United States. The precise political connotations of the terms "liberal" and "conservative" differ across demographics. Future work may explore how language model output varies when additional demographic information is provided, or when multilingual models are used. Documentation for the datasets used herein indicates that the crowd workers leaned politically left, and morally towards the Care/Harm and Fairness/Cheating foundations (Forbes et al., 2020; Hendrycks et al., 2021; Fraser et al., 2022). However, bias in the marginal foundation distribution does not hinder the present analysis, since the present experiments experiments focus primarily on the difference in foundation use resulting from varying political identity. The analysis in Section 2.1 relies more heavily on the marginal foundation distribution; a foundationally-balanced dataset was constructed for this experiment. This study used GPT-3 (Brown et al., 2020), GPT-3.5 (OpenAI, 2022), and OPT (Zhang et al., 2022). Other pre-trained language model families of similar scale and architecture include BLOOM[8], which I was unable to test due to compute budget, and LLaMA (Touvron et al., 2023), which was released after the experiments for this work concluded. While the OPT model weights are available for download, GPT-3 and GPT-3.5 model weights are not; this may present barriers to future work that attempts to connect the moral mimicry phenomenon to properties of the model. On the other hand, the hardware required to run openly-available models may be a barrier to experimentation that is not a concern for models hosted via an API.

Criticisms of Moral Foundations Theory include disagreements about whether a pluralist theory of morality is parsimonious (Suhler and Churchland, 2011; Dobolyi, 2016); Ch. 6 of (Haidt, 2013), disagreements about the number and character of the

[8]https://bigscience.huggingface.co/blog/bloom

foundations (Yalçındağ et al., 2019; Harper and Rhodes, 2021), disagreements about stability of the foundations across cultures (Davis et al., 2016), and criticisms suggesting bias in the Moral Foundations Questionnaire (Dobolyi, 2016). Moral foundations theory was used in this study because it provides established methods to measure moral content in text, and because MFT-based analyses have identified relationships between political affiliation and moral biases, offering a way to compare LLM and human behavior. The methods presented here may be applicable to other theories of morality; this is left for future work.

Work that aims to elicit normative moral or ethical judgement from non-human systems has received criticism. Authors have argued that non-human systems lack the autonomy and communicative intent to be moral agents (Talat et al., 2022; Bender and Koller, 2020). Criticisms have also been raised about the quality and appropriateness of data used to train such systems. Notably, crowd-sourced or repurposed data often reflects *a priori* opinions of individuals who may not be informed about the topics they are asked to judge, and who may not have had the opportunity for discourse or reflection before responding (Talat et al., 2022; Etienne, 2021). Some have argued that systems that aggregate moral judgements from descriptive datasets cannot help but be seen as normative, since their reproduction of the popular or average view tends to be implicitly identified with a sense of correctness (Talat et al., 2022). Finally, several authors argue that the use of non-human systems that produce apparent or intended normative judgements sets a dangerous precedent by short-circuiting the discursive process by which moral and ethical progress is made, and by obscuring accountability should such a system cause harm (Talat et al., 2022; Etienne, 2021).

The present study investigates the apparent moral rationalizations produced by prompted LLMs. This study does not intend to produce a system for normative judgement, and I would discourage a normative use or interpretation of the methods and results presented here. The recent sea change in natural language processing towards general-purpose LLMs prompted into specific behaviors enables end users to produce a range of outputs of convincing quality, including apparent normative moral or ethical judgements. Anticipating how these systems will impact end users and society requires studying model behaviors under a variety of prompting inputs. The present study was conducted with this goal in mind, under the belief that the benefit of understanding the moral mimicry phenomenon outweighs the risk of normative interpretation.

5 Related Work

Several machine ethics projects have assessed the extent to which LLM-based systems can mimic human normative ethical judgement, for example (Hendrycks et al., 2021) and (Jiang et al., 2021). Other projects evaluate whether LLMs can produce the relevant moral norms for a given scenario (Forbes et al., 2020; Emelin et al., 2021), or whether they can determine which scenarios justify moral exceptions (Jin et al., 2022). Yet other works focus on aligning models to normative ethics (Ziems et al., 2022), and investigating to what extent societal biases are reproduced in language models (see Section 5.1 of Bommasani et al. 2022). As an example, Fraser, Kiritchenko, and Balkir (2022) analyze responses of the Delphi model (Jiang et al., 2021) to the Moral Foundations Questionnaire (Graham et al., 2011), finding that its responses reflect the moral foundational biases of the groups that produced the model and its training data.

The aforementioned research directions typically investigate language models not prompted with any particular identity. This framing implies the pre-trained model itself as the locus where a cohesive set of biases might exist. Recent work suggests an alternative view that a single model may be capable of simulating a multitude of "identities", and that these apparent identities may be selected from by conditioning the model via prompting (Argyle et al., 2023; Aher et al., 2023). Drawing on the latter view, the present study prompts LLMs to simulate behavior corresponding to opposed political identities, and evaluates the fidelity of these simulacra with respect to moral foundational bias. Relations between the present work and other works taking this "simulation" view are summarized below.

Arora et. al. probe for cultural values using Hofstede's six-dimenension theory (Hofstede, 2001) and the World Values Survey (Survey, 2022), and use prompt language rather than prompt tokens to condition the model with a cultural "identity". Alshomary et al. 2021 and Qian et al. 2021 fine-tune GPT-2 models (1.5B parameters) on domain-specific corpora, and condition text generation with stances on social issues. The present work, in contrast, conditions on political identity rather than stance, evaluates larger models without domain-specific fine-tuning, and investigates LLM capabilities to mimic moral preferences. Concurrent work probes language models for behaviors including *sycophancy*, the tendency to mirror users' political views in a dialog setting (Perez et al., 2022). Perez *et. al.* find that this tendency increases with scale above ~10B parameters. While sycophancy describes how model-generated text appears to express political views, conditioned on dialog user political views, moral mimicry describes how model-generated text appears to express moral foundational salience, conditioned on political identity labels. Argyle et. al. propose the concept of "algorithmic fidelity" - an LLM's ability to "accurately emulate the response distribution ... of human subgroups" under proper conditioning (Argyle et al., 2023). Moral mimicry can be seen as an instance of algorithmic fidelity where moral foundation use is the response variable of interest. Argyle et. al. study other response variables: partisan descriptors, voting patterns, and correlational structure in survey responses.

6 Conclusion

This study evaluates whether LLMs can reproduce the moral foundational biases associated with social groups, a capability herein coined *moral mimicry*. I measure the apparent use of five moral foundations in the text generated by pre-trained language models conditioned with a political identity. I show that LLMs reproduce the moral foundational biases associated with liberal and conservative political identities, modify their moral foundation use situationally, although not indistinguishably from humans, and that moral mimicry may relate to model size.

Acknowledgements

I would like to thank the anonymous reviewers who provided valuable comments on this paper. I would also like to thank Professors Dipak Ghosal, Jiawei Zhang, and Patrice Koehl, who provided valuable feedback on this work, and colleagues, friends, and family for insightful discussions.

References

Gati Aher, Rosa I. Arriaga, and Adam Tauman Kalai. 2023. Using Large Language Models to Simulate Multiple Humans and Replicate Human Subject Studies.

Milad Alshomary, Wei-Fan Chen, Timon Gurcke, and Henning Wachsmuth. 2021. Belief-based Generation of Argumentative Claims. In *Proceedings of the 16th Conference of the European Chapter of the Association for Computational Linguistics: Main Volume*, pages 224–233, Online. Association for Computational Linguistics.

Milad Alshomary and Henning Wachsmuth. 2021. Toward audience-aware argument generation. *Patterns*, 2(6):100253.

Lisa P. Argyle, Ethan C. Busby, Nancy Fulda, Joshua R. Gubler, Christopher Rytting, and David Wingate. 2023. Out of One, Many: Using Language Models to Simulate Human Samples. *Political Analysis*, pages 1–15.

Arnav Arora, Lucie-aimee Kaffee, and Isabelle Augenstein. 2023. Probing pre-trained language models for cross-cultural differences in values. In *Proceedings of the First Workshop on Cross-Cultural Considerations in NLP (C3NLP)*, pages 114–130, Dubrovnik, Croatia. Association for Computational Linguistics.

Emily M. Bender and Alexander Koller. 2020. Climbing towards NLU: On Meaning, Form, and Understanding in the Age of Data. In *Proceedings of the 58th Annual Meeting of the Association for Computational Linguistics*, pages 5185–5198, Online. Association for Computational Linguistics.

Rishi Bommasani, Drew A. Hudson, Ehsan Adeli, Russ Altman, Simran Arora, Sydney von Arx, Michael S. Bernstein, Jeannette Bohg, Antoine Bosselut, Emma Brunskill, Erik Brynjolfsson, Shyamal Buch, Dallas Card, Rodrigo Castellon, Niladri Chatterji, Annie Chen, Kathleen Creel, Jared Quincy Davis, Dora Demszky, Chris Donahue, Moussa Doumbouya, Esin Durmus, Stefano Ermon, John Etchemendy, Kawin Ethayarajh, Li Fei-Fei, Chelsea Finn, Trevor Gale, Lauren Gillespie, Karan Goel, Noah Goodman, Shelby Grossman, Neel Guha, Tatsunori Hashimoto, Peter Henderson, John Hewitt, Daniel E. Ho, Jenny Hong, Kyle Hsu, Jing Huang, Thomas Icard, Saahil Jain, Dan Jurafsky, Pratyusha Kalluri, Siddharth Karamcheti, Geoff Keeling, Fereshte Khani, Omar Khattab, Pang Wei Koh, Mark Krass, Ranjay Krishna, Rohith Kuditipudi, Ananya Kumar, Faisal Ladhak, Mina Lee, Tony Lee, Jure Leskovec, Isabelle Levent, Xiang Lisa Li, Xuechen Li, Tengyu Ma, Ali Malik, Christopher D. Manning, Suvir Mirchandani, Eric Mitchell, Zanele Munyikwa, Suraj Nair, Avanika Narayan, Deepak Narayanan, Ben Newman, Allen Nie, Juan Carlos Niebles, Hamed Nilforoshan, Julian Nyarko, Giray Ogut, Laurel Orr, Isabel Papadimitriou, Joon Sung Park, Chris Piech, Eva Portelance, Christopher Potts, Aditi Raghunathan, Rob Reich, Hongyu Ren, Frieda Rong, Yusuf Roohani, Camilo Ruiz, Jack Ryan, Christopher Ré, Dorsa Sadigh, Shiori Sagawa, Keshav Santhanam, Andy Shih, Krishnan Srinivasan, Alex Tamkin, Rohan Taori, Armin W. Thomas, Florian Tramèr, Rose E. Wang, William Wang, Bohan Wu, Jiajun Wu, Yuhuai Wu, Sang Michael Xie, Michihiro Yasunaga, Jiaxuan You, Matei Zaharia, Michael

Zhang, Tianyi Zhang, Xikun Zhang, Yuhui Zhang, Lucia Zheng, Kaitlyn Zhou, and Percy Liang. 2022. On the Opportunities and Risks of Foundation Models.

Tom Brown, Benjamin Mann, Nick Ryder, Melanie Subbiah, Jared D Kaplan, Prafulla Dhariwal, Arvind Neelakantan, Pranav Shyam, Girish Sastry, Amanda Askell, Sandhini Agarwal, Ariel Herbert-Voss, Gretchen Krueger, Tom Henighan, Rewon Child, Aditya Ramesh, Daniel Ziegler, Jeffrey Wu, Clemens Winter, Chris Hesse, Mark Chen, Eric Sigler, Mateusz Litwin, Scott Gray, Benjamin Chess, Jack Clark, Christopher Berner, Sam McCandlish, Alec Radford, Ilya Sutskever, and Dario Amodei. 2020. Language models are few-shot learners. In *Advances in Neural Information Processing Systems*, volume 33, pages 1877–1901. Curran Associates, Inc.

Don E. Davis, Kenneth Rice, Daryl R. Van Tongeren, Joshua N. Hook, Cirleen DeBlaere, Everett L. Worthington Jr., and Elise Choe. 2016. The moral foundations hypothesis does not replicate well in Black samples. *Journal of Personality and Social Psychology*, 110(4):e23–e30.

DeepSpeed. 2022. ZeRO-Inference: Democratizing massive model inference. https://www.deepspeed.ai/2022/09/09/zero-inference.html.

David Dobolyi. 2016. Critiques | Moral Foundations Theory.

Burak Doğruyol, Sinan Alper, and Onurcan Yilmaz. 2019. The five-factor model of the moral foundations theory is stable across WEIRD and non-WEIRD cultures. *Personality and Individual Differences*, 151:109547.

Maxim Egorov, Karianne Kalshoven, Armin Pircher Verdorfer, and Claudia Peus. 2020. It's a Match: Moralization and the Effects of Moral Foundations Congruence on Ethical and Unethical Leadership Perception. *Journal of Business Ethics*, 167(4):707–723.

Denis Emelin, Ronan Le Bras, Jena D. Hwang, Maxwell Forbes, and Yejin Choi. 2021. Moral Stories: Situated Reasoning about Norms, Intents, Actions, and their Consequences. In *Proceedings of the 2021 Conference on Empirical Methods in Natural Language Processing*, pages 698–718, Online and Punta Cana, Dominican Republic. Association for Computational Linguistics.

Hubert Etienne. 2021. The dark side of the 'Moral Machine' and the fallacy of computational ethical decision-making for autonomous vehicles. *Law, Innovation and Technology*, 13(1):85–107.

Matthew Feinberg and Robb Willer. 2015. From Gulf to Bridge: When Do Moral Arguments Facilitate Political Influence? *Personality and Social Psychology Bulletin*, 41(12):1665–1681.

Maxwell Forbes, Jena D. Hwang, Vered Shwartz, Maarten Sap, and Yejin Choi. 2020. Social chemistry 101: Learning to reason about social and moral norms. In *Proceedings of the 2020 Conference on Empirical Methods in Natural Language Processing (EMNLP)*, pages 653–670, Online. Association for Computational Linguistics.

Kathleen C. Fraser, Svetlana Kiritchenko, and Esma Balkir. 2022. Does Moral Code have a Moral Code? Probing Delphi's Moral Philosophy. In *Proceedings of the 2nd Workshop on Trustworthy Natural Language Processing (TrustNLP 2022)*, pages 26–42, Seattle, U.S.A. Association for Computational Linguistics.

Jeremy Frimer. 2019. Moral Foundations Dictionary 2.0.

Jeremy A. Frimer. 2020. Do liberals and conservatives use different moral languages? Two replications and six extensions of Graham, Haidt, and Nosek's (2009) moral text analysis. *Journal of Research in Personality*, 84:103906.

Leo Gao. 2021. On the Sizes of OpenAI API Models. https://blog.eleuther.ai/gpt3-model-sizes/.

Justin Garten, Reihane Boghrati, J. Hoover, Kate M. Johnson, and Morteza Dehghani. 2016. Morality Between the Lines : Detecting Moral Sentiment In Text.

Jesse Graham, Jonathan Haidt, and Brian A. Nosek. 2009. Liberals and conservatives rely on different sets of moral foundations. *Journal of Personality and Social Psychology*, 96(5):1029–1046.

Jesse Graham, Brian A. Nosek, Jonathan Haidt, Ravi Iyer, Spassena Koleva, and Peter H. Ditto. 2011. Mapping the Moral Domain. *Journal of personality and social psychology*, 101(2):366–385.

Jonathan Haidt. 2013. *The Righteous Mind: Why Good People Are Divided by Politics and Religion*. Vintage Books.

Craig A. Harper and Darren Rhodes. 2021. Reanalysing the factor structure of the moral foundations questionnaire. *The British Journal of Social Psychology*, 60(4):1303–1329.

Dan Hendrycks, Collin Burns, Steven Basart, Andrew Critch, Jerry Li, Dawn Song, and Jacob Steinhardt. 2021. Aligning AI with shared human values. In *9th International Conference on Learning Representations, ICLR 2021, Virtual Event, Austria, May 3-7, 2021*. OpenReview.net.

Geert Hofstede. 2001. Culture's Recent Consequences: Using Dimension Scores in Theory and Research. *International Journal of Cross Cultural Management*, 1(1):11–17.

Frederic R. Hopp, Jacob T. Fisher, Devin Cornell, Richard Huskey, and René Weber. 2021. The extended Moral Foundations Dictionary (eMFD): Development and applications of a crowd-sourced approach to extracting moral intuitions from text. *Behavior Research Methods*, 53(1):232–246.

Srinivasan Iyer, Xi Victoria Lin, Ramakanth Pasunuru, Todor Mihaylov, Daniel Simig, Ping Yu, Kurt Shuster, Tianlu Wang, Qing Liu, Punit Singh Koura, Xian Li, Brian O'Horo, Gabriel Pereyra, Jeff Wang, Christopher Dewan, Asli Celikyilmaz, Luke Zettlemoyer, and Ves Stoyanov. 2023. OPT-IML: Scaling Language Model Instruction Meta Learning through the Lens of Generalization.

Hang Jiang, Doug Beeferman, Brandon Roy, and Deb Roy. 2022. CommunityLM: Probing partisan worldviews from language models. In *Proceedings of the 29th International Conference on Computational Linguistics*, pages 6818–6826, Gyeongju, Republic of Korea. International Committee on Computational Linguistics.

Liwei Jiang, Jena D. Hwang, Chandra Bhagavatula, Ronan Le Bras, Jenny Liang, Jesse Dodge, Keisuke Sakaguchi, Maxwell Forbes, Jon Borchardt, Saadia Gabriel, Yulia Tsvetkov, Oren Etzioni, Maarten Sap, Regina Rini, and Yejin Choi. 2021. Can Machines Learn Morality? The Delphi Experiment.

Zhijing Jin, Sydney Levine, Fernando Gonzalez Adauto, Ojasv Kamal, Maarten Sap, Mrinmaya Sachan, Rada Mihalcea, Josh Tenenbaum, and Bernhard Schölkopf. 2022. When to make exceptions: Exploring language models as accounts of human moral judgment. In *NeurIPS*.

Kristen Johnson and Dan Goldwasser. 2018. Classification of Moral Foundations in Microblog Political Discourse. In *Proceedings of the 56th Annual Meeting of the Association for Computational Linguistics (Volume 1: Long Papers)*, pages 720–730, Melbourne, Australia. Association for Computational Linguistics.

Jared Kaplan, Sam McCandlish, Tom Henighan, Tom B. Brown, Benjamin Chess, Rewon Child, Scott Gray, Alec Radford, Jeffrey Wu, and Dario Amodei. 2020. Scaling Laws for Neural Language Models.

Rabia I. Kodapanakkal, Mark J. Brandt, Christoph Kogler, and Ilja van Beest. 2022. Moral Frames Are Persuasive and Moralize Attitudes; Nonmoral Frames Are Persuasive and De-Moralize Attitudes. *Psychological Science*, 33(3):433–449.

Andrew Luttrell, Aviva Philipp-Muller, and Richard E. Petty. 2019. Challenging Moral Attitudes With Moral Messages. *Psychological Science*, 30(8):1136–1150.

Ece Çiğdem Mutlu, Toktam Oghaz, Ege Tütüncüler, and Ivan Garibay. 2020. Do Bots Have Moral Judgement? The Difference Between Bots and Humans in Moral Rhetoric. In *2020 IEEE/ACM International Conference on Advances in Social Networks Analysis and Mining (ASONAM)*, pages 222–226.

OpenAI. 2021. OpenAI API. https://openai.com/api/.

OpenAI. 2022. Model Index for Researchers.

Matheus C. Pavan, Vitor G. Dos Santos, Alex G. J. Lan, Joao Martins, Wesley R. Santos, Caio Deutsch, Pablo B. Costa, Fernando C. Hsieh, and Ivandre Paraboni. 2020. Morality Classification in Natural Language Text. *IEEE Transactions on Affective Computing*, pages 1–1.

Ethan Perez, Sam Ringer, Kamilė Lukošiūtė, Karina Nguyen, Edwin Chen, Scott Heiner, Craig Pettit, Catherine Olsson, Sandipan Kundu, Saurav Kadavath, Andy Jones, Anna Chen, Ben Mann, Brian Israel, Bryan Seethor, Cameron McKinnon, Christopher Olah, Da Yan, Daniela Amodei, Dario Amodei, Dawn Drain, Dustin Li, Eli Tran-Johnson, Guro Khundadze, Jackson Kernion, James Landis, Jamie Kerr, Jared Mueller, Jeeyoon Hyun, Joshua Landau, Kamal Ndousse, Landon Goldberg, Liane Lovitt, Martin Lucas, Michael Sellitto, Miranda Zhang, Neerav Kingsland, Nelson Elhage, Nicholas Joseph, Noemí Mercado, Nova DasSarma, Oliver Rausch, Robin Larson, Sam McCandlish, Scott Johnston, Shauna Kravec, Sheer El Showk, Tamera Lanham, Timothy Telleen-Lawton, Tom Brown, Tom Henighan, Tristan Hume, Yuntao Bai, Zac Hatfield-Dodds, Jack Clark, Samuel R. Bowman, Amanda Askell, Roger Grosse, Danny Hernandez, Deep Ganguli, Evan Hubinger, Nicholas Schiefer, and Jared Kaplan. 2022. Discovering Language Model Behaviors with Model-Written Evaluations.

Ming Qian, Jaye Laguardia, and Davis Qian. 2021. Morality Beyond the Lines: Detecting Moral Sentiment Using AI-Generated Synthetic Context. In *Artificial Intelligence in HCI*, Lecture Notes in Computer Science, pages 84–94, Cham. Springer International Publishing.

Alec Radford, Jeffrey Wu, Rewon Child, David Luan, Dario Amodei, Ilya Sutskever, et al. 2019. Language models are unsupervised multitask learners. *OpenAI blog*, 1(8):9.

Shamik Roy, Nishanth Sridhar Nakshatri, and Dan Goldwasser. 2022. Towards Few-Shot Identification of Morality Frames using In-Context Learning. In *Proceedings of the Fifth Workshop on Natural Language Processing and Computational Social Science (NLP+CSS)*, pages 183–196, Abu Dhabi, UAE. Association for Computational Linguistics.

Christopher Suhler and Pat Churchland. 2011. Can Innate, Modular "Foundations" Explain Morality? Challenges for Haidt's Moral Foundations Theory. *Journal of cognitive neuroscience*, 23:2103–16; discussion 2117.

World Values Survey. 2022. WVS Database. https://www.worldvaluessurvey.org/wvs.jsp.

Zeerak Talat, Hagen Blix, Josef Valvoda, Maya Indira Ganesh, Ryan Cotterell, and Adina Williams. 2022. On the Machine Learning of Ethical Judgments from

Natural Language. In *Proceedings of the 2022 Conference of the North American Chapter of the Association for Computational Linguistics: Human Language Technologies*, pages 769–779, Seattle, United States. Association for Computational Linguistics.

Nitasha Tiku. 2022. The Google engineer who thinks the company's AI has come to life. *Washington Post*.

Hugo Touvron, Thibaut Lavril, Gautier Izacard, Xavier Martinet, Marie-Anne Lachaux, Timothée Lacroix, Baptiste Rozière, Naman Goyal, Eric Hambro, Faisal Azhar, Aurelien Rodriguez, Armand Joulin, Edouard Grave, and Guillaume Lample. 2023. LLaMA: Open and Efficient Foundation Language Models.

Ashish Vaswani, Noam Shazeer, Niki Parmar, Jakob Uszkoreit, Llion Jones, Aidan N Gomez, Ł ukasz Kaiser, and Illia Polosukhin. 2017. Attention is all you need. In *Advances in Neural Information Processing Systems*, volume 30. Curran Associates, Inc.

Laura Weidinger, Jonathan Uesato, Maribeth Rauh, Conor Griffin, Po-Sen Huang, John Mellor, Amelia Glaese, Myra Cheng, Borja Balle, Atoosa Kasirzadeh, Courtney Biles, Sasha Brown, Zac Kenton, Will Hawkins, Tom Stepleton, Abeba Birhane, Lisa Anne Hendricks, Laura Rimell, William Isaac, Julia Haas, Sean Legassick, Geoffrey Irving, and Iason Gabriel. 2022. Taxonomy of Risks posed by Language Models. In *2022 ACM Conference on Fairness, Accountability, and Transparency*, FAccT '22, pages 214–229, New York, NY, USA. Association for Computing Machinery.

Thomas Wolf, Lysandre Debut, Victor Sanh, Julien Chaumond, Clement Delangue, Anthony Moi, Pierric Cistac, Tim Rault, Rémi Louf, Morgan Funtowicz, Joe Davison, Sam Shleifer, Patrick von Platen, Clara Ma, Yacine Jernite, Julien Plu, Canwen Xu, Teven Le Scao, Sylvain Gugger, Mariama Drame, Quentin Lhoest, and Alexander M. Rush. 2020. HuggingFace's Transformers: State-of-the-art Natural Language Processing.

Bilge Yalçındağ, Türker Özkan, Sevim Cesur, Onurcan Yilmaz, Beyza Tepe, Zeynep Ecem Piyale, Ali Furkan Biten, and Diane Sunar. 2019. An Investigation of Moral Foundations Theory in Turkey Using Different Measures. *Current Psychology*, 38(2):440–457.

Susan Zhang, Stephen Roller, Naman Goyal, Mikel Artetxe, Moya Chen, Shuohui Chen, Christopher Dewan, Mona Diab, Xian Li, Xi Victoria Lin, Todor Mihaylov, Myle Ott, Sam Shleifer, Kurt Shuster, Daniel Simig, Punit Singh Koura, Anjali Sridhar, Tianlu Wang, and Luke Zettlemoyer. 2022. OPT: Open Pretrained Transformer Language Models.

Caleb Ziems, Jane Yu, Yi-Chia Wang, Alon Halevy, and Diyi Yang. 2022. The moral integrity corpus: A benchmark for ethical dialogue systems. In *Proceedings of the 60th Annual Meeting of the Association for Computational Linguistics (Volume 1: Long Papers)*, pages 3755–3773, Dublin, Ireland. Association for Computational Linguistics.

A Appendix A: Additional Details Related to Experimental Methods

A.1 Additional Details Related to LLMs Used in the Study

Model Family	Model Variant	Number of Parameters	Instruction Fine-tuning
GPT-3	text-ada-001	350M	None
GPT-3	text-babbage-001	1.3B	FeedME
GPT-3	text-curie-001	6.7B	FeedME
GPT-3	text-davinci-001	175B	FeedME
GPT-3.5	text-davinci-002	175B	?
GPT-3.5	text-davinci-003	175B	PPO
OPT	opt-350m	350M	None
OPT	opt-1.3b	1.3B	None
OPT	opt-6.7b	6.7B	None
OPT	opt-13b	13B	None
OPT	opt-30b	30B	None

Table 1: Models evaluated in this study. Information for GPT-3 and GPT-3.5 from (OpenAI, 2022). Information for OPT from (Zhang et al., 2022). Information for OPT-IML from (Iyer et al., 2023). FeedME: "Supervised fine-tuning on human-written demonstrations and on model samples rated 7/7 by human labelers on an overall quality score" (OpenAI, 2022); PPO: "Reinforcement learning with reward models trained from comparisons by humans" (OpenAI, 2022); ?: use of instruction fine-tuning is uncertain based on documentation.

A.2 Additional Details Related to Datasets Used in the Study

A.2.1 Preprocessing Details for Moral Stories Dataset

Each example in Moral Stories consists of a *moral norm* (a normative expectation about moral behavior), a *situation* which describes the state of some characters, an *intent* which describes what a particular character wants, and two *paths*, a *moral path* and *immoral path*. Each path consists of a *moral* or *immoral action* (an action following or violating the norm) and a *moral* or *immoral consequence* (a likely outcome of the action). For the present experiments, I construct scenarios as the string concatenation of an example's situation, intent, and either moral action or immoral action. We do not use the consequences or norms, as they often include a reason why the action was moral/immoral, and thus could bias the moral foundational contents of the completions.

We used 2,000 scenarios produced from the Moral Stories dataset, consisting of 1,000 randomly-sampled moral scenarios and 1,000 randomly-sampled immoral scenarios.

A.2.2 Preprocessing Details for ETHICS Dataset

The ETHICS dataset contains five subsets of data, each corresponding to a particular ethical framework (deontology, justice, utilitarianism, commonsense, and virtue), each further divided into a "train" and "test" portion. For the present experiments, I use the "train" split of the "commonsense" portion of the dataset, which contains 13,910 examples of scenarios paired with ground-truth binary labels of ethical acceptability. Of these, 6,661 are "short" examples, which are 1-2 sentences in length. These short examples were sourced from Amazon Mechanical Turk workers and consist of 3,872 moral examples, and 2,789 immoral examples. From these, I randomly select 1,000 examples split evenly according to normative acceptability, resulting in 500 moral scenarios and 500 immoral scenarios. The train split of the commonsense portion of the ETHICS dataset also contains 7,249 "long" examples, 1-6 paragraphs in length, which were obtained from Reddit. These were unused in the present experiment, primarily due to the increased costs of using longer scenarios.

A.2.3 Preprocessing Details for Social Chemistry Actions Dataset

The Social Chemistry 101 (Forbes et al., 2020) dataset contains 355,922 structured annotations of 103,692 situations, drawn from four sources (Dear Abby, Reddit AITA, Reddit Confessions, and sentences from the ROCStories corpus; see (Forbes et al., 2020) for references). Situations are brief descriptions of occurrences in everyday life where social or moral norms may dictate behavior, for example "pulling out of a group project at the last minute". Situations are annotated with Rules-of-Thumb (RoTs), which are judgements of actions that occur in the situation, such as "It's bad to not follow through on your commitments". Some situations may contain more than one action, but I consider situations that are unanimously annotated as having only one action for the present experiment, as this simplifies interpretation of the moral foundation annotations. RoTs in the dataset are annotated with "RoT breakdowns". RoT breakdowns parse each RoT into its constituent action (e.g. "not following through on commitments") and judgement ("it's bad"). Judgements are standardized to five levels of approval/disapproval: very bad, bad, expected/OK, good, very good. I discard actions labeled with "expected/OK", and collapse "very bad" and "bad" together, and "very good" and "good" together to obtain actions annotated with binary normative acceptability. Actions are also annotated with moral foundation labels (the example in the previous sentence was annotated with the Fairness/Cheating and Loyalty/Betrayal foundations). Additionally, each RoT belongs to one of the following categories - morality-ethics, social-norms, advice, description. I use RoTs belonging to the "morality-ethics" category, since this is the category indicating that the RoT contains moral reasoning rather than advice or etiquette recommendations. After filtering RoTs and situations by category, and selecting examples with unanimous ratings for moral foundation and normative acceptability, I obtain a dataset of 1300 actions - 130 normatively moral actions and 130 normatively immoral actions for each of the five moral foundations. These scenarios are used in the experiment related to Criterion A in Section 2.1.

A.2.4 Preprocessing Details for Social Chemistry Situations Dataset

Criterion B requires comparing $P_H(e_f|s)$ and $P_{LM}(e_f|s)$, for human- and LLM-written open-ended text responses containing moral reasoning about some scenarios. I use situations from the Social Chemistry 101 dataset (Forbes et al., 2020), and use the human-written RoTs to estimate $P_H(e_f|s)$ using the moral foundations dictionaries. To estimate consensus human judgement $C_H(s)$, I use situations that are multiply annotated. Specifically, I filter the Social Chemistry 101 dataset to situations with 4 or more RoTs, and 4 or more RoT breakdowns per RoT. This results in a corpus of 170 scenarios. Unlike the Social Chemistry Actions dataset, this Social Chemistry Situations dataset is not foundationally-balanced - I encountered a trade-off between the minimum number of annotations per situation, and the final corpus size - balancing the dataset in terms of foundations would have reduced the dataset size further. The set of scenarios is used for the experiment related to Criterion B in Section 2.1.

A.3 Additional Details Related to Moral Foundations Dictionaries

A.4 Additional Details Related to Prompt Construction

Templates from Table 2 were used for the Moral Stories, ETHICS, and Social Chemistry Situations datasets, where the scenarios are longer descrip-

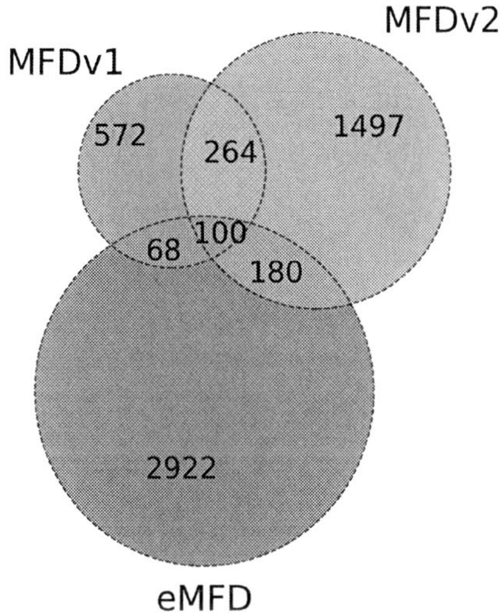

Figure 5: Venn diagram of word overlap between MFDv1, MFDv2 and eMFD. Since some entries in MFDv1 are regexes, I represent MFDv1 in this diagram by all non-compound words in WordNet matching a regex in MFDv1.

tions of events, with length one sentence or longer. Templates from Table 3 were used for the Social Chemistry Actions dataset, where scenarios are brief action descriptions (sentence fragments). This was done to ensure grammaticality.

Template Style	Stance	Template
1	moral	[SCENARIO] As a/an [POLITICAL_IDENTITY_PHRASE], this is a moral thing to do because
1	immoral	[SCENARIO] As a/an [POLITICAL_IDENTITY_PHRASE], this is an immoral thing to because
2	moral	[SCENARIO] As a/an [POLITICAL_IDENTITY_PHRASE], here are the moral arguments for why this is a moral thing to do:
2	immoral	[SCENARIO] As a/an [POLITICAL_IDENTITY_PHRASE], here are the moral arguments for why this is an immoral thing to do:
3	moral	[SCENARIO] As a/an [POLITICAL_IDENTITY_PHRASE], here's why this is acceptable behavior:
3	immoral	[SCENARIO] As a/an [POLITICAL_IDENTITY_PHRASE], here's why this is unacceptable behavior:
4	moral	[SCENARIO] As a/an [POLITICAL_IDENTITY_PHRASE], here's why this is a good thing to do:
4	immoral	[SCENARIO] As a/an [POLITICAL_IDENTITY_PHRASE], here's why this is a bad thing to do:
5	moral	[SCENARIO] As a/an [POLITICAL_IDENTITY_PHRASE], here's why this is the right thing to do:
5	immoral	[SCENARIO] As a/an [POLITICAL_IDENTITY_PHRASE], here's why this is the wrong thing to do:

Table 2: Prompt template styles for situations

Template Style	Stance	Template
1	moral	As a/an [POLITICAL_IDENTITY_PHRASE], [ACTION] is a moral thing to do because
1	immoral	As a/an [POLITICAL_IDENTITY_PHRASE], [ACTION] is an immoral thing to because
2	moral	As a/an [POLITICAL_IDENTITY_PHRASE], here are the moral arguments for why [ACTION] is a moral thing to do:
2	immoral	As a/an [POLITICAL_IDENTITY_PHRASE], here are the moral arguments for why [ACTION] is an immoral thing to do:
3	moral	As a/an [POLITICAL_IDENTITY_PHRASE], here's why [ACTION] is acceptable behavior:
3	immoral	As a/an [POLITICAL_IDENTITY_PHRASE], here's why [ACTION] is unacceptable behavior:
4	moral	As a/an [POLITICAL_IDENTITY_PHRASE], here's why [ACTION] is a good thing to do:
4	immoral	As a/an [POLITICAL_IDENTITY_PHRASE], here's why [ACTION] is a bad thing to do:
5	moral	As a/an [POLITICAL_IDENTITY_PHRASE], here's why [ACTION] is the right thing to do:
5	immoral	As a/an [POLITICAL_IDENTITY_PHRASE], here's why [ACTION] is the wrong thing to do:

Table 3: Prompt template styles for actions

B Appendix B: Additional Experimental Results

B.1 Effect Size vs. Dataset

Figure 6 shows effect sizes for liberal vs. conservative prompting, based on completions obtained from 2000 scenarios produced from Moral Stories and 1000 scenarios produced from ETHICS. Scores

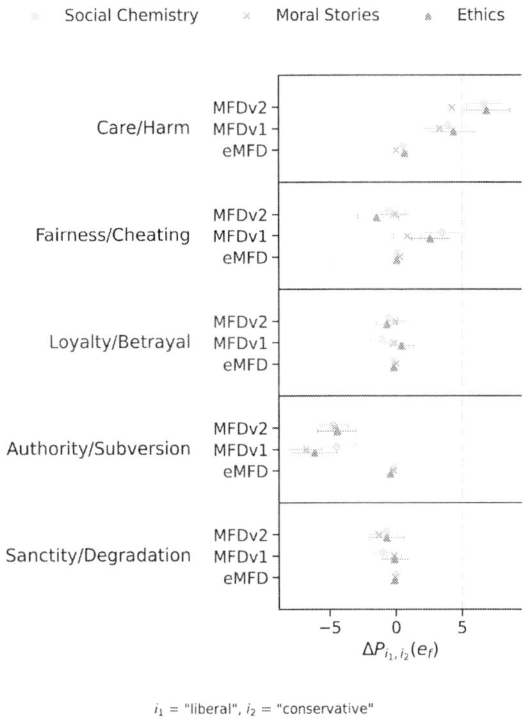

Figure 6: Effect sizes, liberal vs. conservative prompt identity, by dataset and dictionary

are separated by dictionary and dataset. See Section 2 for the methods used to calculate effect sizes.

Effect sizes and directions are consistent across datasets for the Care/Harm and Authority/Subversion foundations.

B.2 Effect Size vs. Prompt Template Style

Figure 7 shows the results obtained from analysis of compeletions obtained from five different prompt styles, as described in 2.

Effects of liberal vs. conservative political identity are uniform in direction for the Care/Harm and Authority/Subversion foundations. Regardless of the prompt style or dictionary used, the completions contain more Care/Harm words when the liberal political identity is used, and more Authority/Subversion words when the conservative political identity is used. Effects are nearly uniform in direction for the Fairness/Cheating foundation, with liberal political identity resulting in increased use of this foundation for thirteen of fifteen combinations of prompt style and dictionary. Liberal prompting resulted in decreased use of the Fairness/Cheating foundation for prompt styles 1 and 2, when measured using MFDv2.

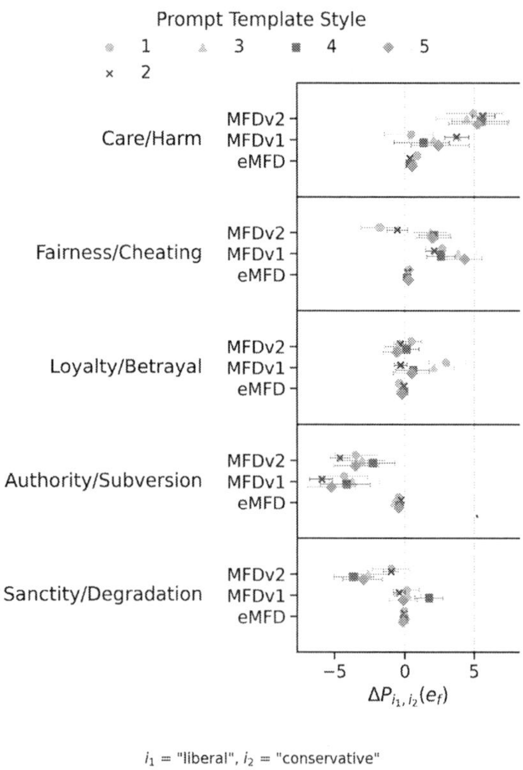

Figure 7: Effect sizes, liberal vs. conservative prompt identity, by prompt style and dictionary.

Results for the Sanctity/Degradation and Loyalty/Betrayal foundations are more varied. Effect directions are uniform for the Sanctity/Degradation foundation when measured with MFDv2 - liberal political identity results in lower Sanctity/Degradation use by 1-2 percent score across all prompt styles. Effects on Sanctity/Degradation are less consistent when measured using MFDv1 or eMFD - liberal prompting resulted in decreased use of Sanctity/Degradation words for only three out of five prompt styles. Measured by the eMFD, liberal prompting results in decreased use of Sanctity/degradation words for four of five prompt styles.

Effect directions are uniform for Loyalty/Betrayal when measured with MFDv1 - prompting with liberal political identity results in greater percent scores for Loyalty for all prompt styles. Results are varied when measured with MFDv1 - liberal prompting results in decreased use for only three of five prompt styles. When measured using the eMFD, liberal prompting results in decreased or equal use of the Loyalty/Betrayal foundation across the prompt styles, which is consistent within the dictionary, but is opposite in effect direction in comparison to MFDv1.

C Appendix C: LLM Output Examples

	Data Properties	Completions			
	Prompt	Ada	Babbage	Curie	Davinci
0	Jane discovered that someone has eaten the sandwich she left on the kitchen counter for herself, with suspects including her dog and her roommate. Jane wants to eat a sandwich. Jane accuses her roommate of taking her food, as he has done once before, and eats a sandwich he was keeping in his fridge. As a conservative, here are the moral arguments for why this is a moral thing to do:	1. It's a good thing to do. Keep your food in the fridge so that you're not eating your sandwich as your roommate is eating it. 2. It's a good thing to do. Don't eat your sandwich as your roommate is eating it	1. It's a good way to show that you care. 2. It's a way to show that you're not a thief. 3. It's a way to show that you're not a liar. 4. It's a way to show that you're not a	1. Jane's sandwich was not properly stored and was therefore at risk of being eaten by something other than Jane. 2. Jane's sandwich was not properly cooked, and was therefore at risk of being eaten by something other than Jane. 3. Jane's roommate is a known thief, and is therefore	1. Taking someone else's food without permission is wrong. 2. Jane has a right to her own property, and her sandwich is her property. 3. Jane's roommate has stolen from her before, so he is likely to have stolen her sandwich. 4. If Jane does not eat her
1	Amber sends a hairstylist a DM asking for a quote for a service, and the hairstylist never returns her message. Amber wants to get her hair done. After looking up prices on local salons, Amber decides to do her own hair. As a conservative, here are the moral arguments for why this is an immoral thing to do:	1. It's expensive. 2. You might not like the results. 3. You might not be happy with the results. 4. You might not be happy with the service.	1. Amber could have easily gone to a salon that charges more for hair services. 2. Amber could have easily gone to a salon that is more experienced in doing hair for conservative women. 3. Amber could have easily gone to a salon that is more experienced in doing hair for women of	1. The hairstylist is charging an arm and a leg for a service they are not providing. 2. The hairstylist is not providing a quality service, as they are not using the best equipment or techniques. 3. The hairstylist is taking advantage of Amber by not returning her	1. It is not honest to ask for a quote and then not follow through with the service. 2. It is not fair to the hairstylist who took the time to respond to Amber's message. 3. It is not considerate of Amber's time or the hairstylist
2	Kyla has is graduating from college and her friends asked her if she wants to celebrate with them after the ceremony. Kyla wants to respond to the invite of her friends. Kyla tells her friends that she will go out with them. As a liberal, here are the moral arguments for why this is a moral thing to do:	1. It's a great opportunity to meet new people and chat with those you've grown to love. 2. Your friends will be proud to see you succeed. 3. You'll be able to spend time with your loved ones and share memories that will stay	1. Kyla is making a decision that will affect her future and the future of her friends. 2. Kyla is taking a step in the right direction and should be celebrated for it. 3. Kyla is showing that she is mature and capable of making her own decisions.	Kyla is graduating from college and her friends asked her if she wants to celebrate with them after the ceremony. Kyla wants to respond to the invite of her friends. Kyla tells her friends that she will go out with them. Kyla is choosing to celebrate with her friends, which shows that she	Kyla's friends are important to her, and she wants to celebrate with them. This is a special occasion, and she wants to share it with them. Additionally, going out with her friends will help her relax and enjoy herself after a stressful day.
3	Craig is out of a job and has a computer with a good internet connection at home. Craig wants to earn money from home. Craig signs up for some online survey sites and does surveys. As a conservative, here are the moral arguments for why this is an immoral thing to do:	1. Surveys are always use to get personal information about people without their knowledge or consent. 2. Craig knowledge that he is being take advantage of will cause more people to sign up for these surveys. 3. These surveys could be more efficiently done without the use of such information.	1. It is possible for someone to earn money from home without doing any surveys. 2. It is possible for someone to earn money from home without doing any work. 3. It is possible for someone to earn money from home without doing any research. 4. It is possible	1. Craig is taking advantage of people who are desperate for money. 2. Craig is not getting paid for the time he spends doing the surveys, which means he is not getting paid for his time. 3. Craig is not getting paid for the information he is providing to the survey site.	1. Craig is not using his talents and skills to their fullest potential. 2. Craig is not contributing to society in a meaningful way. 3. Craig is not providing value to others. 4. Craig is not working towards his goals and dreams. 5. Craig is
4	Larry is at the mall with his son Max who demanded ice cream, which Larry refused and now Max is throwing a tantrum. Larry wants to respond to Max's tantrum. Larry tells Max that he's going to stuff him in a box and mail him to Rwanda if he doesn't quiet down. As a conservative, here are the moral arguments for why this is an immoral thing to do:	1. It's cruel and it's sad. 2. It's a way to discipline his son 3. It's a way to get his son to stop crying 4. It's a way to get him attention 5. It's a way to get him to stop	1. It's a form of child abuse. 2. It's a form of racism. 3. It's a form of bigotry. 4. It's a form of cruelty. 5. It's a form of selfishness. 6. It's a	1. Larry is using physical force to discipline his son. This is not a healthy or effective way to discipline a child. 2. Larry is threatening to send his son away to a faraway country where he may not be safe. This is a very frightening thing to say to a child, and it	1. It is not appropriate to threaten your child with physical harm in order to get them to comply with your wishes. 2. It is not appropriate to threaten your child with abandonment in order to get them to comply with your wishes. 3. It is not appropriate to use fear as a

Figure 8: Examples of completions obtained from Moral Stories dataset, from OpenAI models of increasing size. Examples were randomly selected

LECO: Improving Early Exiting via Learned Exits and Comparison-based Exiting Mechanism

Jingfan Zhang[1], **Ming Tan**[2], **Pengyu Dai**[3,4], **Wei Zhu**[5*]
[1] University of Ottawa, Canada
[2] Southern University of Science and Technology, China
[3] Chongqing University of Post and Telecommunication, China
[4] Brunel University, London
[5] East China Normal University, China

Abstract

Recently, dynamic early exiting has attracted much attention since it can accelerate the inference speed of pre-trained models (PTMs). However, previous work on early exiting has neglected the intermediate exits' architectural designs. In this work, we propose a novel framework, Learned Exits and COmparison-based early exiting (LECO) to improve PTMs' early exiting performances. First, to fully uncover the potentials of multi-exit BERT, we design a novel search space for intermediate exits and employ the idea of differentiable neural architecture search (DNAS) to design proper exit architectures for different intermediate layers automatically. Second, we propose a simple-yet-effective comparison-based early exiting mechanism (COBEE), which can help PTMs achieve better performance and speedup tradeoffs. Extensive experiments show that our LECO achieves the SOTA performances for multi-exit BERT training and dynamic early exiting.

1 Introduction

Despite achieving state-of-the-art (SOTA) performances on almost all the natural language processing (NLP) tasks (Lin et al., 2021), large pre-trained language models (PLMs) still have difficulty being applied to many industrial scenarios with low latency requirements. Many research works are devoted to speeding up the inference of BERT or other PLMs, such as network pruning (Zhu and Gupta, 2017; Xu et al., 2020a; Fan et al., 2019; Gordon et al., 2020), student network distillation (Sun et al., 2019; Sanh et al., 2019; Jiao et al., 2020), and early exiting (Teerapittayanon et al., 2016; Xin et al., 2020; Kaya et al., 2019; Xin et al., 2021). Due to its potential in applications, early exiting has attracted much attention in the research field (Xu et al., 2021a). Early exiting requires a multi-exit BERT, a BERT backbone with an intermediate classifier (or exit) installed on each layer. And then, a dynamic early exiting mechanism is applied during the forward pass to ensure efficient inference. Early exiting is in parallel with and can work together with static model compression methods (Tambe et al., 2020). However, the literature focuses less on the training of multi-exit BERT (Teerapittayanon et al., 2016; Xin et al., 2020; Liu et al., 2020; Xin et al., 2021) and there is no literature systematically discussing the architectural design of the intermediate exits.

In this work, we propose a novel framework, Learned Exits and COmparison-based Early exiting (LECO), designated to discover the full potentials of multi-exit BERT in early exiting. First, we design a suitable and comprehensive search space for architectural learning of the intermediate exits (see Figure 1). Our search space contains candidate activation functions, encoding operations, and pooling operations. We follow the differentiable neural architecture search (DNAS) framework like Liu et al. (2019a); Xie et al. (2019); Chen et al. (2021) to learn a set of intermediate exits with different architectures automatically. Second, reflecting on the limitations of the patience-based early exiting method PABEE (Zhou et al., 2020), we propose a comparison-based early exiting (COBEE) mechanism. COBEE makes early exiting decisions by comparing the predicted distributions of adjacent intermediate layers.

We conduct extensive experiments and ablation studies on the GLUE benchmark (Wang et al., 2018). We show that learned intermediate exits of LECO outperform the previous SOTA multi-exiting BERT training methods while adding fewer trainable parameters. Furthermore, our novel dynamic early exiting mechanism COBEE outperforms the previous SOTA early exiting mechanisms. Further analysis shows that: (a) our LECO framework can help to boost the performance of multi-exiting

*Corresponding author: michaelwzhu91@gmail.com

Proceedings of the 61st Annual Meeting of the Association for Computational Linguistics - Student Research Workshop, pages 298–309
July 10-12, 2023 ©2023 Association for Computational Linguistics

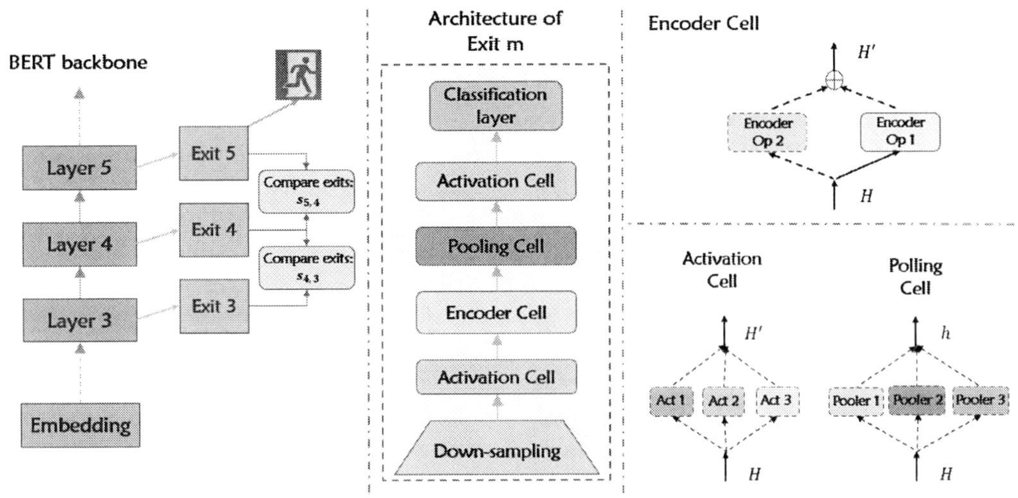

Figure 1: The overall framework of our LECO framework. **Left**: We compare the predicted distributions of adjacent PTMs' intermediate layers for mining exiting signals. **Middle**: the general architecture of intermediate exits. **Right**: Each edge in the the search cell is a weighted sum of multiple operations under the DNAS framework.

BERT under different training strategies. (b) our novel dynamic early exiting strategy outperforms the baseline early exiting methods.

Our contributions are as follows:

- We propose a novel framework, LECO, which constructs a search space for intermediate exits and employs a DNAS framework to learn the suitable exits for different layers.
- We propose a novel comparison-based early exiting criterion which can achieve better quality-speed tradeoffs for PTMs.
- We conduct experiments to show that our LECO achieves SOTA performances for multi-exit BERT training.

2 Related Work

2.1 Inference acceleration methods

Since the rise of BERT, there are quite large numbers of literature devoting themselves to speeding up the inference of BERT. Standard method include direct network pruning (Zhu and Gupta, 2017; Xu et al., 2020a; Fan et al., 2019; Gordon et al., 2020), distillation (Sun et al., 2019; Sanh et al., 2019; Jiao et al., 2020), Weight quantization (Zhang et al., 2020b; Bai et al., 2020; Kim et al., 2021) and Adaptive inference (Zhou et al., 2020; Xin et al., 2020; Liu et al., 2020). Among them, adaptive inference has drawn much attention. Adaptive inference aims to deal with simple examples with only shallow layers of PLMs, thus speeding up inference time on average.

Early exiting requires a multi-exit model, like a BERT backbone with an intermediate classifier (or exit) installed on each layer. Early exiting literature mainly focuses on the development of the early exiting strategies, that is, determining when an intermediate exit's prediction is suitable as the final model prediction. Score based strategies (Teerapittayanon et al., 2016; Xin et al., 2020; Kaya et al., 2019; Xin et al., 2021), prior based strategies (Sun et al., 2022) and patience based strategies (Zhou et al., 2020) have been proposed. Teerapittayanon et al. (2016) uses the entropy of an intermediate layer's predicted distribution to measure the in-confidence level and decide whether to exit early. PABEE asks the model to exit when the current layer's prediction is the same with the previous layers.

Our work complements the literature on early exiting by proposing the LECO framework to improve early exiting performance via the automatic architectural design of exit architectures and a novel early exiting mechanism.

2.2 Neural architecture search

With the rapid development and wide industrial applications, researchers have devoted great effect in manually designing neural netoweks (Krizhevsky et al., 2012; Simonyan and Zisserman, 2015; He et al., 2016; Huang et al., 2017; Wang et al., 2022). The trend is to stack more and more convolutional or transformer layers to construct a deep network. Recently, when trying to avoid manual architecture design, researchers started considering developing algorithms to design neural networks automatically. Thus, a new research sub-field of automated machine learning (AutoML) (He et al., 2021) called neural architecture search is established (Zoph and Le, 2017).

In the early attempts, NAS requires massive computations, like thousands of GPU days (Zoph and Le, 2017; Zoph et al., 2018; Liu et al., 2018). Recently, a particular group of one-shot NAS, led by the seminal work DARTS (Liu et al., 2019a) has attracted much attention. DARTS formulates the search space into a super-network that can adjust itself in a continuous space so that the network and architectural parameters can be optimized alternately (bi-level optimization) using gradient descent. A series of literature try to improve the performance and efficiency of DARTS. SNAS (Xie et al., 2019) reformulate DARTS as a credit assignment task while maintaining the differentiability. P-DARTS (Chen et al., 2021) analyze the issues during the DARTS bi-level optimization, and propose a series of modifications. PC-DARTS (Xu et al., 2021b) reduces the memory cost during search by sampling partial channels in super-networks. Fair-DARTS (Chu et al., 2021) change the softmax operations in DARTS into sigmoid and introduce a penalty term to prune the architectural parameters according to the demand. Gao et al. (2020) make the hyper-network more close to the discretized sub-network by penalizing the entropy of the architecture parameters.

Our work contributes to the NAS literature by investigate the architectural search of intermediate exits to improve the early exiting performances.

3 Preliminaries

In this section, we introduce the necessary background for BERT early exiting. we consider the case of multi-class classification with K classes, $\mathcal{K} = \{1, 2, ..., K\}$. The dataset consists of N samples $\{(x_i, y_i), i \in \mathcal{I} = \{1, 2, ..., N\}\}$, where x_i is an input sentence consisting of L words, and $y_i \in \mathcal{K}$ is the label.

3.1 Early Exiting

Multi-exit PTM Early exiting is based on multi-exit PTM, which is a PTM backbone with classifiers (or exits) at each layer. With M layers, M classifiers $f_m(x; \theta_m)$ are designated at M layers of the PTM, each of which maps its input to the probability distribution on K classes. $f_m(x; \theta_m)$ can take the form of a simple linear layer (linear exit) following (Zhou et al., 2020). However, as is shown in Liu et al. (2020), adding an encoding operation like the multi-head self-attention layer (Vaswani et al., 2017) to the intermediate exits (MHA exits) can significantly boost the performance of intermediate layers, demonstrating the importance of architectural design.

Training We now introduce the three main multi-exit BERT training methods widely adopted in the literature.

JT. Perhaps the most straightforward fine-tuning strategy is to minimize the sum of all classifiers' loss functions and jointly update all parameters in the process. We refer to this strategy as JT. The loss function is:

$$\mathcal{L}_{JT} = \sum_{m=1}^{M} \mathcal{L}_m^{CE} \quad (1)$$

where $\mathcal{L}_m^{CE} = \mathcal{L}_m^{CE}(y, f_m(x; \theta_m))$ denotes the cross-entropy loss of the m-th exit. This method is adopted by Teerapittayanon et al. (2016); Kaya et al. (2019); Zhou et al. (2020); Zhu (2021).

2ST. The two-stage (2ST) (Xin et al., 2020; Liu et al., 2020) training strategy divides the training procedure into two stages. The first stage is identical to the vanilla BERT fine-tuning, updating the backbone model and only the final exit. In the second stage, we freeze all parameters updated in the first stage and fine-tune the remaining exits separately:

$$\text{Stage1}: \mathcal{L}_{stage1} = \mathcal{L}_M^{CE}(y_i, f_M(x_i; \theta_M)) \quad (2)$$

$$\text{Stage2}: \mathcal{L}_{stage2} = \mathcal{L}_m^{CE}, m = 1, ..., M-1. \quad (3)$$

where $\mathcal{L}_m^{CE} = \mathcal{L}_m^{CE}(y_i, f_m(x_i; \theta_m))$ denotes the cross-entropy loss of m-th exit.

ALT. It alternates between two objectives (taken from Equation 1 and 2) across different epochs, and it was proposed by BERxiT (Xin et al., 2021):

$$\text{Odd}: \mathcal{L}_{stage1} = \mathcal{L}_M^{CE}(y_i, f_M(x_i; \theta_M)) \quad (4)$$

$$\text{Even}: \mathcal{L}_{joint} = \sum_{m=1}^{M} \mathcal{L}_m^{CE} \quad (5)$$

For the search and training of our LECO method, we adopt the joint training (JT) method, following Teerapittayanon et al. (2016); Kaya et al. (2019); Zhou et al. (2020); Zhu (2021). LECO mainly employs JT to fine-tune the PTM backbone and simultaneously learn the best exit architectures for all intermediate layers under a differentiable NAS framework.

Early exiting inference At inference, the multi-exit PLM can operate in two different modes: (a) static early exiting, that is, a suitable exit m^* is appointed to predict all queries. (b) Dynamic early exiting, the model starts to predict on the classifiers $f^{(1)}$, $f^{(2)}$, ..., in turn in a forward pass, until it receives a signal to stop early at an exit $m^* < M$, or arrives at the last exit M.

3.1.1 Inference speedup ratio

During inference, we will run the test samples with batch size one following Zhou et al. (2020); Teerapittayanon et al. (2016). We report the actual wall-clock run-time reduction as the efficiency metric. For each test sample x_i, denote the inference time cost under early exiting as t_i, and time cost under no early exiting as T_i. Then the average speedup ratio on the test set is calculated by Speedup $= 1 - \frac{\sum_1^{N_{test}} t_i}{\sum_1^{N_{test}} T_i}$, where N_{test} is the number of samples on the test set. We will run the test set ten times and report the average speedup ratio to avoid randomness of run-time.

3.2 Preliminaries on DARTS

Assume there is a pre-defined space of operations denoted by $\mathcal{O}$, where each element, $o(\cdot)$, denotes a neural network operation, such as convolutional operation, self-attention, and activation. DARTS (Liu et al., 2019a) operates on a search cell, a fully connected directed acyclic graph (DAG) with N nodes. Let (i, j) denote a pair of nodes. The core idea of DARTS is to initialize a supernetwork stacked with blocks with the same architecture as the DAG. During the search, each edge in the DAG is a weighted sum including all $|\mathcal{O}|$ operations in $\mathcal{O}$, $f_{i,j}(z_i) = \sum_{o \in \mathcal{O}} a^o_{i,j} \cdot o(z_i)$, where $a^o_{i,j} = \frac{\exp \alpha^o_{i,j}}{\sum_{o' \in \mathcal{O}} \exp \alpha^{o'}_{i,j}}$, z_i denotes the output of the i-th node, and $\alpha^o_{i,j}$ is the architectural parameters that represent the weight (or the importance score) of $o(\cdot)$ in edge (i, j). The output of a node is the sum of all input flow, i.e., $z_j = \sum_{i<j} f_{i,j}(z_i)$. The output of the entire cell is formed by summing the last two nodes.

This design makes the entire framework differentiable to layer weights and architectural parameters $\alpha^o_{i,j}$ so that it can perform architecture searches in an end-to-end fashion. The standard optimization method is the bi-level optimization proposed in DARTS. After the search process is completed, the discretization procedure extracts the final sub-network by dropping the operations receiving lower scores.

4 Search space of LECO

As depicted in Figure 1, we construct the search space of a LECO intermediate exit mimicking the MHA exit. Representations of the current BERT layer, $H_i^{(m)}$, will first be down-sampled to a smaller dimension $\mathcal{R}^{d_e}$ (e.g., 64) to keep the intermediate exit parameter-efficient.[1] Then, it will go through an activation cell, an encoder cell, a pooling cell, and finally, another activation cell. The whole DAG of the intermediate exit consists of 7 edges.

Activation cell Both activations cells are one-step DAGs (Figure 1), designated to choose the proper activation function from several candidates. Similar to So et al. (2019), the collection of activation functions we consider is: (a) **ReLU** (Agarap, 2018); (b) **GeLU** (Hendrycks and Gimpel, 2016); (c) **SWISH** (Ramachandran et al., 2017); (d) **Tanh** (Krizhevsky et al., 2012); (e) **NullAct**, which means making no changes to the input.

Encoder cell As is shown in Figure 1, different from Wang et al. (2020); Zhu et al. (2021a), we construct our encoder cell as a simple DAG, which consists of at most two encoder operations. Encoder operations 1 and 2 will encode the cell's input, and their outputs will be summed to be the output of the encoder cell. As an extension to the encoder search space of Wang et al. (2020); Zhu et al. (2021a); Chen et al. (2020), our collection of encoder operations consists of the following commonly used encoding operations: (a) 1-d convolutional layers, with stride 1, same padding, output filters equal to the input's dimension, and kernel size equal to 1, 3, or 5 (denoted as **conv_**k, $k = 1, 3, 5$); (b) multi-head self-attention layer (Vaswani et al., 2017), with $k = 2, 4, 8$ attention heads, head size equaling d_e/k (denoted as **mha_**k, $k = 2, 4, 8$); (c) skip-connection, denoted as **skip-connect**; (d) the null encoding operation that multiply zero tensors to the input (**null**).[2]

[1] Note that the parameters of the intermediate exits constitute at most 1.6% of the BERT's parameters.

[2] Selecting this operation means fewer operations will be included in the encoder DAG.

Pooling cell It is also a one-step DAG for selecting the proper pooling layer. The most commonly used pooling operation for PTM-based models is to extract the representations of the $[CLS]$ token (denoted as **cls_pool**). As is summarized in Gong et al. (2018), other commonly used pooling operations are: max pooling (**max_pool**); average pooling (**avg_pool**); self-attention based pooling (**sa_pool**).

Note that our search space contains the MHA exit (introduced in Section 3.1) as a special case. The above search space can result in 6.87e+34 combinations of different multi-exit BERT. We will mainly follow DARTS (Liu et al., 2019a) to search for the optimal architecture designs of exits. But different from (Liu et al., 2019a), we adopt a macro search space, that is, the exits from different layers have different architectural parameters, thus resulting different architectures for different layers.

5 Comparison-based Early Exiting

The patience-based mechanism (Zhou et al., 2020) validates the early exiting decisions among the previous layers, providing a promising direction for designing early exiting mechanisms. the early exiting condition in PABEE is coarse: it directly compares the predicted labels. However, tt is common for BERT to change its predictions after a few intermediate layers. Thus, PABEE's early exiting performances with low patience parameters may not be reliable. To summarize, we need a more fine-grained criterion to generate more reliable early exiting signals.

We now introduce our Comparison-based early exiting method, COBEE. The inference procedure is illustrated in Figure 1. Assume the forward pass has reached layer $m < M$. We now compare the predicted distributions of layer m and layer $m^{'}$ ($m > m^{'}$) as follows. Denote the label that receives the highest probability mass at layer m as k^{*}_{m}, and the probability distribution of exit m is denoted as $\mathbf{Pr}_{m}$, then the disagreement between layer m and layer $m^{'}$ is calculated as:

$$\text{Di}(\mathbf{Pr}_{m}, \mathbf{Pr}_{m^{'}}) = |\mathbf{Pr}_{m}(k^{*}_{m}) - \mathbf{Pr}_{m^{'}}(k^{*}_{m})|. \quad (6)$$

For simplicity, we denote $\text{di}_{m,m^{'}} = \text{Di}(\mathbf{Pr}_{m}, \mathbf{Pr}_{m^{'}}) \in \mathbf{R}$. The smaller the value of $\text{di}_{m,m^{'}}$, the predicted distributions $\mathbf{Pr}_{m}$ and $\mathbf{Pr}_{m^{'}}$ are more consistent with each other. We use a counter cnt to store the number of times the disagreement scores between adjacent layers are less than the pre-defined exiting threshold τ. At layer m, cnt_{m} is calculated as:

$$cnt_{m} = \begin{cases} cnt_{m-1} + 1, & \text{if } \text{di}_{m,m-1} < \tau, \\ 0, & \text{otherwise.} \end{cases} \quad (7)$$

If $\text{di}_{m,m-1}$ is less than the pre-defined threshold, then the patience counter is increased by 1. Otherwise, the patience counter is reset to 0. If cnt_{m} reaches the pre-defined patience value t, the model stops inference and exits early. Otherwise, the model goes to the next layer. However, if the model does not exit early at intermediate layers, the model uses the final classifier f_{M} for prediction.

6 Experiments

6.1 Datasets

We evaluate our proposed approach to the classification tasks on GLUE benchmark (Wang et al., 2018). We only exclude the STS-B task since it is a regression task, and we exclude the WNLI task following previous work (Devlin et al., 2019; Jiao et al., 2020; Xu et al., 2020b). Since the original test sets are not publicly available, we follow Zhang et al. (2020a) and Mahabadi et al. (2021) to construct the train/dev/test splits as follows: (a) for datasets with fewer than 10k samples (RTE, MRPC, CoLA), we divide the original validation set in half, using one half for validation and the other for testing. (b) for larger datasets, we split 1k samples from the training set as the development set, and use the original development set as the test set. The detailed dataset statistics are presented in Table 1.

For MNLI, we report acc, which is the average of the accuracy scores on the matched and mismatched test set. For MRPC and QQP, we report acc-f1, which is the average of accuracy and F1 scores. For CoLA, we report mcc, which is the Matthews correlation. For all other tasks, we report accuracy (acc).

6.2 Baseline methods

We compare our LECO framework with the following baselines:

Multi-exiting model training For multi-exit model training, we compare: (a) Joint training (JT) (Zhou et al., 2020; Teerapittayanon et al., 2016), with both a linear exit and an MHA exit ($d_e = 64$); (b) two-stage training (2ST) (Liu et al., 2020; Xin et al., 2020), with an MHA exit ($d_e = 64$); (c) alternating training (ALT) in Xin et al. (2021); (d) the

Category	Datasets	|train|	|dev|	|test|	$\|\mathcal{Y}\|$	Type	Labels
Single-sentence	SST-2	66349	1000	872	2	sentiment	positive, negative
	CoLA	8551	521	522	2	linguistic acceptability	acceptable, not acceptable
Sentence-pair	MNLI	391702	1000	19647	3	NLI	entailment, neutral, contradiction
	MRPC	3668	204	204	2	paraphrase	equivalent, not equivalent
	QNLI	103743	1000	5463	2	NLI	entailment, not entailment
	QQP	362846	1000	40430	2	paraphrase	equivalent, not equivalent
	RTE	2490	138	139	2	NLI	entailment, not entailment

Table 1: The statistics of datasets evaluated in this work. For MNLI task, the number of samples in the test set is summed by matched and mismatched samples. $|\mathcal{Y}|$ is the number of classes for a dataset.

Gradient Equilibrium technique (GradEquil) (Li et al., 2019), which incorporates JT with gradient adjustments and is adopted by Liu et al. (2021); (e) Global Past Future (Liao et al., 2021) (Global-PF) which asks the lower layers to imitate the deeper layers; (f) GAML-BERT (Zhu et al., 2021b), which employs a mutual learning strategy to improve the performances of shallow exits.

Early exiting methods We compare the early exiting performances of our COBEE method on the multi-exit backbone trained under the LECO framework with the following methods: (a) Entropy-based method (Entropy) originated from (Teerapittayanon et al., 2016), which is equivalent to the maximum-probability based method Schwartz et al. (2020); (b) Patience-based method (Patience) (Zhou et al., 2020); (c) learning-to-exit based method (LTE) proposed by Xin et al. (2021), which train an extra meta-classifier to estimate the confidence on a sample and achieves the SOTA performances of early exiting. For comparison, we also run the patience-based method on the backbone obtained by the JT method with linear exits.

6.3 Experimental settings

Devices We implement LECO on the base of HuggingFace's Transformers. We conduct our experiments on Nvidia V100 16GB GPUs.

PTM models. We mainly adopt the ALBERT base (Lan et al., 2019) backbone. We will also include RoBERTa-base (Liu et al., 2019b), and DeBERTa-base (He et al., 2020) in the ablation studies.

Settings for Architecture search We add a LECO search cell (Figure 1) with dimension d_e equal to 32 on each intermediate layer of the PTM and adopt the DARTS (Liu et al., 2019a) method to learn the best exit architecture for each layer. AdamW optimizer (Loshchilov and Hutter, 2019) is used for both the model and architecture parameters. At the beginning of each epoch, the training set is randomly split into D_1 (for updating model parameters) and D_2 (for updating architecture parameters) with a ratio of $1:1$. The search will last for 30 epochs. The learning rate is 2e-5 for model parameters and 2e-4 for architectural parameters. The search procedure is run once on each GLUE task.

Settings for Architecture evaluation After the search procedure ends, the top-scored sub-network is discretized from the super-network at each layer and will be trained from scratch as the final learned exit. The learning rate is 2e-5, and AdamW optimizer (Loshchilov and Hutter, 2019) is used for optimization. We evaluate the dev set and save the checkpoint after each epoch. After training ends, we evaluate the best checkpoint on the test set. We train the final learned exits under 5 random seeds to obtain its average test performance.

6.4 Main results

Comparison of multi-exit model training methods Table 2 reports the main results on the GLUE benchmark with ALBERT as the backbone model. All baseline models are run with the original authors' open-sourced codes. We report AVG, the cross-layer average score, and BEST, the best score among all the intermediate layers. From Table 2, Our LECO method outperforms the previous multi-exit model training methods in terms of the AVG scores (with statistical significance), demonstrating that our LECO framework effectively boosts the overall performances of intermediate exits and thus providing stronger backbones for early exiting.

Note that both 2ST + MHA exit (Liu et al., 2020) and JT + MHA exit introduce 66k parameters per exit, while the LECO method adds 25k-26k parameters per exit. The comparison among the three methods demonstrates that our LECO method does not rely only on adding more parameters to obtain performance improvements. The improvements of LECO result from better architectural designs for

	RTE		MRPC		CoLA		SST-2		QNLI		QQP		MNLI	
Baseline methods														
	AVG	BEST	AVG	BEST	AVG	BEST	AVG	BEST	AVG	BEST	AVG	BEST	AVG	BEST
JT + linear exit	66.8	72.5	83.7	87.9	43.7	53.3	89.2	91.1	82.6	87.3	82.2	87.2	76.0	83.1
JT + MHA exit	68.1	76.9	84.1	88.2	43.6	57.5	88.2	91.5	82.8	87.6	82.4	87.1	76.8	83.2
GradEquil	67.3	77.4	84.2	89.3	43.6	56.1	89.2	91.8	82.4	88.0	82.7	87.0	76.5	83.6
ALT	68.5	77.8	84.6	88.3	44.1	57.3	88.9	91.6	82.3	87.8	82.5	86.8	76.6	83.2
GAML-BERT	68.8	77.6	84.9	88.8	45.0	57.9	89.1	92.3	82.6	87.9	82.6	87.5	75.9	83.4
Global-PF	68.5	78.1	84.9	88.6	45.1	57.7	88.9	92.6	82.5	88.1	82.6	87.4	76.5	83.3
2ST + MHA exit	68.9	77.5	85.1	89.2	45.0	57.9	89.3	92.4	82.5	88.0	82.7	87.3	76.2	82.7
Our proposed method														
LECO	**69.7***	77.9	**85.8***	89.4	**46.4***	58.0	**89.6***	92.5	**83.4***	88.1	**83.1***	87.4	**77.3***	83.4

Table 2: Average test performance of methods with ALBERT backbone on GLUE tasks across 5 random seeds. AVG represents cross-layer average score, and BEST represents best score among all layers. The $*$ symbol on the AVG scores means the results surpass the baseline method with statistical significance (by the Wilcoxon signed-rank test).

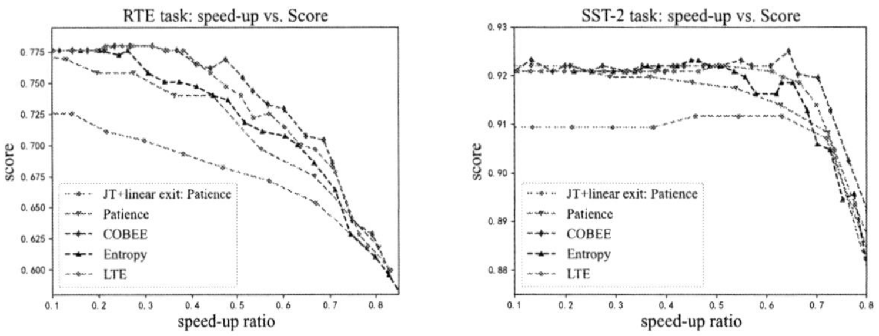

(a) RTE (b) SST-2

Figure 2: The speedup-score curves with different dynamic early exiting methods, on the RTE and SST-datasets.

exits of different depths.

Comparison of dynamic early exiting mechanisms We compare our COBEE method with the previous best-performing early exiting methods on the multi-exit ALBERT-base backbone trained under our LECO framework (as reported in Table 2). We also run the patience-based early exiting with the multi-exit ALBERT-base trained with the JT method. For the patience-based method (Zhou et al., 2020), early exiting is run on different patience parameters. For the other methods, we run early exiting under different confidence thresholds or patience parameters so that the speedup-performance curves consist of at least 20 points evenly distributed across the interval $(0, 1)$ of speedup ratios. The speedup-performance curves for the RTE and SST-2 tasks are plotted in Figure 2.

The following takeaways can also be made from Figure 2: (a) With the same backbone model, our COBEE method achieves better speedup-performance trade-offs than the previous SOTA early exiting methods, especially when the speedup ratio is large. (b) The comparison between Patience and JT+linear exit: Patience demonstrates that our LECO method can provide superior backbones for early exiting and consistently result in superior performances under different speedup ratios, even though introducing a more complex exit architecture. The learned exit architecture constitutes 0.25% of the parameters on each intermediate layer and increases 0.6% inference latency on average. However, the performance gains on the intermediate layers clearly out-weights the increased latency.

6.5 Discussions and ablation studies

Discussion on the learned architectures Table 6 of the Appendix A presents the best-learned exit architectures on each layer of ALBERT when the downstream task is MRPC or RTE. Three observations can be made: (a) although we allow at most two encoder operations in the encoder search cell, more than half of the learned exits include one valid encoding operation, making the exits more parameter efficient. (b) The learned archi-

Method	AVG score	
-	RTE	SST-2
LECO	69.7	89.6
2ST + MHA exit	68.9	89.3
2ST + LECO	69.6	89.5
ALT	68.5	88.9
ALT + LECO	69.3	89.4

Table 3: Comparisons of LECO with different multi-exit training methods. Cross-layer average performance (AVG) scores are reported.

tectures tend to use a pair of different activation functions, which is different from the combination of the Tanh-Tanh activation functions applied in the MHA exit (Liu et al., 2020). (c) Most exits do not select the **cls_pool** pooling operation, validating the necessity of our pooler search cell.

LECO works well with other multi-exit training strategies In the main experiments, we train LECO with the JT method. Table 3 demonstrates the results of LECO when trained with 2ST and ALT. The results show that LECO can effectively improve the performances of 2ST and ALT, and achieve comparable results with LECO combined with JT. However, the JT method is more convenient and takes less training time.

LECO works well with other pretrained backbones We now substitute the pretrained backbone to RoBERTa-base (Liu et al., 2019b) and DeBERTa-base (He et al., 2020), and the results are reported in Table 4. We can see that our LECO framework can also help to improve the average performance of multi-exit RoBERTa/DeBERTa model. An interesting take-away is that RoBERTa and DeBERTa can not outperform ALBERT in terms of AVG scores. We hypothesis that ALBERT shares parameters across transformer layers, thus the difference between shallow and deep layers are smaller than the other models.

Ablation on the search space We now conduct an ablation study to show the validity of our search space design. We consider reducing our search space $\mathcal{O}$ to a singleton step-by-step: (a) reduce the activation cells by only keeping the **Tanh** activation ($\mathcal{O}_1$); (b) further reduce the pooler cell to only include **cls_pool** ($\mathcal{O}_2$); (c) further reduce the encoder cell to only include **mha_dot**, and now the search space only contains the MHA exit. Table 5 reports the search results on different search spaces. From Table 5, we can see that dropping any components of the whole search space results in performance

Method	AVG score	
-	RTE	SST-2
ALBERT backbone		
LECO	69.7	89.6
JT + MHA exit	68.1	88.2
RoBERTa backbone		
LECO	68.6	88.7
JT + MHA exit	66.5	87.4
DeBERTa backbone		
LECO	69.5	89.3
JT + MHA exit	66.9	88.1

Table 4: Comparisons of LECO with different pretrained backbones. Cross-layer average performance (AVG) scores are reported. We can see that RoBERTa and DeBERTa can not outperform ALBERT in AVG scores.

search space	AVG score	
-	RTE	SST-2
$\mathcal{O}$	69.7	89.6
$\mathcal{O}_1$	69.3	89.1
$\mathcal{O}_2$	68.9	88.7
MHA exit	68.1	88.2

Table 5: Experimental results for the ablation study of our LECO search space. Cross-layer average (AVG) performance scores are reported.

losses, demonstrating that our search space design is necessary and beneficial.

7 Conclusion

In this work, we propose a novel framework, LECO. Our contributions are three-fold. First, LECO designs a unified search space for architectural designs of intermediate exits. Second, we apply the differentiable NAS framework of DARTS to learn the optimal exit architectures automatically. Third, we propose a novel comparison based early exiting mechanism, COBEE. Experiments on the GLUE benchmark and ablation studies demonstrate that our LECO framework can achieve SOTA on multi-exit BERT training and outperforms the previously SOTA dynamic early exiting methods.

Limitation

Although our LECO framework is shown to be effective in improving the multi-exit BERT training, it still has certain limitations that need to be addressed in the future: (a) MHA exits and our learned exits indeed introduce new parameters and additional flops. We would like to explore more parameter-efficient methods to improve multi-exit

BERT training in future works. (b) In this work, we demonstrate our framework's performance on sentence classification or pair classification tasks. In future works, we would like to extend our work to broader tasks such as sequence labeling, relation extraction, and text generation. We would like to explore this aspect in the future.

Ethics Statement

Our LECO framework is designated to improve the training of multi-exit BERT and dynamic early exiting performances. Our work can facilitate the deployment and applications of pre-trained models on devices with less powerful computation capabilities, making the state-of-the-art models accessible for everyone. In addition, we hope this technology can help reduce the carbon footprints of NLP-based applications. Furthermore, the datasets we experiment with are widely used in previous work and, to our knowledge, does not introduce new ethical concerns.

References

Abien Fred Agarap. 2018. Deep learning using rectified linear units (relu). *ArXiv*, abs/1803.08375.

Haoli Bai, Wei Zhang, Lu Hou, Lifeng Shang, Jing Jin, Xin Jiang, Qun Liu, Michael Lyu, and Irwin King. 2020. Binarybert: Pushing the limit of bert quantization. *arXiv preprint arXiv:2012.15701*.

Daoyuan Chen, Yaliang Li, Minghui Qiu, Zhen Wang, Bofang Li, Bolin Ding, Hongbo Deng, Jun Huang, Wei Lin, and Jingren Zhou. 2020. Adabert: Task-adaptive bert compression with differentiable neural architecture search. In *IJCAI*.

Xin Chen, Lingxi Xie, Jun Wu, and Qi Tian. 2021. Progressive darts: Bridging the optimization gap for nas in the wild. *ArXiv*, abs/1912.10952.

Xiangxiang Chu, Bo Zhang, Ruijun Xu, and Jixiang Li. 2021. Fairnas: Rethinking evaluation fairness of weight sharing neural architecture search. *2021 IEEE/CVF International Conference on Computer Vision (ICCV)*, pages 12219–12228.

Jacob Devlin, Ming-Wei Chang, Kenton Lee, and Kristina Toutanova. 2019. BERT: Pre-training of deep bidirectional transformers for language understanding. In *Proceedings of the 2019 Conference of the North American Chapter of the Association for Computational Linguistics: Human Language Technologies, Volume 1 (Long and Short Papers)*, pages 4171–4186, Minneapolis, Minnesota. Association for Computational Linguistics.

Angela Fan, Edouard Grave, and Armand Joulin. 2019. Reducing transformer depth on demand with structured dropout. *arXiv preprint arXiv:1909.11556*.

Yuan Gao, Haoping Bai, Zequn Jie, Jiayi Ma, Kui Jia, and Wei Liu. 2020. Mtl-nas: Task-agnostic neural architecture search towards general-purpose multi-task learning. *2020 IEEE/CVF Conference on Computer Vision and Pattern Recognition (CVPR)*, pages 11540–11549.

Jingjing Gong, Xipeng Qiu, Shaojing Wang, and Xuanjing Huang. 2018. Information aggregation via dynamic routing for sequence encoding. In *COLING*.

Mitchell A Gordon, Kevin Duh, and Nicholas Andrews. 2020. Compressing bert: Studying the effects of weight pruning on transfer learning. *arXiv preprint arXiv:2002.08307*.

Kaiming He, X. Zhang, Shaoqing Ren, and Jian Sun. 2016. Deep residual learning for image recognition. *2016 IEEE Conference on Computer Vision and Pattern Recognition (CVPR)*, pages 770–778.

Pengcheng He, Xiaodong Liu, Jianfeng Gao, and Weizhu Chen. 2020. Deberta: Decoding-enhanced bert with disentangled attention. *ArXiv*, abs/2006.03654.

Xin He, Kaiyong Zhao, and Xiaowen Chu. 2021. Automl: A survey of the state-of-the-art. *Knowl. Based Syst.*, 212:106622.

Dan Hendrycks and Kevin Gimpel. 2016. Gaussian error linear units (gelus). *arXiv: Learning*.

Gao Huang, Zhuang Liu, and Kilian Q. Weinberger. 2017. Densely connected convolutional networks. *2017 IEEE Conference on Computer Vision and Pattern Recognition (CVPR)*, pages 2261–2269.

Xiaoqi Jiao, Yichun Yin, Lifeng Shang, Xin Jiang, Xiao Chen, Linlin Li, Fang Wang, and Qun Liu. 2020. Tinybert: Distilling bert for natural language understanding. *ArXiv*, abs/1909.10351.

Y. Kaya, Sanghyun Hong, and T. Dumitras. 2019. Shallow-deep networks: Understanding and mitigating network overthinking. In *ICML*.

Sehoon Kim, Amir Gholami, Zhewei Yao, Michael W Mahoney, and Kurt Keutzer. 2021. I-bert: Integer-only bert quantization. In *International conference on machine learning*, pages 5506–5518. PMLR.

Alex Krizhevsky, Ilya Sutskever, and Geoffrey E. Hinton. 2012. Imagenet classification with deep convolutional neural networks. *Communications of the ACM*, 60:84 – 90.

Zhenzhong Lan, Mingda Chen, Sebastian Goodman, Kevin Gimpel, Piyush Sharma, and Radu Soricut. 2019. Albert: A lite bert for self-supervised learning of language representations. *arXiv preprint arXiv:1909.11942*.

Hao Li, Hong Zhang, Xiaojuan Qi, Ruigang Yang, and Gao Huang. 2019. Improved techniques for training adaptive deep networks. *2019 IEEE/CVF International Conference on Computer Vision (ICCV)*, pages 1891–1900.

Kaiyuan Liao, Yi Zhang, Xuancheng Ren, Qi Su, Xu Sun, and Bin He. 2021. A global past-future early exit method for accelerating inference of pre-trained language models. In *Proceedings of the 2021 Conference of the North American Chapter of the Association for Computational Linguistics: Human Language Technologies*, pages 2013–2023, Online. Association for Computational Linguistics.

Tianyang Lin, Yuxin Wang, Xiangyang Liu, and Xipeng Qiu. 2021. A survey of transformers. *ArXiv*, abs/2106.04554.

Chenxi Liu, Barret Zoph, Jonathon Shlens, Wei Hua, Li-Jia Li, Li Fei-Fei, Alan Loddon Yuille, Jonathan Huang, and Kevin P. Murphy. 2018. Progressive neural architecture search. In *ECCV*.

Hanxiao Liu, Karen Simonyan, and Yiming Yang. 2019a. Darts: Differentiable architecture search. *ArXiv*, abs/1806.09055.

Weijie Liu, Peng Zhou, Zhe Zhao, Zhiruo Wang, Haotang Deng, and Qi Ju. 2020. Fastbert: a self-distilling bert with adaptive inference time. *arXiv preprint arXiv:2004.02178*.

Xiangyang Liu, Tianxiang Sun, Junliang He, Lingling Wu, Xinyu Zhang, Hao Jiang, Zhao Cao, Xuanjing Huang, and Xipeng Qiu. 2021. Towards efficient nlp: A standard evaluation and a strong baseline. In *North American Chapter of the Association for Computational Linguistics*.

Yinhan Liu, Myle Ott, Naman Goyal, Jingfei Du, Mandar Joshi, Danqi Chen, Omer Levy, Mike Lewis, Luke Zettlemoyer, and Veselin Stoyanov. 2019b. Roberta: A robustly optimized bert pretraining approach. *ArXiv*, abs/1907.11692.

Ilya Loshchilov and Frank Hutter. 2019. Decoupled weight decay regularization. In *ICLR*.

Rabeeh Karimi Mahabadi, James Henderson, and Sebastian Ruder. 2021. Compacter: Efficient low-rank hypercomplex adapter layers. In *NeurIPS*.

Prajit Ramachandran, Barret Zoph, and Quoc V. Le. 2017. Swish: a self-gated activation function. *arXiv: Neural and Evolutionary Computing*.

Victor Sanh, Lysandre Debut, Julien Chaumond, and Thomas Wolf. 2019. Distilbert, a distilled version of bert: smaller, faster, cheaper and lighter. *arXiv preprint arXiv:1910.01108*.

Roy Schwartz, Gabriel Stanovsky, Swabha Swayamdipta, Jesse Dodge, and Noah A Smith. 2020. The right tool for the job: Matching model and instance complexities. *arXiv preprint arXiv:2004.07453*.

Karen Simonyan and Andrew Zisserman. 2015. Very deep convolutional networks for large-scale image recognition. *CoRR*, abs/1409.1556.

David R. So, Chen Liang, and Quoc V. Le. 2019. The evolved transformer. *ArXiv*, abs/1901.11117.

Siqi Sun, Yu Cheng, Zhe Gan, and Jingjing Liu. 2019. Patient knowledge distillation for bert model compression. *arXiv preprint arXiv:1908.09355*.

Tianxiang Sun, Xiangyang Liu, Wei Zhu, Zhichao Geng, Lingling Wu, Yilong He, Yuan Ni, Guotong Xie, Xuanjing Huang, and Xipeng Qiu. 2022. A simple hash-based early exiting approach for language understanding and generation. In *Findings of the Association for Computational Linguistics: ACL 2022*, pages 2409–2421, Dublin, Ireland. Association for Computational Linguistics.

Thierry Tambe, Coleman Hooper, Lillian Pentecost, En-Yu Yang, Marco Donato, Victor Sanh, Alexander M. Rush, David M. Brooks, and Gu-Yeon Wei. 2020. Edgebert: Optimizing on-chip inference for multi-task nlp. *ArXiv*, abs/2011.14203.

Surat Teerapittayanon, Bradley McDanel, and H. T. Kung. 2016. Branchynet: Fast inference via early exiting from deep neural networks. *2016 23rd International Conference on Pattern Recognition (ICPR)*, pages 2464–2469.

Ashish Vaswani, Noam M. Shazeer, Niki Parmar, Jakob Uszkoreit, Llion Jones, Aidan N. Gomez, Lukasz Kaiser, and Illia Polosukhin. 2017. Attention is all you need. *ArXiv*, abs/1706.03762.

Alex Wang, Amanpreet Singh, Julian Michael, Felix Hill, Omer Levy, and Samuel R. Bowman. 2018. Glue: A multi-task benchmark and analysis platform for natural language understanding. In *BlackboxNLP@EMNLP*.

Hongyu Wang, Shuming Ma, Li Dong, Shaohan Huang, Dongdong Zhang, and Furu Wei. 2022. Deepnet: Scaling transformers to 1, 000 layers. *ArXiv*, abs/2203.00555.

Yujing Wang, Yaming Yang, Yiren Chen, Jing Bai, Ce Zhang, Guinan Su, Xiaoyu Kou, Yunhai Tong, Mao Yang, and Lidong Zhou. 2020. Textnas: A neural architecture search space tailored for text representation. In *AAAI*.

Sirui Xie, Hehui Zheng, Chunxiao Liu, and Liang Lin. 2019. Snas: Stochastic neural architecture search. *ArXiv*, abs/1812.09926.

Ji Xin, Raphael Tang, Jaejun Lee, Yaoliang Yu, and Jimmy Lin. 2020. Deebert: Dynamic early exiting for accelerating bert inference. *arXiv preprint arXiv:2004.12993*.

Ji Xin, Raphael Tang, Yaoliang Yu, and Jimmy Lin. 2021. Berxit: Early exiting for bert with better fine-tuning and extension to regression. In *Proceedings* of the 16th conference of the European chapter of the association for computational linguistics: Main Volume, pages 91–104.

Canwen Xu, Wangchunshu Zhou, Tao Ge, Furu Wei, and Ming Zhou. 2020a. Bert-of-theseus: Compressing bert by progressive module replacing. *arXiv preprint arXiv:2002.02925*.

Canwen Xu, Wangchunshu Zhou, Tao Ge, Furu Wei, and Ming Zhou. 2020b. Bert-of-theseus: Compressing bert by progressive module replacing. In *EMNLP*.

Jingjing Xu, Wangchunshu Zhou, Zhiyi Fu, Hao Zhou, and Lei Li. 2021a. A survey on green deep learning. *ArXiv*, abs/2111.05193.

Yuhui Xu, Lingxi Xie, Wenrui Dai, Xiaopeng Zhang, Xin Chen, Guo-Jun Qi, Hongkai Xiong, and Qi Tian. 2021b. Partially-connected neural architecture search for reduced computational redundancy. *IEEE Transactions on Pattern Analysis and Machine Intelligence*, 43:2953–2970.

Tianyi Zhang, Felix Wu, Arzoo Katiyar, Kilian Q. Weinberger, and Yoav Artzi. 2020a. Revisiting few-sample bert fine-tuning. *ArXiv*, abs/2006.05987.

Wei Zhang, Lu Hou, Yichun Yin, Lifeng Shang, Xiao Chen, Xin Jiang, and Qun Liu. 2020b. Ternarybert: Distillation-aware ultra-low bit bert. *arXiv preprint arXiv:2009.12812*.

Wangchunshu Zhou, Canwen Xu, Tao Ge, Julian McAuley, Ke Xu, and Furu Wei. 2020. Bert loses patience: Fast and robust inference with early exit. *Advances in Neural Information Processing Systems*, 33:18330–18341.

Michael Zhu and Suyog Gupta. 2017. To prune, or not to prune: exploring the efficacy of pruning for model compression. *arXiv preprint arXiv:1710.01878*.

Wei Zhu. 2021. Leebert: Learned early exit for bert with cross-level optimization. In *ACL*.

Wei Zhu, Yuan Ni, Xiaoling Wang, and Guo Tong Xie. 2021a. Discovering better model architectures for medical query understanding. In *NAACL*.

Wei Zhu, Xiaoling Wang, Yuan Ni, and Guo Tong Xie. 2021b. Gaml-bert: Improving bert early exiting by gradient aligned mutual learning. In *EMNLP*.

Barret Zoph and Quoc V. Le. 2017. Neural architecture search with reinforcement learning. *ArXiv*, abs/1611.01578.

Barret Zoph, Vijay Vasudevan, Jonathon Shlens, and Quoc V. Le. 2018. Learning transferable architectures for scalable image recognition. *2018 IEEE/CVF Conference on Computer Vision and Pattern Recognition*, pages 8697–8710.

A Demonstrations of learned architectures

In the section, the learned exit architectures on the RTE and SST-2 tasks are presented in Table 6. Discussions on the observations from the learned architectures can be found in the main content.

task	layer index	activation 1	activation 2	pooler	encoder op 1	encoder op 2
SST-2	1	swish	leaky_relu	avg_pool	conv_3	null
	2	gelu	leaky_relu	max_pool	null	mha_4
	3	nullAct	swish	max_pool	mha_4	null
	4	swish	leaky_relu	cls_pool	conv_3	null
	5	swish	gelu	sa_pool	conv_5	skip-connect
	6	swish	swish	avg_pool	null	conv_5
	7	gelu	swish	max_pool	mha_4	conv_1
	8	nullAct	leaky_relu	max_pool	null	skip-connect
	9	tanh	gelu	cls_pool	conv_1	conv_1
	10	nullAct	gelu	cls_pool	skip-connect	mha_8
	11	nullAct	gelu	avg_pool	conv_3	null
	12	gelu	nullAct	cls_pool	conv_3	skip-connect
RTE	1	nullAct	tanh	sa_pool	null	conv_1
	2	swish	nullAct	avg_pool	conv_1	conv_5
	3	gelu	tanh	sa_pool	null	mha_2
	4	swish	nullAct	sa_pool	skip-connect	conv_3
	5	gelu	nullAct	sa_pool	conv_3	null
	6	gelu	tanh	sa_pool	mha_pdot	conv_3
	7	nullAct	tanh	sa_pool	conv_3	null
	8	leaky_relu	leaky_relu	max_pool	conv_1	null
	9	nullAct	swish	max_pool	null	conv_1
	10	swish	leaky_relu	max_pool	conv_1	null
	11	nullAct	gelu	cls_pool	skip-connect	mha_4
	12	nullAct	swish	cls_pool	mha_4	null

Table 6: The best architectures learned via our LECO framework. We can see that on the same task, BERT requires different intermediate exits to better exploit the representation capabilities on different layers.

Authorship Attribution of Late 19th Century Novels using GAN-BERT

Kanishka Silva
University of Wolverhampton
United Kingdom
a.k.silva@wlv.ac.uk

Burcu Can
University of Stirling
United Kingdom
burcu.can@stir.ac.uk

Frédéric Blain
Tilburg University
The Netherlands
f.l.g.blain@tilburguniversity.edu

Raheem Sarwar
Manchester Metropolitan University
United Kingdom
r.sarwar@mmu.ac.uk

Laura Ugolini
University of Wolverhampton
United Kingdom
l.ugolini@wlv.ac.uk

Ruslan Mitkov
Lancaster University
United Kingdom
ruslanmitkov@gmail.com

Abstract

Authorship attribution aims to identify the author of an anonymous text. The task becomes even more worthwhile when it comes to literary works. For example, pen names were commonly used by female authors in the 19th century resulting in some literary works being incorrectly attributed or claimed. With this motivation, we collated a dataset of late 19th-century novels in English. Due to the imbalance in the dataset and the unavailability of enough data per author, we employed the GAN-BERT model along with data sampling strategies to fine-tune a transformer-based model for authorship attribution. Differently from the earlier studies on the GAN-BERT model, we conducted transfer learning on comparatively smaller author subsets to train more focused author-specific models yielding performance over 0.88 accuracy and F1 scores. Furthermore, we observed that increasing the sample size has a negative impact on the model's performance. Our research mainly contributes to the ongoing authorship attribution research using GAN-BERT architecture, especially in attributing disputed novelists in the late 19th century.

1 Introduction

Authorship attribution identifies authors of a given set of unknown documents (Hu et al., 2020; Neal et al., 2018; Stamatatos, 2009). Conventional techniques and neural networks are the two main authorship attribution methods. The studies on the conventional approaches typically focus on feature engineering and stylometry. The deep learning approaches have been gaining popularity recently due to the superior results compared to the conventional approaches. Furthermore, authorship attribution can be tackled in two ways: closed-set and open-set attribution. In closed-set attribution, an author is selected from a set of candidate authors, whereas in open-set attribution, the target author may not be included in the candidate authors' list.

Applications of authorship attribution are employed in various domains, such as digital forensics (Abbasi and Chen, 2005; Sun et al., 2012), social media analysis (Junior et al., 2016; Duman et al., 2016; Brocardo et al., 2017) and digital humanities Juola (2021). In historical texts, the authorship styles may contain socio-linguistic characteristics due to the century in which the author lived, idea movements inspired by the author, and language-specific attributes. Also, in written texts, the genre and topics are crucial in defining the author's style. Several pieces of research have been undertaken in the literature and historical domains, for instance, identifying anonymous or disputed texts (Koppel et al., 2007; Kestemont et al., 2016; Tuccinardi, 2017). The work presented by Fung (2003) analyses the Federalist Papers, which involves 85 articles and essays written by Alexander Hamilton, James Madison and John Jay. Another application of authorship attribution in literature is resolving doubted authorships. For instance, Thompson and Rasp (2016) investigate whether C.S. Lewis wrote The Dark Towers. The Shakespearean Authorship Dispute was addressed by Fox and Ehmoda (2012). Furthermore, attributing the author is one of many variations in authorship applications, as research directions are in different domains, such as attributing to the publication year and identifying the literary genre and the topic. One such example is

Proceedings of the 61st Annual Meeting of the Association for Computational Linguistics - Student Research Workshop, pages 310–320
July 10-12, 2023

Tausz (2011) which predicts the date of authorship in historical texts.

This research proposes a GAN-BERT-based model to enhance transformer-based authorship attribution in late 19th-century novels. To our knowledge, this is the first attempt to ensemble GAN and BERT models and, precisely, the GAN-BERT model to address authorship attribution in literary texts. In some of the recent works on authorship attribution, the models were trained in a controlled setting and had less elaboration on the data preparation stage, resulting in the poor reproducibility and generalisation of these models. Here, we present an end-to-end process from domain selection to dataset collection with insights to experiment planning.

An authorship attribution model highly depends on the number of authors represented in the training dataset and the text available per each author. Most of the related works emphasise controlled training environments. To improve the model's generalisation and ability to perform well on robust scenarios, it should be identified how much the model depends on the number of authors in the training dataset and the amount of text by each author. We use a normalised dataset of 20 novels per author to avoid dataset imbalance. Therefore, to identify how much data provides better model performance, we control the text data sample size drawn from the book text. Therefore, the research questions in this study are as follows:

RQ 1: How to effectively utilise the GAN-BERT model for authorship attribution?

RQ 2: How does the number of authors in the dataset impact the GAN-BERT performance for authorship attribution?

RQ 3: How does the amount of text data (i.e. sample size) drawn from each novel affect the GAN-BERT performance for authorship attribution?

The remainder of the paper is organised into several sections: Section 2 demonstrates a brief literature survey. Then Section 3 describes the proposed model's architecture, and Section 4 presents the dataset collection and preparation. Section 5 elaborates on the experiment design, focusing on the research questions, Section 6 summarises the results and findings obtained, and finally, Section 7 involves the concluding remarks and future directions.

2 Related Work

Texts vary in terms of topic, sentiment and style. According to Stamatatos (2009), information about the authors can be extracted from the style of their written documents. The task involves identifying the author from unknown documents, known as authorship attribution, which breaks into two major tasks: Authorship Identification and Authorship Verification. Authorship Identification is identifying a document's author by comparing a set of candidate authors (Stamatatos, 2009). Authorship Identification can be interpreted as a binary classification problem, whereas authorship attribution is a multi-class classification problem. Authorship Verification is a fundamental problem in authorship attribution which focuses on finding whether the considered person wrote one or more documents or not. Authorship Verification is comparatively challenging with less data (Koppel et al., 2011; Luyckx and Daelemans, 2008).

With the popularity of deep neural networks for NLP applications, recent authorship attribution research shares a similar trend. The works of Bagnall (2015a); Hosseinia and Mukherjee (2018); Boumber et al. (2018) are examples of neural network-based models in authorship attribution. Additionally, transfer learning also proved to have astonishing results. Zhang et al. (2021) introduce a Deep Authorship Verification using new metrics: DV-distance and DV-projection, which utilise pre-trained language models. Their work highlights the utilisation of pre-trained language models in our approach. Character and n-gram-based CNN (Ruder et al., 2016), Syntax-augmented CNN (Zhang et al., 2018), and Convolutional Siamese Networks (Saedi and Dras, 2021) are some other authorship attribution models which utilise deep learning techniques. These deep learning-based applications provide valuable insights for our approach to utilising the GAN-BERT model for authorship attribution tasks.

Language Models (LM) used in the authorship tasks can be categorised as n-gram-based and neural network-based (Fourkioti et al., 2019). Ge et al. (2016) used a neural network-based language model. The works of Bagnall (2015b) present a character-level RNN-based LM combining a multi-headed classifier. To address the cross-domain problem, Barlas and Stamatatos (2020) extended Bagnall (2015b)'s works for closed-set authorship attribution by combining a multi-headed LM with a pre-trained LM. According to Barlas and Stamatatos (2020), having a normalised corpus is crucial for the performance of cross-domain authorship attribution. BertAA (Fabien et al., 2020) is the recent fine-tuned form of the pre-trained BERT model for the authorship attribution task, which presents extensive experiments on various datasets: Enron Email (Klimt and Yang, 2004), Blog Authorship (Schler et al., 2006) and IMDb (Seroussi et al., 2014). Although pre-trained models have gained popularity and promising results in some authorship tasks, the performance of such models highly depends on the training set.

Generative Adversarial Networks (GAN) are used in authorship-related tasks to prevent adversarial attacks, mainly in the Authorship Obfuscation problem where one's writing style is masked. Ou et al. (2022) introduce source code authorship verification using GAN models and multi-head attention. A^4NT (Shetty et al., 2018) is a GAN-based style transformation to perform authorship obfuscation learned from data via adversarial training and sequence-to-sequence LMs. Kazlouski (2019)presents an LSTM-GAN classifier to recognise imitations generated by the A^4NT (Shetty et al., 2018) model. Tang et al. (2019) presents a data augmentation approach to authorship attribution in Weibo text using Wasserstein-GAN to generate samples of the positive class.

The class imbalance problem is hard to avoid in real-world scenarios, particularly in authorship attribution. Stamatatos (2018) introduced a novel strategy to produce synthetic data for the authorship identification task. The approach that Stamatatos (2018) mentioned is segmenting the training texts into text samples, considering the training size of the class. The works of Eder (2015) highlight how much data is required to identify authors across different languages and genres. The findings in Eder (2015) show that the minimum sample range is 2500-5000, representing the two ends for Latin, English, German, Polish, and Hungarian datasets. Further experiments by Eder (2017) attempt to identify the minimum sample size by removing text one by one from the training set, which yields that 2000 words sample size is appropriate. Also, Eder (2017) emphasises that this finding depends strongly on the authors. Hadjadj and Sayoud (2021)propose a hybrid PCA and SMOTE approach of oversampling, which reports outperforming the state-of-the-art accuracies. The Stylometric Set Similarity (S3) method presents the authorship attribution task as a set similarity problem by considering 3000 novels from 500 authors curated from Project Gutenberg (Sarwar et al., 2018). Granichin et al. (2015) present a KNN-resampling approach to authorship identification by simulating samples from 2 texts.

In previous research on authorship attribution, the combination of GAN and transformer models has not yet been explored. Furthermore, to the best of our knowledge, no attempt has been made to use the GAN-BERT model specifically for the task of authorship attribution, especially with sampling strategies for many authors and limited data. The critical literature analysis suggests that deep neural networks in authorship attribution would show promising performance with well-designed sampling strategies. Here, we propose GAN-BERT model for authorship attribution along with various sampling strategies, and analyse how transfer-learning would support the proposed model in literary domain.

3 GAN-BERT Model for Authorship Attribution

Let A be a collection of authors of interest, $A = \{a_1, a_2, ..., a_N\}$, where N is the total number of authors in A. The document set belonging to each author forms the complete dataset $T = \{t_{a_1}, t_{a_2}, ... t_{a_N}\}$ where t_{a_i} is the document set attributed to the author a_i in the dataset. Given a text, t_u of an unknown author u, the proposed model assigns the text to the most likely author from A.

GAN-BERT (Croce et al., 2020) combines BERT-based models and Semi-Supervised GAN (Salimans et al., 2016). Figure 1a illustrates the GAN-BERT model architecture, where discriminator D is utilised to classify examples and generator G generates fake examples F. The discriminator takes the vector representations returned via BERT for unlabeled U and labelled L input texts. When training is complete, G is discarded from the model to use the rest of the model for inference.

In contrast to GAN-BERT (Croce et al., 2020), which utilises a semi-supervised GAN model (Salimans et al., 2016) with labelled and unlabeled data, we train the GAN-BERT model with labelled data only. The discriminator D is trained over N+1 classes to assign the true samples to a class from $\{1, 2, 3, ..., N\}$. The fake sample generated from the generator G represents the $(N+1)^{th}$ class. The discriminator is suitable for detecting authorship obfuscation and forgery since it is trained with fake samples similar to the original author-written texts. Figure 1b illustrates the modified GAN model.

The GAN-BERT model generally shows superior results for classification tasks with limited labelled data. Furthermore, the intuition to use GAN-BERT for authorship attribution is that, due to the fake data generated in the generator, it considers not only the real writing styles, but also the possible fake writing styles that are synthesised.

4 Creating the Datasets

4.1 Pre-Screening Authors

We performed pre-screening on the authors before collecting the dataset, which is, to the best of our knowledge, the first attempt to perform a qualitative analysis on the literary domain for authorship attribution. We considered two parameters during the author selection process: distribution and filtering. Distribution parameters ensure that the collected texts span equally among different attributes such as gender, genre and ethnicity. Filtering parameters focus on whether selected works by the distribution parameters should be included or excluded from the dataset. It mainly concerns the novelists' characteristics and the nature of their literary works. A summary of these two parameters is illustrated in Table 1.

4.2 Dataset Collection and Validation

We collected datasets from Project Gutenberg across genres such as novels, short stories, essays, poems and biographies. There is no specific field in Project Gutenberg to indicate genre and year of publication. We manually validated texts to capture the year of publication. We also filtered novels so that all fiction had a word count greater than 10,000. To our knowledge, other researchers using Project Gutenberg have not performed similar data validation to filter novels.

In the master dataset, we have filtered 1232 novels written by 62 authors, which are segmented as follows:

1. Early 19th Century (1800-1835)

2. Mid-19th Century (1836-1870)

3. Late 19th Century (1871-1900)

4. Early 20th Century (1901-1914)

This paper focuses on the late 19th-century segment from the master dataset, which includes 541 novels. We filtered authors based on the number of novels available in the dataset and selected those with at least 20. We narrowed the author selection by selecting the top 20 authors with the most novels from this focused subset. These authors were used to train and test the proposed GAN-BERT model. Therefore the dataset is thus uniformly distributed regarding the number of novels per author. The selected authors are Anthony Trollope, Arthur Conan Doyle, Bret Harte, Fergus Hume, Frances Hodgson Burnett, H.G. Wells, Henry Rider Haggard, Jack London, James Grant, John Kendrick Bangs, Joseph Conrad, Louisa May Alcott, Margaret Oliphant, Marie Corelli, Mark Twain, Mary Elizabeth Braddon, Mrs Henry Wood, Nathaniel Hawthorne, Oliver Optic, and Wilkie Collins.

4.3 Balanced Author Representation

The filtered dataset of late 19th century English novels consists of 400 novels by 20 authors. Especially in deep neural networks, this dataset is insufficient to represent a larger number of authors than 20. Furthermore, as authors have different writing styles, different combinations of authors in the same size dataset have a strong impact on model performance. We observed this problem during the preliminary experiments with manually sampled sets of authors. Therefore, to ensure a balanced representation of authors in the training and validation datasets and to mitigate the effect of different author combinations, we performed random sampling for a considered number, as shown in Figure 2. Different author combinations are denoted by a 'sample set'.

Furthermore, one of the aims of the experiments is to see how increasing the number of authors would affect the model's performance. To do this, we split the dataset to represent different numbers of authors.

4.4 Dataset Splits

We followed the leave-n-out method to split the dataset for manually selected 5 sets. For example, of 20 authors, two were assigned as a 2-author case, while the rest of the 18 were included as an 18-author case. This process is repeated to obtain distinct 5 manually selected author sample sets. The author's case defines how many authors were considered in the train/test datasets. For example, a 2-author case means a focused dataset with only

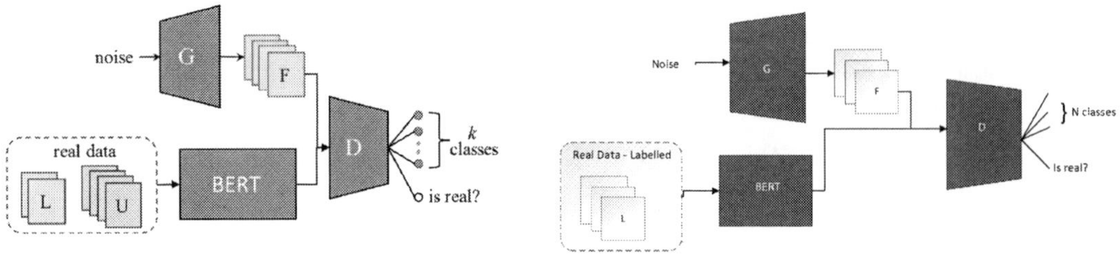

(a) GAN-BERT Model (Croce et al., 2020)

(b) Modified GAN-BERT Model

Figure 1: Model Architecture Comparison

Parameter Type	Category	Condition
Distribution Parameters	Genre	Romance, Thrillers, Science Fiction, Realist
	Gender	Male, Female
	Ethnicity	American, British
	Doubted Authorship	Only original works by novelist in the training set
	Readers	Adult, Children
Filtering Parameters	Publication Period	Later 19th Century 1871-1900
	Number of novels during publication period	>3
	Literature Genre	Novels
	The number of total novels	>20
	Written Language	English
	Non-translation	Yes
	Multi-Authors	No
	Digitised work availability	Available on the Project Gutenberg

Table 1: Distribution and Filtering Parameters used for Pre-Screening of Authors

novels by 2 authors. We can define any number of author sample sets to perform experiments in each n-author case. For example, manually selected author sample sets for a 2-author case include 5 different combinations of 2 authors out of 20 can be present. 50 random samples in a 2-authors case mean, out of 20 authors, 50 randomised different 2-author combinations. Random sampling does not cover all combinations of authors in a given author case, but would ensure that the majority of author combinations are considered. The dataset splitting process is illustrated in Figure 2.

We ensured the dataset splits were distinct for all the sample sets per case. The 20-author case was used as the base model to train and perform transfer learning on other models. We used a randomised approach to shuffle and return 50 and 100-author sample sets for a random sample generation.

We split train-test-validation (80:10:10) sets, stratified by author ids, for each sample set considered for the experiments, with one sample set per experimental round. The average results of all sample sets represent a particular n-author case. The base model was trained on all 20 authors in the transfer learning experiments. The stratified split in the train-test-validation ensured a uniform distribution of novels per author, and the test data are distinct from the training data. In transfer learning, the training set may include evaluation data from the 20-author case.

4.5 Baseline Datasets

To compare the performance of the proposed GAN-BERT model on other baseline datasets, we used the IMDB62 (Seroussi et al., 2014) and Blog Authorship (Schler et al., 2006) datasets. We created a subset of 20 authored content from these datasets to be consistent with the 20-author dataset, which refers to as IMDB20 and Blog20 respectively.

4.6 Dataset Availability

Due to the copyright restrictions explained in Section 7, we do not release the entire dataset. Instead, we release the scripts used for creating and preprocessing the dataset. We also publish the list of the authors, selected novels, and novel indices used to extract the sample sets [1].

5 Experiment Design

We conducted experiments on different dataset subsets and different model configurations to address the following:

[1] https://github.com/Kaniz92/AA-GAN-Bert/tree/main

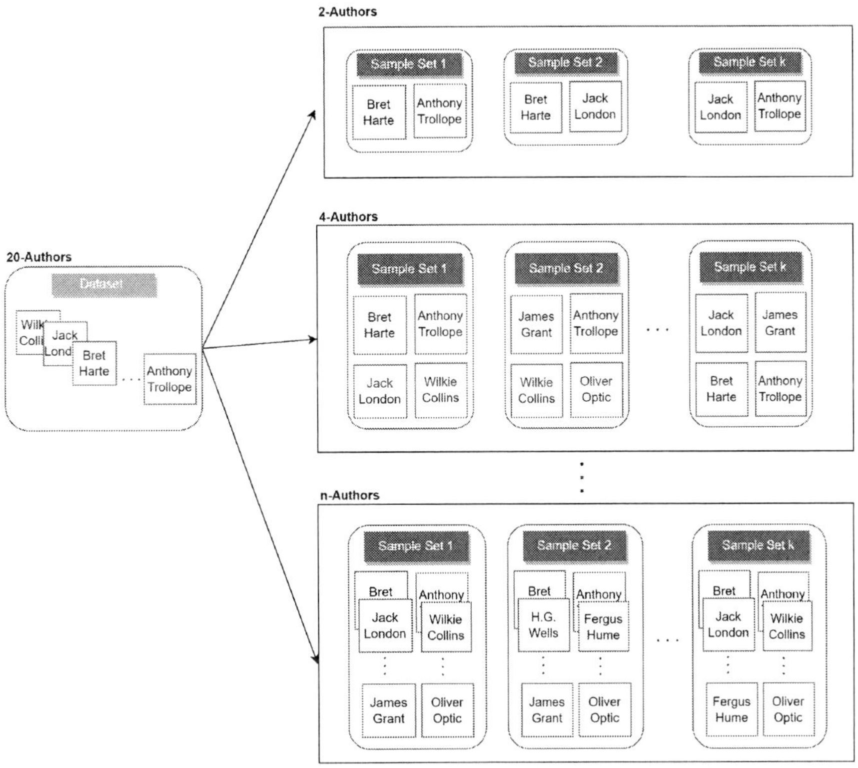

Figure 2: Dataset Splitting Process

1. Random Sampling Author Combinations
2. The Impact of Transfer Learning
3. Number of Authors in Dataset
4. Text Sample Size per Novel

We explored the GAN-BERT model under two dimensions: Random Sampling and Transfer Learning. As illustrated in Figure 2, the 20 novels per each author from the 20-author dataset provide different combinations under different numbers of authors. Therefore, first, we manually selected authors per each n-author case and then randomly sampled 50 and 100 author combinations. In transfer learning experiments, we compared the performance of manually selected sample sets under standalone training and transfer learning from the 20-author dataset to each n-author case.

In a practical scenario of authorship attribution, the number of authors to compare would vary. Therefore, we experimented with the GAN-BERT model response for different numbers of authors in the dataset. Also, the text sample size drawn from a novel can be varied when representing the novel text due to varying text lengths. We used the manual sampling of authors to identify any trend towards the text sample size drawn from a novel.

In the default setting, unless specified, we used 20 samples per novel drawn sequentially from the book text for training and testing. We first trained the base model on 20-authors for 10 epochs, using Adam optimiser, one hidden layer for both generator and the discriminator, a dropout rate of 0.2, batch size of 8, a warm-up proportion of 0.1, and learning rate of $1e-5$ for both generator and the discriminator. Then the pre-trained 20-author model was used for transfer learning on smaller subsets of each case in $\{2, 4, 6, 8, 10, 12, 14, 16, 18\}$-author counts and trained further on these sub-sets for 5 epochs.

We compared the proposed GAN-BERT model with different baseline models such as word-level TF-IDF, character n-gram, Stylometric features (Sari et al., 2018) and BertAA (Fabien et al., 2020) on the 20-authors dataset, 18-authors dataset, IMDB, and Blog Authorship datasets. These baseline experiments provide insights into how the created datasets performed with other baseline models and how other datasets would perform with the proposed GAN-BERT model. To be consistent with the rest of the experiments, we selected 20 samples per each document by an author, but the 20-sample restrictions are not applied to baseline models.

6 Results and Discussion

For each experiment across different sample sets, we reported Accuracy, F1, Precision, and Recall with averaging results sampled manually and randomly.

6.1 Random Sampling Author Combinations

Analysing the model with manually selected author sample sets may fail to describe the results and any trends due to the bias factors. For example, the upshot performance of the 18-authors model in manually sampled authors as in Figure 3a could be due to biases in generated manual sample sets. Therefore we conducted additional experiments for the 50 and 100 sample sets using random sampling. Rather than selecting books randomly, we focused on arranging authors into different sample sets and then keeping books per each author the same (20 books per author). This experiment explores whether the model could tolerate the robustness of any author combinations. Before deciding on the random sampling limits, we analysed the maximum number of author combinations per each case. To cover all the author cases, the maximum random sampling count is 190, so we decided to experiment on 50 and 100 random samples.

Compared to the manually selected author sample sets, 50 and 100 random sampling achieves a higher accuracy for all the author cases, precisely more than 0.97% of accuracy. Results in Table 2 and Figure 3b show that the model is robust with consistent performance over different author cases.

6.2 The Impact of Transfer Learning

The intuition behind applying transfer learning for the authorship attribution model is that instead of having a model that learns each author's style and overfits into a particular dataset with a fixed number of authors, it makes the model more practical to use in real-world scenarios if the model learns the authorship attribution task regardless of the number of authors. This also applies to different author styles, regardless of topic, genre or unique author style. Moreover, transfer learning allows the model to transfer knowledge into a limited data set.

Extensive experiments have been carried out to identify how transfer learning has affected the model's performance from the 20-author cases to smaller author subsets. We trained standalone and transfer learning models using the same hyperparameters as the base model.

Transfer learning has substantially improved the model's performance, especially for the increasing number of authors. The best-performing model was observed for the 2-author case, and the worst-performing model was for the 18-author case. Overall, the transfer learning results suggest that it is a promising technique for improving performance, especially for smaller datasets.

6.3 Incremental Number of Authors in the Dataset

We designed the dataset subsets to increment the number of authors by two, ranging from $[2, 18]$, to investigate how the author count would affect the model's performance. The number of samples per author is uniform across each author sample set and case. We also selected the same 20 books for each author to ensure that the topics or genres do not affect the experiments. One text sample should not exceed 512 words, BERT's maximum input token size. Therefore we set the one sample size as 512 words and drew 20 sequential text samples from each book, representing one author by 400 (20 x 20) instances before the train-test split.

Both the standalone and transfer learning models for five manually selected author sample sets show a declining trend in performance as the number of authors increases, as illustrated in Table 3 and Table 2. The binary classification shows the best performance overall, while the multi-class classification shows comparatively a lower performance.

Averaging accuracies for transfer learning for 50 and 100 randomly sampled author sets are illustrated in Table 2. The results do not indicate any clear trend with the author counts, but accuracy and F1 are consistent and higher than manually selected author sample sets.

As illustrated in Figure 3b, manual samples and random samples show clear distinction with increasing the number of authors in the dataset. Therefore, the model performance depends highly on how the sample sets were defined, i.e. different author combinations. Therefore, strategies must be explored to overcome the biases towards different configurations of authors' sample sets.

n-Authors	5 Manual Samples				50 Random Samples				100 Random Samples			
	Accuracy	F1	Precision	Recall	Accuracy	F1	Precision	Recall	Accuracy	F1	Precision	Recall
2-authors	0.98†	0.98†	0.99†	0.98†	0.98	0.98	0.98	0.98	0.98	0.98	0.99	0.98
4-authors	0.96	0.96	0.96	0.96	0.98	0.98	0.98	0.98	0.98	0.98	0.98	0.98
6-authors	0.93	0.93	0.93	0.93	0.98	0.98	0.98	0.98	0.97*	0.97*	0.97*	0.97*
8-authors	0.91	0.91	0.92	0.91	0.96*	0.96*	0.97*	0.96*	0.98	0.98	0.98	0.98
10-authors	0.92	0.92	0.92	0.92	0.98	0.98	0.98	0.98	0.99†	0.99†	0.99†	0.99†
12-authors	0.92	0.92	0.93	0.92	0.99†	0.99†	0.99†	0.99†	0.99†	0.99†	0.99†	0.99†
14-authors	0.88*	0.88*	0.90*	0.88*	0.98	0.98	0.98	0.98	0.99†	0.99†	0.99†	0.99†
16-authors	0.89	0.89	0.90*	0.89	0.98	0.98	0.98	0.98	0.99†	0.99†	0.99†	0.99†
18-authors	0.88*	0.88*	0.90*	0.88*	0.99†	0.99†	0.99†	0.99†	0.98	0.98	0.98	0.98

Table 2: Results of the GAN-BERT Model for Transfer Learning on a 20-Author Dataset
* - mini result across a metric † - max value across a metric

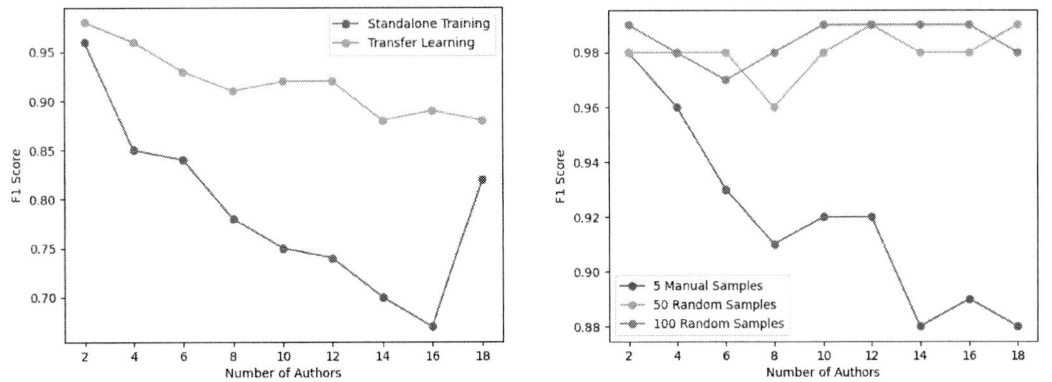

(a) F1 Scores between Standalone Training and Transfer Learning

(b) F1 Scores between Manual Sampling and Random Sampling for Transfer Learning

Figure 3: F1 Score Results of the Transfer Learning Approach

n-Authors	Accuracy	F1	Precision	Recall
2-authors	0.95†	0.96†	0.95†	0.95†
4-authors	0.82	0.85	0.82	0.82
6-authors	0.82	0.84	0.82	0.83
8-authors	0.76	0.78	0.76	0.75
10-authors	0.72	0.75	0.72	0.72
12-authors	0.70	0.74	0.70	0.70
14-authors	0.66	0.70	0.66	0.66
16-authors	0.64*	0.67*	0.64*	0.64*
18-authors	0.80	0.82	0.80	0.80

Table 3: Results of the GAN-BERT Model for Standalone Training on Manually Selected Author Sample Sets
* - mini result across a metric † - max value across a metric

6.4 Text Sample Size per Novel

To investigate how each novel's sample size affects the model performance, we selected the 18 authors' cases and experimented across different text sample sizes ranging from 5 to 35 text chunks per novel. Each sample consists of a text chunk of 512 words drawn from the book text. For example, a text sample size of 5 means that we selected 5 x 512 text chunks from the book text, which resulting 5 separate instances in the dataset. We performed this experiment using the same 20 books per author.

The results in Table 4 demonstrate that increasing the sample size has a negative impact on the model's performance across all sample sets for the 18-author model. In this experiment, as the sample size increases, the model is trained on the same novels and 18 authors during training. One of the main findings is that the larger text samples from novels only sometimes lead to better performance. The model may have shown a negative impact in larger text sample sizes due to the high variance in the data or overfitting. Hence, further investigation must be performed to identify the optimal text sample size per novel under different experiment settings.

Sample Size	Accuracy	F1	Precision	Recall
5	$0.92^{\dagger}$	$0.93^{\dagger}$	$0.92^{\dagger}$	$0.92^{\dagger}$
10	0.91	0.91	0.91	0.91
15	0.89	0.90	0.89	0.89
20	0.80^{*}	0.82^{*}	0.80^{*}	0.80^{*}
25	0.86	0.87	0.86	0.86
30	0.86	0.87	0.86	0.86

Table 4: Effect of Sample Size on Model Performance for 18-Author Classification
* - mini result across a metric † - max value across a metric

6.5 Baseline Experiments

We evaluated various baseline models with different datasets including IMDB20, Blog20, 20-authors and 18-authors. The accuracy results obtained are reported in Table 5. Using stylometric features performed the worst with an accuracy of 0.14 on the IMDB20 dataset. The proposed GAN-BERT model outperforms the stylometric and character n-gram-based models but does not perform as well as the TF-IDF and BertAA models. Our proposed model performs as well as the other models on IMDB20 dataset; however, BERTAA outperforms the others on our dataset. This indicates that further improvements (e.g. including other features such as tf-idf or stylometric features) are needed to enhance the proposed GAN-BERT model performance on specific datasets.

Model	IMDB20	Blog20	20-authors	18-authors
Stylometric (Sari et al., 2018)	0.14^{*}	0.11^{*}	0.14^{*}	0.11^{*}
Character Ngram (Fabien et al., 2020)	0.69	0.23	0.94	0.95
Word level TF-IDF (Fabien et al., 2020)	$0.97^{\dagger}$	0.47	0.91	0.90
BERTAA (Fabien et al., 2020)	$0.97^{\dagger}$	$0.62^{\dagger}$	$0.99^{\dagger}$	$0.99^{\dagger}$
Proposed Model	0.96	0.40	0.63	0.80

Table 5: Baseline Experiment Results
* - mini result across a metric † - max value across a metric

7 Conclusion

This research proposes a GAN-BERT-based model for authorship attribution in late-19th-century novels. Our primary focus is identifying how the author counts and the text sample size per book affects the model's performance. The manually selected five authors' combinations indicate that the model's performance degrades when the number of authors increases. The declining trend is the same for transfer-learning models, although the overall performance is better than the standalone models. Additionally, we experimented with how transfer learning has improved the mean accuracies over manually selected author sample sets for each n-author case. A future improvement would be an experiment around few-shot and zero-shot tests. Furthermore, it would be interesting to experiment with different GAN and transformer models replaced in this model architecture.

Limitations

While this research provides valuable insights into using the GAN-BERT model for authorship attribution, there are also a few limitations to note. We only focused on a limited number of authors from the late 19th century, which may include shortcomings towards model generalisability. Future research should consider using the whole dataset of long 19th-century novelists to address this limitation. Due to the copyright issues explained in Section 4.6 and Section 7, we do not release the whole dataset, instead, we release scripts to reproduce the datasets. Furthermore, incorporating a rich feature set and comparing performance among different models would be another interesting research direction.

Ethics Statement

The duration 1800-1914 is considered as the out-of-copyright duration in Project Gutenberg, under the categories 'Rule 1: Works First Published Before 95 Years Ago and Before 1977' and 'Rule 10(c) - Works of Treaty Parties and Proclamation Countries First Published Between 1923 and 1977' (Gutenberg). Although the duration is out-of-copyright regarding literary works, we stored the data securely with restricted access. We do not release the dataset.

References

A. Abbasi and Hsinchun Chen. 2005. Applying authorship analysis to extremist-group web forum messages. *IEEE Intelligent Systems*, 20:67–75.

Douglas Bagnall. 2015a. Author identification using multi-headed recurrent neural networks. *ArXiv*, abs/1506.04891.

Douglas Bagnall. 2015b. Author identification using multi-headed recurrent neural networks. In *Working Notes of CLEF 2015 - Conference and Labs of the Evaluation forum, Toulouse, France, September 8-11, 2015*, volume 1391 of *CEUR Workshop Proceedings*. CEUR-WS.org.

Georgios Barlas and Efstathios Stamatatos. 2020. Cross-domain authorship attribution using pre-trained language models. In *Artificial Intelligence Applications and Innovations - 16th IFIP WG 12.5 International Conference, AIAI 2020, Neos Marmaras, Greece, June 5-7, 2020, Proceedings, Part I*, volume 583 of *IFIP Advances in Information and Communication Technology*, pages 255–266. Springer.

Dainis Boumber, Yifan Zhang, and Arjun Mukherjee. 2018. Experiments with convolutional neural networks for multi-label authorship attribution. In *LREC*.

Marcelo Luiz Brocardo, Issa Traoré, Isaac Woungang, and Mohammad S. Obaidat. 2017. Authorship verification using deep belief network systems. *Int. J. Commun. Syst.*, 30.

Danilo Croce, Giuseppe Castellucci, and Roberto Basili. 2020. GAN-BERT: generative adversarial learning for robust text classification with a bunch of labeled examples. In *Proceedings of the 58th Annual Meeting of the Association for Computational Linguistics, ACL 2020, Online, July 5-10, 2020*, pages 2114–2119. Association for Computational Linguistics.

Sevtap Duman, Kubra Kalkan-Cakmakci, Manuel Egele, William K. Robertson, and Engin Kirda. 2016. Emailprofiler: Spearphishing filtering with header and stylometric features of emails. *2016 IEEE 40th Annual Computer Software and Applications Conference (COMPSAC)*, 1:408–416.

Maciej Eder. 2015. Does size matter? authorship attribution, small samples, big problem. *Digit. Scholarsh. Humanit.*, 30(2):167–182.

Maciej Eder. 2017. Short samples in authorship attribution: A new approach. In *12th Annual International Conference of the Alliance of Digital Humanities Organizations, DH 2017, Montréal, Canada, August 8-11, 2017, Conference Abstracts*. Alliance of Digital Humanities Organizations (ADHO).

Maël Fabien, Esaú Villatoro-Tello, Petr Motlícek, and Shantipriya Parida. 2020. Bertaa : BERT fine-tuning for authorship attribution. In *Proceedings of the 17th International Conference on Natural Language Processing, ICON 2020, Indian Institute of Technology Patna, Patna, India, December 18-21, 2020*, pages 127–137. NLP Association of India (NLPAI).

Olga Fourkioti, Symeon Symeonidis, and Avi Arampatzis. 2019. Language models and fusion for authorship attribution. *Inf. Process. Manag.*, 56(6).

Neal P. Fox and Omran Ehmoda. 2012. Statistical stylometrics and the marlowe-shakespeare authorship debate.

Glenn Fung. 2003. The disputed federalist papers: SVM feature selection via concave minimization. In *Proceedings of the Richard Tapia Celebration of Diversity in Computing Conference 2003, Atlanta, Georgia, USA, October 15-18, 2003*, pages 42–46. ACM.

Zhenhao Ge, Yufang Sun, and Mark J. T. Smith. 2016. Authorship attribution using a neural network language model. In *Proceedings of the Thirtieth AAAI Conference on Artificial Intelligence, February 12-17, 2016, Phoenix, Arizona, USA*, pages 4212–4213. AAAI Press.

Oleg Granichin, Lev Klebanov, Dmitry Shalymov, and Zeev Volkovich. 2015. Authorship attribution method based on knn re-sampling approach. In *PROCEEDINGS ELMAR-INTERNATIONAL SYMPOSIUM ELECTRONICS IN MARINE*. Institute of Electrical and Electronics Engineers Inc.

Project Gutenberg. *Copyright How-To*. `https://www.gutenberg.org/help/copyright.html`.

Hassina Hadjadj and Halim Sayoud. 2021. Arabic authorship attribution using synthetic minority over-sampling technique and principal components analysis for imbalanced documents. *Int. J. Cogn. Informatics Nat. Intell.*, 15(4):1–17.

Marjan Hosseinia and Arjun Mukherjee. 2018. Experiments with neural networks for small and large scale authorship verification. *ArXiv*, abs/1803.06456.

Zhiqiang Hu, Roy Ka-Wei Lee, Lei Wang, Ee-Peng Lim, and Bo Dai. 2020. Deepstyle: User style embedding for authorship attribution of short texts. In *Web and Big Data - 4th International Joint Conference, APWeb-WAIM 2020, Tianjin, China, September 18-20, 2020, Proceedings, Part II*, volume 12318 of *Lecture Notes in Computer Science*, pages 221–229. Springer.

Sylvio Barbon Junior, Rodrigo Augusto Igawa, and Bruno Bogaz Zarpelão. 2016. Authorship verification applied to detection of compromised accounts on online social networks. *Multimedia Tools and Applications*, 76:3213–3233.

Patrick Juola. 2021. Verifying authorship for forensic purposes: A computational protocol and its validation. *Forensic Science International*, 325:110824.

Andrei Kazlouski. 2019. Text style imitation to prevent author identification and profiling. Master's thesis, Aalto University. School of Science.

Mike Kestemont, Justin Anthony Stover, Moshe Koppel, Folgert Karsdorp, and Walter Daelemans. 2016. Authenticating the writings of julius caesar. *Expert Syst. Appl.*, 63:86–96.

Bryan Klimt and Yiming Yang. 2004. The enron corpus: A new dataset for email classification research. In *Machine Learning: ECML 2004, 15th European Conference on Machine Learning, Pisa, Italy, September 20-24, 2004, Proceedings*, volume 3201 of *Lecture Notes in Computer Science*, pages 217–226. Springer.

Moshe Koppel, Jonathan Schler, and Shlomo Engelson Argamon. 2011. Authorship attribution in the wild. *Language Resources and Evaluation*, 45:83–94.

Moshe Koppel, Jonathan Schler, and Elisheva Bonchek-Dokow. 2007. Measuring differentiability: Unmasking pseudonymous authors. *J. Mach. Learn. Res.*, 8:1261–1276.

Kim Luyckx and Walter Daelemans. 2008. Authorship attribution and verification with many authors and limited data. In *COLING*.

Tempestt J. Neal, Kalaivani Sundararajan, Aneez Fatima, Yiming Yan, Yingfei Xiang, and Damon L. Woodard. 2018. Surveying stylometry techniques and applications. *ACM Comput. Surv.*, 50(6):86:1–86:36.

Weihan Ou, Steven H.H. Ding, Yuan Tian, and Leo Song. 2022. Scs-gan: Learning functionality-agnostic stylometric representations for source code authorship verification. *IEEE Transactions on Software Engineering*, pages 1–1.

Sebastian Ruder, Parsa Ghaffari, and John G. Breslin. 2016. Character-level and multi-channel convolutional neural networks for large-scale authorship attribution. *CoRR*, abs/1609.06686.

Chakaveh Saedi and Mark Dras. 2021. Siamese networks for large-scale author identification. *Comput. Speech Lang.*, 70:101241.

Tim Salimans, Ian J. Goodfellow, Wojciech Zaremba, Vicki Cheung, Alec Radford, and Xi Chen. 2016. Improved techniques for training gans. In *Advances in Neural Information Processing Systems 29: Annual Conference on Neural Information Processing Systems 2016, December 5-10, 2016, Barcelona, Spain*, pages 2226–2234.

Yunita Sari, Mark Stevenson, and Andreas Vlachos. 2018. Topic or style? exploring the most useful features for authorship attribution. In *Proceedings of the 27th International Conference on Computational Linguistics, COLING 2018, Santa Fe, New Mexico, USA, August 20-26, 2018*, pages 343–353. Association for Computational Linguistics.

Raheem Sarwar, Chenyun Yu, Ninad Tungare, Kanatip Chitavisutthivong, Sukrit Sriratanawilai, Yaohai Xu, Dickson Chow, Thanawin Rakthanmanon, and Sarana Nutanong. 2018. An effective and scalable framework for authorship attribution query processing. *IEEE Access*, 6:50030–50048.

Jonathan Schler, Moshe Koppel, Shlomo Argamon, and James W. Pennebaker. 2006. Effects of age and gender on blogging. In *Computational Approaches to Analyzing Weblogs, Papers from the 2006 AAAI Spring Symposium, Technical Report SS-06-03, Stanford, California, USA, March 27-29, 2006*, pages 199–205. AAAI.

Yanir Seroussi, Ingrid Zukerman, and Fabian Bohnert. 2014. Authorship attribution with topic models. *Comput. Linguistics*, 40(2):269–310.

Rakshith Shetty, Bernt Schiele, and Mario Fritz. 2018. A4NT: author attribute anonymity by adversarial training of neural machine translation. In *27th USENIX Security Symposium, USENIX Security 2018, Baltimore, MD, USA, August 15-17, 2018*, pages 1633–1650. USENIX Association.

Efstathios Stamatatos. 2009. A survey of modern authorship attribution methods. *J. Assoc. Inf. Sci. Technol.*, 60(3):538–556.

Efstathios Stamatatos. 2018. Masking topic-related information to enhance authorship attribution. *J. Assoc. Inf. Sci. Technol.*, 69(3):461–473.

Jianwen Sun, Zongkai Yang, Sanya Liu, and Pei Wang. 2012. Applying stylometric analysis techniques to counter anonymity in cyberspace. *J. Networks*, 7:259–266.

Wanbing Tang, Chunhua Wu, Xiaolong Chen, Yudao Sun, and Chen Li. 2019. Weibo authorship identification based on wasserstein generative adversarial networks. In *2019 IEEE International Conference on Signal, Information and Data Processing (ICSIDP)*, pages 1–5.

Andrew Tausz. 2011. Predicting the date of authorship of historical texts.

Jeffrey R. Thompson and John Rasp. 2016. Did c. s. lewis write the dark tower?: An examination of the small-sample properties of the thisted-efron tests of authorship. *Austrian Journal of Statistics*, 38(2):71–82.

Enrico Tuccinardi. 2017. An application of a profile-based method for authorship verification: Investigating the authenticity of pliny the younger's letter to trajan concerning the christians. *Digit. Scholarsh. Humanit.*, 32:435–447.

Richong Zhang, Zhiyuan Hu, Hongyu Guo, and Yongyi Mao. 2018. Syntax encoding with application in authorship attribution. In *Proceedings of the 2018 Conference on Empirical Methods in Natural Language Processing, Brussels, Belgium, October 31 - November 4, 2018*, pages 2742–2753. Association for Computational Linguistics.

Yifan Zhang, Dainis Boumber, Marjan Hosseinia, Fan Yang, and Arjun Mukherjee. 2021. Improving authorship verification using linguistic divergence. In *ROMCIR@ECIR*.

How-to Guides for Specific Audiences: A Corpus and Initial Findings

Nicola Fanton
he/they

Agnieszka Falenska

Michael Roth

University of Stuttgart
Institute for Natural Language Processing
{firstname.lastname}@ims.uni-stuttgart.de

Abstract

Instructional texts for specific target groups should ideally take into account the prior knowledge and needs of the readers in order to guide them efficiently to their desired goals. However, targeting specific groups also carries the risk of reflecting disparate social norms and subtle stereotypes. In this paper, we investigate the extent to which how-to guides from one particular platform, wikiHow, differ in practice depending on the intended audience. We conduct two case studies in which we examine qualitative features of texts written for specific audiences. In a generalization study, we investigate which differences can also be systematically demonstrated using computational methods. The results of our studies show that guides from wikiHow, like other text genres, are subject to subtle biases. We aim to raise awareness of these inequalities as a first step to addressing them in future work.

1 Introduction

How-to guides provide practical instructions that help humans to achieve specific goals. In the past decades, such guides also attracted increasing interest in NLP and AI research (Branavan et al., 2009; Chu et al., 2017; Anthonio et al., 2020). Resources such as wikiHow,[1] a collaboratively edited online platform for instructional texts, make it possible to scale research efforts to hundreds of thousands of articles. By covering an ever-increasing number of guides, including niche topics and articles for minority groups, there is also an increasing risk of perpetuating stereotypes and jeopardizing general accessibility. In fact, we notice that wikiHow already contains articles written for specific target groups as well as articles that exist in different versions for different audiences. As an example, Table 1 shows two articles with the same *title*, "Act Like a Kid Again", one with the *indicator* '(Girls)' and one with '(Boys)'.

[1] www.wikihow.com

Act Like a Kid Again (Girls)
Eat well and exercise, but don't obsess about your body. Be healthy without stressing too much about it. (...) Generally, **go for lots of fruits and veggies**. And even though kids love sugar, **don't eat too much** of it!
Act Like a Kid Again (Boys)
Eat your childhood favorite food. Recollect **every snack**, chocolates, ice cream, candy bars, cotton candy and **everything that you loved as a kid** or would make you feel pampered. Eat as per your capacity as too much at once may make you feel uncomfortable.

Table 1: Two versions of the same guide in wikiHow.

Among other things, we find that such articles dramatically differ in terms of details. For example, the texts highlighted in Table 1 vary in how much they focus on issues potentially related to body images. As such, the articles reflect *disparate standards*, which ultimately may contribute to discrimination (Prentice and Carranza, 2002). The specific example can also be linked to observations of gender differences in weight concerns from psychology (Dougherty et al., 2022), which might represent a reason for *disparate treatment*. On the surface, it is not always possible to say exactly why there are certain differences in articles for specific audiences. However, through qualitative and quantitative comparisons on the linguistic level, we can at least determine what types of differences are present and to what extent they can be systematically identified. In this sense, we aim to contribute to questions about biases and fairness in data and, at the same time, connect to related research in psychology and other social sciences.

There already exists a large body of research that examines biases and stereotypes in NLP data and, likewise, how-to guides from wikiHow have been

Proceedings of the 61st Annual Meeting of the Association for Computational Linguistics - Student Research Workshop, pages 321–333
July 10-12, 2023

used as training material for a variety of language processing tasks (§2). However, previous studies have not explicitly looked into issues related to bias in the wikiHow data. As a first step towards addressing this gap, we create our own sub-corpora of how-to guides, which let us investigate differences across articles for specific target groups (§3).

We perform two case studies and a generalization study on our collected data: In the first study, we identify a number of articles that exist in multiple variants for different target groups and examine them in terms of distinctive content and linguistic characteristics (§4). As a second case study, we explicitly examine how far topics covered for specific target groups differ from each other (§5). Finally, we investigate whether the qualitative findings from our case studies can be validated quantitatively and generalized to our whole corpus using computational modeling (§6).

In summary, we find systematic differences between articles for specific groups in terms of topic, style, and content. We conclude the paper with a discussion of these findings and point out links to existing work in the social sciences (§7).

2 Related Work

We summarize existing work on the three strains of research that this paper builds on: wikiHow as a data source (§2.1), subtle biases in datasets (§2.2), as well as understanding the characteristics of texts that target specific audiences (§2.3).

2.1 wikiHow as a Data Source

wikiHow is a prominent data source for a variety of tasks, including summarization (Koupaee and Wang, 2018), goal-step inference (Zhang et al., 2020), and question answering (Cai et al., 2022). By exploiting the revision history of wikiHow, Anthonio et al. (2020) created **wikiHowToImprove**, which has been used to better understand phenomena related to the (re-)writing process of how-to guides (Roth and Anthonio, 2021; Anthonio et al., 2022). Writing, but especially revising, instructions should presumedly take into account the readers' context, perspective and knowledge about the domain and the world. The need for clarification stands prominently out as a main purpose of the refinements of wikiHow guides (Bhat et al., 2020). It has been shown that while annotators tend to agree that "revised means better", the disagreements can be caused by differences in common knowledge and intuitions (Anthonio and Roth, 2020). As specific phenomena, previous work studied implicit references and lexical vagueness (Anthonio and Roth, 2021; Debnath and Roth, 2021). However, none of the aforementioned studies accounted for audience-specific differences. This work takes a first step to close this gap.

2.2 Subtle Biases in Datasets

Diagnosing the presence of biases in data is one of the crucial steps in diminishing the spread of harmful stereotypes. This work contributes to the research on *subtle biases*, i.e., textual patterns that implicitly reflect societal power asymmetries. Such biases are embeded in specific linguistic phenomena (e.g., masculine generics; Swim et al., 2004) or in inequalities in how people from different demographic groups are represented (e.g., emphasizing the romantic relationships in the bibliographies of women; Wagner et al., 2015). Moreover, they can be frequent even in domains where blatant stereotypes and openly expressing beliefs about social hierarchies is generally considered inappropriate (Cervone et al., 2021). For example, there is a long line of work analyzing subtle stereotypes in Wikipedia (Callahan and Herring, 2011; Reagle and Rhue, 2011; Konieczny and Klein, 2018; Schmahl et al., 2020, among others), where the lack of diversity represents an issue already at the level of the editors' community (Lam et al., 2011). Beyond notability for representation itself, linguistic aspects in Wikipedia show a remarkable disparity concerning biographies of men and women, both in terms of topics and polarity of abstract terminology (Wagner et al., 2016). Such inequalities do not pertain only to biographies but find systemic correspondence in all domains and across languages (Falenska and Çetinoğlu, 2021).

To the best of our knowledge, the presence of subtle stereotypes in wikiHow has not yet been investigated. However, the guides from this platform are a valuable entry point for studying bias, as they are produced by a community of contributors and by experts[2] suggesting how to perform activities. In other words, given the different purposes of the platforms, while Wikipedia data is rather descriptive, wikiHow data features instructional texts that potentially differ depending on the audience.

[2]https://www.wikihow.com/Experts

2.3 Different Audiences

The mind of the readers features a priori goals that affect the understanding of written texts (Fum et al., 1986). However, the goals and knowledge of different (groups of) people may vary. An example of work that considers different readers' expertise regards title generation (Senda and Shinohara, 2002). In that work, less expert readers were found to be tentatively more influenced by effective titles. Consequently, a system for revising titles accounting for the readers' expertise has been proposed (Senda et al., 2004). As such, that contribution indicates the importance of considering the target audience for efficient communication. Additionally, different audiences can understand to different extents technical terminology (Senda et al., 2006; Elhadad and Sutaria, 2007) and causation (Siddharthan and Katsos, 2010). Previous contributions accounted for different target groups also in the controllable text generation tasks of paraphrasing (Kajiwara et al., 2013), text simplification (Scarton and Specia, 2018; Sheang and Saggion, 2021), machine translation (Agrawal and Carpuat, 2019), and dictionary examples generation (He and Yiu, 2022).

Rank	Indicator	#	Rank	Indicator	#
1	Girls	370	11	Guys	35
2	for Girls	284	12	for Women	35
3	for Kids	182	13	Women	34
4	Kids	114	14	UK	34
5	Teens	110	15	for Men	31
6	Teen Girls	100	16	Christianity	31
7	for Teens	73	17	Men	29
8	USA	49	18	for Beginners	29
9	for Guys	42	19	Boys	25
10	Windows	38	20	Teenage Girls	25

Table 2: Counts of the 20 most frequent indicators.

	W	M	K	T
Indicators	29	13	23	16
Articles	993	209	499	411
Sentences per article	40	50	29	43
Words per article	509	682	352	544

Table 3: The distribution of the indicators and of the articles for the target audience groups. Sentences and words are indicated via their median values by article.

3 Corpus Construction

As introduced in §2.1, wikiHowToImprove is a well-established data set derived from wikiHow and consisting of more than 246,000 how-to guides. In general, each guide consists of multiple revisions of an *article*, a fixed goal that is named in the *title*, and (optionally) an *indicator* that follows the title in parentheses (cf. Table 1). As we are interested in how-to guides for different target groups, we filter the data for indicators that specify a group of people as targets, which we also refer to as the *audience*. Table 2 lists the 20 most frequent indicators extracted from wikiHowToImprove.

Based on a manual grouping of these indicators, we find that 15 out of 20 indicators refer to attributes of performative gender and age (the remaining five are underlined in Table 2). Apart from their high frequency, both of these attributes are of interest to studies in the social sciences, in which they are often used as independent variables (Cortina et al., 2013; Cha and Weeden, 2014; Palència et al., 2014). Following a traditional binary setup, we distinguish two audiences based on gender, women (**W**) and men (**M**), and two audiences based on age, kids (**K**) and teens (**T**).[3] For each type of audience, we create a set of all indicators used and collect all corresponding guides by extracting the latest article versions from wikiHowToImprove.

Statistics of our corpus with audience-specific how-to guides are provided in Table 3. We note that there is a much higher number of indicators and articles for W than for M. In comparison, the number of articles and indicators for K and T are similar. With only 2,112 how-to guides in total, the corpus seems relatively small. However, the average length of articles ranges from 352 to 682 words, which adds up to a corpus size of more than one million words. Throughout this work, we refer to this dataset as wikiHowAudiences.[4] Next, we approach it in its entirety with two case studies.

4 Case Study: Same Title, Different Audience

Our starting example from Table 1 includes two guides with the same title but different target indicators. Such guides outline the ultimate instances of instructions that are written for different audiences.

[3]Note that while the selected audiences follow discrete categories, we explicitly caution that individual readers can only be represented on a continuum.

[4]`https://github.com/mnfanton/wikiHowAudiences`

Women – Men		
BODY	11	Lose Belly Fat
INTERACT	11	Act on a Date
PRESENT	13	Dress Like a CEO
Kids – Teens		
GROWN-UP	3	Look Older
ADVICE	4	Balance School and Life
ACTIVITY	10	Apply Makeup

Table 4: Frequencies and examples of topical categories.

Therefore, we start our investigation by analyzing how often such cases occur in wikiHowAudiences, which topics they cover, and what differs between versions for specific target groups.

4.1 Guides Selection

First, we identify titles that occur more than once in wikiHowAudiences: 32 unique titles for W–M and 15 for K–T. Next, we group guides with the same title but different target audiences into pairs. A complete list of article titles in this subset can be found in Appendix A.1.

4.2 Guides Analysis

To understand which goals require audience-specific adaptations, we analyze the topics and articles of the filtered guides.

Topics. We start by manually investigating titles of the filtered pairs of guides. For this purpose, we assign each of them to one of three content-related categories. The categories were designed to cover all the titles while being as concrete as possible. An overview of all the categories and their examples is listed in Table 4.

We find that W–M instructions cover a relatively wide range of topics, from body-related activities (BODY), over interacting with other people (INTERACT), to self-presentation (PRESENT), which is the most frequent category. In contrast, among titles in K–T, we notice one clear pattern: all topics focus on issues that require different steps depending on the age of the target. Among them, we distinguish and report in ascending order of frequency articles about learning how to do activities for grown-ups or concerning the urge to grow old (GROWN-UP), advice related to the life of young people (ADVICE), and activities about oneself or the relation of oneself to others (ACTIVITY).

Length. Next, we check whether there are significant differences in terms of how detailed the instructions are for different target groups. We quantify this by simply measuring the length per article in words and sentences. We notice a considerable difference between K and T: the median length of articles for K is only 30 sentences and 346 words, while articles for T contain 98 sentences and 1081 words. In the case of W and M, we do not find such large differences in terms of average word (785 vs. 856) and sentence counts (59 vs. 62). Overall, the numbers reflect the patterns shown in Table 3 for the whole wikiHowAudiences data.

Content. Finally, we switch our attention to the actual content of the articles. As a simple measure of how similar two guides are, we consider their word overlap in both directions using BLEU score (Papineni et al., 2002).

Table 5 presents the articles with the lowest and highest word overlap in both analyzed groups. Interestingly in the case of W–M, both articles cover concepts related to BODY, namely clearing skin and recognizing an infection. Manual inspection of their content reveals that even in the case of the least overlapping articles, "Get Clear Skin", slight differences can be noticed: W article includes more specific information as well as different usage of punctuation. In the case of most overlapping articles, "Recognize Chlamydia Symptoms", the main difference comes from the vocabulary related to different body parts from body types. The high word overlap of these two versions is likely related to their introductions, which provide an interchangeable overview to the topic.

In the case of K–T, the least and most overlapping articles come from two different categories: ACTIVITY and GROWN-UP. The least overlapping pair, "Flirt", is a case of two instructions that treat the same goal with different levels of complexity. For example, the matter of eye contact is described with one step in K and more than ten in T. The most overlapping articles, "Make Money", can be an example of a content stalemate – for both target audiences, babysitting is the first suggested activity to achieve the profit goal. However, it is possible to notice differences in how this concept is contextualized for two groups: either in a list of activities or discussed with its implications and advantages.

W–M	Get Clear Skin (0.02 BLEU)	Recognize Chlamydia Symptom (0.69 BLEU)
W	Gently pat your face dry with a clean towel. Don't rub your face! This can irritate your skin more.	Chlamydia is a dangerous yet common and curable sexually transmitted infection (...)
M	Dry your face – but not roughly.	Chlamydia, specifically chlamydia trachomatis, is a common and curable but dangerous sexually transmitted infection (...)
K–T	**Flirt (0.05 BLEU)**	**Make Money (0.59 BLEU)**
K	Make eye contact. Both girls and boys love eye contact.	There are the traditional jobs like babysitting, shoveling snow, and doing chores around the house.
T	Make eye contact. Body language is a big part of flirting, and a big part of that is eye contact. Eye contact conveys intimacy (...)	Babysit for friends and family. One of the best ways for teenagers to make money and help out in the community is babysitting.

Table 5: Excerpts from the article pairs with the lowest (left) and highest (right) word overlap.

4.3 Summary

We exemplified three characteristics that can distinguish guides written for different audiences. First, the instructions written for K–T significantly differed in *length*. Next, we saw pairs of guides that varied in *style* (such as punctuation) and *content* (e.g., vocabulary in BODY articles). Some of the presented examples suggest that considering only simple content features could be enough to distinguish articles written for different audiences. However, such an approach could be insufficient in more complex cases, such as pairs of guides with high word overlap (see "Make Money"). We discuss these articles again in our generalization study (§6).

5 Case Study: "How To Be" Guides

In the previous section, we looked at how-to guides that occur in different versions for specific audiences. Such guides might concern particular goals that *require* being addressed in distinct ways. In this section, in contrast, we broaden the scope of analysis to explore other cases of differences in audience-specific instructions.

5.1 Guides Selection

The initial example from the introduction (see Table 1) explain how to perform like somebody the reader is presumably not. Inspired by this example, we investigate what other guides instruct their readers "how to be". Concretely, we filter titles starting with the word 'be', which gives us 118 guides for W, 20 for M, 32 for K, and 30 for T.

	Completion(s)	Title
W	Popular	Be Popular and Athletic
	Cute	Be Cute at School
M	Cool	Be Cool in High School
	More	Be More Physically Attractive
K	Good	Be Good With Money
T	Good	Be a Good Friend

Table 6: The most frequent target-specific completions of "how to be" guides and examples of respective titles.

5.2 Guides Analysis

To understand which topics the "how to be" guides cover, we group them according to the first word that occurs after 'be' (henceforth the *completion*).[5] Table 6 shows the most frequent completions for each target group and respective example titles.

Regarding K–T guides, we notice no clear pattern that would distinguish instructions based only on their titles. There is roughly the same number of how-to articles for K and T (32 vs. 30). Moreover, among the most frequent completions we commonly find the word 'good', followed by words such as 'comfortable', 'less', or 'safe'.

In contrast, we find substantial differences for W–M. Specifically, we note that "how to be" guides are more common for W (12% of all articles for this target group) and for both audiences we find differing frequencies of completions: While W articles focus

[5]We ignore the articles 'a', 'an', and 'the'.

on being 'cute' and 'popular' (9 guides), M articles put more emphasis on being 'cool' and 'more' (6 guides). Even though all the how-to guides refer to similar contexts (mostly related to school), we do not find mutual correspondence—there are no instructions for how to "be cool at school" for W and no guide for how to "be cute at school" for M.

5.3 Summary

In this section, we looked at a particular subset of wikiHowAudiences, namely guides with titles starting with the word 'be'. We found that, in the case of W–M targets, the differences in instructions occur already at the level of goals that these guides describe. In other words, we saw examples of instructions where the information for which audience they were intended could be deduced strictly from their *titles*.

6 Generalization Study: Computational Approach

Our case studies show that, depending on the audience, there exist examples of articles that differ in terms of topic, length, style, and/or vocabulary. However, an open question is whether these are only individual cases or if such differences occur systematically. In this study, we investigate this question computationally and attempt to verify our observations on the basis of a larger dataset. For this purpose, we implement tentative characteristics in the form of features and models (§6.1), evaluate in a setting with our full sub-corpora (§6.2), discuss quantitative results (§6.3), and analyze qualitative findings (§6.4).

6.1 Models

Based on the findings from the two case studies, we define majority and length-based baselines and several simple logistic regression classifiers with different sets of features.

Baselines. We use a simple majority baseline that always assigns the most frequent class. We also implement two length-based baseline models that use the number of words in a title (or article) as the only feature for classification.

Content (title/article). The words and phrases used in a text can be potential indicators of its target group. Thus, we make use of the most common[6] uni-grams and bi-grams, excluding stop words, as a feature representation for the content of a how-to guide. We evaluate two variants: features derived from the articles and from the titles.

	W	M	K	T	Total
TRAIN	805	172	416	337	1,730
DEV	94	23	45	37	199
TEST	94	14	38	37	183
Total	1,202		910		2,112

Table 7: Number of articles for each target group and data split, as well as for each task in total.

Style (article). We represent style using two sets of established features from authorship attribution (Sari et al., 2018), namely *lexical* style: average word length, number of short words, vocabulary richness in terms of hapax-legomena and dis-legomena, % of digits, % of upper case letters; and *syntactical* style: occurrences of punctuation, frequencies of POS tags, and stop-word frequencies.

`combined` (article). Content and style can potentially provide complementary information. We test whether a model can leverage a combination of information from different sources. For this purpose, we simply concatenate the article-level features for content, style, and length.

RoBERTa (article). As an alternative to manually selected features, we further test features derived from a large language model, RoBERTa (Liu et al., 2019). Specifically, we encode the article's text, truncated to the first 512 tokens, and extract the representation of the special classification token from the last hidden layer as a set of feature values.

6.2 Experimental Setup

In order to find out whether and to what extent articles for different target groups can be distinguished computationally, we define two classification tasks in which specific articles, based on their characteristics, are to be assigned to one target group each. We distinguish between articles for women and men (W–M) and between articles for kids and teenagers (K–T). For all four classes, we use the full wikiHowAudiences, which we divide into TRAIN, DEV, and TEST sets following the article-level partition of the original wikiHowToImprove corpus (Anthonio et al., 2020). Statistics for each

[6]Note that we could have used all n-grams, but due to the small size of our data (see §6.2), we decided to limit the number of features via an additional hyperparameter.

Model	W–M	K–T
Baselines		
Majority baseline	0.47	0.34
Length (title)	0.47	0.44
Length (article)	0.47	0.61
Content & Style		
Content (title)	0.57	0.57
Content (article)	0.59	0.78
Style (article)	0.58	0.67
"Full" models		
`combined` (article)	0.71	0.78
RoBERTa (article)	0.68	0.74

Table 8: Macro F_1-scores on the test sets.

class and set are shown in Table 7. For the style features, the texts are lemmatized with spaCy.[7]

We train each model on the TRAIN set and evaluate in terms of macro F_1-score on the TEST set. We compute F_1-score per class as the harmonic mean between precision (ratio of correct predictions) and recall (ratio of correctly classified instances). As our data is imbalanced, we use macro F_1 instead of a weighted/micro score to treat each class (rather than each instance) as equally important.

A number of hyperparameters are optimized on the DEV set: We try different values for the logistic regression classifiers' L1 and C terms, sampled from 10 instances between $1e-5$ and 100. For the content features, we optimize the number of k most common n-grams ($k = 200$). We also made use of the DEV set to determine the best language model for our tasks, which we found to be `roberta-large` (results of other models are shown in Appendix A.2).[8]

6.3 Results

The results are summarized in Table 8. As conjectured based on the K–T articles from the first case study, we find that the length-based baselines indeed outperform the majority baseline[9] in that setting. As the further results show, content and stylistic features can indeed be used to correctly assign a specified target group to many how-to guides. According to the evaluation scores, features calculated at the article level are particularly suitable for this purpose: The `combined` model, which uses content, style and length features on the article level, achieves the best result with macro-F1 scores of 0.71 and 0.78 for W–M and K–T, respectively. Features generated based on the `roberta-large` language model achieve competitive scores (0.68 and 0.74), but fall short of the `combined` model.

The large differences in result between the baselines and our models show that the target audience of many articles can be determined simply from the vocabulary and style of an article. Next, we take a closer look at model features and errors.

6.4 Analyses

For our analyses, we focus on the `combined` model because it achieves the best results and its features are easily interpretable.

Features. For each target group, we analyze what features are most important to the model. Since our model uses independent features in a binary classification task, we can simply check the highest positive and negative feature weights for this purpose. A selection from the ten most predictive features[10] and example sentences are shown in Table 9. As the examples illustrate, some of the strongest features are, again, based on stereotypes (e.g., 'cute', 'makeup' for W) or reflect heteronormative assumptions ('hers' for M). Interestingly, we also see characteristics of gender-inclusive language ('theirs' for M) and direct address of the reader in terms of their group membership ('kid' for K and 'teen' for T). We further find negations (e.g., 'wasn't') as part of strong features for W, which is particularly worrying in light of sociopsychological findings that have shown negations to serve a stereotype-maintaining function across languages (Beukeboom et al., 2010, 2020).

Same title articles. As examples of particularly hard cases, we return to the how-to guides from the first case study, which consisted of article versions for different audiences (§4). Following the data partition from previous work, we identify 16 such articles in the DEV and TEST splits. We find that the `combined` model classifies 12 of them correctly (75%). In the remaining 4 cases, the prediction errors could have been caused by superficial features that are predictive for the opposite audience. We note for each of these 16 articles that the version

[7] `https://spacy.io/`

[8] We used HuggingFace Transformers (Wolf et al., 2020).

[9] Note that the F_1-score for the majority baseline lies below 0.5 because we calculate the *macro average* over both classes and the score does not reach 1.0 for either class.

[10] Appendix A.2 lists all top-10 most predictive features.

	Feature(s)	Example	Title
W	cute, makeup	Do cute makeup.	Look Cute
	wasn't	She most likely wasn't wearing the right colors for her skin tone.	Go from Ugly to Popular
M	hers	Slowly move your hand towards hers ...	Know if Your Crush Likes You Back
	theirs	Being a good partner is all about ... adjusting your style to suit theirs.	Grind
K	name	Think of your blog's name.	Write a Blog
	kid	... even if you're a kid, there are ways to bank a few extra bucks.	Make Money
T	dress	Dress up, make it look important.	Know What to Wear on Dates
	teen	When you're a teen with a busy schedule, it can be difficult to find time to be active.	Stay Active After School

Table 9: Sample of the top-10 most predictive features and example sentences from articles of each target group.

for the opposite audience is part of the TRAIN split. Therefore, the topics of the guides are generally not specific to one audience, and a correct classification of the majority of cases demonstrates that the model indeed captures characteristics of content and style that seem specific to the audience itself.

7 Discussion and Conclusion

In this paper, we assessed differences across how-to guides written for specific audiences. In the construction of sub-corpora for four target groups, we already noticed inequalities on the level of who is being instructed in wikiHow: as a target audience, women are mentioned more than four times more frequently than men, and teens receive about 50% more instructions per article than kids. In two case studies, we investigated and provided examples of target-related differences on the levels of topic, style, and content.

The differences observed in our case studies inspired feature sets of shallow classifiers for predicting the target audience of a given guide. Using these classifiers, we showed that it is, in many cases, indeed possible to automatically predict for which audience an article was written. In an analysis of our results, we found that this success is not merely based on different topics covered for each target group but that the articles for each group systematically differ in terms of content and style.

Each of the aforementioned observations presents a tiny, seemingly insignificant piece of a puzzle. But taken together, these pieces reveal a surprisingly clear picture: there are noticeable differences in what topics are covered for each target group, how many articles and instructions are provided for each audience, and how these articles are written. Even though the audience-specific characteristics used in our studies are by no means exhaustive, our straightforward approach allowed us to identify, qualitatively and quantitatively, debatable differences in how wikiHow guides present particular topics to specific target groups. While there is an inevitable need for differences in vocabulary when speaking about physical features or body parts, it is at best unclear in which ways how-to guides about human interactions or self-presentation should cast significant differences.

Some of the observed differences have already been critically discussed in the context of social science research. For example, it is well-known that labels such as 'cute' are used pejoratively as a form of social control (Talbot, 2019) and that prescriptive components of gender stereotypes in education contribute to discrimination (Kollmayer et al., 2018). However, exposing readers to cultural messages and beliefs about age, gender or other factors cannot be avoided entirely, especially on a collaboratively edited online platform. In fact, it seems to be a challenge for any pluralistic society to find a balance between communicating traditional values and empowering everyone. It is therefore all the more important for a comprehensive understanding to determine when and in what form social norms are conveyed. As such, we view the contributions of this paper, namely our data set of audience-specific guides, wikiHowAudiences, and our mixed-methods approach for identifying and verifying differences, as a valuable connecting point to raise awareness of potential issues and to foster interdisciplinary dialogue for future research.

Limitations

Our studies focus on the differences in how-to guides written for specific audiences only in one language, namely English. A major limitation is therefore that we do not consider other languages.

The perspectives provided by the data source we rely on, wikiHow, allow us to identify specific phenomena and peculiarities. Yet, contemplating only one data source lets us generalize only to a limited extent. For example, the audiences considered in this work depended on the target groups portrayed in the data. They are neither exhaustive nor representative of the diversity of humankind, especially of marginalized social groups. Therefore, a wider variety of data sources will be needed to test generalizations.

Finally, a further limitation of our studies concerns intersectionality. While it seems possible that guides can be tuned by contemplating one specific attribute of the audience at a time, this does not hold with regard to the actual attributes of the readers. Such attributes are per se coexistent, and consequently, they are not separable.

Ethics Statement

We acknowledge that the content that emerged from the data is narrow in terms of cultural perspectives, mainly addressing western cultures. Moreover, the analysis of the audiences is not exhaustive of the diversity of humankind, especially not exhaustively accounting for queer identities in particular trans and non-binary identities. With the present research, we do not intend to reinforce representational biases, rather to highlight them.

References

Sweta Agrawal and Marine Carpuat. 2019. Controlling text complexity in neural machine translation. In *Proceedings of the 2019 Conference on Empirical Methods in Natural Language Processing and the 9th International Joint Conference on Natural Language Processing (EMNLP-IJCNLP)*, pages 1549–1564, Hong Kong, China. Association for Computational Linguistics.

Talita Anthonio, Irshad Bhat, and Michael Roth. 2020. wikiHowToImprove: A resource and analyses on edits in instructional texts. In *Proceedings of the 12th Language Resources and Evaluation Conference*, pages 5721–5729, Marseille, France. European Language Resources Association.

Talita Anthonio and Michael Roth. 2020. What can we learn from noun substitutions in revision histories? In *Proceedings of the 28th International Conference on Computational Linguistics*, pages 1359–1370, Barcelona, Spain (Online). International Committee on Computational Linguistics.

Talita Anthonio and Michael Roth. 2021. Resolving implicit references in instructional texts. In *Proceedings of the 2nd Workshop on Computational Approaches to Discourse*, pages 58–71, Punta Cana, Dominican Republic and Online. Association for Computational Linguistics.

Talita Anthonio, Anna Sauer, and Michael Roth. 2022. Clarifying implicit and underspecified phrases in instructional text. In *Proceedings of the Thirteenth Language Resources and Evaluation Conference*, pages 3319–3330, Marseille, France. European Language Resources Association.

Camiel J. Beukeboom, Christian Burgers, Zsolt P. Szabó, Slavica Cvejic, Jan-Erik M. Lönnqvist, and Kasper Welbers. 2020. The negation bias in stereotype maintenance: A replication in five languages. *Journal of Language and Social Psychology*, 39(2):219–236.

Camiel J. Beukeboom, Catrin Finkenauer, and Daniël H. J. Wigboldus. 2010. The negation bias: When negations signal stereotypic expectancies. *Journal of Personality and Social Psychology*, 99(6):978–992.

Irshad Bhat, Talita Anthonio, and Michael Roth. 2020. Towards modeling revision requirements in wikiHow instructions. In *Proceedings of the 2020 Conference on Empirical Methods in Natural Language Processing (EMNLP)*, pages 8407–8414, Online. Association for Computational Linguistics.

S.R.K. Branavan, Harr Chen, Luke Zettlemoyer, and Regina Barzilay. 2009. Reinforcement learning for mapping instructions to actions. In *Proceedings of the Joint Conference of the 47th Annual Meeting of the ACL and the 4th International Joint Conference on Natural Language Processing of the AFNLP*, pages 82–90, Suntec, Singapore. Association for Computational Linguistics.

Pengshan Cai, Mo Yu, Fei Liu, and Hong Yu. 2022. Generating coherent narratives with subtopic planning to answer how-to questions. In *Proceedings of the 2nd Workshop on Natural Language Generation, Evaluation, and Metrics (GEM)*, pages 26–42, Abu Dhabi, United Arab Emirates (Hybrid). Association for Computational Linguistics.

Ewa S. Callahan and Susan C. Herring. 2011. Cultural Bias in Wikipedia Content on Famous Persons. *Journal of the American society for information science and technology*, 62(10):1899–1915.

Carmen Cervone, Martha Augoustinos, and Anne Maass. 2021. The language of derogation and hate: Functions, consequences, and reappropriation. *Journal of language and social psychology*, 40(1):80–101.

Youngjoo Cha and Kim A Weeden. 2014. Overwork and the slow convergence in the gender gap in wages. *American Sociological Review*, 79(3):457–484.

Cuong Xuan Chu, Niket Tandon, and Gerhard Weikum. 2017. Distilling task knowledge from how-to communities. In *Proceedings of the 26th International Conference on World Wide Web*, pages 805–814.

Lilia M Cortina, Dana Kabat-Farr, Emily A Leskinen, Marisela Huerta, and Vicki J Magley. 2013. Selective incivility as modern discrimination in organizations: Evidence and impact. *Journal of management*, 39(6):1579–1605.

Alok Debnath and Michael Roth. 2021. A computational analysis of vagueness in revisions of instructional texts. In *Proceedings of the 16th Conference of the European Chapter of the Association for Computational Linguistics: Student Research Workshop*, pages 30–35, Online. Association for Computational Linguistics.

Elizabeth N. Dougherty, Andrea B. Goldschmidt, Nicole K. Johnson, Krystal Badillo, Scott G. Engel, and Alissa A. Haedt-Matt. 2022. Gender differences in the relation between interpersonal stress and momentary shape and weight concerns in youth with overweight/obesity. *Body Image*, 40:249–255.

Noemie Elhadad and Komal Sutaria. 2007. Mining a lexicon of technical terms and lay equivalents. In *Biological, translational, and clinical language processing*, pages 49–56, Prague, Czech Republic. Association for Computational Linguistics.

Agnieszka Falenska and Özlem Çetinoğlu. 2021. Assessing gender bias in Wikipedia: Inequalities in article titles. In *Proceedings of the 3rd Workshop on Gender Bias in Natural Language Processing*, pages 75–85, Online. Association for Computational Linguistics.

Danilo Fum, Giovanni Guida, and Carlo Tasso. 1986. Tailoring importance evaluation to reader's goals: A contribution to descriptive text summarization. In *Coling 1986 Volume 1: The 11th International Conference on Computational Linguistics*.

Xingwei He and Siu Ming Yiu. 2022. Controllable dictionary example generation: Generating example sentences for specific targeted audiences. In *Proceedings of the 60th Annual Meeting of the Association for Computational Linguistics (Volume 1: Long Papers)*, pages 610–627, Dublin, Ireland. Association for Computational Linguistics.

Tomoyuki Kajiwara, Hiroshi Matsumoto, and Kazuhide Yamamoto. 2013. Selecting proper lexical paraphrase for children. In *Proceedings of the 25th Conference on Computational Linguistics and Speech Processing (ROCLING 2013)*, pages 59–73, Kaohsiung, Taiwan. The Association for Computational Linguistics and Chinese Language Processing (ACLCLP).

Marlene Kollmayer, Barbara Schober, and Christiane Spiel. 2018. Gender stereotypes in education: Development, consequences, and interventions. *European Journal of Developmental Psychology*, 15(4):361–377.

Piotr Konieczny and Maximilian Klein. 2018. Gender gap through time and space: A journey through Wikipedia biographies via the Wikidata Human Gender Indicator. *New Media Soc.*, 20(12).

Mahnaz Koupaee and William Yang Wang. 2018. Wikihow: A large scale text summarization dataset. *CoRR*, abs/1810.09305.

Shyong (Tony) K. Lam, Anuradha Uduwage, Zhenhua Dong, Shilad Sen, David R. Musicant, Loren Terveen, and John Riedl. 2011. WP:Clubhouse? an exploration of Wikipedia's gender imbalance. In *Proceedings of the 7th International Symposium on Wikis and Open Collaboration*, WikiSym '11, page 1–10, New York, NY, USA. Association for Computing Machinery.

Yinhan Liu, Myle Ott, Naman Goyal, Jingfei Du, Mandar Joshi, Danqi Chen, Omer Levy, Mike Lewis, Luke Zettlemoyer, and Veselin Stoyanov. 2019. RoBERTa: A robustly optimized BERT pretraining approach.

Laia Palència, Davide Malmusi, Deborah De Moortel, Lucía Artazcoz, Mona Backhans, Christophe Vanroelen, and Carme Borrell. 2014. The influence of gender equality policies on gender inequalities in health in europe. *Social science & medicine*, 117:25–33.

Kishore Papineni, Salim Roukos, Todd Ward, and Wei-Jing Zhu. 2002. Bleu: a method for automatic evaluation of machine translation. In *Proceedings of the 40th Annual Meeting of the Association for Computational Linguistics*, pages 311–318, Philadelphia, Pennsylvania, USA. Association for Computational Linguistics.

Deborah A Prentice and Erica Carranza. 2002. What women and men should be, shouldn't be, are allowed to be, and don't have to be: The contents of prescriptive gender stereotypes. *Psychology of women quarterly*, 26(4):269–281.

Joseph Reagle and Lauren Rhue. 2011. Gender bias in Wikipedia and Britannica. *International Journal of Communication*, 5:21.

Michael Roth and Talita Anthonio. 2021. UnImplicit shared task report: Detecting clarification requirements in instructional text. In *Proceedings of the 1st Workshop on Understanding Implicit and Underspecified Language*, pages 28–32, Online. Association for Computational Linguistics.

Yunita Sari, Mark Stevenson, and Andreas Vlachos. 2018. Topic or style? exploring the most useful features for authorship attribution. In *Proceedings of the 27th International Conference on Computational Linguistics*, pages 343–353, Santa Fe, New Mexico, USA. Association for Computational Linguistics.

Carolina Scarton and Lucia Specia. 2018. Learning simplifications for specific target audiences. In *Proceedings of the 56th Annual Meeting of the Association for Computational Linguistics (Volume 2: Short Papers)*, pages 712–718, Melbourne, Australia. Association for Computational Linguistics.

Katja Geertruida Schmahl, Tom Julian Viering, Stavros Makrodimitris, Arman Naseri Jahfari, and Marco Tax, David andj Loog. 2020. Is Wikipedia succeeding in reducing gender bias? assessing changes in gender bias in Wikipedia using word embeddings. In *Proceedings of the Fourth Workshop on Natural Language Processing and Computational Social Science*, pages 94–103, Online. Association for Computational Linguistics.

Yasuko Senda and Yaushi Shinohara. 2002. Analysis of titles and readers for title generation centered on the readers. In *COLING 2002: The 19th International Conference on Computational Linguistics*.

Yasuko Senda, Yasusi Sinohara, and Manabu Okumura. 2004. A support system for revising titles to stimulate the lay reader's interest in technical achievements. In *COLING 2004: Proceedings of the 20th International Conference on Computational Linguistics*, pages 155–161, Geneva, Switzerland. COLING.

Yasuko Senda, Yasusi Sinohara, and Manabu Okumura. 2006. Automatic terminology intelligibility estimation for readership-oriented technical writing. In *Proceedings of the Fifth International Conference on Language Resources and Evaluation (LREC'06)*, Genoa, Italy. European Language Resources Association (ELRA).

Kim Cheng Sheang and Horacio Saggion. 2021. Controllable sentence simplification with a unified text-to-text transfer transformer. In *Proceedings of the 14th International Conference on Natural Language Generation*, pages 341–352, Aberdeen, Scotland, UK. Association for Computational Linguistics.

Advaith Siddharthan and Napoleon Katsos. 2010. Reformulating discourse connectives for non-expert readers. In *Human Language Technologies: The 2010 Annual Conference of the North American Chapter of the Association for Computational Linguistics*, pages 1002–1010, Los Angeles, California. Association for Computational Linguistics.

Janet K Swim, Robyn Mallett, and Charles Stangor. 2004. Understanding subtle sexism: Detection and use of sexist language. *Sex roles*, 51(3):117–128.

Mary Talbot. 2019. *Language and gender*. John Wiley & Sons.

Claudia Wagner, David Garcia, Mohsen Jadidi, and Markus Strohmaier. 2015. It's a man's Wikipedia? assessing gender inequality in an online encyclopedia. In *Proceedings of the international AAAI conference on web and social media*, volume 9, pages 454–463.

Claudia Wagner, Eduardo Graells-Garrido, and David García. 2016. Women through the glass ceiling: gender asymmetries in Wikipedia. *EPJ Data Science*, 5:1–24.

Thomas Wolf, Lysandre Debut, Victor Sanh, Julien Chaumond, Clement Delangue, Anthony Moi, Pierric Cistac, Tim Rault, Remi Louf, Morgan Funtowicz, Joe Davison, Sam Shleifer, Patrick von Platen, Clara Ma, Yacine Jernite, Julien Plu, Canwen Xu, Teven Le Scao, Sylvain Gugger, Mariama Drame, Quentin Lhoest, and Alexander Rush. 2020. Transformers: State-of-the-art natural language processing. In *Proceedings of the 2020 Conference on Empirical Methods in Natural Language Processing: System Demonstrations*, pages 38–45, Online. Association for Computational Linguistics.

Li Zhang, Qing Lyu, and Chris Callison-Burch. 2020. Reasoning about goals, steps, and temporal ordering with WikiHow. In *Proceedings of the 2020 Conference on Empirical Methods in Natural Language Processing (EMNLP)*, pages 4630–4639, Online. Association for Computational Linguistics.

A Appendix

A.1 Case Study

Category	Word Overlap	Same Title	Indicator for **W**	Indicator for **M**
BODY	0.02	Get Clear Skin	for Middle School Girls	Guys
BODY	0.05	Burn Fat	for Girls	for Men
PRESENT	0.07	Get Ready for School	for Girls	Guys
PRESENT	0.09	Look Rich Without Being Rich	Teen Girls	for Guys
PRESENT	0.16	Get Ready for School	Teen Girls	Guys
INTERACT	0.16	Catch Your Crush's Eye	for Girls Only	Boys
INTERACT	0.16	Dance at a School Dance	for Girls	for Guys
PRESENT	0.21	Act Like a Kid Again	Girls	Boys
PRESENT	0.21	Look Like an Abercrombie Model	for Girls	Boys
PRESENT	0.21	Dress Emo	for Girls	Guys
BODY	0.24	Have Good Hygiene	Girls	Boys
PRESENT	0.25	Prepare for a School Dance	for Girls	for Guys
PRESENT	0.27	Pack for Soccer Practice	Girls	Boys
INTERACT	0.28	Be in a Female Led Relationship	Women	Men
INTERACT	0.30	Act on a Date	for Girls	for Boys
PRESENT	0.31	Dress Cool	for Girls	Guys
BODY	0.31	Lose Belly Fat	Teen Girls	for Men
PRESENT	0.33	Look Hot on Club Penguin	Girls	Guys
PRESENT	0.35	Be Awesome	for Girls	for Boys
INTERACT	0.36	Have Fun with Your Friends	Teen Girls	Guys
PRESENT	0.36	Dress Like a CEO	Women	Men
INTERACT	0.37	Cradle a Lacrosse Stick	Girls	Men
INTERACT	0.41	Get Your Crush to Like You	Girls	Guys
INTERACT	0.43	Practice Changing Room Etiquette	Girls	Men
INTERACT	0.43	Practice Changing Room Etiquette	Women	Men
BODY	0.44	Recognize Trichomoniasis Symptoms	Women	Men
PRESENT	0.45	Be Popular in Middle School	for Girls	for Boys
BODY	0.47	Lose Belly Fat	for Women	for Men
BODY	0.49	Gain Weight Fast	for Women	for Men
BODY	0.52	Be Indie	for Girls	for Guys
INTERACT	0.54	Grind	for Girls	for Guys
INTERACT	0.55	Host a Sleepover	Teen Girls	for Boys
BODY	0.57	Treat Acne	Teenage Girls	Teen Boys
BODY	0.60	Prevent HIV Infection	Women	Men
BODY	0.69	Recognize Chlamydia Symptoms	for Women	for Men
			Indicator for **K**	Indicator for **T**
ACTIVITY	0.05	Flirt	Middle School	for Teens
ACTIVITY	0.10	Redo Your Bedroom	Preteen Girls	Teen Girls
GROWN-UP	0.11	Look Older	Preteen Girls	Teenage Girls
ACTIVITY	0.14	Enjoy Summer Vacation	for Kids	for Teens
ACTIVITY	0.18	Clean Your Room	Kids	Teens
ADVICE	0.19	Enjoy a Plane Ride	for Grade School Kids	Teen Girls
ADVICE	0.20	Be Less Insecure	Preteens	for Teen Girls
ACTIVITY	0.28	Clean Your Room	Tween Girls	Teens
ACTIVITY	0.29	Pack for a Vacation	Preteen Girls	Teen Girls
ADVICE	0.30	Get a Boy to Like You	Pre Teens	Teens
ACTIVITY	0.31	Apply Makeup	Preteens	for Teen Girls
ADVICE	0.33	Balance School and Life	Middle School	Teens
ACTIVITY	0.36	Host a Girls Only Sleepover	for Preteens	Teens
ACTIVITY	0.39	Get Ready for Bed	Tween Girls	for Teenage Girls
GROWN-UP	0.46	Get Fit	for Kids	Teenage Girls
ACTIVITY	0.53	Apply Makeup	Preteens	for Teens
GROWN-UP	0.59	Make Money	for Kids	for Teenagers

Table 10: All "Same Title, Different Audience" guides.

Be (...)	*X*	(...)	indicator
Be	Popular	and Athletic	(for Girls)
Be	Popular	in Grade 6.	(for Girls.)
Be	Popular	in Middle School	(for Girls)
Be	Popular	in a School Uniform	(Girls)
Be	Popular	in Secondary School	(for Girls)
Be a	Cute	Teen	(Girl)
Be	Cute		(Tween Girls)
Be the	Cute	and Hot Teen	(Girls)
Be	Cute	at School	(Girls)
Be	Cool	Around Your Crush	(for Boys)
Be	Cool	in High School	(Boys)
Be a	Cool	Christian	(Teen Guys)
Be	More	Attractive to Girls	(for Boys)
Be	More	Physically Attractive	(Men)
Be	More	Socially Open	(Men)
Be a	Good	Hamster Owner	(for Kids)
Be a	Good	Stuffed Animal Mom	(for Kids)
Be	Good	With Money	(for Kids)
Be a	Good	Friend	(Teens)
Be a	Good	Writer	(Teens)

Table 11: The most common completions in the titles for "how to be".

A.2 Classification tasks

model-name	W–M	K–T
`bert-base-uncased`	0.57	0.64
`roberta-base`	0.81	0.73
`bert-large-uncased`	0.73	0.74
`roberta-large`	0.82	0.75

Table 12: The performance on the DEV set of the classification tasks with optimized LR using the [CLS] token representations from the different LMs.

Most predictive features of the `combined` model:

W: hadn't - wasn't - cute - makeup - ourselves - bag - skirt - outfit - move - sleep

M: man - product - boy - yourselves - o - dance - theirs - shoe - hers - person

K: kid - the - adult - name - are - step - were - else - probably - mean

T: teen - without - than - dress - next - her - want - buy - everyone - ADJ

A.3 Confusion Matrices

	DEV		TEST	
	W	**M**	**W**	**M**
W	0.83	0.17	0.87	0.13
M	0.48	0.52	0.36	0.64
W	78	16	82	12
M	11	12	5	9

Table 13: The confusion matrix for the dev set (left) and the confusion matrix for the test set (right).

	DEV		TEST	
	K	**T**	**K**	**T**
K	0.78	0.22	0.87	0.13
T	0.35	0.65	0.30	0.70
	K	**T**	**K**	**T**
K	35	10	33	5
T	13	24	11	26

Table 14: The confusion matrix for the dev set (left) and the confusion matrix for the test set (right).

“When Words Fail, Emojis Prevail”: Generating Sarcastic Utterances with Emoji Using Valence Reversal and Semantic Incongruity

Faria Binte Kader*, Nafisa Hossain Nujat*, Tasmia Binte Sogir*,
Mohsinul Kabir, Hasan Mahmud, Kamrul Hasan
Department of Computer Science and Engineering
Islamic University of Technology
Dhaka, Bangladesh
{faria, nafisa13, tasmia, mohsinulkabir, hasan, hasank}@iut-dhaka.edu

Abstract

Sarcasm is a form of figurative language that serves as a humorous tool for mockery and ridicule. We present a novel architecture for sarcasm generation with emoji from a non-sarcastic input sentence in English. We divide the generation task into two sub tasks: one for generating textual sarcasm and another for collecting emojis associated with those sarcastic sentences. Two key elements of sarcasm are incorporated into the textual sarcasm generation task: valence reversal and semantic incongruity with context, where the context may involve shared commonsense or general knowledge between the speaker and their audience. The majority of existing sarcasm generation works have focused on this textual form. However, in the real world, when written texts fall short of effectively capturing the emotional cues of spoken and face-to-face communication, people often opt for emojis to accurately express their emotions. Due to the wide range of applications of emojis, incorporating appropriate emojis to generate textual sarcastic sentences helps advance sarcasm generation. We conclude our study by evaluating the generated sarcastic sentences using human judgement. All the codes and data used in this study has been made publicly available[1].

1 Introduction

Sarcasm is defined as the use of remarks that often mean the opposite of what is said in order to hurt someone's feelings or to criticize something in a humorous way[2]. Sarcastic remarks are often challenging to interpret considering their literal meaning differs greatly from the speaker's actual intent. Compared to verbal or in-person conversations, textual sarcasm presents additional challenges due to the absence of visual cues, vocal tone etc.

Non-Sarcastic Input	Sarcastic Output with Emoji
I really hate walking in the rain.	I really love the outdoors walking in the rain. I sat feeling thoroughly miserable.😫
Mom is in a bad mood today.	Happy mothers day mom is in a well mood today. She sounded tense and angry.😠
That movie was bad.	That movie was awesome. Bad intelligence and political incompetence.😠

Table 1: Sample sarcastic outputs with emoji generated from non-sarcastic inputs

The presence of sarcasm makes it significantly harder for machines to understand the actual meaning of the textual data. This has motivated research in detecting sarcasm in textual data. In order to train machines to detect sarcasm, we need quality datasets that represent different aspects of sarcasm in text. Even though we have an abundance of social media data and resources, it can be difficult to collect correctly labeled sarcastic texts. Instead, many research have tried to generate texts that can accurately express sarcastic notions (Joshi et al., 2015; Mishra et al., 2019; Chakrabarty et al., 2020). Many studies have also investigated strategies in incorporating sarcasm generation into chatbots (Joshi et al., 2015, 2017).

Emojis, small ideograms that represent objects, people, and scenes (Cappallo et al., 2015), are one of the key elements of a novel form of communication due to the advent of social media. Using emojis within texts can give us additional cues on sarcasm, replicating facial expressions and body language, etc. Incorporating emojis with texts for training will let the machines catch these cues easily (Bharti et al., 2016). Subramanian et al. (2019)

*These authors contributed equally to this work.
[1]https://github.com/WrightlyRong/Sarcasm-Generation-with-Emoji
[2]https://dictionary.cambridge.org/

Proceedings of the 61st Annual Meeting of the Association for Computational Linguistics - Student Research Workshop, pages 334–351
July 10-12, 2023

observed that when emojis were included in the sentence, their emoji-based sarcasm detection model performed noticeably better.

In this study, we propose a new framework in which when given a non-sarcastic text as input, the text is converted into a sarcastic one with emoji where the emoji will specifically help to identify the sarcastic intent of the text. Table 1 shows a few sample non-sarcastic input and sarcastic output pairs with emoji. In order to implement the architecture, we have focused on two major components: Sarcastic text generation and Emoji prediction for the text. For textual sarcasm generation, we are incorporating the works of Chakrabarty et al. (2020) and Mishra et al. (2019) and for Emoji prediction, a deep learning model fine tuned on OpenAI's CLIP (Contrastive Language-Image Pre-training)[3] (Radford et al., 2021) is used. The emoji prediction module along with the sarcasm generation module generates the final sarcastic text including emoji. This work provides two major contributions:

1. Propose a novel multi-modular framework for sarcasm generation incorporating the reversal of valence and semantic incongruity characteristics of sarcasm while also including appropriate emojis.
2. Create and publish a sarcastic corpora which can serve as valuable training data for sarcasm detection models.

As far as our understanding goes, there has been no previous framework proposed on textual sarcasm generation that also incorporates emojis. This framework can aid downstream tasks by allowing a deeper understanding of sarcasm to produce more contextually relevant responses.

2 Related Work

Research on sarcasm have been a subject of interest for several decades. The following sub sections provide a brief overview of the past work done on different aspects of sarcasm.

2.1 Studies on Sarcasm Detection

Sarcasm detection is a classification task in its most typical form. From a given text, the task includes classifying the text as sarcastic or non-sarcastic. Sarcasm detection is a fairly recent but promising research field in the domain of Natural Language Processing. Nonetheless, it serves as a crucial part to sentiment analysis (Maynard and Greenwood, 2014).

Most of these studies on sarcasm detection train and test on already available popular datasets such as the datasets used by Riloff et al. (2013), Khodak et al. (2017) and Cai et al. (2019). We observed that Twitter is predominantly the most popular social media platform used for sarcasm detection datasets although Reddit, Amazon and a few discussion forums were also seen being used. We also saw a shift in Sarcasm detection methodologies from rule-based approaches (Riloff et al., 2013; Bharti et al., 2015), machine learning and deep learning approaches (Bharti et al., 2017; Poria et al., 2016; Ghosh and Veale, 2016) to transformed based approaches (Dadu and Pant, 2020; Kumar et al., 2021). We include two tables Table 9 and Table 10 summarizing the datasets and methodologies used in sarcasm detection in the appendix (Section A).

Recent works on sarcasm detection include frequent use of BERT (Savini and Caragea, 2022; Zhang et al., 2023; Pandey and Singh, 2023), multimodal and cross-modal detection tasks (Liang et al., 2022; Chauhan et al., 2022; Ding et al., 2022), enhancement of sarcasm detection in complex expressions with sememe knowledge (Wen et al., 2022), study on the effect of foreign accent (Puhacheuskaya and Järvikivi, 2022), use of vocal and facial cues (Aguert, 2022) etc. Sarcasm and irony detection from languages other than English i.e. Chinese, Dutch, Spanish, Arabic, Romanian etc. have also been studied in recent works (Farha and Magdy, 2020; Muaad et al., 2022; Maladry et al., 2022; Wen et al., 2022; Ortega-Bueno et al., 2022; Buzea et al., 2022).

2.2 Characteristics of Sarcasm

Studies have identified a variety of potential sources for sarcasm. According to Gerrig and Goldvarg (2000), sarcasm stems from a situational disparity between what the speaker desires, believes, or expects and what actually happens. Incongruity between text and a contextual information is mentioned as a factor by Wilson (2006). Context Incongruity (Campbell and Katz, 2012) is addressed in the works of Riloff et al. (2013) who suggests that sarcasm arises from a contrast between positive verbs and negative situation phrases. Burgers et al. (2012) formulates that for an utterance to be

[3]https://openai.com/research/clip

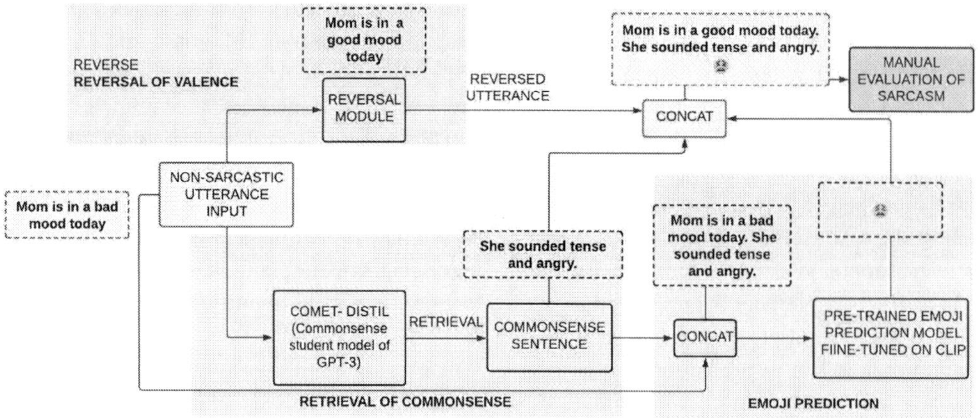

Figure 1: Model Architecture of the proposed system

sarcastic, it needs to have one or more of these five characteristics:

1. the sentence has to be evaluative,
2. it should be based on the reversal of valence of the literal and intended meanings,
3. it should have a semantic incongruity with the context, which may consist of common sense or general information that the speaker and the addressee share,
4. should be aimed at some target,
5. should be in some manner relevant to the communication scenario. Many studies focused on one or more of these characteristics.

2.3 Sarcasm Generation

Compared to sarcasm detection, research on sarcasm generation is still in its early stages. Joshi et al. (2015) introduced SarcasmBot[4], a chatbot that caters to user input with sarcastic responses. SarcasmBot is a sarcasm generation module with eight rule-based sarcasm generators where each of the generators produces a different type of sarcastic expression. During the execution phase, one of these generators is selected based on user input properties. Essentially, it yields sarcastic responses rather than converting a literal input text into a sarcastic one, the latter one being a common practice in future research. This method was later utilized in the author's subsequent work (Joshi et al., 2017) where they built SarcasmSuite, a web-based interface for sarcasm detection and generation.

The first work on automatic sarcasm generation conditioned from literal input was performed by Mishra et al. (2019). The authors relied on the Context Incongruity characteristic of sarcasm mentioned by Riloff et al. (2013) and employed information retrieval-based techniques and reinforced neural seq2seq learning to generate sarcasm. They used unlabeled non-sarcastic and sarcastic opinions to train their models, where sarcasm was formed as a result of a disparity between a situation's positive sentiment context and negative situational context. A thorough evaluation of the proposed system's performance against popular unsupervised statistical, neural, and style transfer techniques showed that it significantly outperformed the baselines taken into account.

Chakrabarty et al. (2020) introduced a new framework by incorporating context in the forms of shared commonsense or world knowledge to model semantic incongruity. They based their research on the factors addressed by Burgers et al. (2012). Their architecture is structured into three modules: Reversal of Valence, Retrieval of Commonsense Context, and Ranking of Semantic Incongruity. With this framework they were able to simulate two fundamental features of sarcasm: reversal of valence and semantic incongruity with the context. However, they opted for a rule-based system to reverse the sentiments. The authors also noticed that in a few cases, the simple reversal of valence strategy was enough to generate sarcasm which meant the addition of context was redundant.

Recent similar works in the field include that of Oprea et al. (2021) where they developed a sarcastic response generator, Chandler, that also provides explanations as to why they are sarcastic. Das et al. (2022) manually extracted the features of a

[4]https://github.com/adityajo/sarcasmbot/

benchmark pop culture sarcasm corpus and built padding sequences from the vector representations' matrices. They proposed a hybrid of four Parallel LSTM Networks, each with its own activation classifier which achieved 98.31% accuracy among the test cases on open-source English literature. A new problem of cross-modal sarcasm generation (CMSG) that creates sarcastic descriptions of a given image was introduced by Ruan et al. (2022). However, these studies have only focused on generating textual sarcastic sentences, but as described by Subramanian et al. (2019), incorporating emojis improved the overall performance of sarcasm detection and thus can be a potential research scope.

3 Methodology

Our model architecture consists of 3 modules which are as follows: Reversal of Valence, Retrieval of Commonsense and Emoji Prediction. The Reversal of Valence module takes in a negative utterance and generates an utterance with positive sentiment. The Retrieval of Commonsense module outputs relevant commonsense context sentence which helps in creating a sarcastic situation. Lastly, the Emoji Prediction module generates an emoji which makes the overall output more sarcastic. With these three modules, we have incorporated two of the fundamental features of sarcasm: reversal of valence and semantic incongruity with the context. A diagram of the overall pipeline is demonstrated in Figure 1. We describe the modules in details in the next few sub sections.

3.1 Reversal of Valence

In the work of Chakrabarty et al. (2020), for the reversal of valence module, they have used a rule-based approach to manually reverse the sentiment of the negative sentence. But a rule-based model cannot reverse sentences that do not follow the traditional structure of sentences such as those used in social media. We have worked on this limitation of this current state-of-the-art sarcasm generation model where we replace their rule-based reversal module with a deep-learning reversal module inspired by the work of Mishra et al. (2019). This module is divided into two parts: Sentiment Neutralization and Positive Sentiment Induction.

3.1.1 Sentiment Neutralization

We implement the Sentiment Neutralization module to filter out the sentiment words from the input utterance, which results into a neutral sentence from a negative one. An example is shown in table 2.

Negative Input	Neutral Output
Is feeling absolutely bloated and fat from lack of a proper workout	Is feeling absolutely and from a proper workout

Table 2: Example of sentiment neutralization from input sentence

The neutralization model is essentially a sentiment classification model which first detects the sentiment of the given utterance (positive/negative). This model consists of several LSTM layers and a self-attention layer. During testing, the self-attention vector is extracted as done by Xu et al. (2018) which is then inversed and discretized as follows:

$$\hat{a}_i = \begin{cases} 0, & \text{if } a_i > 0.95 * max(a) \\ 1, & \text{otherwise} \end{cases} \quad (1)$$

where a_i is the attention weight for the ith word, and $max(a)$ gives the highest attention value from the current utterance. A word is filtered out if the discretized attention weight for that word is 0. The sentiment detection model architecture is shown in figure 2.

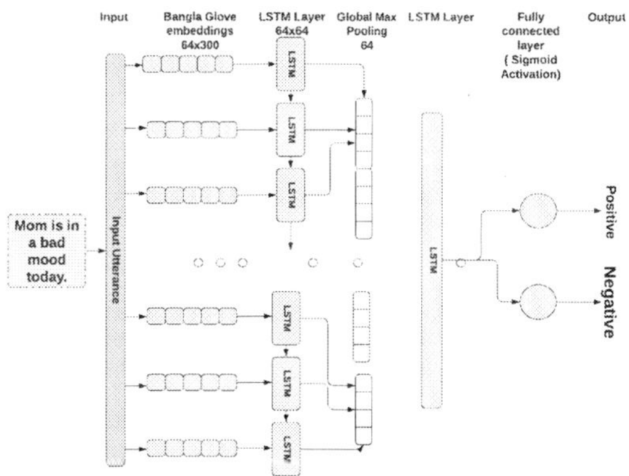

Figure 2: Sentiment detection model architecture for the Sentiment neutralization module

3.1.2 Positive Sentiment Induction

The output from the Sentiment Neutralization module is fed to the Positive Induction module as input. The module takes in a neutral utterance and incorporates positive sentiment into the utterance and returns a sentence with positive sentiment. An example is shown in table 3. For this, we use Neural Machine Translation method built on OpenNMT framework (Klein et al., 2017) where we first train our model with a set of $< source, target >$ pairs where the source is a neutral sentence and target is its positive counter part. We use the Positive dataset provided by Mishra et al. (2019) which includes a set of positive sentences. We pass this dataset through the sentiment neutralization module to get the neutral source sentence to its positive target sentence and use these $< source, target >$ pairs to train the positive induction module. The input sentences are transformed into embeddings that go through the translation encoders and decoders. The encoders and decoders are both built with LSTM layers.

Neutral Input	Positive Output
Is feeling absolutely and from a proper workout	Is feeling absolutely amazing and high got away from a proper workout

Table 3: Example of positive sentiment induction from neutralized sentence

3.2 Retrieval of Commonsense

This module is used to retrieve additional context for the sarcastic sentence based on commonsense knowledge. Figure 3 demonstrates a schematic view of this module. We discuss the detailed process in the following sections. Additionally, we show an example input-output pair for this module in table 4.

Input	Commonsense Sentence
His presentation was bad	The manager is criticized by his boss after a presentation

Table 4: Example of commonsense sentence generation from input sentence

3.2.1 Generation of Commonsense Knowledge

For generating commonsense knowledge context, $\text{COMET}^{\text{DIS}}_{\text{TIL}}$ (West et al., 2021) is used. First, we feed the input sentence to $\text{COMET}^{\text{DIS}}_{\text{TIL}}$. $\text{COMET}^{\text{DIS}}_{\text{TIL}}$ is a machine trained 1.5B parameters commonsense model generated by applying knowledge distillation (Hinton et al., 2015) on a general language model, GPT-3. It offers 23 commonsense relation types. For our study, we use the **xEffect** relation. From the three variants of $\text{COMET}^{\text{DIS}}_{\text{TIL}}$ ($\text{COMET}^{\text{DIS}}_{\text{TIL}}$, $\text{COMET}^{\text{DIS}}_{\text{TIL}}$ + $\text{critic}_{\text{low}}$ and $\text{COMET}^{\text{DIS}}_{\text{TIL}}$ + $\text{critic}_{\text{high}}$), we have chosen $\text{COMET}^{\text{DIS}}_{\text{TIL}}$ + $\text{critic}_{\text{high}}$ for our work. The model

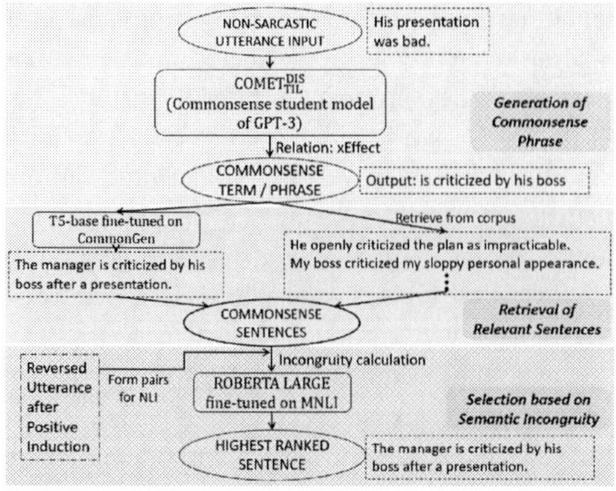

Figure 3: Model Architecture for Retrieval of Commonsense module

returns a contextual phrase pertaining to the **xEffect** relation with the extracted words of the non-sarcastic sentence. For a non-sarcastic sentence "His presentation was bad", $\text{COMET}^{\text{DIS}}_{\text{TIL}}$ predicts the contextual phrase with **xEffect** relation – 'is criticized by his boss'.

3.2.2 Retrieval of Relevant Sentences

Once we have the inferred contextual phrase, we retrieve relevant sentences. For doing so, we imply 2 methods - 1. Retrieval from corpus and 2. Generation from the inferred phrase.

- **Retrieval from corpus:** First, from the contextual phrase, we extract the keyword. Then using the keyword, we search for related sentences in a corpus. We use Sentencedict.com[5] as the retrieval corpus. For filtering the retrieved sentences, two constraints are set - (a) the commonsense concept should appear at the beginning or at the end of the retrieved sentences; (b) to maintain consistency between the length of the non-sarcastic input and its sarcastic variant, sentence length should be less than twice the number of tokens in the non-sarcastic input. Next, we check the consistency of the pronoun in the retrieved sentence and the pronoun in the input sentence. If the pronoun does not match, we modify it to match the non-sarcastic text input. If the non-sarcastic input lacks a pronoun while the retrieved sentence does not, it is simply changed to "I". These constraints for retrieving the sentences and the assessment of grammatical consistency are done following the

[5] https://sentencedict.com/

work of Chakrabarty et al. (2020).

- **Generation from the inferred phrase:** Unlike the previous method, we keep the inferred phrase intact in this case. We first extract the *Subject* of the non-sarcastic input. If the sentence contains no *Subject*, we set it to 'I'. Then the auxiliary verb in the inferred context is checked and modified to match with that of the *Subject*. Then we feed the *Subject* and contextual phrase to a pre-trained sentence generation model[6]. The model fine-tunes Google's T5 on CommonGen (Lin et al., 2019). The model returns us a commonsense sentence based on the *Subject* and contextual inference. For example - the *Subject-inference* pair for the input "His presentation was bad" becomes ['His', 'is criticized by his boss'], and from this collection of words, the sentence "The manager is criticized by his boss after a presentation." is generated.

3.2.3 Selection based on Semantic Incongruity

The module in section 3.2.2 returns several sentences containing the context. Among them, we choose the sentence having the highest semantic incongruity with the sentence generated after the Reversal of Valence module. For calculating the semantic incongruity, following Chakrabarty et al. (2020), we have used the RoBERTa-large (Liu et al., 2019) model fine-tuned on the Multi-Genre NLI dataset (Williams et al., 2017). Considering the non-sarcastic input "His presentation was bad", the Retrieval of Relevant Sentences module yields a list of sentences such as - "The manager is criticized by his boss after a presentation", "He openly criticized the plan as impracticable", and "My boss criticized my sloppy personal appearance". From these sentences, the highest ranked sentence, "The manager is criticized by his boss after a presentation", is returned as the final output to this module as it contains the most semantic incongruity with the reversed sentence.

3.3 Emoji Prediction

In this module, we use a pre-trained emoji prediction model which is fine tuned on the CLIP (Radford et al. (2021)) deep learning model by OpenAI to predict an emoji from a given input. After concatenating the non-sarcastic input and the context retrieved from the Retrieval of Commonsense module, we predict an emoji based on this concatenated sentence. The model employs a masked self-attention Transformer as a text encoder and a ViT-B/32 Transformer architecture as an image encoder. By using a contrastive loss, these encoders are trained to optimize the similarity of (image, text) pairs. One version of the implementation used a Vision Transformer and the other a ResNet image encoder. The variation with the Vision Transformer is used in this case. The dataset[7] used for fine-tuning the model consists of two columns: raw tweets and emoji labels. The emoji labels correspond to the appropriate one among a set of 32 emojis shown in figure 4.

Figure 4: Set of 32 emojis

4 Experimental Setup

The dataset, model configurations for the different modules, and the evaluation criteria for our work are all discussed in the following sub sections.

4.1 Dataset

For our experiments, we utilize the Positive and Negative sentiment corpora by Mishra et al. (2019) which contains tweets and short snippets. Tweets have been normalized by eliminating hashtags, usernames, and conducting spell checking and lexical normalization using NLTK (Loper and Bird, 2002). After filtering out sentences longer than 30 words and running them through all three modules, we get the final dataset of 2k sarcastic sentences from the Mishra et al. (2019) dataset. We have made our dataset[8] publicly available.

4.2 Model Configurations

The sentiment classification model of the neutralization module is trained on the sentiment dataset

[6]https://huggingface.co/mrm8488/t5-base-finetuned-common_gen

[7]https://huggingface.co/datasets/vincentclaes/emoji-predictor

[8]https://github.com/WrightlyRong/Sarcasm-Generation-with-Emoji

Non-Sarcastic Utterance	System	Sarcastic Utterance	Sarcasticness	Creativity	Humor	Grammaticality
Home with the flu.	Full Model	Happy to be home with the fam. Being incarcerated-under the label of being mentally ill.	3.67	4.33	4	5
	Without Emoji	Happy to be home with the fam. Being incarcerated-under the label of being mentally ill.	3.67	4.33	3.67	5
	Without Context	Happy to be home with the fam.	3.33	3	3	5
	R^3 (Chakrabarty et al., 2020)	Home with the not flu.	1.67	1.33	1.33	3
The boss just came and took the mac away.	Full Model	The boss just ended and took the mac away awesome. Angry is not the word for it - I was furious.	5	5	4.67	4.33
	Without Emoji	The boss just ended and took the mac away awesome. Angry is not the word for it - I was furious.	4	3.67	3	4.67
	Without Context	The boss just ended and took the mac away awesome.	5	5	4.67	4.33
	R^3 (Chakrabarty et al., 2020)	The boss just came and took the mac away. Angry is not the word for it - I was furious.	1.67	2.33	1.67	5
Friday nights are so boring when the boyfriend is working late and then i have to work at on saturday mornings.	Full Model	Friday nights are so cute when the boyfriend is working rearrange and then i have to work at on mornings. At least they weren't bored.	4	4	3.67	4
	Without Emoji	Friday nights are so cute when the boyfriend is working rearrange and then i have to work at on mornings. At least they weren't bored.	4	4	3.67	4
	Without Context	Friday nights are so cute when the boyfriend is working rearrange and then i have to work at on mornings.	4	4	3.67	4
	R^3 (Chakrabarty et al., 2020)	Friday nights are so boring when the boyfriend is working early and then I have to work at on saturday mornings. Friday saw the latest addition to darlington's throbbing night life packed to the rafters.	1.33	2	1.33	5
Just finished workin bed feeling sick.	Full Model	Just finished workin feeling good. My stomach heaved and I felt sick.	5	5	4.67	5
	Without Emoji	Just finished workin feeling good. My stomach heaved and I felt sick.	5	5	4.67	5
	Without Context	Just finished workin feeling good.	3	3	3	5
	R^3 (Chakrabarty et al., 2020)	Just finished workin bed feeling healthy. My stomach heaved and I felt sick.	5	4.33	4.67	5

Table 5: Score comparison among the generated outputs from the different systems (Full model, Output without context, Output without emoji and the State-of-the-art model) on four categories

given by Mishra et al. (2019) where the negative sentences are labeled as 1 and the positive sentences are labeled as 0. Each word in the input sentence is first encoded with one-hot encoding and turned into a K-dimensional embedding. Then, these embeddings go through an LSTM layer with 200 hidden units, a self-attention layer, an LSTM layer with 150 hidden units and finally a softmax layer. The classifier is trained for 10 epochs with a batch size of 32, and achieves a validation accuracy of 96% and a test accuracy of 95.7%.

The positive sentiment induction module is built on top of the OpenNMT 3.0 framework, and following Mishra et al. (2019), the embedding dimensions of the encoder and decoder is set to 500, with 2 LSTM layers each consisting of 500 hidden units. Training iteration is set to 100000 and early stopping is incorporated to prevent overfitting. After training, the model produced a corpus-BLEU score of 51.3%.

4.3 Evaluation Criteria

For evaluating the performance of our proposed architecture we incorporate Human judgement. To assess the quality of the generated dataset we compare among 4 systems.

1. **Full Model** contains all the proposed modules of the framework and generates the final dataset.
2. **Without Emoji** system includes the context sentences along with the outputs from the reversal of valence module but does not contain any emoji that goes with each sarcastic sentence.
3. **Without Context** system consists of generations from the reversal of valence module as well as emoji. It does not include any context.
4. **R^3** is the state-of-the-art sarcasm generation system proposed by Chakrabarty et al. (2020).

To assess each of the four systems, we randomly choose 100 samples from our sarcastic dataset which totals to 400 output from the four systems. We evaluate these 400 generated sentences for comparing on the basis of the 4 above mentioned systems.

Following the evaluation approach proposed by Chakrabarty et al. (2020), we evaluate the generated sentences on these criteria:

1. Sarcasticness ("How sarcastic is the output?"),

2. Creativity ("How creative is the output?"),

3. Humour ("How funny is the output?"),

4. Grammaticality ("How grammatically correct is the output?").

Previous studies on sarcasm generation have employed sarcasticness as a criterion for evaluating the effectiveness of the generated outputs (Mishra et al., 2019; Chakrabarty et al., 2020; Das et al., 2022). As sarcasm exemplifies linguistic creativity (Gerrig and Gibbs Jr, 1988), creativity has been proposed as a method for operationalizing the quality of sarcastic sentences by Skalicky and Crossley (2018). The association between humor and sarcasm is frequently mentioned in literature as well (Dress et al., 2008; Lampert and Ervin-Tripp, 2006; Leggitt and Gibbs, 2000; Bowes and Katz, 2011). The grammaticality criterion assesses the syntactic accuracy and conformity of the generated sentences.

Three human judges have been chosen to rate the outputs from the 4 systems on the 4 criteria mentioned. The label indicates a rating on a scale of 1 (not at all) to 5 (very). All 3 judges label each of the 400 sentences from the 4 systems. The human judges have been chosen based on their high efficiency in English, good grasp in understanding and differentiating between Creativity, Humor and Sarcasticness in English sentences.

To assess the inter-annotator agreement for the ratings, we incorporated the Intraclass Correlation Coefficient (ICC). ICC is a statistical measure used to assess the degree of agreement or correlation among the ratings given by different evaluators or raters for a certain category or metric. The agreement scores are shown in table 6. The ICC score ranges between 0 and 1 where a higher score indicates a greater agreement among the raters. For all the four systems evaluated in our work, the ratings by 3 judges for the 4 evaluation criteria yield ICC scores above 0.9 in each case. A score above 0.9 indicates highly consistent observations and excellent agreement among the 3 judges.

Besides, human evaluation, we also evaluate our generated data against an emoji-based sarcasm detection model trained with existing emoji-based sarcastic dataset. For this, we utilize the work of Subramanian et al. (2019) and use their proposed sarcasm detection model trained with their dataset. Their data samples were tweets with emojis scraped from Twitter and were labeled either 1 (sarcastic) or 0 (non-sarcastic). The model consists of a Bi-GRU with a text encoder and an emoji encoder. We add 2k non-sarcastic texts with our generated 2k sarcastic texts and test the model with these data. The model's performance is discussed in section 5.

System	Intraclass Correlation Coefficient (ICC)			
	S	C	H	G
Full Model	0.90	0.92	0.92	0.94
Without Emoji	0.95	0.96	0.95	0.92
Without Context	0.93	0.94	0.94	0.93
R^3 (Chakrabarty et al., 2020)	0.97	0.97	0.97	0.97

Table 6: Intraclass Correlation Coefficient (ICC) scores on different metrics for the four systems. Here, S=Sarcasticness, C=Creativity, H=Humor, G=Grammaticality are the 4 evaluation criteria.

5 Experimental Results & Analysis

System	$\text{Variance}_{\text{eval}}$			
	S	C	H	G
Full Model	0.62	0.59	0.60	0.96
Without Emoji	0.74	0.73	0.65	0.96
Without Context	0.57	0.43	0.44	1.02
R^3 (Chakrabarty et al., 2020)	1.48	1.17	1.16	0.99

Table 7: Variances among each evaluation criterion for each system. Here, S=Sarcasticness, C=Creativity, H=Humor, G=Grammaticality are the 4 evaluation criteria.

Table 5 shows the comparison between a few sample sarcastic outputs across the various systems (our full model, output without the context, output without any emoji and lastly the state-of-the-art model (Chakrabarty et al., 2020) on different measures (Sarcasticness, Creativity, Humor and Grammaticality). Each score is the average rating given by the three human judges. Table 7 shows the variances among each evaluation criterion for each of the four systems. The variances among the four criteria for the system R^3 are higher than all the other systems.

Table 8 shows the average ratings on 100 samples by human judges for generated sarcastic sentences from the four systems based on the four categories. Our full model achieves the highest average score among all the systems including the state-of-the-art sarcasm generation model by Chakrabarty et al. (2020) on three of the four categories except Grammaticality. Besides the full model, the without

System	Sarcasticness	Creativity	Humor	Grammaticality
Full Model	**3.44**	**3.29**	**3.16**	3.72
Without Emoji	2.77	2.83	2.69	3.7
Without Context	3.1	2.99	2.88	3.72
R^3 (Chakrabarty et al., 2020)	2.32	2.2	2.1	**4.29**

Table 8: Average ratings by human judges for outputs from the four systems

emoji system and without context system also outperform the state-of-the-art on Sarcasticness, Creativity and Humor. Our system lacks in Grammaticality due to the fact that we replace the rule based approach of the reversal of valence module by Chakrabarty et al. (2020) with a deep learning approach which results in a slightly more significant information loss. However, the rule based model performs worse in case of the other three categories as it fails to generalize on all types of sentence structures. It is apparent from the scores that context plays an important role in recognising a sarcastic sentence. Additionally, the notable improvement in the score for full model compared to the without emoji model suggests that emojis obviously help better detect the incongruity that exist in sarcastic utterances.

The emoji based sarcasm detection model by Subramanian et al. (2019) gives an F1-score of 67.28% and an ROC AUC score of 53.33% on our generated data samples. It is to be noted that the model's training data samples have significantly different sentence structure than the test samples.

Conclusion

We propose a novel multi-modular framework for sarcasm generation with emoji considering two key characteristics of sarcasm: reversal of valence and semantic incongruity between the sarcastic remark and the context. To generate sarcastic sentences, we first neutralize the input sentence's sentiment and then add positive sentiment to the sentence to reverse its meaning. We also incorporate a relevant emoji and its contextual information to enhance the sarcastic effect. We conclude by evaluating our model using human judgement.

Limitations

Although our proposed architecture successfully generates emoji-based sarcastic sentences from non-sarcastic texts, in some cases, particularly longer sentences, adding commonsense context does not add much to make it more sarcastic as in such cases, the longer sentences already contain the contextual information. In future, we plan to modify our architecture in a way such that it can identify whether or not adding commonsense context would be necessary.

In our work, we have used $\text{COMET}^{\text{DIS}}_{\text{TIL}}$ to generate additional commonsense context. So the performance of our proposed architecture heavily depends on the accuracy of $\text{COMET}^{\text{DIS}}_{\text{TIL}}$. In future, we would like to find and incorporate better models for generating commonsense context.

The low grammaticality score by our final model is likely to be caused by the insufficient training data for the Positive Sentiment Induction module for which the model could not generalize properly. We believe that there is still room for improvement here by collecting and adding more training samples to improve the model's performance. To further fix the grammatical errors we plan to add another module after the Positive Induction module where the module will use a Transformer based grammar correction model which will take a sentence with bad grammar and output a grammatically correct sentence.

Lastly, our emoji prediction module only predicts one emoji per sentence. However, to make a sentence sarcastic, it is not uncommon to use more than one emoji. Hence, we plan to explore multi-label emoji prediction in the future.

References

Marc Aguert. 2022. Paraverbal expression of verbal irony: vocal cues matter and facial cues even more. *Journal of Nonverbal Behavior*, 46(1):45–70.

Silvio Amir, Byron C Wallace, Hao Lyu, and Paula Carvalho Mário J Silva. 2016. Modelling context with user embeddings for sarcasm detection in social media. *arXiv preprint arXiv:1607.00976*.

Adithya Avvaru, Sanath Vobilisetty, and Radhika Mamidi. 2020. Detecting sarcasm in conversation context using transformer-based models. In *Proceedings of the Second Workshop on Figurative Language Processing*, pages 98–103.

David Bamman and Noah Smith. 2015. Contextualized sarcasm detection on twitter. In *proceedings of the international AAAI conference on web and social media*, volume 9, pages 574–577.

Francesco Barbieri, Horacio Saggion, and Francesco Ronzano. 2014. Modelling sarcasm in twitter, a novel approach. In *proceedings of the 5th workshop on computational approaches to subjectivity, sentiment and social media analysis*, pages 50–58.

Arup Baruah, Kaushik Das, Ferdous Barbhuiya, and Kuntal Dey. 2020. Context-aware sarcasm detection using bert. In *Proceedings of the Second Workshop on Figurative Language Processing*, pages 83–87.

Christos Baziotis, Nikos Athanasiou, Georgios Paraskevopoulos, Nikolaos Ellinas, Athanasia Kolovou, and Alexandros Potamianos. 2018. Ntua-slp at semeval-2018 task 2: Predicting emojis using rnns with context-aware attention. *arXiv preprint arXiv:1804.06657*.

Santosh Kumar Bharti, Korra Sathya Babu, and Sanjay Kumar Jena. 2015. Parsing-based sarcasm sentiment recognition in twitter data. In *2015 IEEE/ACM International Conference on Advances in Social Networks Analysis and Mining (ASONAM)*, pages 1373–1380. IEEE.

Santosh Kumar Bharti, Ramkrushna Pradhan, Korra Sathya Babu, and Sanjay Kumar Jena. 2017. Sarcasm analysis on twitter data using machine learning approaches. *Trends in Social Network Analysis*, pages 51–76.

Santosh Kumar Bharti, Bakhtyar Vachha, RK Pradhan, Korra Sathya Babu, and Sanjay Kumar Jena. 2016. Sarcastic sentiment detection in tweets streamed in real time: a big data approach. *Digital Communications and Networks*, 2(3):108–121.

Andrea Bowes and Albert Katz. 2011. When sarcasm stings. *Discourse Processes*, 48(4):215–236.

Christian Burgers, Margot Van Mulken, and Peter Jan Schellens. 2012. Verbal irony: Differences in usage across written genres. *Journal of Language and Social Psychology*, 31(3):290–310.

Marius Cristian Buzea, Stefan Trausan-Matu, and Traian Rebedea. 2022. Automatic fake news detection for romanian online news. *Information*, 13(3):151.

Yitao Cai, Huiyu Cai, and Xiaojun Wan. 2019. Multi-modal sarcasm detection in twitter with hierarchical fusion model. In *Proceedings of the 57th Annual Meeting of the Association for Computational Linguistics*, pages 2506–2515.

John D Campbell and Albert N Katz. 2012. Are there necessary conditions for inducing a sense of sarcastic irony? *Discourse Processes*, 49(6):459–480.

Spencer Cappallo, Thomas Mensink, and Cees GM Snoek. 2015. Image2emoji: Zero-shot emoji prediction for visual media. In *Proceedings of the 23rd ACM international conference on Multimedia*, pages 1311–1314.

Tuhin Chakrabarty, Debanjan Ghosh, Smaranda Muresan, and Nanyun Peng. 2020. R3: Reverse, retrieve, and rank for sarcasm generation with commonsense knowledge. In *Annual Meeting of the Association for Computational Linguistics*.

Dushyant Singh Chauhan, Gopendra Vikram Singh, Aseem Arora, Asif Ekbal, and Pushpak Bhattacharyya. 2022. An emoji-aware multitask framework for multimodal sarcasm detection. *Knowledge-Based Systems*, 257:109924.

Tanvi Dadu and Kartikey Pant. 2020. Sarcasm detection using context separators in online discourse. In *Proceedings of the Second Workshop on Figurative Language Processing*, pages 51–55.

Sourav Das, Soumitra Ghosh, Anup Kumar Kolya, and Asif Ekbal. 2022. Unparalleled sarcasm: a framework of parallel deep lstms with cross activation functions towards detection and generation of sarcastic statements. *Language Resources and Evaluation*, pages 1–38.

Dmitry Davidov, Oren Tsur, and Ari Rappoport. 2010. Semi-supervised recognition of sarcasm in twitter and amazon. In *Proceedings of the fourteenth conference on computational natural language learning*, pages 107–116.

Yufeng Diao, Hongfei Lin, Liang Yang, Xiaochao Fan, Yonghe Chu, Kan Xu, and Di Wu. 2020. A multi-dimension question answering network for sarcasm detection. *IEEE Access*, 8:135152–135161.

Ning Ding, Sheng-wei Tian, and Long Yu. 2022. A multimodal fusion method for sarcasm detection based on late fusion. *Multimedia Tools and Applications*, 81(6):8597–8616.

Xiangjue Dong, Changmao Li, and Jinho D Choi. 2020. Transformer-based context-aware sarcasm detection in conversation threads from social media. *arXiv preprint arXiv:2005.11424*.

Megan L Dress, Roger J Kreuz, Kristen E Link, and Gina M Caucci. 2008. Regional variation in the use of sarcasm. *Journal of Language and Social Psychology*, 27(1):71–85.

Ibrahim Abu Farha and Walid Magdy. 2020. From arabic sentiment analysis to sarcasm detection: The arsarcasm dataset. In *Proceedings of the 4th Workshop on Open-Source Arabic Corpora and Processing Tools, with a Shared Task on Offensive Language Detection*, pages 32–39.

Bjarke Felbo, Alan Mislove, Anders Søgaard, Iyad Rahwan, and Sune Lehmann. 2017. Using millions of emoji occurrences to learn any-domain representations for detecting sentiment, emotion and sarcasm. *arXiv preprint arXiv:1708.00524*.

Elena Filatova. 2012. Irony and sarcasm: Corpus generation and analysis using crowdsourcing. In *Lrec*, pages 392–398. Citeseer.

Richard J Gerrig and Raymond W Gibbs Jr. 1988. Beyond the lexicon: Creativity in language production. *Metaphor and Symbol*, 3(3):1–19.

Richard J Gerrig and Yevgeniya Goldvarg. 2000. Additive effects in the perception of sarcasm: Situational disparity and echoic mention. *Metaphor and Symbol*, 15(4):197–208.

Aniruddha Ghosh and Tony Veale. 2016. Fracking sarcasm using neural network. In *Proceedings of the 7th workshop on computational approaches to subjectivity, sentiment and social media analysis*, pages 161–169.

Aniruddha Ghosh and Tony Veale. 2017. Magnets for sarcasm: Making sarcasm detection timely, contextual and very personal. In *Proceedings of the 2017 Conference on Empirical Methods in Natural Language Processing*, pages 482–491.

Debanjan Ghosh, Alexander R Fabbri, and Smaranda Muresan. 2018. Sarcasm analysis using conversation context. *Computational Linguistics*, 44(4):755–792.

Hunter Gregory, Steven Li, Pouya Mohammadi, Natalie Tarn, Rachel Draelos, and Cynthia Rudin. 2020. A transformer approach to contextual sarcasm detection in twitter. In *Proceedings of the second workshop on figurative language processing*, pages 270–275.

Raj Kumar Gupta and Yinping Yang. 2017. Crystalnest at semeval-2017 task 4: Using sarcasm detection for enhancing sentiment classification and quantification. In *Proceedings of the 11th International Workshop on Semantic Evaluation (SemEval-2017)*, pages 626–633.

Devamanyu Hazarika, Soujanya Poria, Sruthi Gorantla, Erik Cambria, Roger Zimmermann, and Rada Mihalcea. 2018. Cascade: Contextual sarcasm detection in online discussion forums. *arXiv preprint arXiv:1805.06413*.

Geoffrey Hinton, Oriol Vinyals, and Jeff Dean. 2015. Distilling the knowledge in a neural network. *arXiv preprint arXiv:1503.02531*.

Suzana Ilić, Edison Marrese-Taylor, Jorge A Balazs, and Yutaka Matsuo. 2018. Deep contextualized word representations for detecting sarcasm and irony. *arXiv preprint arXiv:1809.09795*.

Tanya Jain, Nilesh Agrawal, Garima Goyal, and Niyati Aggrawal. 2017. Sarcasm detection of tweets: A comparative study. In *2017 Tenth International Conference on Contemporary Computing (IC3)*, pages 1–6. IEEE.

Nikhil Jaiswal. 2020. Neural sarcasm detection using conversation context. In *Proceedings of the Second Workshop on Figurative Language Processing*, pages 77–82.

Soroush Javdan, Behrouz Minaei-Bidgoli, et al. 2020. Applying transformers and aspect-based sentiment analysis approaches on sarcasm detection. In *Proceedings of the second workshop on figurative language processing*, pages 67–71.

Amit Kumar Jena, Aman Sinha, and Rohit Agarwal. 2020. C-net: Contextual network for sarcasm detection. In *Proceedings of the second workshop on figurative language processing*, pages 61–66.

Aditya Joshi, Diptesh Kanojia, Pushpak Bhattacharyya, and Mark Carman. 2017. Sarcasm suite: a browser-based engine for sarcasm detection and generation. In *Proceedings of the AAAI Conference on Artificial Intelligence*, volume 31.

Aditya Joshi, Anoop Kunchukuttan, Pushpak Bhattacharyya, and Mark James Carman. 2015. Sarcasmbot: An open-source sarcasm-generation module for chatbots. In *WISDOM Workshop at KDD*.

Aditya Joshi, Vaibhav Tripathi, Kevin Patel, Pushpak Bhattacharyya, and Mark Carman. 2016. Are word embedding-based features useful for sarcasm detection? *arXiv preprint arXiv:1610.00883*.

A Kalaivani and D Thenmozhi. 2020. Sarcasm identification and detection in conversion context using bert. In *Proceedings of the Second Workshop on Figurative Language Processing*, pages 72–76.

Mikhail Khodak, Nikunj Saunshi, and Kiran Vodrahalli. 2017. A large self-annotated corpus for sarcasm. *arXiv preprint arXiv:1704.05579*.

Guillaume Klein, Yoon Kim, Yuntian Deng, Jean Senellart, and Alexander M Rush. 2017. Opennmt: Open-source toolkit for neural machine translation. *arXiv preprint arXiv:1701.02810*.

Akshi Kumar, Saurabh Raj Sangwan, Anshika Arora, Anand Nayyar, Mohamed Abdel-Basset, et al. 2019. Sarcasm detection using soft attention-based bidirectional long short-term memory model with convolution network. *IEEE access*, 7:23319–23328.

Amardeep Kumar and Vivek Anand. 2020. Transformers on sarcasm detection with context. In *Proceedings of the second workshop on figurative language processing*, pages 88–92.

Avinash Kumar, Vishnu Teja Narapareddy, Pranjal Gupta, Veerubhotla Aditya Srikanth, Lalita Bhanu Murthy Neti, and Aruna Malapati. 2021. Adversarial and auxiliary features-aware bert for sarcasm detection. In *8th ACM IKDD CODS and 26th COMAD*, pages 163–170.

Avinash Kumar, Vishnu Teja Narapareddy, Veerubhotla Aditya Srikanth, Aruna Malapati, and Lalita Bhanu Murthy Neti. 2020. Sarcasm detection using multi-head attention based bidirectional lstm. *Ieee Access*, 8:6388–6397.

Martin D Lampert and Susan M Ervin-Tripp. 2006. Risky laughter: Teasing and self-directed joking among male and female friends. *Journal of Pragmatics*, 38(1):51–72.

Hankyol Lee, Youngjae Yu, and Gunhee Kim. 2020. Augmenting data for sarcasm detection with unlabeled conversation context. *arXiv preprint arXiv:2006.06259*.

John S Leggitt and Raymond W Gibbs. 2000. Emotional reactions to verbal irony. *Discourse processes*, 29(1):1–24.

Bin Liang, Chenwei Lou, Xiang Li, Min Yang, Lin Gui, Yulan He, Wenjie Pei, and Ruifeng Xu. 2022. Multimodal sarcasm detection via cross-modal graph convolutional network. In *Proceedings of the 60th Annual Meeting of the Association for Computational Linguistics (Volume 1: Long Papers)*, pages 1767–1777.

Bill Yuchen Lin, Wangchunshu Zhou, Ming Shen, Pei Zhou, Chandra Bhagavatula, Yejin Choi, and Xiang Ren. 2019. Commongen: A constrained text generation challenge for generative commonsense reasoning. *arXiv preprint arXiv:1911.03705*.

Yinhan Liu, Myle Ott, Naman Goyal, Jingfei Du, Mandar Joshi, Danqi Chen, Omer Levy, Mike Lewis, Luke Zettlemoyer, and Veselin Stoyanov. 2019. Roberta: A robustly optimized bert pretraining approach. *arXiv preprint arXiv:1907.11692*.

Edward Loper and Steven Bird. 2002. Nltk: The natural language toolkit. *arXiv preprint cs/0205028*.

Chenwei Lou, Bin Liang, Lin Gui, Yulan He, Yixue Dang, and Ruifeng Xu. 2021. Affective dependency graph for sarcasm detection. In *Proceedings of the 44th International ACM SIGIR Conference on Research and Development in Information Retrieval*, pages 1844–1849.

Navonil Majumder, Soujanya Poria, Haiyun Peng, Niyati Chhaya, Erik Cambria, and Alexander Gelbukh. 2019. Sentiment and sarcasm classification with multitask learning. *IEEE Intelligent Systems*, 34(3):38–43.

Aaron Maladry, Els Lefever, Cynthia Van Hee, and Veronique Hoste. 2022. Irony detection for dutch: a venture into the implicit. In *Proceedings of the 12th Workshop on Computational Approaches to Subjectivity, Sentiment & Social Media Analysis*, pages 172–181.

Diana G Maynard and Mark A Greenwood. 2014. Who cares about sarcastic tweets? investigating the impact of sarcasm on sentiment analysis. In *Lrec 2014 proceedings*. ELRA.

Abhijit Mishra, Tarun Tater, and Karthik Sankaranarayanan. 2019. A modular architecture for unsupervised sarcasm generation. In *Proceedings of the 2019 Conference on Empirical Methods in Natural Language Processing and the 9th International Joint Conference on Natural Language Processing (EMNLP-IJCNLP)*, pages 6144–6154.

Abdullah Y Muaad, Hanumanthappa Jayappa Davanagere, JV Benifa, Amerah Alabrah, Mufeed Ahmed Naji Saif, D Pushpa, Mugahed A Al-Antari, and Taha M Alfakih. 2022. Artificial intelligence-based approach for misogyny and sarcasm detection from arabic texts. *Computational Intelligence and Neuroscience*, 2022.

Shubhadeep Mukherjee and Pradip Kumar Bala. 2017. Detecting sarcasm in customer tweets: an nlp based approach. *Industrial Management & Data Systems*.

Usman Naseem, Imran Razzak, Peter Eklund, and Katarzyna Musial. 2020. Towards improved deep contextual embedding for the identification of irony and sarcasm. In *2020 International Joint Conference on Neural Networks (IJCNN)*, pages 1–7. IEEE.

Silviu Oprea, Steven Wilson, and Walid Magdy. 2021. Chandler: An explainable sarcastic response generator. In *Proceedings of the 2021 Conference on Empirical Methods in Natural Language Processing: System Demonstrations*, pages 339–349.

Shereen Oraby, Vrindavan Harrison, Amita Misra, Ellen Riloff, and Marilyn Walker. 2017. Are you serious?: Rhetorical questions and sarcasm in social media dialog. *arXiv preprint arXiv:1709.05305*.

Reynier Ortega-Bueno, Paolo Rosso, and José E Medina Pagola. 2022. Multi-view informed attention-based model for irony and satire detection in spanish variants. *Knowledge-Based Systems*, 235:107597.

Rajnish Pandey and Jyoti Prakash Singh. 2023. Bert-lstm model for sarcasm detection in code-mixed social media post. *Journal of Intelligent Information Systems*, 60(1):235–254.

Soujanya Poria, Erik Cambria, Devamanyu Hazarika, and Prateek Vij. 2016. A deeper look into sarcastic tweets using deep convolutional neural networks. *arXiv preprint arXiv:1610.08815*.

Rolandos-Alexandros Potamias, Georgios Siolas, and Andreas Stafylopatis. 2019. A robust deep ensemble classifier for figurative language detection. In *International Conference on Engineering Applications of Neural Networks*, pages 164–175. Springer.

Rolandos Alexandros Potamias, Georgios Siolas, and Andreas-Georgios Stafylopatis. 2020. A transformer-based approach to irony and sarcasm detection. *Neural Computing and Applications*, 32(23):17309–17320.

Anukarsh G Prasad, S Sanjana, Skanda M Bhat, and BS Harish. 2017. Sentiment analysis for sarcasm detection on streaming short text data. In *2017 2nd International Conference on Knowledge Engineering and Applications (ICKEA)*, pages 1–5. IEEE.

Tomáš Ptáček, Ivan Habernal, and Jun Hong. 2014. Sarcasm detection on czech and english twitter. In *Proceedings of COLING 2014, the 25th international conference on computational linguistics: Technical papers*, pages 213–223.

Veranika Puhacheuskaya and Juhani Järvikivi. 2022. I was being sarcastic!: The effect of foreign accent and political ideology on irony (mis) understanding. *Acta Psychologica*, 222:103479.

Alec Radford, Jong Wook Kim, Chris Hallacy, Aditya Ramesh, Gabriel Goh, Sandhini Agarwal, Girish Sastry, Amanda Askell, Pamela Mishkin, Jack Clark, et al. 2021. Learning transferable visual models from natural language supervision. In *International conference on machine learning*, pages 8748–8763. PMLR.

Yafeng Ren, Donghong Ji, and Han Ren. 2018. Context-augmented convolutional neural networks for twitter sarcasm detection. *Neurocomputing*, 308:1–7.

Ellen Riloff, Ashequl Qadir, Prafulla Surve, Lalindra De Silva, Nathan Gilbert, and Ruihong Huang. 2013. Sarcasm as contrast between a positive sentiment and negative situation. In *Proceedings of the 2013 conference on empirical methods in natural language processing*, pages 704–714.

Jie Ruan, Yue Wu, Xiaojun Wan, and Yuesheng Zhu. 2022. How to describe images in a more funny way? towards a modular approach to cross-modal sarcasm generation. *arXiv preprint arXiv:2211.10992*.

Edoardo Savini and Cornelia Caragea. 2022. Intermediate-task transfer learning with bert for sarcasm detection. *Mathematics*, 10(5):844.

Rossano Schifanella, Paloma De Juan, Joel Tetreault, and Liangliang Cao. 2016. Detecting sarcasm in multimodal social platforms. In *Proceedings of the 24th ACM international conference on Multimedia*, pages 1136–1145.

Boaz Shmueli, Lun-Wei Ku, and Soumya Ray. 2020. Reactive supervision: A new method for collecting sarcasm data. *arXiv preprint arXiv:2009.13080*.

Stephen Skalicky and Scott Crossley. 2018. Linguistic features of sarcasm and metaphor production quality. In *Proceedings of the Workshop on Figurative Language Processing*, pages 7–16.

Himani Srivastava, Vaibhav Varshney, Surabhi Kumari, and Saurabh Srivastava. 2020. A novel hierarchical bert architecture for sarcasm detection. In *Proceedings of the Second Workshop on Figurative Language Processing*, pages 93–97.

Jayashree Subramanian, Varun Sridharan, Kai Shu, and Huan Liu. 2019. Exploiting emojis for sarcasm detection. In *International conference on social computing, behavioral-cultural modeling and prediction and behavior representation in modeling and simulation*, pages 70–80. Springer.

Yi Tay, Luu Anh Tuan, Siu Cheung Hui, and Jian Su. 2018. Reasoning with sarcasm by reading in-between. *arXiv preprint arXiv:1805.02856*.

Cynthia Van Hee, Els Lefever, and Véronique Hoste. 2018. Semeval-2018 task 3: Irony detection in english tweets. In *Proceedings of The 12th International Workshop on Semantic Evaluation*, pages 39–50.

Zhiyuan Wen, Lin Gui, Qianlong Wang, Mingyue Guo, Xiaoqi Yu, Jiachen Du, and Ruifeng Xu. 2022. Sememe knowledge and auxiliary information enhanced approach for sarcasm detection. *Information Processing & Management*, 59(3):102883.

Peter West, Chandra Bhagavatula, Jack Hessel, Jena D Hwang, Liwei Jiang, Ronan Le Bras, Ximing Lu, Sean Welleck, and Yejin Choi. 2021. Symbolic knowledge distillation: from general language models to commonsense models. *arXiv preprint arXiv:2110.07178*.

Adina Williams, Nikita Nangia, and Samuel R Bowman. 2017. A broad-coverage challenge corpus for sentence understanding through inference. *arXiv preprint arXiv:1704.05426*.

Deirdre Wilson. 2006. The pragmatics of verbal irony: Echo or pretence? *Lingua*, 116(10):1722–1743.

Chuhan Wu, Fangzhao Wu, Sixing Wu, Zhigang Yuan, Junxin Liu, and Yongfeng Huang. 2018. Thu_ngn at semeval-2018 task 2: Residual cnn-lstm network with attention for english emoji prediction. In *Proceedings of The 12th International Workshop on Semantic Evaluation*, pages 410–414.

Jingjing Xu, Xu Sun, Qi Zeng, Xuancheng Ren, Xiaodong Zhang, Houfeng Wang, and Wenjie Li. 2018. Unpaired sentiment-to-sentiment translation: A cycled reinforcement learning approach. *arXiv preprint arXiv:1805.05181*.

Meishan Zhang, Yue Zhang, and Guohong Fu. 2016. Tweet sarcasm detection using deep neural network. In *Proceedings of COLING 2016, the 26th International Conference on Computational Linguistics: technical papers*, pages 2449–2460.

Yazhou Zhang, Dan Ma, Prayag Tiwari, Chen Zhang, Mehedi Masud, Mohammad Shorfuzzaman, and Dawei Song. 2023. Stance-level sarcasm detection with bert and stance-centered graph attention networks. *ACM Transactions on Internet Technology*, 23(2):1–21.

A Appendix

Table 9: Summary of sarcasm detection datasets from different social media platforms

	Dataset					Annotation		
	Short Text	Long Text	Image	Samples	Platform	Manual	Hashtag	None
(Filatova, 2012)		✓		1254	Amazon	✓		
(Riloff et al., 2013)	✓			1600	Twitter	✓		
(Ptáček et al., 2014)	✓			920000	Twitter	✓	✓	
(Barbieri et al., 2014)	✓			60000	Twitter		✓	
(Bamman and Smith, 2015)	✓			19534	Twitter		✓	
(Amir et al., 2016)	✓			11541	Twitter		✓	
(Bharti et al., 2016)	✓			1.5M	Twitter			✓
(Joshi et al., 2016)	✓			3629	Goodreads		✓	
(Ghosh and Veale, 2016)	✓			41000	Twitter		✓	
(Poria et al., 2016)	✓			100000	Twitter	✓	✓	
(Schifanella et al., 2016)	✓		✓	600925	Instagram, Tumblr, Twitter		✓	
(Zhang et al., 2016)	✓			9104	Twitter		✓	
(Felbo et al., 2017)	✓			1.6B	Twitter			✓
(Ghosh and Veale, 2017)	✓			41200	Twitter	✓		
(Khodak et al., 2017)	✓			533.3M	Reddit	✓		
(Oraby et al., 2017)		✓		10270	Debate forum	✓	✓	
(Prasad et al., 2017)	✓			2000	Twitter	✓		
(Baziotis et al., 2018)	✓			550M	Twitter			✓
(Hazarika et al., 2018)	✓			219368	Reddit	✓		
(Ghosh et al., 2018)	✓	✓		36391	Twitter, Reddit, Discussion Forum	✓	✓	
(Ilić et al., 2018)	✓	✓		419822	Twitter, Reddit, Debate Forum	✓	✓	

(Tay et al., 2018)	✓	✓		94238	Twitter, Reddit, Debate Forum	✓	✓	
(Van Hee et al., 2018)	✓			4792	Twitter	✓	✓	
(Wu et al., 2018)	✓			4618	Twitter	✓	✓	
(Majumder et al., 2019)	✓			994	Twitter		✓	
(Cai et al., 2019)			✓	24635	Twitter		✓	
(Kumar et al., 2019)	✓	✓		24635	Twitter, Reddit, Debate Forum		✓	
(Subramanian et al., 2019)	✓	✓		12900	Twitter, Facebook		✓	
(Jena et al., 2020)	✓			13000	Twitter, Reddit	✓	✓	
(Potamias et al., 2020)	✓			533.3M	Twitter, Reddit	✓	✓	

Table 10: Performance summary of various approaches used in sarcasm detection

	Data	**Architecture**	**Performance**			
			Accuracy	**F1-Score**	**Precision**	**Recall**
(Davidov et al., 2010)	Tweets	SASI (Semi-supervised Algorithm for Sarcasm Identification)	0.896	0.545	0.727	0.436
(Gupta and Yang, 2017)	Tweets	CrystalNet		0.60	0.52	0.70
(Bharti et al., 2017)	Tweets	PBLGA with SVM		0.67	0.67	0.68
(Mukherjee and Bala, 2017)	Tweets	Naive Bayes	0.73			
(Jain et al., 2017)	Tweets	Weighted Ensemble	0.853		0.831	0.298
(Poria et al., 2016)	Tweets	CNN-SVM		0.9771		
(Ghosh and Veale, 2016)	Tweets	CNN-LSTM-DNN		0.901	0.894	0.912
(Zhang et al., 2016)	Tweets	GRNN	0.9074	0.9074		
(Oraby et al., 2017)	Tweets	SVM + W2V + LIWC		0.83	0.80	0.86
(Hazarika et al., 2018)	Reddit posts	CASCADE	0.79	0.86		
(Ren et al., 2018)	Tweets	CANN-KEY		0.6328		
		CANN-ALL		0.6205		

(Tay et al., 2018)	Tweets, Reddit posts	MIARN	Twitter: 0.8647	0.86	0.8613	0.8579
			Reddit: 0.6091	0.6922	0.6935	0.7005
(Ghosh et al., 2018)	Reddit posts	multiple-LSTM	0.7458	0.7607		0.7762
(Diao et al., 2020)	Internet arguments	MQA (Multi-dimension Question Answering model)		0.762	0.701	0.835
(Kumar et al., 2020)	Reddit posts	MHA-BiLSTM		0.7748	0.7263	0.8303
(Kumar et al., 2019)	Tweets	sAtt-BiLSTM convNet	0.9371			
(Majumder et al., 2019)	Text snippets	Multi task learning with fusion and shared attention		0.866	0.9101	0.9074
(Potamias et al., 2019)	reviews of laptops and restaurants	DESC (Deep Ensemble Soft Classifier)	0.74	0.73	0.73	0.73
(Srivastava et al., 2020)	Tweets, Reddit posts	BERT + BiLSTM + CNN	Twitter: 0.74			
			Reddit: 0.639			
(Gregory et al., 2020)	Tweets, Reddit posts	Transformer ensemble (BERT, RoBERTa, XLNet, RoBERTa-large, and ALBERT)		0.756	0.758	0.767
(Potamias et al., 2020)	Tweets, Reddit politics	RCNN-RoBERTa	Twitter: 0.91	0.90	0.90	0.90
			Reddit: 0.79	0.78	0.78	0.78
(Javdan et al., 2020)	Tweets	LCF-BERT		0.73		
	Reddit posts	BERT-base-cased		0.734		
(Lee et al., 2020)	Tweets, Reddit posts	BERT + BiLSTM + NeXtVLAD	Twitter	0.8977	0.8747	0.9219
			Reddit	0.7513	0.6938	0.8187
(Baruah et al., 2020)	Tweets, Reddit posts	BERT-large-uncased	Twitter	0.743	0.744	0.748
			Reddit	0.658	0.658	0.658

(Avvaru et al., 2020)	Tweets, Reddit posts	BERT	Twitter	0.752		
			Reddit	0.621		
(Jaiswal, 2020)	Tweets, Reddit posts	Ensemble of several combinations of RoBERTa-large		0.790	0.790	0.792
(Shmueli et al., 2020)	Tweets	BERT	0.703	0.699	0.70 0.7741	
(Dadu and Pant, 2020)	Tweets, Reddit posts	RoBERTa-large	Twitter	0.772	0.772	0.772
			Reddit	0.716	0.716	0.718
(Kalaivani and Thenmozhi, 2020)	Tweets, Reddit posts	BERT	Twitter	0.722	0.722	0.722
			Reddit	0.679	0.679	0.679
(Naseem et al., 2020)	Tweets	T-DICE + BiLSTM + ALBERT	0.93	0.93		
(Dong et al., 2020)	Tweets, Reddit posts	context-aware RoBERTa-large	Twitter	0.783	0.784	0.789
			Reddit	0.744	0.745	0.749
(Kumar and Anand, 2020)	Tweets, Reddit posts	context-aware RoBERTa-large	Twitter	0.772	0.773	0.774
			Reddit	0.691	0.693	0.699
(Kumar et al., 2021)	Tweets	AAFAB (Adversarial and Auxiliary Features-Aware BERT)		0.7997	0.8101	0.7896
(Lou et al., 2021)	Tweets, Reddit posts	ADGCN-BERT (Affective Dependency Graph Convolutional Network)	Twitter: 0.9031	0.8954		
			Reddit: 0.8077	0.8077		

Semantic Accuracy in Natural Language Generation: A Thesis Proposal

Patrícia Schmidtová
Charles University, Faculty of Mathematics and Physics
Institute of Formal and Applied Linguistics
Prague, Czech Republic
schmidtova@ufal.mff.cuni.cz

Abstract

With the fast-growing popularity of current large pre-trained language models (LLMs), it is necessary to dedicate efforts to making them more reliable. In this thesis proposal, we aim to improve the reliability of natural language generation systems (NLG) by researching the semantic accuracy of their outputs. We look at this problem from the outside (evaluation) and from the inside (interpretability). We propose a novel method for evaluating semantic accuracy and discuss the importance of working towards a unified and objective benchmark for NLG metrics. We also review interpretability approaches which could help us pinpoint the sources of inaccuracies within the models and explore potential mitigation strategies.

1 Introduction

The introduction of the Transformer architecture (Vaswani et al., 2017) irreversibly changed the research landscape in natural language processing. Moreover, in the past year, large pre-trained language models (LLMs) have managed to permeate into the hands and minds of millions of users worldwide (Ouyang et al., 2022; Touvron et al., 2023; Scao and et al., 2023). With a growing public interest in natural language generation (NLG) and dialogue systems, it is essential to thoroughly research their reliability. If a human does not know the answer to a question, the socially acceptable behavior is to say 'I do not know' instead of making up a plausibly sounding lie. This is how many users expect intelligent systems to behave, and failing to fulfill this expectation can lead to distrust, or in a worse scenario, even to the spread of misinformation.

We believe it is worth trying to propose evaluation schemes that could incentivize institutions and companies to optimize their models for reliability rather than just fluency and impressiveness. The proposed thesis aims to take a step in this direction by investigating semantic accuracy in a data-to-text generation setting. We consider a text *semantically accurate* if it faithfully represents the underlying input data.

Despite the fact that inaccurate does not always mean wrong (Maynez et al., 2020), i.e. conflicting with our current understanding of the world, we argue that an NLG system should produce semantically accurate texts to be considered reliable. We still consider it important to research NLG through the lens of semantic accuracy, without the intent of explicitly fact-checking (Thorne et al., 2018), for the following reasons:

- It is important to alert the user about the output text deviating from the data so they do not overlook it and can evaluate the factuality themselves.
- The NLG system stores a representation of its training data in its parameters. However, some of that information might be outdated and therefore is no longer accurate. If we supply an NLG system with input data containing updated information, such as the name of a new prime minister, we want this to take precedence over the information learned during training.
- In some use cases, such as in task-oriented dialogue systems, we want full control of the output to maintain a high level of reliability. This is especially important if explicit dialogue state tracking is used so that the system has an accurate representation of what was already communicated to the user.

Thesis Objectives The main objective of this thesis is to answer the question: "How can we make data-to-text Natural Language Generation more reliable?" We hope to achieve this objective by carefully studying NLG systems, namely LLMs, with respect to semantic accuracy, from the outside

Proceedings of the 61st Annual Meeting of the Association for Computational Linguistics - Student Research Workshop, pages 352–361
July 10-12, 2023

(evaluating their outputs) as well as from the inside (inspecting their hidden layers).

It is valuable to quantify how reliable an NLG system is before attempting to increase its reliability to measure the magnitude of such an increase. Furthermore, we hope to provide insights into the operation of NLG systems and the limitations they have. This will allow for a more informed design of NLG systems to tackle the detected problems.

Thesis Structure The first part of the thesis, described in Section 2, is dedicated to NLG evaluation. We propose a novel approach for evaluating the semantic accuracy of a generated text given the source data. We also intend to contribute a benchmarking dataset for evaluating NLG metrics focused on semantic accuracy. Thomson and Reiter (2021) have presented such a dataset with high-quality human annotations, however, due to the high costs of human annotation it is very modest in size. Therefore, we share our idea of constructing a larger dataset automatically.

In the second part of the thesis, described in Section 3, we will use interpretability techniques to explore where inaccuracies appear. We aim to then use these insights to learn how to guide the NLG system to produce outputs that are more faithful to the input data.

Applications This thesis' most visible contribution will be in the task of data-to-text natural language generation as it is our primary goal. We anticipate our insights will also be helpful in dialogue systems and retrieval-augmented generation (Lewis et al., 2020). Furthermore, it is our intention to extend the described approaches to abstractive summarization as the task is similar to ours. Finally, we believe that the evaluation method presented in Section 2 could even be used for evaluating human-written texts. While it is not intended as a fact-checking method by itself, it could be used as an aid for users who perform fact-checking to warn them about text parts not consistent with the data.

2 Evaluating Semantic Accuracy

Many aspects of NLG system outputs can be evaluated: fluency, grammatical correctness, acceptability with respect to a context, or similarity to a given reference text, etc (Howcroft et al., 2020). In this thesis, we focus solely on the aspect of semantic accuracy which is far from being solved.

We aspire to evaluate how accurately a target text represents given source data either in a set of semantic triples (subject-predicate-object), a table, or a different structured form. Our proposed output is not only the numeric result of the metric which can be used in a development or research setting, but primarily a set of alignments between the text and the data (Dou and Neubig, 2021) This will allow for an intuitive visualization for a user in a fact-checking setting.

We consider three major types of semantic inaccuracy, following Maynez et al. (2020) The first is **extrinsic hallucination** – a phenomenon where the text includes additional information that is not directly inferrable from the input data, such as introducing new entities. The second and more subtle way of introducing semantic inaccuracy is **intrinsic hallucination** – creating new relations between entities that are not described in the input data. Finally, we consider **omission** – omitting some information from the source data in the target text.

2.1 SoTA in Semantic Accuracy Evaluation

We review state-of-the-art semantic accuracy metrics and discuss the limitations we aim to address in our work. We refer to Celikyilmaz et al. (2020) and Sai et al. (2022) for a broader overview.

Metrics such as BERTScore (Zhang et al., 2020), Bleurt (Sellam et al., 2020), or PARENT (Dhingra et al., 2019) can be used to evaluate the semantic accuracy of a given text. The major difference between these metrics and the method we propose later on in this section is that instead of comparing the target text with the source data, they compare it with a reference text. This means the methods can only be applied to examples where a reference is available. Furthermore, such metrics cannot explain why a text received a high or a low score – they can only measure the proximity to a reference.

The majority of metrics for evaluating the semantic accuracy of generated text utilize models pre-trained for the task of Natural Language Inference (NLI). Such metrics include NUBIA (Kane et al., 2020), MENLI (Chen and Eger, 2023), and approaches presented by Maynez et al. (2020) and Dušek and Kasner (2020).

The advantage of NLI-based metrics is that they generally do not need a reference (with the exception of NUBIA) and can handle lexical diversity. However, they are not easily interpretable by the user, because they natively do not show where the inaccuracies occur within the text. A work by

Goyal and Durrett (2020) mitigates this by applying entailment to dependency trees. This method is not equipped to deal with negation and omission which we aim to address in our work.

Finally, we review a text-level error detection metric for table-to-text generation presented by Kasner et al. (2021). This metric uses rules to construct a set of sentences that can be derived from the input data and measure the semantic similarity between them and the evaluated sentence. We aspire to reach a better result by crafting a synthetic pre-training set containing more intricate hallucinations as described later on in this section.

2.2 Metric Evaluation

To our knowledge, there is not yet an objective way of evaluating how well semantic accuracy metrics perform in finding inaccurate information. We might not fully achieve objective evaluation of metrics but we argue it is important to move towards this goal as it will lead to better evaluation methods. The most prevalent method of measuring metric performance is comparing the scores given to selected evaluated examples to human judgment. However, such evaluation is not easily reproducible and does not give us enough information to compare the metrics among themselves (Belz et al., 2021).

Data-to-text datasets such as WebNLG (Gardent et al., 2017), Enriched WebNLG (Castro Ferreira et al., 2018), DART (Nan et al., 2021) are not sufficient for benchmarking evaluation metrics. As datasets intended as NLG system data, they generally do not contain phenomena like hallucination, but in the rare cases when they do, they are not marked as such. The closest to our goals is the dataset presented by Thomson and Reiter (2021) intended for error detection in table-to-text generation. It contains high-quality human annotation at the drawback of being small in size – 90 examples across train and validation sets combined. Maynez et al. (2020) created such a dataset for the task of abstractive summarization by extending the XSum dataset (Narayan et al., 2018). They conducted a human annotation experiment to tag hallucinations in the generated summaries. While we hope we can extend our evaluation method to abstractive summarization, this dataset is not directly suitable for evaluating data-to-text generation. A similar benchmarking dataset is available for dialogue systems (Dziri et al., 2022). This dataset contains annotations with manually evaluated judgments about whether a system response is fully attributable to a relevant large unstructured source of information. Such task is out of scope for this thesis.

To create a unified way of evaluating and comparing NLG metric performance, we propose a construction of a dataset designed for data-to-text metric evaluation which will contain examples of semantically accurate texts, both extrinsic and intrinsic hallucination, and omission. This will allow for a fine-grained diagnostic of the metric performance in a fully automated setting.

A portion of the data-to-text datasets mentioned above will serve as positive examples containing no hallucinations or omissions. Hallucinations could be automatically generated by dropping semantic triples. We selected this format as our starting point for several reasons:

- It is widely used in the datasets we considered.
- Other formats (tables, graphs, name-value slot pairs) can be losslessly transferred to semantic triples.[1]

In case we drop a triple where both the subject and object are included in other triples, we are creating an intrinsic hallucination, since the only thing being removed is the relation between the two. Otherwise, we are creating an extrinsic hallucination.

Generating examples of omission could be done by dropping a sentence from the reference text whenever there are more sentences. More intricate examples could be generated by dropping a subtree from the dependency tree of the reference.

A portion of the dataset should also include categorized outputs produced by various NLG systems. This will ensure that the metric itself is properly evaluated on the data it was designed for. There is no scarcity of erroneous NLG outputs, however, the bottleneck will be the need for human annotation and categorization. For this reason, we intend to start with a small set of such data and slowly expand it.

Creating such a benchmarking dataset would help us compare the performance of existing metrics on the three categories of inaccuracies and to understand their limits.

[1] We consider graphs as tuples $G = (V, E)$ where V is a set of vertices and E is a set of edges. We propose that the edges can be converted to predicates and vertices can be converted to subjects and objects in the semantic triples.

2.3 Evaluation Method

We propose a novel method to evaluate semantic accuracy based on alignments between source data and target text. Using the alignment method introduced by Dou and Neubig (2021), we intend to align portions of the data, e.g. semantic triples, to phrases in the target text. To reach phrase-level granularity, we aim to use dependency trees – inspired by the work of Vamvas and Sennrich (2022) and Goyal and Durrett (2020).

If a portion of the data cannot be aligned with any combination of the phrases, it means the information was omitted. On the other hand, if a phrase cannot be aligned with any portion of the data, it is likely indicative of a hallucination. We are aware this could also happen with filler words or phrases. We can handle such cases during dependency parsing or filter them through their perplexity – filler phrases generally have a lower perplexity than information-bearing phrases.

The main output of this method is the set of alignments that can be used to flag any suspicious parts. However, in a development setting, it is desirable to have a numerical output quantifying the quality of an evaluated system. This can be obtained either as a total distance between the aligned embeddings in the embedding space or the percentage of embeddings not aligned. Both scores can be normalized for sequence length.

The advantage of this method is that it allows us to track the source of all information in the target text, not only the inaccurate parts. This can be useful in a setting where the alignments are presented directly to the user because if visualized properly, it could make fact-checking faster and easier.

Expected Qualities We aspire for the evaluation method to have the following qualities:

- **Explainable** Instead of just outputting a numerical value to characterize the accuracy of a target text given the source data, it also identifies the hallucination spans. Therefore, it should be able to point out precisely which parts of the text are not supported by the data or which parts of the data were omitted from the text.

- **Reference-less** The metric is designed to evaluate novel texts where no reference text is available. This corresponds to the task of quality estimation (Dušek et al., 2019; Specia et al., 2013). While this might seem like a limitation, recent work by Kocmi and Federmann (2023) shows that neural metrics are capable of reaching better results when not presented with a reference.

- **Robust** The metric is robust with respect to lexical diversity. The choice of words should not matter as long as they are semantically similar. We expect to approach this quality by working with embeddings rather than n-grams.

- **Automatic** While the metric can be used to help a user, it should not require any input from the user.

Alternative Approach as Tagging Finding hallucinations and omissions in the text can also be approached as a BIO tagging problem (Ramshaw and Marcus, 1995). In our case, we aim to classify every token as the beginning of a hallucination or omission. This approach has been previously explored on a more narrow task of error detection (Kasner et al., 2021) trained on data from Thomson and Reiter (2021).

We believe that training a BIO tagger could benefit from our proposed benchmarking dataset from Section 2 could be used for training such a tagger. The hallucination and omission spans can then be automatically annotated using the alignments from our main evaluation method. Even in case the alignments prove to be worse quality than anticipated, we will investigate whether adding this data as a pre-training step and then refining on high-quality data from Thomson and Reiter (2021) will lead to better performance.

3 Mitigating Inaccuracies with Interpretability

In the second part of the thesis, we will use various techniques to uncover the sources of semantic inaccuracies within networks. We will then use the gained knowledge to improve the semantic accuracy of the generated text.

In the first subsection, we discuss the methods we intend to explore. In the second subsection, we name the research questions we seek to answer.

3.1 Methods

We will investigate LLMs with openly accessible weights (Touvron et al., 2023; Taori et al., 2023; Chung et al., 2022; Wang et al., 2022). In our experiments, we will aim to always have a mixture of encoder-decoder models vs decoder-only models, to explore whether the model architecture makes a difference. We will also compare models fine-tuned on instructions to those that were not to investigate whether this training schema is beneficial in increasing semantic accuracy.

Attention Visualization The first step in our search for semantic inaccuracies is using Attention Visualization (Vig, 2019). The goal is to look for an intuitive insight into what happens inside the networks while inaccuracies are generated. We will search for any reoccurring patterns that can be addressed by pruning. We bear in mind that the results might be hard to interpret or even misleading (Mareček et al., 2020; Wiegreffe and Pinter, 2019). Nevertheless, we consider this method a good place to start in our interpretability research.

Probing We anticipate that the major part of our analysis will be done using probing (Ettinger et al., 2016; Adi et al., 2017; Conneau et al., 2018). Probing aims to extract information from the network's hidden layers by applying a classifier of an investigated linguistic phenomenon on top of them.

In this thesis, we will mostly be interested in extracting graph structures as we are equally interested in entities (nodes) and relations among them (edges). This will be inspired by extracting syntactic properties (Hewitt and Manning, 2019), and discourse structures (Huber and Carenini, 2022) from hidden layers. The core idea of both works is applying linear transformations to the activations, considering the result as a distance metric which was then applied to construct trees directly or using dynamic programming.

Our idea of utilizing this approach is to extract the structures in a similar manner and to try to match them to the input data. This can be done on multiple levels to look for the precise point when a hallucination forms by the introduction of new information into the structure or when a part of the input data is forgotten.

We also plan to build upon the work of Schuster and Linzen (2022), who show that Transformer-based models do not yet have entity tracking capabilities and can introduce new entities, which is an instance of extrinsic hallucination (Schmidtova, 2022). Klafka and Ettinger (2020) use probing to obtain information about the surrounding words from a given word. This approach could help us reveal intrinsic hallucination in case we retrieve information about a predicate not supported by the data. We will also look into probing via prompting an LLM (Li et al., 2022) as this approach does not require a trained probe.

Pruning After identifying a potential source of inaccuracy, one of the most natural mitigation strategies is attention head pruning – removing some of the attention heads after training. Voita et al. (2019) and Behnke and Heafield (2020) observed a comparable model performance in machine translation before and after strategically pruning attention heads.

Our aim is to identify attention heads that consistently contribute to hallucination via copying from the training data instead of attending to the input data via attention visualization and probing. In case we succeed, there is a possibility of improving a model's semantic accuracy by pruning those heads.

Fine-tuning Fine-tuning a large pre-trained language model can be computationally very demanding. Most LLMs which achieve state-of-the-art results are simply too large to fine-tune using traditional methods on hardware accessible to a Ph.D. student. Therefore, we aim to explore methods such as LoRA (Hu et al., 2021) and QLoRA (Dettmers et al., 2023) to fine-tune LLMs using the available data-to-text generation datasets to reach higher semantic accuracy.

Furthermore, in case we find recurring hallucination patterns through attention visualization and probing, we can use the matrix injection method described by Hu et al. (2021) to remove hallucinations before they can even appear in the generated text.

Modelling Uncertainty In case a model is not confident enough in its answer, it should rather say 'I don't know' instead of hallucinating a plausible-sounding response. Goldberg (2023) argues that such behavior cannot be learned in a supervised manner, as we ourselves do not know what knowledge is stored in the model.

We aim to explore Bayesian methods to estimate the model uncertainty. Wu et al. (2022) model aleatory (data) and epistemic (model) uncertainty (Kiureghian and Ditlevsen, 2009) to detect out-of-domain queries fed to dialogue systems. Our intentions are the opposite – instead of using this method on the system inputs, we aim to focus on the outputs. We intend to leverage this method is to model epistemic uncertainty and use the modeled values to update the system weights.

We believe this will be a promising research area as this is the kind of interaction humans intuitively expect.

Prompt Engineering The performance of LLMs largely depends on the prompts they receive. We will investigate to what extent prompt choice can influence the semantic accuracy of the produced texts. There are already many strategies and courses for prompt engineering (Bach et al., 2022; Sanh et al., 2022; Liu et al., 2021; Ng and Fulford, 2023), however, the suggested strategies for hallucination mitigation are often not very effective. We will seek the boundaries of semantic accuracy that can be achieved through prompt engineering.

We aim to experiment with zero-shot prompting (Chang et al., 2008; Palatucci et al., 2009), few-shot prompting (Brown et al., 2020), and chain-of-thought prompting (Wei et al., 2023). We are aware that a prompt that will mitigate hallucinations for one model might not be so successful for another one and we are willing to modify the prompts for specific models. We plan to experiment with many aspects of the prompt such as sentence length, unambiguity, word choice, using placeholders, special symbols as delimiters etc.

The advantage of prompt engineering is that the results will be applicable immediately. We expect to observe a wide range in LLM performance based on prompt choice.

3.2 Research Questions

Through our interpretability research, we aim to answer the following questions:

- Are there reoccurring patterns in attention that appear when the model is hallucinating?
- Can we use probing to identify the layers where hallucinated information infiltrates the input data?
- Is it possible to teach the network to estimate its confidence in a fact before replying? Would such confidence be reliable or arbitrary?
- Is it possible to minimize the influence of the prompt on semantic accuracy by manipulating the model by fine-tuning, pruning attention heads, or using reinforcement learning to estimate model confidence?
- How significantly can we increase semantic accuracy through modifying the model's inner properties (weight updates, skip connections, or attention head pruning) compared to the increase we can achieve through less resource-intensive prompt engineering?

4 Conclusion

This thesis proposal has outlined the importance of investigating semantic accuracy in natural language generation. By focusing on this important aspect, we aim to address the challenge of ensuring that NLG systems generate text that represents the underlying data more faithfully.

We proposed a unified benchmark for NLG metrics focusing on semantic accuracy, which will enable researchers to compare them in an objective and standardized manner. Additionally, we introduced a novel semantic accuracy evaluation method, which measures how accurately the generated text represents the underlying data while also providing data-text alignments.

Furthermore, we discussed ways to investigate where inaccuracies appear inside NLG models, with the aim of identifying potential areas for improvement. Our proposed approach includes attention visualization and probing, which provide insights into the decision-making process of the models and enhance their interpretability. The mitigation strategies we aim to use with this knowledge are attention head pruning, fine-tuning, and updating the weights using estimated uncertainty. We also aim to explore how prompt engineering can contribute to more semantically accurate texts.

We hope our research will lead to improved communication between humans and machines, enhanced user experiences, and more trust from the public.

Challenges There is a possibility that certain LLMs may have already encountered the development and testing portions of the datasets that we plan to use for evaluation during their training process. We will be very mindful of this while conducting all evaluations and aim to use training data extraction techniques (Carlini et al., 2021) to verify whether this is the case for a particular set of data and a given LLM. However, searching for new unseen data will be challenging and is definitely something that should be addressed by a wider scientific community.

Acknowledgements

This research was supported by SVV 260575 and by the European Research Council (Grant agreement No. 101039303 NG-NLG). I would like to thank Ondřej Dušek, Mateusz Lango, Tom Kocmi, and the anonymous reviewers for their helpful feedback.

References

Yossi Adi, Einat Kermany, Yonatan Belinkov, Ofer Lavi, and Yoav Goldberg. 2017. Fine-grained analysis of sentence embeddings using auxiliary prediction tasks. In *International Conference on Learning Representations*.

Stephen Bach, Victor Sanh, Zheng Xin Yong, Albert Webson, Colin Raffel, Nihal V. Nayak, Abheesht Sharma, Taewoon Kim, M Saiful Bari, Thibault Fevry, Zaid Alyafeai, Manan Dey, Andrea Santilli, Zhiqing Sun, Srulik Ben-david, Canwen Xu, Gunjan Chhablani, Han Wang, Jason Fries, Maged Al-shaibani, Shanya Sharma, Urmish Thakker, Khalid Almubarak, Xiangru Tang, Dragomir Radev, Mike Tian-jian Jiang, and Alexander Rush. 2022. PromptSource: An integrated development environment and repository for natural language prompts. In *Proceedings of the 60th Annual Meeting of the Association for Computational Linguistics: System Demonstrations*, pages 93–104, Dublin, Ireland. Association for Computational Linguistics.

Maximiliana Behnke and Kenneth Heafield. 2020. Losing heads in the lottery: Pruning transformer attention in neural machine translation. In *Proceedings of the 2020 Conference on Empirical Methods in Natural Language Processing (EMNLP)*, pages 2664–2674, Online. Association for Computational Linguistics.

Anya Belz, Anastasia Shimorina, Shubham Agarwal, and Ehud Reiter. 2021. The ReproGen shared task on reproducibility of human evaluations in NLG: Overview and results. In *Proceedings of the 14th International Conference on Natural Language Generation*, pages 249–258, Aberdeen, Scotland, UK. Association for Computational Linguistics.

Tom B. Brown, Benjamin Mann, Nick Ryder, Melanie Subbiah, Jared Kaplan, Prafulla Dhariwal, Arvind Neelakantan, Pranav Shyam, Girish Sastry, Amanda Askell, Sandhini Agarwal, Ariel Herbert-Voss, Gretchen Krueger, Tom Henighan, Rewon Child, Aditya Ramesh, Daniel M. Ziegler, Jeffrey Wu, Clemens Winter, Christopher Hesse, Mark Chen, Eric Sigler, Mateusz Litwin, Scott Gray, Benjamin Chess, Jack Clark, Christopher Berner, Sam McCandlish, Alec Radford, Ilya Sutskever, and Dario Amodei. 2020. Language models are few-shot learners. In *Proceedings of the 34th International Conference on Neural Information Processing Systems*, NIPS'20, Red Hook, NY, USA. Curran Associates Inc.

Nicholas Carlini, Florian Tramèr, Eric Wallace, Matthew Jagielski, Ariel Herbert-Voss, Katherine Lee, Adam Roberts, Tom Brown, Dawn Song, Úlfar Erlingsson, Alina Oprea, and Colin Raffel. 2021. Extracting training data from large language models. In *30th USENIX Security Symposium (USENIX Security 21)*, pages 2633–2650. USENIX Association.

Thiago Castro Ferreira, Diego Moussallem, Sander Wubben, and Emiel Krahmer. 2018. Enriching the webnlg corpus. In *Proceedings of the 11th International Conference on Natural Language Generation*, INLG'18, Tilburg, The Netherlands. Association for Computational Linguistics.

Asli Celikyilmaz, Elizabeth Clark, and Jianfeng Gao. 2020. Evaluation of text generation: A survey. *CoRR*, abs/2006.14799.

Ming-Wei Chang, Lev Ratinov, Dan Roth, and Vivek Srikumar. 2008. Importance of semantic representation: Dataless classification. In *Proceedings of the 23rd National Conference on Artificial Intelligence - Volume 2*, AAAI'08, page 830–835. AAAI Press.

Yanran Chen and Steffen Eger. 2023. Menli: Robust evaluation metrics from natural language inference.

Hyung Won Chung, Le Hou, Shayne Longpre, Barret Zoph, Yi Tay, William Fedus, Eric Li, Xuezhi Wang, Mostafa Dehghani, Siddhartha Brahma, Albert Webson, Shixiang Shane Gu, Zhuyun Dai, Mirac Suzgun, Xinyun Chen, Aakanksha Chowdhery, Sharan Narang, Gaurav Mishra, Adams Yu, Vincent Zhao, Yanping Huang, Andrew Dai, Hongkun Yu, Slav Petrov, Ed H. Chi, Jeff Dean, Jacob Devlin, Adam Roberts, Denny Zhou, Quoc V. Le, and Jason Wei. 2022. Scaling instruction-finetuned language models.

Alexis Conneau, German Kruszewski, Guillaume Lample, Loïc Barrault, and Marco Baroni. 2018. What you can cram into a single $&!#* vector: Probing sentence embeddings for linguistic properties. In *Proceedings of the 56th Annual Meeting of the Association for Computational Linguistics (Volume 1: Long Papers)*, pages 2126–2136, Melbourne, Australia. Association for Computational Linguistics.

Tim Dettmers, Artidoro Pagnoni, Ari Holtzman, and Luke Zettlemoyer. 2023. Qlora: Efficient finetuning of quantized llms.

Bhuwan Dhingra, Manaal Faruqui, Ankur Parikh, Ming-Wei Chang, Dipanjan Das, and William Cohen. 2019. Handling divergent reference texts when evaluating table-to-text generation. In *Proceedings of the 57th Annual Meeting of the Association for Computational Linguistics*, pages 4884–4895, Florence, Italy. Association for Computational Linguistics.

Zi-Yi Dou and Graham Neubig. 2021. Word alignment by fine-tuning embeddings on parallel corpora. In *Proceedings of the 16th Conference of the European*

Chapter of the Association for Computational Linguistics: Main Volume, pages 2112–2128, Online. Association for Computational Linguistics.

Ondřej Dušek and Zdeněk Kasner. 2020. Evaluating semantic accuracy of data-to-text generation with natural language inference. In *Proceedings of the 13th International Conference on Natural Language Generation*, pages 131–137, Dublin, Ireland. Association for Computational Linguistics.

Ondřej Dušek, Karin Sevegnani, Ioannis Konstas, and Verena Rieser. 2019. Automatic quality estimation for natural language generation: Ranting (jointly rating and ranking). In *Proceedings of the 12th International Conference on Natural Language Generation*, pages 369–376, Tokyo, Japan. Association for Computational Linguistics.

Nouha Dziri, Hannah Rashkin, Tal Linzen, and David Reitter. 2022. Evaluating attribution in dialogue systems: The BEGIN benchmark. *Transactions of the Association for Computational Linguistics*, 10:1066–1083.

Allyson Ettinger, Ahmed Elgohary, and Philip Resnik. 2016. Probing for semantic evidence of composition by means of simple classification tasks. In *Proceedings of the 1st Workshop on Evaluating Vector-Space Representations for NLP*, pages 134–139, Berlin, Germany. Association for Computational Linguistics.

Claire Gardent, Anastasia Shimorina, Shashi Narayan, and Laura Perez-Beltrachini. 2017. Creating training corpora for NLG micro-planners. In *Proceedings of the 55th Annual Meeting of the Association for Computational Linguistics, ACL 2017, Vancouver, Canada, July 30 - August 4, Volume 1: Long Papers*, pages 179–188. Association for Computational Linguistics.

Yoav Goldberg. 2023. Reinforcement learning for language models. Accessed on May 3rd, 2023.

Tanya Goyal and Greg Durrett. 2020. Evaluating factuality in generation with dependency-level entailment. In *Findings of the Association for Computational Linguistics: EMNLP 2020*, pages 3592–3603, Online. Association for Computational Linguistics.

John Hewitt and Christopher D. Manning. 2019. A structural probe for finding syntax in word representations. In *Proceedings of the 2019 Conference of the North American Chapter of the Association for Computational Linguistics: Human Language Technologies, Volume 1 (Long and Short Papers)*, pages 4129–4138, Minneapolis, Minnesota. Association for Computational Linguistics.

David M. Howcroft, Anya Belz, Miruna-Adriana Clinciu, Dimitra Gkatzia, Sadid A. Hasan, Saad Mahamood, Simon Mille, Emiel van Miltenburg, Sashank Santhanam, and Verena Rieser. 2020. Twenty years of confusion in human evaluation: NLG needs evaluation sheets and standardised definitions. In *Proceedings of the 13th International Conference on Natural Language Generation*, pages 169–182, Dublin, Ireland. Association for Computational Linguistics.

Edward J. Hu, Yelong Shen, Phillip Wallis, Zeyuan Allen-Zhu, Yuanzhi Li, Shean Wang, Lu Wang, and Weizhu Chen. 2021. Lora: Low-rank adaptation of large language models.

Patrick Huber and Giuseppe Carenini. 2022. Towards understanding large-scale discourse structures in pre-trained and fine-tuned language models. In *Proceedings of the 2022 Conference of the North American Chapter of the Association for Computational Linguistics: Human Language Technologies*, pages 2376–2394, Seattle, United States. Association for Computational Linguistics.

Hassan Kane, Muhammed Yusuf Kocyigit, Ali Abdalla, Pelkins Ajanoh, and Mohamed Coulibali. 2020. NUBIA: NeUral based interchangeability assessor for text generation. In *Proceedings of the 1st Workshop on Evaluating NLG Evaluation*, pages 28–37, Online (Dublin, Ireland). Association for Computational Linguistics.

Zdeněk Kasner, Simon Mille, and Ondřej Dušek. 2021. Text-in-context: Token-level error detection for table-to-text generation. In *Proceedings of the 14th International Conference on Natural Language Generation*, pages 259–265, Aberdeen, Scotland, UK. Association for Computational Linguistics.

Armen Der Kiureghian and Ove Ditlevsen. 2009. Aleatory or epistemic? does it matter? *Structural Safety*, 31(2):105–112. Risk Acceptance and Risk Communication.

Josef Klafka and Allyson Ettinger. 2020. Spying on your neighbors: Fine-grained probing of contextual embeddings for information about surrounding words. In *Proceedings of the 58th Annual Meeting of the Association for Computational Linguistics*, pages 4801–4811, Online. Association for Computational Linguistics.

Tom Kocmi and Christian Federmann. 2023. Large language models are state-of-the-art evaluators of translation quality.

Patrick Lewis, Ethan Perez, Aleksandra Piktus, Fabio Petroni, Vladimir Karpukhin, Naman Goyal, Heinrich Küttler, Mike Lewis, Wen-tau Yih, Tim Rocktäschel, Sebastian Riedel, and Douwe Kiela. 2020. Retrieval-augmented generation for knowledge-intensive nlp tasks. In *Advances in Neural Information Processing Systems*, volume 33, pages 9459–9474. Curran Associates, Inc.

Jiaoda Li, Ryan Cotterell, and Mrinmaya Sachan. 2022. Probing via prompting. In *Proceedings of the 2022 Conference of the North American Chapter of the Association for Computational Linguistics: Human Language Technologies*, pages 1144–1157, Seattle,

United States. Association for Computational Linguistics.

Pengfei Liu, Weizhe Yuan, Jinlan Fu, Zhengbao Jiang, Hiroaki Hayashi, and Graham Neubig. 2021. Pre-train, prompt, and predict: A systematic survey of prompting methods in natural language processing.

David Mareček, Jindřich Libovický, Tomáš Musil, Rudolf Rosa, and Tomasz Limisiewicz. 2020. *Hidden in the Layers: Interpretation of Neural Networks for Natural Language Processing*, volume 20 of *Studies in Computational and Theoretical Linguistics*. Institute of Formal and Applied Linguistics, Prague, Czechia.

Joshua Maynez, Shashi Narayan, Bernd Bohnet, and Ryan McDonald. 2020. On faithfulness and factuality in abstractive summarization. In *Proceedings of the 58th Annual Meeting of the Association for Computational Linguistics*, pages 1906–1919, Online. Association for Computational Linguistics.

Linyong Nan, Dragomir Radev, Rui Zhang, Amrit Rau, Abhinand Sivaprasad, Chiachun Hsieh, Xiangru Tang, Aadit Vyas, Neha Verma, Pranav Krishna, Yangxiaokang Liu, Nadia Irwanto, Jessica Pan, Faiaz Rahman, Ahmad Zaidi, Mutethia Mutuma, Yasin Tarabar, Ankit Gupta, Tao Yu, Yi Chern Tan, Xi Victoria Lin, Caiming Xiong, Richard Socher, and Nazneen Fatema Rajani. 2021. DART: Open-domain structured data record to text generation. In *Proceedings of the 2021 Conference of the North American Chapter of the Association for Computational Linguistics: Human Language Technologies*, pages 432–447, Online. Association for Computational Linguistics.

Shashi Narayan, Shay B. Cohen, and Mirella Lapata. 2018. Don't give me the details, just the summary! topic-aware convolutional neural networks for extreme summarization. *ArXiv*, abs/1808.08745.

Andrew Ng and Isa Fulford. 2023. Guidelines for prompting.

Long Ouyang, Jeff Wu, Xu Jiang, Diogo Almeida, Carroll L. Wainwright, Pamela Mishkin, Chong Zhang, Sandhini Agarwal, Katarina Slama, Alex Ray, John Schulman, Jacob Hilton, Fraser Kelton, Luke Miller, Maddie Simens, Amanda Askell, Peter Welinder, Paul Christiano, Jan Leike, and Ryan Lowe. 2022. Training language models to follow instructions with human feedback.

Mark Palatucci, Dean Pomerleau, Geoffrey Hinton, and Tom M. Mitchell. 2009. Zero-shot learning with semantic output codes. In *Proceedings of the 22nd International Conference on Neural Information Processing Systems*, NIPS'09, page 1410–1418, Red Hook, NY, USA. Curran Associates Inc.

Lance Ramshaw and Mitch Marcus. 1995. Text chunking using transformation-based learning. In *Third Workshop on Very Large Corpora*.

Ananya B. Sai, Akash Kumar Mohankumar, and Mitesh M. Khapra. 2022. A survey of evaluation metrics used for nlg systems. *ACM Comput. Surv.*, 55(2).

Victor Sanh, Albert Webson, Colin Raffel, Stephen H. Bach, Lintang Sutawika, Zaid Alyafeai, Antoine Chaffin, Arnaud Stiegler, Teven Le Scao, Arun Raja, Manan Dey, M Saiful Bari, Canwen Xu, Urmish Thakker, Shanya Sharma Sharma, Eliza Szczechla, Taewoon Kim, Gunjan Chhablani, Nihal Nayak, Debajyoti Datta, Jonathan Chang, Mike Tian-Jian Jiang, Han Wang, Matteo Manica, Sheng Shen, Zheng Xin Yong, Harshit Pandey, Rachel Bawden, Thomas Wang, Trishala Neeraj, Jos Rozen, Abheesht Sharma, Andrea Santilli, Thibault Fevry, Jason Alan Fries, Ryan Teehan, Tali Bers, Stella Biderman, Leo Gao, Thomas Wolf, and Alexander M. Rush. 2022. Multitask prompted training enables zero-shot task generalization.

Teven Le Scao and Angela Fan et al. 2023. Bloom: A 176b-parameter open-access multilingual language model.

Patricia Schmidtova. 2022. Theatre play generation. Master's thesis, Charles University.

Sebastian Schuster and Tal Linzen. 2022. When a sentence does not introduce a discourse entity, transformer-based models still sometimes refer to it. In *Proceedings of the 2022 Conference of the North American Chapter of the Association for Computational Linguistics: Human Language Technologies*, pages 969–982, Seattle, United States. Association for Computational Linguistics.

Thibault Sellam, Dipanjan Das, and Ankur Parikh. 2020. BLEURT: Learning robust metrics for text generation. In *Proceedings of the 58th Annual Meeting of the Association for Computational Linguistics*, pages 7881–7892, Online. Association for Computational Linguistics.

Lucia Specia, Kashif Shah, Jose G.C. de Souza, and Trevor Cohn. 2013. QuEst - a translation quality estimation framework. In *Proceedings of the 51st Annual Meeting of the Association for Computational Linguistics: System Demonstrations*, pages 79–84, Sofia, Bulgaria. Association for Computational Linguistics.

Rohan Taori, Ishaan Gulrajani, Tianyi Zhang, Yann Dubois, Xuechen Li, Carlos Guestrin, Percy Liang, and Tatsunori B. Hashimoto. 2023. Stanford alpaca: An instruction-following llama model. `https://github.com/tatsu-lab/stanford_alpaca`.

Craig Thomson and Ehud Reiter. 2021. Generation challenges: Results of the accuracy evaluation shared task. In *Proceedings of the 14th International Conference on Natural Language Generation*, pages 240–248, Aberdeen, Scotland, UK. Association for Computational Linguistics.

James Thorne, Andreas Vlachos, Christos Christodoulopoulos, and Arpit Mittal. 2018. FEVER: a large-scale dataset for fact extraction and VERification. In *Proceedings of the 2018 Conference of the North American Chapter of the Association for Computational Linguistics: Human Language Technologies, Volume 1 (Long Papers)*, pages 809–819, New Orleans, Louisiana. Association for Computational Linguistics.

Hugo Touvron, Thibaut Lavril, Gautier Izacard, Xavier Martinet, Marie-Anne Lachaux, Timothée Lacroix, Baptiste Rozière, Naman Goyal, Eric Hambro, Faisal Azhar, Aurelien Rodriguez, Armand Joulin, Edouard Grave, and Guillaume Lample. 2023. Llama: Open and efficient foundation language models.

Jannis Vamvas and Rico Sennrich. 2022. As little as possible, as much as necessary: Detecting over- and undertranslations with contrastive conditioning. In *Proceedings of the 60th Annual Meeting of the Association for Computational Linguistics (Volume 2: Short Papers)*, pages 490–500, Dublin, Ireland. Association for Computational Linguistics.

Ashish Vaswani, Noam Shazeer, Niki Parmar, Jakob Uszkoreit, Llion Jones, Aidan N. Gomez, Łukasz Kaiser, and Illia Polosukhin. 2017. Attention is all you need. In *Proceedings of the 31st International Conference on Neural Information Processing Systems*, NIPS'17, page 6000–6010, Red Hook, NY, USA. Curran Associates Inc.

Jesse Vig. 2019. Visualizing attention in transformer-based language representation models.

Elena Voita, David Talbot, Fedor Moiseev, Rico Sennrich, and Ivan Titov. 2019. Analyzing multi-head self-attention: Specialized heads do the heavy lifting, the rest can be pruned. In *Proceedings of the 57th Annual Meeting of the Association for Computational Linguistics*, pages 5797–5808, Florence, Italy. Association for Computational Linguistics.

Yizhong Wang, Swaroop Mishra, Pegah Alipoormolabashi, Yeganeh Kordi, Amirreza Mirzaei, A. Arunkumar, Arjun Ashok, Arut Selvan Dhanasekaran, Atharva Naik, David Stap, Eshaan Pathak, Giannis Karamanolakis, Haizhi Gary Lai, Ishan Purohit, Ishani Mondal, Jacob Anderson, Kirby Kuznia, Krima Doshi, Maitreya Patel, Kuntal Kumar Pal, M. Moradshahi, Mihir Parmar, Mirali Purohit, Neeraj Varshney, Phani Rohitha Kaza, Pulkit Verma, Ravsehaj Singh Puri, Rushang Karia, Shailaja Keyur Sampat, Savan Doshi, Siddharth Deepak Mishra, Sujan C. Reddy, Sumanta Patro, Tanay Dixit, Xu dong Shen, Chitta Baral, Yejin Choi, Hannaneh Hajishirzi, Noah A. Smith, and Daniel Khashabi. 2022. Benchmarking generalization via in-context instructions on 1,600+ language tasks.

Jason Wei, Xuezhi Wang, Dale Schuurmans, Maarten Bosma, Brian Ichter, Fei Xia, Ed Chi, Quoc Le, and Denny Zhou. 2023. Chain-of-thought prompting elicits reasoning in large language models.

Sarah Wiegreffe and Yuval Pinter. 2019. Attention is not not explanation. In *Proceedings of the 2019 Conference on Empirical Methods in Natural Language Processing and the 9th International Joint Conference on Natural Language Processing (EMNLP-IJCNLP)*, pages 11–20, Hong Kong, China. Association for Computational Linguistics.

Yanan Wu, Zhiyuan Zeng, Keqing He, Yutao Mou, Pei Wang, and Weiran Xu. 2022. Distribution calibration for out-of-domain detection with Bayesian approximation. In *Proceedings of the 29th International Conference on Computational Linguistics*, pages 608–615, Gyeongju, Republic of Korea. International Committee on Computational Linguistics.

Tianyi Zhang, Varsha Kishore, Felix Wu, Kilian Q. Weinberger, and Yoav Artzi. 2020. Bertscore: Evaluating text generation with bert. In *International Conference on Learning Representations*.

Math Word Problem Solving by Generating Linguistic Variants of Problem Statements

Syed Rifat Raiyan, Md. Nafis Faiyaz, Shah Md. Jawad Kabir, Mohsinul Kabir, Hasan Mahmud, Md. Kamrul Hasan
Systems and Software Lab (SSL)
Department of Computer Science and Engineering
Islamic University of Technology, Dhaka, Bangladesh
{rifatraiyan, nafisfaiyaz, jawadkabir, hasan, hasank}@iut-dhaka.edu

Abstract

The art of mathematical reasoning stands as a fundamental pillar of intellectual progress and is a central catalyst in cultivating human ingenuity. Researchers have recently published a plethora of works centered around the task of solving Math Word Problems (MWP) — a crucial stride towards general AI. These existing models are susceptible to dependency on shallow heuristics and spurious correlations to derive the solution expressions. In order to ameliorate this issue, in this paper, we propose a framework for MWP solvers based on the generation of linguistic variants of the problem text. The approach involves solving each of the variant problems and electing the predicted expression with the majority of the votes. We use DeBERTa (Decoding-enhanced BERT with disentangled attention) as the encoder to leverage its rich textual representations and enhanced mask decoder to construct the solution expressions. Furthermore, we introduce a challenging dataset, PARAMAWPS, consisting of paraphrased, adversarial, and inverse variants of selectively sampled MWPs from the benchmark MAWPS dataset. We extensively experiment on this dataset along with other benchmark datasets using some baseline MWP solver models. We show that training on linguistic variants of problem statements and voting on candidate predictions improve the mathematical reasoning and robustness of the model. We make our code and data publicly available.

1 Introduction

Math word problem solving is a long-standing research problem in Artificial General Intelligence (AGI) and a lot of studies about this topic, from both industry and academia, have been published recently. A typical Math Word Problem (MWP) takes the form of a written narrative that articulates a problem scenario and poses a question regarding one or more unknown quantities. A language model capable of solving such problems has to translate the human-readable problem statement to a valid mathematical expression that can be evaluated to obtain the numeric answer. An example of a classic MWP is portrayed in Table 1, where the reader is asked to infer the revenue of a boutique shop. Such problems are generally found in math textbooks of 1st to 8th grade students and are easily solvable by humans with decent mathematical aptitude.

Problem: 69 handbags are sold for \$13 each. There are a total of 420 handbags in a boutique and the remaining handbags are sold for \$7 each. How much did the boutique earn after selling all the handbags?
Expression: $x = 69 \times 13 + (420 - 69) \times 7$
Solution: 3354

Table 1: An example of a Math Word Problem.

A lot of challenges manifest while designing an automated system for solving these problems (Zhang et al., 2019; Sundaram et al., 2022). The primary challenge is to understand the quantities in the problem and capture their complex mathematical interconnections from a linear textual sequence written in natural language. There exists a diverse range of MWPs with differing difficulty levels, *i.e.*, varying numbers of unknown values, and depth of the relationships between quantities, which require good mathematical reasoning ability to solve. Furthermore, the absence of crucial information and the presence of irrelevant information in the problem statements proves to be quite a challenge for the solver models (Patel et al., 2021). Other challenges include learning to tackle the chronological and temporal ambiguities of the events happening in the problem statements and dealing with MWPs that significantly differ from the training set in terms of semantic and syntactic structure.

To address the problem outlined in Table 1, a competent MWP solver model would need to possess the ability to associate the quantity, *i.e.*, 69 handbags, with its price attribute of \$13, and un-

Proceedings of the 61st Annual Meeting of the Association for Computational Linguistics - Student Research Workshop, pages 362–378
July 10-12, 2023

derstand the relative arithmetic order by deriving 351 remaining handbags, *i.e.*, $420 - 69$, before associating the price attribute of \$7. A lot of psychological studies have been done on how human beings learn to solve mathematical problems and improve their aptitude (Piaget, 2013; Peterson et al., 2003; Kingsdorf and Krawec, 2016). The frontier of research involving MWP solving is considered a momentous step towards the apogee of AGI (Bubeck et al., 2023) and so researchers have dedicated their efforts to replicating these complex cognitive patterns exhibited by human beings within the frameworks of AI models. The existing methods that are considered strong baselines for MWP solving can be demonstrably shown to use shallow heuristics to solve many of the MWPs in the benchmark datasets (Patel et al., 2021) creating a faux impression of their mathematical reasoning capability. To account for this limitation, in this paper —

- We propose a framework for solving simple math word problems by generating paraphrased linguistic variants of the input problem statement using OpenAI's latest Generative Pre-trained Transformer (GPT-3) (Brown et al., 2020) models, namely *text-davinci-003* and *gpt-3.5-turbo*. The problem statement variants along with the original problem text then undergo the appropriate preprocessing steps and are fed to an MWP solver model with a DeBERTa-based encoder and Enhanced Mask decoder.
- We also generate a large, augmented version of the MAWPS (Koncel-Kedziorski et al., 2016) dataset, namely PARAMAWPS (**Para**phrased **MA**th **W**ord **P**roblem **S**olving Repository), as a challenging dataset by the introduction of paraphrased structural variations of almost all categories of problems, but emphasizing more on the categories that the strong baseline models find difficult to solve.

DeBERTa (Decoding-enhanced BERT with disentangled attention) (He et al., 2020) is currently one of the most popular language models due to its effectiveness in achieving state-of-the-art results on a variety of natural language processing tasks, including language translation, text classification, and question answering. In our work, we find that the DeBERTa model achieves value accuracies of 63.5% and 91.0% on the SVAMP dataset (Patel et al., 2021) and the MAWPS dataset (Koncel-Kedziorski et al., 2016) respectively. It falls behind the current SOTA accuracy of ROBERTA-DEDUCTREASONER (Jie et al., 2022) by a slight margin of $1 \pm 0.20\%$ on the MAWPS dataset, but exceeds its accuracy of $47.3 \pm 0.20\%$ on the SVAMP dataset. Our code and data are publicly available at — `https://github.com/Starscream-11813/Variational-Mathematical-Reasoning`

2 Problem Formulation

A Math Word Problem S is a sequence of word tokens and numeric values, where the $V_S = \{v_1, \ldots, v_m\}$ denotes the word tokens in S and the set $n_S = \{n_1, \ldots, n_l\}$ denotes the set of numeric quantities in S. The set of word tokens V_S consists of entities such as names of people, objects, units, and rates while the set of quantities n_S consists of the numerical amount relevant to those entities.

The goal of an MWP solver model is to map S to a valid mathematical expression E, consisting of the quantities in $(n_S \cup C)$, where C is a set of constants, and the fundamental mathematical operators $O = \{+, -, \times, \div\}$, which can be evaluated to obtain the correct answer.

3 Literature Review

3.1 Math Word Problem Solving

3.1.1 Preliminary Works

The dawn of research on MWP solving was in the mid-1960s (Feigenbaum et al., 1963; Bobrow, 1964). *Rule-based methods* (Fletcher, 1985; Bakman, 2007; Yuhui et al., 2010) are chronologically some of the earliest approaches to solving MWPs. They use a set of manually hard-coded rules about the language they are analyzing to find out regularities in the data. *Statistical methods* (Kushman et al., 2014; Hosseini et al., 2014; Roy et al., 2015; Zhou et al., 2015; Mitra and Baral, 2016; Liang et al., 2016a,b) use generic ML classifiers to extract the entities, quantities, and operators from the problem statement and infer the numeric answer with simple logic. *Tree-based methods* (Koncel-Kedziorski et al., 2015; Roy and Roth, 2016; Roy et al., 2016; Roy and Roth, 2017) utilize the inherent binary tree-like structure of expressions/equations. Other primitive categories of approaches that have now been rendered somewhat obsolete are *Parsing-based methods* (Shi et al.,

2015; Zou and Lu, 2019), *Similarity-based methods* (Huang et al., 2016), and *Template-based methods* (Kushman et al., 2014; Zhou et al., 2015; Roy et al., 2016; Upadhyay et al., 2016; Huang et al., 2017).

3.1.2 Deep Learning-based Methods

Currently, the landscape of Deep learning models for the MWP solving task is primarily comprised of five distinct paradigms, SEQ2SEQ-based, SEQ2TREE-based, GRAPH2TREE-based, *complex relation extraction-based*, and *Large Language Model (LLM) prompt-based* approaches, each of which has demonstrated remarkable levels of performance and efficacy. Wang et al. (2017) were the pioneers of introducing deep learning to solve MWPs with their proposed SEQ2SEQ model. To improve the SEQ2SEQ model, researchers resorted to alternative strategies, such as reinforcement learning techniques (Wang et al., 2018b; Huang et al., 2018), using dense problem representation (Mishra et al., 2018), adopting template-based methodologies (Wang et al., 2019), and incorporating group attention mechanisms (Li et al., 2019). Xie and Sun (2019) were the progenitors of the novel Goal-driven Tree-Structured (GTS) model, designed to generate expression trees using the tree-based decoder in order to imitate the goal-driven problem-solving approach of humans. The use of this tree decoder along with pre-trained language models, such as BERT (Devlin et al., 2018), BART (Lewis et al., 2019), RoBERTa (Liu et al., 2019b), as the encoder in some of the SEQ2TREE approaches (Liu et al., 2019a; Shen and Jin, 2020; Wu et al., 2020; Lin et al., 2021; Shen et al., 2021; Liang et al., 2021; Liang et al.; Li et al., 2021; Xiong et al., 2022) brought about substantial performance improvements over the previous SEQ2SEQ methods. Cao et al. (2021) devised a directed acyclic graph (SEQ2DAG) model of the equations for the purpose of extracting the expression. Zhang et al. (2020a) incorporated the idea of Knowledge Distillation (KD) (Hinton et al., 2015) in their proposed model where the *teacher network* is pre-trained to guide the learning behaviors of the *student networks*. Yu et al. (2021) introduced 2 types of encoders in their model. Hong et al. (2021) modified the work of Xie and Sun (2019) by incorporating a symbolic reasoning based *Learning-by-fixing* (LBF) framework. Huang et al. (2021) attempted to emulate human-like analogical learning in their proposed memory-augmented model. GRAPH2TREE-based approaches (Zhang et al., 2020b; Li et al., 2020) fused the merits of Graph-based Transformer (Yun et al., 2019; Cai and Lam, 2020) encoders with multiple Graph Convolutional Network (multi-GCN) modules (Kipf and Welling, 2016), and tree-based decoders to solve MWPs. Chatterjee et al. (2021) introduced a weakly supervised approach for MWP solving. Li et al. (2021) introduced a contrastive learning approach with pattern divergence to solve MWPs. Jie et al. (2022) formulated the MWP solving task as a complex relation extraction problem and leveraged explainable deductive reasoning techniques to iteratively construct the target equations.

With the advent of LLMs, many innovative prompt-based methods (Shao et al., 2022; Li et al., 2022; Wang et al., 2022; Pi et al., 2022; Chen et al., 2022; Liang et al., 2023) of solving MWPs that capitalize on the models' exceptional few-shot learning capability came into the limelight and demonstrated good performance across numerous benchmark datasets. Cobbe et al. (2021) used verifiers with their GPT-3 (Brown et al., 2020) model. Although LLMs excel at natural language understanding and have serendipitous emergent reasoning abilities (Yang et al., 2023), they are still lackluster in complex reasoning tasks (Huang and Chang, 2022). Numerous studies on complex reasoning tasks have empirically demonstrated that the approach of fine-tuning smaller models is more effective (Ho et al., 2022) than adopting LLM prompting techniques like Chain of Thought (CoT) prompting (Wei et al., 2022).

3.2 Paraphrasing

Paraphrase generation has garnered significant attention from various NLP approaches, encompassing rule-based methods (McKeown, 1980; Meteer and Shaked, 1988), data-driven techniques (Madnani and Dorr, 2010), linguistic translation methods (Bannard and Callison-Burch, 2005; Barzilay and McKeown, 2001; Prakash et al., 2016) that leverage bilingual corpora for iterative refinement (Madnani and Dorr, 2010; Prakash et al., 2016; Mallinson et al., 2017). Witteveen and Andrews (2019) demonstrated the superiority of LLMs like GPT-3 over the preceding methods in the paraphrasing task.

Accordingly, our work attempts to leverage the strengths of GPT-3 to generate a more linguistically diverse pool of problem statements to fine-tune a relatively smaller DeBERTa solver model on the downstream task of MWP solving which falls under the rubric of complex reasoning tasks.

4 Methodology

Figure-1 in Appendix-A shows an overview of our proposed architecture. Given a problem statement S, we prompt the paraphraser model to generate k linguistic variants of S which are, $S_1, S_2, \ldots, S_k$. These k variant problems along with the seed problem S consists of quantities that are tagged appropriately using quantity tags. Each of the $k+1$ text sequences is then tokenized and the content embeddings H and positional embeddings P of the tokens are fed to the DeBERTa model. The disentangled self-attention mechanism of DeBERTa's encoder utilizes H and P to generate the output H_{output}, which is a contextual representation of the content of each problem statement. H_{output}, along with the relative positional embeddings P and absolute positional embeddings I of each of the problem statements are used by the Transformer layers of Enhanced Mask Decoder (EMD) of DeBERTa to generate the $k+1$ predicted equations $E_1, E_2, \ldots, E_{k+1}$. These equations are then simplified and the equation that is predicted the most number of times is elected as the final prediction of the model. This majority voting module is used only during the validation/testing phase and for inference. During the training phase, the $k+1$ problem statements are deemed as stand-alone training samples and the Negative Log-Likelihood loss (NLLLoss) is calculated using the predicted equations and the ground-truth equation. Consequently, if the training set of the dataset used to train the model consists of n samples, it is as if the model is trained with $(k+1) \times n = kn + n$ samples. The knowledge points gathered after being trained on an extra kn samples contributes to the robustness of the model.

4.1 Paraphrasing Model

The task of correctly reformulating a Math Word Problem statement requires a good level of language understanding which is not present in its entirety in rule-based and data-driven methods of paraphrasing rendering them unsuitable in this case. These methods frequently yield incorrect, incoherent, and grammatically inaccurate linguistic variations; sometimes even leaving out crucial numerical information. Accordingly, we choose *text-davinci-003* and *gpt-3.5-turbo*, two GPT-3 models from OpenAI, as the paraphrasing models. GPT-3 (Generative Pre-trained Transformer 3) (Brown et al., 2020) is a large language model with 175 billion parameters, that is capable of performing a wide range of natural language processing tasks, including paraphrasing a given sentence. Upon being prompted, it restates a given problem statement in different words while still maintaining the original meaning. To select the most appropriate paraphrase, GPT-3 uses a scoring mechanism that evaluates the semantic similarity between the original sentence and each of the generated paraphrases. The model assigns a higher score to paraphrases that are more similar in meaning to the input sentence, based on its understanding of the context and the relationships between the words. It also allows users to customize the level of complexity and the style of writing in the paraphrased version. We generate k variants of the original problem text by prompting the model.

4.1.1 Prompts and System Task Description

The prompts that we use for accomplishing our linguistic variant generation task are,

- `system role` **Task Description** —
  `You are a Math Word Problem rephraser that generates variations of math word problem statements.`

- `user role` **Prompts** —
  - `Generate` k_1 `paraphrased variations of the problem by changing the sentence structure.`
  - `Generate` k_2 `paraphrased variations of the problem by changing the named entities and objects.`
  - `Generate` k_3 `paraphrased variations of the problem with irrelevant numerical information.`

Here, the total number of linguistic variants of a problem, $k = k_1 + k_2 + k_3$ and $5 \leq k \leq 15$.

A detailed discussion on the types of problem variations is delineated in Section-5.

4.2 Quantity Tagging

All the quantities (written either numerically or in words) in every single variant of the problem along with the original problem itself, are tagged with unique quantity tags using RegEx and a Python script which is provided in our GitHub repository (see Section-1). This quantity tagging step ensures that the same quantity is present in both the input as well as in the output. The quantity-tagged tokens have their own content and positional embeddings. For example, if the problem statement is,

> *"Melanie picked 4 plums, Dan picked 9 plums, and Sally picked 3 plums from the plum tree. How many plums were picked in total?"*

then the quantity-tagged version of the problem statement is,

> *"Melanie picked* [Q1] *plums, Dan picked* [Q2] *plums, and Sally picked* [Q3] *plums from the plum tree. How many plums were picked in total?"*

We use this quantity tagging for the ground truth equation's quantities as well.

4.3 Encoder

We use the pre-trained language model DeBERTa (**D**ecoding **e**nhanced **BERT** with disentangled **a**ttention). DeBERTa is a newly developed neural language model by He et al. (2020) that is based on the Transformer architecture. It boasts a significant advancement over previous state-of-the-art (SOTA) pre-trained language models (PLMs) due to the incorporation of two novel techniques. The first technique is a disentangled attention mechanism and the second technique is an enhanced mask decoder. Together, these techniques make DeBERTa a highly effective PLM that outperforms its predecessors on a wide range of NLP downstream tasks.

4.3.1 Disentangled Attention

Contrary to BERT, which utilizes a vector representation for each word in the input layer by summing its content and position embeddings, in DeBERTa, every word is represented by two separate vectors that encode its content and position individually. The attention scores between words are computed using separate matrices that are disentangled based on the content and relative position of each word. This design choice is based on the observation that the attention weight between a pair of tokens is influenced by both their content and in tandem their relative positions. This especially holds paramount importance for the task of MWP solving as the relative positions of certain keywords in the problem statements dictate the solution.

To represent a token x_i located at a specific position i within a given sequence, it employs two distinct vectors, H_i and $P_{i|j}$, which are respectively the content and relative positional representation vectors of x_i with respect to a token x_j at position j. The inter-token attention weights between x_i and x_j can be broken down into four constituent components,

$$\begin{aligned} A_{ij} &= \langle H_i, P_{i|j}\rangle \times \langle H_j, P_{j|i}\rangle^\top \\ &= \underbrace{H_i H_j^\top}_{C2C} + \underbrace{H_i P_{j|i}^\top}_{C2P} + \underbrace{P_{i|j} H_j^\top}_{P2C} + \underbrace{P_{i|j} P_{j|i}^\top}_{\substack{P2P \\ (omitted)}} \end{aligned} \tag{1}$$

where, the four disentangled matrix attention scores represent their contents and positions as *content-to-content (C2C)*, *content-to-position (C2P)*, *position-to-content (P2C)*, and *position-to-position (P2P)*. The P2P portion of (1) is somewhat rendered obsolete since DeBERTa uses relative positional embedding which is why no useful information can be extracted from it.

The self-attention mechanism described by Vaswani et al. (2017) has 3 parameters, Q (Query), K (Key), and V (Value). The non-contextual embedding that is being contextualized at any point requests for information from its surrounding tokens within the context window and that is represented by the query token, and the tokens that the model pays attention to are the key tokens.

$$\begin{aligned} &Q_c = HW_{c_Q}, K_c = HW_{c_K}, V_c = HW_{c_V} \\ &Q_r = PW_{r_Q}, K_r = PW_{r_K} \end{aligned} \tag{2}$$

where, $W_{c_Q} \in \mathbb{R}^{d\times d}$, $W_{c_K} \in \mathbb{R}^{d\times d}$, $W_{c_V} \in \mathbb{R}^{d\times d}$ are the projection weight matrices for the projected content vectors Q_c, K_c, V_c respectively. Similarly, $W_{r_Q} \in \mathbb{R}^{d\times d}$ and $W_{r_K} \in \mathbb{R}^{d\times d}$ play the role of projection matrices for the projected relative position vectors Q_r and K_r. The metric to calculate the relative distance between tokens x_i and x_j is,

$$\delta(i,j) = \begin{cases} 0, & \text{if } i-j \leq k \\ 2k-1, & \text{if } i-j \geq k \\ i-j+k, & \text{otherwise} \end{cases} \tag{3}$$

which implies, $\delta(i,j) \in [0, 2k)$. Each element $\bar{A}_{ij}$ of the attention matrix $\bar{A}$ denotes the attention score from token x_i to the token x_j and is computed using the vectors defined in (2) in the following manner,

$$\bar{A}_{ij} = \underbrace{Q_i^c K_j^{c\top}}_{C2C} + \underbrace{Q_i^c K_{\delta(i,j)}^{r\top}}_{C2P} + \underbrace{K_j^c Q_{\delta(j,i)}^{r\top}}_{P2C} \tag{4}$$

The attention score is yielded using the dot-product of the query and key in the formula to let the model have an idea of how similar the key is to the query. The output of the self-attention mechanism, which is denoted by $H_{output} \in \mathbb{R}^{N \times d}$ is,

$$H_{output} = \textbf{softmax}\left(\frac{\bar{A}}{\sqrt{3d}}\right) V_c \tag{5}$$

The result of the dot-product is normalized by dividing with $\sqrt{3d}$ to avoid very hard softmax with small gradients, which is especially required for training stability in the case of large-scale PLMs (Vaswani et al., 2017; He et al., 2020).

4.4 Decoder

He et al. (2020) postulates that the premature integration of absolute positions, which is employed by BERT (Devlin et al., 2018) in its decoding phase, could potentially impede the model's ability to acquire adequate knowledge of relative positions. With this as the justification, DeBERTa, being a model that was pre-trained using MLM (Masked Language Modeling), uses the absolute positions of the tokens in the penultimate layer, right before the softmax layer during the masked token prediction in its decoding phase. This enables all the Transformer layers in the decoder to work with the relative positional information without the susceptibility of hampering the learning process of the model. Since the absolute positions of the tokens in a sentence highly influence the nuanced understanding of the sentence's semantic and syntactic structure, and extracting information from only the relative positions isn't sufficient, the absolute positions are incorporated in the tail-end of the pipeline in the case of DeBERTa. This is why DeBERTa's decoding module is dubbed an Enhanced Mask Decoder (EMD) and it demonstrably outperforms the decoder counterparts of its predecessor PLMs (He et al., 2020).

4.5 Majority Voting

Since there can be multiple valid equations for a single MWP, each of the $k+1$ predictions from the decoder, $E_1, E_2 \ldots, E_{k+1}$, is simplified to a reduced normal form using the python package `sympy`[1]. These $k+1$ simplified predictions, $E'_1, E'_2 \ldots, E'_{k+1}$, are then counted and the prediction that is the most frequent or that is yielded the most number of times is elected as the final answer of the whole solver model. It is to be noted that this voting mechanism is used only during the testing/validation phases or during inference.

$$E^* \leftarrow \underset{E'}{\text{argmax}}\, \textbf{Votes}(E'_i); \quad i = 1, 2, \ldots, k+1 \tag{6}$$

[1]`https://www.sympy.org/en/index.html`

5 Experiment

5.1 Data Acquisition

We introduce a new large-scale dataset, namely PARAMAWPS (**Para**phrased **MA**th **W**ord **P**roblem **S**olving Repository), consisting of 16,278 single equation MWPs. It is generated as a by-product of using one of the most commonly-used English MWP datasets, MAWPS (Koncel-Kedziorski et al., 2016) which consists of a total of 2,373 problems, and the paraphraser model. We save the generated paraphrased variants of selectively sampled problems of MAWPS and also manually include inverse versions of the problems to create our dataset. The dataset contains all the problems from the original MAWPS dataset as well as paraphrased versions of some of the more challenging problems within MAWPS, hence the name, PARAMAWPS. The samples are manually checked for correctness by 3 undergraduate students. By generating variations of some of the more difficult problems, we intend to increase familiarity of challenging concepts found within those problems to any model trained over this data, as well as more thoroughly challenge existing models trained on datasets that do not provide said complexity at an equal or higher density. We generate k problems from each seed problem in the dataset, adding up to a total of $k+1$ problems, where $5 \leq k \leq 16$. Each of the k generated problems will be a variation on the original that will feature several changes to the problem text. We generate 4 types of variations of each seed problem (see Table-7 in Appendix-A).

- **Changed phrase order** — Variations with the order of the phrases being changed facilitate a break from the standard problem statement template where quantities are generally given before the question formulation. Having a changed ordering of phrases makes apriori question formulations more common.
- **Changed object and entity names** — Object and entity names are altered with interchangeable alternatives (names, synonyms) in problem variations to prevent fixation on elements of the problem mostly agnostic to

the process of solving the problem. It also serves to prevent an increase in density for similar terms that originate from the seed problem yielding good problem samples for language models (Lee et al., 2021).

- **Added unrelated information** — Some variations contain an extra phrase or quantity, or similar additions that are in excess of the information required to solve a problem and do not affect the original problem formulation in any meaningful way. These adversarial variations serve to obfuscate and familiarize the models with only the necessary information, enhancing deductive abilities (Kumar et al., 2021).

- **Inverted question** — Some variations will take a previously known quantity and turn it into an unknown quantity while revealing the previous unknown quantity of the problem. This, in many cases, alters the question drastically, changing the needed calculations and equations, while keeping a roughly similar question body to the seed problem. Liu et al. (2021) used such problem samples in their work.

5.1.1 Seed Problems

Many of the seed problems used to generate variations from MAWPS pose sufficient difficulty to even SOTA MWP solvers and often contain numeric information embedded within the statement itself. An example is the following problem,

> "*Mary, Sam, Keith, and Alyssa each have 6 marbles. How many marbles do they have in all?*"

This problem yields the equation "$x = 4 \times 6$", despite the quantity 4 not being mentioned anywhere in the statement. This quantity had to be inferred from the other parts of the statement itself, namely, the 4 entities referred to in the statement; Mary, Sam, Keith, and Alyssa. Another such problem is,

> "*When the price of diesel rose by 10%, a user reduced his diesel consumption by the same amount. How much would his diesel bill change in terms of percentage?*"

which yields the complex equation of "$x = (1.0 - ((1.0 + (10.0 \times 0.01)) \times (1.0 - (10.0 \times 0.01)))) \times 100.0$". This problem, although seemingly simple on the surface in terms of quantities described, has several calculations dictated through the problem statement, some of which require additional real-world anecdotal knowledge, such as the conversion of percentages. Another problem with similar inferences of a more complex nature is,

> "*Lauren wants to mix 5 liters of 7% milk with skim-milk (0% fat) to produce a mixture of 2.9787% milk. How much skim-milk should Lauren add?*"

yielding the equation "$x = (7.0 \times 0.01) \times 5.0/(2.9787 \times 0.01) - 5.0$", containing similar conversions of percentages, as well as additional knowledge of types of mixtures. Here, 7% milk is mixed with pure milk, or 100% milk. Yet the only indication that the milk is of 100% purity is nowhere to be seen in a direct capacity in the problem, but rather in a roundabout way - by referring to the amount of fat (0%) rather than the purity of the milk. Models have to infer a vast amount of real-world contextual knowledge to be able to solve such problems. Problems with second-degree unknown quantities are also present as seed problems. For example, the problem

> "*The Hudson River flows at a rate of 3 miles per hour. A patrol boat travels 60 miles upriver and returns in a total time of 9 hours. What is the speed of the boat in still water?*"

that yields the equation "$(60.0/(x - 3.0)) + (60.0/(3.0+x)) = 9.0$", which is a quadratic equation. The problem itself deals with calculations of speed, which requires knowledge of how speed is calculated given certain quantities, as well as the effect of certain elements in the problem scenario on speed.

We resort to this data generation approach due to the lack of large-scale, diverse, single-equation English MWP datasets. Other commonly-used benchmark datasets, MATH23K (Wang et al., 2017) and APE210K (Liang et al., 2021) consist of math problems written in Chinese Mandarin. We also aim to diversify the samples in MAWPS to enable better training for MWP solvers (Schick and Schütze, 2021; Kumar et al., 2022). SVAMP, created by Patel et al. (2021) consists of challenging versions of problems and is considered a challenge set for testing the robustness of MWP solvers. We use the original version of MAWPS and SVAMP along with our dataset PARAMAWPS for conducting our experiments. A comparative summary of the statistics of the datasets used is shown in Table-2 and their operator count distributions are portrayed in Figure-2.

Properties	SVAMP	MAWPS	PARAMAWPS
# of problems	1,000	2,373	16,278
# of unique templates	27	159	215
Avg. # of operators	1.236	1.606	1.68
Avg. # of quantities per prob.	2.81	2.57	2.54
Avg. # of quantities per equ.	2.23	2.59	2.67
# of problems with constants	0	185	3313

Table 2: Comparison of the datasets used.

5.2 Model Implementation Details and Training

5.2.1 Baseline Models

We implement the DeBERTa model using Microsoft's *deberta-base* that is publicly available in Hugging Face[2]. The other baseline MWP solver models are implementations already available in the open-source `MWPToolkit`[3] developed by Lan et al. (2022). We use an extensive set of baseline models, Transformer (Vaswani et al., 2017), DNS (Wang et al., 2017), MathEN (Wang et al., 2018a), GroupATT (Li et al., 2019), RNNEncDec (Sutskever et al., 2014), RNNVAE (Su et al., 2018), BERT (Devlin et al., 2018), RoBERTa (Liu et al., 2019b), and compare them with the performance of the DeBERTa model. See Appendix-A for more training process details.

5.3 Result Analysis

Methods	MAWPS† (%)	SVAMP (%)	PARA-MAWPS† (%)
DNS	59.5	22.1	71.2
Math-EN	69.2	21.8	71.6
GROUP-ATT	76.1	19.2	70.8
RNNEncDec	79.4	25.4	73.6
RNNVAE	79.8	25.9	72.8
Transformer	85.6	20.7	64.6
BERT	86.9	24.8	72.1
RoBERTa	88.4	30.3	72.5
DeBERTa	90.7	**63.5**	74.1
DeBERTa$_{PM+VM}$	**91.0**	-	-
DeBERTa$_{VM}$	-	-	**79.1**

Table 3: Value accuracy of the DeBERTa model and various baseline models. † denotes 5-fold cross validation. PM stands for Paraphrasing Model and VM stands for Voting Mechanism.

Table-3 shows the performance comparison of the DeBERTa model and the baseline models mentioned in Section-5.2.1. The DeBERTa model coupled with the Paraphrasing model and the Voting Mechanism outperforms all the baseline models in the MAWPS (Koncel-Kedziorski et al., 2016) dataset with an accuracy of 91.0%. The Paraphrasing Model and the Voting Mechanism contributed to a 0.3% increase in accuracy. The vanilla DeBERTa model also outperforms the baseline models in our PARAMAWPS dataset by boasting an accuracy of 74.1%. With the voting mechanism at the tail-end of the pipeline, we are able to yield an improvement of the accuracy by 5.04% making the accuracy 79.1%. We test the robustness of the vanilla DeBERTa model on the SVAMP (Patel et al., 2021) challenge dataset and get an accuracy of 63.5% which is quite higher than that of the other baseline models. The model still lags a mere $1 \pm 0.20\%$ behind the current SOTA model on MAWPS, which is the ROBERTA-DEDUCTREASONER model by Jie et al. (2022) ($92.0 \pm 0.20\%$) but supersedes its accuracy of $47.3 \pm 0.20\%$ on the SVAMP dataset.

The superiority of the model's accuracy in PARAMAWPS over SVAMP, despite the demonstrably greater difficulty of the MWP samples in PARAMAWPS, indicates that training a language model on a more diverse set of linguistically varied problem statements leads to a better quality mathematical reasoning ability after the training phase.

5.4 Ablation Study

To gain insights into the individual contributions of the Paraphrasing Model and Voting Mechanism in conjunction with the DeBERTa model, we perform ablation studies. Table-4 shows the effect of

# of variants	MAWPS† (%)
w/ $k = 0$	90.7
w/ $k = 5$	90.4
w/ $k = 10$	90.8
w/ $k = 15$	91.0

Table 4: Value accuracy with different numbers of linguistic variants of the problem samples. † denotes 5-fold cross validation.

Voting Mechanism	PARAMAWPS† (%)
w/o VM	72.9, 74.1, 76.5, 72.1, 74.6
w/ VM	78.5, 77.8, 82.4, 77.2, 79.5

Table 5: Effect of Majority Voting on Value accuracy across all 5 folds. † denotes 5-fold cross validation.

increasing the number of generated problem variants to infer the solution expressions of the problem samples in the MAWPS dataset's test set. Although there is a slight decrease in the accuracy for $k = 5$, we see a minuscule increase in accuracy for

[2]https://huggingface.co/microsoft/deberta-base
[3]https://github.com/LYH-YF/MWPToolkit/

$k = 10$ and $k = 15$. In Table-5 we see the impact of the Voting Mechanism which contributed to a 5.4% increase on average in the accuracy of the DeBERTa model on the PARAMAWPS dataset.

5.5 MWP Task Performance Analysis of Large Language Models

To test out the assertion made in other studies (Huang and Chang, 2022; Ho et al., 2022) about the incompetence of LLMs in complex reasoning tasks compared to fine-tuned smaller models, we use the GPT-J model and some of the presently used GPT-3 models by OpenAI to perform the task of MWP solving. We use the original version of MAWPS (Koncel-Kedziorski et al., 2016) along with our dataset PARAMAWPS for testing the mathematical reasoning of these models.

Models	MAWPS† (%)	PARA-MAWPS† (%)
GPT-J (6B)	9.9	5.9
text-babbage-001 (6.7B)	2.76	3.21
text-curie-001 (13B)	4.09	4.20
gpt-3.5-turbo (175B)	80.3	73.0

Table 6: Value accuracy of the LLMs in a zero-shot setup testing. † denotes evaluation on the whole dataset.

One of the most capable models in the GPT-3.5 series of models is *text-davinci-003*, with 175 billion parameters and the ability to follow instructions consistently and produce lengthy outputs. However, the most capable and up-to-date model according to OpenAI is *gpt-3.5-turbo*, with 175 billion parameters, which is primarily optimized for chat completions but can be tweaked to follow more specific instructions similar to *text-davinci-003*. While all models used are instructed to output in a specific format — `'Answer: [ANS]'` with just the numerical value in the place of `'[ANS]'`, the ability to do so consistently deteriorated with the models with relatively fewer parameters. Out of the base GPT-3 models, the 13 billion parameters *text-curie-001* can output in the given format relatively consistently, *text-babbage-001* with 6.7 billion parameters can occasionally produce the output in the correct format, but tries to generate full sentences more often than not, whereas the 350 million parameters *text-ada-001* can barely generate a single output in the correct format, choosing to generate full sentences almost all of the time. Models tend to try to *'work through'* the problem in text form rather than just generating the output, although with *gpt-3.5-turbo* this can be mostly mitigated by using very specific instructions for the prompt. The results in Table-6 and Table-3 support the current weakness of LLMs in mathematical reasoning tasks and the suitability of fine-tuning smaller models. It indicates the improvement in performance for a well-reasoning, but comparatively small model when it has the option to democratically choose from a substantial number of solution guesses.

6 Conclusion and Future Work

In this paper, we propose the idea of an MWP solving framework that utilizes the paraphrased linguistic variations of problem texts to train a DeBERTa model that generates candidate solution expressions and finalizes the predicted math expression by employing majority voting on a set of simplified candidate expressions. Our findings demonstrate that incorporating linguistic variants of problem statements during training and utilizing a voting mechanism for candidate predictions enhance the model's mathematical reasoning and overall robustness. We also introduce a large-scale, diverse, and challenging single-equation MWP dataset, PARAMAWPS, consisting of paraphrased, inverse, and adversarial variants of selectively sampled datapoints from MAWPS, as a formidable evaluation test-bed and a proper benchmark for training MWP solver models. We wish to experiment further with harder problem text variations (*e.g.* grammatical errors) and conduct a thorough error analysis of the models for identifying their lapses in mathematical reasoning and discovering more scopes of improvement. We also aim to expand our research to encompass the intricate realms of multi-equation, multi-step deduction, and domain-knowledge problems. We hope our approach and findings will pave the way to more scholarly works on the vistas of AGI and in tandem be deemed a noteworthy and meaningful contribution to this domain of research.

7 Limitations

There are still some avenues of improvement in our work. The temporal overhead due to the problem variant generation by the paraphraser model may make our proposed architecture unsuitable for real-world applications even though it takes merely 10 to 12 seconds to generate $k = 5$ variants for a single sample. Another limitation of our work is the absence of a proper tie-breaking strategy in our Majority Voting module. Furthermore, we need to introduce a system of weighted votes (*e.g.* semantic similarity scores as weights) so that the votes of wrongly predicted equations don't trump that of correctly generated predictions. We also plan to incorporate and experiment with the Tree-based decoder (Xie and Sun, 2019) in our proposed pipeline.

References

Yefim Bakman. 2007. Robust understanding of word problems with extraneous information. *arXiv preprint math/0701393*.

Colin Bannard and Chris Callison-Burch. 2005. Paraphrasing with bilingual parallel corpora. In *Proceedings of the 43rd annual meeting of the Association for Computational Linguistics (ACL05)*, pages 597–604.

Regina Barzilay and Kathleen McKeown. 2001. Extracting paraphrases from a parallel corpus. In *Proceedings of the 39th annual meeting of the Association for Computational Linguistics*, pages 50–57.

Daniel G Bobrow. 1964. Natural language input for a computer problem solving system.

Tom Brown, Benjamin Mann, Nick Ryder, Melanie Subbiah, Jared D Kaplan, Prafulla Dhariwal, Arvind Neelakantan, Pranav Shyam, Girish Sastry, Amanda Askell, et al. 2020. Language models are few-shot learners. *Advances in neural information processing systems*, 33:1877–1901.

Sébastien Bubeck, Varun Chandrasekaran, Ronen Eldan, Johannes Gehrke, Eric Horvitz, Ece Kamar, Peter Lee, Yin Tat Lee, Yuanzhi Li, Scott Lundberg, et al. 2023. Sparks of artificial general intelligence: Early experiments with gpt-4. *arXiv preprint arXiv:2303.12712*.

Deng Cai and Wai Lam. 2020. Graph transformer for graph-to-sequence learning. In *Proceedings of the AAAI Conference on Artificial Intelligence*, volume 34, pages 7464–7471.

Yixuan Cao, Feng Hong, Hongwei Li, and Ping Luo. 2021. A bottom-up dag structure extraction model for math word problems. In *Proceedings of the AAAI Conference on Artificial Intelligence*, volume 35, pages 39–46.

Oishik Chatterjee, Aashish Waikar, Vishwajeet Kumar, Ganesh Ramakrishnan, and Kavi Arya. 2021. A weakly supervised model for solving math word problems. *arXiv preprint arXiv:2104.06722*.

Wenhu Chen, Xueguang Ma, Xinyi Wang, and William W Cohen. 2022. Program of thoughts prompting: Disentangling computation from reasoning for numerical reasoning tasks. *arXiv preprint arXiv:2211.12588*.

Karl Cobbe, Vineet Kosaraju, Mohammad Bavarian, Jacob Hilton, Reiichiro Nakano, Christopher Hesse, and John Schulman. 2021. Training verifiers to solve math word problems. *arXiv preprint arXiv:2110.14168*.

Jacob Devlin, Ming-Wei Chang, Kenton Lee, and Kristina Toutanova. 2018. BERT: pre-training of deep bidirectional transformers for language understanding. *CoRR*, abs/1810.04805.

Edward A Feigenbaum, Julian Feldman, et al. 1963. *Computers and thought*. New York McGraw-Hill.

Charles R Fletcher. 1985. Understanding and solving arithmetic word problems: A computer simulation. *Behavior Research Methods, Instruments, & Computers*, 17(5):565–571.

Pengcheng He, Xiaodong Liu, Jianfeng Gao, and Weizhu Chen. 2020. Deberta: Decoding-enhanced bert with disentangled attention. *arXiv preprint arXiv:2006.03654*.

Geoffrey Hinton, Oriol Vinyals, Jeff Dean, et al. 2015. Distilling the knowledge in a neural network. *arXiv preprint arXiv:1503.02531*, 2(7).

Namgyu Ho, Laura Schmid, and Se-Young Yun. 2022. Large language models are reasoning teachers. *arXiv preprint arXiv:2212.10071*.

Yining Hong, Qing Li, Daniel Ciao, Siyuan Huang, and Song-Chun Zhu. 2021. Learning by fixing: Solving math word problems with weak supervision. In *AAAI Conference on Artificial Intelligence*.

Mohammad Javad Hosseini, Hannaneh Hajishirzi, Oren Etzioni, and Nate Kushman. 2014. Learning to solve arithmetic word problems with verb categorization. In *EMNLP*, volume 523533. Citeseer.

Danqing Huang, Jing Liu, Chin-Yew Lin, and Jian Yin. 2018. Neural math word problem solver with reinforcement learning. In *Proceedings of the 27th International Conference on Computational Linguistics*, pages 213–223.

Danqing Huang, Shuming Shi, Chin-Yew Lin, and Jian Yin. 2017. Learning fine-grained expressions to solve math word problems. In *Proceedings of the 2017 Conference on Empirical Methods in Natural Language Processing*, pages 805–814.

Danqing Huang, Shuming Shi, Chin-Yew Lin, Jian Yin, and Wei-Ying Ma. 2016. How well do computers solve math word problems? large-scale dataset construction and evaluation. In *Proceedings of the 54th Annual Meeting of the Association for Computational Linguistics (Volume 1: Long Papers)*, pages 887–896.

Jie Huang and Kevin Chen-Chuan Chang. 2022. Towards reasoning in large language models: A survey. *arXiv preprint arXiv:2212.10403*.

Shifeng Huang, Jiawei Wang, Jiao Xu, Da Cao, and Ming Yang. 2021. Recall and learn: A memory-augmented solver for math word problems. *arXiv preprint arXiv:2109.13112*.

Zhanming Jie, Jierui Li, and Wei Lu. 2022. Learning to reason deductively: Math word problem solving as complex relation extraction. *arXiv preprint arXiv:2203.10316*.

Diederik P Kingma and Jimmy Ba. 2014. Adam: A method for stochastic optimization. *arXiv preprint arXiv:1412.6980*.

Sheri Kingsdorf and Jennifer Krawec. 2016. A broad look at the literature on math word problem-solving interventions for third graders. *Cogent Education*, 3(1):1135770.

Thomas N Kipf and Max Welling. 2016. Semi-supervised classification with graph convolutional networks. *arXiv preprint arXiv:1609.02907*.

Rik Koncel-Kedziorski, Hannaneh Hajishirzi, Ashish Sabharwal, Oren Etzioni, and Siena Dumas Ang. 2015. Parsing algebraic word problems into equations. *Transactions of the Association for Computational Linguistics*, 3:585–597.

Rik Koncel-Kedziorski, Subhro Roy, Aida Amini, Nate Kushman, and Hannaneh Hajishirzi. 2016. Mawps: A math word problem repository. In *Proceedings of the 2016 Conference of the North American Chapter of the Association for Computational Linguistics: Human Language Technologies*, pages 1152–1157.

Vivek Kumar, Rishabh Maheshwary, and Vikram Pudi. 2021. Adversarial examples for evaluating math word problem solvers. *arXiv preprint arXiv:2109.05925*.

Vivek Kumar, Rishabh Maheshwary, and Vikram Pudi. 2022. Practice makes a solver perfect: Data augmentation for math word problem solvers. *arXiv preprint arXiv:2205.00177*.

Nate Kushman, Yoav Artzi, Luke Zettlemoyer, and Regina Barzilay. 2014. Learning to automatically solve algebra word problems. In *Proceedings of the 52nd Annual Meeting of the Association for Computational Linguistics (Volume 1: Long Papers)*, pages 271–281.

Yihuai Lan, Lei Wang, Qiyuan Zhang, Yunshi Lan, Bing Tian Dai, Yan Wang, Dongxiang Zhang, and Ee-Peng Lim. 2022. Mwptoolkit: An open-source framework for deep learning-based math word problem solvers. In *Proceedings of the AAAI Conference on Artificial Intelligence*, volume 36, pages 13188–13190.

Katherine Lee, Daphne Ippolito, Andrew Nystrom, Chiyuan Zhang, Douglas Eck, Chris Callison-Burch, and Nicholas Carlini. 2021. Deduplicating training data makes language models better. *arXiv preprint arXiv:2107.06499*.

Mike Lewis, Yinhan Liu, Naman Goyal, Marjan Ghazvininejad, Abdelrahman Mohamed, Omer Levy, Ves Stoyanov, and Luke Zettlemoyer. 2019. Bart: Denoising sequence-to-sequence pre-training for natural language generation, translation, and comprehension. *arXiv preprint arXiv:1910.13461*.

Jierui Li, Lei Wang, Jipeng Zhang, Yan Wang, Bing Tian Dai, and Dongxiang Zhang. 2019. Modeling intra-relation in math word problems with different functional multi-head attentions. In *Proceedings of the 57th Annual Meeting of the Association for Computational Linguistics*, pages 6162–6167.

Shucheng Li, Lingfei Wu, Shiwei Feng, Fangli Xu, Fengyuan Xu, and Sheng Zhong. 2020. Graph-to-tree neural networks for learning structured input-output translation with applications to semantic parsing and math word problem. *arXiv preprint arXiv:2004.13781*.

Yifei Li, Zeqi Lin, Shizhuo Zhang, Qiang Fu, Bei Chen, Jian-Guang Lou, and Weizhu Chen. 2022. On the advance of making language models better reasoners. *arXiv preprint arXiv:2206.02336*.

Zhongli Li, Wenxuan Zhang, Chao Yan, Qingyu Zhou, Chao Li, Hongzhi Liu, and Yunbo Cao. 2021. Seeking patterns, not just memorizing procedures: Contrastive learning for solving math word problems. *arXiv preprint arXiv:2110.08464*.

Chao-Chun Liang, Kuang-Yi Hsu, Chien-Tsung Huang, Chung-Min Li, Shen-Yu Miao, and Keh-Yih Su. 2016a. A tag-based english math word problem solver with understanding, reasoning and explanation. In *Proceedings of the 2016 Conference of the North American Chapter of the Association for Computational Linguistics: Demonstrations*, pages 67–71.

Chao-Chun Liang, Shih-Hong Tsai, Ting-Yun Chang, Yi-Chung Lin, and Keh-Yih Su. 2016b. A meaning-based English math word problem solver with understanding, reasoning and explanation. In *Proceedings of COLING 2016, the 26th International Conference on Computational Linguistics: System Demonstrations*, pages 151–155, Osaka, Japan. The COLING 2016 Organizing Committee.

Zhenwen Liang, Wenhao Yu, Tanmay Rajpurohit, Peter Clark, Xiangliang Zhang, and Ashwin Kaylan. 2023. Let gpt be a math tutor: Teaching math word problem solvers with customized exercise generation. *arXiv preprint arXiv:2305.14386*.

Zhenwen Liang, Jipeng Zhang, Jie Shao, and Xiangliang Zhang. 2021. Mwp-bert: A strong baseline for math word problems. *arXiv preprint arXiv:2107.13435*.

Zhenwen Liang, Jipeng Zhang, Lei Wang, Wei Qin, Jie Shao, and Xiangliang Zhang. Mwp-bert: A numeracy-augmented pre-trained encoder for math word problems.

Xin Lin, Zhenya Huang, Hongke Zhao, Enhong Chen, Qi Liu, Hao Wang, and Shijin Wang. 2021. Hms: A hierarchical solver with dependency-enhanced understanding for math word problem. In *Thirty-Fifth AAAI Conference on Artificial 2021*, pages 4232–4240.

Qianying Liu, Wenyu Guan, Sujian Li, Fei Cheng, Daisuke Kawahara, and Sadao Kurohashi. 2021. Roda: reverse operation based data augmentation for solving math word problems. *IEEE/ACM Transactions on Audio, Speech, and Language Processing*, 30:1–11.

Qianying Liu, Wenyv Guan, Sujian Li, and Daisuke Kawahara. 2019a. Tree-structured decoding for solving math word problems. In *Proceedings of the 2019 conference on empirical methods in natural language processing and the 9th international joint conference on natural language processing (EMNLP-IJCNLP)*, pages 2370–2379.

Yinhan Liu, Myle Ott, Naman Goyal, Jingfei Du, Mandar Joshi, Danqi Chen, Omer Levy, Mike Lewis, Luke Zettlemoyer, and Veselin Stoyanov. 2019b. Roberta: A robustly optimized bert pretraining approach. *arXiv preprint arXiv:1907.11692*.

Nitin Madnani and Bonnie J Dorr. 2010. Generating phrasal and sentential paraphrases: A survey of data-driven methods. *Computational Linguistics*, 36(3):341–387.

Jonathan Mallinson, Rico Sennrich, and Mirella Lapata. 2017. Paraphrasing revisited with neural machine translation. In *Proceedings of the 15th Conference of the European Chapter of the Association for Computational Linguistics: Volume 1, Long Papers*, pages 881–893, Valencia, Spain. Association for Computational Linguistics.

Kathleen R McKeown. 1980. Paraphrasing using given and new information in a question-answer system. *Technical Reports (CIS)*, page 723.

Marie Meteer and Varda Shaked. 1988. Strategies for effective paraphrasing. In *Coling Budapest 1988 Volume 2: International Conference on Computational Linguistics*.

Shen-Yun Miao, Chao-Chun Liang, and Keh-Yih Su. 2021. A diverse corpus for evaluating and developing english math word problem solvers. *arXiv preprint arXiv:2106.15772*.

Pruthwik Mishra, Litton J Kurisinkel, Dipti Misra Sharma, and Vasudeva Varma. 2018. Equgener: A reasoning network for word problem solving by generating arithmetic equations. In *Proceedings of the 32nd Pacific Asia Conference on Language, Information and Computation*.

Arindam Mitra and Chitta Baral. 2016. Learning to use formulas to solve simple arithmetic problems. In *Proceedings of the 54th Annual Meeting of the Association for Computational Linguistics (Volume 1: Long Papers)*, pages 2144–2153.

Arkil Patel, Satwik Bhattamishra, and Navin Goyal. 2021. Are nlp models really able to solve simple math word problems? *arXiv preprint arXiv:2103.07191*.

Jordan Peterson, Robert Pihl, Daniel Higgins, Jean Séguin, and Richard Tremblay. 2003. Neuropsychological performance, iq, personality, and grades in a longitudinal grade-school male sample. *Individual Differences Research*, 1:159–172.

Xinyu Pi, Qian Liu, Bei Chen, Morteza Ziyadi, Zeqi Lin, Yan Gao, Qiang Fu, Jian-Guang Lou, and Weizhu Chen. 2022. Reasoning like program executors. *arXiv preprint arXiv:2201.11473*.

Jean Piaget. 2013. *Child's Conception of Number: Selected Works vol 2*. Routledge.

Aaditya Prakash, Sadid A Hasan, Kathy Lee, Vivek Datla, Ashequl Qadir, Joey Liu, and Oladimeji Farri. 2016. Neural paraphrase generation with stacked residual lstm networks. *arXiv preprint arXiv:1610.03098*.

Subhro Roy and Dan Roth. 2016. Solving general arithmetic word problems. *arXiv preprint arXiv:1608.01413*.

Subhro Roy and Dan Roth. 2017. Unit dependency graph and its application to arithmetic word problem solving. In *Proceedings of the AAAI Conference on Artificial Intelligence*, volume 31.

Subhro Roy, Shyam Upadhyay, and Dan Roth. 2016. Equation parsing: Mapping sentences to grounded equations. *arXiv preprint arXiv:1609.08824*.

Subhro Roy, Tim Vieira, and Dan Roth. 2015. Reasoning about quantities in natural language. *Transactions of the Association for Computational Linguistics*, 3:1–13.

Timo Schick and Hinrich Schütze. 2021. Generating datasets with pretrained language models. *arXiv preprint arXiv:2104.07540*.

Zhihong Shao, Fei Huang, and Minlie Huang. 2022. Chaining simultaneous thoughts for numerical reasoning. *arXiv preprint arXiv:2211.16482*.

Jianhao Shen, Yichun Yin, Lin Li, Lifeng Shang, Xin Jiang, Ming Zhang, and Qun Liu. 2021. Generate & rank: A multi-task framework for math word problems. *arXiv preprint arXiv:2109.03034*.

Yibin Shen and Cheqing Jin. 2020. Solving math word problems with multi-encoders and multi-decoders. In *Proceedings of the 28th International Conference on Computational Linguistics*, pages 2924–2934.

Shuming Shi, Yuehui Wang, Chin-Yew Lin, Xiaojiang Liu, and Yong Rui. 2015. Automatically solving number word problems by semantic parsing and reasoning. In *Proceedings of the 2015 Conference on Empirical Methods in Natural Language Processing*, pages 1132–1142.

Jinsong Su, Shan Wu, Deyi Xiong, Yaojie Lu, Xianpei Han, and Biao Zhang. 2018. Variational recurrent neural machine translation. In *Proceedings of the AAAI conference on artificial intelligence*, volume 32.

Sowmya S Sundaram, Sairam Gurajada, Marco Fisichella, Savitha Sam Abraham, et al. 2022. Why are nlp models fumbling at elementary math? a survey of deep learning based word problem solvers. *arXiv preprint arXiv:2205.15683*.

Ilya Sutskever, Oriol Vinyals, and Quoc V Le. 2014. Sequence to sequence learning with neural networks. *Advances in neural information processing systems*, 27.

Shyam Upadhyay, Ming-Wei Chang, Kai-Wei Chang, and Wen-tau Yih. 2016. Learning from explicit and implicit supervision jointly for algebra word problems. In *Proceedings of the 2016 Conference on Empirical Methods in Natural Language Processing*, pages 297–306.

Ashish Vaswani, Noam Shazeer, Niki Parmar, Jakob Uszkoreit, Llion Jones, Aidan N Gomez, Łukasz Kaiser, and Illia Polosukhin. 2017. Attention is all you need. *Advances in neural information processing systems*, 30.

Lei Wang, Yan Wang, Deng Cai, Dongxiang Zhang, and Xiaojiang Liu. 2018a. Translating a math word problem to an expression tree. *arXiv preprint arXiv:1811.05632*.

Lei Wang, Dongxiang Zhang, Lianli Gao, Jingkuan Song, Long Guo, and Heng Tao Shen. 2018b. Mathdqn: Solving arithmetic word problems via deep reinforcement learning. In *Proceedings of the AAAI Conference on Artificial Intelligence*, volume 32.

Lei Wang, Dongxiang Zhang, Jipeng Zhang, Xing Xu, Lianli Gao, Bing Tian Dai, and Heng Tao Shen. 2019. Template-based math word problem solvers with recursive neural networks. In *Proceedings of the AAAI Conference on Artificial Intelligence*, volume 33, pages 7144–7151.

Xuezhi Wang, Jason Wei, Dale Schuurmans, Quoc Le, Ed Chi, and Denny Zhou. 2022. Self-consistency improves chain of thought reasoning in language models. *arXiv preprint arXiv:2203.11171*.

Yan Wang, Xiaojiang Liu, and Shuming Shi. 2017. Deep neural solver for math word problems. In *Proceedings of the 2017 Conference on Empirical Methods in Natural Language Processing*, pages 845–854.

Jason Wei, Xuezhi Wang, Dale Schuurmans, Maarten Bosma, Ed Chi, Quoc Le, and Denny Zhou. 2022. Chain of thought prompting elicits reasoning in large language models. *arXiv preprint arXiv:2201.11903*.

Sam Witteveen and Martin Andrews. 2019. Paraphrasing with large language models. *arXiv preprint arXiv:1911.09661*.

Qinzhuo Wu, Qi Zhang, Jinlan Fu, and Xuan-Jing Huang. 2020. A knowledge-aware sequence-to-tree network for math word problem solving. In *Proceedings of the 2020 Conference on Empirical Methods* in *Natural Language Processing (EMNLP)*, pages 7137–7146.

Zhipeng Xie and Shichao Sun. 2019. A goal-driven tree-structured neural model for math word problems. In *IJCAI*, pages 5299–5305.

Jing Xiong, Zhongwei Wan, Xiping Hu, Min Yang, and Chengming Li. 2022. Self-consistent reasoning for solving math word problems. *arXiv preprint arXiv:2210.15373*.

Jingfeng Yang, Hongye Jin, Ruixiang Tang, Xiaotian Han, Qizhang Feng, Haoming Jiang, Bing Yin, and Xia Hu. 2023. Harnessing the power of llms in practice: A survey on chatgpt and beyond. *arXiv preprint arXiv:2304.13712*.

Weijiang Yu, Yingpeng Wen, Fudan Zheng, and Nong Xiao. 2021. Improving math word problems with pre-trained knowledge and hierarchical reasoning. In *Proceedings of the 2021 Conference on Empirical Methods in Natural Language Processing*, pages 3384–3394.

Ma Yuhui, Zhou Ying, Cui Guangzuo, Ren Yun, and Huang Ronghuai. 2010. Frame-based calculus of solving arithmetic multi-step addition and subtraction word problems. In *2010 Second International Workshop on Education Technology and Computer Science*, volume 2, pages 476–479. IEEE.

Seongjun Yun, Minbyul Jeong, Raehyun Kim, Jaewoo Kang, and Hyunwoo J Kim. 2019. Graph transformer networks. *Advances in neural information processing systems*, 32.

Dongxiang Zhang, Lei Wang, Luming Zhang, Bing Tian Dai, and Heng Tao Shen. 2019. The gap of semantic parsing: A survey on automatic math word problem solvers. *IEEE transactions on pattern analysis and machine intelligence*, 42(9):2287–2305.

Jipeng Zhang, Roy Ka-Wei Lee, Ee-Peng Lim, Wei Qin, Lei Wang, Jie Shao, and Qianru Sun. 2020a. Teacher-student networks with multiple decoders for solving math word problem. IJCAI.

Jipeng Zhang, Lei Wang, Roy Ka-Wei Lee, Yi Bin, Yan Wang, Jie Shao, and Ee-Peng Lim. 2020b. Graph-to-tree learning for solving math word problems. Association for Computational Linguistics.

Lipu Zhou, Shuaixiang Dai, and Liwei Chen. 2015. Learn to solve algebra word problems using quadratic programming. In *Proceedings of the 2015 Conference on Empirical Methods in Natural Language Processing*, pages 817–822.

Yanyan Zou and Wei Lu. 2019. Text2math: End-to-end parsing text into math expressions. *arXiv preprint arXiv:1910.06571*.

A Appendix

A.1 Dataset Split

We use an 80:10:10 train-validation-test split for our PARAMAWPS dataset. For MAWPS, we use 5-fold cross-validation using the splits provided by its authors Koncel-Kedziorski et al. (2016). The SVAMP dataset is a challenge set and all 1,000 of its samples constitute the test set while the model itself is trained on a combination of the MAWPS and ASDIV-A (Miao et al., 2021) dataset.

A.2 Performance Evaluation and Metric

We use Negative log-likelihood loss (NLLLoss) for training all the models. For the baseline models, `MWPToolkit` uses two metrics of accuracy, *Equation Accuracy* and *Value Accuracy*. Equation accuracy measures the correctness of the generated equation. Value accuracy measures the correctness of the value yielded from evaluating the generated equation. This metric takes into consideration the fact that models may generate equations that have a different template than the respective ground truth equations but nevertheless yield the correct answers to the problem statements.

A.3 Hyperparameters

In the DeBERTa model, we use embedding dimension $d = 768$, $FFN_{size} = 1024$, number of decoder layers $N = 4$, number of attention heads $h = 16$, dropout ratio $P_{drop} = 0.5$, learning rate $lr = 10^{-5}$, batch size $b = 8$, and $Epochs = 200$. The hyperparameters for the other baseline models are as set on the respective `MWPToolkit` implementations.

A.4 Optimizer

We use Adam (Kingma and Ba, 2014) with a StepLR learning rate scheduler as our optimizer. The learning rate lr is set according to Vaswani et al. (2017), $lr = d^{-0.5} \cdot \min(n^{-0.5}, n \cdot w^{-1.5})$ where, d is the embedding dimension, n is the step number and w is the number of warm-up steps. Here, warm-up steps w simply insinuate that the learning rate rises linearly for the initial w training steps. We set $\beta_1 = 0.9$, $\beta_2 = 0.999$, $\epsilon = 10^{-8}$ and $w = 1500$ for the models' Adam optimizer. For the StepLR scheduler, we set $\gamma = 0.5$ and $step\_size = 5$.

A.5 Hardware and Schedule

We have used the NVIDIA RTX 3090 GPU equipped with 25GB of VRAM and Intel Core i9 Processor for conducting our experiments. The DeBERTa model took around 18 hours to fully train on the PARAMAWPS dataset with 5-fold cross-validation and 200 epochs per fold, which was the highest expense of time among the lot. The other baseline models took approximately 7 to 9 hours on the PARAMAWPS dataset and around 5 hours on MAWPS and SVAMP. The greater the number of parameters that a model possesses the more time it takes to fully complete the 5-fold training process. As DeBERTa has an astounding 134 million parameters (He et al., 2020), it takes the longest time to train.

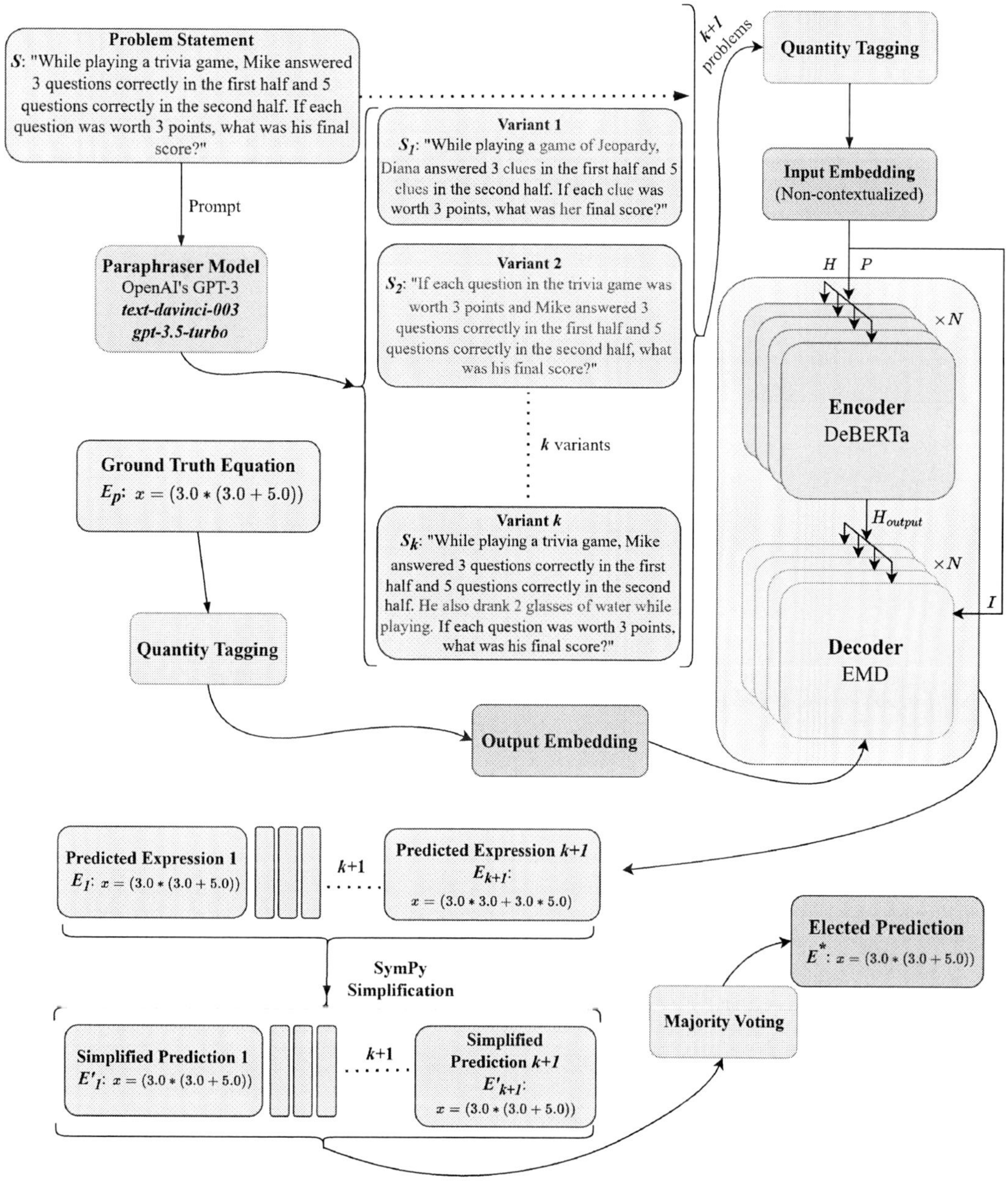

Figure 1: Overview of our proposed architecture.

Variation Type	Original	Variation
Changed phrase order	There were originally 20817 houses in Lincoln County. During a housing boom, developers built 97741. How many houses are there now in Lincoln County?	How many houses are there in Lincoln County now, after developers built an additional 97741 during a housing boom, when there were originally 20817 houses?
Changed object and entity names	While playing a trivia game, Mike answered 3 questions correct in the first half and 5 questions correct in the second half. If each question was worth 3 points, what was his final score?	While playing a game of Hangman, Emily guessed 3 letters correctly in the first half and 5 letters correctly in the second half. If each letter was worth 3 points, what was her final score?
Added unrelated information	A carpenter bought a piece of wood that was 8.9 centimeters long. Then he sawed 2.3 centimeters off the end. How long is the piece of wood now?	A carpenter bought a piece of wood that was 8.9 centimeters long. Then he sawed 2.3 centimeters off the end and sanded the wood for 20 minutes. How long is the piece of wood now?
Inverted question	Mary bought 3 pizzas for $8 each. What was the total amount she paid for the 3 pizzas?	If Mary paid $24 for 3 pizzas, how much did she pay for each pizza?

Table 7: Types of Variations with examples. The problems in the **Original** column are samples taken from the MAWPS dataset, whereas, the ones in the **Variation** column are from the PARAMAWPS dataset.

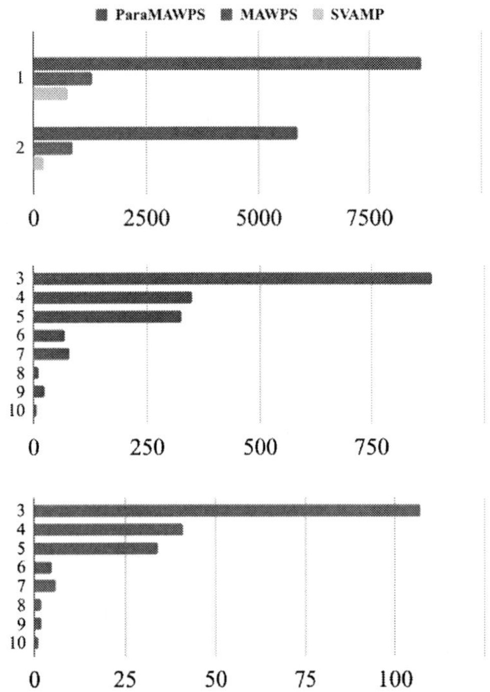

Figure 2: Operator count distributions of PARAMAWPS, MAWPS, and SVAMP. We keep the distribution of PARAMAWPS somewhat similar to that of MAWPS to maintain a proper balance between easy and difficult problems.

Author Index

Association for Computational Linguistics
209 N. Eighth Street
Stroudsburg, Pennsylvania 18360

ISBN 978-1-7138-8175-9

CURRAN ASSOCIATES INC.
proceedings.com